An Inventory of the
Historical Monuments in the

COUNTY OF
NORTHAMPTON

ROYAL COMMISSION ON HISTORICAL MONUMENTS
ENGLAND

An Inventory of the Historical Monuments in the

COUNTY OF NORTHAMPTON

Volume IV
Archaeological Sites in South-West Northamptonshire

LONDON · HER MAJESTY'S STATIONERY OFFICE

© Crown copyright 1982

First published 1982

ISBN 0 11 700994 6* (Red binding)

ISBN 0 11 700997 0* (Grey binding)

TABLE OF CONTENTS

MAP showing the parishes described in the Inventory, in pocket at the end of volume

LIST OF ILLUSTRATIONS

(The prefixed numerals in brackets refer to the monument numbers in the text)

FOREWORD

This, the fourth volume of an Inventory of the earthworks of Northamptonshire, describes the archaeological sites within the south-western part of the county. Of the 530 or so monuments which are described, many have not hitherto been recognised.

The archaeological sites recorded in this volume have been examined by our staff, but much original material was gathered from published records and manuscript notes and from verbal information supplied by local archaeologists and historians; the Commission is conscious of the debt which it owes for the help received from these sources. It is hoped that this Inventory will be of use not only to archaeologists but also to those concerned with planning decisions or with conservation. This volume also includes Addenda, in which are briefly listed those sites and finds which have come to light since the completion of the first three Inventories.

ADEANE
Chairman

COMMISSIONERS

The Right Honourable the Lord Adeane, P.C., G.C.B., G.C.V.O.
Her Majesty's Lieutenant of Northamptonshire (*ex officio*)
Sheppard Sunderland Frere, Esq., C.B.E.
Richard John Copland Atkinson, Esq., C.B.E.
George Zarnecki, Esq., C.B.E.
John Kenneth Sinclair St Joseph, Esq., C.B.E.
Arthur Richard Dufty, Esq., C.B.E.
Christopher Nugent Lawrence Brooke, Esq.
Andrew Colin Renfrew, Esq.
Mrs. Irene Joan Thirsk
Peter Kidson, Esq.
Maurice Warwick Beresford, Esq.
Robert Angus Buchanan, Esq.
Albert Lionel Frederick Rivet, Esq.
Sir Harry Thurston Hookway
John Kerry Downes, Esq.,

Secretary
Peter Jon Fowler, Esq.

ROYAL COMMISSION ON THE ANCIENT AND HISTORICAL MONUMENTS AND CONSTRUCTIONS OF ENGLAND

REPORT *to the Queen's Most Excellent Majesty*

MAY IT PLEASE YOUR MAJESTY

We, the undersigned Commissioners, appointed to make an Inventory of the Ancient and Historical Monuments and Constructions connected with or illustrative of the contemporary culture, civilisation and conditions of life of the people of England from the earliest times to the year 1714, and such further Monuments and Constructions subsequent to that year as may seem in our discretion to be worthy of mention therein, and to specify those which seem most worthy of preservation, do humbly submit to Your Majesty the following Report, being the thirty-ninth Report on the work of the Commission since its first appointment.

2. We have to record the loss to the Commission by resignation of Doctor Mark Girouard, for whose advice and assistance over a period of five years we are deeply grateful.

3. We have to thank Your Majesty for the appointment to the Commission of Sir Harry Thurston Hookway, Knight, and Professor John Kerry Downes, Fellow of the Society of Antiquaries, under Your Majesty's Royal Sign Warrant dated 27th March, 1981.

4. We have pleasure in reporting the completion of our recording of archaeological sites in the south-western part of the County of Northampton, an area comprising sixty-nine parishes containing 536 monuments.

5. Following our usual practice we have prepared an illustrated Inventory of these monuments, which will be issued as a non-Parliamentary publication entitled *Northamptonshire IV*. As in recent Inventories, the Commissioners have adopted the terminal date of 1850 for the monuments included in the Inventory.

6. The method of presentation of material has in general followed that adopted in the previous Inventories.

7. The descriptions of the more important monuments have been submitted to specialist authorities. We are satisfied that no significant monument which survived until 1978 has been omitted.

8. Our special thanks are due to owners and occupiers who have allowed access by our staff to the monuments in their charge. We are indebted to the Directors and Curators of many Institutions for their ready assistance to us and in particular to Mr. P. I. King, the Northamptonshire County Archivist. We have to record our indebtedness to the Director-General of the Ordnance Survey for access to his archaeological records and for valuable work carried out by the field surveyors of his Department. We wish to record our gratitude to Professor J. K. S. St Joseph, lately Director in Aerial Photography in the University of Cambridge, for permission to use a large number of air photographs. We further wish to express our thanks to those persons and organizations who have given particular help to our executive staff during the field investigation; their co-operation is greatly appreciated. They include Mr. D. J. Barrett who has supplied records of his detailed fieldwork in Marston St. Lawrence and neighbouring parishes and Mr. A. E. Brown who has

contributed much of his unpublished material on flint-working sites in the north-west of the county (included in the Addendum) and the account of the Roman town at Towcester, as well as Mr. W. N. Terry and Mr. W. R. G. Moore (respectively Curator and Keeper of Archaeology, Northampton Central Museum and Art Gallery).

We gratefully acknowledge permission to reproduce a number of maps and plans belonging to His Grace the Duke of Grafton, Sir Hereward Wake, Bart., the Peterborough Diocesan Registrar and Abthorpe and Rothersthorpe Parish Councils.

9. As a result of the limitations imposed on us by the continuing need for economy, only two members of our staff have been available to carry out work in the field.

10. We humbly recommend to Your Majesty's notice the following monuments in south-western Northamptonshire as being most worthy of preservation:

Roman, prehistoric and undated monuments:

CHIPPING WARDEN
(2) Iron Age Fort

COLD HIGHAM
(2) Enclosures and Ditches

GAYTON
(1) Roman Villa

HARTWELL
(1) Enclosure

KING'S SUTTON
(5) Prehistoric and Roman Settlement

NEWBOTTLE
(1) Hill Fort

PAULERSPURY
(3) and (4) Roman Buildings

ROTHERSTHORPE
(8) Enclosure

Medieval and later earthworks

ABTHORPE
(5) Deserted Hamlet of Charlock

ASTON LE WALLS
(1) Deserted Village of Appletree
(3) Fishponds and Hollow-way

BLISWORTH
(6) Tramway

CHACOMBE
(3) Site of Manor House

CULWORTH
(1) Ringwork

EASTON NESTON
(4) Site of Manor House

EVENLEY
(9) Deserted Village of Astwick

FARTHINGHOE
(18) Deserted Village of Steane

GRAFTON REGIS
(5) and (6) Motte, Site of Manor House and Garden Remains

HELMDON
(4) Site of Manor House and Settlement Remains

RADSTONE
(2) Deserted Village of Lower Radstone

SULGRAVE
(3) Ringwork

WOODEND
(1) Deserted Village of Kirby

11. In compiling the foregoing list, our criteria have been archaeological or historical importance and rarity, not only in the national but in the local field, and the degree of loss to the nation that would result from destruction. The list is based on academic considerations and does not take into account the problems of preservation.

However, destruction of field monuments continues to be rapid and widespread, and the increasing rarity of these monuments makes it desirable that as many as possible of those listed in the Inventory should be preserved. Also, the extent and impressiveness of surface remains are not the only indications of archaeological importance; their significance can often only be appreciated after excavation. Destruction should therefore not be permitted before archaeological investigation has taken place.

12. We desire to express our acknowledgement of the good work accomplished by our executive staff in the production of this volume, particularly by Mr. C. C. Taylor and Mrs. F. M. Brown who carried out the fieldwork and the preparation of the Inventory, by the editor Mr. S. D. T. Spittle, by Dr. B. E. A. Jones who carried out research in the Public Record Office, by our illustrators Mr. R. E. Beeton and Mr. P. N. Hammond and by our photographers Mr. J. Parkinson, Mr. R. Braybrook, and Mr. H. Marsden. We are also grateful for the work done by our chief photographer Mr. R. E. W. Parsons and by Mr. J. N. Hampton who assisted with the aerial photography.

13. Since the publication of our 38th Report Your Majesty has appointed Mr. S. D. T. Spittle and Mr. E. Barbour-Mercer, members of the executive staff of the Commission, Officers of Your Most Excellent Order of the British Empire.

14. Mr. Robert William McDowall, C.B.E., M.A., F.S.A., retired from the Secretaryship of the Royal Commission in 1979, and Dr. Peter Jon Fowler, M.A., F.S.A., was appointed to succeed him.

15. We desire to add that our Secretary and General Editor, Dr. P. J. Fowler, has afforded us constant assistance.

16. The next Inventory in the Northamptonshire series will record archaeological sites within Northampton.

Signed:

Adeane (*Chairman*)

John Chandos-Pole	A. C. Renfrew
Sheppard Frere	I. Joan Thirsk
R. J. C. Atkinson	P. Kidson
G. Zarnecki	Maurice Beresford
J. K. S. St Joseph	R. A. Buchanan
Paul Ashbee	A. L. F. Rivet
A. R. Dufty	J. K. Downes
Christopher Brooke	H. T. Hookway

P. J. Fowler (*Secretary*)

LIST OF PARISHES IN THE INVENTORY

The parish boundaries, shown in red on the map in the pocket at the end of the volume, were those in effect when the Inventory was compiled.

ABBREVIATIONS AND SHORTENED TITLES
OF WORKS OF REFERENCE

Ant. J.	*Antiquaries Journal.*
Arch. J.	*Archaeological Journal.*
Ass. Arch. Soc. Reps.	*Reports and Papers of the Associated Architectural Societies.*
Beds. Arch. J.	*Bedfordshire Archaeological Journal.*
BM	British Museum.
BNFAS	*Bulletin of the Northamptonshire Federation of Archaeological Societies.*
Bridges, *Hist. of Northants.*	John Bridges, *History and Antiquities of Northamptonshire* (1791).
Brit. Num. J.	*British Numismatic Journal.*
Cal. Inq. Misc.	*Calendar of Miscellaneous Inquisitions.*
Cal. IPM	*Calendar of Inquisitions Post Mortem.*
Cal. Pat.	*Calendar of Patent Rolls.*
Cambridge Museum	University of Cambridge Museum of Archaeology and Ethnology
CBA	Council for British Archaeology.
CUAP	Cambridge University Air Photographs.
Current Arch.	*Current Archaeology.*
DMVRG	Deserted Medieval Village Research Group.
DOE	Department of Environment.
FSL	Fairey Surveys Limited.
Gent's Mag.	*Gentleman's Magazine.*
JBAA	*Journal of the British Archaeological Association.*
J. Northants. Mus. and Art Gall.	*Journal of the Northampton Museum and Art Gallery.*
J. Northants. Natur. Hist. Soc. and FC	*Journal of the Northamptonshire Natural History Society and Field Club.*
JRS	*Journal of Roman Studies.*
KM	Kettering Museum
Margary	I. D. Margary, *Roman Roads in Britain* (1973).
Meaney, *Gazetteer*	A. Meaney, *Gazetteer of Early Anglo-Saxon Burial Sites* (1964).
Med. Arch.	*Medieval Archaeology.*
Morton, *Nat. Hist. of Northants.*	J. Morton, *Natural History of Northamptonshire* (1712).
MOW	Ministry of Works.
MPBW	Ministry of Public Buildings and Works.
NCAU	Northamptonshire County Archaeological Unit.
NM	Northampton Museum.
NMR	National Monuments Record.
Northants. Ant. Soc. Rep.	*Northamptonshire Antiquarian Society Reports and Papers.*
Northants. Archaeol.	*Northamptonshire Archaeology.*
Northants. Archit. and Arch. Soc. Reps.	*Northamptonshire Architectural and Archaeological Society Reports.*
Northants. N. and Q.	*Northamptonshire Notes and Queries.*
Northants. P. and P.	*Northamptonshire Past and Present.*
Northants. SMR	Northamptonshire Sites and Monuments Record.
NRO	Northamptonshire Record Office.
Num. Chron.	*Numismatic Chronicle.*
OS	Ordnance Survey.
PM	Peterborough Museum.
PN Northants.	J. E. B. Gover, A. Mawer and F. M. Stenton, *The Place-Names of Northamptonshire* (1933).
PPS	*Proceedings of the Prehistoric Society.*
PRO	Public Record Office.
Procs. Cambs. Ants. Soc.	*Proceedings of the Cambridge Antiquarian Society.*
PSA	*Proceedings of the Society of Antiquaries of London.*
RAF VAP	Royal Air Force Vertical Air Photographs.
RCHM	Royal Commission on Historical Monuments.
Trans. Anc. Mons. Soc.	*Transactions of the Ancient Monuments Society.*
VCH	Victoria History of the Counties of England
Whellan, *Dir.*	F. Whellan, *History, Topography and Directory of Northamptonshire* (1874).

INTRODUCTION

This Inventory of the earthworks of Northamptonshire covers parishes in the south-western part of the county. In it the policy regarding content and scope largely follows that of earlier Inventories.

Apart from Roman Roads (Appendix), the monuments are listed in the following order, under the names of the Civil Parishes in which they lie:

(1) Prehistoric and Roman Monuments
(2) Medieval and Later Earthworks
(3) Undated Earthworks, etc.

Each parish entry has a short introductory note, summarizing the physical topography, major monuments and history.

National Grid references are given for all monuments; a map of the whole area is in the pocket inside the back cover. A superior letter before a monument number refers to the sheet number in the OS 1:10000 map series, as listed at the head of the parish.

The entries in the Inventory are necessarily much compressed and where a site has been adequately described elsewhere few details are given and the reader is directed to the relevant publication.

Many of the plans included in the text have been prepared from air-photographic evidence. Every attempt has been made to avoid inaccuracy, but a number of drawings showing crop or soil-marks have been plotted from oblique air photographs only and therefore the locations shown may in some cases differ slightly from the actual, although general comparative sizes are correct. Furthermore, crop and soil conditions prevailing when the air photographs were taken have sometimes made interpretation difficult. Only those features considered as being archaeologically significant have been included in the illustrations. No attempt has been made to show the correct widths of ditches. Pit alignments and other arrangements of pits are shown conventionally; the precise number of pits, and variations in their size and shape, have not been reproduced.

The present locations of finds are, if known, indicated in the Inventory. Chance finds which are unrelated to monuments have not been included except when their importance warrants it or when it is likely that one of the monuments described in the Inventory was their provenance.

Roman roads in the area are described together in an Appendix, and are identified by the numbers given to them by I. D. Margary in *Roman Roads in Britain*, 3rd ed. (1973).

All earthworks listed in the Inventory have been inspected by our Investigator, and those which are of major importance, or have proved difficult of analysis, have been re-examined on a number of occasions. Some monuments have been destroyed since their investigation, but these have been included in the Inventory. Most of the recording was carried out in 1977–78 and alterations to the monuments occurring since 1979 have not been described.

The Addenda comprise lists of those sites and finds which have come to light in those parts of the county covered by the previous Inventories since their publication, but no material found after 1979 has been included.

Work of this nature can seldom escape the inclusion of some errors, but it is believed that those in this survey are neither numerous nor serious. Any corrections may be sent to the Secretary with a view to their inclusion in the National Monuments Record.

The present rate both of destruction and of discovery of monuments renders unlikely the finality of any inventory, particularly with regard to prehistoric and Roman remains. New sites discovered since the publication of Volumes I to III of the Inventory, together with new information about known sites, are listed in the Addenda to the present volume (p. 184). The four Inventories, Volumes I to IV, thus provide a complete account of all known archaeological sites and finds recorded before the end of 1979. Volume V, the City of Northampton, will be published at a later date.

SECTIONAL PREFACE

TOPOGRAPHY AND GEOLOGY

The part of Northamptonshire described in this volume covers an area of some 750 square kilometres in the S.W. of the county. Topographically the region is a plateau dipping very gently eastwards and composed largely of rocks of the Jurassic Series. The down-cutting of the four major river systems, the Cherwell in the N., the Great Ouse in the S., the Nene in the N. and the Tove in the E. and centre, has produced a rolling landscape of open valleys and flat-topped ridges. Only in the extreme S.W. does the Oolite Limestone form large areas of level ground and even here erosion has produced a number of deep valleys. Most of the higher land, except in the extreme W. of the area, is covered by Boulder Clay and other glacially-derived deposits, and the solid geology is only exposed in the valleys. In the W., and to a lesser extent in the N., clays, limestones and sands form the greater part of the surface geology.

Apart from the higher limestone plateau, the region is well timbered, with numerous small woods and copses; larger tracts of woodland in the S. and S.E. are survivals of the medieval forests of Whittlewood and Salcey. There are ample water supplies throughout most of the area and building stone of varying quality has been available from the limestone strata. Today the greater part of the land is arable except for the old woodlands.

Rural settlement is evenly distributed over the area and the only towns are Towcester and Brackley, both relatively small. The former has Roman origins but the latter is a planned medieval town created sometime before 1173. No major extractive industries continue at present, though in the recent past extensive ironstone-mining has occurred between Gayton and Blisworth in the N.E. and at King's Sutton in the S.W.

PREHISTORIC AND ROMAN SETTLEMENT (Figs. 1–13)

Compared with the other parts of the county, the area covered by this Inventory is poor in prehistoric and Roman remains and relatively few standing monuments of these periods have survived. The lack of material is largely due to insufficient archaeological research, just as the density of known sites in the E. and N.E. of the county is more a reflection of the amount of archaeological work there than of any outstanding importance in prehistoric and Roman times. This explanation is supported by the exceptional amount of material found at Marston St. Lawrence, Thenford and in parts of the adjoining parishes of Farthinghoe and Greatworth, almost all of which has been discovered during intensive fieldwork by D. J. Barrett over the last twenty years. With such detailed work, the relationship between the distribution of the archaeological material and the existing land-use becomes apparent and this is of considerable significance in assessing the validity of distribution patterns elsewhere (Fig. 85). There can be little doubt that the same quantity of material could be found throughout this part of Northamptonshire if the same level of field examination were carried out.

Few crop and soil-marks have been recorded in this area, partly as a result of concentration of archaeological air reconnaissance in the centre and N.E. of the county, though this imbalance is now being rectified. Many sites doubtless await discovery, especially on the limestone tableland in the S.W. of this area. There is reason to believe that almost every part of this section of the county was settled and cultivated throughout most of the later prehistoric times and in the Roman period, and few conclusions can be drawn from the distribution maps at present available.

PREHISTORIC REMAINS

As in earlier Inventories, it is difficult to establish a chronology for the prehistoric period. Few sites have produced pottery, except for a small number of Iron Age settlements, and though numerous flint-working areas have been found it is still not possible to date them. Similarly, the majority of the cropmark sites cannot be dated without excavation. Some of them may indeed be of post-Roman origin. The cropmarks inevitably occur on the lighter soils, but prehistoric settlements which have been discovered by fieldwork, notably in Marston St. Lawrence and Thenford, indicate that the heavier clay soils were also occupied. Especially important is the survival, until recent destruction, of earthworks, of Iron Age settlements within Whittlewood Forest (Whittlebury (1–3)). One Iron Age enclosed settlement does survive in Salcey Forest (Hartwell (1)). These sites show that areas regarded as marginal or waste in medieval or later times were occupied at least in late prehistoric times. No excavations have been carried out on prehistoric sites except at the Iron Age hill fort at Rainsborough (Newbottle (1)).

Palaeolithic and Mesolithic Periods

Only two Palaeolithic axes have been found in the area, one at Marston St. Lawrence and the other at Towcester. Two Mesolithic sites are recorded at Marston St. Lawrence (1) and (2) and three at Thenford (1), (2) and (6), and isolated tools attributable to the period have been noted at Newbottle and Paulerspury. The lack of Mesolithic material must be due in large part to the difficulty of recognition. A more careful examination of the numerous flint-working sites would almost certainly reveal the presence of flints of Mesolithic type, as has been shown in south-east England (CBA *Research Report*, 21 (1978), 75), and many other sites must be as yet undiscovered.

Neolithic Period

A number of stone or flint axes has been found in the area but their distribution appears to be random. Many of the stone axes are of Group VI. The marked concentration around Marston St. Lawrence is again only the result of the intensive fieldwork there. No Neolithic site has been excavated though there are said to be settlements at King's Sutton (5), Marston St. Lawrence (1) and Helmdon (1). Many of the known flint-working sites seem to be of late Neolithic or early Bronze Age date although more work is needed on these. Some of them, notably at Thenford (1), Middleton Cheney (2) and Marston St. Lawrence (2), cover considerable areas and lie on heavy clayland. More difficult to explain are the small scatters of worked flints which, in places where fieldwork has been intensive, have been found in almost every field. For example in Marston St. Lawrence, in addition to the major flint-working sites and numerous isolated arrowheads, no less than seventeen small areas of flints are listed. Indeed the true nature of late Neolithic occupation and land-use is far from being understood.

The Bronze Age

Almost as little is known of the Bronze Age as of the earlier periods in the area under review. A number of stray finds is listed in the Inventory, such as the palstaves from Thenford, Stoke Bruerne and Aston le Walls. Bronze axes are known from Chipping Warden and stone tools of Bronze Age type have also been recorded (e.g. Potterspury and Harpole). A major hoard at Thenford is of interest because, although not accurately located, it may have been found within or near the possible defended hilltop settlement which is generally assumed to be of Iron Age date (Thenford (2)).

No definite Bronze Age settlements are known, though there is some evidence for one beneath the Roman villa at Cosgrove and for another at King's Sutton (6). As with the Neolithic period,

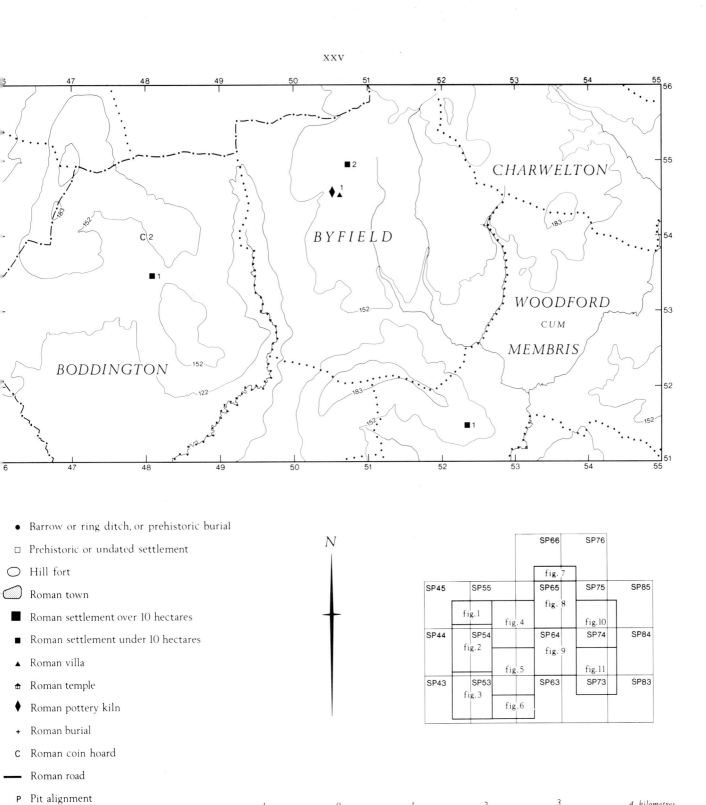

Fig. 1 Prehistoric and Roman sites and finds

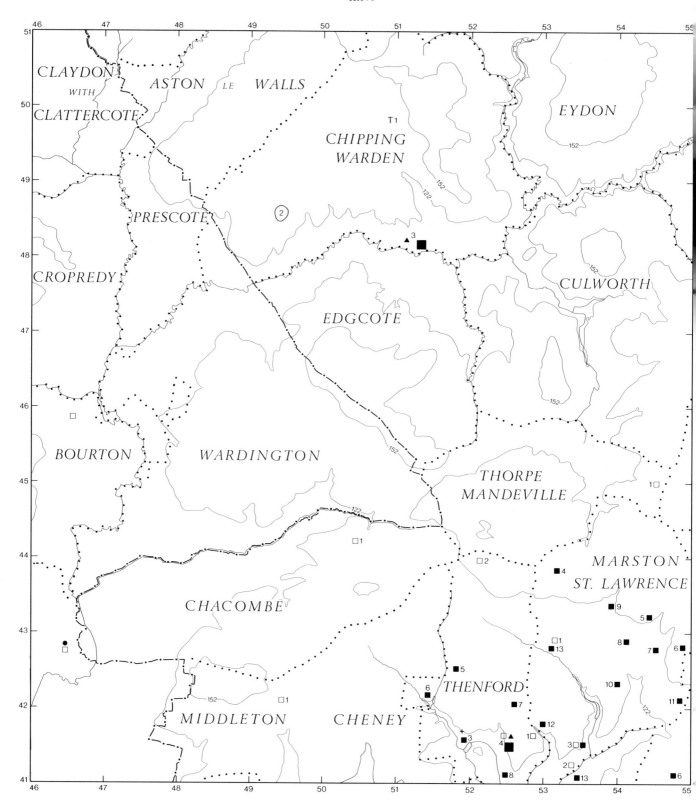

Fig. 2 Prehistoric and Roman sites and finds (for key see fig. 1)

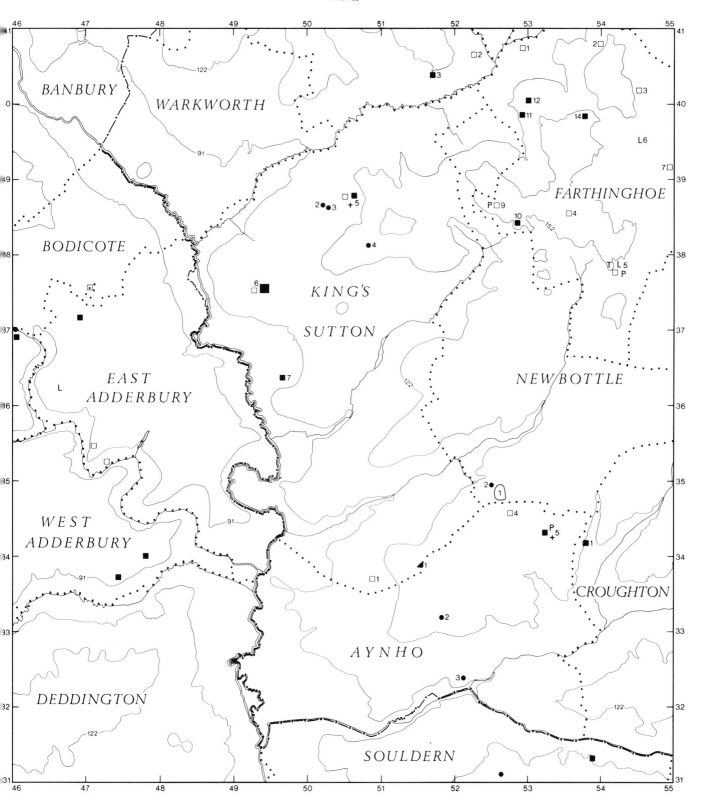

Fig. 3   Prehistoric and Roman sites and finds (for key see fig. 1)

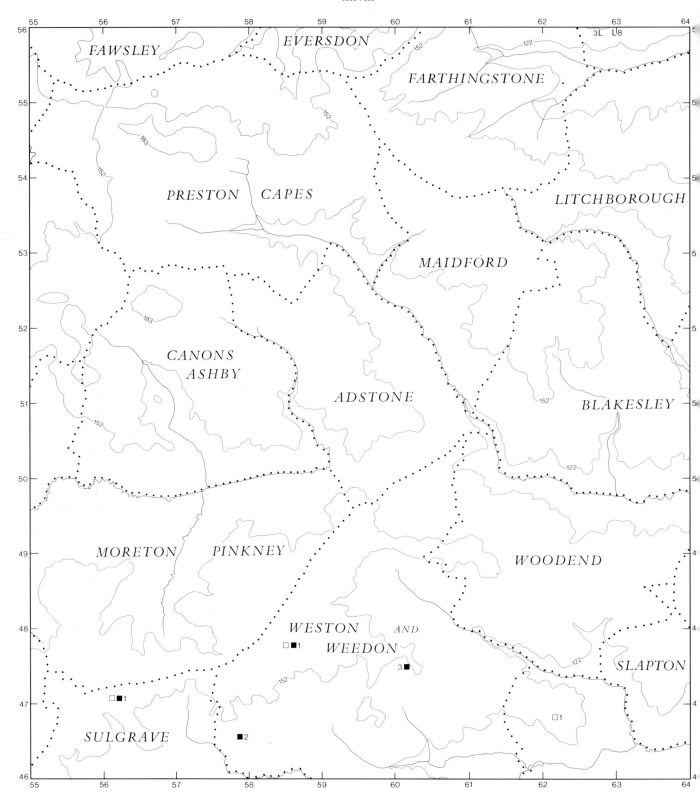

Fig. 4 Prehistoric and Roman sites and finds (for key see fig. 1)

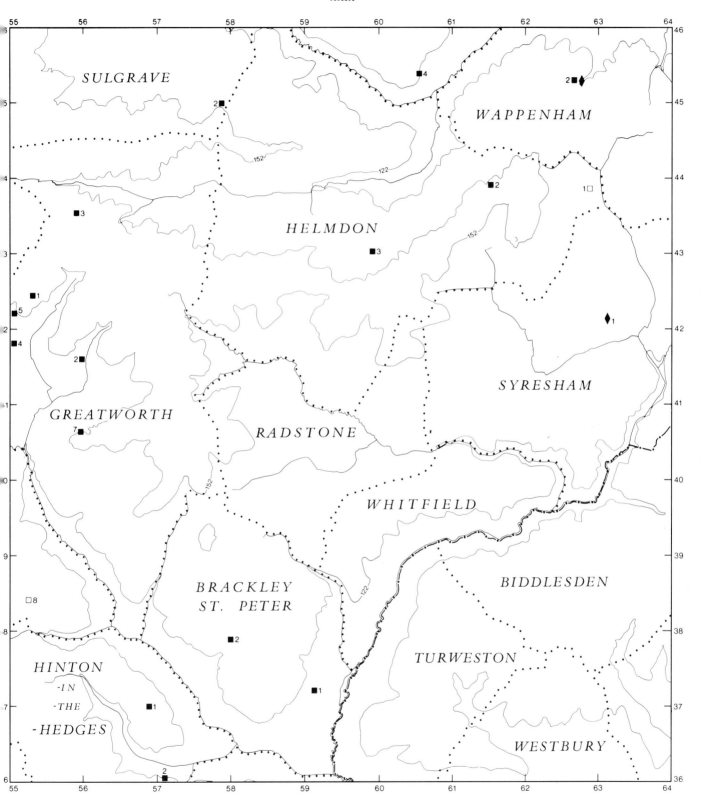

Fig. 5 Prehistoric and Roman sites and finds (for key see fig. 1)

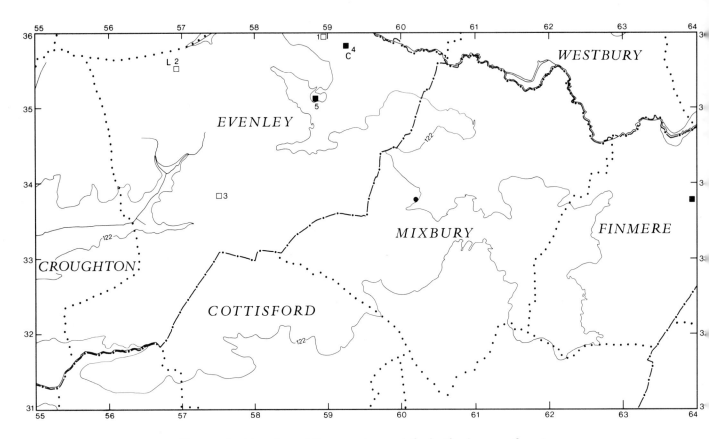

Fig. 6 Prehistoric and Roman sites and finds (for key see fig. 1)

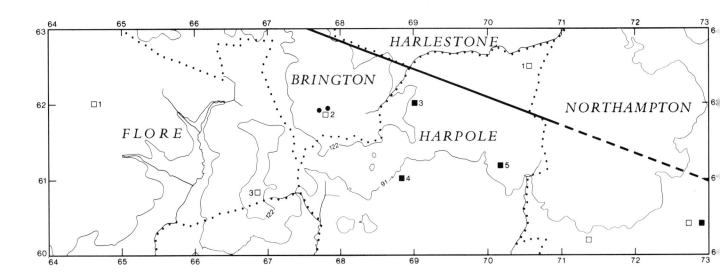

Fig. 7 Prehistoric and Roman sites and finds (for key see fig. 1)

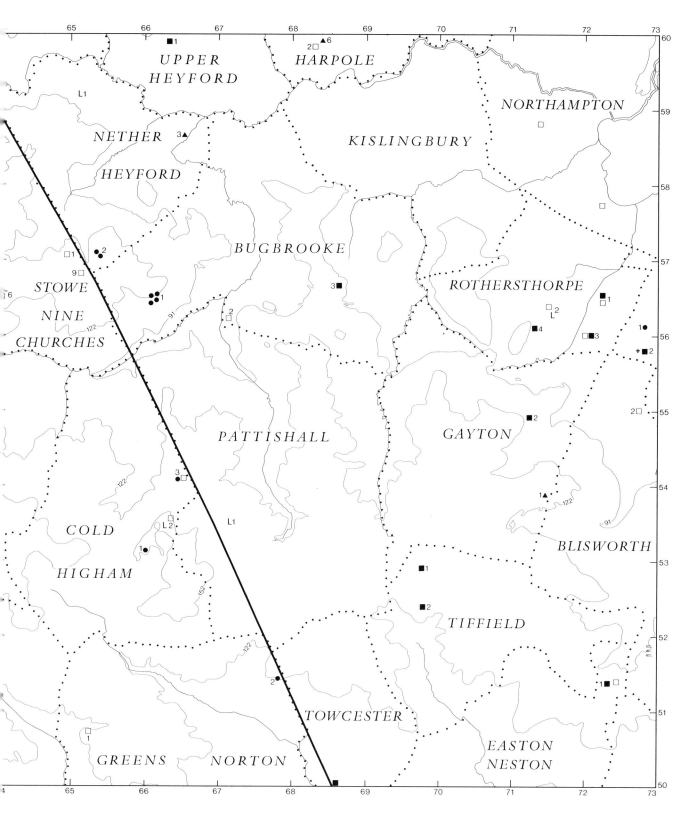

Fig. 8 Prehistoric and Roman sites and finds (for key see fig. 1)

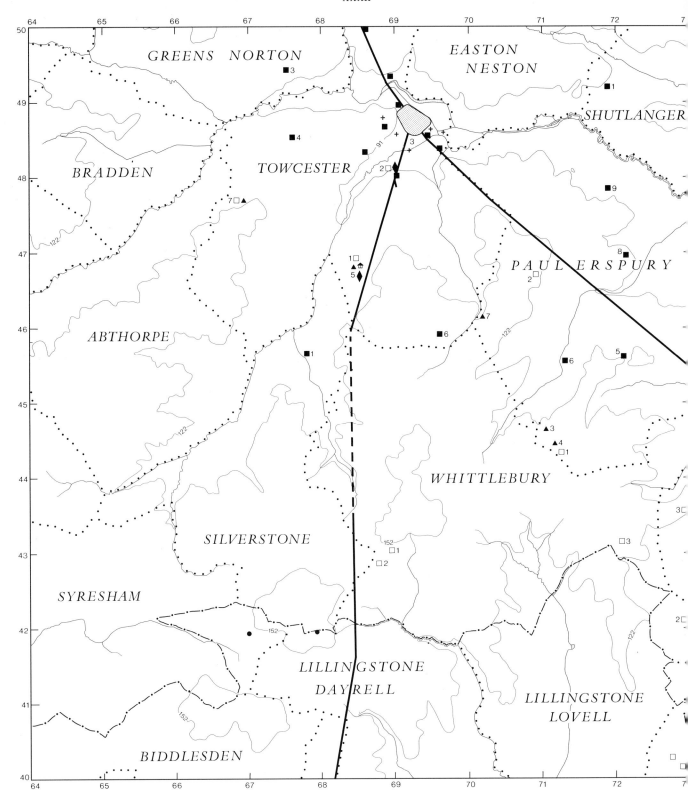

Fig. 9 Prehistoric and Roman sites and finds (for key see fig. 1)

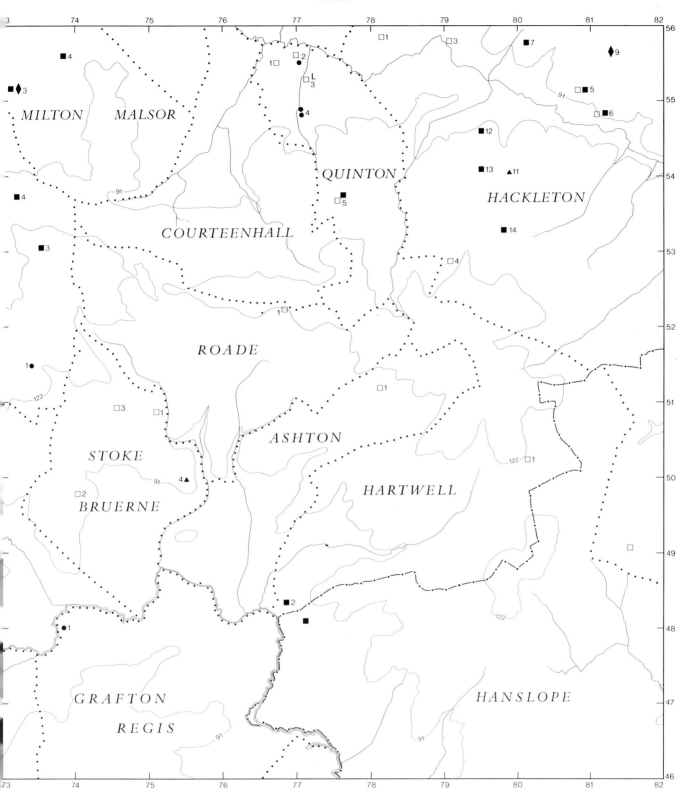

Fig. 10 Prehistoric and Roman sites and finds (for key see fig. 1)

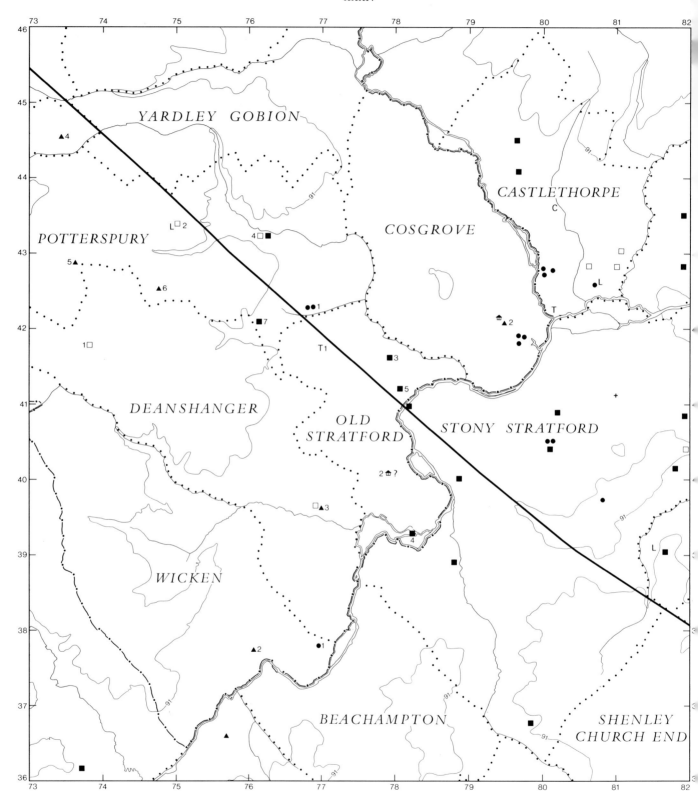

Fig. 11 Prehistoric and Roman sites and finds (for key see fig. 1)

the existence of flint-working sites which appear to be partly of Bronze Age date, and the numerous cropmark sites of enclosures which are at the moment undated, need to be borne in mind in assessing the pattern of Bronze Age settlement.

Flat burials are known from Aynho (1–3) and Milton Malsor (1) and burials within round barrows are listed at King's Sutton (2–4). Several mounds may be barrows, or are barrows reused as windmill mounds in the medieval period (e.g. Blisworth (1), Slapton (3) and Sulgrave (8)), but only excavation can prove their true character. There are very few ring ditches which can be interpreted as ploughed out barrows (e.g. Quinton (2)). Those at Cosgrove and Old Stratford are now known to be former anti-aircraft gun emplacements.

The Iron Age

Only 23 settlements broadly attributable to the Iron Age have been noted in the Inventory, but these include some of considerable interest and importance, for example the hill fort of Rainsborough (Newbottle (1)) and another fort known as Arbury Banks (Chipping Warden (2)). The former has been extensively excavated, but the latter has not been closely studied. The hilltop settlement at Thenford, though it survived into this century, has now been largely destroyed. Finds from the area indicate a long period of occupation, originating before the Iron Age. At least two other settlements (Whittlebury (1) and (2)) remained as earthworks until the 1950s in the former Whittlewood Forest, and one which still survives in Salcey Forest (Hartwell (1)) is an important reminder of what has gone. These settlements have an additional significance in terms of Iron Age occupation in that they lie on land that was waste or forest throughout medieval times. Their existence thus implies a pattern of settlement and land-use very different from that of the historical period. They also suggest a much larger population than has hitherto been presumed.

Other Iron Age settlements are known only from concentrations of pottery found on modern arable land or in quarry faces. Little can be made of the overall distribution and the marked lack of sites in the centre of the area is more likely to be due to lack of fieldwork there than to any real absence of Iron Age occupation. No excavations have been carried out on these sites and thus it is not clear what they represent in terms of settlement type. A few coins, almost all isolated finds, are listed in the Inventory (e.g. Blisworth, Brackley, Farthinghoe and Gayton) but they are too few to form a basis for distributional analysis.

Examples of pit alignments, which are now regarded as being of late Iron Age date, have been found at Aynho (5) and Farthinghoe (9). The former is unrelated to any other archaeological feature but the latter is associated with some undated enclosures. The existence of these and many other cropmarks of undated enclosures and ditches must not be ignored in any discussion of the Iron Age in this area.

ROMAN REMAINS

Almost a hundred Roman settlements of various types are recorded from the area under review. This is less than in the three previous Inventories, but still a considerable number and many more than are known for the Iron Age in the same area. This contrast may be the result of the greater durability of Roman material and its ease of recognition rather than of any real difference in the density of settlement in the two periods, though it is noteworthy that at Thenford and Marston St. Lawrence where intensive fieldwork has taken place nineteen Roman settlements are known but only three Iron Age ones. As has been noted in the earlier Inventories, the density of Roman settlement appears to be the result of an intensification of occupation in a landscape already well populated in late Iron Age times. A number of the Roman sites listed yield evidence of Iron Age occupation as well, suggesting continuity at least in the general area and probably of a particular habitation.

The distribution of known Roman sites in the area cannot reflect the true pattern of settlement. As with the Iron Age and earlier material, there is a gap across the centre of south-west Northamptonshire which certainly results from the lack of fieldwork there. To the E. of Watling Street, and on both sides of it immediately S. of Towcester, there is a fairly even spread of settlements and there is a regular scatter in the extreme S.W. of the county. Elsewhere, except in the parishes of Farthinghoe, Thenford, Marston St. Lawrence, Greatworth, Sulgrave and Weston and Weedon, all of which have been subjected to intensive fieldwork, only two Roman sites are recorded. There is certainly no obvious explanation for this distribution in terms of soils, or indeed modern land-use. It must reflect only a lack of archaeological work there. It would be dangerous, for example, to assume that the concentration of sites to the S.E. of Towcester is entirely due to the proximity of the Roman town.

As with some of the Iron Age sites in the S. of the area, it is of interest to note the existence of Roman settlements within or close to what was to become the medieval Whittlewood Forest. These include not only minor agricultural settlements but at least two major villas (Whittlebury (4) and Potterspury (5)). As with Rockingham Forest in the N.E. of the county, the implications are that the woodland either did not exist or was considerably less extensive in the late prehistoric and Roman periods than it later became.

Most of the small rural sites are only known from scatters of pottery, and those that have associated cropmarks (e.g. Helmdon (2)) show the familiar pattern of interlocked and overlapping rectangular enclosures. Of these only the site at Quinton (5) has been excavated to modern standards; a late Iron Age and early Roman farmstead, with at least one circular wooden house, had been replaced in the late 1st century by a rectangular stone building. The small finds at this site are of interest for they indicate not only a varied agricultural economy but a way of life of some sophistication.

A number of important villas are recorded in the Inventory and many of them have been excavated, to various standards, a situation which is in marked contrast to that in other parts of the county. None of the excavations was complete, but together they indicate the variety of structures loosely defined as villas. They range from the simple corridor building at Towcester (7), which seems to have been largely unaltered throughout its life, to the complicated building at Thenford (4) which underwent a process of enlargement, alteration and rebuilding. There is evidence of large, sophisticated villas at Gayton (1) and Towcester (5) where parts of porticos are recorded; buildings arranged round courtyards include those at Whittlebury (4) and Deanshanger (3). To judge from surface finds, there was an extensive villa or a large settlement at Chipping Warden (3), but only the bath block has been excavated. A similar settlement, which must have comprised much more than a single farm, has been recognised at King's Sutton (6) but the exact nature of this type of occupation remains speculative.

The only Roman town in the area was Lactodurum (Towcester (3)) which lay astride Watling Street where the latter crossed the River Tove and a tributary stream. Although numerous finds have been made within the walled area, no major buildings have yet been recognised and the details of the town's history remain unknown. The general outline of the defences has been recovered, as well as some details of their development. It is the extra-mural occupation that is best understood, in part as a result of railway construction and building work in the 19th century as well as of excavation in advance of modern housing development. The latter has resulted in particular in the discovery of an industrial suburb to the S.W. of the town. The position of Easton Neston Park which extends to the edge of Towcester on the E. has resulted in a complete absence of evidence of occupation on this side of the town, and has also prevented the discovery of at least one other Roman road which may be assumed to have run N.E. towards Northampton.

Other important Roman structures include possible temples at Towcester (5) and Cosgrove (2) and, perhaps, pottery kilns at Milton Malsor (3) and Wappenham (2). Among the more interesting chance finds listed in the Inventory are a celebrated glass beaker from Stoke Bruerne and pewter plates from Croughton and Newbottle. By far the most remarkable discovery is the hoard of unusual silver plaques and bronze head-dresses from Old Stratford (2) which may be from an undiscovered temple.

PAGAN SAXON REMAINS

Important Saxon cemeteries are listed in the Inventory as are other isolated burials and finds. An analysis of the material from burials throughout the county is much needed, but this task is not within the Commission's terms of reference.

The major cemeteries do not appear necessarily to relate either to the preceding late Roman occupation pattern or to the medieval one. For example the large cemetery at Marston St. Lawrence (14) lies at some distance not only from the medieval village but also from the great wealth of earlier material found in the parish. The same is true in the adjacent parish of Thenford (9). However the cemetery at Passenham (Old Stratford (6)) lies within the medieval village, and the one at Milton Malsor (6) has produced evidence of Roman occupation. The burials at King's Sutton were remote from the village but on a site apparently occupied from late Neolithic times onwards. The single burial from Stoke Bruerne lay very close to the village.

In contrast to the previous volumes the present area is notable for the lack of early Saxon settlements; only one certain settlement, at Milton Malsor (5), is recorded. This clearly reflects lack of fieldwork in the area as well as the difficulty of recognition of early Saxon pottery. A possible mid Saxon site is listed in Marston St. Lawrence and a late Saxon one at Farthinghoe (15), both at a distance from later settlements.

MEDIEVAL AND LATER SETTLEMENT

The earliest record of the pattern of medieval settlement is found in Domesday Book of 1086. It indicates a regular scatter of nucleated villages, from 2 km. to 4 km. apart, over the whole region. Many of these villages lay within a unit of land which has survived to the present time as an ecclesiastical parish. A more complicated pattern is recorded in other parishes where minor settlements isolated from the main village appear always to have had their own land units entirely separate from the land of the main village. These settlements have, in the past, usually been regarded as secondary or daughter hamlets of the primary or mother village but this now seems doubtful. There is no evidence that the minor settlements are later than the major ones and they could be interpreted as elements of a system of late Saxon settlement fitted into a pre-existing arrangement of land units of great antiquity. The best example in the area under review is seen in King's Sutton and Newbottle parishes (Fig. 82).

Also of interest are the parishes of Blakesley, Woodend and Abthorpe. Blakesley and Woodend were once a single ecclesiastical parish but the villages of Blakesley and Woodend each had its own associated land unit and so did the now deserted villages of Kirby (Woodend (1)) and Seawell (Blakesley (2)) and the hamlet of Foxley (Blakesley (3)). At Abthorpe the hamlets of Foscote and Charlock (Abthorpe (3) and (5)) both had clearly defined areas of land associated with them. Elsewhere it is not clear whether settlements now within a single parish ever had separate lands. It is not known whether the hamlet and land of Heathencote in Paulerspury (18) were once separate from the rest of the parish, or whether Crowfield (Syresham (4)) was separate from

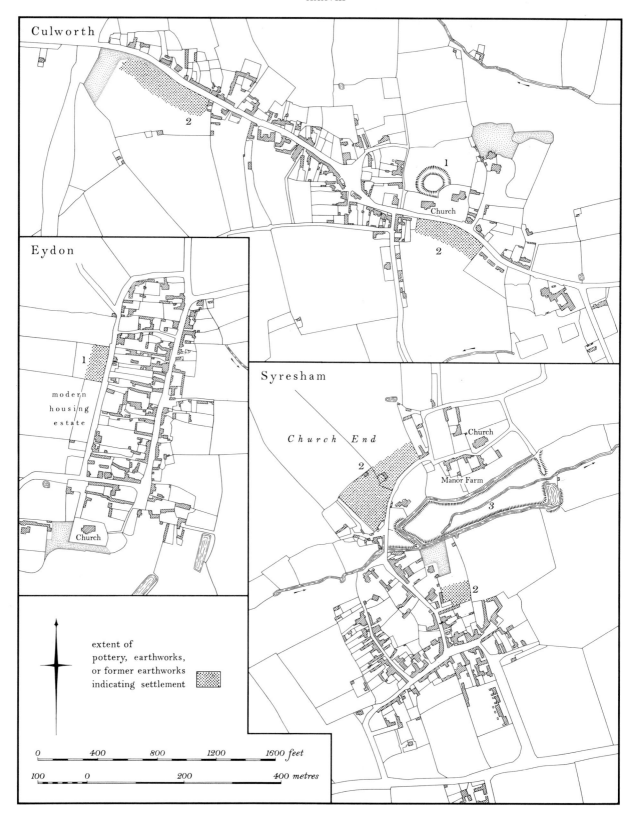

Fig. 12 CULWORTH, EYDON and SYRESHAM Village plans

Syresham. Similarly Astcote, Eastcote and Dalscote (Pattishall (3–5)) may never have had land units separate from that of Pattishall. In all these examples the lack of early documentation makes firm conclusions impossible.

Further questions arise from fieldwork evidence. For example, the old parish of Stoke Bruerne contained the present parish of Shutlanger and clearly included the two separate settlements and their lands. However, an undocumented third medieval settlement of unknown name has been identified at Stoke Bruerne (7) and this makes it difficult to reconstruct exactly the pattern of medieval settlement there. Similarly, the deserted village of Furtho (Potterspury (9)) appeared to have been the only settlement in the medieval parish of Furtho until the discovery of a second medieval settlement formerly in Furtho parish (Old Stratford (9)), the name and history of which are apparently totally unrecorded.

The system of multiple settlements and estates within ecclesiastical parishes also poses problems in the interpretation of surviving documents. The population statistics recorded in the various medieval national taxation returns are of limited value for they rarely make clear whether the figures refer to one settlement or to several. Indeed it appears from these taxation returns that the medieval administrators also failed to understand the overall relationships between groups of settlements for it is common to find successive returns which fail to agree on which settlements were to be taxed together.

Topographical studies taking into account any traceable earthworks have continued to throw light on the origins and development of settlements in Northamptonshire. The period of establishment of villages still remains unknown, place-names suggesting pre-Saxon origins are almost entirely absent, although Walton (King's Sutton (10)) may be one example. Several villages appear to have been created or extended by deliberate planning, for example the W. part of Stoke Bruerne (6) is laid out in a neat grid pattern, and at Eydon (1) and Farthinghoe (16) there are plans of equally regular appearance. The single-street village with greens at either end is another recurring type which may have been the result of planning. Of these, it is possible that Wappenham (3) and Yardley Gobion (1) could have developed gradually, but Weston (Weston and Weedon (8)) has additional features which indicate some degree of deliberate arrangement. The first phase of the deserted village of Astwick (Evenley (9)) also appears to be planned. Another recurring village type, already noted in other parts of the county, has buildings only on one side of a single street. It cannot always be shown that these villages had this form from the beginning (e.g. Warkworth (1) and Walton (King's Sutton (10)), but at the ploughed-out deserted village which probably once represented one of the manors of Furtho (Old Stratford (9)) field evidence shows that there were never buildings on both sides of the street. Such asymmetrical layouts presumably indicate planning.

Evidence of polyfocal villages, settlements which have developed into their later form from two or more discrete centres, has also been noted. Moreton Pinkney (1) seems to have been a double village with two parts each centred on a green. Culworth (2) also may have originated as two settlements, with different names at least in 1086. Quinton (7–9) appears once to have had two or possibly three separate centres and Helmdon (4) had two quite distinct parts before later additions were made. Syresham (2) still retains two distinct parts. Perhaps the best example of a village of this type is Paulerspury. There the present large sprawling settlement can be seen to have been made up of at least five centres. In contrast, the two villages of Purston (King's Sutton (11) and Newbottle (4)) lay side by side and apparently used the single main street between them, but each had its own land unit and each lay in a different parish.

Villages once established were subject to many changes throughout the medieval period; some grew larger, others declined or were abandoned and many underwent changes of location. All these processes have been tentatively identified in the area under review, although in most examples lack of firm documentation makes it difficult to establish a chronology. Some villages certainly had planned additions. The best example is Helmdon (4) where a neat rectangular area, bounded by a bank and ditch and containing the church, manor house and other dwellings, appears to have been added to one of the earlier parts of the village. The two parts of Culworth may have been linked together by the creation of a market place, possibly in the 13th century. Upper Boddington (Boddington (3)) also has indications that a rectangular arrangement of streets and lanes was added to a single-street village, and the same process is perhaps visible at Maidford (1). Evenley too appears to be a small, single-street village to which has been added a very large square green. Blakesley (1) is more complicated; not only is there an obvious planned addition, but it is also possible that the present green is an insertion between two older parts. A striking example of alteration is evident at the deserted village of Astwick (Evenley (9)) where the surviving earthworks show clearly that the original rectangular layout of the village was overlaid by a less regular street pattern associated with buildings of late medieval form.

The forest-edge village of Silverstone is another example of a village with several discrete centres. These may originally have been separate units but here secondary growth on the waste is an alternative explanation. All the interpretations of village development given here are tentative. In the final analysis only excavation within and around these villages will elucidate their origins and growth.

The reasons for other changes, movement, decline and desertion, are often obscure. They usually took place over many centuries, through a combination of circumstances and rarely as a sudden response to a single cause. At Edgcote (1) for example, though the village was finally cleared for emparking in the 18th century, it had apparently been declining in size for centuries. Most of the villages that were deliberately removed, whether for sheep-farming in the late medieval period or for landscape parks in the post-medieval period, were always small and very susceptible to the pressures of major land-owners or economic changes. The same applies to those villages which seem to have been reduced to hamlets by the 19th century.

It is difficult to understand decline or desertion when the process took place in the medieval period. The lack of detailed documentation giving population statistics over a continuous period makes it almost impossible to isolate either general or specific conditions or events which caused changes in individual villages, or in the overall pattern of settlement. Few of the national taxation returns are comparable even for the best-documented villages and many villages, especially the smaller places, are almost entirely undocumented. There appears to have been depopulation in many villages between the late 14th century and the early 16th century and this is usually explained as being the result of clearance for sheep. Stuchbury and Halse (Greatworth (10) and (13)), Caswell and Field Burcote (Greens Norton (5) and (6)), Newbottle (3) and the two Purstons (King's Sutton (11) and Newbottle (4)) are examples. However, the earlier history of all these is either unknown or incomplete and the conditions which led to their final abandonment are not fully known.

The post-medieval changes to villages are better understood, as a result of improved documentation. Those cleared for emparking, such as Edgcote (1) and Courteenhall (2), are fairly closely dated. Elsewhere the process of continuous shrinkage or movement can to some extent be established though it is rarely obvious why it took place. At Greens Norton (4) 18th or 19th-century shrinkage or abandonment can be identified and the same is true of Upper Heyford (2), Rothersthorpe (5), Passenham (Old Stratford (7)) and Foscote (Abthorpe (3)). At all these places however, it is clear that early movement or shrinkage, quite undatable without excavation, had already occurred. At Hulcote (Easton Neston (3)) the early 19th-century replanning of the whole village to produce the pretty estate hamlet is of some interest.

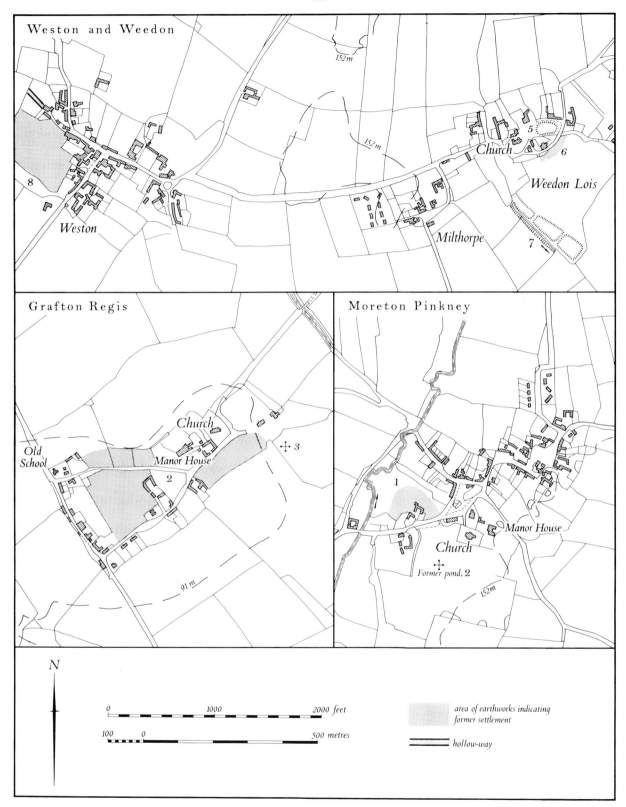

Fig. 13 GRAFTON REGIS, MORETON PINKNEY and WESTON AND WEEDON Village plans

MEDIEVAL EARTHWORKS
Settlement Remains

Thirty-one deserted hamlets and villages are recorded in the Inventory: Foscote and Charlock (Abthorpe (3) and (5)), Appletree (Aston le Walls (1)), Seawell and Foxley (Blakesley (2) and (3)), Trafford (Chipping Warden (10)), Potcote (Cold Higham (5)), Courteenhall (2), Easton Neston (2), Edgcote (1), Astwick (Evenley (9)), Steane (Farthinghoe (18)), Stuchbury and Halse (Greatworth (10) and (13)), Caswell and Field Burcote (Greens Norton (5) and (6)), Hartwell (3), Bozenham (Hartwell (6)), Falcutt and Astwell (Helmdon (5) and (6)), Walton and Purston (King's Sutton (10) and (11)), Moreton Pinkney (3), Newbottle (3), Purston (Newbottle (4)), Old Stratford (9), Furtho (Potterspury (9)), Lower Radstone (Radstone (2)), Hyde (Roade (2)), Stoke Bruerne (7) and Kirby (Woodend (1)).

Most of the sites have been damaged or altered by later activity, much of it in the present century. Bozenham and the Purston in Newbottle were ploughed over and largely destroyed in antiquity. Astwell was partly obliterated by 17th and 18th-century gardens and emparking and Furtho also had a later garden laid across parts of it. In recent years Caswell, Seawell, Walton, Hartwell and Potcote have been mainly or completely destroyed by industry or agriculture and Hyde by housing estates. Others such as Astwick, Stuchbury and Trafford have been partly damaged by other modern agricultural activities.

Despite this destruction there is still sufficient evidence from existing earthworks, air photographs or early maps and plans for certain features to be identified. Most deserted villages, at least in their final stages, lay either along single streets or around more complicated street systems, all later reduced to hollow-ways. Impressive hollow-ways still remain at Appletree, Astwick, Stuchbury, Halse, Lower Radstone and Kirby and less well-defined ones at Trafford, Foscote, Astwell and Purston. Air photographic evidence shows the same features at Walton and Furtho in Old Stratford. Well-preserved house-sites survive at Astwick, Stuchbury and Kirby. At Astwick clearly defined traces of stone buildings remain up to 0.5 m. high. Less well-defined house-sites in the form of raised or sunken platforms are visible at Foxley, Charlock, Trafford, Steane and Purston in King's Sutton. Villages which were abandoned or cleared at a late date are notable for their lack of good house-sites or indeed closes and paddocks. The best example of this is Courteenhall where after clearance most of the former settlement area appears to have been deliberately flattened; the same process seems to have taken place at Edgcote and Foscote.

By far the most important deserted village in the area in terms of surviving earthworks is Astwick in Evenley where a complete alteration of the village's layout is visible. Another important site is Charlock in Abthorpe where the small hamlet appears to have been laid out within, and at the end of, a pre-existing common-field furlong.

As elsewhere in the county, the remains of shrunken and moved villages are common. Nearly seventy sites are recorded in the Inventory and almost every village has some place where houses formerly stood. Some of the remaining earthworks are well preserved and of considerable interest. These include a hollow-way at Upper Boddington (Boddington (3)), house-sites at Alderton (Grafton Regis (7)) and Passenham (Old Stratford (7)) and abandoned closes at Weston (Weston and Weedon (8)). Modern destruction has been on a large scale. The recent loss of the earthworks at Plumpton (Weston and Weedon (10)) is particularly unfortunate as they indicate that the village had a planned extension to its original nucleus. The continuing process of destruction of earthworks by modern development in many villages is a great loss to scholarship. The remains are often slight and of little apparent interest and so are easily destroyed. They often contain the only clues to the physical history of a village. For example, the remains at Kislingbury (1) are unimpressive, but their excavation could confirm or disprove the theory put forward in the Inventory that they represent the older part of the village and that the settlement was subsequently extended to the E.

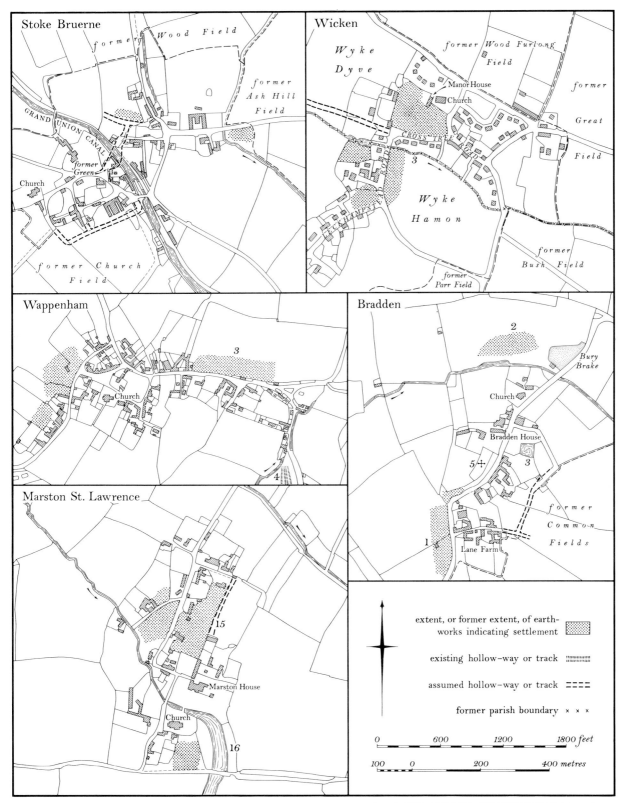

Fig. 14   BRADDEN, MARSTON ST. LAWRENCE, STOKE BRUERNE, WAPPENHAM and
WICKEN   Village plans

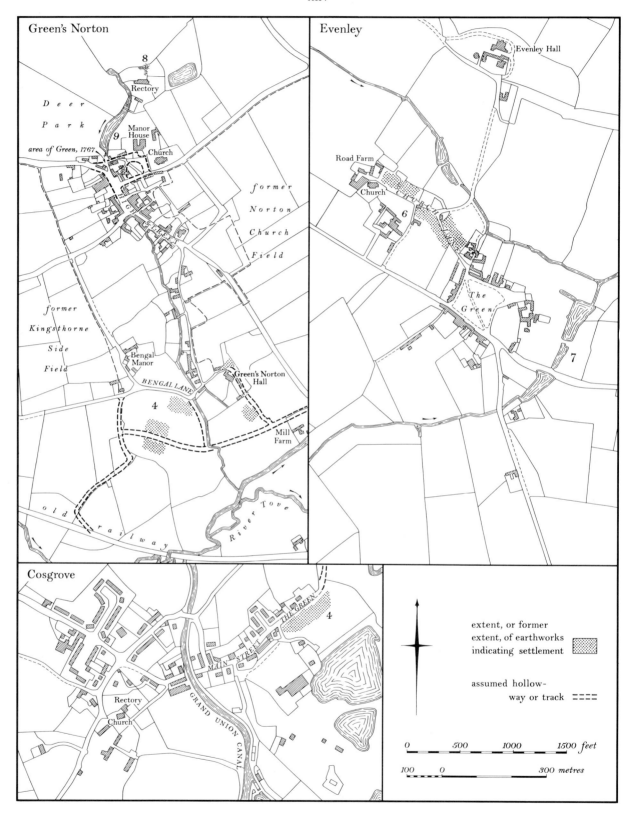

Fig. 15 COSGROVE, EVENLEY and GREENS NORTON Village plans

Castles

The remains of a number of large mottes or ringworks have been recorded. The most notable of these are the ringworks at Sulgrave (3), Culworth (1) and Weedon Lois (Weston and Weedon (5)) which appear to have been constructed by the tenant-in-chief, recorded in Domesday Book. However, despite excavations at Sulgrave, the exact sequence of development of the ringworks is not understood. Another ringwork or motte survives at Alderton (Grafton Regis (5)) but the only true motte, that at Towcester (8), has been altered to form part of a garden in the post-medieval period.

Moated Sites

Several earthworks which have at some time been described as moated sites are listed in the Inventory. Two of these are probably 18th or 19th-century landscape features (Cosgrove (3) and Woodend (3)). Of the others those at Caldecote (Towcester (12)), Yardley Gobion (2), Hinton-in-the-Hedges (3), Harpole (7) and Chipping Warden (5) have been totally destroyed either recently or in the past, and those at Easton Neston (6), Milton Malsor (7) and Moor End (Yardley Gobion (3)) have all been partly destroyed, damaged or altered in post-medieval times to such an extent that future work on them would be of limited value. The interesting circular moat at Ashton (2) has a standing building within it. Only those at Helmdon (11), Passenham (Old Stratford (8)), Potterspury (8) and Wicken (5) are relatively undamaged. All the certain medieval moats are comparatively small though some had outer enclosures and fishponds attached to them. Most were constructed around medieval manor houses, e.g. Yardley Gobion, Caldecote, Hinton-in-the-Hedges, Harpole, Milton Malsor and Passenham. The one at Helmdon is likely to have been a park-keeper's lodge, but the other isolated ones, for example at Wicken and Potterspury, are more difficult to explain unless they represent outlying farms established in the parochial wastes or woodlands.

Only one moat, at Quinton (6), has been excavated to modern standards. It appears to have been a manor house site as the remains of a 12th-century stone hall, solar and kitchen range were discovered. The outer paddocks and enclosures have not been investigated.

Manor House Sites

In addition to moated manor houses, the Inventory lists several other sites of large houses. These vary considerably in their history and physical form. The earthworks at Aston le Walls (2) are the remains of paddocks and closes around the extant manor house, but those at Greatworth (9), Thorpe Mandeville (3), Alderton (Grafton Regis (6)) and Warkworth (2) are the sites of post-medieval houses demolished or destroyed at a late date. The first three are associated with the remains of contemporary gardens. Little trace remains on the sites of the medieval manor houses at Thenford (10) and Litchborough (1) as a result of destruction. The earthworks at Helmdon (4), Bradden (2) and Chacombe (3) are well preserved and the last is also associated with a series of medieval fishponds (5). The best earthworks are those at Hulcote (Easton Neston (4)), where the house-site is surrounded by closes, some with ridge-and-furrow within them, and there are fishponds. At Grafton Regis (4) excavations have shown that a small monastic site was remodelled in the late medieval period to become a manorial dwelling which in turn was abandoned in the late 15th century when the whole area was ploughed over and incorporated into the common fields of the parish.

Monastic Sites

The sites of five small monastic houses are known from the area under review. Of these, no trace remains of the Benedictine Priory of Luffield which lay in the S. of Silverstone parish, astride the Buckinghamshire county boundary. Only some fishponds remain at Weedon (Weston and Weedon (7)) and the only earthworks of the Augustinian Priory of Chacombe (2) appear to be part of the precinct boundary and the much modified fishponds. At the site of the Cistercian Priory at Showsley (Easton Neston (8)) again only the fishponds survive, though some coffin slabs were discovered in the 19th century. The excavation of an assumed manor-house site at Grafton Regis (4) revealed an early monastic site about which little is known. The structural remains discovered during excavation are important and unusual.

Deer Parks

Several medieval deer parks have been identified though not all have been located on the ground; the position of the park at Silverstone remains quite unknown and the one at Greatworth (12) is not located with any certainty. The boundaries of the park at Wicken (6) have not been identified and those around Gayton Park (Gayton (8)) are hardly recoverable. On the other hand the well-preserved boundary at Helmdon (12) appears to belong to a deer park which is undocumented. Among the parks with surviving early boundaries are those at Stoke Bruerne (8) and Paulerspury (20). A notable aspect of the medieval deer parks in the area under review is the evidence for their enlargement in the 16th century. Such enlargements, usually as a result of royal instructions, have been recognised at Hartwell (8), Grafton Regis (8) and Yardley Gobion (8). These, though still termed deer parks, may have been the result of Crown policy of the period to encourage the breeding of horses (J. Thirsk, *Horses in Early Modern England* (1978)). All the medieval deer parks contain areas of ridge-and-furrow though it is not clear whether this pre-dates the establishment of the parks. The 16th-century enlargements also include ridge-and-furrow and some can be proved to have been enclosed from former arable land.

Fishponds

Numerous medieval fishponds are included in the Inventory but other possible ones which have been radically altered in recent times have been omitted. Most of the well-preserved fishponds can be assigned to the various types described in the second Northamptonshire Inventory (*Northants.* II (1979), lvii–lix) on the basis of their physical characteristics.

Type A. These ponds are formed by the construction of a simple earth dam across a valley. The best example is at Silverstone (2) and there is another at Moreton Pinkney (2).

Type B. Ponds in this category are formed by the construction of a dam, as in type A, but in addition large quantities of spoil have been removed to make them deeper and flat-bottomed. They are characterized by steep artificial scarps along one or both sides where the valley slopes have been cut away. Such ponds exist at Weedon (Weston and Weedon (7)), Thorpe Mandeville (4) and Paulerspury (15).

Type C. These are set on valley sides with dams along the sides of the ponds and the ponds themselves formed by removal of spoil from the hillside. This type is usually placed on a spring line. Some of the ponds at Aston le Walls (3) can be assigned to this category.

Type D. These ponds, constructed on relatively level ground, are entirely surrounded by banks made of spoil from the interior or from the side leats. The large pond at Radstone (3) and those at Stuchbury (Greatworth (11)) and Astwell (Helmdon (7)) are of this type.

Type E. These are simple sunken ponds, usually of small size, and with no real dams or embankments, for example at Culworth (4).

No ponds of Types F and G have been recorded in this area.

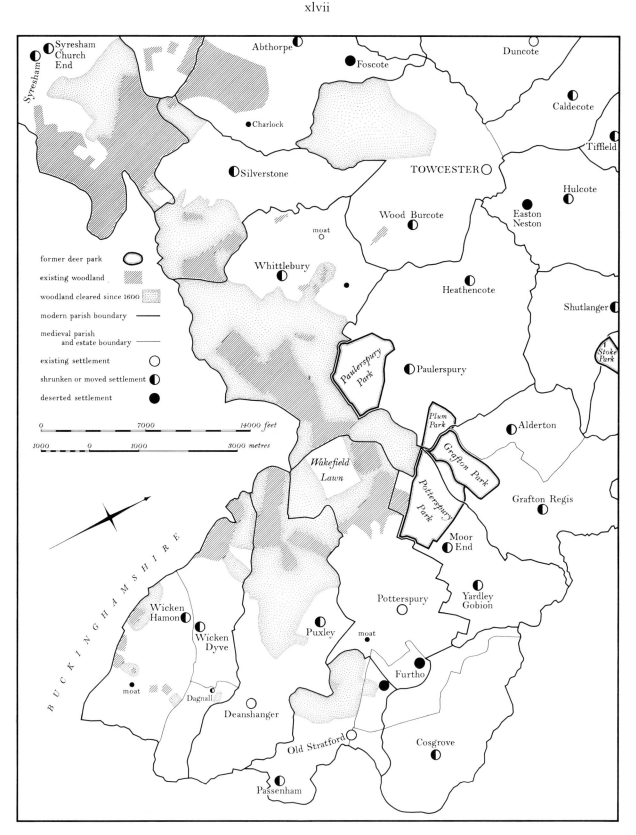

Fig. 16 WHITTLEWOOD FOREST Medieval settlements and estates

Many fishponds occur in groups of up to four, often set one below the other along a valley. These probably relate to intensive fish-breeding where each pond has a separate function. Such groups of ponds occur at Chacombe (5), Chipping Warden (6), Evenley (7), Greatworth (11) and Weston and Weedon (7). The largest group of fishponds is at Aston le Walls (3) where no less than 20 ponds are identifiable. This site is of interest also because some of the ponds appear to have been constructed across a hollow-way and thus to have prevented its use.

Two features already noted elsewhere in the county have been recorded, islands and ridge-and-furrow within ponds. Islands in fishponds may be low and rectangular or tall and conical as at Aston le Walls (3), or flat-topped and circular as at Radstone (3). The pond at Radstone has recently been restored and the island has regained its medieval appearance. An 'island' of unusual shape in the fishponds at Stuchbury (Greatworth (11)) is inexplicable as it appears to have lain below the water-level of the original ponds. No new functions for these islands have been suggested (RCHM *Northants.*, II (1979), lix).

One fishpond at Paulerspury (16) has ridge-and-furrow within it and it is possible that this is comparable with examples at Dingley and Braybrooke (RCHM *Northants.*, II (1979), Dingley (3), Braybrooke (1)) where the ridge-and-furrow represents medieval ploughing of the bottom of the pond as part of a rotation of fish-breeding and arable cultivation.

The most important fishponds in the area are those at Silverstone (2). The smaller ones are probably breeding ponds, the largest the main fishery. The latter was doubtless the most extensive area of artificial water in the county in medieval times. As they were in royal ownership these ponds are extremely well documented and a number of interesting details of their management has emerged. It also appears that the earlier parish boundary between Silverstone and Abthorpe was moved N. outside the pond, presumably to ensure that the pond lay within one parish for ease of administration.

Several post-medieval ponds are recorded. The most extensive, at Thorpe Mandeville (7), are probably of 18th-century date and may have been constructed for fishing, boating and wild-fowling as well as to enhance the landscape. They contain features which could relate to any of these activities.

Watermills
Of the numerous watermills that once existed in the area only those of special interest are recorded in the Inventory. These include the dam of a very large mill pond at Upper Boddington (Boddington (4)) and the complex series of leats and ponds of the mill at Astwell (Helmdon (10)).

Windmills
As with watermills, the number of documented windmills in the area is considerable and the recording of the mounds which often remain after the demolition of mills has been selective. Mounds which are definitely the sites of mills but which may be misinterpreted in the future as possible barrows, for example those at Old Stratford (10), Radstone (4) and Thenford (12), have been included, as have mounds where there is considerable doubt as to whether they are the sites of mills or barrows, for example Sulgrave (8) and Thorpe Mandeville (9). Windmill mounds of special interest are also listed including a mound at Chipping Warden (7) which lies over earlier ridge-and-furrow that in turn overlies the ramparts of the Iron Age fort there.

CULTIVATION REMAINS
Ridge-and-furrow in Open Fields
Large areas of south-west Northamptonshire bear traces of ridge-and-furrow. Indeed more survives here than elsewhere in the county and in certain parishes, notably Moreton Pinkney and

Weston and Weedon, the pattern of ridge-and-furrow is almost completely recoverable. In medieval times part at least of every economic land-unit associated with a settlement seems to have been cultivated. Thus in Abthorpe parish each of the three settlements, Abthorpe, Foscote and Charlock, had its own field system. In some parishes almost the entire area seems to have been in strip cultivation at some time (e.g. Moreton Pinkney (4)) but elsewhere there were large expanses which were always woodland or waste, or that were cultivated by other means. This is particularly true of parishes such as Syresham, Whittlebury and Silverstone which lay on the edges of Whittlewood Forest, or Hartwell which lay close to Salcey Forest.

In some areas the lack of ridge-and-furrow is due to modern cultivation, on light soils which never produced well-developed ridges. The higher areas of Oolite Limestone and Northampton Sand in the parishes of Aynho, Croughton and Thorpe Mandeville have very little ridge-and-furrow on them. In contrast, the only part of Nether Heyford which has no ridge-and-furrow is the Heyford Hills, an outcrop of Northampton Sand in the S.W. of the parish.

There are several dated maps which show the detailed layout of the former common fields. These include maps of Blisworth (1808), Brackley (1840), Bradden (1803) and Weston and Weedon (1593). They confirm the accepted view that the ridges were 'lands' or 'selions', groups of which made up the units of property (individual strips). The strips themselves had no physical demarcation. Other maps show the general area of arable land at the time of enclosure, but examination of the ridge-and-furrow on the ground shows that at various times this cultivation was more widespread than the maps indicate. Most of the medieval deer parks have ridge-and-furrow within their boundaries (e.g. Gayton (9) and Stoke Bruerne (9)) but its date is unknown. At Quinton (11) and Bradden (7) ridge-and-furrow lies on land which is depicted as meadow on maps of 1815 and 1803 respectively.

Enclosure of the common fields was carried out over a long period of time. The fields of a number of deserted villages were enclosed, usually for sheep, in the late 15th and early 16th centuries. These included Potcote (Cold Higham (6)) in 1499, Walton (King's Sutton (13)) in 1487, Purston (King's Sutton (13) and Newbottle (7)) in 1495, and Caswell (Greens Norton (10)) in 1509. There was little enclosure in the latter part of the 16th century and it was not until the first half of the 17th century that further enclosures took place, usually by agreement between major land owners. Among the parishes enclosed then were Furtho (Potterspury (17)) in 1600, Culworth (6) in 1612, Greatworth (14) in 1634 and part of Litchborough (5) in 1647. Very little enclosure is recorded for the late 17th century. The first Parliamentary Act of Enclosure, for Grafton Regis (9), was passed in 1727, and only one other, for Chipping Warden (11) in 1733, became law before the main flood of Parliamentary Enclosures commenced in 1758. Between 1758 and 1800 no less than 26 parishes were formally enclosed; the remaining 17 lost their common fields between 1800 and 1840.

Many minor details of ridge-and-furrow already noted elsewhere in the county have again been recorded. Among the most notable are features related to alterations of the layout of the fields, probably in the post-medieval period. For example the joining up of two, three or even four adjacent ridges into a single ridge has been noted at Aston le Walls (4), Radstone (5), Chacombe (6) and Gayton (9), though the exact reason for this is unknown. A more common procedure is the joining up of adjacent end-on furlongs by ploughing over the headlands, so producing unusually long ridges of double or, in one case (King's Sutton (13)), triple reversed-S curves. This probably results from the change over from ox to horse traction, which allowed longer plough runs. The considerable tenurial changes implied by the relatively simple agricultural alterations to the fields are not apparently documented. The abandonment of parts of ridges, so that a new headland is created on top of the older ridge leaving them and the original headland with an uneven and disturbed appearance, is particularly well marked at Warkworth (3).

The remains of cultivation on steep slopes which have been subject to land-slips have again been noted, all on unstable Upper Lias Clay deposits. Small areas exist at Gayton (9) and Purston (Newbottle (7)); at Farthinghoe (20) part of an area of land-slips was cultivated in ridge-and-furrow, but the rest was apparently too steep, and too disturbed by slumping, for ploughing to be undertaken. The most notable example of ploughing on land-slips is at Edgcote (2) where ridge-and-furrow occurs on the treads of massive terraces formed by the collapse of the hillside, and is also visible over and around stabilized mudflows on the lower slopes.

The most interesting piece of ridge-and-furrow in the area under review is at Kirby (Woodend (4)) where there is evidence, within one field, of over-ploughing of land-slips, shortening of furlongs, and even the formation of ridges over and at right angles to older ridges.

Ridge-and-Furrow in 'old enclosures'

Ridge-and-furrow can often be traced in fields described as 'old enclosures' on 19th-century and earlier maps. This type of ridge-and-furrow sometimes appears to have a direct relationship with other earthworks and indicates changes of land use at some period. The deserted village of Charlock (Abthorpe (5)) seems to have been inserted into the end of an earlier furlong, the curved boundaries of which are still reflected in the form of the settlement. At Paulerspury (10) the opposite process is visible, with ridge-and-furrow riding over and destroying earlier house-sites, and at the deserted village of Kirby (Woodend (1)) almost all the surviving earthworks have been ploughed over at some time after the abandonment of the site. Another example of a change in land-use of this kind is at Grafton Regis where the site of the manor house (4), previously a monastic building, was completely ploughed over and almost obliterated by ridge-and-furrow some time after the area was abandoned in the late 15th century. In this case the land was incorporated into the common fields which existed until enclosure in 1727.

Nineteenth-Century Ridge-and-Furrow

In a number of places, especially around and within the former Whittlewood Forest, there are large rectangular fields which bear traces of broad, exactly straight ridge-and-furrow up to 7 m. wide. This is presumably of 19th-century date and was perhaps formed by steam-ploughing in the latter part of that century. It occurs in the parishes of Syresham, Silverstone and Deanshanger and some of it must date from after 1853 when a Disafforestation Act was passed for Whittlewood and large areas of land were cleared for cultivation.

POST-MEDIEVAL EARTHWORKS

Garden Remains

The remains of post-medieval gardens, often elaborate, associated with important houses, have continued to be recognised; eleven have been recorded in the Inventory, all but one of late 16th or 17th-century date. None covers an extensive area except the site at Purston (Newbottle (5)) which appears never to have been completed, though it was planned on a large scale. The gardens at Furtho (Potterspury (9)), Shutlanger (3), Farthinghoe (17) and (19) and Greens Norton (8) have all been damaged by subsequent activity, but the terraces of the 17th-century garden at Astwell (Helmdon (9)) are virtually complete as are those at Thorpe Mandeville (3). The best example is at Alderton (Grafton Regis (6)) where the original layout of terraces, ponds and a mount are all well preserved. The only late garden is the small 18th-century terraced and walled area at Greatworth (9) which belonged to a house destroyed in 1793. An unusual site is the medieval motte at Towcester (8) which has been modified to form part of a post-medieval garden.

Tramways

Two tramways, both associated with the construction of canals, have been recorded. The one at Rothersthorpe (6) has now been destroyed but the one at Blisworth (6), which was built in 1800 to carry goods between Stoke Bruerne and Blisworth during the delayed construction of Blisworth Tunnel, remains virtually complete. It is an unusual and important survival from the early canal era.

Undated Earthworks

Without excavation the purpose and date of a number of earthworks listed in the Inventory must remain speculative. The most important of these is the large fortified enclosure known as The Bury at Rothersthorpe (8). Though apparently in use in the medieval period it may well be prehistoric in origin. The earthwork known as Wallow Bank at Chipping Warden (12) has been the subject of much speculation in the past but no convincing explanation for it has been propounded.

Miscellaneous Earthworks

As in the previous volumes earthworks associated with woodland management in medieval and later times have been omitted from the Inventory. The innumerable banks and ditches which bound and cross the areas of surviving woodland are important but little understood and would repay detailed study. The tramways associated with the ironstone-mining of the late 19th and 20th century in the Blisworth and King's Sutton area have also been omitted and these too warrant investigation before an important aspect of the industrial archaeology of the county can be understood.

AN INVENTORY OF
THE ARCHAEOLOGICAL MONUMENTS
IN SOUTH-WESTERN NORTHAMPTONSHIRE
Arranged alphabetically by Parishes

1   ABTHORPE

(OS 1:10000 [a] SP 64 NW, [b] SP 64 SW, [c] SP 64 NE, [d] SP 64 SE)

The small parish occupies about 790 hectares on the S. side of the R. Tove. Its W. and E. boundaries are defined by small streams. The village is situated close to the river on a small deposit of glacial sands and gravels sloping N.W., but the greater part of the parish, between 135 m. and 145 m. above OD, is covered by Boulder Clay.

No remains of prehistoric or Roman date have been noted in the parish but there are earthworks of two medieval settlements, Foscote (3) and Charlock (5), as well as within the village of Abthorpe (1).

MEDIEVAL AND LATER

The handle of a medieval jug with stamped lettering on it was found in Abthorpe village in 1964 (NM; *Med. Arch.*, 11 (1967), 233–4).

[a](1) SETTLEMENT REMAINS (SP 647466; Fig. 18), lie immediately N. of Abthorpe village, on land sloping N., on Upper Lias Clay and glacial gravels between 100 m. and 110 m. above OD. The earthworks are typical of the abandoned closes and paddocks that surround many villages in the county and consist of shallow ditches and low scarps which mark the lines of former hedges. Some of these closes have traces of ridge-and-furrow within them. Two other features in the area are worthy of note. In the centre of the remaining earthworks ('a' on plan) an area of disturbed ground represents the remains of a farmstead which still stood in 1823 (map in NRO). A more regular pattern of closes further S.W., around Abthorpe Manor ('b' on plan), probably indicates the paddocks of the manor house. A rectangular sunken area ('c' on plan) may be the remains of part of a 17th-century garden. (RAF VAP CPE/UK/1926, 1228–9; CUAP, AWN70; air photographs in NMR)

[c](2) PONDS (SP 652466; Fig. 18), lie immediately N.E. of Abthorpe village, on Upper Lias Clay at 104 m. above OD. Today there are two irregular ponds, but originally there was a single rectangular one. A dam up to 1.5 m. high still survives at the downstream end and returns along the E. side as a bank between 1.5 m. and 0.5 m. high. (RAF VAP CPE/UK/1926, 1229–30)

[c](3) DESERTED HAMLET OF FOSCOTE (SP 660473; Figs. 17, 19, 20, 21 and 22), lies in a small combe in the E. of the parish, on clay at 107 m. above OD. In medieval times the hamlet was the centre of a unit of land with its own field system entirely separate from Abthorpe. Foscote is not recorded in documents until 1200 (PN *Northants.*, 90) but is doubtless much older. It rarely occurs in the national taxation records as it was usually included with Abthorpe or Towcester. However, in 1301 ten people paid the Lay Subsidy (PRO, E179/155/31), and in 1488 80 acres of land were enclosed and 12 people were evicted from one of the two manors there (K. J. Allison *et al.*, *The Deserted Villages of Northants.* (1966), 40); in 1525 five people paid the Lay Subsidy (PRO, E179/155/130). The earliest depiction of the hamlet is a map of 1726 (NRO; Fig. 20) which shows an irregular green with five houses and two farmsteads arranged around it, and two other houses lying on the N. side of a lane to the N.E. Another farmstead, the present Hill Farm, lay to the E. On a map of 1823 associated with the enclosure of the parish (NRO; Fig. 21) the green is shown, although its S. end had by then been encroached upon by the grounds of the two houses there. One of the farmsteads still stood, but the other farm and one of the cottages both shown on the 1726 map had been abandoned, as had a lane running S.E. from the green. The lane to the N.E. and the two houses there still existed and a third building is shown in the area. Hill Farm also remained to the E. The Enclosure Map of two or three years later (NRO; Fig. 22) shows the changes effected by enclosure. The green had been reduced to a track leading N.W. to one farmstead and a house, though Hill Farm, the two houses at the S.E. end of the green and those to the N.E. all remained. The map also shows in outline the present

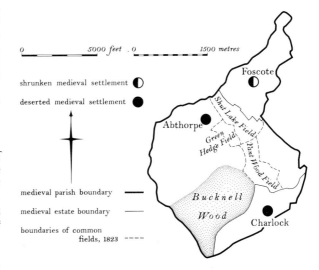

Fig. 17   ABTHORPE
Medieval settlements and estates

Foscote House which was presumably built soon afterwards. By the early 19th century, therefore, the hamlet of Foscote was probably no smaller than it had been 400 years earlier and the main contraction of settlement did not occur until later. During the second half of the 19th century all the buildings at Foscote except the new Foscote House, Hill Farm and one of the cottages at the S.E. end of the old green were removed though it is possible that the two buildings N.W. of Hill Farm actually remained standing until well into this century. Most of the earthworks of this settlement are thus the result of recent desertion or are the boundaries of closes shown on the various maps.

Immediately W. of Hill Farm, in the bottom of the valley, is a group of roughly rectangular ponds set in one corner of a generally rectangular area bounded by low banks and ditches ('a' on plan). Not all the ditches are contemporary; some are relatively recent drains. The disturbed nature of the ground here suggests that it is the site of a large building or group of buildings, probably the medieval manor of Foscote. The village earthworks are in poor condition. The outlines of the original green ('b' on plan) can be identified from the existing hedges or by low banks and scarps, but the sites of the buildings on the 1726 and 1823 maps are now only disturbed ground. No trace exists of the lane which ran N.E. from the green and again only disturbed ground marks the sites of the cottages which stood there. To the S.W. ('c' on plan), a ditch represents the line of a hedge shown on the 1726 map but which had been removed by 1823. (RAF VAP CPE/UK/1926, 1229–31; CUAP, AWO61; air photographs in NMR)

Fig. 18 ABTHORPE (1) Settlement remains (2) Ponds

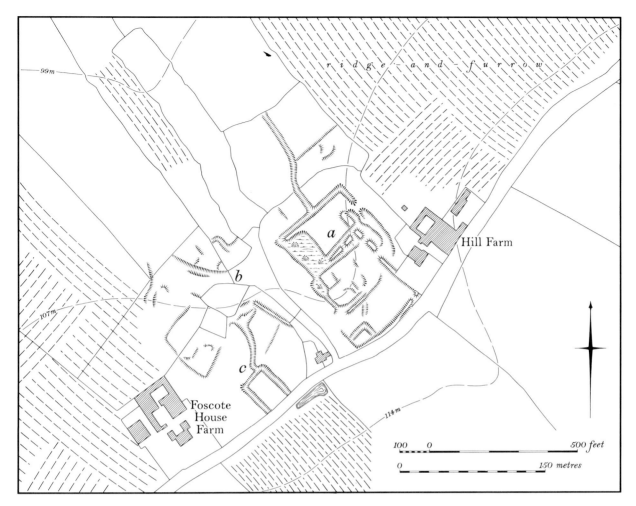

Fig. 19   ABTHORPE (3)   Deserted hamlet of Foscote

[c](4) MOUND (SP 65674684), lies S.W. of Foscote, on the top of a low hill, on Boulder Clay at 122 m. above OD. The mound is circular, 15 m. in diam. and only 0.3 m. high, with a shallow depression in the centre, and is surrounded by a very slight ditch 3 m. wide. Beyond the ditch are traces of an outer bank. The adjacent ridge-and-furrow appears to avoid the mound. It is not shown on any known map but in 1726 (map in NRO) the field in which it lies was called Moor Close. On a map of 1823 (NRO) the field, which had by then been enlarged to the N.E., was called the Moat and Fullers Close. The mound is likely to be the site of a windmill though it has been suggested that it may have been a cock-pit (OS Record Cards). (RAF VAP CPE/UK/1926, 1229–30; air photographs in NMR)

[d](5) DESERTED HAMLET OF CHARLOCK (SP 662447; Figs. 17 and 23), lies in the S. of the parish, S. of Charlock Farm and E. of the site of a former farm known as Old Charlock, on Boulder Clay at 122 m. above OD. Nothing is known of the history of the site. It is not recorded by name until 1250 (PN *Northants.*, 90) though it is probably much older. It is presumably included with Abthorpe in the national taxation records, though it was the centre of a separate land unit occupying the S. of the modern parish and appears to have had its own field system (6). The principal interest of the remains is that they appear to have been fitted into the end of a pre-existing furlong of ridge-and-furrow and thus must post-date the field system of the area.

The remains consist of a roughly rectangular area bounded by shallow ditches on the S.E. Two ditches on the N.E. appear to continue the furrows of the furlong to the S.E., as does another ditch crossing the interior. Within the enclosed area are a number of small paddocks, bounded by shallow ditches or low scarps. In the W. corner is a low circular mound and on the N.W. side are two adjacent depressions, perhaps once ponds. Traces of a hollow-way are visible on the N.E. (RAF VAP CPE/UK/1926, 3230–1; air photographs in NMR)

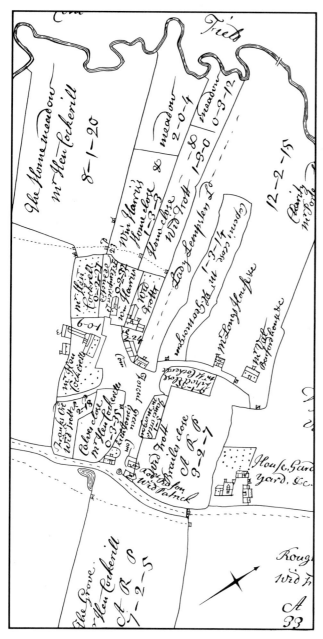

Fig. 20 ABTHORPE (3) Deserted hamlet of Foscote. Part of a plan of 1726 (NRO)

(6) CULTIVATION REMAINS (Fig. 17). The surviving parts of the common fields of Abthorpe, some 130 hectares, were enclosed by an Act of Parliament of 1823 (NRO, Enclosure Map; G. Baker, *Hist. of Northants.*, II (1836–41), 271). This area was divided into three fields, Shutlake Field to the E. and S.E. of the village, Green Hedge Field to the S. and Yant Wood Field further S.E.

Ridge-and-furrow of these fields exists on the ground or can be traced on air photographs only in the former Shutlake and Green Hedge Fields, where it agrees exactly with the furlongs shown on the Enclosure Map. It is arranged in end-on and interlocked furlongs of reversed-S form. Ridge-and-furrow also survives in the area of Abthorpe which had been enclosed before 1823, and in areas which were already enclosed in 1726, notably along the edges of Bucknell Wood (SP 655458) and in the W. of the parish (SP 640456 and 646456).

The date of the enclosure of the common fields of the now deserted hamlet of Foscote (3) is unknown, though 80 acres of land were enclosed in 1488 (K. J. Allison *et al.*, *The Deserted Villages of Northants.* (1966), 40). Ridge-and-furrow exists on the ground or can be traced on air photographs over much of the land attributable to Foscote, particularly in pasture around the site of the village. It is arranged in normal end-on and interlocked furlongs.

The date of the enclosure of the common fields of the deserted hamlet of Charlock (5) is also unknown but was before 1726 (map in NRO), and was probably much earlier than that. A little ridge-and-furrow remains or can be traced on air photographs in the S. of the parish around the site of the hamlet. (RAF VAP CPE/UK/1926, 1227–31, 3228–30)

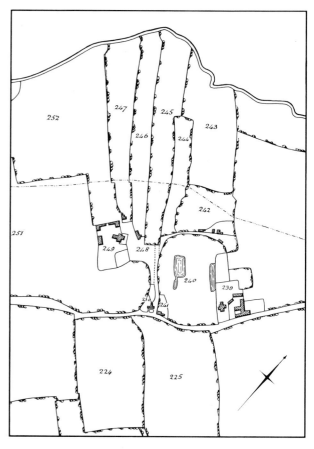

Fig. 21 ABTHORPE (3) Deserted hamlet of Foscote. Part of a plan of 1823 (NRO)

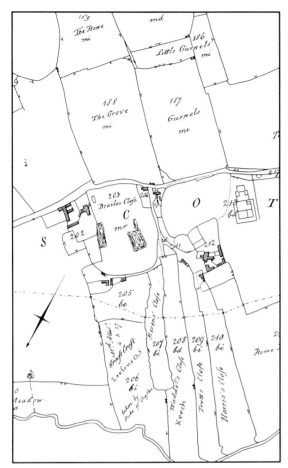

Fig. 22   ABTHORPE (3)
Deserted hamlet of Foscote.
Part of the Enclosure Map (NRO)

2   ADSTONE

(OS 1:10000 [a] SP 55 SE, [b] SP 55 SW, [c] SP 54 NE)

The rectangular parish occupies only 574 hectares on a spur projecting S. between two S.S.E.-flowing streams. Much of the higher ground, rising to a maximum height of 173 m. above OD, is covered by Boulder Clay, but there are patches of Northampton Sand where the land falls into the valleys and expanses of glacial sands and gravels alongside the stream in the N.E.

No prehistoric or Roman remains have been found in the parish but the settlement remains (1) of the medieval village are of interest.

MEDIEVAL AND LATER

[a](1) SETTLEMENT REMAINS (SP 595515), formerly part of Adstone, lie in and around the village, on Boulder Clay and Northampton Sand, between 150 m. and 170 m.

above OD. The village is small and stands at the junction of a number of roads which meet at a triangular green. The latter may once have been much larger, perhaps extending further S.E., although there is no proof of this. The parish church would then have stood in the S. corner of the green.

On the S.W. side of the village, alongside the road to Blakesley, is an area of earthworks covering some 3 hectares, but most of these remains have been dug into by large quarries and it is difficult to interpret what now exists. There are probable house-sites in the form of roughly rectangular sunken areas 10 m. by 6 m., with closes bounded by low banks and ditches extending up the slope behind them. There is also a short length of hollow-way running W. at the S. end. At the N.E. end of the village, further closes lie on the N. side of the Maidford Road but these too have later quarries cut through them. To the E. of the village are other abandoned closes. (RAF VAP CPE/UK/1994, 4093–4; CPE/UK/1926, 3053–4; air photographs in NMR)

(2) CULTIVATION REMAINS. The date of the enclosure of the common fields of Adstone is unknown, but was probably earlier than the late 18th century; a map of 1780 (NRO) covering only a small group of fields in the N. of the parish suggests this.

Ridge-and-furrow of these fields exists on the ground or can be traced on air photographs over much of the parish, arranged in end-on and interlocked furlongs of normal medieval forms, usually with reversed-S curves. (RAF VAP CPE/UK/1926, 1051–5, 3051–7; CPE/UK/1994, 4093–5, 4163–5)

3   ASHTON

(OS 1:10000 [a] SP 75 SE, [b] SP 74 NE)

The long narrow parish covers just over 450 hectares and extends N.E. from the R. Tove on the S.W. boundary, at 75 m. above OD, to the edges of Salcey Forest, at 130 m. above OD. The N.E. half is covered by Boulder Clay but in the S. bands of Oolitic Limestone and patches of Upper Lias Clay are exposed. The settlement remains (3) are of interest in that they suggest that the village has had a history much more complex than appears at first sight.

PREHISTORIC AND ROMAN

Three Roman coins were found near the manor house in about 1948. One was silver, of Vespasian, and the others were bronze (OS Record Cards).

[a](1) ENCLOSURE (SP 782512), lies in the E. of the parish immediately N. of Rowley Wood, on Boulder Clay, at about 116 m. above OD. Air photographs (CUAP, BGC69, and in NMR) show cropmarks of a sub-rectangular enclosure with rounded ends, covering about 0.5 hectares. To the E. at least one other enclosure is faintly visible on some of the available air photographs. (Northants. Archaeol., 10 (1975), 173)

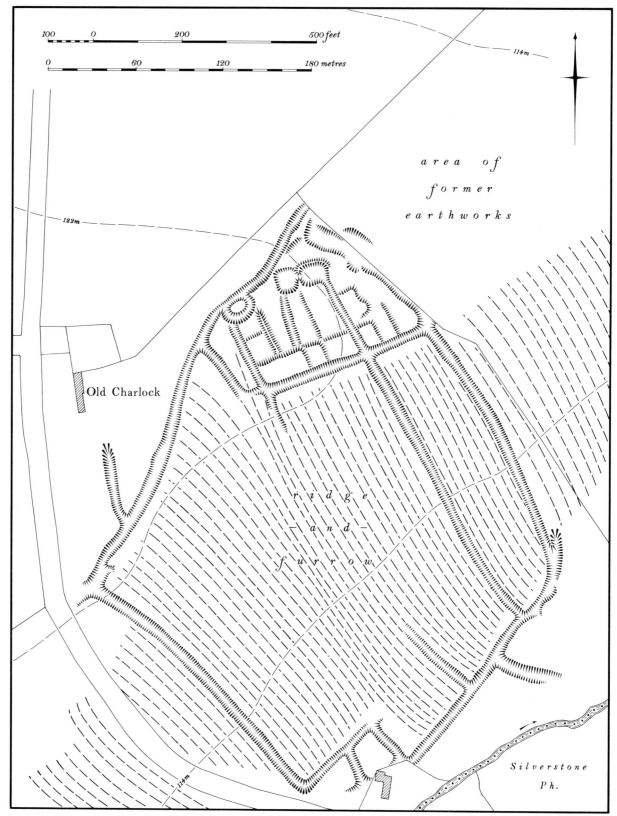

100　　0　　　　　200　　　　　　500 *feet*

0　　　　　60　　　　　120　　　　　180 *metres*

114m

area of former earthworks

122m

Old Charlock

ridge -and- furrow

114m

Silverstone Ph.

Fig. 23　ABTHORPE (5)　Deserted hamlet of Charlock

MEDIEVAL AND LATER

[ab](2) MOAT (SP 764500; Fig. 24), lies immediately N. of the village, on land sloping steeply S., on Oolitic Limestone and Upper Lias Clay at 90 m. above OD. In 1874 Whellan (*Dir.*, 561) recorded that the manor house had stood 'north of the church . . . surrounded by a broad deep moat' but the remains have been badly damaged and the ditch partly filled. A level, oval platform, about 45 m. by 40 m., is bounded on the W., S. and E. by a wide ditch, 2 m. deep on the downhill side but only 1 m. deep on the uphill side. On the N. the original ditch and platform appear to have been cut back into the hillside but the ditch has apparently been filled in at this point. Only a scarp 0.25 m. high marks its outer edge. The manor house standing within the moat appears to be of 16th and 17th-century date but the earliest depiction of the site is on a map of 1768 (NRO); the moat was then water-filled on the S. and E. sides. The map also shows a long narrow pond running E.-W. on the line of, but detached from, the S. part of the moat (SP 76515002–76575001), and a second pond to the S. (SP 76404994–76454994). Both have been destroyed but a low scarp marks the N. edge of the southernmost pond.

[ab](3) SETTLEMENT REMAINS (centred SP 765500), formerly part of the village of Ashton, lie in and around the village, on Upper Lias Clay between 75 m. and 90 m. above OD. The village now has a rather amorphous plan, made difficult to understand by the massive embankment of the London-Birmingham railway which cuts through the village. However, early maps (NRO, 1729, 1768 and 1819) show a more understandable though still complex plan made up of two distinct parts. In the N.E., set around the moated manor house (2) and the church, was an irregular arrangement of streets, now Roade Hill and Stoke Road. To the S. and E. was a separate part of the village, with a generally L-shaped plan, made up of streets and lanes laid out at right angles to each other and bounded on the S.E. by the present Hartwell Road. On the N.W. side was a small green. Construction of the railway and other changes in the 19th century led to the abandonment of part of this rectangular pattern and to encroachment over most of the green. Traces of one of the original lanes in this part of the village, still in use in 1819, survive on either side of the railway line (SP 76744988 and 76854995) but only as a degraded hollow-way partly occupied by a stream. Disturbed areas of ground, the sites of buildings still standing in 1729 or 1819, exist in a number of places (e.g. SP 78484988, 76055003). (RAF VAP CPE/UK/1926, 1245–6)

[b](4) SITE OF WATERMILL (?) AND PONDS (SP 769501), lie immediately N.E. of the village, in the bottom of a small valley draining S.E., on Upper Lias Clay at 85 m. above OD. The valley is spanned by the remains of a large earthen dam, up to 20 m. wide and 2 m. high, which formerly created a trapezoidal pond nearly 2 hectares in extent. The present stream flows through a gap in the centre of the dam; on either side of it, below the dam, an area of uneven ground marks the site of a building, perhaps a watermill, shown there in 1729 (map in NRO). (RAF VAP CPE/UK/1926, 1245–6)

[b](5) EARTHWORKS (SP 761501), lie immediately N.W. of the village, in a steep-sided valley drained by a S.-flowing stream, on limestone between 83 m. and 90 m. above OD. On both sides of the valley, covering some 6 hectares, is a system of low banks and ditches extending down the slope and forming a pattern resembling abandoned closes of deserted villages or settlement remains. However, there are no indications of occupation within these closes or of any obvious trackway approaching them. There are extensive later quarry pits in the area. No function or date can be assigned to these earthworks, but they may be potentially important in the history of Ashton village. (RAF VAP CPE/UK/1926, 1244–5; air photographs in NMR)

(6) CULTIVATION REMAINS. The common fields of the parish were enclosed by an Act of Parliament of 1816 (NRO, Draft Enclosure Map, 1817–18). The map shows four named fields, Warren Field in the N.W., Breach Field in the N.E., South Field in the S.W. and Bossenham Field in the S.E.; the latter included a small part of the parish which is now in Hartwell. The same four fields are shown on an earlier map (NRO, 1768). Very little of the ridge-and-furrow of these fields survives or can be traced from air photographs. There is one block W. of Ashton Lodge (SP 771508) known as Nether Furlong on the 19th-century map, and another N. of Bozenham Mill (SP 767484). Of a small group of end-on and interlocked furlongs W. of the village, some were on land shown as old enclosures in both 1768 and 1817 (SP 761498). (RAF VAP CPE/UK/1926, 1243–6, 1019–26; 106G/UK/1562, 4086–9; FSL 6565, 1001–5)

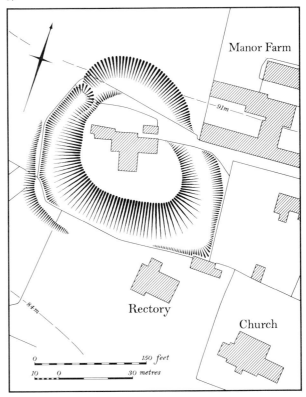

Fig. 24 ASHTON (2) Moat

4 ASTON LE WALLS
(OS 1:10000 [a] SP 44 NE, [b] SP 45 SE, [c] SP 55 SW)

The parish is roughly rectangular and covers about 650 hectares. The S.W. boundary lies against Oxfordshire and the N.W. boundary follows a tributary of the R. Cherwell; from there the land rises across a narrow S.W.-N.E. scarp of Lower and Middle Lias Clay and Marlstone Rock, between 110 m. and 145 m. above OD, to a flat area of Upper Lias Clay in the S.E. There is an outcrop of Northampton Sand in the N.E. of the parish. The main monuments in the parish are the site of the manor house of Aston le Walls (2) with its extensive fishponds (3) and the deserted village of Appletree (1). The latter had its own lands separate from those of Aston Fig. 25).

PREHISTORIC AND ROMAN

A looped bronze palstave was found in the parish in the 19th century (J. Evans, *Ancient Bronze Implements* (1881), 89; *BAR*, 31 (ii) (1976), No. 808; NM). An urn, described as Roman, was dug up in the N. side of the chancel of the church before 1845 but it was destroyed and the suggested date is by no means certain (*JBAA*, 1 (1845), 337; VCH *Northants.*, I (1902), 216).

MEDIEVAL AND LATER

[a](1) DESERTED VILLAGE OF APPLETREE (SP 483497; Figs. 25 and 26; Plate 2), lies on a steep N.W.-facing scarp, on Middle Lias clays and silts, between 145 m. and 120 m. above OD. The village was one of two medieval settlements in the parish, each with its own land (Fig. 25; NRO, Tithe Map, 1850). Appletree was not recorded by name until 1175 (PN *Northants.*, 32) but was presumably included in the large six-hide manor of Aston le Walls listed in Domesday Book with a recorded population of 25 (VCH *Northants.*, I (1902), 345). It was noted as a separate place in the *Nomina Villarum* of 1316, but thereafter was always taxed with Aston. In the 15th century nine people were documented as holding land in the common fields of Appletree, but in 1509 one of the two manors there, held by Chacombe Priory, was let apparently without undertenants. In 1539 eight able-bodied men are listed in the Muster Rolls for Appletree. (K. J. Allison *et al.*, *The Deserted Villages of Northants.* (1966), 34)

The remains of the village have been damaged by later activity and are in poor condition. No coherent plan is visible and the main feature is a deeply cut hollow-way up to 2 m. deep ('a'-'b' on plan) climbing the hillside. At its S.E. end this forks and fades out. It was still used as a track in the 19th century (OS 1st ed. 1 in. map, 1834). Another hollow-way ('c'-'d' on plan) runs down the hill to the S.W. and probably once joined the first. On both sides of these hollow-ways are slight traces of embanked and scarped closes, as well as some large level platforms edged by scarps up to 2.5 m. high, but few certain house-sites can be identified. One area at the N. end of the site has been ploughed in low ridge-and-furrow. A small quantity of green-glazed pottery, probably of late medieval date, has been found on the S.W. side of the main hollow-way. (RAF VAP CPE/UK/1926, 3072; CUAP, AWO40, AZX39, NU66)

[b](2) SITE OF MANOR HOUSE (SP 494508; Fig. 27), lies immediately N.W., N. and E. of the existing manor house of Aston le Walls, at the W. end of the village, on Marlstone Rock and Middle Lias Clay, at 137 m. above OD. The manor house is traditionally said to have had a moat around it but now only a 19th-century ha-ha bounds it on the N., E. and S. sides. To the N.W. ('a' on plan) are fragments of at least two enclosures bounded by low banks and shallow ditches, and to the E. and N.E. are other indeterminate hollows, scarps and banks forming no distinct pattern. The remains are probably old paddocks and sites of buildings connected with the manor house. The earthworks may perhaps be associated with the 'foundation walls' which Bridges records as having been dug up on this side of the village in the early 18th century, and which he took to indicate that the village had once been much larger than it was in his day (*Hist. of Northants.*, I (1791), 100). In 1850 (NRO, Tithe Map) the area had already been abandoned and was part of a large field called Cow Close. (RAF VAP CPE/UK/1994, 4105–6)

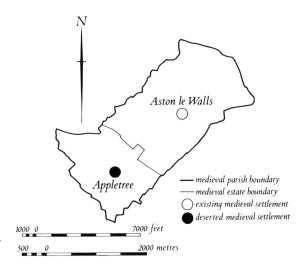

Fig. 25   ASTON LE WALLS
Medieval settlements and estates

[b](3) FISHPONDS AND HOLLOW-WAY (centred SP 493511; Fig. 27), lie on either side of a shallow valley cut back into the steep Middle Lias Clay escarpment, between 137 m. and 113 m. above OD. Bridges, writing in about 1720 (*Hist. of Northants.*, I (1791), 100), recorded that there had been 52 fishponds here in the early 17th century and that 'some still remain', as well as 'vestiges of others now disused'. Some of the earthworks visible on air photographs taken in 1947 (RAF VAP CPE/UK/1994, 4105–6) have been destroyed but it is very doubtful whether there were ever as many as 52 ponds, though the sites of at least 20 can be detected.

The earliest feature of the site is a *Hollow-way* which was largely destroyed by the construction of the ponds. It

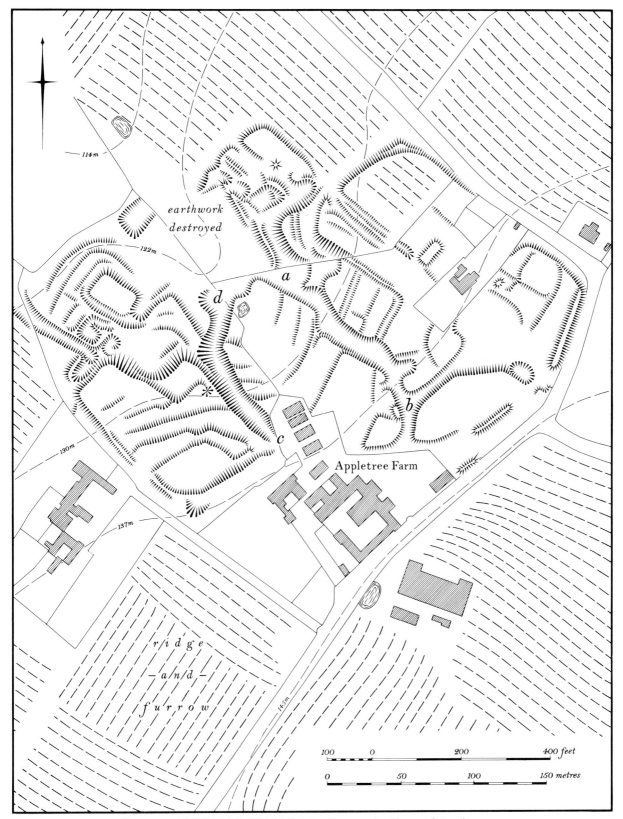

earthwork destroyed

114m

122m

130m

137m

145m

a

d

c

b

Appletree Farm

r/i d g e

– a/n/d –

f u r r o w

| 100 | 0 | 200 | 400 *feet* |

| 0 | 50 | 100 | 150 *metres* |

Fig. 26 ASTON LE WALLS (1) Deserted village of Appletree

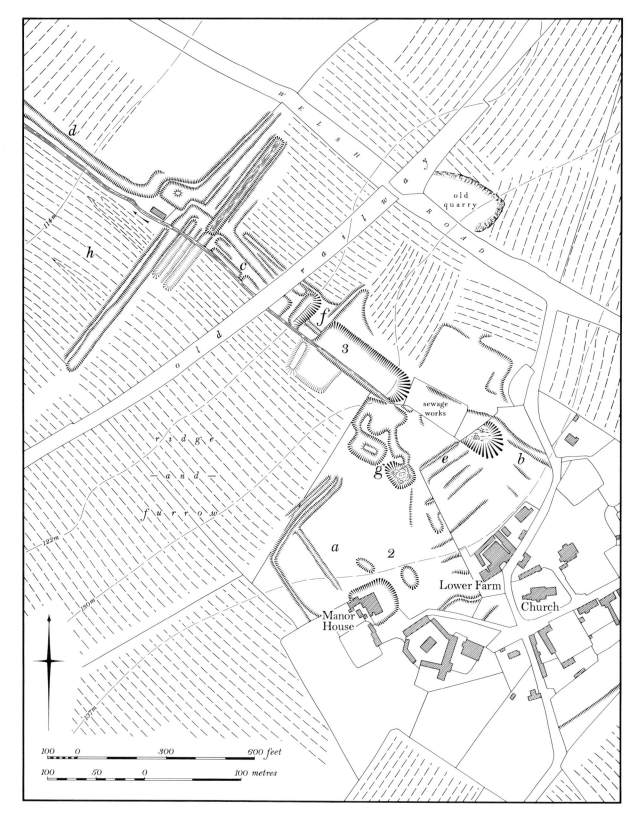

Fig. 27 ASTON LE WALLS (2) Site of manor house, (3) Fishponds and hollow-way

is traceable at the S.E. end of the site as a broad depression 0.5 m. deep ('b' on plan) running up the hillside to the existing village street; clearly it once crossed the latter and ran on eastwards. This part of the hollow-way is cut at its N.W. end by a deep, marshy hollow, one of the main feeders for the later ponds. On the N.W. side of the old railway track it again appears as a broad depression between 1 m. and 0.5 m. deep, traceable for some 80 m. ('c' on plan), after which it has again been destroyed by ponds. Beyond the north-westernmost of the ponds the hollow-way has survived, 1.5 m.–0.5 m. deep, and runs N.W., as far as the small stream which forms the parish boundary with Boddington ('d' on plan). North of the stream its line is taken up by an access-way leading to Lower Boddington village (see Boddington (7)). This hollow-way appears to have been an alternative to the present road to the E., an ancient drove road usually known as the Welsh Road, and may have been put out of use by the construction of the fishponds. The *Fishponds* themselves are very complex and cannot be completely understood. The uppermost ('e' on plan) is merely a shallow depression 0.25 m. deep, possibly with another similar one to the S. reduced to two parallel scarps. To the N.E. of this is a large marshy depression cut back 3 m. into the hillside which appears to have been the main source of water for the ponds below. The first of these ponds is now occupied by a modern sewage plant and is almost totally destroyed. On OS maps made before the construction of the plant, as well as on air photographs, it is shown as a large rectangular depression. Below it is a large pond with a maximum depth of 2 m., cut back into the hillside. There was once a small, roughly circular pond above it to the S.W. but this has been ploughed out. At the N.W. end of the surviving pond the water passes through a shallow channel cut into the top of a massive dam 12 m. wide and 2 m. high ('f' on plan). At its N.E. end this dam continues, first as a narrow steep-sided bank 1.5 m. high, and then as a headland between ridge-and-furrow; the function of this bank is not clear. Below the dam is a smaller rectangular pond, orientated N.E.–S.W., and below that lie two very small ponds or tanks set at right angles to each other. Beyond the old railway track which crosses the site at this point and to the S.W. of the hollow-way ('c' on plan) are three long narrow ponds and below them are the N.E. ends of two more long ponds which formerly extended S.W. across the modern stream but which have been destroyed. To the N.W. of these is a very large pond, over 200 m. long, but only 12 m. wide. This has been damaged but at its N.E. end, which still survives, it turned S.E. at right angles. To the N.E. are two other long narrow ponds. The upper one, now the only pond still holding water, is embanked on both sides. The lower one is similar, but at its N.E. end it fades out and, at its S.W. end it turns and opens into a subsidiary rectangular pond in the centre of which is a conical mound or island 1.2 m. high.

Immediately to the S.W. of the present sewage plant is another set of ponds, apparently filled by separate springs on the hillside ('g' on plan). The southernmost is a marshy rectangular depression with an outfall-channel leading from its N.E. corner into another larger rectangular pond. The latter was also fed by water from a rectangular pond to the S.W. which has in its centre a flat-topped mound

1.5 m. high with square ends.

(4) CULTIVATION REMAINS (Fig. 27). The dates of the enclosure of Aston le Walls and Appletree are unknown but there were common fields at Appletree in the 15th century (see (1) above). Ridge-and-furrow of the fields of both villages exists on the ground or can be traced on air photographs over parts of the parish, though the construction of the large wartime airfield S.E. of Aston village has removed much of the evidence. On the flat ground in the N.W. and S.E. of the parish the ridge-and-furrow is mainly arranged in interlocked blocks but along the Middle Lias Clay escarpment it is all in end-on furlongs running across the contours. In this area there is evidence of the over-ploughing of ancient landslips (SP 487503), and of the joining up of former end-on furlongs (SP 489506). To the N.W. of the fishponds (3) (SP 491511; 'h' on plan) one furlong has more ridges in its S. half than it has in the N.; groups of the S. ridges join in the centre of the furlong to become single ridges. This must be the result of the joining of two once separate end-on furlongs where the existing ridges could not be matched. Another similar example lies to the S. (SP 491508).

Along the N.W. boundary of the parish there are considerable areas which appear never to have had ridge-and-furrow on them, but these may have been extensive patches of very wet ground close to the small stream which could not have been ploughed. (RAF VAP CPE/UK/1926, 3068–74, 5067–70; CPE/UK/1994, 4104–7, 4152–4; 106G/UK/ 721, 3003–4, 4002–4)

5 AYNHO
(OS 1:10000 [a] SP 43 SE, [b] SP 53 SW)

The large, rectangular parish occupies 930 hectares of land in the extreme S.W. of the county and is bounded by Oxfordshire on the S. and W. The N. and N.E. part of the parish is an almost level tableland of Great Oolite Limestone at about 145 m. above OD. From there the land slopes steeply to the S.W. and more gently to the S. across deposits of Northampton Sand and Upper and Middle Lias Clay to the valleys of the Ockley Brook on the S. and the R. Cherwell on the W. The latter, flowing in a broad open valley at around 80 m. above OD, has extensive spreads of alluvium alongside it.

PREHISTORIC AND ROMAN

A bronze flanged axe is recorded from Aynho (NM; *BAR*, 31 (ii) (1976), No. 262).

[b](1) BRONZE AGE BURIAL (?) (perhaps SP 514340), found close to the N. boundary of the parish, and possibly within Kings Sutton parish. Baker (*Hist. of Northants.*, I (1822–30), 558), said that 'near the portion of the Portway north of (Aynho) village a grooved brass celt was found a few years since with a number of skeletons laying north to south'. The 'celt' was a bronze looped palstave (J. Evans, *Ancient Bronze Implements* (1881), 73) and is in private hands (*BAR*, 31 (ii) (1976), No. 809).

^b(2) PREHISTORIC BURIAL (?) (around SP 518332), found in the early 19th century, in Aynho Park, E. of the village. Baker (*Hist. of Northants.*, I (1822–30), 558) records the discovery of a crouched inhumation in a stone cist when the ancient trackway known as The Port Way was being levelled. It has been suggested that this was a Saxon burial (A. Meaney, *Gazetteer*, 186) but a prehistoric origin is more likely (VCH *Northants.*, I (1902), 139).

^b(3) PREHISTORIC BURIAL (?) (around SP 521323), near the parish boundary, on the S. side of Aynho Park, and perhaps in Souldern parish, Oxfordshire. Baker (*Hist. of Northants.*, I (1822–30), 558) noted that discoveries similar to those at (2) above had been made in the early 19th century near the Portway, S. of the village. Beesley (*Hist. of Banbury* (1841), 37) specifically mentions a skeleton 'lying at full length . . . discovered at the declivity of the hill between Aynho and Souldern'. These burials, if there were indeed more than one, may have been Saxon (Meaney, *Gazetteer*, 186).

^b(4) ENCLOSURES AND DITCHES (SP 527346; Fig. 87), lie in the extreme N. of the parish, immediately S. of Rainsborough hill fort (Newbottle (1)), on limestone at 146 m. above OD. On air photographs taken in 1964 (*PPS*, 33 (1967), Plate XXIII) some indeterminate ditches, perhaps forming a series of overlapping enclosures, are visible. These may be associated with the occupation of the fort.

^b(5) ROMAN SETTLEMENT AND BURIALS (?) AND PIT ALIGNMENT (SP 533343), lie in the N.W. corner of the parish on Oolite Limestone at 137 m. above OD. In 1872 a line of stones 10 m. long, possibly the foundations of a wall, was ploughed up in a field called Spitchel. Soon afterwards, in 1874, a Roman urn placed upright with stones on top of it was discovered. It was surrounded by an area of burnt stones, animal bones and fragments of Roman pottery. In 1884 5 stone cists, each containing a skeleton but with no datable finds, were found in the vicinity (*The Antiquary*, 4 (1884), 78). The name Spitehill Common is shown for this area on a late 18th-century map of the parish (NRO) and the land to the S. where the find spot is located by the OS is called The Warren on the same map. If the location given here is correct then these finds must have been discovered close to a pit alignment visible on air photographs in the same field (SP 534344 *Northants. Archaeol.*, 9 (1974), 44, listed under Croughton). Further Roman material, possibly from the eastern extension of this site, has been found in Croughton parish (Croughton (1)).

For Roman Road 161a, The Port Way, see Appendix.

MEDIEVAL AND LATER

For possible Saxon burials, see (2) and (3) above.

^b(6) SETTLEMENT REMAINS AND HOLLOW-WAYS (centred SP 511332), formerly part of Aynho, lie on the W. side of the village, on Northampton Sand and Upper Lias Clay between 105 m. and 120 m. above OD. Some of the remains result from the alteration of the road system on this side of the village following the enclosure of the common fields in 1793, but the rest represent earlier changes. The remains fall into three parts:

(a) At SP 510334, along the S. side of the present main A41 road N.W. of the village, is a large broad bank now ploughed over, 10 m.–12 m. across and 0.5 m. high. This is the S. side of the hollow-way of the pre-enclosure road which was straightened and moved a little to the N. in 1793. The bank is also the headland on which adjacent ridge-and-furrow ended.

(b) At SP 511330, S.W. of the village and W. of Aynho House, in the N.W. corner of the park, are the remains of a broad hollow-way up to 15 m. wide and 2.5 m. deep at its W. end. This was the original road out of Aynho to the S.W. which, until the late 18th century, continued the line of the existing road on the S. side of the village alongside Aynho House in a S.W. direction, until it met the present road some distance beyond the village (at SP 508330). This original road is shown on the Enclosure Map of 1793 (NRO), but on a slightly later map (NRO, undated but before 1807) it is depicted as having been abandoned, presumably because Aynho Park had been extended shortly before and the road stopped up.

(c) At SP 511332, on the S. and S.W. sides of College Farm are other earthworks. To the W. of the farm is a broad hollow-way, 15 m. wide and 1 m. deep, running down the hillside and fading out at the head of a stream near a large rectangular pond. This hollow-way had already been abandoned by 1793. At its W. end, within and S.W. of the garden of the farm, are several low banks and scarps. Some of these represent buildings existing in the late 18th century, but others are perhaps the remains

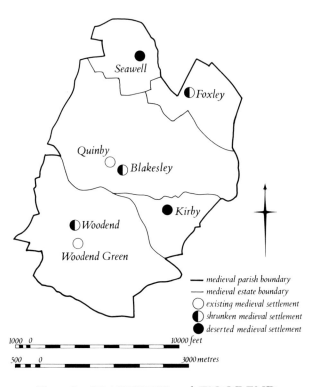

Fig. 28   BLAKESLEY and WOODEND
Medieval settlements and estates

of older structures and property boundaries. They may represent, at least in part, the site of a separate medieval settlement, known as Cotnam, which is said to have comprised the S.W. end of the village (J. Bridges, *Hist. of Northants.*, I (1791), 134). (RAF VAP CPE/UK/1926, 4208–9; CPE/UK/1929, 2168–70, 3167–9)

(7) CULTIVATION REMAINS. The common fields of the parish were finally enclosed by an Act of Parliament of 1792. By that date however, the greater part of the W. half of the parish was already divided into hedged fields while along the E. boundary lay areas known as Spitehill Common, The Warren and Old Down (NRO, Enclosure Map, 1793). Bridges (*Hist. of Northants.*, I (1791), 134), writing in about 1720, stated that extensive areas were already enclosed, including The Warren.

Ridge-and-furrow of the common fields exists on the ground or can be traced on air photographs over most of the area already enclosed in 1793; these are almost entirely on the Upper and Middle Lias Clay deposits. Here there are rectangular interlocked and end-on furlongs, mainly of reversed-S form, with well-marked headlands or access-ways between them, especially in Aynho Park. To the W. of the village (SP 505330) the existing rectangular field pattern reflects almost exactly the end-on furlongs of ridge-and-furrow, suggesting that the individual furlongs were enclosed as separate fields. Elsewhere in the parish, on the lighter sandstone or limestone soils, no ridge-and-furrow remains and only in a few areas close to the village (e.g. SP 519335) can it be traced on air photographs. This is probably the result of post-enclosure ploughing, which has destroyed the ridge-and-furrow there more easily than on the heavier land. (RAF VAP CPE/UK/1926, 4208–10; CPE/UK/1929, 2165–74, 3165–73; 106G/UK/1488, 3228–35)

6 BLAKESLEY
(OS 1:10000 [a] SP 65 SW, [b] SP 64 NW)

The modern parish covers about 1050 hectares and contains the land of the medieval settlement of Blakesley itself and of the now deserted settlements of Seawell (2) and Foxley (3) (Fig. 28). The medieval parish included what is now the parish of Woodend. Blakesley parish lies on land sloping generally S., drained by several streams which join, on the S. boundary, an E.-flowing tributary of the R. Tove. Upper Lias Clay, Northampton Sand and small outcrops of limestones are exposed on the valley sides. On the higher ridges, above 120 m. above OD, there are patches of Boulder Clay.

PREHISTORIC

A late Neolithic flint chisel was found in 1978 (SP 64685113; NM; *Northants. Archaeol.*, 14 (1979), 102).

MEDIEVAL AND LATER

There are references to a medieval deer park at Blakesley (*Northants. P. and P.*, 5 (1975), 220) but this has not been located.

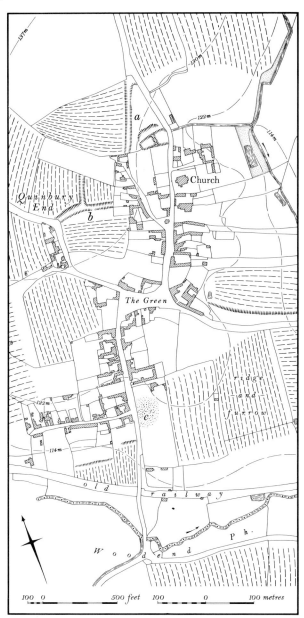

Fig. 29   BLAKESLEY (1)
Settlement remains and hollow-ways

[a](1) SETTLEMENT REMAINS AND HOLLOW-WAYS (centred 625502; Fig. 29), formerly part of Blakesley, lie in and around the existing village, on Jurassic Clay and Boulder Clay between 122 m. and 130 m. above OD.

The village of Blakesley has a plan which is unique in the county. Before modern development it consisted of two almost completely separate units joined by a central green. In the N. was a straight street extending N.E., with the church on its E. side and a minor lane running N. from the centre of its W. side. In the S. was a neat L-shaped arrangement of streets. The origins of this plan are obscure and it is possible to interpret it in a number of ways. The streets in the N. around the church may be the oldest part, and the S. part a planned extension, with the green being created even later. On the other hand it may have been a polyfocal village with two original centres, later joined by the green. A further possibility is that the green may be the old centre and that there was later expansion to the N. and S. A further complication is the small group of houses known as Quinbury End which lies immediately N.W. of the green and until recently was quite separate from the rest of the village.

The surviving earthworks and other material noted here do not help to elucidate the problem to any great extent. Only three features are of note. At the N. end of the village ('a' on plan) a hollow-way continues the line of the minor lane and runs N.E. to meet the existing lane N. of the village. In the triangular area left between the hollow-way

and the modern road there are no indications of former buildings, though later quarrying may have obscured any. In the S.E. corner are two small embanked ponds. To the W. of the hollow-way ridge-and-furrow survives undamaged. The existence of the hollow-way means that there was once a diamond-shaped area edged by roads in this part of the village, which might be interpreted as a former green, now partly abandoned and partly built over. If so this part of the village might be the older centre. Further support for this is the existence of a second hollow-way ('b' on plan) which continues the line of the Maidford Road E. towards the assumed green, from the point where the road turns S. at Quinbury End on its way to the present green. This may indicate that the road from Maidford once entered the N. part of the village and was later diverted.

In the S. part of the village, construction work at the

Fig. 30   BLAKESLEY (2)   Deserted village of Seawell

time when the Commission was carrying out its survey led to the discovery of considerable quantities of medieval pottery, all apparently of 12th to 14th-century date including some Potterspury wares. These finds were made on the previously empty plot at the S.E. end of the main street ('c' on plan). (RAF VAP CPE/UK/1926, 1047–9; air photographs in NMR)

[a](2) DESERTED VILLAGE OF SEAWELL (SP 630525; Figs. 28 and 30), lay in the N. of the parish, N.E. of the present Seawell Farm, in the bottom of a small E.-draining valley, on Northampton Sand and Upper Lias Clay at 137 m. above OD. The village had its own land unit occupying the N. part of Blakesley parish (Fig. 28). It is first mentioned in 1086 when Domesday Book lists it as a single manor with a recorded population of 13 (VCH Northants., I (1902), 333), but thereafter nothing is known of its size until the early 18th century. It is mentioned by name in the Nomina Villarum of 1316 and in late medieval times Seawell was divided into two manors, both held by non-resident families. By 1547 400 sheep were grazed on its land (K. J. Allison et al., The Deserted Villages of Northants. (1966), 45). Bridges, writing about 1720 (Hist. of Northants., I (1791), 235), said that it was 'an hamlet only of two houses, but was formerly a more considerable place'. These two houses are marked on a map of Seawell of 1726 (NRO), one lying on the edge of the village but the other, a large farm, well to the S. and apparently on top of earlier ridge-and-furrow (SP 63105228). On a plan of 1837 (NRO) these two buildings are shown, with a third, perhaps only a barn, to the N.E. The farm was demolished in the mid 19th century and replaced by the present Seawell Farm to the W. By 1883 (1st ed. OS 25 in. plan, Northants. L16) another cottage, the present Seawell Cottage, had been erected on the site of the village, but the building to the N.E. had gone. The other house shown on the 1726 map was demolished early in this century.

Apart from Seawell Cottage and the stone foundations of the house to the W. nothing remains on the site of the village. No earthworks are visible on air photographs taken in 1947 (RAF VAP CPE/UK/1926, 3046–7) and in 1970 only a mutilated dam of a former pond was noted (OS Record Cards). Since then the area has been landscaped and a series of small ponds have been constructed in the valley bottom. A few sherds of late medieval pottery have been found in the area.

[a](3) DESERTED VILLAGE OF FOXLEY (SP 640518; Figs. 28 and 31), lies in the N.E. corner of the parish, on the N.E. side of a small S.E.-flowing stream, on Northampton Sand and Upper Lias Clay between 120 m. and 137 m. above OD. Foxley was once a settlement with its own land unit and fields (Fig. 28) but its history is largely unknown. It is not mentioned as a holding by name in Domesday Book although it certainly existed at that time for its name was then given to the hundred which was later known as Greens Norton Hundred. The earliest reference to Foxley as a settlement is in 1190 (PN Northants., 40). Although it is named in some national taxation records, it is always included in Cold Higham and no indication of its size can be ascertained until the early 18th century when Bridges (Hist. of Northants., I (1791), 234) stated that there were

only three houses there. (K. J. Allison et al., Deserted Villages of Northants. (1966), 40)

The earliest map of the village, dated 1819 (NRO), shows the two groups of farm buildings and the cottage on the S.W. which remains today, but it also shows two buildings within a small paddock to the S.W. of the cottage. By the late 19th century these had gone but a new farm had been erected to the N. (OS 1st ed. 25 in. plan, Northants. L16) apparently on the site of older houses (see below). The farm has since been demolished.

The remains of the village are very slight and fragmentary. From the small green on the N. side of the remaining farm traces of a hollow-way extend down the hillside, following the bed of a small stream ('a'-'b' on plan). On the N. side of the hollow-way, but set curiously askew to it, are the remains of seven small closes, separated by low scarps and with a well-marked boundary ditch on the N.W. Two of these closes contain irregular depressions which may be the sites of former houses, but the later farm, now demolished, has destroyed any trace of earlier buildings in the N.E. closes. These earthworks are probably the remains of a row of houses and paddocks which once lay along the hollow-way, but their unusual arrangement and the fact that the close boundaries continued the line of the unusually short ridge-and-furrow to the N.W. suggest that the ridge-and-furrow once extended as far as the hollow-way and that the houses were erected on former arable land.

Some disturbed ground immediately S.E. of the existing cottage ('c' on plan) is the only other indication of houses on the site. Other earthworks lie in a large pasture field to the S. and S.W. but none of them appear to be part of the village and they may be associated with a manor house site. The main feature is a roughly triangular embanked pond with a small low island in it ('d' on plan). The island is depicted on the 1819 map. The pond is approached from the N.E. by a narrow channel, leading from another pond now mainly filled in, higher up a small valley. A second channel leaves the main pond at its W. corner, runs down the hillside and enters a long narrow depression embanked on its W. side. This feature ('e' on plan) may also once have been a pond. On the S.E. edge of the site, a ditch with a large bank on its N.W. side runs down the hillside, along the present hedge-line, from the former pond to the N.E. as far as the stream in the valley bottom. This appears to be a water channel but its function is obscure.

On the N.W. part of the site are the fragmentary remains of ditched closes, the largest of which has traces of ridge-and-furrow within it. At their S. ends, near the present road, is a disturbed area much of which appears to be later quarrying. (RAF VAP CPE/UK/1926, 1044–5, 3045–7; CUAP, XT43–6, AKS3; air photographs in NMR)

(4) CULTIVATION REMAINS (Fig. 31). The common fields of Blakesley were enclosed by an Act of Parliament of 1760 but nothing is known of their layout. Ridge-and-furrow of these fields exists on the ground or can be traced on air photographs over much of the part of the parish attributable to the village of Blakesley. It is arranged mainly in interlocked furlongs, often showing careful adaptation to the broken ground and thus ensuring that, where possible, the ridges run across the contours.

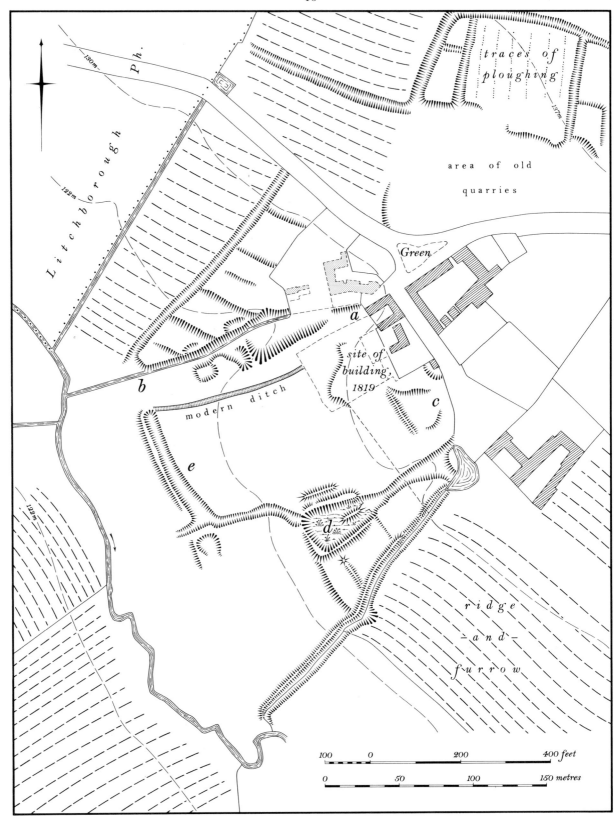

traces of ploughing

area of old quarries

Litchborough Ph.

130m

122m

Green

a

site of building, 1819

b

c

modern ditch

e

d

ridge -and- furrow

122m

| 100 | 0 | | 200 | 400 feet |

| 0 | 50 | 100 | 150 metres |

Fig. 31 BLAKESLEY (3) Deserted village of Foxley

The common fields of the deserted village of Seawell (2) had been enclosed by the 16th century, but the exact date is not known. Very little ridge-and-furrow remains in the land of Seawell because of destruction by modern agriculture. Some survives E. of Seawell Farm (SP 627521) and air photographs show a more extensive area of interlocked furlongs. The names Banky Meadow on a map of 1837 (NRO) and Banky Close on a map of 1726 (NRO), refer to a low-lying field in the N. of the parish where ridge-and-furrow was presumably once well marked (SP 627531).

The date of enclosure of the common fields of the deserted village of Foxley (3) is also unknown but enclosure had certainly taken place by 1819 (NRO, map) and probably by the 16th century. Ridge-and-furrow of these fields exists on the ground, especially around the site of the village, and can be traced elsewhere on air photographs. It is arranged in interlocked furlongs, except along the valley sides of a stream to the S.W. of Foxley where the ridges run across the contours to the valley bottom. Even where the ridge-and-furrow has been destroyed, well-marked headlands survive as low ridges (e.g. SP 646511 and 646513). As at Seawell, the map of 1837 (NRO) records three fields as Banky Ground or Banky Close. All still have well-marked ridge-and-furrow within them (SP 635515 and 647512). (RAF VAP CPE/UK/1926, 1043–51, 3044–7; CPE/UK/1944, 2083–7, 4167–70)

7 BLISWORTH
(OS 1:10000 [a] SP 75 NW, [b] SP 75 SW)

The parish is of irregular shape, covering almost 800 hectares. The N. part is a rather flat area of Upper Lias Clay, glacial sands and gravels and alluvium, all at about 84 m. above OD, but from there the land rises steeply, exposing narrow bands of Northampton Sand, Blisworth Limestone and other Oolitic deposits, to a high ridge covered by Boulder Clay with a maximum height of 130 m. above OD. A N.-flowing stream has cut a steep-sided, narrow valley, now occupied by the Grand Union Canal which then passes below the ridge in a tunnel.

PREHISTORIC AND ROMAN

A gold stater of Tasciovanus (Mack, 167) was found in the S.W. of the parish around 1950 (SP 720524; NM; S. S. Frere (ed.), *Problems of the Iron Age in S. Britain* (1958), 223; NM Records). Another, listed under Gayton, may have come from Blisworth. Part of a quern, possibly Roman, was found in 1969 (SP 71935404; NM; *BNFAS*, 4 (1970), 6).

[b](1) ROUND BARROW (?) (SP 73435160), on Blisworth Hill in the S. of the parish, on Boulder Clay at 125 m. above OD. The mound is situated in a field called Bury Hill in 1729 (map in NRO); it is circular, 16 m. in diam. and 0.25 m. high, with slight traces of a surrounding ditch about 3 m. across. The field has slight traces of ridge-and-furrow in it but it is impossible to say if this pre-dates

the mound. The mound may be a barrow, but could also be a medieval windmill mound. (*BNFAS*, 5 (1971), 1; RAF VAP CPE/UK/1926, 1029–30)

[ab](2) ENCLOSURE (SP 727550), lies in the N. of the parish, on Upper Lias Clay at 80 m. above OD. Air photographs (not seen by RCHM) are said to show a rectangular enclosure of just under 1 hectare, perhaps with other enclosures attached to it on the N. (*BNFAS*, 6 (1971), 3).

[b](3) ROMAN SETTLEMENT (unlocated but possibly around SP 735530), believed to have been discovered in the 19th century during ironstone-quarrying S.E. of the village, on Blisworth Limestone at just over 122 m. above OD. Roman coins, pottery and 'ornaments', some from wells or pits, are recorded from the parish (VCH *Northants.*, I (1902), 216; T. J. George, *Arch. Survey of Northants.* (1904), 10). Worked flints are also documented.

[b](4) ROMAN SETTLEMENT (?) (SP 733536), in a restored quarry E. of the village, on Northampton Sand, at 145 m. above OD. Roman pottery has been found on reclaimed land, in soil taken from the adjacent area (inf. D. N. Hall).

For Roman settlement at SP 712529, see Gayton (3).

MEDIEVAL AND LATER

[b](5) SETTLEMENT REMAINS (SP 726537), formerly part of Blisworth, lay at the N. end of the village, immediately N. of Chapel Lane and Little Lane. The earthworks, in existence until at least 1947 (RAF VAP CPE/UK/1926, 3030–1), have now been destroyed, but consisted of a group of small rectangular paddocks bounded by low banks, presumably the gardens of houses that once stood along the lane. Some of the houses remained until after 1810 for they are depicted on the draft Enclosure Map of that date (NRO) as well as on a map of the parish of 1729 (NRO).

[b](6) TRAMWAY (SP 743500–724533; Fig. 32), extends for 3.8 km. over Blisworth Hill, between Blisworth and Stoke Bruerne. It was build in 1800–1 to carry the freight of the Grand Junction Canal over the hill during the construction of Blisworth Tunnel. The construction of the tunnel started in 1793, but difficulties with flooding and contractors continually held up the work. By the end of 1796, when there was still no prospect of the tunnel's early completion, it was proposed that a road be constructed over the hill to join the two already complete sections of the canal. The road was not a success and in March 1799, it was decided that it should be replaced by a tramway. This was finished by 1801 and was in use until February 1805 when the tunnel was finally completed. The tramway was then abandoned and its track was reused on the Northampton Tramway (see Rothersthorpe (6)). The rails used for the line were L-shaped in section and were fixed to stone sleepers with the horizontal flange facing outwards (examples in Stoke Bruerne Waterways Museum). The wagons therefore had flangeless wheels and elaborate sidings were not necessary as wagons could simply be run off the track and parked. The gauge of the track was probably 4 ft. 2 in. Although no record survives it seems likely that the N. end of the tramway was later used to carry stone from the Blisworth quarries to the canal wharves. (A. H. Faulkner, *The Grand Junction Canal* (1972), 42–60; *Northants. Ant. Soc. Rep.*, 64 (1962–3), 14–26).

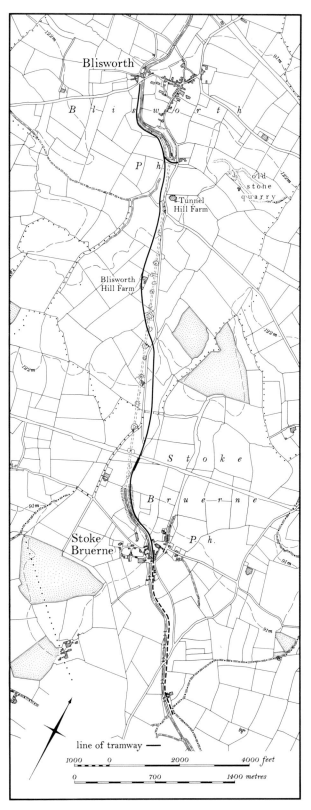

Fig. 32   BLISWORTH   (6) Tramway

The S. end of the tramway lay S.E. of Stoke Bruerne, on the E. side of the canal where the Northampton to Stony Stratford road crosses it (SP 74894919). No trace of it survives for the first 1200 m. to the N., but it probably ran N.W. alongside the existing towpath. At the point where the canal enters the cutting leading to the S. entrance of Blisworth Tunnel (SP 74135006) the line of the tramway is visible as a ledge or terrace, 4 m.–5 m. wide, climbing the hillside, parallel to the cutting. This terrace continues beyond the tunnel entrance until it meets a lane running S. from the Blisworth-Stoke Bruerne Road (SP 73885033). For the next 300 m. the lane takes the original line of the tramway as it ascends the steep S. side of the hill and no trace of the tramway exists. Then (at SP 73865070) the lane swings N.W. and in a small triangular copse the tramway is again visible as a terrace 5 m. wide. Beyond the copse, as the top of the hill is reached, no trace of the tramway can be seen except for a line of stones 5 m.–6 m. wide across an arable field.

At the point where it enters Blisworth parish (SP 73765094) the tramway appears as a broad stony ridge 10 m. wide and 0.25 m. high crossing a green lane. This ridge continues N.N.W. for 350 m. in a pasture field. At the N. end of this field it cuts across an area of rather narrow ridge-and-furrow. Beyond the field it continues for a further 140 m. until it reaches the Blisworth-Stoke Bruerne Road. Along this section the remains have been ploughed over but survive partly as a low embankment and partly as a shallow cutting 15 m. across. At the point where it crossed the road (SP 73525141) the tramway turned N.W. and the line continues as a low embankment 0.25 m. high and 12 m. wide for a distance of 230 m. Midway along this section (SP 73425155) the embankment is partly overlaid by the tail of one of the spoil heaps from the canal tunnel which lies directly below. From this point the tramway starts to descend the N. side of Blisworth Hill and for the next 200 m. the remains take the form of a shallow cutting, crossing two adjacent furlongs of reversed-S ridge-and-furrow. At Blisworth Hill Farm (SP 73195189) the tramway turned N. but any trace has been obscured by farm buildings. To the N. of the farm, for some 500 m., the remains of the tramway have been ploughed over and only a broad cutting up to 20 m. wide and 1.5 m. deep survives, in a very degraded form. Immediately S.W. of Tunnel Hill Farm (SP 73005253) the alignment again turns N.N.W. and is visible for 230 m. as a broad cutting passing between piles of spoil from the canal tunnel. Beyond, the tramway survives as a massive embankment over 3 m. high and some 70 m. long crossing a small valley after which it passes on to the level summit of another spoil heap (SP 72905282). This point probably marks the position of winding machinery which drew the wagons up the very steep incline to the N. The incline can be traced as a cutting or terrace running in a broad curve N.W. and then W. above and roughly parallel to the canal as it enters the N. portals of the tunnel. To the S. of the village (SP 72505307) the tramway reached the level of the canal and continued along the W. side of it until it reached wharves at Blisworth (SP 72385335). Along this section it survives as a broad embankment.

In 1969 an excavation was carried out on the line of the tramway in the extreme S. of Blisworth parish (SP 736513).

Four rows of stone sleeper blocks, two rows for each track, were found (*BNFAS*, 4 (1970), 30).

Although there is no documentary proof, a section of the tramway to the N. of the tunnel entrance to Blisworth may have had a later use. At its S. end, above the tunnel, a secondary cutting runs S.E. and then E. and appears to be heading towards the stone quarries further E. and N.E. In addition the discovery, during fieldwork on the incline, of a cast iron chair to take a rail of conventional type suggests that a later track had at some time replaced that of 1800–5. (RAF VAP CPE/UK/1926, 1029–30, 1242–3, 3029–1)

(7) CULTIVATION REMAINS. The common fields of the parish were enclosed by an Act of Parliament of 1808 (NRO, Draft Enclosure Map, 1808). By that time the whole of the S. part of the parish centred on Blisworth Hill was already enclosed, as well as a large area N.W. of the village and a narrow strip N. of the village on the W. side of the main A43 road. Until enclosure the remaining land was divided into four open fields. Windmill Field lay to the N.E. of the village, Nether Field to the N.W., Long Stockin Field to the S.E. and Wood Field to the S.W. An earlier map, of 1729 (NRO) shows exactly the same situation except that in the extreme S.W. a small area was named Wooley Field. Ridge-and-furrow of these and earlier fields exists on the ground or can be traced on air photographs over parts of the parish. Most of the traceable remains lie on the summit and slopes of Blisworth Hill, which was already enclosed by 1729. Here as elsewhere, the ridge-and-furrow is arranged in end-on and interlocked furlongs, and it would appear that most of this area was under normal strip-field cultivation at some time. Similar ridge-and-furrow is traceable in other areas of old enclosures to the W. and N. of the village. Ridge-and-furrow in the area covered by the four open fields up to 1808 survives in a few places and where it is complete it agrees exactly with the furlongs and direction of strips shown on the draft Enclosure Map. It is notable that in the N.E. of the parish, against the Milton Malsor parish boundary (SP 731542), the location as well as the furlong names, Lower, Middle and Upper Breach Furlongs, would suggest a late intake of land. The ridge-and-furrow is laid out in large blocks neatly related to adjacent furlongs and does not appear to be the result of infilling of small irregular areas left uncultivated at an earlier period. (RAF VAP CPE/UK/1926, 1028–31, 3029–33, 5028–31; FSL 6565, 1796–8, 1997–9, 2015–9)

8 BODDINGTON
(OS 1:10000 [a] SP 45 NE, [b] SP 45 SE)

The oval parish, which covers 1265 hectares, lies with its W. boundary adjoining parts of Oxfordshire and Warwickshire. It is mainly on flat or gently undulating Lower Lias Clay between 100 m. and 150 m. above OD, but in the centre around Upper Boddington and in the N.W. the land rises steeply to a maximum of 180 m. above OD, based on an outcrop of Middle Lias clays and silts. There are two separate villages in the parish, Upper and Lower Boddington, each of which had, in medieval times, its own land and field system (Fig. 33).

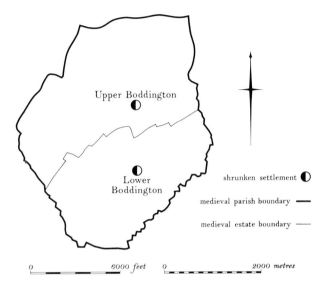

Fig. 33   BODDINGTON
Medieval settlements and estates

PREHISTORIC AND ROMAN

Part of a Neolithic polished stone adze was found in Upper Boddington in 1978 (SP 48125371; NM; *Northants. Archaeol.*, 14 (1979), 102).

[b](1) ROMAN SETTLEMENT (?) (SP 481534), within the village of Upper Boddington, on clays and silts at 145 m. above OD. A quantity of Roman pottery has been found in this area over a number of years (NM; OS Record Cards).

[b](2) ROMAN COIN HOARD (SP 480540), N. of Upper Boddington. In 1873 a brown-glazed red pot was discovered in this area. It contained 360 Roman coins dating mainly from the second half of the 3rd century, all 'third brass'. (NM; *Northants. N. and Q.*, 1st Ser., 3 (1890), 151; OS Record Cards)

MEDIEVAL AND LATER

[b](3) SETTLEMENT REMAINS (centred SP 482535; Fig. 34), formerly part of Upper Boddington, lie within and around the existing village, on clays and silts between 125 m. and 152 m. above OD. The plan of Upper Boddington consists of two separate elements lying to the W. of an undoubtedly ancient trackway known as the Welsh Road. The S. part is a simple N.-S. street with the church and manor house at its southern, higher end. To the N. is a more complex arrangement of streets and lanes arranged in an irregular grid. A possible interpretation of this plan is that the N.-

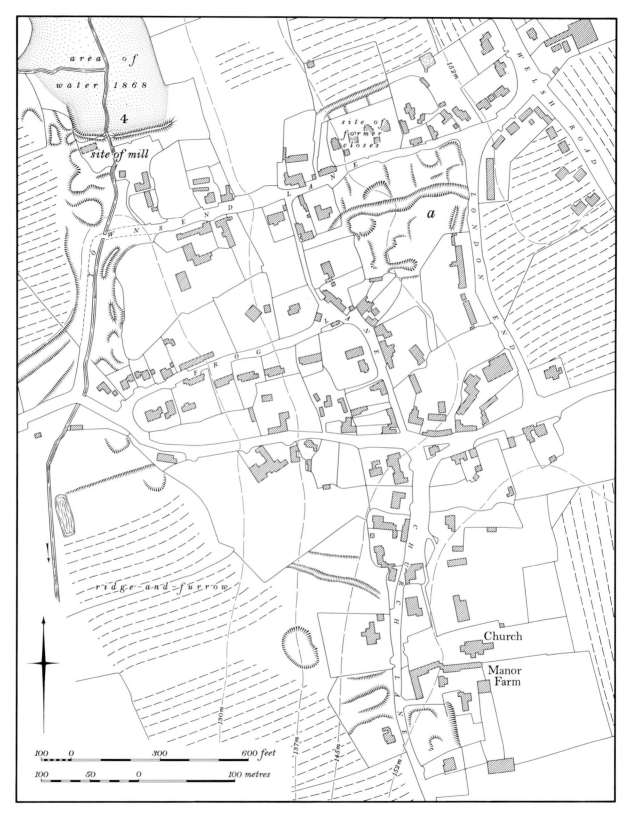

area of water 1868

4

site of mill

site of former closes

a

ridge-and-furrow

Church

Manor Farm

100   0   300   600 feet

100   50   0   100 metres

Fig. 34   BODDINGTON (3)   Settlement remains at Upper Boddington, (4)   Dam

S. street was the earlier and that the N. part grew up, or was deliberately added, at a later date. The surviving earthworks go some way to supporting this idea.

The main earthworks lie in the N.E. of the village, S. of Townsend Lane ('a' on plan). They consist of a broad irregular hollow-way extending E.-W. parallel to Townsend Lane and forming a link between London End and the hollowed footpath N. of Frog Lane. On either side of this hollow-way are earthworks, very disturbed, but with some indications that there was formerly a series of closes bounded by low scarps. A number of large depressions may represent former buildings. A little late-medieval pottery has been found in the side of the hollow-way.

A further set of abandoned closes, probably the sites of former houses, lay along the N. side of Townsend Lane (SP 481537). These have been destroyed by recent housing development, except for a short section of another E.-W. hollow-way, perhaps the N. boundary of the village at one time, and the ends of three closes. Fragments of an early medieval pot were found in this area in 1975 (SP 48155370; NM; *Northants. Archaeol.*, 13 (1978), 186).

At the S. end of the village there are some indeterminate banks and scarps S. of Manor Farm; on the steep hillside to the W. of the farm, two wide, rounded depressions extend down the hillside, perhaps old tracks to the fields below. There is probably another hollow-way further N. All the earthworks were already abandoned by the mid 19th century (NRO, map of Upper Boddington, said to be of 1868, but probably before 1831). (RAF VAP CPE/UK/ 1926, 5071; 106G/UK/1698, 5283–4)

b(4) DAM (SP 478537; Fig. 34), lies in the N.W. corner of the village, N. of Townsend Lane, spanning the valley of a small S.-flowing brook, on Lower Lias Clay at 132 m. above OD. On a mid 19th-century map (NRO) a large pond covering almost 2.5 hectares is shown though there is no indication of its purpose. The dam is 15 m. wide and up to 2.5 m. high, with a break in the centre through which the stream now passes. Below the dam, to the W. of the stream, are the foundations of a stone building which certainly existed until 1947 and which are perhaps the remains of a mill. An irregular watercourse further W. and N.W. between the assumed mill and the adjacent ridge-and-furrow appears to be an overflow channel around the W. end of the dam. (RAF VAP 106G/UK/1698, 5284–5)

b(5) SETTLEMENT REMAINS (centred SP 482523; Fig. 35), formerly part of Lower Boddington, lie in and around the existing village, on Lower Lias Clay between 120 m. and 140 m. above OD. The present village lies along two streets, Banbury Road and Hill Road, which meet at a crossroads in the N.W. corner; another street, Owl End Lane, runs parallel to Hill Road. The remains of an L-shaped hollow-way now 3 m. deep show that Owl End Lane, now a *cul-de-sac*, once extended N.E. to meet Hill Road ('a' on plan). Other earthworks elsewhere appear to be sites of former houses and gardens. (RAF VAP CPE/UK/ 1926, 5070–1)

b(6) ENCLOSURES (SP 482518; Fig. 35), lie immediately S. of Lower Boddington village, around Paradise Farm, on Lower Lias Clay at 115 m. above OD. All the fields around the farm contain small enclosures bounded by low scarps

or shallow ditches. A hollow-way passes through them to the S.E. of the farm and the fragmentary remains of another run S.W. The date and purpose of the enclosures is unknown but they may be abandoned paddocks of the farm. (RAF VAP CPE/UK/1926, 5070–1)

(7) CULTIVATION REMAINS (Fig. 33). Upper and Lower Boddington appear each to have had separate common fields, but both were enclosed under the same Act of Parliament of 1758. Ridge-and-furrow of these fields exists on the ground or can be traced on air photographs over almost the whole parish except in a small area N. of Upper Boddington known as Little Common (NRO, 19th-century map of Boddington). However, on the higher land in the extreme N.W. of the parish known as Short Down Leys ridge-and-furrow is still visible. On the lower, flatter ground in the S. and S.W. the ridge-and-furrow is arranged mainly in large rectangular interlocked furlongs, but on the higher land in the N. and N.W., and especially on the steep slopes there, end-on furlongs are more common.

Several minor details of the common fields are of interest. To the S.W. of Lower Boddington (SP 480511) two large end-on furlongs of reversed-S form have been ploughed as one, with the result that the ridges twist as they rise over the older underlying headlands. This also occurs in other places for example W. of Lower Boddington (SP 469522) and W. of Upper Boddington (SP 475532). The most notable of the access-ways or roads through the ridge-and-furrow is a long lane extending from the parish boundary with Aston le Walls (SP 488512) to the S.E. corner of Lower Boddington (SP 484518). This appears to be an alternative route of the ancient drove road, known as the Welsh Road, and once continued S.E. to Aston le Walls village until blocked by the later fishponds (Aston le Walls (3)). (RAF VAP CPE/UK/1926, 5067–74; CPE/UK/1994, 4105–7, 4152–4; 106G/UK/1698, 5281–6)

9 BRACKLEY
(OS 1:10000 SP 53 NE)

The generally diamond-shaped parish, covering less than 700 hectares, is bounded by the Great Ouse on the S.E. and by smaller watercourses on the other three sides. Boulder Clay covers the higher land in the N. rising to 152 m. above OD, and wide bands of Oolite Limestone and Upper Lias Clay are exposed along the valley sides. The town of Brackley was a deliberate plantation, laid out before 1173 along the existing main Northampton–Oxford road at some distance from the earlier village of Brackley (3) to the N.E.

PREHISTORIC AND ROMAN

One barbed-and-tanged arrowhead has been found in the W. of the parish (SP 572382; *BNFAS*, 5 (1971), 1) and an Iron Age gold coin of the Dobunni is also recorded (Mack, 386; S. S. Frere (ed.), *Problems of the Iron Age in S. Britain* (1958), 251; Fitzwilliam Museum). A few Roman

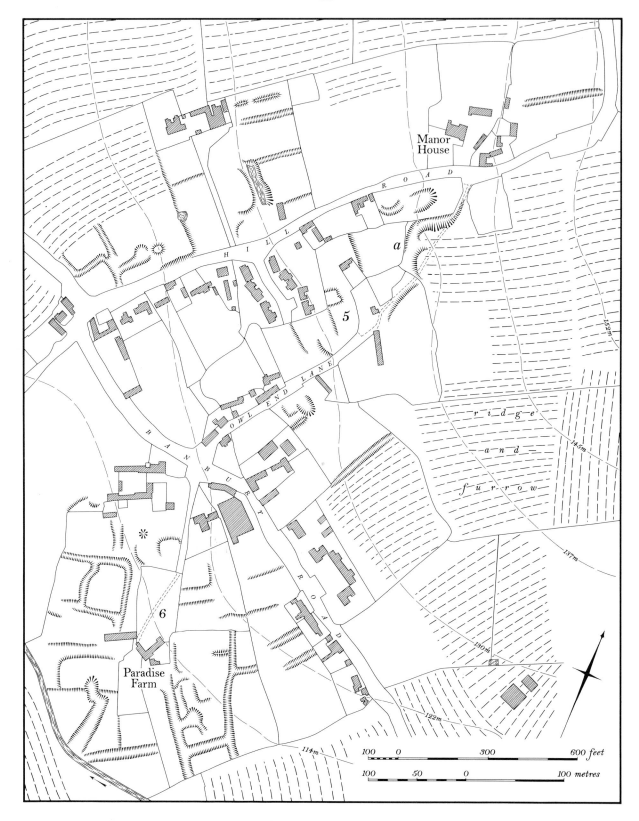

Fig. 35 BODDINGTON (5) Settlement remains at Lower Boddington, (6) Enclosures

sherds and one scraper have been found at SP 573378 and other Roman sherds at SP 58403677 (Northants. SMR).

(1) ROMAN SETTLEMENT (centred SP 592372), lies S.S.E. of Brackley church, at 107 m. above OD. Building work between 1971 and 1974 revealed evidence of an extensive Roman settlement. Finds included: (a) (SP 594370) pottery and roof tiles (*BNFAS*, 5 (1971), 6); (b) (SP 592373) samian ware, roof and flue tiles, tesserae, plaster and much coarse ware indicating late Roman occupation, as well as coins of Severus Alexander, Tetricus I, Gallienus and Crispus, foundations of walls, a cobbled floor and a covered stone gully (*Northants. Archaeol.*, 8 (1973), 5; 9 (1974), 86; *Britannia*, 4 (1973), 294; Northants. SMR).

(2) ROMAN SETTLEMENT (?) (SP 580378), N.W. of the town at 125 m. above OD. Evidence of a Roman settlement was noted before 1977 but no details are known. (Northants. SMR)

MEDIEVAL AND LATER

The site of the poorly documented Brackley Castle is said to have been S.W. of the town (SP 581346), but no trace of a castle has been discovered (J. Bridges, *Hist. of Northants.*, I (1791), 143; OS Record Cards). A sceatta in NM was perhaps found in Brackley before 1902 (VCH *Northants.*, I (1902), 255; *Brit. Num. J.*, 47 (1977), 34).

A penny of Ethelred was found in a garden at Brackley before 1866 (*JBAA*, 22 (1866), 245). A Saxon spearhead and perhaps part of a shield boss were found in a pond somewhere in the parish before 1904 (T. J. George, *Arch. Survey of Northants.* (1904), 11; NM) and a late Saxon dagger said to be from Brackley is in the Ashmolean Museum. Medieval pottery has been noted over the years on the S. side of the town, near Bridge Street (SP 585366, 584365; Ashmolean Museum; Northants. SMR).

(3) SETTLEMENT REMAINS (centred SP 591372), formerly part of the village of Brackley, lie S. and W. of St. Peter's Church, in the area known as Old Town. Brackley is first mentioned in 1086 when Domesday Book lists it as a small manor of two hides with a recorded population of 24 (VCH *Northants.*, I (1902), 330). By 1173 the new town of Brackley appears to have been laid out along the Oxford-Northampton road to the S.W. of the earlier village (M. W. Beresford, *New Towns of the Middle Ages* (1967), 468–9). The old village with its parish church remained separate from the new town and even in the early 18th century it only contained 20 houses (Bridges, op. cit.). Similarly the Enclosure Map of 1830 (NRO) shows only a few houses to the N. and E. of the church. In recent years most of the area has been built over and little of the earlier village survives. Pottery of the 12th to 14th centuries, has been found in two places within the area of the village, in the allotment and graveyard extensions immediately S. of the church and further to the W. on the N. side of Pebble Lane (SP 589372).

Leland, writing in the 16th century, said that the town was then in decline and that there were the remains of abandoned streets (*Itinerarium*, II (1744), 36), but as a result of later growth no trace of these remains survives.

(4) FISHPOND (SP 580366), formerly lay S.W. of the town in the valley of a small S.E.-flowing stream, at 105 m. above OD. The area N. of the stream was known as The Duke's Fishpond in the early 19th century (NRO, Enclosure Map, 1830). In 1978 large blocks of masonry, perhaps from the original dam, were discovered (Northants. SMR).

(5) CULTIVATION REMAINS. The common fields of Brackley were enclosed by an Act of Parliament of 1829 (NRO, Enclosure Map, 1830). At that date there were five open fields lying N. and W. of the town, with extensive old enclosures occupying the area immediately S.W. of the town and in the N.W. along the Greatworth parish boundary. Ridge-and-furrow of these fields exists on the ground or can be traced on air photographs and appears to correspond with the strips shown on the Draft Enclosure Map (NRO). It lies in end-on furlongs running across the contours on the valley sides in the S.W. and W. of the parish, except where small tributary valleys occur. Here the ridge-and-furrow is arranged at right angles to the minor stream and an interlocked pattern results (SP 570381 and 576374). This area lay in the former Castle and Middle Castle Fields in 1829. The same pattern of ridge-and-furrow occurs immediately N. of the Old Town, along another valley side, in the former Old Town and Middle Old Town Fields (SP 594384, 594378 and 593372). On the higher flatter ground N. of the town, in the former High Field, a pattern of rectangular furlongs set at right angles to each other is traceable (SP 582388). Ridge-and-furrow is also visible within the former old enclosures in the N.W. of the parish. (*Northants. P. and P.*, 6 (1975), 33–48; RAF VAP CPE/UK/1926, 2217–20, 4216–21; CPE/UK/1929, 1320–2; CPE/UK/2097, 3157–8)

10 BRADDEN
(OS 1:10000 [a] SP 64 NW, [b] SP 64 NE)

The small, rectangular parish, covering only 420 hectares, is bounded on the S.E. by the R. Tove and on the N.E. by a tributary stream. Apart from small outcrops of Northampton Sand and Oolitic Limestone the area is almost entirely covered by glacial sands, gravels and clays. No pre-medieval monuments are recorded.

MEDIEVAL AND LATER

[a](1) SETTLEMENT REMAINS (centred SP 645480; Fig. 14), formerly part of Bradden, lie in and around the village, on Boulder Clay and glacial sands and gravels, between 132 m. and 122 m. above OD.

Bradden was first documented in Domesday Book, as two small manors with a recorded population of six (VCH *Northants.*, I (1902), 336, 355). In 1301 23 people paid the Lay Subsidy Tax (PRO, E179/155/31) and in the same tax of 1334 Bradden together with Slapton paid 79 shillings (PRO, E179/155/3). The Poll Tax Returns of 1377 (PRO, E179/155/28) indicate that at least 52 people over the age of 14 were living at Bradden. Thereafter there is no record of the size of the village until about 1720 when there were

25 families (J. Bridges, *Hist. of Northants.*, I (1791), 236). In 1801 the population of the parish was 156.

The modern village consists of a single winding street running N.E.-S.W. with two short lanes E. and S.E. from it. Most of the houses lie on the S.E. side of the main street, the N.W. side being occupied by Bradden House and its garden, the church, the rectory and a row of cottages. However, the surviving earthworks and a map of 1740 (NRO) suggest that there were once houses along most of the N.W. side of the street, as well as the manor house (2). At the S.W. end of the village (SP 644481) there are some rather indeterminate earthworks lying along the street and separated from the ridge-and-furrow to the W. by a well-marked bank about 1 m. high, with an outer ditch. These appear to be house-sites and closes already abandoned by 1740; at that date they lay in two fields which still exist, then called Higher and Middle Conigree. To the N.E. the map of 1740 depicts three buildings edging the street (SP 64434825, 64634830 and 64674838), between the street and the formal gardens (5) of Bradden House. These were still standing in 1803 (NRO, Enclosure Map) but were removed later in the 19th century when the garden was extended. No trace of them remains in the present shrubbery, although stone-rubble foundations of a small barn or shed associated with one of them still survive.

The 1740 map shows that the two lanes to the S.E. of the main street were continuous, forming a loop road on that side of the village. This road still existed in 1803, although the Enclosure Map shows a field boundary cutting across it. Part of the road still survives as a hollow-way immediately N.E. of Lane Farm (SP 647481), running N.E. down the hillside to meet the S.W. end of Lower End Road. (RAF VAP CPE/UK/1994, 2083–4, 3087–8; air photographs in NMR)

ᵃ(2) MANOR HOUSE SITE (SP 647486; Fig. 14), lies immediately N. of the church, on the side of a shallow valley, on Boulder Clay at 122 m. above OD. The present Bradden House to the S.W. is traditionally the site of a manor house of the Knights Hospitallers who held land in Bradden; the existing building certainly incorporates a late medieval structure. The earthworks described here may therefore be the site of another medieval manor house of the village.

The earthworks consist of a large rectangular area 120 m. long, bounded on the N. and E. by a bank up to 1.5 m. high with an outer ditch 0.25 m. deep, and on the S. by a scarp. There is no evidence of a W. side. The interior is uneven and has two low scarps along the N. side. In the centre of the S. side are broad rectangular terraces edged by low scarps which may be the remains of a garden. The site was already abandoned by 1740 (map in NRO) when the field was called Bury; the copse to the E. is still called Bury Brake. (RAF VAP CPE/UK/1994, 2083–4; air photographs in NMR)

ᵃ(3) FISHPONDS (SP 647483), at the head of a small stream on the E. side of the village street, on glacial deposits, at 120 m. above OD. A rectangular pond 30 m. by 25 m., with a large dam up to 2 m. high at its E. end, is the only survivor of a system of ponds which in 1740 (map in NRO) lay in a small field called Fishpond Close. To the S. of the surviving pond there was a much larger rectangular pond with a small rectangular island within it; another smaller pond lay to the N.W. By 1803 (NRO, Enclosure Map) the two main ponds still existed though they are depicted as circular. The smaller one had been replaced by a group of five other small ponds. All these were presumably destroyed in the 19th century.

ᵃ(4) PONDS (SP 645493), lay in the extreme N. of the parish on Boulder Clay at 110 m. above OD. On a map of 1740 (NRO) two large rectangular ponds are shown here. They appear to have been ornamental. Both have now been totally destroyed and even on air photographs taken in 1947 only very slight traces are visible. (RAF VAP CPE/UK/1994, 2083–4)

ᵃ(5) GARDEN REMAINS (SP 645483), associated with Bradden House, lie immediately S.W. of the house, on level ground at 125 m. above OD. The original gardens are depicted on a map of 1740 (NRO). The house was then L-shaped with, to the S.E., a pair of rectangular flower beds separated by a drive. To the S.W. of the house the main garden extended for some 170 m. and was divided into three separate parts. The N.E. part, closest to the house, is shown on the map as four rectangular areas, probably flower beds, arranged in two pairs along the axis of the garden. Beyond were two other rectangular areas lying side by side and planted with trees. To the S.W. lay a triangular wooded area through which passed seven intersecting straight walks. From the map it is possible to suggest that this garden was of 17th or early 18th-century date. By 1803 (NRO, Enclosure Map) the garden had been altered. The central and S.W. parts formed an area called The Wilderness and that part close to the house consisted of terraces and flower beds. Since then further alterations have taken place around the house.

A circular mound 15 m. in diam. and 1.5 m. high which lies on the edge of the modern shrubbery at the S. end of the garden (SP 64544827) may be the only surviving part of the 17th-century garden. The mound would have been situated at the junction of the central and S.W. parts of that garden, on the edge of the triangular wooded area. A mound in such a position would not be unusual for a garden of this period (see RCHM *Northants.*, I (1975) Barnwell (9)). Several scarps remain from the 19th-century garden.

ᵃ(6) MOUND (SP 643479), lies on the summit of a hill S.W. of the village, on Boulder Clay at 137 m. above OD. It consists of a low, flat-topped mound 15 m. in diam. and 0.25 m. high, completely surrounded by a water-filled ditch up to 10 m. wide. It certainly existed in its present form in 1740 (map in NRO) when it was depicted as tree-covered. At that time it lay between two fields called West and Middle Conigree. Its date and purpose are not known but it may have originated as the base of a windmill or have been connected with a rabbit warren as the field name suggests.

(7) CULTIVATION REMAINS. The common fields of Bradden were enclosed by an Act of Parliament of 1803 (NRO, Enclosure Map). All the land to the N. and W. of the

village had already been enclosed at least as early as 1740 (map in NRO) and by 1803 there were three open fields, North Field in the N.E. of the parish, Middle Field in the E. and Upper Field in the S.

Ridge-and-furrow of these fields exists on the ground or can be traced on air photographs over much of their former area arranged in end-on and interlocked furlongs, many of reversed-S form. It can be correlated exactly with the individual strips shown on the Draft Enclosure Map.

Ridge-and-furrow can also be traced close to the R. Tove and to its tributary on the N. edge of the parish on land which had become permanent meadow or pasture by 1803. It is well marked, for example, in the extreme N. of the parish (SP 646495) in what was Flitwell Cow Pasture and in the E. (at SP 660480) in what was Foscote Cow Pasture in 1803.

Ridge-and-furrow also survives in the N.W. in the area already enclosed in 1740, in the same form and layout as elsewhere in the parish. (RAF VAP CPE/UK/1926, 1043–4, 1230–28; CPE/UK/1994, 2080–5, 3085–9)

11 BUGBROOKE
(OS 1:10000 SP 65 NE)

The parish, of irregular form, covers some 910 hectares of land on the S. side of the R. Nene which forms its short N. boundary. Most of the parish is an undulating plain of clay between 70 m. and 90 m. above OD, across which the Bug Brook flows N.E. and then N. to join the R. Nene. In the extreme S. of the parish the land rises steeply to Bugbrooke Downs which are capped by Northampton Sand at 120 m. above OD.

PREHISTORIC AND ROMAN

A polished stone axe of Group VI (Langdale) type was found in the parish before 1904 (NM; T. J. George, *Arch. Survey of Northants.* (1904), 11; *PPS*, 28 (1962), 262, No. 982). A quartzite pebble with a central hour-glass perforation, probably a mace, was found in 1973 (SP 67675768; NM; *Northants. Archaeol.*, 9 (1974), 83). A large saucer quern was discovered during ploughing in 1973 (SP 65415662; *Northants. Archaeol.*, 13 (1978), 178).

(1) RING DITCHES (SP 661566), in the S.W. of the parish, on the S.E. edge of a high flat-topped plateau of Northampton Sand at 125 m. above OD. Air photographs (NCAU) show one ring ditch 15 m. in diam. and indistinct traces of at least three others in the immediate area.

(2) ENCLOSURES AND DITCHES (SP 671562), in the S. of the parish, close to a small N.-flowing stream, on Marlstone Rock at 80 m. above OD. Air photographs (NCAU) show very indistinctly two small circular conjoined enclosures 10 m. in diam., possibly hut-sites, set inside an incomplete circular feature 50 m. wide. Traces of linear ditches are visible around and intersecting the circular feature.

(3) ROMAN SETTLEMENT (SP 686567), S.E. of the village, on Upper Lias Clay at 94 m. above OD. A scatter of Roman pottery, fragments of tile and building stone, some dressed, was found in 1975 (*Northants. Archaeol.*, 11 (1976), 186).

For Roman Road 1f, Watling Street, see Appendix.

MEDIEVAL AND LATER

No medieval earthworks have been recorded in the village of Bugbrooke but the village plan is unusual with a single street on the E. of the stream and an almost isolated church on the W. (NRO, Enclosure Map, 1779). The area around the church, still mainly permanent pasture, might well repay excavation in the future in order to establish the origins of the village.

(4) FISHPONDS (SP 675576), lie N. of the village, immediately W. of the manor house, on the E. side of the Bug Brook, on Middle Lias Clay at 76 m. above OD. Three sunken rectangular ponds 1.5 m. deep, set roughly at right angles to each other and linked by narrow channels, lie close to the brook. The northernmost is 20 m. by 8 m., the central one 40 m. by 12 m. and the southernmost 22 m. by 20 m. The latter has a large outer bank on its S. and W. sides. A broad curving bank 12 m. wide and 1.5 m. high lies immediately to the S. At the N. end of the area two parallel ditches up to 10 m. wide, 1.5 m. deep and 15 m.–20 m. apart extend up the valley sides. The earthworks must be associated with Manor Farm and the fishponds are presumably medieval in date. (Air photographs in NMR)

(5) CULTIVATION REMAINS. The common fields of the parish were enclosed by an Act of Parliament of 1779 (NRO, Enclosure Map). Ridge-and-furrow of these fields exists on the ground or can be traced on air photographs over almost the entire parish with the exception of a wide strip of floodable meadowland along the R. Nene in the N. and on the high parts of Bugbrooke Downs in the S.E. No doubt it once existed in the latter area but modern cultivation has removed all traces from the light sandy soils.

On the gently undulating land which makes up most of the parish the ridge-and-furrow is arranged in end-on or interlocked furlongs, many of markedly reversed-S form. Some extremely large headlands up to 12 m. wide and 0.5 m. high survive (e.g. SP 679584), and at least two of them between end-on furlongs have been over-ploughed at some time in order to make the two furlongs into one (SP 673580 and 678568). A small area of narrow ridge-and-furrow presumably of the 18th or 19th century formerly lay immediately N. of the manor house (SP 677577). (RAF VAP CPE/UK/1926, 4035–7, 5034–40; CPE/UK/1994, 1172–6, 3161–6; 3G/TUD/UK/118, 6030–5, 6047–53; FSL6603, 2379–84)

UNDATED

(6) BURIALS (unlocated, but apparently in the village), found about 1840 during the 'levelling of a hill'. Several human skulls, 'together with a crocodile in a petrified state' were discovered as well as horseshoes. A human skeleton

with a severed head is also recorded (Whellan, *Dir.*, 303). No date or function can be suggested for these oddly assorted finds, though the site has been interpreted as a 'tumulus' (T. J. George, *Arch. Survey of Northants.* (1904), 11).

12 CHACOMBE
(OS 1:10000 [a] SP 44 SE, [b] SP 54 SW)

The long narrow parish covering some 680 hectares lies E. of the R. Cherwell which forms the short W. boundary. The much longer N. boundary follows a W.-flowing tributary stream. Apart from a flat alluvial area in the N.W. at about 100 m. above OD most of the parish lies on a steep N.W.-facing scarp rising across Lias Clay and Marlstone Rock to a maximum height of 152 m. above OD.

PREHISTORIC OR ROMAN

[b](1) ENCLOSURE (SP 504442), lies in the E. of the parish, on Marlstone Rock at 130 m. above OD. Air photographs (CUAP, ABW89, 90) show the cropmark of part of a large, perhaps rectangular enclosure with an entrance in the S. side. The only side which is completely visible is almost 100 m. long.

MEDIEVAL AND LATER

[a](2) SITE OF AUGUSTINIAN PRIORY (centred SP 488439), lies immediately W. of the village, on river gravel and alluvium at 100 m. above OD. The priory was founded by Hugh de Chacombe, lord of the manor of Chacombe in the reign of Henry II. Little is known of its early history, although some details of its later life are recorded. It was dissolved in 1536 (VCH *Northants.*, II (1906), 133–5).

The present house is partly of early 17th-century date but there are many later additions and alterations. Only one medieval structure, containing some 13th-century features, and said to be a chapel, exists at the E. end of the house. The S. and E. boundaries of the grounds around the house are defined by a continuous water-filled ditch with a total length of about 500 m. In its present form this is an 18th-century landscape feature. At its N.E. corner the line of the pond is continued N. and W. by two rectangular depressions 10 m. wide and up to 1 m. deep linked by a short channel and further W., along the N. and W. sides of the priory grounds, there is a wide ditch or pond 10 m. wide and 1 m. deep. These channels, forming a continuous line of water along the N. and W. sides of the priory grounds, lie beyond the landscape gardens of the existing house, and have not been altered; they indicate that the whole of the medieval priory precinct was bounded by a wide, water-filled ditch or fishpond.

Within the precinct, immediately N. and N.W. of the house, are two further ponds, one rectangular, the other of more irregular shape. They are both ornamental, but may have originated as medieval fishponds of the priory. At least three medieval coffin slabs have been found in the grounds of the priory, including one of 13th-century date (*Arch. J.*, 1 (1845), 393; 15 (1858), 88). (RAF VAP CPE/UK/1926, 1205–7; F21 58/RAF/1567, 0080–1; F21 58/RAF/3963, 0010–11)

[a](3) SITE OF MANOR HOUSE (SP 491439), lies at the N.W. edge of the village, within a large pasture field known as the Berry Close immediately E. of the church (NRO, Tithe Map, 1840), on Lower Lias Clay at 114 m. above OD. The site, with the church, occupies a low rounded hill which dominates the village. A roughly rectangular enclosure, orientated N.E.-S.W., 50 m. by 25 m., is bounded on all but the S.W. corner by a scarp up to 2 m. high at the N.E. end, but elsewhere only 1 m.–1.5 m. In a few places there are slight indications of an external ditch but quarry pits along the outer edge of the scarp, as well as within the enclosure itself, have removed most traces of the ditch and any interior features. Although the site is in poor condition the topographical relationship of manor house, church and village is of interest. To the E., within the same field, are other remains associated with the village (see (4) below). (RAF VAP CPE/UK/1926, 1205–7; F21 58/RAF/3963, 0010–11)

[a](4) SETTLEMENT REMAINS (SP 491439), formerly part of Chacombe village, lie immediately E. and N.E. of (3), in a similar situation. The village consists of two conjoined loops from which radiate several roads or tracks, some now abandoned. One track runs N. down the valley side from the N.E. corner of the N. loop. The S. part of it is still a street, Silver Street North, with houses on its E. side; a hollow-way 15 m. across and up to 1.5 m. deep continues its line for some 100 m. into the valley bottom. On the W. side of the hollow-way and of the existing street are the very fragmentary remains of rectangular closes bounded by shallow ditches or low scarps. Disturbed areas at their E. ends suggest former buildings. The southernmost closes end just below the massive scarp which bounds the E. side of the manor house site (3). The area was already devoid of buildings in 1840 (NRO, Tithe Map). There is no evidence in any of the surviving medieval or post-medieval national taxation records of a decline in the size of the village at any time.

On the S. side of the village another of the radiating lanes, now used as the drive to Chacombe House, runs on as a hollowed track through the adjacent ridge-and-furrow (SP 492435). (RAF VAP CPE/UK/1926, 1205–7; F21 58/RAF/3963, 0010–11)

[a](5) FISHPONDS (SP 490441–493442), lie along the S. side of the small stream which forms the parish and county boundary, immediately to the N. of the village, on Lower Lias Clay between 103 m. and 106 m. above OD. At the upper, N.E. end there was formerly a large pond, some 180 m. long and 20 m. wide, slightly curved in plan, cut back into the valley side on the S. and embanked on the N. side above the stream. This has now been largely destroyed by a sewage works; only its N.E. corner and part of the W. end survive. Downstream to the W. is a similar but smaller pond, 80 m. long and 20 m. across, cut back into the hillside on the S. and bounded on the N. by a large bank 10 m. wide and 1.5 m. high. What appears to be a later leat has been cut along its S. side and continues W. beyond the pond. This and other damage make it impossible to be certain about the original form of the W. end of the pond. The purpose of the leat is unknown. (RAF VAP CPE/UK/1926, 1205–7; F21 58/RAF/3963, 0010–11)

(6) CULTIVATION REMAINS. The exact date of the enclosure of the common fields of the parish is not known, but Bridges (*Hist. of Northants.*, I (1791), 153), writing in about 1720, said that the whole lordship was then enclosed and had been so 'for near a 100 years'. Ridge-and-furrow of these fields exists on the ground or can be traced on air photographs over much of the parish arranged in end-on or interlocked furlongs. Much of it is still well preserved and good examples of hollow-ways and headlands are visible in a number of places running between end-on furlongs (e.g. SP 474428 and 487435). Elsewhere end-on furlongs have been joined together; the point of junction is indicated by a sudden change in direction of the ridges and in some places by the merging of two or more ridges into a single one (e.g. SP 482431 and 477429). On the low-lying ground in the extreme W. of the parish where a number of small streams meet the R. Cherwell large areas of permanent grassland have no trace of ridge-and-furrow on them and appear always to have been meadowland. One area (SP 472433) was known as Burston Meadow in 1840 (NRO, Tithe Map). To the N. are two small 'islands' of ridge-and-furrow, on areas slightly raised above the low-lying flood-plain (at SP 468434 and 472435). These suggest that every suitable piece of land was taken into cultivation at some time in the medieval period. (RAF VAP CPE/UK/1926, 1203–11; F21 58/RAF/1567, 0080–4; F21 58/RAF/3963, 0009–11)

13 CHIPPING WARDEN

(OS 1:10000 [a] SP 44 NE, [b] SP 54 NW, [c] SP 55 SW, [d] SP 45 SE)

The modern parish covers more than 950 hectares; the R. Cherwell forms its S. and E. boundaries, and the Oxfordshire boundary its S.W. side. From the river, here flowing at about 110 m. above OD, the ground rises across bands of Lower and Middle Lias Clay and Marlstone Rock to an area of Upper Lias Clay at 125 m. above OD. Northampton Sand outcrops in the E. on Warden Hill over 155 m. above OD.

There is evidence for both Iron Age and Roman occupation in the parish including the fortified site known as Arbury Banks (2) and the Roman villa (3). The modern parish includes the land of the deserted village of Trafford (10), formerly an extra-parochial part of Byfield parish. The medieval parish of Chipping Warden had a detached part to the N., now in Aston le Walls parish (Fig. 38) and a further detached area centred on the abandoned village of Stoneton, now in Warwickshire.

PREHISTORIC AND ROMAN

The major portion of a large flint implement was found in 1961 in the N. of the parish (SP 517508; OS Record Cards; lost) and two bronze axes of unknown provenance have also been discovered (NM). A looped palstave and a

socketed axe are said to have been found in 1977 N.W. of the village (SP 495497; Banbury Museum; *Northants. Archaeol.*, 14 (1979), 102). Several Iron Age coins have been found in the parish; some are said to have come from the Iron Age site (2) or from the Roman villa (3) but these attributions seem uncertain. The coins include a British 'Remic' gold stater (Mack, 59) said to be from (2), a bronze coin of Tasciovanus, three bronze coins of Cunobelinus and an inadequately recorded gold quarter stater (S. S. Frere (ed.), *Problems of the Iron Age in Southern Britain* (1958), 223, 233, 284; OS Record Cards).

[b](1) DITCHED TRACKWAY (?) (SP 509498), in the centre of the parish, N.E. of the village, on Upper Lias Clay at 137 m. above OD. Air photographs (NCAU) show two parallel ditches 12 m. apart orientated N.-S. and visible for 90 m. It is not clear whether the feature is overlaid by ridge-and-furrow; it may be recent.

[a](2) IRON AGE FORT (SP 494486; Fig. 36), known as Arbury Camp, lies on the flat summit of a low rounded hill S.W. of Chipping Warden village, mainly on Marlstone Rock at 134 m. above OD. The monument is of considerable interest not only as a rare survival of an upstanding prehistoric site in this part of the county but also because of the medieval land use; the ramparts have been incorporated into the headlands of the common field system of the parish (11) and a windmill (7) stood on a mound on part of the outer bank. The E. part and the S.W. corner are now arable land, but the rest is permanent grassland.

The site was described by Bridges in the early 18th century (*Hist. of Northants.*, I (1791), 111) who said: 'It is certain that no Roman coins or other marks of antiquity have ever been discovered there, though the ground is now ploughed up'. The absence of finds from the site is still notable, though one gold Iron Age coin, a British 'Remic' stater (Mack, 59; in private hands) is said to have come from the site. Five other Iron Age coins are recorded from the parish but were perhaps found on the Roman site (3) and not here (S. S. Frere (ed.), op. cit.). The site was described in the 19th century by A. Beesley (*Hist. of Banbury* (1841), 30); he interpreted it as circular with a large outer enclosure attached to it on the W. This idea was elaborated by the Ordnance Survey (OS Record Cards, 1968) who said that the site consisted of a hexagonal enclosure, probably Belgic in date because of its shape, a rectangular annex or extension to the W., a further annex to the N., and a bank of unknown purpose further W. again. These interpretations can be discounted as all the banks of the suggested annexes are simply well-marked headlands between ridge-and-furrow and have no connection with the fort itself. Moreover the fort is now hexagonal in plan almost certainly because its original ramparts have also been used as headlands of the medieval fields and have been pulled out of shape by ploughing. There is no reason to doubt that, in its original form, the enclosure was roughly circular.

The main enclosure covers just under 3 hectares and was presumably once bounded by a massive bank and external ditch, perhaps with an original entrance in the S.E. corner. The whole of the E. part is now under permanent arable and the surviving rampart is no more than 10 cm. high with no trace of a ditch. Air photographs (CUAP AKS10; RAF

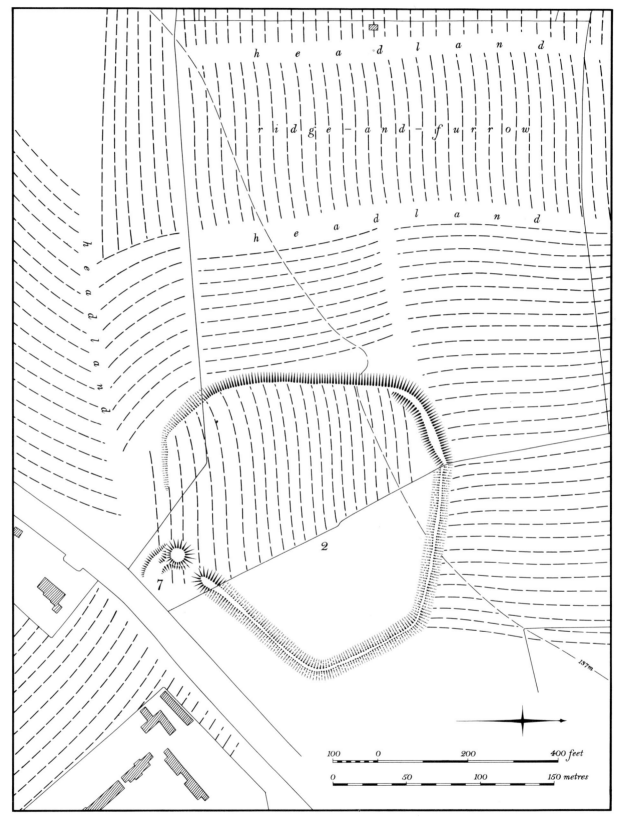

Fig. 36 CHIPPING WARDEN (2) Iron Age fort, (7) Windmill mound

VAP 106G/UK/721, 3002–4; in NMR) show three alignments of the rampart here, two of which, on the N. and E., have been straightened by being used as headlands in medieval times. All trace of the ridge-and-furrow has now disappeared except on the N. side. A short section of the rampart in the N.W. has been less damaged as the ridge-and-furrow to the N. stopped short of it and to the S. ran E.-W. below it. Here the rampart is 1.5 m. high above the land to the N. and 1 m. high above the interior. There is no ditch, any trace presumably having been destroyed by the adjacent ridge-and-furrow. The W. side is now reduced to a broad slightly curving scarp 2.5 m. high. The assumed outer ditch does not survive, again obliterated by the adjacent ridge-and-furrow, here running N.-S. The scarp itself has been used as a headland during the ploughing of the interior of the fort and its top is extremely uneven where the ridge-and-furrow rides over it.

The S.W. corner of the fort is now only a simple scarp 1 m.–1.5 m., curving first S.E. and then E. before fading out. The mound to the S. of it shown on OS 1:2500 maps is part of another medieval headland (as shown on plan). The S. side of the fort now hardly exists, for the W. part has been ploughed down into ridge-and-furrow which in turn has had a windmill mound (7) built over it. Immediately to the E. of the windmill mound is a small gap which may be an original entrance, for beyond it to the N.E. is the end of an original bank, 0.5 m. high. The W. half of the interior of the fort is covered by well-marked ridge-and-furrow running approximately E.-W., up to 0.5 m. high, and obscuring any original feature.

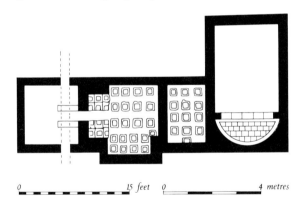

0   15 feet   0   4 metres

Fig. 37   CHIPPING WARDEN (3)
Roman bath house
(from a plan in VCH, *Northants.* I)

^b(3) ROMAN VILLA (SP 510482; Fig. 37), lies S.E. of the village, on a valley side close to the R. Cherwell, on Lias Clay at about 110 m. above OD. The site was known in the early 18th century, for Morton (*Hist. of Northants.* (1712), 526) records the ploughing up of foundation stones, ashes and Roman coins, but the main finds were made in the early 19th century. The ploughing of a field called Black Grounds revealed dark earth, foundations, dressed stone and Roman coins; in 1826 an urn containing human bones was discovered. Drainage work close to the river in 1849 produced much pottery, including samian, as well as

four skeletons without grave goods apart from a small finger ring. This work also led to the discovery of a detached bath house near the river, consisting of three rooms and a stoke hole (Fig. 37). Subsequent ploughing across the whole area revealed extensive stone foundations and large quantities of Roman pottery from the 1st to the 4th century including much samian, coins and other small objects. Some of the Iron Age coins listed above may have come from this site. A small well is also recorded (G. Baker, *Hist. of Northants.*, I (1822–30), 530–2; A. Beesley, *Hist. of Banbury* (1841), 27; *JBAA*, 5 (1850), 83, 168; VCH *Northants.*, I (1902), 200; OS Record Cards).

For Anglo-Saxon finds from this site, see below.

MEDIEVAL AND LATER

Anglo-Saxon objects found in the parish include sceattas said to have come from the site of the Roman villa (3) (*JBAA*, 2 (1847), 346; VCH *Northants.*, I (1902), 255; *Brit. Num. J.*, 47 (1977), 38) and a 6th-century francisca of unknown provenance, probably from a male grave (*J. Northants. Mus. and Art Gall.*, 6 (1969), 47). An iron bolt-head with hinged barbs discovered on Warden Hill in 1836 has been interpreted as a relic of the Battle of Danesmoor (1469) (OS Record Cards; see (4)).

^a(4) CEMETERY (around SP 499485), S. of the church. In the early 19th century many burials were discovered, including large pits full of bones with a quantity of spurs, and single interments apparently laid out in lines. These remains have been associated with the Battle of Danesmoor (1469) which took place in the neighbouring parish of Edgcote (*JBAA*, 1 (1845), 56; OS Record Cards; A. Beesley, *Hist. of Banbury* (1841), 28).

^b(5) MOAT (SP 501483), lay on the S.E. side of the village, close to the R. Cherwell, on Lower Lias Clay at 105 m. above OD. The moat has been almost completely destroyed by ploughing and the ground returned to pasture. From plans made before destruction, the site appears to have been a simple moated enclosure of roughly rectangular form (OS 1:2500 plan, Northants. LIV 7; G. Baker, *Hist. of Northants.*, I (1822–30), 527). Air photographs (RAF VAP 106G/UK/721, 3002–3; CPE/UK/1926, 1069–70, and in NMR) show slight traces of what appears to be ridge-and-furrow on the island. Water entered the moat near its N.E. corner and returned to the R. Cherwell by a large ditch on the S.E. side. In 1809 (NRO, map of Chipping Warden) the area was known as Castle Yard but nothing is known of its history.

^d(6) FISHPONDS (SP 501486), lie 200 m. N.W. of (5) and immediately S.E. of the village, in a shallow valley at the N. end of Edgcote Park, on Middle Lias Clay at 122 m. above OD. They consist of a line of three flat-bottomed ponds, each cut down 2 m. into the valley floor. The two upper northernmost ponds are small and have been much altered by later activity but the lower one is larger, 120 m. by 50 m. All have earthen dams up to 1.5 m. high. The ponds were filled by springs above the upper pond and water still runs from the lower pond down the valley towards the moated site (5) which it once filled. Immediately to the W. of the lower pond there are other earth-

works including large scarps up to 2.5 m. high. These have no coherent plan but may be the sites of houses removed when the park was made, perhaps in the 18th century (G. Baker, *Hist. of Northants.*, I (1822–30), 527; air photographs in NMR).

[a](7) WINDMILL MOUND (SP 49434847; Fig. 36), lies on the edge of a low rounded hill S.W. of the village, on Marlstone Rock at 134 m. above OD. The mound lies on top of the S. rampart of the Iron Age fort known as Arbury Banks (2). It is roughly circular, 20 m. in diam. and 2.25 m. high, with a flat top 9 m. across, and has a slight cross-shaped depression in the centre. There are traces of a ramp leading on to the mound from the S.E. The mill was constructed on the S. rampart of the fort, which had already been diminished by ploughing. The plough ridges can be seen to underlie the mound. Two ridges approach the mound from the W. The northernmost passes under the mound but was later reploughed short of it and thus has a secondary headland on the edge of the mound. The southernmost ridge also passes under the mound, but has not been reploughed. In the 19th century (NRO, Tithe Map, 1837) the field in which the mound lay was known as Windmill Bank, but no mill then existed. (CUAP, AKS10; RAF VAP CPE/UK/1926, 1070–1)

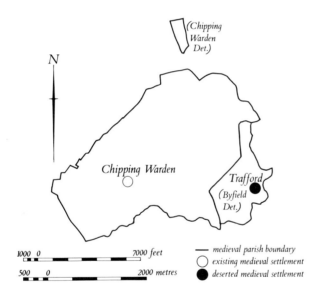

Fig. 38 CHIPPING WARDEN
Medieval settlements and estates

[a](8) FISHPOND (SP 497484), lies 225 m. S.W. of the church, in the bottom of a small S.-draining valley, on Middle Lias Clay at 120 m. above OD. It is roughly rectangular, 40 m. by 65 m., cut back into the adjacent hillside to a depth of 2 m., with a massive earthen dam 15 m. wide and 2.5 m. high at the S. end. Nothing is known of its date or history. (RAF VAP 106G/UK/721, 3002–4; air photographs in NMR)

[a](9) SETTLEMENT REMAINS (SP 497486), formerly part of Chipping Warden village, lay W. of the church in the angle between the Banbury Road and Mill Lane. Air photographs taken in 1947, before the area was built over, show a series of rectangular closes or paddocks bounded by low scarps. More closes to the S. (at SP 497484) had already been partly destroyed when the air photographs were taken. No definite building sites are visible and the earthworks may have been small fields. (RAF VAP CPE/UK/1926, 1069–70)

[b](10) DESERTED VILLAGE OF TRAFFORD (SP 527486; Figs. 38 and 39), lies in the E. of the parish, on the W. side of the R. Cherwell, on Marlstone Rock and Lias Clay at 112 m. above OD. The village lay at the S. end of a long narrow strip of land bounded by the R. Cherwell, which was a detached part of Byfield parish until the late 19th century (NRO, Tithe Map of Byfield, (1837)).

The village is first mentioned in Domesday Book when it was listed as a small manor with a recorded population of six (VCH *Northants.*, I (1902), 332). In 1301 13 taxpayers paid the Lay Subsidy (PRO, E179/155/31) but this is the last record of its population. Trafford is mentioned by name in the *Nomina Villarum* of 1316 but thereafter it was always taxed with Byfield. By 1547 600 sheep were kept on the manor which suggests that it was already depopulated. By the early 19th century only the present farmhouse and the existing cottages to the N. remained, though at least part of the E.-W. hollow-way appears still to have been used as a track (OS 1st ed. 1 in. map, 1834; K. J. Allison, *et al., The Deserted Villages of Northants.* (1966), 47).

The remains of the village are in poor condition but certain features are clear. A very damaged hollow-way up to 1 m. deep runs from the W. end of the site to immediately S. of Trafford Farm where it turns sharply S. and runs down the hillside to the R. Cherwell ('a'-'b' on plan). To the W. of the farm this hollow-way widens into a roughly triangular depression from the N. end of which another hollow-way extends N. and becomes a headland between rather narrow ridge-and-furrow. On the S. side of the main hollow-way lie the very degraded remains of a series of closes, with long boundaries surviving as scarps. At their N. ends, adjacent to the hollow-way, are several rounded or irregular platforms, possibly the sites of former buildings. A third, narrower hollow-way runs N.E. and then N.W. from the point where the first meets the river. Below it to the E., in the bend of the river, are two rectangular fishponds, set at right angles to each other and up to 1.5 m. deep ('c' on plan). Immediately N. of the farm are traces of at least one enclosure bounded by low scarps. To the S.W. of the village remains there was formerly a large rectangular pond, but this has recently been altered and extended to the E. and filled with water. (RAF VAP CPE/UK/1926, 1065–6)

(11) CULTIVATION REMAINS. The common fields of Chipping Warden were enclosed by an Act of Parliament of 1733, but no details of the fields are known. Ridge-and-furrow exists on the ground or can be traced on air photographs over much of the land attributable to Chipping Warden village, arranged in end-on or interlocked

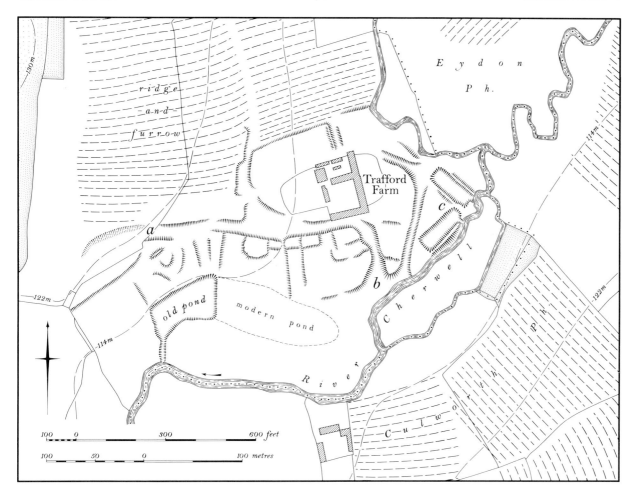

Fig. 39   CHIPPING WARDEN (10)   Deserted village of Trafford

furlongs. In a few places, for example in and around Arbury Camp (2) to the W. of the village, the ridge-and-
furrow is preserved in permanent pasture and is of a considerable height, up to almost 0.75 m. high in places. The
headlands in the area of Arbury Camp are especially notable, not only for their size but also because they have in
the past been interpreted as part of the Iron Age camp (Fig.
36).

Elsewhere headlands survive as broad ridges in permanent arable land (e.g. SP 504495). Ridge-and-furrow is
traceable on the higher broken land in the N.E. of the
parish around Warden Hill, indicating that almost the
whole parish has been under cultivation at some time.
There is one exception to this E. of Warden Hill Farm (SP
519497) where, though there is ridge-and-furrow in the
bottom and along the N. side of a steep-sided valley, the
S. side shows no evidence of ploughing. This is due to the
fact that the unstable clay has formed landslips which have
not been ploughed. Further N. (SP 517499) there is a large
area of narrow-rig ploughing, presumably of late 18th or
19th-century date.

Although the exact date is not known, the enclosure of
the common fields of the now deserted village of Trafford

(10) had presumably taken place by 1547 when sheep were
being grazed there in some numbers. Ridge-and-furrow of
these fields exists on the ground or can be traced on air
photographs over the whole of the small area of land
attributable to Trafford (Fig. 38). Except for the high land
to the N.W. of the village itself (SP 523488) where the
furlongs are interlocked, all the ridge-and-furrow is orientated E.-W., extending down the W. side of the Cherwell
valley. (RAF VAP CPE/UK/1926, 1064–71, 3065–8; CPE/UK/
1994, 2101–7, 4102–5; 106G/UK/721, 3301–4)

UNDATED

[a](12) BANK (SP 49924910), known as Wallow Bank, lies
on the N.W. edge of the village immediately N.E. of
Manor Farm, on the N. side of the Byfield Road. It is on
flat ground, on Marlstone Rock, at 132 m. above OD.

Probably because of the existence of Arbury Camp (2)
to the S.W. and of the large Roman settlement to the E.
(3), as well as the name Aston le Walls to the N., the bank
has been interpreted in a number of ways, all unsubstan-
tiated. It was first mentioned by Morton in the early 18th
century (Hist. of Northants. (1712), 525) and Bridges (Hist.
of Northants., I (1791), 111) writing in about 1720 described

it as an earthen rampart '24 paces in length (with) a narrow ridge; the west side of it is almost perpendicularly steep, the east is gradually sloped; from the foot to the ridge is 9 paces'. It was apparently dug into in 1824 when it was found to be of simple earth construction and in 1841 it was recorded as being about 28 m. long and about 2 m. high (A. Beesley, *Hist. of Banbury* (1841), 29). A skeleton was found within the bank in 1883 (Dryden Collection, Central Library, Northampton). The earthwork now consists of a broad bank, orientated N.N.W.-S.S.E., 32 m. long and 13 m. wide, much spread by gardening. Its N. end is rounded, and its S. end has been cut short and damaged by walls and hedges. No date or function can be assigned to the remains.

14   COLD HIGHAM
(OS 1:10000 [a] SP 65 SW, [b] SP 65 SE, [c] SP 65 NE, [d] SP 65 NW)

The parish, covering just over 700 hectares, lies W. of Watling Street (A5) which forms the N.E. boundary, and is drained by several small streams flowing generally N.E. and S.E. A large outcrop of Northampton Sand with small patches of Oolitic Limestone occupies much of the central and S. part, with a blanket of Boulder Clay in the S.W. and S.E. where the land rises to a maximum height of 162 m. above OD. A N.-facing scarp in the N., between 120 m. and 90 m. above OD, is on Upper Lias Clay and Marlstone Rock.

The parish contains three medieval settlements (Fig. 41) one of which, Potcote (5), is now largely deserted. The village of Cold Higham itself is very small, and only Grimscote (4) is of any size.

PREHISTORIC AND ROMAN

A Roman sestertius, probably of the 2nd century, was found in 1966 at Grimscote (SP 653535; *Northants. Archaeol.*, 12 (1977), 211).

[b](1) RING DITCH (?) (SP 660531), 500 m. S.W. of Cold Higham church, on Northampton Sand at 152 m. above OD. Air photographs (NCAU) show a possible ring ditch some 15 m. in diam.

[b](2) ENCLOSURES AND DITCHES (centred SP 663535; Fig. 40), S. and N.E. of Cold Higham church, on Northampton Sand between 142 m. and 152 m. above OD. Air photographs (NCAU) show an area of complicated cropmarks covering some 12 hectares. Most of these are indistinct and almost impossible to understand. The plan given here should be regarded as an interim interpretation. The numerous overlapping enclosures and ditches presumably indicate a long period of occupation.

[b](3) ENCLOSURES AND RING DITCH (SP 665541), 200 m. N. of Foster's Booth and immediately W. of Watling Street, on Northampton Sand at 142 m. above OD. Air photographs (NCAU) show very indistinctly a rectangular arrangement of at least six small elongated paddocks or

closes only 50 m. by 10 m.–20 m., orientated E.-W. and not aligned on the Roman road. A ring ditch 12 m. in diam. is just visible inside one of them.

For Roman Road 1f, Watling Street, see Appendix.

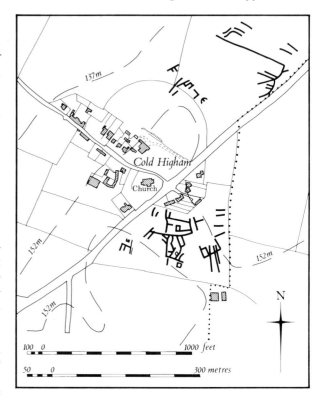

Fig. 40   COLD HIGHAM (2)
Enclosures and ditches

MEDIEVAL AND LATER

[b](4) SETTLEMENT REMAINS (SP 654535; Fig. 41), formerly part of Grimscote, lie in and around the hamlet, on Northampton Sand between 122 m. and 140 m. above OD. The hamlet is the largest centre of population in the parish and already was so in the early 18th century (J. Bridges, *Hist. of Northants.*, I (1791), 259). Little is known of its history, but extensive earthworks around it might suggest that it was once much larger than it is now. Indeed even in the mid 19th century Baker (*Hist. of Northants.*, II (1836–41), 291) said that Grimscote 'abounds in abrupt inequalities of surface'.

Most of the surviving earthworks are of little archaeological interest as they appear to be relatively modern and unconnected with settlement. For example, there are extensive stone quarries immediately S. and S.W. of Manor Farm (SP 654535) and broad bench or terrace features on the valley side to the N. of the farm (SP 654537) also appear to be old quarries. Banks to the N.E. and S.E. of the farm (SP 655637 and 655534) are at least in part the lines of old hedges bounding paddocks which were still in existence in 1812 (NRO, Enclosure Map). Elsewhere the banks appear to be old close boundaries, which had already been abandoned by 1726 (Map in NRO), for example on both sides of Mill Lane, behind Home Farm, Goffs Farm and Ivybank (SP 649535, 651534 and 651535). The only possible former house-sites lie in two small embanked closes on the E. side of Manor Road and immediately S. of Manor Farm (SP 653535); the E. ends of these have been cut by the later quarries. (RAF VAP CPE/UK/1926, 3041–3; CUAP, AKS2; air photographs in NMR)

b(5) DESERTED HAMLET OF POTCOTE (SP 658526; Fig. 41), lies S.W. of Cold Higham, around Potcote Farm, on limestone and sand at 137 m. above OD. The hamlet was the centre of a discrete unit of land which occupied the S. part of the modern parish of Cold Higham, the boundaries of which are shown on a map of 1726 (NRO). In addition, it appears that a small area of land at the N. end of Greens Norton parish also belonged to Potcote, and there is still a farm called Potcote there (at SP 662518). It is not clear how or why this land in Greens Norton became part of Potcote. Either there were originally two places both called Potcote, or the unit of land belonging to Potcote predates the establishment of the Cold Higham-Greens Norton parish boundary.

Potcote is not recorded in documents until 1202 (PN Northants., 91–2), but is almost certainly much older. In the 12th-century Survey of Northamptonshire (VCH Northants., I (1902), 373) there is a reference to an otherwise unidentified place called Potton in Towcester Hundred and this may by Potcote. The hamlet is mentioned by name in the 1316 Nomina Villarum, but thereafter there is no indication of its size until 1499 when Sir Thomas Green of Greens Norton, whose family had acquired the manor before 1428, destroyed four houses and enclosed 304 acres of land, converting it to pasture (K. J. Allison et al., The Deserted Villages of Northants. (1966), 45). Nothing is then known of Potcote until 1726; a map of that date shows a single farmstead there, with another farm to the S. within Greens Norton. The same situation existed in 1812 (NRO, Enclosure Map of Cold Higham). Since then, except for the rebuilding of the main Potcote Farm on a new site to the N.W. of the old one, nothing has changed.

There is little trace of the hamlet on the ground and the modern farm may have destroyed any former earthworks. An area of some 8 hectares around the farm is devoid of ridge-and-furrow and this may mark the overall extent of the hamlet. There are some very slight, indeterminate banks and scarps forming no coherent pattern to the S.E. of the modern farm, while to the S.W. are the fragmentary remains of what appear to be three sides of an embanked enclosure of about 2 hectares. A small quantity of pottery, mainly of 13th or 14th-century date but including some post-medieval sherds, has been found in the fields to the S. of the farm (SP 658525).

At the Potcote Farm to the S., in Greens Norton parish, are some slight banks lying to the W. of the present buildings. These may be the boundaries of paddocks abandoned relatively recently. (RAF VAP CPE/UK/1926, 3041–3; CPE/UK/1994, 4171–2)

(6) CULTIVATION REMAINS (Fig. 41). The common fields of Cold Higham and Grimscote were enclosed by an Act of Parliament of 1812 (NRO, Enclosure Map), and it is not certain whether each settlement had its own field system. An earlier map of 1726 (NRO) shows the common fields, but the furlongs and strips on it appear to be schematic.

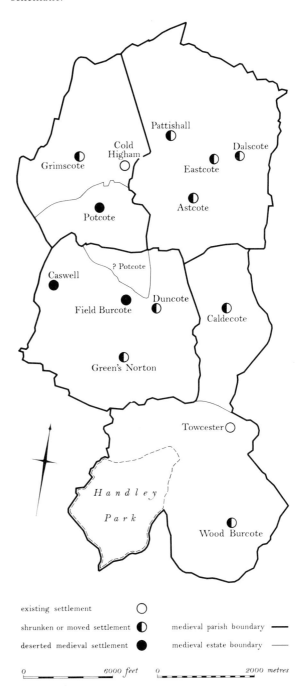

existing settlement　○

shrunken or moved settlement　◑　　medieval parish boundary　——

deserted medieval settlement　●　　medieval estate boundary　——

0　　　　6000 feet　　　0　　　　2000 metres

Fig. 41　COLD HIGHAM, GREENS NORTON, PATTISHALL and TOWCESTER
Medieval settlements and estates

Ridge-and-furrow of these fields exists on the ground or can be traced on air photographs over much of that part of the parish associated with Grimscote and Cold Higham. It is arranged in end-on and interlocked furlongs, many of reversed-S form. There are examples of the overploughing of headlands in order to make two end-on furlongs into one (e.g. at SP 651532) and in places where the ridge-and-furrow has been ploughed out the original headlands survive as broad low ridges in the modern arable (e.g. at SP 649540).

The common fields of Potcote were apparently at least partly enclosed in 1499 when Sir Thomas Green converted 304 acres there to pasture (K. J. Allison et al., *The Deserted Villages of Northants.* (1966), 45). Certainly the whole area was enclosed by 1726. Ridge-and-furrow of these fields exists on the ground or can be traced on air photographs over much of the land attributable to Potcote, arranged in end-on and interlocked furlongs of normal medieval form. (RAF VAP CPE/UK/1926, 3040–5, 5039–43; CPE/UK/1994, 4168–74)

15 COSGROVE
(OS 1:10000 [a] SP 74 SE, [b] SP 74 NE)

The parish, covering some 700 hectares, is roughly oval and lies on a broad spur bounded by the R. Tove on the E., the Great Ouse on the S.E., and the Dogsmouth Brook on the S.W. From the wide alluvial valleys of the two rivers at about 64 m. above OD the land rises across Oolitic limestones and clays; the higher ground, above 85 m., in the central, N. and W. areas is covered by Boulder Clay.

The most important archaeological remains in the parish are the Roman villa, bath house and temple (2). The modern parish is the result of both ancient and recent adjustments. Baker (*Hist. of Northants.*, II (1836–41), 128) wrote that 'this parish, prior to the inclosures, was inconveniently and inexplicably intermingled with Potterspury', and maps show that it included at least two detached areas now in Potterspury. In 1954 the creation of Old Stratford parish involved the transfer of the S.W. part of Cosgrove.

PREHISTORIC AND ROMAN

A few late Neolithic or Bronze Age flints and some pottery, perhaps sherds of a beaker, were discovered during the excavation of the Roman buildings (2) (*BNFAS*, 4 (1970), 8) and a bronze spearhead was found in about 1967 close to the R. Ouse in the E. of the parish (SP 80104206; Bucks. County Museum).

[a](1) RING DITCHES (?) (centred SP 795419), on river gravel, between 64 m. and 71 m. above OD. Air photographs (not seen by RCHM) are said to show the cropmarks of two ring ditches (SP 79564190 and 79584188), with a third 250 m. to the W. (OS Record Cards). From the description it is possible that these are the ploughed out remains of a wartime anti-aircraft emplacement (see also Old Stratford, p. 108).

[a](2) ROMAN VILLA, BATH HOUSE AND TEMPLE (SP 795421), S. of the village, on limestone, at 70 m. above OD. The discovery of an urn containing 60 silver denarii (*Gent's. Mag.*, 1 (1801), 76) and of many other Roman coins including silver medallions of Constantine I, Valentinian II and Magnus Maximus, as well as coins of Diocletian, Constans, Magnentius, Julian, Valens and Gratian (Baker, *Hist. of Northants.*, 2 (1836–41), 136; VCH *Northants.*, I (1902), 216; OS Record Cards), all probably found during the construction of the canal, suggested the presence of a Roman settlement in the area. An undated burial had also been discovered in the vicinity. Excavations in the 1950s revealed a well-preserved bath house and in 1969 the main buildings of a villa were investigated. These covered more than 1 hectare and were arranged around a large courtyard. The main building, a double-corridor villa, was built in about AD 100 and survived for about 200 years. The bath buildings constructed in about 150 went out of use before 300. Another less sophisticated double-winged building was occupied about 100–150. A small temple built in about 300 may have replaced earlier ones. Other walls and buildings were also found. (*BNFAS*, 1 (1966), 7; 4 (1970), 7–8; *JRS*, 48 (1958), 140; 49 (1959), 115; *Wolverton and District Arch. Soc. Newsletter*, 4 (1959), 7; 7 (1962), 2–4; *Britannia*, 1 (1970), 288; CBA *Summaries of Excavations* (1969), 11; MOPBW *Arch. Excavations 1969* (1970), 21; OS Record Cards)

MEDIEVAL AND LATER

[a](3) MOAT (?) (SP 796432), lies on the N.E. side of The Priory, close to the R. Tove, on river gravel at 64 m. above OD. An L-shaped ditch with a maximum depth of 1.3 m. is correctly shown on OS 1:2500 plan SP 7943. There is no trace of other sides and it is uncertain whether the feature is a genuine medieval moat or a later landscape feature. The latter is more likely.

[a](4) SETTLEMENT REMAINS (SP 796427; Fig. 15), formerly part of Cosgrove, lie at the extreme N.E. end of the village, on river gravel, at 65 m. above OD. Faint traces of a hollow-way, continuing the line of Main Street and The Green, are visible running N.E. towards Castlethorpe, Buckinghamshire. To the S.E. of The Green and cut into by later gravel-pits are very indeterminate earthworks which may be the sites of former houses. Though these remains are slight, they emphasize the relatively simple layout of the village before it was disrupted by the construction of the Grand Junction Canal in 1800. Until then the village probably consisted of a single street extending from the church in the S.W. to The Green. The Main Street was blocked by the canal, except for pedestrian use, and traffic was diverted in a broad loop to the N. on which all subsequent development has been based. The Rectory garden and the new graveyard have obliterated any trace of the original street between the canal and the church but a modern footpath follows the approximate line. (RAF VAP CPE/UK/1926, 4248–9)

(5) CULTIVATION REMAINS. The common fields of the parish were enclosed by an Act of Parliament of 1767 (NRO, Enclosure Map). No details are known of the

arrangement or the names of the fields before that date. Ridge-and-furrow of these fields exists on the ground or can be traced from air photographs in a few places, mainly alongside the R. Tove and the Great Ouse, arranged in end-on and interlocked furlongs, many of reversed-S form. Some exceptionally well-preserved ridge-and-furrow remains immediately N. of the village (SP 793427), where it is cut by both the canal and Bridge Road, and to the S.W. of The Priory (SP 795429). Another common field, a detached part of the parish the exact location of which is unknown, was enclosed with the fields of Potterspury in 1775. (Baker, *Hist. of Northants.*, II (1836–41), 128). (RAF VAP CPE/UK/1926, 2245–9, 4246–9; F21 58/RAF/5517, 0029–32; F22 58/RAF/5517, 0030–2; air photographs in NMR)

For the cultivation remains of the deserted village of Furtho, some of which lie in this parish, see Potterspury (17).

UNDATED

[a](6) BURIALS (SP 781427), W. of Rectory Farm, on glacial gravel at 85 m. above OD. Several skeletons were found in a gravel-pit in about 1893–4 (OS Record Cards).

16 COURTEENHALL

(OS 1:10000 [a] SP 75 NE, [b] SP 75 SE, [c] SP 75 SW)

The roughly triangular parish of 550 hectares lies on land sloping gently N., from a ridge on the S. boundary at about 220 m. above OD to a W.-flowing tributary of the R. Nene on the short N. boundary. Much of the N. and the S. of the area is covered by Boulder Clay and glacial sands and gravels; to the N.W. of the village bands of limestone and Upper Lias Clay are exposed.

PREHISTORIC AND ROMAN

A Neolithic axe was found in the parish before 1902 (T. J. George, *Arch. Survey of Northants.* (1904), 13; VCH *Northants.*, I (1902), 139).

[b](1) ROMAN SETTLEMENT (?) (unlocated). A coin of Antoninus Pius was found somewhere in the parish before 1860 and pottery is recorded from the same location but no details are known (NM Records).

MEDIEVAL AND LATER

[c](2) DESERTED VILLAGE OF COURTEENHALL (SP 762530; Figs. 42 and 43), lies within and to the E. of Courteenhall Park, on the sides of a shallow N.-draining valley, on Great Oolite Limestone between 107 m. and 114 m. above OD. Though it is clear that the village was deliberately removed for emparking in the late 18th century, the actual process is not understood.

The village of Courteenhall is first documented in 1086 when Domesday Book describes it as being divided into two manors. One was of 3½ hides with a recorded population of 15, including a priest; the other was only of half a hide and half a virgate and no population is given (VCH *Northants.*, I (1902), 337, 339). In 1334 the vill paid 44s. 2d.

for the Lay Subsidy (PRO, E179/155/3), a sum which is about average for the area. Nothing is known of the size of the village in later medieval times until 1524 when 17 people paid tax (PRO, E179/155/142). Some desertion seems to have taken place after the enclosure of the common fields (5) in the mid 17th century for Bridges (*Hist. of Northants.*, I (1791), 353), writing in about 1720, said that the parish church then stood 'at the upper end of the town, but within the memory of man had houses standing beyond and about it, which since the enclosure of the parish had been destroyed'. Forty-three householders paid the Hearth Tax in 1673 (PRO, E179/254/14).

A plan made in 1766 (Fig. 43; original at Courteenhall, copy in NRO) showed the village to be made up of three distinct parts. To the E. of the church was a single row of buildings on the N. side of the street, as there is today. To the W. of the church, in the area of the present park, lay the main part of the village, arranged along a N.-S. street with a triangular green at the S. end and the manor house and its garden S. and S.E. again. The manor house is depicted as a long straight range with multiple chimneys and was certainly that described by Bridges (op. cit.) as an Elizabethan building with the date 1580 on it. Further W., to the W. of the present House was another group of buildings on the S. side of the road, including the late 17th-century school which still stands.

It is possible that at this time plans were already being prepared to empark the area, for a note on the 1766 map included the details of a 'New Intended Road' which seems to have been designed to replace the S. end of the main village and its continuation S.W. as far as the church. Sir William Wake, 7th baronet, owned Courteenhall at that time. This plan or a modification of it was presumably carried out soon afterwards and the whole village, except for the manor house, the church and the houses E. of the church, was removed and the area emparked. The magnificent stable block which now lies to the S.W. of the present House was probably erected at the same time. This is usually said to be of around 1750 and to have been built by Sir Charles Wake-Jones, 6th baronet, who died in 1755. However, the stables did not exist in 1766 and must have been built by his successor.

By 1791 Repton's 'Red Book' of the estate (at Courteenhall) shows the manor house standing alone in the park with the stables away on the hill to the W. The manor house, however, seems very different from that shown on the 1766 plan for the old 16th-century range has an L-shaped structure attached to its E. end, apparently with symmetrical 18th-century elevations. It is likely that the 7th baronet carried out the removal of the village, the erection of the stables and the enlargement of the old manor house, all of which were completed well before 1790 and perhaps as early as 1770.

In 1791 Sir William Wake, 9th baronet, who had succeeded in 1785, removed the old manor house completely, and employed Samuel Saxon to design and build the present house on the hilltop to the W. and Humphrey Repton to alter the park. Thus by 1793 the park, house and stables existed in their present form, and the village of Courteenhall was only a few houses to the E. of the church. A map of 1792 (NRO) which only covers the area to the S. and E. of the church shows that the present rectory had been

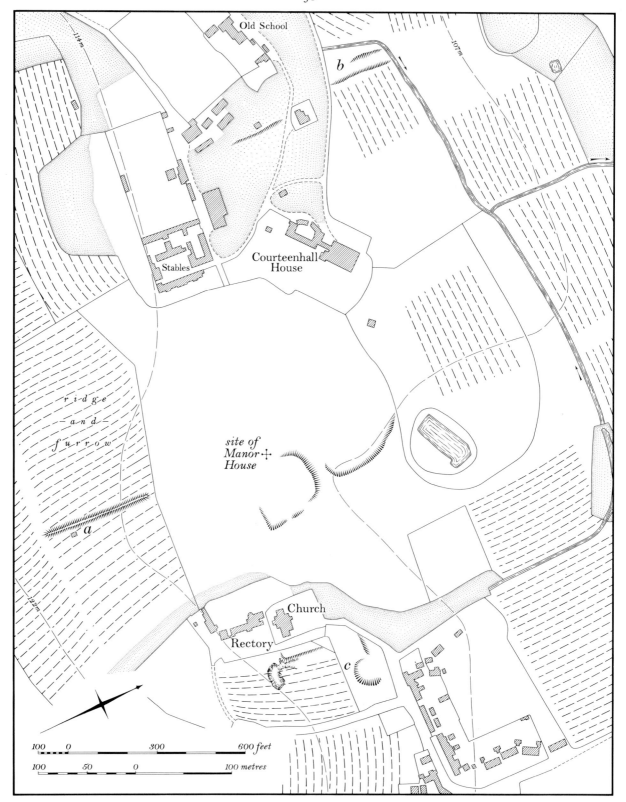

Old School

b

Courteenhall
House

Stables

r i d g e
– a n d –
f u r r o w

site of
Manor
House

a

Church

Rectory

c

100   0   300   600 feet

100   50   0   100 metres

Fig. 42   COURTEENHALL (2)   Deserted village

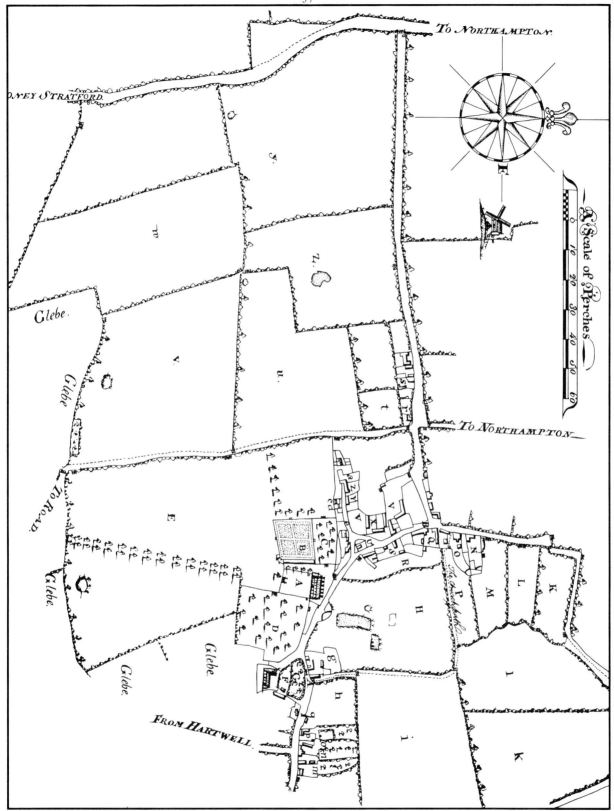

Fig. 43   COURTEENHALL (2)   Deserted village, (3)   Windmill mound (based on a plan of 1766, in Courteenhall House)

built, but probably very recently (Whellan, *Dir.*, 258). A map of the parish of 1794 (NRO) shows the village consisting of no more than six houses or farmsteads N.E. of the church. By 1839 (NRO, Tithe Map) at least one of these houses, immediately N.E. of the church, had been demolished and the rest had been at least partly rebuilt. In recent years the village has expanded again, with new houses along the road to Quinton.

The remains of the village fall into three parts. Of that section which was between the house and the church, almost nothing survives. Its area can be established accurately by the limits of the ridge-and-furrow, but no earthworks of the village itself remain. The whole area appears to have been flattened, probably by ploughing, after the destruction of the village and before being grassed over. The occupation-areas are marked by dark soil in the molehills but only three features are identifiable. Part of the site of the manor house (SP 76325300) is marked by a large N.-facing scarp about 1.5 m. high. To the S.E. (at SP 76355296) is an L-shaped scarp only 0.25 m. high which appears to have lain inside the area of an orchard in 1766. Further S.S.W. and S. of the manor house site, is a massive bank running almost N.-S., 8 m. wide and 1 m. high, lying on top of ridge-and-furrow ('a' on plan). In part it coincides with an avenue of trees on the 1766 map which was part of a view from the manor house. The bank has large depressions in its sides, presumably the holes where the trees stood. It is not a drive to the manor house, but a raised ridge in which trees were planted. The second area of remains lies N.E. of the Old School ('b' on plan) where a short section of a shallow hollow-way running N.-S. appears to be the road marked 'to Northampton' on the 1766 map. Another low scarp to the S., though approximately on the line of the E. edge of this road, may be the result of later landscaping. The only other earthworks of the village are those immediately N.E. of the church ('c' on plan) where indeterminate remains represent the site of a farm and outbuildings which stood there in 1766. (RAF VAP CPE/UK/1926, 3024–6; FSL6565, 2011–5; air photographs in NMR)

[b](3) WINDMILL MOUND (SP 75635325), lies in the N. corner of a triangular spinney, N. of the main drive to Courteenhall House, on the summit of a hill, on Boulder Clay at 115 m. above OD. The 1766 map of the village (Fig. 43; original at Courteenhall, copy in NRO) depicts a post mill here, standing on a low mound; on the Tithe Map of 1839 (NRO), the mill is no longer shown but the area is called Windmill Hill. An oval mound survives, 20 m. by 16 m. and 0.25 m. high, with a ditch 5 m. across and 0.25 m. deep on the N. and S. sides. It has been much damaged by the removal of trees in recent years.

[b](4) SITE OF WATERMILL (?) (SP 753534), in the N.W. corner of Courteenhall Park, in the bottom of a N.-draining valley at 90 m. above OD. The area is occupied by a small wood now called Windmill Spinney but on earlier maps called Old Mill Spinney (NRO, maps of Courteenhall, 1794 and 1839). Within the spinney are three small rectangular ponds with a larger roughly E.-shaped one further upstream. To the S.W., in a side valley, is another sub-rectangular pond bounded on the W. by a low stone-rubble dam. They are shown exactly as now on the 1839 map. None of the surviving ponds appears to be the site of a watermill, but they may have been altered as part of the landscaping of the park in the 18th century.

(5) CULTIVATION REMAINS. The common fields of the parish were probably enclosed in 1631 (*Northants. P. and P.*, 1 (1949), 271). Ridge-and-furrow of these fields exists on the ground or can be traced on air photographs over much of the parish, arranged in end-on and interlocked furlongs, many of reversed-S form. Some pre-enclosure features are still visible, including part of the original road from Quinton to Courteenhall, N.E. of the park (SP 763534), which remained in use until the late 18th century (map of 1776, copy in NRO). It is now a broad depression 30 m. wide and almost ploughed out passing between end-on furlongs. Ridge-and-furrow survives in fine condition in the park around the site of the original village of Courteenhall (2). Of particular interest are two former end-on furlongs on the S. side of the park (SP 762526) which appear to have been later ploughed as one. The earlier headland between the two original furlongs is a massive scarp at least 200 m. long and 1.5 m. high, now cut into by the later ridges. This scarp is of a nature to suggest that it may pre-date the medieval field system and represent an earlier land boundary. (RAF VAP CPE/UK/1926, 3020–3, 5021–5; FSL6565, 1001–3, 2011–5, 1800–4)

17 CROUGHTON

(OS 1:10000 [a] SP 53 SW, [b] SP 53 SE, [c] SP 53 NW, [d] SP 53 NE)

The roughly rectangular parish lies in the S.W. of the county, with its S. boundary adjoining Oxfordshire. It covers 860 hectares, and the higher parts in the N. and S. are an almost level tableland of Oolite Limestone between 134 m. and 144 m. above OD. The down-cutting of three small W. and S.W.-flowing streams has exposed the underlying Northampton Sand which occupies most of the parish between 100 m. and 140 m. above OD.

ROMAN

Two late Roman pewter plates were discovered during ploughing in Croughton before 1975 (Plate 8; *Northants. Archaeol.*, 11 (1976), 191; CBA Group 9, *Newsletter*, 6 (1976), 191; NM). Unspecified Roman finds were recorded from the parish in about 1879 (NM Records).

[a](1) ROMAN SETTLEMENT (?) (SP 538343), lies in the W. of the parish, N.W. of the village, on Northampton Sand at 115 m. above OD. Roman pottery, mainly late colour-coated wares, was found in 1947–8 (*Oxoniensia*, 13 (1948), 66) but no recent finds have been made. The settlement, if such it is, may be a continuation of the one to the W. in Aynho parish (Aynho (5)).

MEDIEVAL AND LATER

[a](2) SETTLEMENT REMAINS (SP 545335), formerly part of Croughton, lie on the S. side of the main village street, on

sand at 114 m. above OD. A long narrow paddock immediately N.W. of the church extends S. from the street, bounded on its W. and S. sides by a low scarp up to 0.5 m. high presumably marking the original boundary of an abandoned garden. The site of the assumed former house at its N. end is occupied by a later quarry pit. Further S.E. and to the W. of the manor house (at SP 544334) is an enclosure bounded on the S. and W. by a low bank and external ditch. This appears to be the end of a close which once belonged to the existing buildings to the N. (RAF VAP CPE/UK/1929, 2173–4, 3173–4)

(3) CULTIVATION REMAINS. The common fields of Croughton were enclosed by an Act of Parliament of 1807. On the Draft Enclosure Map of 1807 (NRO) furlongs and strips are shown, and these agree exactly with the recoverable pattern of ridge-and-furrow. Very little ridge-and-furrow exists on the ground or can be traced on air photographs, as post-enclosure cultivation on the light soil of the parish has removed the ridges almost completely. Apart from indeterminate traces on air photographs of rectangular furlongs N.E. of the village (SP 547338), W. of the village (SP 558333) and in the S.W. of the parish (SP 539318), the only visible remains lie along the valley of the small brook N.W. of the village (SP 534336) and in an area of damp ground N. of The Moors (SP 551337). (RAF VAP CPE/UK/1929, 2173–7, 3172–7; 106G/UK/1488, 3226–30, 4264–8)

18 CULWORTH

(OS 1:10000 [a] SP 54 NW, [b] SP 54 NE)

The parish occupies an area of over 920 hectares. It lies across the valleys of three small streams flowing N.W. to the R. Cherwell on the N. boundary. Two of these tributaries form the W. and N.E. boundaries. From the Cherwell, at about 115 m. above OD, the land rises across Upper Lias Clay and Northampton Sand to a plateau of Oolite Limestone over 160 m. above OD in the S.E. of the parish. The main monument is the medieval ringwork (1) in the centre of the village. The recorded village of Brime, thought to be lost, may in fact be part of the existing village of Culworth (2).

ROMAN

A 3rd-century Roman coin, of Quintillus, was found in the parish before 1841 (A. Beesley, *Hist. of Banbury* (1841), 30).

For possible Roman Road 56a, see Appendix.

MEDIEVAL AND LATER

[a](1) RINGWORK (SP 544470; Figs. 12 and 44; Plate 5), known as Berry Hill, lies immediately N. of the church, towards the S.E. end of the village, on Northampton Sand at 165 m. above OD. The modern village of Culworth is made up of at least two discrete settlements, Culworth and Brime (see (2)). Brime has been identified as the S.E. part of the village which includes the church and the ringwork.

In 1086 Brime was held by Landric of Gilo (VCH *Northants.*, I (1902), 344). Landric also held part of Sulgrave of Gilo and Gilo himself held Weedon Lois. These three adjacent villages have similar ringworks (Sulgrave (3), Weston and Weedon (5)) and all may date from the same period. Only the one at Sulgrave has been excavated.

The site consists of a simple ringwork with no visible outer bailey. It is almost exactly circular, surrounded by a wide ditch up to 1.75 m. deep below the natural ground surface outside and up to 3.5 m. deep below the inner ramparts. The Old Rectory garden has encroached upon the ditch on the S.E. and largely destroyed it. The circular flat top of the mound is bounded, except on the W., by an inner bank or rampart, nowhere more than 0.5 m. high. In the S.E. corner this rampart has been cut away, apparently in the mid 19th century, as part of the improvements to the garden of the adjoining Old Rectory. The rest of the interior is flat and featureless. The field in which the ringwork stands was known as Bury Close in 1839 (NRO, Tithe Map). (CUAP, ABW93; VCH *Northants.*, II (1906), 404; G. Baker, *Hist. of Northants.*, I (1822–30), 607)

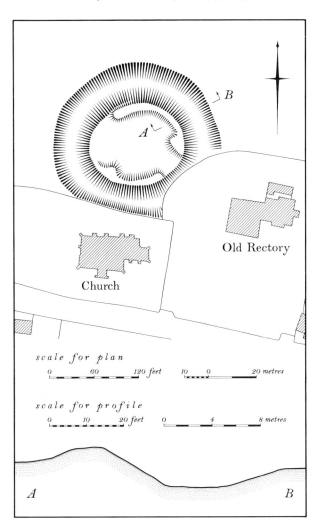

scale for plan
0 — 60 — 120 feet   10 — 0 — 20 metres

scale for profile
0 — 10 — 20 feet   0 — 4 — 8 metres

A   B

Fig. 44   CULWORTH (1)   Ringwork

[a](2) SETTLEMENT REMAINS (SP 538471 and 545468; Fig. 12), formerly part of Culworth village, lay in two places. At the N.W. end of the village, within the allotment gardens on the S. side of the main street, large quantities of medieval and later pottery have been discovered. Some of the more recent pottery may have been brought to the site in refuse used on the allotments, but the 12th to 14th-century material as well as the 17th and 18th-century sherds may indicate the existence of former buildings on this side of the street. At the S.E. end of the village, on the S. side of the street and immediately S. of the church and the Old Rectory, are fragmentary earthworks indicating that buildings once stood there. At least one building still remained in 1839 (NRO, Tithe Map). Although these remains are insignificant in themselves, they may go a little way to help explain the complex history of the village. Culworth is mentioned in Domesday Book as a small manor with a recorded population of 15 (VCH Northants., I (1902), 346). However, Domesday Book notes another place apparently also in Culworth parish, listed as Brime, with a recorded population of 12 including a priest (VCH, op. cit., 344). Brime does not occur by name in later documents and it has thus been identified as a village deserted at an early date (K. J. Allison et al., The Deserted Villages of Northants. (1966), 36). It has been tentatively sited in the N.W. of the parish (at SP 527484) but fieldwork by RCHM and OS (OS Record Cards) has revealed no possible trace of a deserted village there, or indeed elsewhere in the parish. It is possible that Brime was a settlement which now forms part of the existing village and was never deserted but only lost its name. The record of a priest at Brime in 1086 may be of significance in this respect for there is no evidence of any church in the parish apart from the existing one in Culworth village.

Documents record another place in Culworth, also now lost. This is Coten, Cotes, Cotes Culworth or Cotton beside Culworth, first mentioned in about 1200 (PN Northants., 52; J. Bridges, Hist. of Northants., I (1791), 164. The documentary history of the area therefore suggests that Culworth village is made up of more than one settlement, i.e. Culworth and Coten and perhaps Brime, and is thus a settlement of polyfocal type (Med. Arch., 21 (1977), 189).

The present plan of the village fits this theory as it consists of three distinct parts. In the N.W. is a long straight street, now with buildings only on one side but, from the evidence of the pottery noted above, once built up on both sides. This part of the village may be the Culworth of Domesday Book or the Coten of later documents, or both of them. In the S.E. is another single street, also apparently once built up on both sides, with the church and the ringwork (1) on the N. side. This, if the Domesday Book record of a priest is correctly interpreted, could have been the original Brime. Between the two streets lies a green, now of irregular shape, but clearly once rectangular and much larger. All the buildings on the E. of it and part of the grounds of the manor house in the N.W. appear to be later encroachments. The origin of this green between the two other settlements may be interpreted in two ways. It could be the original village of Culworth, laid out immediately N.E. of the ringwork (1) and from which the other settlement expanded, or it could be a deliberately planned infill to provide a market place between two existing settlements. The grant of a weekly market and an annual fair to Richard de Coleworth in 1264 may be connected with the establishment of this market place. (RAF VAP CPE/UK/1994, 1099)

[a](3) PONDS (SP 534471), lie W. of the village, in the bottom of a narrow valley draining N., on Upper Lias Clay at about 120 m. above OD. There is a long narrow pond with, a little to the N., two small rectangular ones; the northernmost has an island in it. In 1839 (NRO, Tithe Map) these ponds were called Osier Beds.

[a](4) PONDS (SP 541475), lie N. of the village, in the bottom of a valley draining W., on Upper Lias Clay at 132 m. above OD. There are slight traces of two rectangular ponds lying within and S. of a loop in the stream. In 1839 both lay in a field called Pond Close (NRO, Tithe Map).

[a](5) PONDS (SP 547466), lie S. of Culworth House, at the extreme S.E. of the village, in the valley of a small W.-flowing stream, on clay at 152 m. above OD. A large rectangular pond, with a massive dam 1.5 m. high, has a smaller embanked pond to the N.E. In 1839 another long narrow pond lay immediately to the N. (NRO, Tithe Map). The site was then a watermill.

(6) CULTIVATION REMAINS. The common fields of the parish were enclosed by agreement in 1612 (notes on Northants. enclosures, Central Library, Northampton). Ridge-and-furrow of these fields exists on the ground or can be traced on air photographs over most of the parish. On the lower flatter ground it is arranged in interlocked furlongs, many of reversed-S form, but on the edges of the rising ground it is in end-on furlongs running across the contours. One exception to this is in the N. of the parish, beside the R. Cherwell, where there are long sweeps of end-on furlongs parallel to the contours on the sloping valley sides. In the same area (SP 541489) one of these furlongs is set below a steep natural scarp caused by landslips. Here the ridge-and-furrow narrows, the ridges joining together and curving markedly to avoid the lower projections of the landslip. Other details are of interest. For example, on a steep N.-facing slope immediately N. of the village (SP 542473) a broad hollow-way passes between the furlongs and links the W. part of Culworth with the ponds (4) and the meadowland along the stream. (RAF VAP CPE/UK/1926, 1061–8; CPE/UK/1994, 1099–1101, 2096–7, 3099–103; 106G/UK/721, 4000–2)

UNDATED

[a](7) BURIALS (SP 548468), at the E. end of the village, on Northampton Sand at 167 m. above OD. Two shallow graves containing inhumations were found in 1953 when council houses were being built. There were no grave goods except for an object said to resemble 'a thin cylinder of coal'. (Cake and Cockhorse, 2 (1965), 110)

19 DEANSHANGER
(OS 1:10000 [a] SP 73 NE, [b] SP 74 SE, [c] SP 74 SW)

The large modern parish, formerly a chapelry of Passenham, covers about 1000 hectares and extends from the Great Ouse on the S.E. boundary into Whittlewood Forest in the N. Most of the N. and W. of the parish, between 100 m. and 120 m. above OD, is covered by Boulder Clay but a large area of limestone is exposed in the valley of the small stream on which the village stands, and the lowland in the E., at about 65 m. above OD, is gravel and alluvium. A number of Iron Age and Roman settlements are recorded in the parish.

PREHISTORIC AND ROMAN

An axe of banded tuff has been found in the village (SP 76263980; NM Records). Roman material, including pottery, floor tiles, wall-plaster, tesserae, glass and animal bones (in BM) said to have come from an excavation of a villa before 1940 may be from a site now lost or from the known villa (3). However, the material is described as from 'near Wakefield Lodge' and may thus be associated with Potterspury (5).

[c](1) IRON AGE SETTLEMENT (SP 73704178), lies in the forested area in the extreme W. of the parish, on Boulder Clay at 118 m. above OD. A quantity of Iron Age pottery was discovered in this area in 1959 (OS Record Cards).

[c](2) IRON AGE AND ROMAN SETTLEMENT (SP 72914204), lies 850 m. N.W. of (1) and in a similar situation. Forest clearance in 1959 revealed a Roman settlement, apparently of late Iron Age origin, covering an area of 30 m. by 90 m. The site was badly damaged but a number of floors were recognised and finds included samian and coarse wares, stone, ash, wall-plaster and coins of Constantine and Valens. (NM; *Wolverton and District Arch. Soc. Newsletter*, 6 (1961), 3; *BNFAS*, 1 (1966), 7; OS Record Cards)

[a](3) IRON AGE SETTLEMENT (?) AND ROMAN VILLA (SP 770396), lie S.E. of the village, on river gravels at 70 m. above OD. The first excavations on the site, in 1957, revealed a stone-built corridor villa about 30 m. by 15 m. and a group of other buildings around a courtyard. This yard, 75 m. by 60 m., contained a stone-lined pond and evidence of fencing. Some late Iron Age pottery, associated with post-holes of a circular structure, was found to the N. of the villa. Further excavations in 1972 to the E. of the earlier one revealed ditches and gullies containing early Roman pottery, domestic refuse and 1st-century brooches. Other recorded features included three 3rd-century circular structures, between 5 m. and 12 m. in diam., paddocks and compounds, a pond, a T-shaped corn-drying oven, a metal-working hearth and a large barn about 13 m. by 21 m. A silver denarius of Sallustia Barbia Orbiana was found on the site in 1963. (*JRS*, 48 (1958), 140; *Northants. Archit. and Arch. Soc. Reps.*, 63 (1960–6), 22–8; *Britannia*, 4 (1973), 294; DOE *Arch. Excavations 1972* (1973), 61–62;

Northants. Archaeol., 9 (1974), 89; 11 (1976), 191; *Milton Keynes J. of Arch. and Hist.*, 3 (1974), 8–9; OS Record Cards)

MEDIEVAL AND LATER

A medieval bronze spout in the form of an animal's head was found in the village in 1972 (NM; *Northants. Archaeol.*, 8 (1973), 20).

[b](4) SETTLEMENT REMAINS (SP 757415; Fig. 16), formerly part of the hamlet of Puxley, lie in the N. of the parish, on Boulder Clay and limestone between 90 m. and 98 m. above OD. The settlement is first mentioned in Domesday Book where it is described as two very small estates with a total recorded population of three (VCH *Northants.*, I (1902), 307, 308, 374). There is then no indication of its size as it was always included under Deanshanger and Passenham in the medieval national taxation records except in 1525 when three people in Puxley paid the Lay Subsidy (PRO, E179/155/130). Bridges, writing in about 1720, described Puxley as 'an hamlet of four mean houses on the borders of the forest . . . but formerly a much greater number with one considerable mansion-house called Pokel to which the wardenship of Whittlewood Forest was annexed' (J. Bridges, *Hist. of Northants.*, I (1791), 309). By 1874 the hamlet contained three farm-houses (Whellan, *Dir.*, 574) and it now consists of ten farms and cottages, mostly of recent date, scattered along the road for about 1 km. The evidence suggests that Puxley was always a small dispersed forest-edge settlement with no obvious centre.

No earthworks survive but finds from the area include medieval pottery, part of a medieval gilt-bronze book fastening and a 13th-century gilt-bronze pendant (NM; *Northants. Archaeol.*, 10 (1975), 166; 11 (1976), 191). (RAF VAP CPE/UK/1926, 4243–4)

(5) CULTIVATION REMAINS (Fig. 16). The common fields of the parish were enclosed by an Act of Parliament of 1772. No details of the open fields are known at that date, but on a map of 1600 (NRO) four named fields are shown, South Field to the S.E. of the village, North Field to the N., King's Hill Field to the E. and Deanshanger Field to the W. The N. part of the parish was part of Whittlewood Forest, except around Puxley (4) where there was a group of old enclosures. Ridge-and-furrow of these fields exists on the ground or can be traced from air photographs over wide areas in the S. of the parish. In the former South Field are large expanses of rectangular furlongs set at right angles to each other (SP 765392 and 771384). Similar ridge-and-furrow exists in the S. part of the former King's Hill Field on either side of the present Stratford Road (SP 772395), but only small fragments survive in the former North and Deanshanger Fields (SP 763404 and 757398).

Ridge-and-furrow is also traceable in a field immediately S. of Grange Farm at Puxley (SP 759413) which was already an old enclosure in 1600. A much larger area of furlongs is visible to the S.E. (SP 765412) in an area which was woodland in 1600. Although one block appears to be exactly straight, lying within the field boundaries, and is thus probably of post-enclosure date, there are also three curved interlocked furlongs of open field form. (RAF VAP CPE/UK/ 1926, 2241–4, 4233–45; CPE/UK/1929, 1183–9, 3183–94; CPE/UK/2097, 3180–5; F21 58/RAF/5517, 0024–9; 2F41, 534/ RAF/1426, 0365–6)

20   EASTON NESTON
(OS 1:10000 [a] SP 75 SW, [b] SP 74 NW, [c] SP 65 SE, [d] SP 64 NE)

The modern parish covers about 700 hectares and is of irregular shape, incorporating the land of two medieval settlements, Easton Neston itself, now deserted (2), and Hulcote (3). Part of the interest of Hulcote is its 19th-century rebuilding. The area is bounded on the S. by the R. Tove here flowing in a wide alluvial valley at 84 m. above OD. Boulder Clay covers the higher W. part of the parish and from there the land slopes gently E. across bands of Oolitic Limestone to an area of Upper Lias Clay.

PREHISTORIC AND ROMAN

A quernstone, perhaps prehistoric or Roman, was ploughed up somewhere in the parish between 1860 and 1870 and a complete Roman 'flagon' was discovered in 1889, during the construction of the railway 'near Showsley' (Dryden Collection, Central Library, Northampton).

[a](1) IRON AGE AND ROMAN SETTLEMENT (SP 724514), lies in the N.E. projection of the parish, on Boulder Clay at 122 m. above OD. A scatter of Roman material extending over 2 hectares, including samian, colour-coated and grey wares as well as some possible Iron Age sherds, a coin of

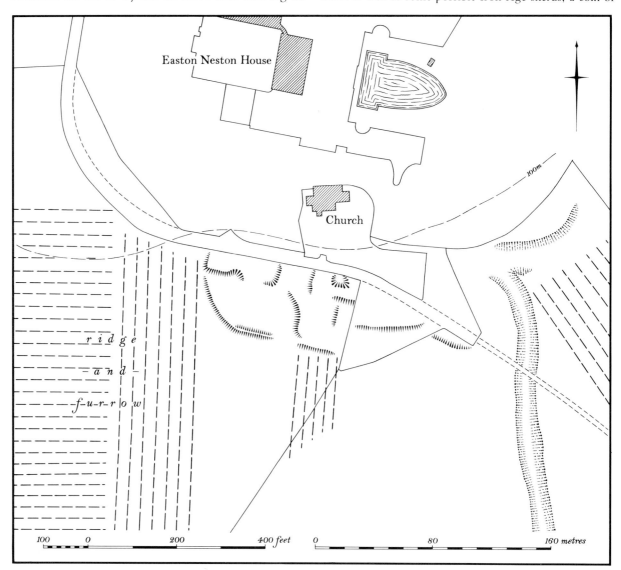

Fig. 45   EASTON NESTON (2)   Deserted village

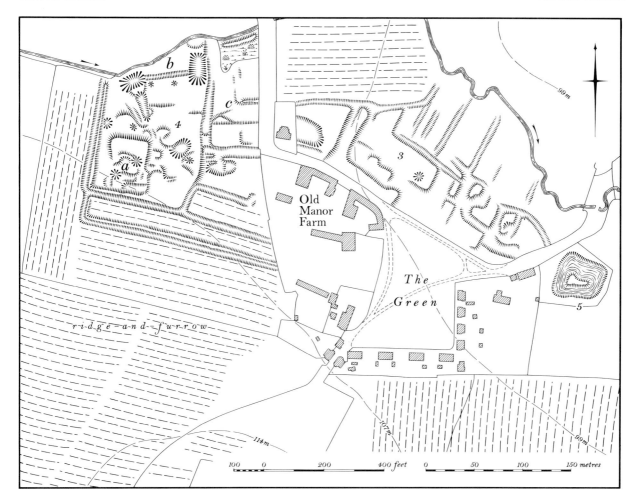

Fig. 46 EASTON NESTON (3) Settlement remains at Hulcote, (4) Site of manor house, (5) Pond

Constans and a brooch, is recorded from this site (*BNFAS*, 4 (1970), 13).

MEDIEVAL AND LATER

b(2) DESERTED VILLAGE OF EASTON NESTON (SP 701490; Fig. 45), lies S. of Easton Neston House and immediately S. of the isolated church, on Boulder Clay at 100 m. above OD. The village is first mentioned in 1086, when Domesday Book lists two small manors under Easton Neston, with a total recorded population of 14. However a further holding, listed under Ashton with a recorded population of six, has also been identified as part of Easton Neston (*VCH Northants.*, I (1902), 326, 342, 348). The village is noted in the *Nomina Villarum* of 1316 but thereafter was always taxed with Hulcote (3). In 1307, 65 people from Hulcote and Easton paid the Lay Subsidy (PRO, E179/155/31) and the two places together paid a total of £4–0–3d in tax in 1334, a relatively large sum for the area (PRO, E179/155/3). The Poll Tax Returns of 1377 indicate that 117 people over the age of 14 lived in the two villages (PRO, E179/155/28), and the 1523 and 1525 Lay Subsidy Returns respectively list 33 and 29 people paying tax (PRO,

E179/155/122 and 130). Only 27 people paid the Hearth Tax in 1673 (PRO, E179/254/14) but it is likely that most of these lived at Hulcote and that Easton Neston was by then deserted. A small park had been created at Easton Neston in 1499 by Sir Richard Empson, who made it from 64 acres of former pasture and arable land. Empson also converted a further 24 acres of arable to pasture at the same time. In 1531 the estate was purchased by Richard Fermor and by 1541 only the manor house is mentioned in a survey (K. J. Allison *et al.*, *The Deserted Villages of Northants.* (1966), 38). This house stood S. of the church according to Bridges (*Hist. of Northants.*, I (1791), 289) but was presumably pulled down in the late 17th century when the present house was built for Sir William Fermor.

The remains of the village are very fragmentary and in poor condition, having been much damaged by landscaping. Nothing survives N., W. and E. of the church in the gardens of Easton Neston House. Immediately S. of the church are a few low banks and scarps, some of which are likely to represent the site of the old manor house. Further E. are slight traces of a curving hollow-way, running N.-S. The surrounding area is devoid of ridge-and-furrow, and appears recently to have been levelled. (RAF VAP CPE/UK/1926, 1236–7; air photographs in NMR)

[ab](3) SETTLEMENT REMAINS (SP 705500; Figs. 46, 47 and 48), formerly part of Hulcote, lie on the N. side of the present village green, on clay at 100 m. above OD. The village is first mentioned in 1086 when Domesday Book listed it as a small manor with a recorded population of only seven (VCH Northants., I (1902), 348). In the later medieval period it was always taxed with Easton Neston; the relevant figures are given in (2) above. In 1673, 27 people at Hulcote and Easton paid the Hearth Tax (PRO, E179/254/14) and it is probable that most of these lived at Hulcote. Bridges (Hist. of Northants., I (1791), 295), writing in about 1720, described Hulcote as 'a considerable hamlet'.

The earliest map of the village, dated 1806 (NRO; Fig. 47), shows three farmsteads and four other houses or cottages in addition to the two lodges to Easton Park, all set around a triangular green. Between 1812 and 1849 (NRO, Tithe Map; Fig. 48) most of the buildings on the N. and S.E. sides of the green were removed, the three small farm-houses were rebuilt and two rows of brick cottages of gothic design were erected to the S. of the green. The exact date of this alteration is unknown but the old school house in the S.W. corner of the green, which is built of similar brick to the cottages and farm-houses, bears the date 1816. Hulcote was evidently the estate village for Easton Neston House, a function which it still performs. Since 1849 the only changes have been the removal, in the late 19th century, of the sole surviving house on the N. side of the green and the enlargement of the green southwards to the cottages to give it a rectangular form. The earthworks associated with the village lay to the N. of the green until 1977 when they were ploughed over and largely destroyed. They consisted of a series of ditched or scarped closes and building-platforms with long narrow ditched closes extending to the stream behind them. The recent ploughing revealed large areas of stone-rubble and brick, associated with post-medieval pottery, tiles, glass and bone, in the places where buildings are shown on the 1806 map. Elsewhere large quantities of earlier pottery including 12th-century Stamford ware and 13th and 14th-century sherds of Olney, Lyveden and Potterspury types were exposed. Other closes, possibly the sites of former houses, lie immediately E. of the manor house site (4) ('c' on plan). (Air photographs in NMR)

[a](4) MANOR HOUSE SITE (SP 702501; Figs. 46 and 48), lies immediately W. of Hulcote village, on clay at 107 m. above OD. The field it occupies is called Hall Close (G. Baker, Hist. of Northants., II (1836–41), 153; NRO, Tithe Map, 1849), and the earthworks are presumably the site of

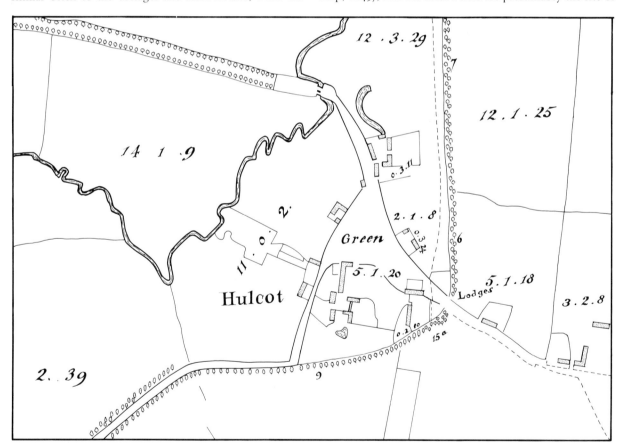

Fig. 47 EASTON NESTON (3)   Settlement remains at Hulcote, (4)   Site of manor house (based on a map of 1806, NRO)

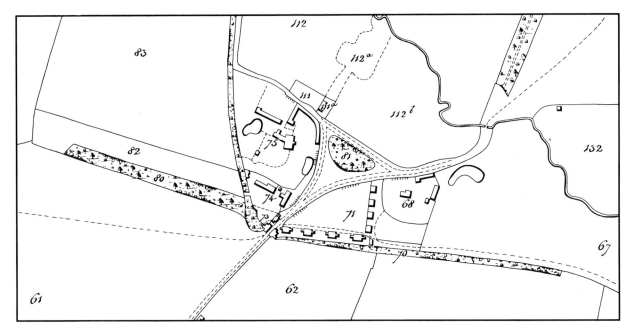

Fig. 48   EASTON NESTON (3)   Settlement   remains at Hulcote,
(4)   Site of manor house (based on the   Tithe Map of Easton Neston, 1849, NRO)

the medieval manor house of Hulcote. A large sub-rectangular enclosure is bounded on the W., S. and E. by a shallow ditch; on the E. this has been cut into and flattened by later activities. The N. side is defined by a small E.-flowing stream. A rectangular raised platform ('a' on plan), bounded on the N. by a scarp 1.7 m. high lies in the S.W. corner of the enclosure. This may be the site of the manor house itself. The platform has a number of depressions and low banks on it. At the N. end of the main enclosure, close to the stream, are two rectangular fishponds, both now dry, linked by a shallow ditch ('b' on plan). Elsewhere within the main enclosure are depressions, some of which may be later quarry pits, and banks and scarps forming no coherent pattern. To the E. of the enclosure are other closes bounded by slight scarps ('c' on plan), these may be sites of houses and gardens. On the S. side of the enclosure and to the S.E. are two long narrow paddocks bounded by ditches and containing ridge-and-furrow. A small quantity of medieval and post-medieval pottery was found in the N.E. corner of the site in 1977 (Northants. SMR). (Air photographs in NMR)

[b](5) POND (SP 706499; Figs. 46 and 48), lies immediately E. of Hulcote, on clay at 100 m. above OD. The pond is roughly circular, with an island in the centre. No function can be assigned to it but it did not exist in its present form in 1849 when the Tithe Map (NRO) shows it only as a semicircular ditch.

[b](6) MOAT, FISHPONDS AND WATERMILL (SP 703487; Fig. 49), lie in the S. of the parish, close to the R. Tove, on river gravel and alluvium at 85 m. above OD. The area is known as Waterhall but its history is unknown. It may

have been the site of a medieval manor house though by the 17th century the manor house of Easton Neston certainly stood immediately S. of Easton Neston church within the area of the former village (2). The earthworks consist of a trapezoidal island surrounded by a broad ditch up to 1.5 m. deep. The island is featureless and overgrown. Immediately to the S.W. are two long narrow ponds and a larger rectangular one; these and the moat are surrounded entirely by an outer rectangular ditch which was supplied with water from two inlet leats running N.E. from the R. Tove. The water continued N.E. along a single leat which passes through the site of a watermill. Part of the dam and the foundations of the mill building still survive, as does the mill pond below them. A channel runs S.W., back to the river. The mill still stood in the 19th century (NRO, maps of 1806, 1844 and 1849) but the moat was then unoccupied. The general appearance of the moat and fishponds suggests that they have been altered in post-medieval times as part of the landscaping of the park.

[b](7) MOUND (SP 70534883), lies in the S. of the parish, N.E. of (6) within the park, on alluvium at 86 m. above OD. A flat-topped circular platform 40 m. across and only 0.25 m. high, surrounded by a ditch 10 m. wide and 0.25 m. deep except on the S. where the ditch has been mutilated, appears to cut ridge-and-furrow approaching it from the N. It is probably a landscape feature of 18th or 19th-century origin; a tree about 100 years old stands in the centre. (Air photographs in NMR)

[a](8) SITE OF CISTERCIAN PRIORY (SP 717508), lies around Showsley Grounds Farm, in the N.E. of the parish, on limestone at 120 m. above OD. Richard de Lister founded

a small house of Cistercian nuns at Showsley or Sewardsley sometime in the reign of Henry II. It seems always to have been very small and poor and at its suppression in 1536 there were only four nuns and the prioress. In 1459–60 the House was appropriated to the Cluniac Abbey of Delapré in Northampton, which then became responsible for its upkeep (VCH *Northants.*, II (1906), 125–7; J. Bridges, *Hist. of Northants.*, I (1791), 295; D. Knowles and R. N. Hadcock, *Medieval Religious Houses* (1957), 225; U. H. Brooks, *Manuscript History of Sewardsley Priory* (1856), Central Library, Northampton).

Little now remains of the priory. The present house, though much altered especially in the mid 19th century, appears to include some parts of a medieval building. In 1852 during the alteration of the house at least three graves associated with elaborately carved coffin lids of the 14th century were discovered under and immediately E. of the E. wing of the house. These remain in the garden. A number of wall foundations, glass and decorated floor tiles were also recorded (*Ass. Arch. Soc. Reps.*, 4 (1857), 139–40; *PSA*, 4 (1859), 121). More recently another plain coffin lid and at least two more burials have been found in the garden E. of the farm-house.

To the S. of the farm, in the bottom of a shallow S.W.-draining valley on Upper Lias Clay (SP 717507), are the remains of a small rectangular *fishpond* 40 m. by 20 m. and only 0.25 m. deep with a low dam at its S.W. end.

There are traces of an inlet channel at its N.E. end, and below the dam to the S.W. are several other shallow ditches and an irregular depression which may mark the site of another pond. The main pond and others in the area are said to have been filled in soon after 1850 (*Ass. Arch. Soc. Reps.*, op. cit.).

Immediately N. of the farm (SP 717509) there were, until recent destruction, some rectangular enclosures bounded by banks (RAF VAP CPE/UK/1926, 1030–5; FSL6565, 1997; air photographs in NMR). No trace of these now exists but large quantities of limestone rubble and 18th and 19th-century material as well as a few medieval sherds remain. The closes probably represent post-medieval buildings unrelated to the priory.

(9) CULTIVATION REMAINS. The date of enclosure of the common fields of Hulcote and Easton Neston is not known, nor whether each had a separate field system, though this seems likely. Some small-scale enclosure is recorded at Easton Neston in the 16th century and the existence of Easton Neston Park indicates that the S. part of the parish had been enclosed by the 18th century. The N. part of the parish was enclosed by 1780; it is described as Old Enclosures on a map of Tiffield of that date (NRO).

Ridge-and-furrow survives on the ground or is visible on air photographs over much of the parish though in the W. it has mainly been destroyed by modern cultivation.

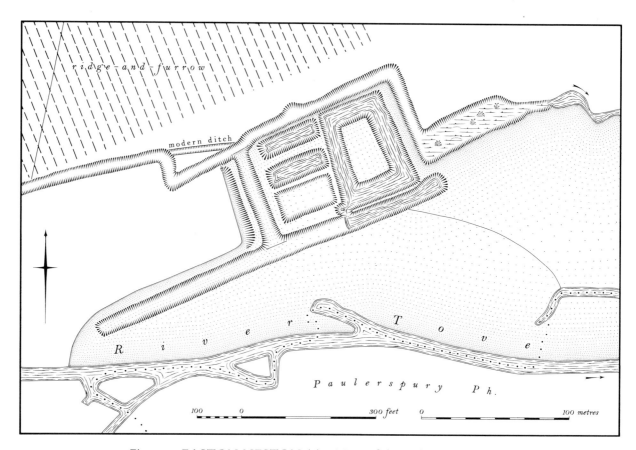

Fig. 49   EASTON NESTON (6)   Moat, fishponds and watermill

The pattern of interlocked and end-on furlongs is traceable on air photographs around the site of Showsley Priory (8) (SP 717507) as well as further S.W. towards Hulcote (SP 712504). There are also considerable areas of ridge-and-furrow around Hulcote village. However ridge-and-furrow is best preserved in the S. of the parish within Easton Neston Park where broad tracts still survive. Here many interlocked and end-on furlongs together with headlands and access-ways are preserved in permanent pasture. (RAF VAP CPE/UK/1926, 1030–5, 1235–8; air photographs in NMR)

21 EDGCOTE
(OS 1:10000 ª SP 44 NE, ᵇ SP 54 NW)

The parish, of only 530 hectares, lies against the Oxfordshire boundary, with the R. Cherwell to the N. and a small tributary of that river on the E. The highest part is in the S.W. where a flat-topped hill of Northampton Sand, capped by rocks of the Lower Estuarine Series, reaches a height of 175 m. above OD. From this hill the land slopes N. and E. to the Cherwell and its tributary, across gently undulating country and in some places steep scarps, on Lias clay and Marlstone Rock between 150 m. and 100 m. above OD. The major monument in the parish is the deserted village of Edgcote (1).

ROMAN

A large quantity of Roman pottery said to range in date across the whole of the Roman period has been found somewhere in the parish (OS Record Cards). It is perhaps to be associated with the Roman villa on the other side of the R. Cherwell (Chipping Warden (3)).

MEDIEVAL AND LATER

The Battle of Danesmoor took place in the W. of the parish in 1469, but has left no visible remains. The site was said to be marked by three small mounds (Whellan, *Dir.*, 453) but these do not now exist (see also Chipping Warden (4)).

ᵇ(1) DESERTED VILLAGE OF EDGCOTE (SP 503480; Fig. 50; Plate 4), lies immediately W. and N.W. of Edgcote House, on Middle Lias Clay between 113 m. and 125 m. above OD. Edgcote is first mentioned in Domesday Book where it is listed as a two-hide manor held by Walchelin of the Bishop of Coutances, with a recorded population of 25 (VCH *Northants.*, I (1902), 310). In 1301 57 people paid the Lay Subsidy (PRO, E179/155/31) and Edgcote is mentioned by name in the *Nomina Villarum* of 1316. The village paid 71 shillings in tax in 1334, one of the largest amounts in the county for villages later to be deserted (PRO, E179/155/3), and 95 people over the age of 14 paid the Poll Tax in 1377 (PRO, E179/155/128). In 1502 240 acres of arable and pasture land were enclosed and nine houses destroyed,

and by 1547 500 sheep were grazing on the manor. However, in 1524 there were still 16 taxpayers in the village (PRO, E179/254/14). Bridges (*Hist. of Northants.*, I (1791), 117), writing in about 1720, said that some 18 families lived at Edgcote. The present Edgcote House was built in 1747–52 on the site of an older one and, it is said, within the village. However a plan of 1710 (in Edgcote House) showing the house with gardens to the E. depicts the church within the garden. Unfortunately the map does not include the land to the S.W. of the house and church and thus no details of the village at that time are known. Between 1761 and 1788 the village was demolished by the Lord of the Manor, to make way for the landscaped park to the W. of the house; two new farms and seven cottages were erected elsewhere in the parish (G. Baker, *Hist. of Northants.*, I (1822–30), 405). By 1801 the parish had a population of 66. (K. J. Allison *et al., The Deserted Villages of Northants.* (1966), 38)

The rather fragmentary remains of the village support the evidence from documents and suggest that the village was a relatively large one with some abandonment at an early date followed by deliberate clearance in the 18th century. The site can be divided into four separate parts. Immediately W. of Edgcote House and the church ('a' on plan) is an area of indeterminate earthworks. These are very faint, perhaps because they represent that part of the village which was deliberately moved in the 18th century. A broad depression extending N.W. in the S. part of the area may be a former hollow-way. Further N., on either side of the drive to Chipping Warden ('b' on plan), the earthworks are better preserved. To the W. of the drive is a series of rectangular closes bounded by scarps up to 1 m. high, and to the E. of the drive is another possible hollow-way, running N. and blocked by a later scarp. The rather uneven land to the S.E. appears to be at least in part spoil dumped in the area, perhaps as a result of the 18th-century clearance.

Further E. again ('c' on plan) a broad hollow-way 1 m.– 1.5 m. deep extends N.E. down the hillside and then divides into three separate trackways before fading out. On the S.W. of the site ('d' on plan) there was formerly an extensive area of earthworks but these have now been destroyed by modern cultivation. Air photographs taken before this destruction (RAF VAP CPE/UK/1926, 1068–70; F21 58/RAF/3963, 0008–9; in NMR) suggest that the hollow-way noted above, S. of 'a', continued N.W., with a number of closes on its S.W. side. However, the details are not clear. When this area is ploughed it produces considerable amounts of stone-rubble, animal bones and pottery ranging in date from the 12th to the 18th century.

(2) CULTIVATION REMAINS (Fig. 51). The final date of enclosure of the common fields of Edgcote is unknown. In 1502, 120 acres of arable land together with another 120 of pasture were enclosed (K. J. Allison *et al., The Deserted Villages of Northants.* (1966), 38) and the parish had been completely enclosed before 1720 (J. Bridges, *Hist of Northants.*, I (1791), 117). Ridge-and-furrow of these fields remains on the ground or can be traced on air photographs over large areas. On the lower, flatter ground close to the R. Cherwell and the tributary stream which forms the E.

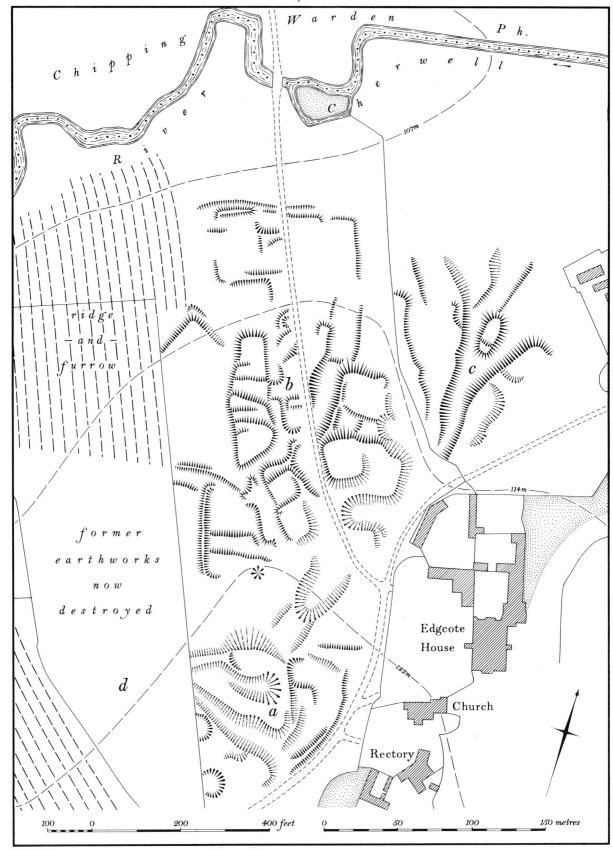

Chipping Warden Ph.

C h i p p i n g *River* *Ch* *e* *r w e l l*

107m

c

R

r i d g e
— a n d —
f u r r o w

b

c

f o r m e r
e a r t h w o r k s
n o w
d e s t r o y e d

114m

d

a

122m

Edgcote
House

Church

Rectory

100   0   200   400 feet   0   50   100   150 metres

Fig. 50   EDGCOTE (1)   Deserted village

boundary of the parish the furlongs are rectangular and interlocked. On the sloping ground further S. and S.W., along the E. and S.E. sides of Edgcote Hill, the furlongs radiate outwards across the contours. In the permanent pasture around Edgcote House and in the parkland to the S. the ridge-and-furrow is very well preserved in spite of a large area of later shallow quarrying. Here high ridges with marked reversed-S curves, headlands and access-ways all still exist. In the W. of the parish, in and around Ladshill Spinney and Hay Spinney (SP 502470), the underlying Upper Lias Clay has slipped down the hillside to produce a rippled appearance on the ground (Fig. 51). In most places the adjacent ridge-and-furrow stops short of these landslips, presumably because they were too difficult to cultivate in medieval times, but in two places the ridge-and-furrow runs over the landslips. To the E. of Hay Spinney (SP 499470) ridge-and-furrow running at right angles to the contours rides over the landslips, and to the S.E. (SP 505468) ridge-and-furrow is arranged along the contours on the terraces of two massive parallel landslips. (RAF VAP CPE/UK/1926, 1066–71; 106G/UK/721, 3000–4); CPE/UK/1994, 1102–3; F21 58/RAF/3963, 0008–0011)

22 EVENLEY
(OS 1:10000 [a] SP 53 NE, [b] SP 53 SE, [c] SP 63 NW, [d] SP 63 SW)

The parish is of irregular shape and covers almost 1300 hectares including the land of the medieval village of Astwick (Fig. 52). Much of it is a plateau at about 135 m. above OD, with radiating streams, but in the N. the land slopes down to the Great Ouse and a tributary which forms the N.E. boundary. Most of the higher flatter ground is on Oolitic Limestone but sands and clays are exposed on the valley sides. Apart from some prehistoric finds the main monuments are a large Roman site (4) and the deserted village of Astwick (9). The latter is noteworthy in that its layout suggests that it has been replanned at some time before abandonment.

PREHISTORIC AND ROMAN

Two leaf-shaped arrowheads have been found (SP 601357, 600357; *BNFAS*, 5 (1971), 3; Banbury Museum).

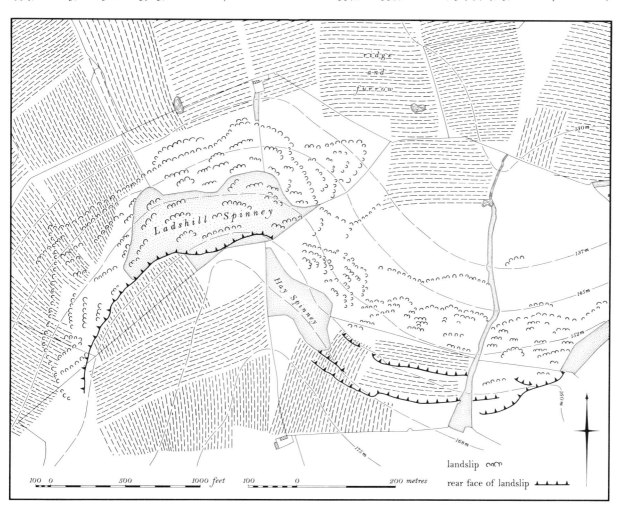

Fig. 51   EDGCOTE (2)   Cultivation remains

Records of Roman coins in 'Astwick Field' in the 18th century cannot be verified (J. Bridges, *Hist. of Northants.*, I (1791), 168; OS Record Cards). Roman pottery found 'at Evenley' before 1862 may have come from the sites described below (2, 3) (PSA, 2 (1862), 75).

[a](1) FLINT-WORKING SITE (centred SP 590362), on both sides of the stream on the N. parish boundary, and partly in Brackley parish, at 107 m. above OD. Field-walking has led to the discovery of worked flints including flakes, blades and a core, as well as some possible Iron Age pottery (*BNFAS*, 5 (1971), 16–17). Mesolithic blades and microliths have been picked up further S.E. (SP 592359; Banbury Museum).

[a](2) ENCLOSURES AND LINEAR DITCH (SP 568355), in the N.W. of the parish, on Great Oolite Limestone at 129 m. above OD. Air photographs (NCAU) show a small trapezoidal enclosure only 20 m. wide apparently lying within a larger enclosure of similar shape and about 0.5 hectare in extent. The larger enclosure is very indistinct. Both enclosures appear to be intersected by a linear ditch running E.-W. and traceable for almost 400 m.

[b](3) ENCLOSURES (SP 575338), lie S.W. of the village, W. of the A43, on limestone, at 132 m. above OD. Air photographs (CUAP, BBK74) show indistinct cropmarks of at least four small conjoined rectangular enclosures covering about 1 hectare.

[a](4) ROMAN SETTLEMENT AND COIN HOARDS (centred SP 593359), lies N. and N.E. of Evenley Hall, between 105 m. and 120 m. above OD. Much Roman material has been found over a wide area and ranging in date from the 1st to the 4th century. It includes pottery, tiles, coins, building stone and a bronze pin. The finds extend from Fox Covert Wood as far as the stream to the N., in the same area as the worked flints and the possible Iron Age sherds described previously (1), and it appears that there was an important building in the area occupied at least throughout the 2nd and 3rd centuries, though no foundations or exact site have yet been identified. In 1826, in the S. of the site, a large hoard was found consisting of several hundred coins of Nero, Domitian, Severus Alexander, Probus, Carausius, Constantine and others. A second hoard, said to comprise over 23,000 coins from the second half of the 3rd century contained in an 'earthenware vase', also came from Evenley before 1854. The exact find spot is unknown. (*BNFAS*, 3 (1969), 9; 5 (1971), 3, 16–17; G. Baker, *Hist. of Northants.*, I (1822–30), 617; *Num. Chron.*, 17 (1854), 38; *Gent's Mag.*, 1 (1854), 55; *Arch. J.*, 49 (1892), 224; VCH *Northants.*, I (1902), 217; *Oxoniensia*, 36 (1971), 112; *BAR*, 40 (1977), 61; Banbury Museum; NM)

[a](5) ROMAN SETTLEMENT (?) (SP 587351), lies immediately N. of the village, at 120 m. above OD. There are vague references to the discovery of Roman pottery in this area (OS Record Cards).

For possible Roman Road 56a, see Appendix.

MEDIEVAL AND LATER

[ab](6) SETTLEMENT REMAINS (SP 586350; Fig. 15), formerly part of Evenley, lie along Church Lane in the N.W. part of the village, on limestone at 120 m. above OD. The village consists of two parts. In the N.W. is Church Lane,

now a cul-de-sac; in the S.E. the rest of the village is arranged around a large rectangular green. Until recent development the parish church together with Road Farm stood in an isolated position at the N.W. end of Church Lane, but the archaeological evidence suggests that in the medieval period the lane was lined with buildings on both sides. The gardens of modern houses on the S. side of the lane have considerable quantities of 13th and 14th-century pottery in them, and on the N. side of the lane, in the only surviving piece of permanent grassland, are two rectangular platforms which probably mark the sites of former buildings. Immediately E. of the church, on the N. side of the lane, there was an L-shaped pond which has now been destroyed by modern houses. In 1780 (NRO, Enclosure Map) this pond was shown as the W. and S. sides of a small rectangular moat with no buildings within it. A long rectangular pond, which also survived until recent times, lay to the N.W. The moat was probably the site of a medieval manor house. The exact chronological relationship of the two parts of the village is not clear but it is possible that Church Lane is the older part and that the green was a later planned addition.

[b](7) FISHPONDS (centred SP 589346; Fig. 15), lie immediately S.E. of Evenley village, in the valley of a small N.E.-flowing stream, on clay, at about 115 m. above OD. Three sub-rectangular ponds, each with a large dam up to 2 m. high, are arranged in a line along the valley bottom. The road to Evenley from Mixbury, Oxfordshire, crosses the dam of the southernmost pond and a farm track uses the dam of the middle pond. This pond has been damaged and much of its W. part has been filled in. The northernmost pond was known as New Pond in 1882 (map in NRO). Two other similar ponds lie N. of the village, within Evenley Park (SP 587352), and although these have been altered by later landscaping they, too, may have originated as medieval fishponds.

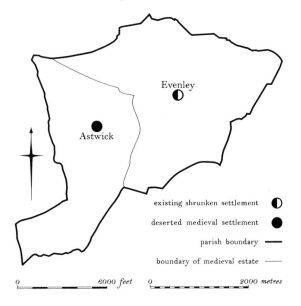

Fig. 52   EVENLEY Medieval settlements and estates

10

Fig. 53   EVENLEY (9)   Deserted village of Astwick, (10)   Enclosure

[a](8) WINDMILL MOUND (?) (SP 583357), lies on the W. side of Evenley Park, immediately W. of Park Lodge, beside the A43, on limestone at 128 m. above OD. A circular flat-topped mound 15 m. in diam. and 1 m. high and much altered by landscape gardening may be the site of a windmill. The area in which it lies was called Windmill Ground on the Enclosure Map of c. 1780 (NRO).

[b](9) DESERTED VILLAGE OF ASTWICK (centred SP 570342; Figs. 52 and 53; Plate 1), lies in the W. of the parish, in the valley of a small S.W.-flowing stream, on limestone and clay at 122 m. above OD. The land associated with the village is now the W. part of Evenley parish.

Astwick is not mentioned by name until 1195 (PN Northants., 53) but it has been identified as the manor of one and three-fifths hides with a recorded population of nine, listed but not named in Domesday Book as pertaining to Evenley (VCH Northants., I (1902), 341). Thereafter no record of its population exists and in all the national taxation returns it is listed with Evenley. However Astwick is mentioned by name in the Nomina Villarum of 1316. In 1510 there were still at least 15 houses there (K. J. Allison et al., The Deserted Villages of Northants. (1966), 35). Bridges (Hist. of Northants., I (1791), 168), writing in about 1720, described it as a village of six houses but he was referring to farms scattered throughout the lands of the former village. He also said that Astwick 'appears to have been formerly a large town, as may be seen from the ruins which are called The Old Town'. By 1839 (NRO, Tithe Map) the whole site was abandoned and the W. part was known as Stoneheap Ground.

Although some modern destruction has occurred the greater part of the village survives as earthworks. These remains suggest that the village once had an L-shaped plan and was later altered; a hollow-way with associated medieval house-sites cuts obliquely across an earlier more regular arrangement of closes. The nearest parallel to this, in terms of both basic plan and later alterations, is Bardolfston in Dorset (RCHM, Dorset, III (1970), Puddletown (21)).

The assumed earlier phase, of L-shaped plan, is well preserved on the E. side of the stream, but on the W. has been almost totally destroyed by modern ploughing. The surviving E. part, divided into numerous rectangular closes, is bounded on the E. by a modern hedge, on the N. and N.W. by the stream and on the W. by an almost continuous line of ditches and scarps. The S. boundary is not clear but the surviving ridge-and-furrow probably defines it. Several of the larger closes in the centre and S. have been overploughed by later ridge-and-furrow though it is not possible to ascertain at which stage in the village's development this took place. The damaged W. part of the earlier village also appears to have had a rectangular layout to judge from the few remaining scarps and banks now only a few centimetres high.

The later phase of the village consists of two hollow-ways. The main one enters the site in the S. and for the first 200 m. follows the general S.S.W.-N.N.E. alignment of the early plan. It then turns sharply N.W. obliquely through some of the older closes and swings W. across the stream. To the W. of the stream it still survives as a shallow depression climbing the valley side; it then turns N.W. and

fades out. The second main hollow-way branches from the first at a point just E. of the stream and curves E. across the older closes. Beyond the hedge on the E. side the route can be traced as a large headland. A low scarp blocks the E.-W. hollow-way at its junction with the main one and this indicates that the latter remained in use after the other hollow-way had been abandoned. Many well-preserved house-sites survive, marked by limestone-rubble walls up to 1 m. high and several showing internal divisions into rooms. Among the most notable are those on the N. side of the E.-W. hollow-way ('a' on plan) where at least six buildings are arranged around a large courtyard. To the S. of the same hollow-way ('b' on plan) is another group of buildings lying on the N. side of and within a broad hollow. Elsewhere there are isolated house-sites beside the hollow-ways and situated in small closes (e.g. 'c' and 'd' on plan). In the damaged W. part at least two house-sites have avoided destruction. To the N. of the site, within the modern arable fields, air photographs show a system of cropmarks; some at least of these are modern drains though others are probably boundaries of former closes. It is unclear what relationship these have with the village. (RAF VAP CPE/UK/1929, 3176-7; 106G/UK/1488, 4264-6; CUAP, AFH92-5, AGV39, BBK77-80)

[b](10) ENCLOSURE (SP 572343; Fig. 53), lies immediately N.E. of the deserted village of Astwick (9), in the bottom of a small valley, on clay at 124 m. above OD. It has been described on various OS maps as 'camp', 'moat' and 'fishpond' but, although it is certainly medieval or later and was perhaps associated with Astwick village, its function is unclear.

The site was first described by Bridges (Hist. of Northants., I (1791), 168) as a 'moat full of water' and the field in which it lay was called Moat Close in 1839 (NRO, Tithe Map). The earthwork consists of a roughly trapezoidal depression in the valley bottom; the original course of the stream is still visible across it. This depression is surrounded by a large bank between 1.7 m. and 2.00 m. high, formerly continuous but with two modern breaks through it. Outside the bank there is an encircling ditch cut back 1.5 m. deep into the hillside on the S., E. and N. and with a low bank on the N.W. There is also an outer bank on the E. (RAF VAP CPE/UK/1929, 3176-7; 106G/UK/1488, 4264-6)

[b](11) ENCLOSURE (SP 577336), lies within a small copse known as The Grove, in the N.W. corner of the crossroads of the A43 and B4031, on clay at 125 m. above OD. A rectangular system of ditches, perhaps originally forming two conjoined enclosures 25 m. across, has been cut by the A43. No date or function can be assigned to the site but the name Le Grofehey is recorded as early as 1275 (PN Northants., 53).

(12) CULTIVATION REMAINS. The common fields of Evenley were enclosed by an Act of Parliament of 1779 (NRO, Enclosure Map). No details of the fields at that time are known except that the greater part of the area to the N. of the village, now Evenley Park, was already enclosed before that date, and that the southern part of the parish was an uncultivated area known as Bayards Green. Bridges (Hist. of Northants., I (1791), 165), writing in about

1720, said that 'about one forth part of Evenle is enclosed' and this presumably refers to the area of the park. Very little ridge-and-furrow survives on the ground or can be traced on air photographs, most of it having been destroyed by modern cultivation of the light limestone soil. Some interlocked furlongs survive within the park.

The date of the enclosure of the common fields of Astwick is unknown, though part of the area had been enclosed before 1535 (K. J. Allison, *et. al.*, *The Deserted Villages of Northants.* (1966), 35). Certainly by 1720 (Bridges, op. cit.) all the land of Astwick was enclosed. Ridge-and-furrow of these fields can be traced only in a few places. Fragments are visible N., S. and W. of the site of Astwick village (9) (SP 572438, 561340 and 569340) though only as single furlongs. Ridge-and-furrow also survives in the closes around and within Astwick village. (RAF VAP CPE/UK/1926, 4217–9; CPE/UK/1929, 1230–2, 2176–7, 3175–7; 106G/UK/1488, 3266–8, 4264–6)

23 EYDON
(OS 1:10000 [a] SP 54 NW, [b] SP 54 NE, [c] SP 55 SW, [d] SP 55 SE)

The roughly oval parish, covering about 650 hectares, occupies a wide spur between the R. Cherwell, here flowing S. on the W. boundary, and a S.W.-flowing stream on the S. boundary. The central part of the parish, rising to 180 m. above OD, is capped by Northampton Sand and the land falls away gently across Lias clays and a narrow band of Marlstone Rock to the streams flowing at about 120 m. above OD.

MEDIEVAL AND LATER

[c](1) SETTLEMENT REMAINS (SP 541502; Fig. 12), formerly part of Eydon village, lie along the W. side of the W. street of the village, on Northampton Sand at 165 m. above OD. Eydon has an unusual plan, based on two almost parallel streets orientated roughly N.-S., with the church in a rather isolated position to the S. It now appears to be a single-street village with a back lane but earthworks suggest that there were once dwellings on both sides of both streets and that the apparent back lane was once of similar importance to the present main street. This indicates that the village may have been deliberately planned with this layout. The area around the church where traces of settlement might be expected is devoid of remains apart from some banks, which do not appear to be old, in the copse W. of the church. The remains along the W. street are now confined to the single field which remains open following modern housing development; a few low scarps and uneven ground are all that is visible, but on air photographs taken before the recent building further scarps and banks suggesting former house-sites are visible to the S. (RAF VAP CPE/UK/1926, 1061–3, 3061–3).

[c](2) QUARRIES (SP 538505), lie N.W. of the village, on Northampton Sand at 174 m. above OD. An area of some 8 hectares is occupied by numerous interlocked pits and spoil heaps resulting from shallow surface quarrying,

probably of medieval date. The W. part has been damaged by modern cultivation, but on the E. edge some isolated quarry pits have been cut into earlier ridge-and-furrow which in turn appears to end at the edge of the main area of quarrying. No date can be assigned to these quarries. (RAF VAP CPE/UK/1926, 3062–4)

(3) CULTIVATION REMAINS. The common fields of the parish were enclosed following an Act of Parliament of 1760. Ridge-and-furrow of these fields exists on the ground or can be traced on air photographs over much of the parish, except on the Northampton Sand deposits where modern cultivation has apparently removed nearly all trace. It is arranged mainly in interlocked and end-on furlongs, often of reversed-S form. A notable feature occurs on landslips in the N.W. of the parish (around SP 533510) where Upper Lias Clay has slumped N.W. into the valley of the Cherwell. Most of the ridge-and-furrow avoids or stops short of the lower edge of the landslips but at one point on Eydon Hill (SP 535512) one block of ridge-and-furrow rides over them. A field in the N. of the parish (SP 540511) is exceptional for the extreme narrowness of the ridges. In places these are less than 2 m. wide but they otherwise appear to be of normal common-field form. (RAF VAP CPE/UK/1926, 1061–6, 3060–6; CPE/UK/1994, 2095–8, 4098–102; 106G/UK/721, 4000–2)

24 FARTHINGHOE
(OS 1:10000 [a] SP 53 NW, [b] SP 53 NE, [c] SP 54 SW, [d] SP 54 SE)

The modern parish, of some 1090 hectares, incorporates the former lands of the deserted village of Steane (18) (Fig. 82). Farthinghoe village is located on a N.-S. ridge of limestone and Northampton Sand at about 152 m. above OD. From this high central ridge the land slopes N.W. and N.E. across Upper and Middle Lias Clay and Marlstone to S.-flowing streams on the N.W. and E. boundaries of the parish.

PREHISTORIC AND ROMAN

A few worked flints have been found in the N. of the area (SP 53754117) and a single flint arrowhead further E. (SP 54054113; inf. D. J. Barrett). An Iron Age gold stater of Whaddon Chase (Mack 138) type was found in the parish in 1847 (*PSA*, 2 (1850), 43; S. S. Frere (ed.), *Problems of the Iron Age in S. Britain* (1958), 186; Ashmolean Museum).

(1–4) FLINT-WORKING SITES. Worked flints of Neolithic and Bronze Age type have been found at four places in the parish during field-walking (inf. D. N. Hall).

[c](1) FLINT-WORKING SITE (SP 529407), in the N.W. of the parish, on the S. side of a small stream, on clay at 107 m. above OD.

[c](2) FLINT-WORKING SITE (SP 540407), in the N. of the parish, on clay at 152 m. above OD.

^c(3) FLINT-WORKING SITE (SP 544402), 600 m. S.S.E. of (2), on Northampton Sand at 150 m. above OD.

^a(4) FLINT-WORKING SITE (SP 535385), in the S. of the parish, on Oolite Limestone at 155 m. above OD.

^a(5) DITCHED TRACKWAY, LINEAR DITCHES, ENCLOSURES AND PIT ALIGNMENT (centred SP 542376; Fig. 54), in the extreme S. of the parish, on the N.W. side of the disused airfield, on Great Oolite Limestone, between 149 m. and 155 m. above OD. Air photographs (NCAU) show numerous features though some have been obscured or destroyed by the buildings and taxi-paths of the airfield. The clearest feature is a ditched trackway running N.W.-S.E. from which extend long linear ditches, perhaps the boundaries of former fields. Further N. there are some ill-defined sinuous ditches and to the S. is a group of small enclosures and a length of pit alignment. Two parallel ditches in the S. may be another ditched trackway.

^a(6) LINEAR DITCHES (SP 545395), S.E. of the village, on limestone at 145 m. above OD. Air photographs (NCAU) show very indistinctly a group of linear ditches.

^a(7) ENCLOSURE (?) (SP 549391), W. of Steane Park, immediately N. of the A422 road, on Great Oolite Limestone at 132 m. above OD. Air photographs (NCAU) show all but the S.E. side of what appears to be a double-ditched enclosure 30 m. by 20 m., orientated S.W.-N.E. The S.W. side, if it existed, has been destroyed by the road. Two roughly parallel linear features to the N. of the enclosure appear to be modern.

^b(8) ENCLOSURE (SP 553384), immediately S. of Steane Park, on Northampton Sand at 138 m. above OD. Air photographs (NCAU) show the W. part of what appears to be a trapezoidal enclosure orientated E.-W. It is 40 m.-45 m. wide and at least 70 m. long.

^a(9) PIT ALIGNMENT AND ENCLOSURE (centred SP 525386), lie immediately W. of Farthinghoe Lodge, in the S. of the parish, on Northampton Sand and Upper Lias Clay at 154 m. above OD. Air photographs (CUAP, ABY83–5) show a clearly marked pit alignment running N.N.E. for 250 m. from SP 525385. Other cropmarks in the vicinity appear to be the result of frost-fracture but there may be a small rectangular enclosure to the W. of the pit alignment (SP 52503865). A little to the S.E. (SP 526383) other air photographs (NCAU) show several indistinct ditches as well as some possible enclosures. The only clear feature is a ring ditch 20 m. in diam.

^a(10) ROMAN SETTLEMENT (SP 528384), lies to the S.E. of an area of cropmarks (9), on Northampton Sand at 152 m. above OD. Much Roman pottery, building stone and a quern have been noted (*Northants. Archaeol.*, 10 (1975), 154).

^a(11) ROMAN SETTLEMENT (?) (SP 527398), lies W. of the village, on Marlstone Rock, at 114 m. above OD. Field-walking has led to the discovery of Roman material (*Northants. Archaeol.*, 10 (1975), 154).

^c(12) ROMAN SETTLEMENT (?) (SP 530401), lies 450 m. N.N.E. of (11), on a small outcrop of Northampton Sand and limestone at about 130 m. above OD. Roman pottery and tile has been found over about 2 hectares (*Northants.*

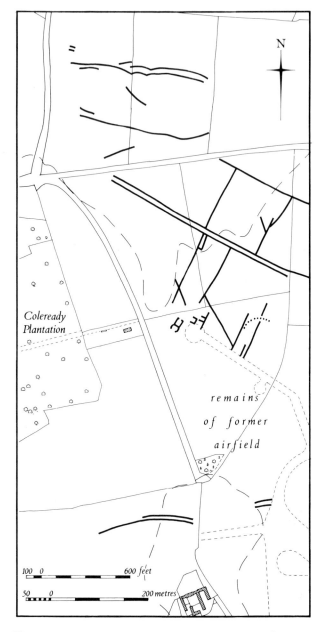

Fig. 54 FARTHINGHOE (5) Ditched trackway, linear ditches, enclosures and pit alignment

Archaeol., 10 (1975), 154).

^c(13) ROMAN SETTLEMENT (?) (SP 53464110), in the N. of the parish on the S. side of a S.W.-flowing stream, on Upper Lias Clay at 110 m. above OD. A small quantity of Roman pottery has been found in the sides of a field drain. As the adjacent fields are under pasture the extent of this possible settlement is not known (inf. D. J. Barrett).

^a(14) ROMAN SETTLEMENT (?) (SP 537398), immediately N.E. of Farthinghoe Church, on limestone at 155 m. above OD. A small scatter of Roman sherds is recorded (inf. D. J. Barrett).

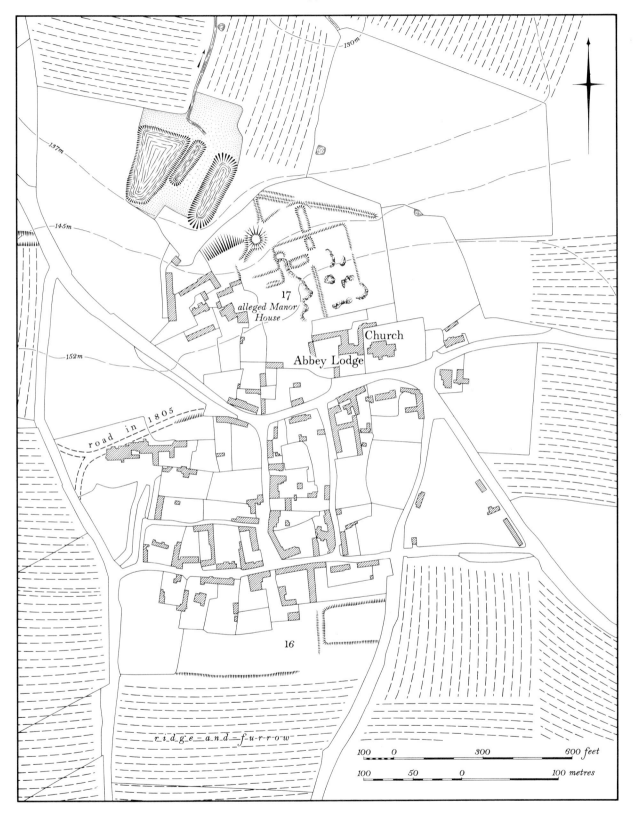

Fig. 55 FARTHINGHOE (16) Settlement remains, (17) Garden remains

MEDIEVAL AND LATER

[a](15) OCCUPATION SITE (SP 53903986), lies 300 m. E. of Farthinghoe church, on limestone at 152 m. above OD. Excavations in 1973 revealed a circular stone structure about 2 m. in diam. and at least 1.5 m. deep. It was burned inside and large quantities of bones, mainly pig, were found. It is likely to have been a well-head. Road works in the following year exposed two ditches in the same area. These contained early medieval pottery, possibly of late Saxon date, as well as fragments of bone and charcoal (*Northants. Archaeol.*, 10 (1975), 166).

[a](16) SETTLEMENT REMAINS (SP 533397 and 535394; Figs. 55 and 83), formerly part of Farthinghoe, lie on the N.W. and S. sides of the village, on Northampton Sand and Upper Lias Clay at just over 152 m. above OD. The present plan of Farthinghoe, although distorted by the main A422 road which runs through it, consists of a basic grid of three or possibly four short N.-S. lanes bounded by two E.-W. roads and with an open space in the N.E. corner near the church. On a map of 1805 (NRO) the W. end of the northern E.-W. street is shown as extending further W., completing the grid pattern of the village. By 1841 (NRO, Tithe Map) this part of the street had been abandoned and the area in which it lay was called 'Old Road'. Most of the line of this street has been built over or destroyed by the later rectory and its garden but one side of a possible hollow-way is still visible as a low scarp 0.5 m. high, close to its junction with the main street. The building-line of an existing row of houses also shows the former line of the street.

On the S. side of the village, behind the houses lining the S. side of the E.-W. street, there are the slight remains of former closes and a hollow-way. These have been largely destroyed but they are visible on air photographs taken in 1947. (RAF VAP CPE/UK/1926, 5212-3)

[a](17) GARDEN REMAINS (SP 534399; Fig. 55), lie on the N. side of the village, N.W. of the church on clay between 137 m. and 153 m. above OD. These remains have not been correctly interpreted previously, partly because of the identification of the mount as a windmill mound (OS Record Cards; CBA Group 9, *Newsletter* 5 (1975), 29) and partly because of damage by quarrying.

The earthworks are certainly the site of a formal garden, perhaps of 17th-century date, and presumably associated with the manor house. The house immediately W. of the church, Abbey Lodge, is usually called the Manor House, although the farmhouse to the N.W. is said locally to be the original one.

The most prominent feature of the site is a large mound, once probably circular but now badly damaged, 2.5 m. high with a flat top 8 m. across and with a ramp on its S.W. side. This mound lies near the N.W. corner of a rectangular area bounded on the N. by a low scarp much altered by a track which runs alongside it, on the E. by a low scarp, and on the S. by the garden of Abbey Lodge. The W. side has been destroyed by quarrying. The interior is also damaged by quarry pits but a low bank and two shallow rectangular former ponds can be identified; a larger pond also now dry lies outside the area to the N. A scarp on the N. side overlies a larger bank which cuts across the

N. of the site. Some slight scarps immediately S. of the mound may be the remains of a tennis court (local inf.). Below the mound on a spring line at the bottom of a steep natural slope are three roughly rectangular ponds. These may be medieval in origin, but have been much altered. The whole area was known as The Park in 1805 (Map in NRO) and Park Hovel and Yard on the Tithe Map of 1841 (NRO). The field to the N. was then called Mount Close. (RAF VAP CPE/UK/1926, 5212-3)

[b](18) DESERTED VILLAGE OF STEANE (SP 551389; Figs. 56 and 83), lies in the S.E. of the parish, on clay and limestone at 137 m. above OD. Steane was once an independent parish with its own land unit and is first recorded in 1086, in Domesday Book, listed as a single manor of two hides with a recorded population of 18 (VCH *Northants.*, I (1902), 344). In 1301 16 people paid the Lay Subsidy (PRO, E179/155/31) and in the 1316 *Nomina Villarum* Steane is mentioned as an independent vill. The village paid 40s. 4d. for the 1334 Lay Subsidy (PRO, E179/155/3) and in 1348 28 tenants are recorded (PRO, E134/102/9). In 1377 51 people over the age of 14 paid the Poll Tax (PRO, E179/155/28) but by 1428 there were less than 10 households in the village (*Feudal Aids*, 4, 51). In 1620 the present chapel was built adjacent to the manor house, but whether it is on the site of the earlier church is not known. Bridges (*Hist of Northants.*, I (1791), 196), writing in about 1720, said that there was only one house in the parish in addition to the manor house, but that 'it is formerly believed . . . that there was once here a flourishing town'. (K. J. Allison et al., *The Deserted Villages of Northants.* (1966), 46)

The remains of the village lie W. and S.W. of the manor house within an area known as Knoll Field. The earthworks are very slight and have been damaged by later quarrying but a generally rectangular arrangement of closes is recognisable. The main identifiable features include a hollow-way 1 m. deep which crosses the S.W. part of the site from N.W. to S.E. ('a'-'b' on plan). At its S.E. end it appears to have met another slight hollow-way running at right angles to it but the latter is not clear. Immediately N.E. of the main hollow-way there is a rectangular enclosure ('c' on plan) bounded by the hollow-way on the S.W. and by scarps and ditches on the other side. It is subdivided by low scarps into about four closes and at least one sunken building platform is visible. The N.W. end of this enclosure is cut by a large quarry from which a few sherds of 13th and 14th-century pottery have come. At the N. end of the site there is another enclosure ('d' on plan) also sub-divided into small closes. (RAF VAP CPE/UK/1926, 2214-5; CUAP SA22-3, AAV 17-18)

[b](19) FISHPONDS AND GARDEN REMAINS (SP 555391; Fig. 57), lie N. of the manor house on the S. side of a broad shallow valley, on Upper Lias Clay at 122 m. above OD. The site was probably once a set of medieval fishponds but has been remodelled, presumably in the early 17th century as part of a garden associated with the manor house.

Part of a late medieval building still remains, but the house was apparently rebuilt in the early 17th century by Sir Thomas Crewe who also rebuilt the chapel in 1620, perhaps on the site of the original medieval church. The land to the N. may have been turned into a formal garden at the same time.

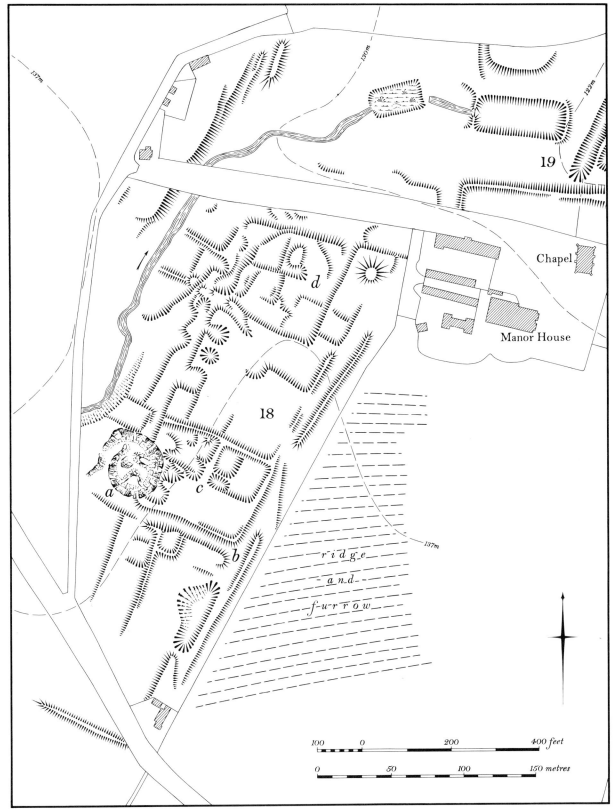

Fig. 56 FARTHINGHOE (18) Deserted village of Steane

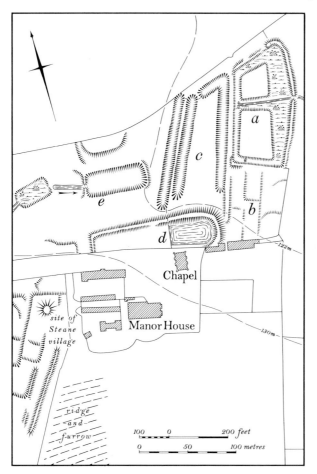

Fig. 57 FARTHINGHOE (19) Fishponds and
garden remains at Steane

The remains can be divided into five parts. The only
surviving earthworks of the medieval fishponds, probably
much altered, lie in the N.E. ('a' on plan). They consist of
two roughly rectangular islands, surrounded by shallow
ditches which widen on the E. to form a pond. The islands
themselves are flat and featureless. The E. side of the broad
pond is edged by a steep-sided flat-topped bank up to 2 m.
high with traces of a dry-stone wall on the inner side in
the N.E. corner. This bank is very similar to terrace walks
in other late 16th or early 17th-century gardens (e.g.
RCHM Northants., III (1981), Canons Ashby (2)) and may
be an addition of that period. To the S. ('b' on plan) is a
roughly rectangular area sloping up gently to the S. with
a number of very slight scarps less than 0.25 m. high across
it. These form no detectable pattern but may be the remains of flower-beds or paths of a formal garden. To the
W. of the medieval ponds are three long narrow ponds up
to 2 m. deep bounding a roughly rectangular area now
ploughed ('c' on plan). Two of the ponds, on the W., lie
parallel and close to each other; the other, which returns
S.W. at its N. end, lies to the E. To the S. again ('d' on

plan) is a large embanked pond which, at its E. end, is
raised 2.5 m. above the adjacent ground. In the N.W. is
another rectangular pond ('e' on plan) with a shallower,
smaller one to the W. These may not have been part of
the formal gardens. (RAF VAP CPE/UK/1926, 2214–5; CUAP
SA22)

(20) CULTIVATION REMAINS. The common fields of Farthinghoe had been enclosed by the early 18th century, for
Bridges (Hist. of Northants., I (1791), 168), writing in about
1720, recorded that the whole lordship was enclosed, but
the exact date is not known. Ridge-and-furrow of these
fields exists on the ground or can be traced on air photographs over much of the old parish of Farthinghoe. It is
arranged in end-on and interlocked furlongs. The most
notable feature is N. of the village on a steep W.-facing
hill of Upper Lias Clay capped with Northampton Sand
(SP 537400–539408); the hillside has collapsed into landslips
and mud-flows. Where the landslips are most marked (SP
538407) the land was never cultivated in medieval times
and the adjacent ridge-and-furrow terminates at the upper
limits of the slip. Further S. the ridge-and-furrow extends
down the hillside over the landslips and as a result has an
unusually uneven appearance both in plan and elevation.

The date of the enclosure of the common fields of the
deserted village of Steane is also unknown, though it was
probably in the late 15th or early 16th century. At least
1000 sheep were being grazed on the land by 1547 (K. J.
Allison, The Deserted Villages of Northants. (1966), 46).
Ridge-and-furrow of these fields exists on the ground or
can be traced on air photographs only in a few places as
modern cultivation has destroyed much of it. Where it
survives it is arranged in end-on furlongs, mainly running
at right angles across the slopes. (RAF VAP CPE/UK/1926,
2211–6, 3212–4, 5211–5)

25 GAYTON
(OS 1:10000 [a] SP 65 NE, [b] SP 65 SE, [c] SP 75 NW,
[d] SP 75 SW)

The roughly rectangular parish, of nearly 700 hectares, lies on land sloping generally N. and is
bounded on the W. and N. by tributaries of the R.
Nene. The village is situated on an outcrop of Northampton Sand at about 114 m. above OD, with
Oolite Limestone and Boulder Clay to the S. and
Upper Lias Clay to the N. sloping steeply down to
82 m. above OD. The major monument is the
Roman villa (1).

PREHISTORIC AND ROMAN

Two worked flints were found in 1974 (SP 699553; Northants. Archaeol., 10 (1975), 150). A silver coin of Tasciovanus (Mack 158) was discovered in 1863 somewhere in the
parish (BM; J. Evans, Coins of the Ancient Britons (1864),
240; S. S. Frere (Ed.), Problems of the Iron Age in S. Britain
(1958), 223).

[d](1) ROMAN VILLA (SP 71455396; Fig. 58), lies in the
extreme E. of the parish in a field known as The Warren,

on Northampton Sand at 130 m. above OD. Parts of a Roman building, including the bases of four columns of a portico with walls at right-angles on each side, were discovered in 1840; the resulting plan is difficult to interpret. Finds included a silver fibula, a small bronze figurine of Cupid, pottery including samian, tiles and 22 coins ranging from Marcus Aurelius to Gratian but mainly of the 4th century. In 1849 more pottery was dug up, 70 m. to the S. of the known building. Stone walls, together with more pottery and a 'road', are also recorded from the face of a sand-pit in the area (*Archaeologia*, 30 (1844), 125 (plan); OS Record Cards).

^a(2) ROMAN SETTLEMENT AND WELL (SP 71275488), E. of the village, on Northampton Sand at 120 m. above OD. A dense scatter of Roman pottery and tiles has been noted in the vicinity of a well. The latter also contained pottery, including samian and grey ware, and pieces of leather. (*J. Northants. Natur. Hist. Soc. and FC*, 34 (1962), 45; OS Record Cards)

^d(3) ROMAN SETTLEMENT (?) (SP 712549), close to the junction of the parishes of Gayton, Blisworth and Tiffield, on Boulder Clay at 130 m. above OD. Roman pottery including colour-coated sherds has been found (OS Record Cards).

MEDIEVAL AND LATER

^d(4) PONDS AND HOLLOW-WAY (SP 704549), lie immediately N. of the village and W. of the manor house, in the bottom and on the steep sides of an N.-draining valley, on Upper Lias Clay at around 120 m. above OD. The area is occupied by earthworks which include some quarry pits near the head of the valley, undated drainage ditches, and considerable spreads of uneven ground caused by natural landslips. In addition there is a hollow-way on the E. side of the valley, extending from the manor house to the uppermost of two rectangular ponds, now dry, which occupy the valley bottom. Both ponds were originally kept full of water by dams which still survive up to 2 m. high at their S. ends. On the Tithe Map of 1841 (NRO) the area is called Springs Orchard. (RAF VAP CPE/UK/1926, 5032–4; FSL6565, 1795–6; air photographs in NMR)

^d(5) POND (SP 708541), lay in the bottom of a small E.-draining valley S.E. of the village, on Upper Lias Clay at 122 m. above OD. A small rectangular pond, with a massive dam at its E. and on which the modern road runs, has recently been destroyed. In 1841 (NRO, Tithe Map) it was described as Fishpond. (RAF VAP CPE/UK/1926, 5032; FSL6565, 1795–6)

^d(6) POND (SP 711534), lies in the S.E. of the parish, immediately N.W. of Gayton Wood House, in the bottom

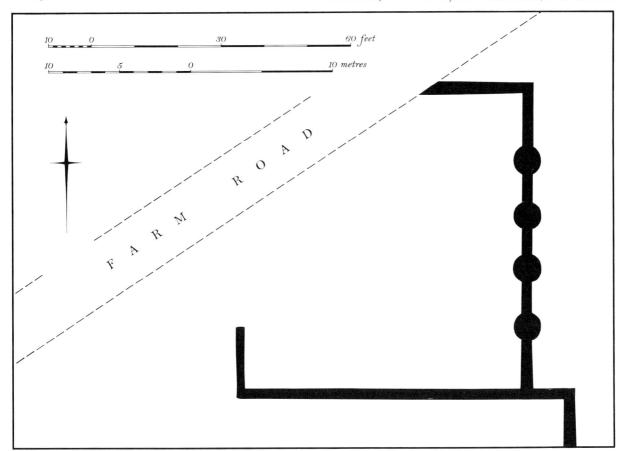

Fig. 58   GAYTON (1)   Roman villa

of a small E.-draining valley, on Upper Lias Clay at 115 m. above OD. A small triangular pond has a large dam 60 m. long, 14 m. wide and up to 2 m. high which carries the track to the house. On the Tithe Map of 1841 (NRO) it is called Fishpond. (RAF VAP CPE/UK/1926, 3032–3)

^c(7) MEDIEVAL SETTLEMENT (?) (SP 720557), lies in the extreme N.E. corner of the parish, near a place known as Oldfield, on Upper Lias Clay at 76 m. above OD. In 1967 a quantity of 13th and 14th century-pottery, together with tiles and bones, was recorded (BNFAS, 3 (1969), 1). No further finds have been made but to judge from the available air photographs the settlement, if such it was, was either very small or had been ploughed over by ridge-and-furrow which once covered almost the entire area. (RAF VAP CPE/UK/1926, 5030–1)

^{ac}(8) DEER PARK (centred SP 700553), lies in the N.W. of the parish, on Upper Lias Clay and Northampton Sand at around 122 m. above OD. The park was created in 1258 by Ingram de Fednes but its later history is unknown. In the early 15th century John Trussel was given permission to empark 300 acres of land in Gayton, called La Hay, though whether this was connected with the earlier park is not certain. (Northants. P. and P., 5 (1975), 224)

The park, covering some 25 hectares, is still bounded by an almost continuous circular hedge, except at the S.E. corner where there is a broad gap. For most of its length this hedge is on a low hedge-bank of no apparent antiquity, though in places it rises to as much as 1.5 m. high and 10 m. wide. Ridge-and-furrow is traceable in the interior of the park and at one point in the N.W. appears to underlie the park boundary (SP 698555). On the Tithe Map of 1841 (NRO) two adjacent fields, one inside the park and one outside it, are called The Park. (RAF VAP CPE/UK/1926, 5032–4)

(9) CULTIVATION REMAINS. The date of the enclosure of the common fields of the parish is unknown. Possibly the early 15th-century reference to the enclosure of 300 acres of land, meadow and pasture may be connected with this (Cal. Chart., 1341–1417, 424). It had certainly taken place by 1841 (NRO, Tithe Map) and a small area of enclosed land in Gayton, shown on a map of Blisworth of 1729 (NRO) implies that at least part of the parish was divided into hedged fields by that date.

Ridge-and-furrow exists on the ground or can be traced on air photographs. Apart from a few fragments of single furlongs, none can be seen in the S. part of the parish, presumably because modern cultivation of the light soil there has removed all trace. However, on the Upper Lias Clay in the lower, N. part of the parish the pattern of interlocked and end-on furlongs is almost complete. Here a number of features of interest can be seen including the overploughing of headlands to make two end-on furlongs into a single large one (e.g. SP 712552 and 712554). In the same area are examples of two narrow ridges merging into one wider ridge without a break. On the steep N.-facing slope of a low hill, on Upper Lias Clay, landslips appear to have occurred after the ridge-and-furrow was created and this has resulted in the distortion and destruction of the ridges over an area of about 4 hectares (SP 700555). (RAF VAP CPE/UK/1926, 3032–7, 5029–35; FSL6565, 1795–9)

26 GRAFTON REGIS
(OS 1:10000 ^a SP 74 NW, ^b SP 74 NE)

The parish, which is roughly rectangular, covers about 930 hectares and includes the village and former parish of Alderton. It lies on the S.W. bank of the R. Tove which defines the N. and E. boundaries; an E.-flowing tributary stream marks the S. boundary. The lower areas in the N. and E. alongside the river are covered by alluvial deposits and Upper Lias Clay at about 75 m. above OD; Oolitic Limestones are exposed on the steep sides and summits of several spurs, and the higher ground in the S.W., with a maximum height of 115 m. above OD, is covered by Boulder Clay.

The parish contains several important medieval monuments, including a motte or ringwork (5) and the site of a later manor house and garden (6) at Alderton, a group of monastic buildings at Grafton Regis (4) and extensive settlement remains at both villages (2) and (7).

PREHISTORIC AND ROMAN

Roman coins, including a gold coin of Antony and Octavia and several silver republican ones, possibly a hoard buried before A.D. 43, were found at Alderton in about 1821 (Wetton, Guide Book to Northampton, (1849), 185; VCH Northants., I (1902), 215; OS Record Cards).

^a(1) RING DITCH (?) (SP 738480), in the extreme N.W. of the parish, close to the R. Tove, on river gravel at 137 m. above OD. Air photographs (NCAU) show an indistinct circular feature which may be a ring ditch.

MEDIEVAL AND LATER

^b(2) SETTLEMENT REMAINS AND MANOR HOUSE SITE (SP 756467; Fig. 13), formerly part of Grafton Regis, lie in and around the village, on a ridge of Great Oolite Limestone, at just over 90 m. above OD.

Grafton Regis, though a small village, has an unusual plan. At its N.E. end there is a single street with only the manor house and the church on the N.W. side. This street once continued further N.E. but is now blocked by two houses; the only through-road turns sharply N.W. and then N.E. to cross the Tove valley towards Ashton. To the S.W. the single street divides and the two branches run back to meet the present Northampton-Old Stratford road.

The surviving earthworks fall into three groups. On the S.E. side of the single street, opposite the manor house, are the very fragmentary remains of small embanked closes with areas of uneven ground within them, probably the sites of former houses. To the S.W. small paddocks along the N. side of the northern branch road probably once had houses within them. The back boundary of these paddocks is continued N.W. by a massive bank up to 1 m. high, suggesting that further houses and gardens once lay to the S. where the present old school and some cottages now stand. A similar line of houses may have stood along the southern branch road though no identifiable remains can be traced.

Fig. 59 GRAFTON REGIS (5) Motte or ringwork, (6) Site of manor house and garden remains,
(7) Settlement remains at Alderton

Within the triangular area formed by the two branch roads and the main Northampton road there is a more extensive area of earthworks. These are in a poor state of preservation, but several small rectangular embanked closes can be identified, surrounding a much larger enclosure which in turn has an irregular embanked area within it. The earthworks may be the site of one of the medieval manor houses of Grafton Regis and the whole of this S.W. part of the village is perhaps an addition to an earlier single-street settlement near the church. (RAF VAP CPE/UK/ 1926, 3244–5; CUAP AWN55; air photographs in NMR)

[b](3) ENCLOSURE (SP 761467), lies 250 m. S.E. of Grafton Regis church, on the S.E. side of a limestone ridge at 90 m. above OD. A small roughly rectangular enclosure 100 m. by 75 m., orientated N.W.–S.E., with a rectangular projection on its S.E. side is bounded by a shallow ditch and low internal bank. It overlies earlier ridge-and-furrow which can still be traced in the interior. A shallow rectangular pond and a number of more indeterminate features lie within the enclosure. No date or function can be assigned to this enclosure. Other earthworks, mainly drainage ditches, and another pond now largely filled in, lie on the lower ground to the N.E. (RAF VAP CPE/UK/1926, 3244–5; CUAP, AWN58; air photographs in NMR)

[b](4) SITE OF PRIORY AND MANOR HOUSE (SP 752467), lies 300 m. W. of Grafton Regis village, on limestone at about 90 m. above OD. The site was fully excavated in 1964–5. Before excavation there was an area of disturbed earthworks, partly overploughed with ridge-and-furrow which terminated on a headland and ditch a little to the S. of the site. Beyond the headland was a hollow-way running W. from the village through the ridge-and-furrow.

It had been assumed that this was the site of one of the two medieval manor houses of Grafton, probably the one held by the Woodville family in the late medieval period. The excavation revealed a range of 13th to 14th-century buildings, apparently of monastic origin, including what was perhaps a small unaisled church with a cloister and other structures on its N. side. Other, detached buildings, probably of the same date, included a barn or hospital, a kitchen and a dovecote. In the 15th century the site seems to have been converted to domestic use. The cloister was removed and replaced by a new building and in the church a new floor was laid which included tiles incorporating the arms of Woodville and the Yorkist rose. The whole site was abandoned soon after the late 15th century and, presumably, converted to arable land.

The excavator identified the site as the beneficed hermitage or small priory of Grafton known to have been supported by the Woodville family in the late 13th and 14th centuries but which apparently ceased to exist at the end of the 14th century. The lands of this priory passed to St. James' Abbey in Northampton, but it is possible that the Woodvilles took over the buildings and altered them. (*Med. Arch.*, 9 (1965), 203; 10 (1960), 202–4; VCH *Northants.*, II (1906), 137; RAF VAP CPE/UK/1926, 3243–4; air photographs in NMR)

[a](5) MOTTE OR RINGWORK (SP 740469; Fig. 59; Plate 3), usually known as The Mount, stands on high ground on the N.E. side of Alderton village, on Great Oolite Lime-

stone at 100 m. above OD. Nothing is known of its history apart from some 13th-century references to it (G. Baker, *Hist. of Northants.*, II (1836–41), 120) but it appears to be of 11th or 12th-century date. It consists of a roughly triangular area raised only about 1 m. above the adjacent land, but surrounded by a very large ditch up to 5 m. deep below a well-marked inner rampart or bank which itself is 1 m.–1.5 m. high above the interior. The ditch has been largely destroyed on the S.W. side and modern houses now occupy its line. However even in the early years of this century no ditch was visible here (VCH *Northants.*, II (1906), 403).

Bridges (*Hist. of Northants.*, I (1791), 280), writing in about 1720, said that 'the entrance . . . seems to have been on the western side'. Presumably he was referring to the gap in the inner rampart in the centre of the S.W. side, but this gap does not appear now to be an entrance. The interior is uneven and very overgrown and no features are visible apart from a sloping platform 0.5 m. high on the S.E. side. On a map of 1726 (NRO) the ditch is shown as filled with water and the area is called Castle Mound.

[a](6) SITE OF MANOR HOUSE AND GARDEN REMAINS (SP 738470; Fig. 59; Plate 3), lie on the W. side of a valley, on land sloping S.W., on limestone and clay at 88 m. above OD. This may have been the site of the medieval manor house of Alderton, but it is certain that William Gorges built 'a very large mansion-house' here in 1582 (J. Bridges, *Hist. of Northants.*, I (1791), 280) and the surviving earthworks must for the most part be the gardens of this house. The house was partly demolished in the early 18th century and the surviving section was then described as 'embattled' (Bridges, op. cit.). On a map of 1726 (NRO) no house is shown on the site but an elaborate gateway is depicted, flanked by two long buildings presumably barns or stables. Baker refers to mullioned windows in the farm buildings (*Hist of Northants.*, II (1836–41), 120).

Nothing remains of the mansion-house; its site, presumably, is occupied by the 19th-century barns and cart-sheds. To the N.E. of these buildings, on gently sloping ground, is a roughly rectangular area bounded on the S.E. by the existing Church Lane, on the N.W. by a low, broad, flat-topped bank or terraced walk and on the N.E. by an old hollow-way (see (7) below). The S.W. part of the area is divided into rectangular blocks, bounded by low scarps nowhere much above 0.5 m. high except on the S.E. side where some of them rise to 1.5 m. These scarps apparently mark the edges of formal flower-beds or terrace-walks which formed part of a small late 16th-century garden. To the N.E. is a large circular mound surrounded by a broad ditch which was once water-filled. The flat top of the mound is level with the adjacent ground to the N. and E. and up to 1.75 m. high above the ground to the S. and W. The ditch is between 1 m. and 2.25 m. deep below the mound. It has been suggested that this mound might be a motte or a moated site (OS Record Cards) but it is much more likely to be a mount, contemporary with the rest of the garden. Such mounts raised above formal gardens were a normal feature of this period.

To the N.W. of the farm buildings there are three rectangular ponds, one large, the other two small and narrow. These may have originated as medieval fishponds, belonging to a manor, but the raised flat-topped terraces that bound them on the N.E. and S.W., suggest that they were either incorporated into the later garden or were first constructed in the late 16th century as part of the overall garden design. (RAF VAP CPE/UK/1926, 3241–2; CUAP, ZJ58, AML68, AWN61; air photographs in NMR)

[a](7) SETTLEMENT REMAINS (centred SP 749468; Fig. 59; Plate 3), formerly part of Alderton, lie in and around the village, on limestone and clay between 83 m. and 103 m. above OD. Alderton is first mentioned in 1086 in Domesday Book where it is listed as two manors with a total recorded population of eight, both held by the Count of Mortain (VCH Northants., I (1902), 322, 328). In 1301, 38 people at Alderton paid the Lay Subsidy (PRO, E179/155/31) but thereafter there is no record of its size until the Lay Subsidy of 1523–4 when 21 people paid tax (PRO, E179/155/40). By the early 18th century there were about 25 houses there (J. Bridges, Hist. of Northants., I (1791), 280) and the village remained much the same size until recent development.

The earliest map of the village is dated 1726 (NRO). It shows the village virtually as it is now, except for three buildings which no longer stand. At the N.E. end of the village was a row of cottages ('a' on plan), immediately S. of the church was a farm house ('b' on plan), and at the N.W. end of Spring Lane, N.W. of the ponds in the garden remains (6), was a house and barn ('c' on plan). Immediately S.W. of the manor house site there was a large triangular green. The Enclosure Map of 1819 (NRO) shows a similar situation, except that most of the green had been enclosed under the Act, the house and barn further N.W. had disappeared and so had the row of cottages. The farm lying S. of the church is shown with a large area of outbuildings around it; this farm was completely demolished later in the 19th century.

The evidence of these maps, together with the surviving earthworks, suggests that there were once two distinct parts to the village of Alderton, along two roughly parallel roads running N.W.-S.E. The road to the N.E. was in part the present E. end of Church Lane. A broad hollow-way up to 1.5 m. runs from the sharp bend in Church Lane ('d' on plan). Ridge-and-furrow edges this hollow-way over most of its length except at its S.E. end where there are at least three small closes. These may once have contained houses, but the area was already devoid of buildings in 1726. On the N.E. side of Spring Lane, the second of the two main streets, S.W. of the church, nothing is visible on the ground or on air photographs taken in 1947 (RAF VAP CPE/UK/1926, 3241–2). However, the area has recently been ploughed and returned to grass and this may have concealed the evidence of earlier occupation here. On the opposite side of the road ('e' on plan) are some disturbed earthworks comprising low banks, scarps and shallow ditches which, though partly quarried into, probably represent an area of former settlement though again any houses had gone by 1726. Similar slight remains lie further N.W. along the S.W. side of Spring Lane ('f' on plan) in an area devoid of buildings in 1726. On the site of the house and barn to the N. ('c' on plan) the well-marked foundation walls of a rectangular stone structure still survive, as well as some other slighter scarps and ditches.

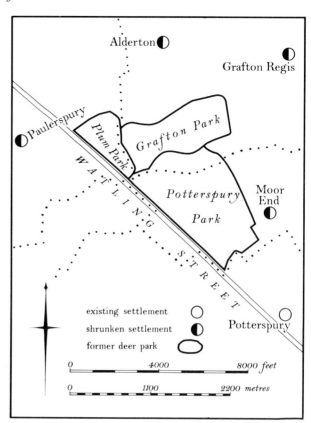

Fig. 60 GRAFTON REGIS (8), PAULERSPURY (21) and YARDLEY GOBION (8) Deer parks

[a](8) DEER PARK (centred SP 740455; Fig. 60), in the S.W. part of the parish, mainly on Boulder Clay, on land sloping S.E. between 114 m. and 99 m. above OD. It lies partly in the old parish of Grafton Regis and partly in the old parish of Alderton. There was a medieval deer park at Grafton though its exact area is unknown and it was probably very small. It was greatly enlarged in 1532 when Henry VIII ordered that 76 acres of land of the fields of Grafton and 70 acres of Alderton should be incorporated into the park. According to Leyland this new park was enclosed partly by pales and partly by a hedge. It was enlarged again in the early 17th century but was finally disparked in 1644 (Northants. P. and P., 5 (1975), 225). The area of the park in its final form is known from a map of 1720 (NRO). At this date it was contiguous with the parks of Yardley Gobion (8) to the S. and Plum Park to the W. (Paulerspury (21)). Nothing remains on the ground of any major boundaries. Most of the park's circuit is marked by normal hedge-banks though part of the S. side follows an old lane, deeply hollowed in places (SP 738453–745454). Much of the interior of the park has ridge-and-furrow and the documented incorporation of part of the fields of Grafton and Alderton within its bounds is proved by the fact that the northern boundary runs obliquely across earlier ridge-and-furrow (SP 742459 and 744461). (RAF VAP CPE/UK/1926, 3242–3, 5241–3)

(9) Cultivation Remains. The common fields of Grafton Regis were finally enclosed by an Act of Parliament of 1727. However, by that time much of the parish was already enclosed and indeed Bridges writing in about 1720 (*Hist. of Northants.*, I (1791), 298) described it as an 'inclosed lordship famous for its meadow-grounds and pastures'. A map of Grafton of 1720 (NRO) shows that only that part of the parish E. of the Northampton–Old Stratford road, together with a small area of land along the S. boundary, remained as open field at that time. The rest of the parish is shown as divided into old enclosures. The date of these is not known though 76 acres of former open field was incorporated into the deer park (8) when it was enlarged in 1532.

Ridge-and-furrow of these fields exists on the ground or can be traced on air photographs over parts of the parish, though the pattern is very incomplete owing to modern destruction. It is arranged mainly in end-on and interlocked furlongs, many of reversed-S form. Considerable areas are still preserved on the low-lying ground in the E. of the parish alongside the R. Tove. A notable feature, now destroyed, was the ridge-and-furrow overlying parts of the monastic and manorial site (4). This ridge-and-furrow, headlands and a hollow-way, all of which bore no relationship to the earlier occupation that lasted until the late 15th century, is an indication of changing land use in the post-medieval period.

The common fields of Alderton were enclosed by an Act of Parliament of 1819 (NRO, Enclosure Map). At that time the deer park (8) and other old enclosures to the N. occupied the S.W. of the parish, but the rest was divided into three large fields, Plumpton Field to the W. and S.W. of the village, Twyford Field to the N. and Burch Field to the E. On an earlier map of 1726 (NRO) the same area of open fields is depicted and though no field names are given all the furlongs are shown and named.

Very little ridge-and-furrow is visible in the former Alderton parish either on the ground or on air photographs. What can be traced appears to be arranged in end-on and interlocked furlongs of normal form and agrees with the furlongs shown on the 1726 map. One small area of ridge-and-furrow in the N.W. of the parish (SP 738478) was known as Windmill Leys in 1726. The best surviving ridge-and-furrow lies immediately N. of the village, along the edge of an abandoned street or hollow-way (SP 739471; partly on Fig. 59). Ridge-and-furrow can also be traced S. of the village in the area already within old enclosures in 1726 as well as within the deer park (8). At the latter site, the park boundary cuts obliquely across the ridge-and-furrow; this supports the documentary record of the enlargement of the park in 1532. (RAF VAP CPE/UK/1926, 1241–4, 3241–6, 5243–5)

Undated

(10) Mounds (?) (centred SP 751463), immediately S.W. of the village, on limestone at 98 m. above OD. There are said to have been at least four 'tumuli of oblong shape', but no trace exists on the ground or on air photographs (Wetton, *Guide to Northampton*, (1849), 184; *Archaeologia*, 35 (1853), map Pl. 16). This may be an incorrect reference to the monastic and manorial site (4) which, before destruction, consisted of an uneven area of earthworks.

27 GREATWORTH
(OS 1:10000 [a] SP 54 SE [b] SP 54 SW [c] SP 53 NE)

The large parish, of some 1570 hectares, incorporates the medieval settlements and parishes of Stuchbury and Halse, both now deserted, as well as Greatworth itself (Fig. 61). The hamlet of Westhorp, which is contiguous with Greatworth village, was formerly in Marston St. Lawrence but is now in Greatworth parish. The parish lies on a watershed between streams flowing to the Rivers Tove, Cherwell and Great Ouse. The higher ground in the E., at about 150 m. above OD, is blanketed by Boulder Clay. Bands of Oolitic Limestone and Northampton Sand as well as expanses of Upper Lias Clay slope down to the stream on the S.W. boundary, at about 115 m. above OD.

The major monuments in the parish are the deserted villages of Stuchbury (10) and Halse (13) and the garden remains (9) at Greatworth.

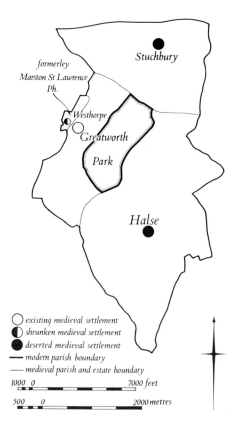

Fig. 61 GREATWORTH Medieval settlements and estates, (12) Deer park

Prehistoric and Roman

A fragment of a perforated disc of silty mudstone has been found in the parish (at SP 549419; NM Records) and small quantities of worked flints of late Neolithic or early Bronze Age type in three places (SP 55904213, 55604186, 55734158; inf. D. J. Barrett).

[a](1) ROMAN SETTLEMENT (?) (SP 553425), immediately N.E. of the village of Greatworth, on limestone at 160 m. above OD. Roman sherds have been noted (OS Record Cards).

[a](2) ROMAN SETTLEMENT (SP 560416), S.E. of the village, on Upper Lias Clay at 132 m. above OD. A large quantity of Roman pottery including samian and mortarium sherds was found in 1978 (Northants. Archaeol., 14 (1979), 105).

[a](3) ROMAN SETTLEMENT (?) (SP 559435), S. of Stuchbury, on Boulder Clay at 168 m. above OD. A small Roman site is recorded (Northants. Archaeol., 11 (1976), 192; CBA Group 9, Newsletter, 6 (1976), 29).

[b](4) ROMAN SETTLEMENT (?) (centred SP 550417), S. of the village, on Upper Lias Clay at about 125 m. above OD. Small scatters of Roman pottery and tile as well as worked flints and one arrowhead have been found dispersed over an area of 10 hectares (inf. D. J. Barrett).

[b](5) ROMAN SETTLEMENT (?) (SP 550422), on the S.W. edge of the village, on limestone and Northampton Sand at 152 m. above OD. A small quantity of Roman pottery and tiles has been discovered (inf. D. J. Barrett).

[b](6) ROMAN SETTLEMENT (?) (SP 549410), E. of Cockley-hill Farm, on Upper Lias Clay at 137 m. above OD. A small quantity of Roman pottery and some worked flints are recorded (inf. D. J. Barrett).

[b](7) ROMAN SETTLEMENT (SP 560406), N.W. of Halse, on limestone at 152 m. above OD. Roman pottery extends over about 6 hectares and a fragment of a flint axe has been found on the S.E. side of the site (inf. D. J. Barrett).

MEDIEVAL AND LATER

An Anglo-Saxon gilt-bronze disc brooch was found in 1957, probably in Greatworth (J. Northants. Mus. and Art Gall., 10 (1974), 18–19; NM).

[b](8) SETTLEMENT REMAINS (SP 549424; Fig. 62), formerly part of Westhorp, lay on the S.E. side of the hamlet, on limestone at 157 m. above OD. Westhorp, though probably always contiguous with the village of Greatworth, was formerly part of Marston St. Lawrence parish and has been transferred to Greatworth only in recent years (NRO, Enclosure Map of Marston St. Lawrence, 1760; OS 1:2500 Northants. LVII 18 and LIX 5 (1925)). The origins and relationship of the hamlet to both Marston St. Lawrence and Greatworth are obscure.

The remains have now been entirely destroyed and the site built over. However on air photographs taken in 1947 (RAF VAP CPE/UK/1926, 3214–5) a small paddock of just over 1 hectare is visible, divided into at least seven rectangular closes bounded by low banks and scarps. No definite house-sites can be recognised.

[a](9) SITE OF MANOR HOUSE AND GARDEN (SP 552421; Fig. 63), lies on the S. side of Greatworth village, immediately S. of the present manor house, on the crest of a S.-facing slope with extensive views, on Northampton Sand at 152 m. above OD. The medieval manor house of Great-

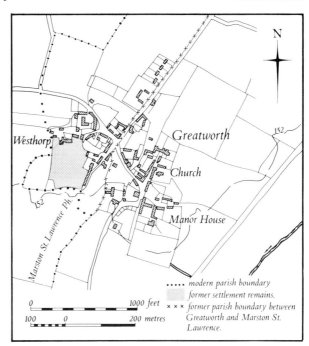

Fig. 62   GREATWORTH (8)   Settlement remains at Westhorp

worth was rebuilt in the early 18th century by Charles Howe (1661–1742). In 1752 the estate was sold to William Higginson who leased the house to George Montagu from 1753 to 1768. The house was destroyed by fire in 1793. (Northants. P. and P., 5 (1976), 311–14)

The present manor house appears to contain fragments of the 18th-century house and to judge from a painting of 1721 this earlier building stood immediately to the S.E. It was a large rectangular building of three storeys with a symmetrical S. elevation surmounted by a balustrade. The original gate piers, topped by elaborate pineapples, survive to the W., as well as parts of the stabling to the N. The site of the house itself is now covered by a modern garden, but below it on the sloping hillside are the remains of the contemporary garden covering about 1 hectare. This is a rectangular area, bounded on most of three sides by a stone wall with shallow pilasters at intervals. In the S.W. corner are the slight remains of a flat-topped terrace-walk only 0.5 m. high which probably extended the whole length of the S. side. Across the centre of the site runs a broad scarp 1.5 m. high but now much degraded, with a rectangular pond at its E. end. The pond still retains fragments of a revetment of dry-stone walling up to 2 m. high. Below the pond, in the S.E. of the garden, is another low scarp only 1 m. high. A track crossing the area from N.W. to S.E. has apparently destroyed further very low scarps visible on air photographs taken in 1947 (RAF VAP CPE/UK/1926, 3214–5). The remains suggest that the garden was of typical early 18th-century type, divided into rectangular compartments but with views over the surrounding country-side to the S.

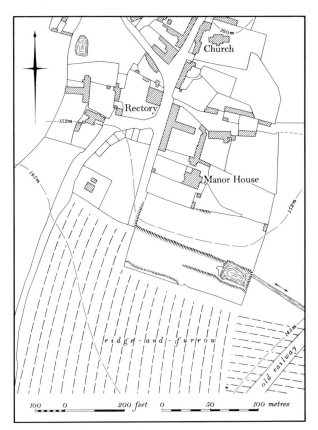

Fig. 63   GREATWORTH (9)   Site of manor
house and garden

ᵃ(10) Deserted Village of Stuchbury (sp 569440; Figs.
61 and 64), lies in the N. of the parish, between 160 m.
and 137 m. above OD. It is situated on the N. side of a
broad valley cut into Upper Lias Clay with, on the higher
slopes, limestone overlaid in places by Boulder Clay. As
a result of this formation springs break out around the site,
producing very marshy ground. Various attempts at drainage both in antiquity and in recent times have resulted in
a considerable number of ditches and the partial destruction
of the remains of the village.

The village had its own lands and field system (Fig. 61),
the boundaries of which are shown on maps of 1634 and
1845 (NRO), and was once an independent parish with its
own church dedicated to St. John.

Stuchbury is first mentioned in 1086 when Domesday
Book lists it as a single manor of two hides with a recorded
population of 13 (VCH Northants., 1 (1902), 344).
Twenty-one people paid the Lay Subsidy of 1301 (PRO,
E179/155/31) and Stuchbury is mentioned by name in the
Nomina Villarum of 1316. The village paid 31s. 4d. for the
Lay Subsidy of 1334 (PRO, E179/155/3) and in 1377 59
people over the age of 14 paid the Poll Tax (PRO, E179/
155/28) but by 1674 only four householders paid the
Hearth Tax (PRO, E179/254/14). Bridges, writing in
about 1720 (Hist. of Northants., 1 (1791), 201), said there
were only four houses at Stuchbury but three of these

would probably be the farms of Stuchbury Manor, Stuchbury Lodge and Stuchbury House which still exist and it
is likely that by then only the present Stuchbury Hall
remained on the village site. By 1801 30 people lived in
the general area.

The village was held by St. Andrew's Priory in Northampton until the Dissolution and it is likely that the
priory cleared the village for sheep at some time after 1377.
It was certainly depopulated by the early 16th century for
no houses or tenants are mentioned when two closes called
West Field and Town Field were let. In 1547 1000 sheep
were being grazed there (K. J. Allison et al., The Deserted
Villages of Northants. (1966), 46).

The remains of the village are poorly preserved as a
result of later ploughing and drainage-works but its general
layout can be ascertained. The main street seems to have
been the lane which runs S. from Stuchbury Hall ('a'-'b'
on plan) which is deeply hollowed over much of its length.
At its N. end ('a' on plan) this street divided into two or
three tracks. One ran N.W. and then N. towards Sulgrave
generally along the line of the existing farm track and part
of the hollowed S.E. end of this is still visible N.E. of the
hall ('c' on plan). Another ran N.E. and its line is marked
by an irregular shallow hollow-way ('d' on plan), now
blocked at its N. end. A third track probably ran S.E.
down the valley side ('e' on plan) where there are traces of
a hollow-way, though its junction with the other tracks is
obscured by later disturbance.

Houses apparently lay on each side of the main street
('a'-'b' on plan). On the E. the present lane is edged by
low earthworks comprising shallow rectangular depressions, probably former house-sites, bounded by low scarps
and banks nowhere above 0.5 m. high. Less well-preserved
earthworks lie on the W. side of the lane, S. of the hall.
Further W. lie three formerly rectangular ponds, now reduced to marshy depressions ('f', 'g' and 'h' on plan) as
well as a number of drainage ditches, low scarps and shallow quarries. Only one of the ponds ('g' on plan) is shown
on the Tithe Map of 1845 (NRO); the area was then known
as Horse Close.

In the N.E. corner of the site, around the hollow-way
('d' on plan), there are numerous large depressions of no
particular form. This land has recently been drained and
ploughed and the surviving earthworks are impossible to
interpret, but local tradition asserts that the parish church
stood here.

Medieval pottery of 13th and 14th-century date has been
found in a modern drain at the N. end of the site and more
is said to have been discovered during earlier drainage-
work in the S.E. corner. In addition Saxon pottery has
been recovered somewhere in the area (CBA Group 9,
Newsletter, 6 (1976), 29). On the edge of the site, in the
valley bottom, is a group of fishponds (11) which were
presumably contemporary with the village. (raf vap cpe/
uk/1926, 1216-7; cpe/uk/1994, 1029-31; cuap, sa31-2,
agv28)

ᵃ(11) Fishponds (sp 568438; Fig. 64), lie in the valley of
a small E.-flowing stream immediately S. of the deserted
village of Stuchbury (10), on Upper Lias Clay at 138 m.
above OD. The stream now flows in an embanked leat on
the S. side of the valley, with the remains of two or three

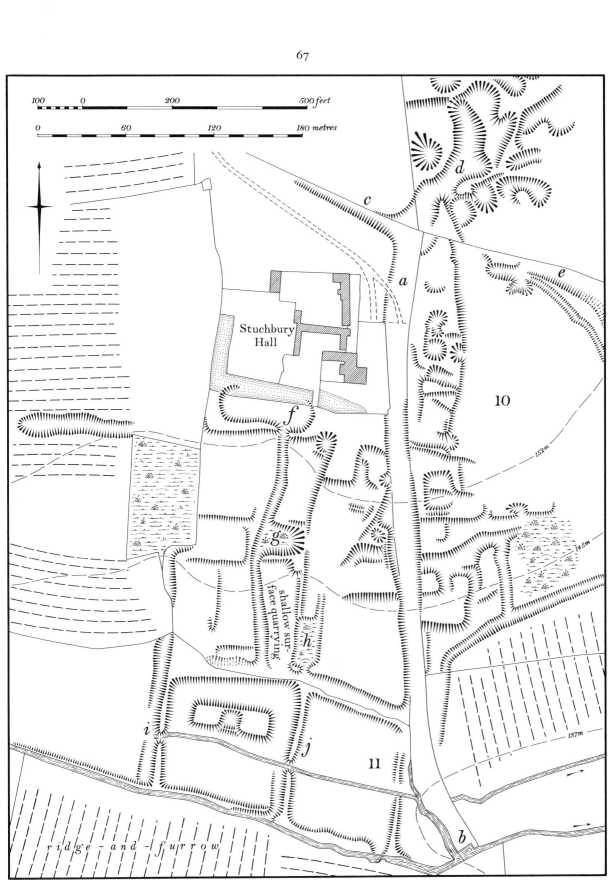

Fig. 64 GREATWORTH (10) Deserted village of Stuchbury, (11) Fishponds

ponds to the N. The W. pond is now identifiable only by its dam ('i' on plan) which consists of a bank 1 m. high, spanning the valley, with a shallow ditch on its W. side from which the material to construct the dam was obtained. The central pond is better defined, with low scarps on the N. and S. and a low bank or dam only 1 m. high at its E. end ('j' on plan). Within this pond, towards its N. edge, are two raised platforms only 0.5 m. high, joined by low banks. These may have been islands in the pond, but if so they would have been very close to the water-level when the pond was full and the depressions between the banks would have been below the water-level. There may have been a third pond to the E., again bounded by low scarps on the N. and S. and by a possible dam at its E. end. The latter is now only a slight limestone-rubble bank, less than 0.5 m. high. It is used as a track across the valley and may originally have been an embanked track rather than a dam. (RAF VAP CPE/UK/1926, 1216–7; CUAP, SA31, AGV28)

a(12) DEER PARK (?) (centred SP 560422; Fig. 61), probably lay S.E. of Greatworth village, on Boulder Clay, limestone and clay between 130 m. and 137 m. above OD. The park is ill recorded in documents, but certainly existed in the mid 13th century (Northants P. and P., 5 (1975), 225) when it was said to be in Halse. A small copse called Park Spinney (SP 554417) and a single field to the N.E. called the Park on the Tithe Map of Greatworth (1845, NRO) provide the only clue to the location of the deer park. No trace remains on the ground of any boundaries, but there are streams along most of its circuit. Elsewhere only low hedge banks are visible. Ridge-and-furrow of normal medieval form is traceable within this assumed park. (RAF VAP CPE/UK/1926, 1215–6)

a(13) DESERTED VILLAGE OF HALSE (SP 566404; Figs. 61 and 65), lies in the S. of the parish, around the source of a small W.-flowing stream, on limestone between 135 m. and 155 m. above OD. Halse was once an independent parish the boundaries of which can still be identified (Fig. 61).

Halse is first mentioned in Domesday Book where it is listed as a single manor gelding for two hides and held by Earl Aubrey together with parts of Brackley and Syresham (VCH Northants., I (1902), 330). Because of the wording of Domesday Book it is impossible to ascertain the population of Halse at this time. The link between Old Brackley (Brackley (3)) and Halse remained throughout medieval and later times and probably originated from the fact that Old Brackley was once a chapelry of Halse. The 1301 Lay Subsidy records 30 taxpayers at Halse (PRO, E179/155/31) but it is likely that Old Brackley is included in this figure, as it certainly is in the 1334 Lay Subsidy when the two places together paid 67s. 3d. (PRO, E179/155/3). This sum is large, however, perhaps suggesting that Halse was still of considerable size at this time. In 1377 107 people at Halse over the age of 14 paid the Poll Tax (PRO, E179/155/27), again a large number but again probably including Old Brackley. Thereafter no firm indication of the size of Halse is recorded until the early 18th century when Bridges (Hist. of Northants., I (1791), 153) said it was a hamlet of nine houses. It remained the same size until the early 19th

century for Baker (Hist. of Northants., I (1822–30), 586) also recorded nine houses there, and by the late 19th century only two farms and three houses stood on the site of the village though one other farm and three other houses lay nearby. This was the situation until recent years but a large number of new houses (not shown on plan) have now been erected in the area between Manor Farm and Halse Grange. The village of Halse had a church or chapel dedicated to St. Andrew (A. Green, Hist. of Brackley (1869), 27).

To judge from the pattern of the surrounding ridge-and-furrow the village was probably situated around Manor Farm, though nothing remains on the ground apart from some slight scarps around a pond cut deeply into the rising ground N. of the farm ('a' on plan). The traditional site of the parish church is said to be at or near Manor Farm and it is recorded that in 1912–13 many skeletons were discovered during alterations to the buildings N.W. of the farmhouse (local inf.). Some fragments of late medieval window tracery are built into the garden wall and an octagonal basin, perhaps a late medieval font, also survives in the garden. A few sherds of medieval pottery are recorded from the area (Northants. Archaeol., 10 (1975), 167).

Surviving earthworks lie in a broad arc S.W., S. and S.E. of Manor Farm but, though clearly related to the village, these are not part of the settlement area. Immediately S. of the farm, in the valley of a stream ('b' on plan), are three rectangular fishponds. The upper, northern one is still filled with water and has traces of a dry-stone revetment on its W. side. It has probably been altered in post-medieval times. The central pond is now dry and the original dam at its S. end is broken through. The third and largest pond, also now dry, is cut back up to 2 m. into the valley sides but only part of the dam at its W. end survives. The water in this pond was apparently supplemented by two catchment drains ('c' and 'd' on plan) which, though reused in modern times, appear to have carried water from adjacent springs.

The main earthworks in the area are a complex system of hollow-ways. The main one is first visible in the S.E. ('e' on plan) as a slightly hollowed feature running S.W. After 60 m. it divides and a branch probably ran N.W. towards Manor Farm, though it now only exists as a narrow gap between the ridge-and-furrow to the N.E. and a bank up to 1 m. high on the S.W. The main hollow-way continues S.W. with two marked curves in its alignment. At its W. end it is cut down 1.75 m. below ground level to the S. and has an almost continuous bank 0.5 m. high on its N. side. This hollow-way meets another at right angles ('f' on plan); the latter runs N.W. until it reaches the stream where it fades out. It apparently once crossed the stream for its continuation, still a broad hollow-way, climbs the opposite hillside and then forks ('g' on plan). The N.W. branch divides again to the N.W., W. and S., apparently to give access to the adjacent ridge-and-furrow, while the main hollow-way continues until it meets the field boundary where it stops abruptly. However, it probably once continued N., for another hollow-way is visible to the N. ('h' on plan) running N.W. to meet a further hollowed trackway which crosses the area from S.W.-N.E.

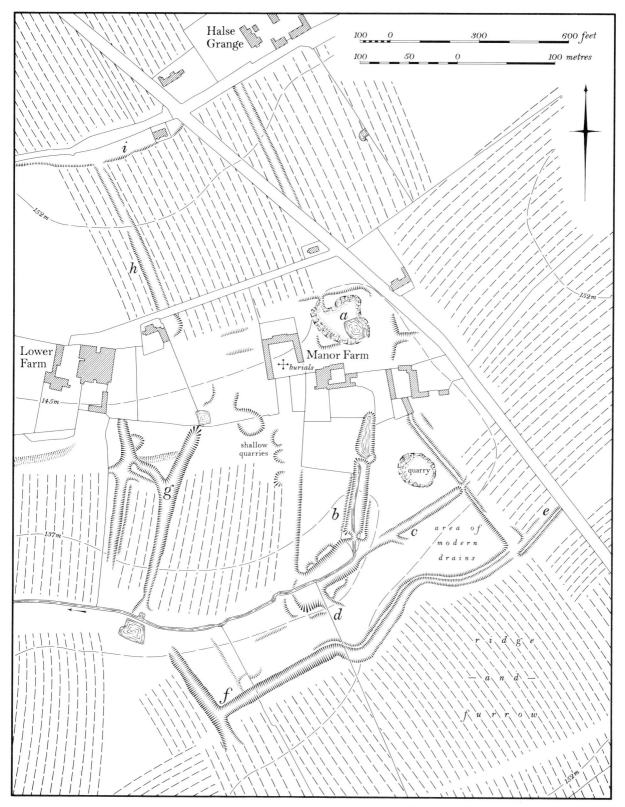

Halse
Grange

100   0   300   600 feet

100   50   0   100 metres

i

152 m

h

Lower
Farm

145 m

a

Manor Farm

+ burials

shallow
quarries

quarry

g

137 m

b

c   area of
modern
drains

e

d

r i d g e

f

— a n d —

f u r r o w

152 m

152 m

Fig. 65   GREATWORTH (13)   Deserted village of Halse

('i' on plan). (RAF VAP CPE/UK/1926, 5214–6; CUAP, LD72, NU97, SA26, ANZ3; air photographs in NMR)

(14) CULTIVATION REMAINS (Fig. 61). The common fields of Greatworth were enclosed by agreement in 1634 (NRO, Enclosure Agreement), but nothing is known of their arrangement. Ridge-and-furrow exists on the ground or can be traced on air photographs over much of the land attributable to Greatworth though it survives best on the lower clay areas in the S.W. of the parish. It is arranged in end-on and interlocked furlongs, many of reversed-S form. To the S. of the village (SP 550418) are runs of end-on furlongs either with deeply hollowed tracks or, in one case, with a modern lane passing between them. Here the ridges terminate on the edges of the tracks in large rounded mounds up to 0.5 m. high.

The date of the enclosure of the common fields of the deserted village of Stuchbury (10) is unknown, but had taken place before the middle of the 16th century when sheep were being grazed within large closes there. It is likely that enclosure took place after 1377 as the village had not been depopulated by that date (K. J. Allison et al., The Deserted Villages of Northants. (1966), 46). Ridge-and-furrow of these fields exists on the ground or can be traced on air photographs over much of the area of land which is attributable to Stuchbury, arranged mainly in rectangular interlocked furlongs. However, modern cultivation has removed much of the generally slight remains except in the clay-floored valley in the S.

The date of the enclosure of the common fields of the deserted village of Halse (13) is also unknown but appears to have been before 1634 (NRO, Enclosure Agreement of Greatworth). Ridge-and-furrow of these fields can be traced in a number of places on air photographs but little now remains on the ground. It is arranged in end-on and interlocked furlongs, many of reversed-S form. To the N.N.E. of the village (SP 567412) there was formerly an unusual arrangement of ridge-and-furrow around the head of a broad W.-facing combe. Here the ridges radiated outwards up the slope in a fan-shaped pattern with the ridges narrowing from 7 m. wide at the top of the slope to under 3 m. near the valley bottom. In the same area there was evidence of overploughing of earlier headlands which produced long ridges of double reversed-S form. (RAF VAP CPE/UK/1926, 1215–9, 2215–7, 3214–9, 5213–8; CPE/UK/1994, 1028–31)

UNDATED

(15) BURIALS (?) (unlocated). At some time before 1712 the discovery was made, during stone-quarrying somewhere in Greatworth parish, of a row of five urns with a smaller vessel inverted in the mouth of one of them; no other information is available (J. Morton, Nat. Hist. of Northants. (1712), 530).

28 GREENS NORTON
(OS 1:10000 [a] SP 65 SE, [b] SP 64 NE, [c] SP 65 SW, [d] SP 64 NW)

The parish, some 980 hectares in area, is bounded on the S. by the R. Tove, on the S.W. and S.E. by S.-flowing tributary streams and on the N.E. by Watling Street (A5). From the alluvium and Upper Lias Clay of the valleys, at about 90 m. above OD, the land rises gently across outcrops of Northampton Sand and Oolitic limestones; outcrops of these formations occur mainly around the village and to the N.E. Patches of Boulder Clay cover the higher land rising to a maximum of 145 m. above OD on the W. boundary.

Very little prehistoric or Roman material has been found in the parish. The main monuments are the remains of the intricate medieval settlement pattern (Fig. 41).

PREHISTORIC AND ROMAN

A polished flint axe was found in the village in the 1950s (SP 66924973; OS Record Cards).

[a](1) FLINT-WORKING SITE (?) (SP 652508), in the N.W. of the parish, S. of the deserted village of Caswell (5), on Upper Lias Clay at 115 m. above OD. Worked flints including at least one barbed-and-tanged arrowhead have been found over a number of years (Northants. Archaeol., 9 (1974), 84).

[a](2) RING DITCH (?) (SP 678515), in the N.E. of the parish, immediately W. of Watling Street, on Great Oolite Limestone at 122 m. above OD. Air photographs (NCAU) show a probable ring ditch 20 m. in diam. with traces of other ill-defined features immediately to the N.

[b](3) ROMAN SETTLEMENT (SP 675494), to the S.E. of the village, on Northampton Sand and Upper Lias Clay at 100 m. above OD. An extensive scatter of Roman pottery has been discovered (NM). It is known that the site has produced other material now in private hands (Northants. Archaeol., 13 (1978), 181).

For Roman Road 1f, Watling Street, see Appendix.

MEDIEVAL AND LATER

A wooden spear with a barbed iron head, probably post-medieval, has been found in the bank of a mill stream in the S. of the parish (SP 67384912; Northants. Archaeol., 10 (1975), 172).

In early post-medieval times there was a deer park in the parish, associated with the manor house. It is not recorded until 1546 (PN Northants., 43) and had been abandoned by the early 18th century (J. Bridges, Hist. of Northants., I (1791), 238). Its exact area is known from the 1726 and 1767 maps of the parish (NRO) which show it as a roughly rectangular area immediately N.W. of the village, between the Bradden and Blakesley roads (centred SP 664504). By the 18th century it was already divided into fields, all with park names. No identifiable boundaries survive apart from the normal hedge-bank around it.

(4)–(7) SETTLEMENT REMAINS (Fig. 41). The parish of Greens Norton, like Cold Higham, Blakesley and Pattishall parishes to the N. and W., had in medieval times a number of discrete settlements in addition to the main village (4): Caswell (5), Field Burcote (6) and Duncote (7). The remains, described below, add little to the documented history of these settlements; their origins and relationship to Greens Norton itself remain obscure. Part of the N. end of the parish apparently once belonged to the hamlet of Potcote in Cold Higham parish.

[b](4) SETTLEMENT REMAINS (SP 668499, 669491 and 671492; Fig. 15), formerly part of Greens Norton, lie in and around the village on limestone, sand and clay between 100 m. and 120 m. above OD. Greens Norton has undergone many changes in the last two centuries and especially in recent years with the addition of large housing estates. The earliest depiction of the village, in the 18th century, (NRO, maps of 1726 and 1767) shows that it was then made up of two parts. In the N. was the main village, lying along the present High Street, with a large rectangular open space or green at the N. end already partly encroached upon; the church stood on the E. side of the green. To the S., linked to the main village by a narrow road and centred on the present hall, was a series of lanes with buildings scattered along them. These lanes are shown as already incomplete in 1726 and large parts of them have since been abandoned. The field evidence indicates that the street system here was once even more complex than is shown on the 18th-century maps. In the 18th century a lane ran S. in a double curve from the small triangular green at Bengal Manor to the R. Tove. This is now traceable as a hollow-way 1.5 m. deep for most of its length. Another hollow-way, also 1.5 m. deep, runs E. from this (from SP 66824913), following a sinuous course until it reaches the stream flowing S. from the main part of the village (SP 67084909). It then turns N.E. and runs straight between blocks of ridge-and-furrow to meet the modern Towcester road just N. of Mill Farm (SP 67354922). Only the E. end of this hollow-way, near Mill Farm, is shown as a road in 1726 and 1767. Near its W. end (SP 66904912) this hollow-way passes through an area of very disturbed ground covering about 0.25 hectares. This is the site of two houses which are shown on the 1726 and 1767 maps but which had gone by 1798 (NRO, Enclosure Map). In the 18th century another road ran N. along the stream from the point where the hollow-way crosses it (SP 67084904) as far as the bend in Bengal Lane, W. of the hall (SP 67014924). This also partly survives as a hollow-way. At its junction with Bengal Lane, and immediately S.W. of it, is another area of disturbed ground which is the site of a house which stood there until after 1798. To the N.E. another track, still just traceable, ran N.E. past the hall and then opened out into a small rectangular area where at least two cottages and a farm stood in the 18th century. These were all cleared away in the 19th century when the hall grounds were extended, but uneven ground in a copse N. of the hall (SP 67104933) marks the site of the cottages. From this point the track turned S.E. and ran to meet the hollow-way to Mill Farm (SP 67244917). A single house stood on the S.W. side of the track in the 18th century and its site is also marked by disturbed ground (SP 672492).

Nothing now remains of the open green at the N. end of the village. It was destroyed in the 19th century when the grounds of Falcon Manor were extended across the E. part, the present New Road was cut across it and the rest was built over. (RAF VAP F21 58/RAF/2316, 0065–7; air photographs in NMR)

[a](5) DESERTED HAMLET OF CASWELL (SP 651510), lay on the N. side of a small W.-flowing brook N.W. of Greens Norton, on Northampton Sand and Upper Lias Clay at 122 m. above OD. The settlement is not recorded in documents until 1200 (PN Northants., 43) but is presumably much older and is perhaps listed silently in Domesday Book under the large royal manor of Greens Norton (VCH Northants., I (1902), 304). In 1301 12 taxpayers are listed in the Lay Subsidy for Caswell (PRO, E179/155/31), and in 1316 the settlement is noted separately in the Nomina Villarum. Thereafter there is no record of its size until 1509 when the five houses which apparently constituted the whole hamlet were destroyed and the area enclosed and converted to pasture. This was carried out by Sir Nicholas Vaux who had inherited the manor of Greens Norton (K. J. Allison et al., The Deserted Villages of Northants. (1966), 36). By the early 18th century only two houses, one presumably the present farm, stood on the site (J. Bridges, Hist. of Northants., I (1791), 238). Traditionally this house is said to have been moated (G. Baker, Hist. of Northants., II (1836–41), 69). The earliest map of the area, dated 1726 (NRO), shows two farms, one called Pinkard's House and the other Grubb's House. The same two houses are shown on a later map of 1767 (NRO).

No earthworks survive at Caswell as a large factory has been built over much of the area. Even in 1947 there were no clearly defined remains in the area (RAF VAP CPE/UK/1926, 1042–3) and the only possible remnant of the settlement is the pond in the valley to the S. of the farm. This is a large triangular pond 1.5 hectares in extent, bounded on the W. by a dam up to 2 m. high. It is possibly the remains of a medieval fishpond, but it has been considerably altered in the post-medieval period.

[a](6) DESERTED HAMLET OF FIELD BURCOTE (SP 667508), lies in the N. of the parish on the S. side of a small S.-flowing stream, on Northampton Sand and Upper Lias Clay at 120 m. above OD. The settlement is not recorded in documents until 1200 (PN Northants., 42) though it is presumably much older and is perhaps listed silently in Domesday Book under the large royal manor of Greens Norton (VCH Northants., I (1902), 304). In 1301 nine taxpayers are listed in the Lay Subsidy for Field Burcote (PRO, E179/155/31) and in 1316 Field Burcote is noted separately in the Nomina Villarum. Thereafter nothing is known of its size until 1499 when Sir Thomas Green destroyed four houses and enclosed the surrounding area and converted it to pasture (K. J. Allison et al., The Deserted Villages of Northants. (1966), 40). The place was termed a hamlet in the early 18th century (J. Bridges, Hist. of Northants., I (1791), 238) though on a map of 1726 (NRO) only two farms are shown there. In the late 19th century these two farm-houses still existed (Whellan, Dir., 519); today Field Burcote consists of a single farm.

No earthworks of the settlement itself now remain but

the limits of the surrounding ridge-and-furrow suggest its original extent. Most of the area is occupied by farm buildings and yards, but a set of uneven hollow-ways cut into a small re-entrant valley immediately N. of the present farm and now ploughed out may be the remains of a road into the settlement. A quantity of medieval pottery, mainly of the 13th century, is said to have been found to the W. of the farm but this report cannot be confirmed (local inf.). (RAF VAP CPE/UK/1926, 1041–2; air photographs in NMR)

^a(7) SETTLEMENT REMAINS (SP 672508), formerly part of the hamlet of Duncote, lie on the N. side of the existing houses, on Upper Lias Clay at 104 m. above OD. The settlement is not recorded until 1227 (PN Northants., 43) but like Caswell and Field Burcote it must be much older. In 1301 eight taxpayers are listed in the Lay Subsidy for Duncote (PRO, E179/155/31) but thereafter nothing is known of its size until the late 19th century. In the early 18th century it was described as a hamlet (J. Bridges, Hist. of Northants., I (1791), 238). In 1874 it was said to contain 18 houses (Whellan, Dir., 519); it is now smaller.

The only earthworks associated with Duncote are some slight traces of abandoned ditched closes behind the farm at the N.W. end of Duncote (SP 67255084) and a group of small rectangular closes bounded by low scarps to the N.W. of the houses on the S.E. side of the settlement (SP 67385079). (RAF VAP CPE/UK/1926, 1040–1; air photographs in NMR)

^a(8) GARDEN REMAINS (SP 669502; Figs. 15 and 66), lie around the present Greens Norton Rectory, in an isolated position N. of the village, on Northampton Sand and Boulder Clay at 112 m. above OD. The main medieval manor house of Greens Norton which was already 'totally destroyed' by the early 18th century (J. Bridges, Hist. of Northants., I (1791), 238) is said to have stood to the N.W. of the church (G. Baker, Hist. of Northants., II (1836–41),

62). The earthworks appear to include the remains of a late 16th or early 17th-century garden associated with this manor house. The garden may relate to the period between 1552 and 1571 when the manor of Greens Norton was held by Sir William Parr (1513–71), later Marquess of Northampton. Maps of 1726 and 1767 and the Enclosure Map of 1798 (NRO) show only one building in the area, presumably the present rectory.

The main surviving feature is a tall conical steep-sided mound, 8 m. in diam. and 5 m. high with a small flat summit only 1 m. across. This stands in the N.E. corner of the present garden and is perhaps a prospect mound. A flat terrace or walk-way 3 m. wide and only 0.25 m. high extends S. from it along the edge of the garden, and a similar one runs W. but has been much damaged by the existing hedge. Outside the garden to the E. a large ditch 3 m. to 7 m. wide and up to 1.5 m. deep which has cut through the adjacent ridge-and-furrow was perhaps the source of material for the adjacent terrace and mound. (RAF VAP F21 58/RAF/2316, 0065–6)

^a(9) PONDS (SP 667500 and 669501; partly on Fig. 66), lie to the E. and S.W. of the rectory, in the valley of two small S.W.-flowing streams, on clay, between 110 m. and 120 m. above OD. In 1767 (map in NRO) there was only a single circular pond immediately S. of the rectory. But by 1798 (Enclosure Map, NRO) a system of ponds had been constructed. To the E. of the rectory a large rectangular pond had been made; it contained two parallel low banks or islands running lengthways. This still remains, 80 m. by 40 m. and orientated N.E.-S.W., cut down at least 2 m. into the valley sides. The earlier circular pond to the S.W. of the rectory had, by 1798, been altered to form a U-shaped pond and below it to the S.W. has a long narrow pond containing two banks or islands end-on to each other down the centre. The U-shaped pond has now disappeared but the long pond remains as two separate ones, with a dam 2 m. high at the S.W. end of the lower one. No purpose can be assigned to these ponds. (RAF VAP F21 58/RAF/2316, 0065–6; air photographs in NMR)

(10) CULTIVATION REMAINS. The common fields of Greens Norton village were enclosed by an Act of Parliament of 1799. Immediately before that date (NRO, Draft Enclosure Map, 1798) there were four open fields around the village. To the W. of the village and immediately S. of the Bradden Road was Upper or Blackridge Field. To the S. of that, extending as far as the R. Tove, was Kingthorne Field. To the N.E. of the village was Church Field, with Lower Field to the S.E. However, an earlier map of 1767 (NRO) shows only three fields. Blackridge and Kingthorne Side Fields were identical to the two similarly named in 1798, but the later Church and Lower Fields were all one, then called Church Field.

Ridge-and-furrow of these fields survives on the ground or can be traced on air photographs over large areas, arranged in end-on and interlocked furlongs which agree exactly with the furlongs marked and named on the Draft Enclosure Map. Where the ridge-and-furrow no longer survives former headlands between furlongs are still visible as long ridges up to 10 m. wide and 0.25 m. high (e.g. SP 673495).

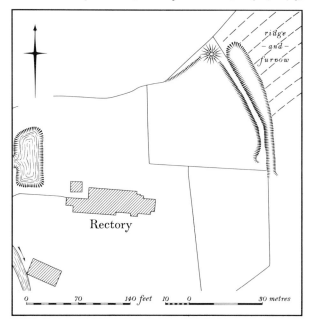

Fig. 66 GREENS NORTON (8) Garden remains

The common fields of Duncote were enclosed by the same Act of Parliament as that for Greens Norton. Before enclosure there were four open fields. East Field lay to the E. of the hamlet and North Field to the N. The area S. and S.E. of Duncote was the Mixt Field and there was a very small Church Field to the W. of the hamlet. As with Greens Norton, the earlier map of 1767 shows only three fields. The East and North Fields already existed but the later Mixt and Church Fields were a single unit called Church Field. Both the 1767 and 1798 maps show a large piece of land called Cow Common N. of Duncote, along the sides of a small S.-flowing stream. Ridge-and-furrow of these fields survives on the ground or can be traced on air photographs over large areas of all the former open fields, arranged in interlocked and end-on furlongs mainly lying at right angles to the contours. Some furlongs are preserved in permanent pasture (e.g. SP 677511). Ridge-and-furrow also exists N. of Duncote in the area of the former Cow Common (SP 674513), indicating that much of it was once under cultivation.

The enclosure of the common fields of Caswell (5) took place in 1509, when the hamlet of Caswell was deserted. The fields of Field Burcote (6) were enclosed in 1499. Both these enclosures were apparently to create sheep walks. Very little ridge-and-furrow of these fields remains on the ground and it is only visible in a few places on air photographs. It appears to be arranged in end-on and interlocked furlongs of normal medieval form, much of it with reversed-S curves.

Ridge-and-furrow also exists in the N. of the parish within land belonging to Potcote (Cold Higham (5)) and in the area of the late medieval deer park (see above). Much of this park is covered by interlocked furlongs, indicating that the park was created from land previously under cultivation. (RAF VAP CPE/UK/1926, 1037–44; F21 58/RAF/2316, 0065–7; air photographs in NMR)

29 HARPOLE

(OS 1:10000 [a] SP 65 NE, [b] SP 66 SE, [c] SP 75 NW, [d] SP 76 SW)

The parish covers about 760 hectares and lies on the N. side of the R. Nene which forms its S. boundary. From the river, here flowing E. at about 60 m. above OD, the land rises gently on Middle Lias Clay and Marlstone Rock and then, beyond the village, more steeply on Upper Lias Clay to an almost level plateau of Boulder Clay at between 107 m. and 122 m. above OD. Apart from the Roman villa (6) little of significance is recorded in the parish.

PREHISTORIC AND ROMAN

A stone, boat-shaped battle-axe (Roe's Group IA; PPS, 32 (1966), 236, No. 144) was found somewhere in the parish in 1937 (NM; J. Northants. Mus. and Art Gall., 6 (1969), 36). The stone adze recorded from 'near Harpole' (NM Records) is an ethnographic item. A bronze socketed axe has also come from the parish (NM; BAR, 31 (ii) (1976), No. 1087).

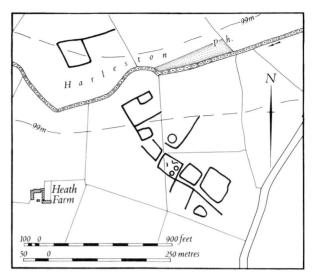

Fig. 67   HARPOLE (1)   Enclosures

[d](1) ENCLOSURES (SP 705625; Fig. 67), lie in the extreme N.E. of the parish, E.N.E. of Heath Farm, on Northampton Sand at 100 m. above OD. Air photographs (in NMR) show cropmarks of a group of ditched enclosures arranged in a rough line N.W.-S.E. No entrances are visible and only one of the enclosures has interior features.

[a](2) BRONZE AGE AND IRON AGE SETTLEMENT (?) (SP 683598), lies on the crest of a hill immediately S. of the Roman villa (6), on Marlstone Rock at 80 m. above OD, and was found in 1966 during excavations in advance of road-works. A circular ditch 54 m. in diam. and 2 m. wide was noted but the details are unsatisfactory. The ditch silt contained a single sherd, said to be of Bronze Age date, pieces of slag and some fragments of a crucible. In the upper silting of the ditch were sherds of late Iron Age date and 'small domestic hearths' overlay the whole area (MOPBW, Arch. Excavations 1966 (1967), 6).

[b](3) ROMAN SETTLEMENT (SP 690620), lies in the N.W. of the parish, on Boulder Clay at 120 m. above OD. Roman pottery, tiles and tesserae were found here in 1967 (BNFAS, 2 (1967), 11). This may be the site of an alleged villa N. of the village (Whellan, Dir. 318; VCH Northants., I (1902), 197). Otherwise the latter is a mislocation of (6).

[b](4) ROMAN SETTLEMENT (SP 688610), lies immediately N.W. of the village on Upper Lias Clay at 93 m. above OD. Pottery of the 2nd and 3rd century, including one sherd of samian, tiles and oyster shell were found on this site in 1971 (BNFAS, 3 (1969), 1).

[d](5) ROMAN SETTLEMENT (SP 702612), lies in the E. of the parish on Upper Lias Clay at 99 m. above OD. A few sherds of Roman pottery were found here in 1968 (BNFAS, 3 (1969), 10). Subsequently more pottery mainly of 2nd to 3rd-century date and of Nene Valley type has been noted (local inf.).

[a](6) ROMAN VILLA (SP 684599), lies S.W. of the village close to the A45 road, on Marlstone Rock at 80 m. above

OD. The site was first discovered in 1846, and in 1849 a mosaic pavement was uncovered. The latter was probably 4 m. by 6 m. and had a central octagon enclosing a medallion with a maltese cross. The rest of the site was not explored but tesserae of other pavements, tiles, bricks and pottery were noted (*JBAA*, 2 (1847), 364; 5 (1850), 375; 6 (1851), 126; VCH *Northants.*, I (1902), 197; A. Rainey, *Mosaics in Roman Britain* (1973), 92–3; P. Corder (ed.), *The Roman Town and Villa at Great Casterton, second interim report* (1954), 35–9). In 1899 the mosaic was uncovered again and some of it was removed (*Annual Report of the Northants. Excavation Society* (1900), 5).

An excavation to the S.E. of the assumed location of this mosaic, prior to road-works in 1966, revealed a stone cistern, 4 m. by 6 m., and a 4th-century 'structure' overlying robbed-out 2nd-century walls (*JRS*, 57 (1967), 186). A large quantity of pottery, mainly 4th-century in date, as well as tiles, tesserae and stone rubble have been found on the site.

For Roman Road 17, see Appendix.

MEDIEVAL AND LATER

A groat of Elizabeth I (1560–1) and sherds of medieval pottery were found in 1969 in the village (SP 693606; *BNFAS*, 5 (1971), 45). Medieval pottery of Lyveden type was found nearby in 1973 (SP 69246057; *Northants. Archaeol.*, 9 (1974), 106).

[b](7) MOAT (?) (SP 688608), lay immediately S. of the rectory, at the W. side of the village, on Upper Lias Clay at 95 m. above OD. The site has been completely destroyed by modern housing and is now occupied by a road called The Motts. On air photographs taken before destruction (RAF VAP CPE/UK/1994, 1259–61; 3G TUD/UK/118, Pt. II, 6114–5) an elongated polygonal enclosure, 60 m. by 30 m., orientated N.-S. and bounded by a dry ditch at least 10 m. wide, is visible. The N.E. part of the ditch had already been partly filled in by 1946. No interior features can be recognised. Baker (*Hist. of Northants.*, I (1822–30), 178) said that this was the site of the house of the Vaux manor which had been long since destroyed.

(8) CULTIVATION REMAINS. The common fields of the parish were enclosed by an Act of Parliament of 1778. Ridge-and-furrow of these fields exists on the ground or can be traced on air photographs over almost the entire parish with the exception of the land in the S. liable to flood along the R. Nene and in the extreme N. of the parish where it may never have existed. On the lower, gently sloping ground in the S. half of the parish it is arranged in markedly rectangular furlongs end-on or at right angles to each other. On the higher, more broken land to the N. the ridge-and-furrow is arranged to run across the contours in a pattern of radiating and interlocking furlongs. Almost everywhere the ridges have marked reversed-S curves. Among the features of interest are well-marked hollowed access-ways running between end-on furlongs (e.g. SP 696610 and 681608–685607). A more unusual feature not noted elsewhere is visible in the S. of the parish close to the R. Nene (SP 683594 and 687595). Two normal rectangular furlongs with ridges running down the slope towards the river each have three curved ridges at their S. end lying parallel to the river.

(RAF VAP CPE/UK/1926, 4032–6; CPE/UK/1994, 1258–62; F21 543/RAF/2409, 0138–41; F22 543/RAF/2409, 0110–4; 3G TUD/UK/118, Pt. II, 6112–7, 6131–3)

UNDATED

[d](9) CROPMARKS (SP 705621), lie in the N.E. of the parish on Lower Estuarine silts and clays at 104 m. above OD. Air photographs (NMR) show a group of at least ten rectangular dark patches, all orientated N.E.-S.W. and varying in size from 5 m. by 2 m. to 20 m. by 10 m., all within an area about 60 m. wide. Some of the patches are surrounded by lighter marks suggesting former banks. They are cut by the cropmarks of an old hedge-line and by a modern farm track. The date and purpose of the site is unknown but it may be relatively recent.

30   HARTWELL
(OS 1:10000 [a] SP 75 SE, [b] SP 74 NE, [c] SP 85 SW, [d] SP 84 NW)

The parish covers nearly 600 hectares and extends from the R. Tove in the S.W., at 74 m. above OD, into Salcey Forest, still largely woodland, in the N.E. at around 126 m. above OD. Boulder Clay covers most of the parish, apart from small outcrops of Oolite Limestone S. and E. of the village. The enclosure (1) within Salcey Forest, which is probably of late prehistoric date, is a rare survival in the Midlands. The settlement remains (3)–(7) are part of an unusual pattern of medieval settlement which is not fully understood.

PREHISTORIC AND ROMAN

A Neolithic polished flint axe was found in 1972 close to Gordon's Lodge in the S.W. of the parish (SP 77394862; *Northants. Archaeol.*, 10 (1975), 151; OS Record Cards).

[c](1) ENCLOSURE (SP 801502; Fig. 68), probably an Iron Age settlement, lies in the S.W. corner of Salcey Forest, within Prentice Copse, on level ground, on Boulder Clay at 122 m. above OD. Few such sites have survived as earthworks, and this one has presumably been saved from destruction because it is situated in an area of medieval and modern woodland. The enclosure is roughly oval, bounded by a continuous bank and external ditch with a single plain inturned entrance in the centre of the E. side. The bank is nowhere much above 0.5 m. high above the interior; the ditch varies between 1.5 m. and 1.75 m. deep. Apart from a later disturbance on the E. side, the bank is complete and undamaged. The surrounding ditch has modern drainage channels in it, and at its S. end and in places along the E. side it has been destroyed by other channels cut across it. The interior is featureless apart from modern drains. Its traditional name is Egg Rings. The site may be compared with similar enclosures in Wessex (e.g. RCHM, *Dorset*, IV (1972), Tarrant Gunville (34)).

[b](2) ROMAN SETTLEMENT (SP 768483), lies in the extreme S.W. of the parish on Boulder Clay at 72 m. above OD,

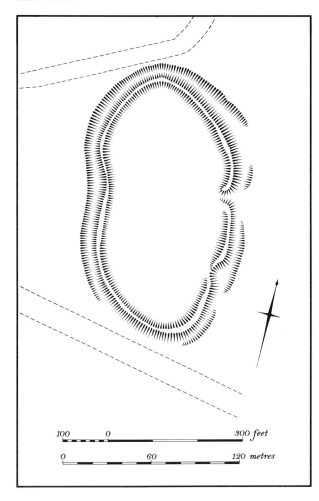

Fig. 68   HARTWELL (1)   Enclosure

and on the same site as a medieval settlement (6). Roman coarse wares and part of a quern thought to be of the same period have been found (OS Record Cards).

MEDIEVAL AND LATER

(3–7) MEDIEVAL SETTLEMENTS (Fig. 69). The modern village of Hartwell, formerly known as Hartwell Green, is a large nucleated settlement lying against the N. boundary of the parish. However there is much evidence to suggest that this situation is relatively recent. Before extensive building in the 19th and 20th centuries this village was little more than a single street, on the S. side of a large rectangular green part of which lay in Roade parish. There was already some encroachment on the green by the mid 18th century (NRO, map of 1768). The village at that time had the appearance of a secondary forest-edge settlement. A parish church was erected in this village on a new site in 1851. Before that there was only a chapel, located in the S. of the parish in the now deserted settlement at Chapel Farm (3) which was known as Hartwell up to 1835 (OS 1st ed. 1 in. map). The modern parish was formerly a chapelry of Roade, though in Domesday Book a priest is listed under Hartwell. It seems likely that the medieval

settlement pattern consisted of a group of hamlets, Bozenham (6), Hartwell (Chapel Farm (3)), Hartwell Green and at least three others at Park Farm (7), Elms Farm (4) and S.E. of Hartwell (5), as well as at Stonepit Farm which lay within an area of old enclosures in 1768. The lost settlement of Wyk Juxta Hertwell (PN *Northants.*, 100) may have been any one of these places.

[b](3) DESERTED VILLAGE OF HARTWELL (centred SP 784489; Figs. 69 and 70, known as Hartwell in the 19th century (OS 1st ed. 1 in. map, 1835), lies around Chapel Farm on the S. side of a shallow valley, on Boulder Clay and limestone between 90 m. and 105 m. above OD. This village must once have been the main settlement in the parish, but all the population records presumably include the other medieval settlements. Hartwell is first mentioned in Domesday Book where it is listed as a single manor with a total recorded population of 26 including a priest (VCH *Northants.*, I (1902), 308, 374). In 1301 49 people paid the Lay Subsidy (PRO, E179/155/31) and for the Lay Subsidy of 1334 Hartwell *cum membris* paid £7–0–13d (sic) (PRO, E179/155/3). This sum was one of the largest paid in the S.W. of the county. In 1377 81 people over the age of 14 paid Poll Tax (PRO, E179/155/27). In 1525 30 taxpayers paid the Lay Subsidy (PRO, E179/155/130) and in 1673 102 people paid the Hearth Tax (PRO, E179/155/130). In 1801 the population of the parish was 357.

The earthworks of this village remained largely intact until 1976 when some of them were destroyed by ploughing. The surviving parts lie N. and N.E. of the farm. In the bottom of the valley ('a' on plan) are the remains of at least two fishponds. The smaller is a simple rectangular depression cut into the lower part of the valley side. Below this and separated from it by a broad ditch is a long rectangular sunken pond with an earthen dam 1.75 m. high at its S.W. end and with a later bank across it. This may be an adaptation from an earlier and much larger pond which may have occupied the whole of the flat valley bottom. On the steep valley side to the S.E. ('b' on plan) is a series of sub-rectangular platforms bounded by scarps of 1 m. high with a broad ditch on their N.W. side. Immediately E. of the ditch is a large rectangular area ('c' on plan), bounded on the S. and E. by a low bank and on the N. by various scarps and ditches and covered with narrow ridge-and-furrow. The footings of a two-cell building abutting on the E. bank appear to be relatively recent and are probably the remains of two cottages which are said to have stood there.

From the S.E. corner of the enclosure a broad hollow-way ('d' on plan) 1 m. deep, extends S.S.E. for 130 m. and then forks. The E. branch runs for 140 m. before fading out. The S.W. branch extends beyond the county boundary into Buckinghamshire. On the E. side of the main hollow-way, as well as in the area between its N. end and the farm itself, are ploughed-down scarps and banks of a series of closes and house platforms. These are associated with dense spreads of limestone rubble and medieval pottery of the 12th to the 14th century and smaller quantities of post-medieval sherds. Immediately W. of the N. end of the main hollow-way a dry stone-lined well 0.75 m. in diam. and about 10 m. deep has been discovered.

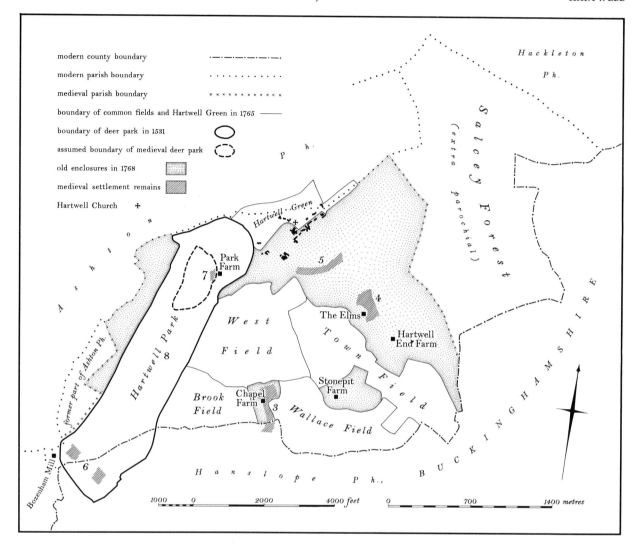

Fig. 69   HARTWELL Plan of the parish showing medieval settlements, fields and deer parks

The fragmentary foundations of the chapel which gives the farm its name survive in the S.E. corner of the farm-yard. It was of late 12th-century date and part of an arcade of that period is incorporated in the existing parish church at Hartwell Green built in 1851. Bridges described the chapel in 1720 (*Hist. of Northants.*, I (1791), 304) as consisting of a nave and a chancel with a north aisle, and later alterations were noted by Baker (*Hist. of Northants.*, II (1836–41), 186).

At the extreme S. of the site, in Buckinghamshire, on either side of the hollow-way there are large areas of stone rubble and medieval and post-medieval pottery, associated with several ponds and depressions ('e' on plan). This is the site of a building called Chantry House which still stood in the 19th century (OS 1st ed. 1 in. map, 1835). (CBA Group 9, *Newsletter*, 5 (1975), 7; RAF VAP CPE/UK/ 1926, 1247–8; air photographs in NMR)

[b](4) SETTLEMENT REMAINS (SP 791497; Figs. 69 and 71),

lie around Elms Farm and Hartwell End Farm on a S.E.-facing slope, on Boulder Clay at about 110 m. above OD. Nothing is known of the history or name of the site; Elms Farm was formerly known as Tythe Farm (OS 1st ed. 1 in. map, 1835) and the adjacent Hartwell End Farm is recorded by that name in 1538 (PN *Northants.*, 100).

The main feature of the site is a system of hollow-ways and tracks, presumably of medieval date. The main track ran E. from the E. end of the village of Hartwell Green and then turned S. to a point just N. of Elms Farm. This part ('a'-'b' on plan) has now been destroyed but it is shown as a road in 1768 (map in NRO) and indeed is still marked as a track on modern OS maps. To the S.E. of Elms Farm ('c' on plan) this road survives as a hollow-way up to 1.5 m. deep running S.E. in a broad curve. It can be traced to the S. of Hartwell End Farm at which point it forks ('d' on plan), one branch continuing E., the other running S. into the area of the former common fields.

A wide L-shaped ditch immediately S.E. of Elms Farm

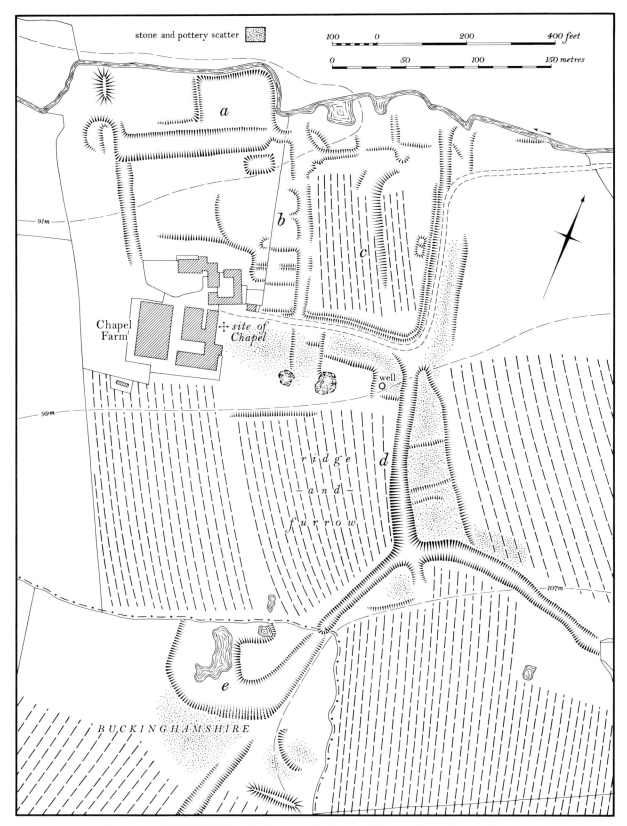

stone and pottery scatter

100   0   200   400 feet

0   50   100   150 metres

a

b

c

Chapel
Farm

site of
Chapel

well

r i d g e

— a n d —

f u r r o w

d

e

B U C K I N G H A M S H I R E

91m

99m

107m

Fig. 70 HARTWELL (3) Deserted village of Hartwell at Chapel Farm

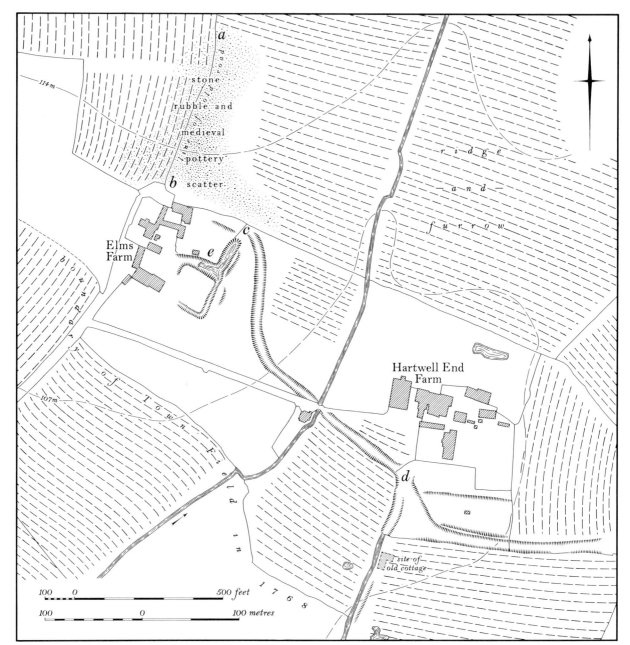

Fig. 71   HARTWELL (4)   Settlement remains at Elms Farm and Hartwell End Farm

with part of a ditched enclosure on its S.W. side may be the remains of a moated site, though later activity has so damaged the E. side that it is no longer possible to be sure ('e' on plan). In the present arable land to the N. of the farm, large quantities of medieval pottery have been found. Most of it is of 13th or 14th-century date, and much is of a form similar to that produced at Olney Hyde, Buckinghamshire. However the occurrence of several fragments of kiln debris on this site suggests that at least some of the pottery was made here. (CBA Group 9, *Newsletter*, 5 (1975), 7; *Northants. Archaeol.*, 12 (1977), 226; RAF VAP CPE/ UK/1926, 1248–9)

[a](5) SETTLEMENT REMAINS (centred SP 788501; Figs. 69 and 72), lie along the valley of a small S.W.-flowing stream immediately S.E. of the present Hartwell village, on Boulder Clay between 110 m. and 120 m. above OD. The earthworks remained until 1976 when all but a small fragment were destroyed by ploughing. The main feature of the site was a long hollow-way up to 1.5 m. deep, running N.E.-S.W. At its S.W. end it used to meet the road from Hartwell Green to Hanslope (Buckinghamshire) but it has now been blocked by modern buildings. At its N.E. end it joined another road which formerly ran S.E. from Hartwell to Elms Farm (4). The hollow-way is marked as a

through road on the map of the parish of 1768 (NRO) and the map also shows at least six buildings along the hollow-way, probably two farm-houses and two cottages. By 1835 (1st ed. 1 in. OS map), although the hollow-way is still shown as a road, only one of the farmsteads and a single house or cottage remained ('a' and 'b' on plan). The cottage survived until recently. On the N.W. side of the hollow-way the sites and closes of the cottages and one of the farmsteads ('a' and 'b') were defined by low banks and scarps until recent destruction. In addition the sites of at least two other buildings removed before 1768 were identifiable ('c' and 'd'). Since ploughing, large areas of stone-rubble, brick, tiles and pottery ranging from the 13th century to the 18th century have been noted along much of the N.W. side of the hollow-way, suggesting that there was an almost continuous line of houses here. To the S.E. of the hollow-way is a larger area of earthworks.

Most appear to be relatively modern drainage ditches, though there is at least one house-site ('e') in addition to the site of the farmstead which was there in 1768 ('f'). The arrangement of some of these house-sites, especially those on the N.W. side of the hollow-way, indicates that they may have been inserted into pre-existing fields or furlongs. (CBA Group 9, *Newsletter*, 5 (1975), 7; (RAF VAP CPE/UK/ 1926. 1248–9; air photographs in NMR)

[b](6) DESERTED HAMLET OF BOZENHAM (SP 768483; Fig. 69), lies immediately N.E. of Bozenham Mill, in an area of permanent arable, on Boulder Clay at 72 m. above OD. Large quantities of 13th-century pottery and limestone-rubble associated with slight depressions which are perhaps former house platforms have been recorded (*BNFAS*, 3 (1969), 19; CBA Group 9, *Newsletter*, 5 (1975), 7. Further S.E., in Buckinghamshire (SP 771481), another area of

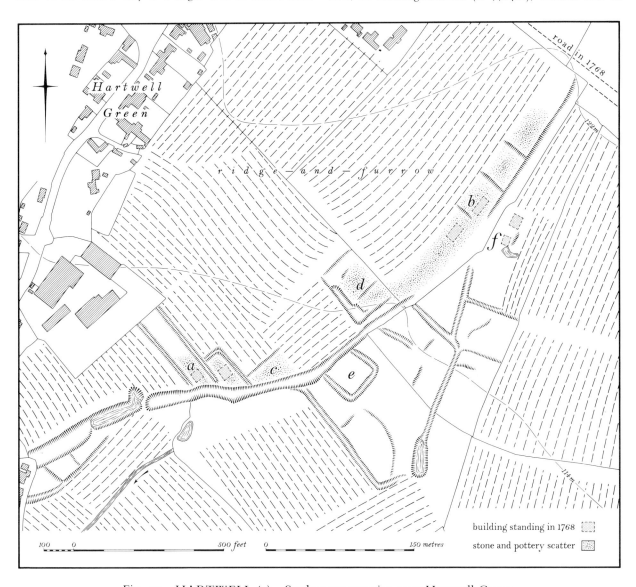

Fig. 72   HARTWELL (5)   Settlement remains near Hartwell Green

13th-century sherds and rubble has been noted. These remains probably represent part of the former hamlet of Bozenham which is first recorded by name in the mid 12th century (PN *Northants.*, 100). Both of these scatters of medieval material lie within the deer park (8) and the site in Buckinghamshire appears to have been overlaid by ridge-and-furrow. (RAF VAP CPE/UK/1926, 1244–5)

[b](7) SETTLEMENT REMAINS (SP 778499; Fig. 69), lie immediately N.W. of Park Farm, on Boulder Clay at 100 m. above OD. No earthworks survive, but air photographs (RAF VAP CPE/UK/1926, 1246–7) show that there was once a disturbed area of some 0.75 hectares. Large quantities of medieval and later pottery have been found in the plough-soil. The status of the site is not clear. The present Park Farm is on the site of the 16th-century park lodge and the remains may represent both this and the medieval lodge, but it is also possible that there may have been a small medieval settlement here.

[b](8) DEER PARK (centred SP 773492; Fig. 69), occupies a long narrow strip of land covering 130 hectares in the W. of the parish, mainly on Boulder Clay between 70 m. and 107 m. above OD. A small park of only 25 acres (about 10 hectares) certainly existed in the medieval period (P. A. J. Pettit, *The Royal Forests of Northants.* (1968), 14). In 1531 Henry VIII enlarged this park, enclosing a further 232 acres (about 100 hectares), and built a new lodge which may have replaced an earlier one (see (7)). In 1699 the park was officially disparked (Pettit, op. cit., 192; *Northants. P. and P.*, 5 (1975), 226).

It is not possible to identify the medieval park with certainty though it may have lain on the S.E. side of a shallow valley immediately S.W. of Park Farm. A hollow-way, visible on air photographs but now destroyed, ran from the S. corner of Park Farm curving gently S.W. and crossing the stream in the valley bottom at SP 77554966. It then ran N.W. towards Ashton. The part of the hollow-way E. of the stream may have formed the S. boundary of the early park and the stream the W. boundary. The N. edge is impossible to determine but it may be represented by the hedge which runs S.E. from the head of the stream towards Park Farm. Within this area there were three furlongs of ridge-and-furrow of medieval type.

The extent of the later park is well known as it is shown in detail on a map of Hartwell of 1768 (NRO). Much of the area was covered by ridge-and-furrow. No substantial boundaries survive apart from normal hedge-banks. The S.E. corner of this park extended into Hanslope parish, Buckinghamshire. (RAF VAP CPE/UK/1926, 1245–7)

(9) CULTIVATION REMAINS (Fig. 69). The common fields of the parish were enclosed by Act of Parliament in 1828. The medieval arrangement of the common fields must have been markedly altered when a formerly cultivated area was enclosed in the 16th century to become a deer park (8). By 1768 (map in NRO) there were four open fields, Town, West, Brook and Wallace Fields, between Hartwell Green and the Buckinghamshire boundary. To the W. of the fields lay the 16th-century deer park with a small area of old enclosures beyond, against the Ashton boundary, and to the E. lay further large areas of old enclosures which extended as far as the edge of Salcey Forest. Within the common fields there were two small areas of old enclosures, one around Chapel Farm (3) and the other around Stonepit Farm to the E.

Very little ridge-and-furrow survives on the ground within the parish although much more can be traced from air photographs. None is visible in the former Town Field and only small fragments are recoverable in West, Brook and Wallace Fields. However, extensive areas of interlocked and end-on furlongs can be traced within both the 16th-century and the assumed medieval deer parks, as well as within the old enclosures along the edge of Salcey Forest, S.E. of Hartwell Green and around Stonepit Farm and Chapel Farm. (RAF VAP CPE/UK/1926, 1018–24, 1245–9; 106G/UK/1562, 3084–9, 4083–7; FLS6565, 1005)

31 HELMDON
(OS 1:10000 [a] SP 54 NE, [b] SP 54 SE, [c] SP 64 NW, [d] SP 64 SW)

The parish is large, covering more than 1550 hectares, and includes the former parish of Falcutt and Astwell. It extends from the headwaters of the R. Tove in the N. to a tributary of the Great Ouse on the S. boundary. The central watershed, rising to 165 m. above OD, is covered by Boulder Clay; Oolitic limestones are exposed along the valley sides and Upper Lias Clay in the valley bottoms. The old parish of Helmdon occupied the W. and N. part of the present parish, and the S.E. part was once the parish of Falcutt and Astwell, which itself was a chapelry of Wappenham. There was formerly a detached part of Helmdon parish lying to the S.E. of Falcutt village (Fig. 117). The present parish contains several important medieval sites, including the deserted villages of Astwell (6) and Falcutt (5). However the most interesting monument is the manor house site and settlement remains of Helmdon (4) which together may indicate that part of the village was deliberately planned.

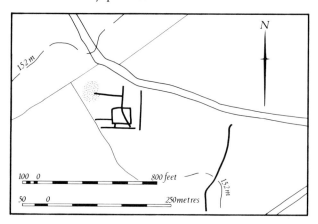

Fig. 73   HELMDON (2)   Roman settlement

PREHISTORIC AND ROMAN

A Roman coin, of Galerius, is recorded from the rectory garden (lost; OS Record Cards).

[d](1) NEOLITHIC SETTLEMENT (SP 628438), N.E. of Astwell, on gravel of 140 m. above OD. A late Neolithic domestic site is recorded, though no details are known (*Northants. Archaeol.*, 11 (1976), 184; CBA Group 9, *Newsletter*, 6 (1976), 28).

[d](2) ROMAN SETTLEMENT (SP 614438; Fig. 73), W. of Astwell Park, on Boulder Clay, at 155 m. above OD. A scatter of Roman occupation-debris has been noted (*Northants. Archaeol.*, 11 (1976), 192; CBA Group 9, *Newsletter*, 6 (1976), 28). On air photographs taken in 1947 (RAF VAP CPE/UK/1926, 3224–5) a small rectangular ditched enclosure is visible, with other ditches joining and intersecting it, and an isolated ditch further S.E.

[b](3) ROMAN SETTLEMENT (SP 599430), E. of Falcutt House, on limestone at 145 m. above OD. Roman material has been found in this area during field-walking (*Northants. Archaeol.*, 11 (1976), 192; CBA Group 9, *Newsletter*, 6 (1976), 28).

MEDIEVAL AND LATER

[b](4) SITE OF MANOR HOUSE AND SETTLEMENT REMAINS (SP 589431; Figs. 74, 75 and 119), lie at the S. end of Helmdon village, on land sloping down to the N., on limestone and Boulder Clay between 128 m. and 155 m. above OD. The earthworks, which are slight and poorly preserved, are probably the site of the main medieval manor house of Overbury, with associated paddocks and ponds, together with some fragments of former house-sites. The significance of the remains is topographical. They appear to be part of a neat rectangular layout, including the church and the existing houses, which forms the long S.E. extension of the modern village. Such a plan indicates that this part of the village may have been deliberately created.

Helmdon is a particularly interesting village, made up of three separate parts (Fig. 74). The N. section lies on the N. side of a small E.-flowing stream and consists of little more than a winding main street which forks at both ends. To the S. of the stream is another short length of street which also forks at its S. end. The S.E. branch climbs the valley side and then turns S. to become the axial road of a rectangular block of closes, houses, church and manor house site (Fig. 75).

The manor house site, fishponds and paddocks are bounded by an almost continuous bank and outer ditch. It is best preserved on the S. and W. where the bank is 0.5 m. high and the ditch 1 m. deep. On the E., to the S. of the church, only the bank survives and in the N.E., to the N.W. of the church, the bank is sinuous and is damaged. The site of the original manor house lies immediately E. of the present one ('a' on plan) and consists of a flat rectangular platform with low banks and ditches attached to it. To the S. there is a long narrow paddock extending the full width of the area, with slight traces of ridge-and-furrow at its W. end, and there are small paddocks further N. around the manor house. The northern part of the area is occupied by three ponds, now dry; the upper two have

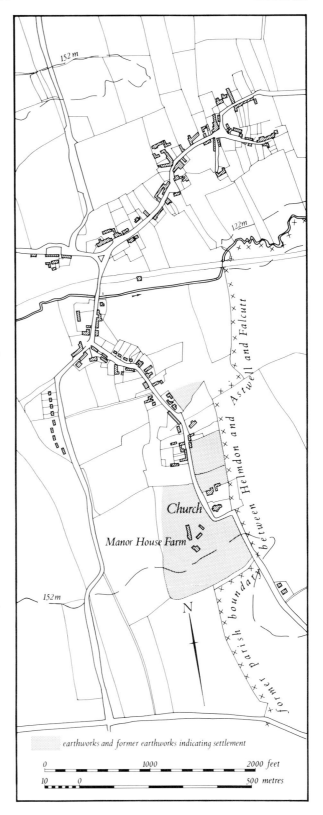

Fig. 74   HELMDON (4)   Village plan

Fig. 75 HELMDON (4) Site of manor house and settlement remains

the fragmentary remains of dams. Until recently some 25 houses and cottages stood in the rectangular area N. of the manor house site but most of the large open spaces between them have now been built over and no earthworks remain. However, on air photographs taken in 1947 (RAF VAP CPE/UK/1926, 3219–20) banks, scarps and ditches indicative of former houses are visible in the area to the N. of the church. On the Enclosure Map (NRO, 1758) a large building is depicted in the N. half of this area and it is clear that the largest of the banks visible on air photographs was the boundary between two closes. The limits of the rectangular area are marked by a modern hedge on a large bank, except at the N.E. corner ('b' on plan) where part of the original N. side survives as a low bank running E.

The tenurial history of Helmdon is complex and it is not clear how this southern extension of the village originated or functioned. Certainly by the early 15th century Helmdon had three manors, Overbury, Middlebury and Netherbury, of which the first and principal manor, through its association with Worcester College, Oxford, can be assigned to the site described here (J. Bridges, *Hist. of Northants.*, I (1791), 172–3; OS Record Cards). There is apparently nothing in the parish church earlier than the 14th century, though its position on the hill-top might suggest an older foundation. In 1086 Helmdon is listed in Domesday Book as a single manor with a recorded population of 11 (VCH *Northants.* I (1902), 322) but in 1301 50 people paid the Lay Subsidy Tax (PRO, E179/155/31) and in 1334 the vill paid 61s. 7¾d., one of the largest amounts in the area (PRO, E179/155/3). The 1377 Poll Tax returns record that 52 people over the age of 14 were living at Helmdon (PRO, E179/155/27) and in 1524 35 people paid the Lay Subsidy (PRO, E179/155/159).

b(5) DESERTED VILLAGE OF FALCUTT (SP 595427; Figs. 76 and 119), lies S.E. of Helmdon village, on either side of a small N.E.-flowing stream, on limestone at 145 m. above OD. Falcutt was one of two separate settlements within the old parish of Falcutt and Astwell and was for a long time associated with Astwell (6), now also deserted. It may once have had its own associated land unit separate from that of Astwell, but this is not proven. Falcutt is first mentioned in 1220 (PN *Northants.*, 47), but is probably included silently in Domesday Book under Astwell which is listed as a single manor with an unusually large recorded population of 17 (VCH *Northants.*, I (1902), 344). It is mentioned by name in the *Nomina Villarum* of 1316 but is usually combined with Astwell in the national taxation records. In 1301 the Lay Subsidy lists 35 taxpayers in the two places (PRO, E179/155/31) and in 1334 they paid a total of 60s. 9d. tax (PRO, E179/155/3). The 1377 Poll Tax Returns record that 57 people over the age of 14 lived at Astwell and Falcutt (PRO, E179/155/28). In 1524 10 people in Falcutt paid the Lay Subsidy (PRO, E179/155/146) and by 1674 only 11 people in the two places paid the Hearth Tax (PRO, E179/254/14). Bridges (*Hist. of Northants.*, I (1791), 214) recorded four houses at Astwell in the early 18th century but described Falcutt as only a hamlet. By the early 19th century Falcutt consisted of five or six houses (1st ed. OS 1 in. map, 1833). Whellan stated (*Dir.*, 502) that it contained 15 houses in 1841, but this presumably included several outlying farms. Whellan also

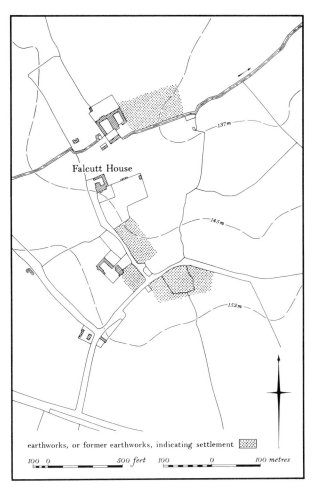

earthworks, or former earthworks, indicating settlement

100 0 500 *feet* 100 0 100 *metres*

Fig. 76 HELMDON (5) Deserted village of Falcutt

noted that there were only nine houses in 1871 as several had been demolished in the previous 20 years. Certainly in 1864 (map in NRO) only the existing Falcutt House and the cottage to the S. remained (K. J. Allison *et al.*, *The Deserted Villages of Northants.* (1966), 39). In 1535 a chapel was recorded at Falcutt, but it had been demolished by 1655 (G. Baker, *Hist. of Northants.*, I (1822–30), 737).

Very little survives of this settlement on the ground. Immediately S.E. of the garden of Falcutt House (SP 59474280) is a paddock with earthworks within it. These include at least one old hedge-bank, several relatively recent drainage ditches and some shallow areas of quarrying. No former house-sites can be clearly identified, though it is said that in about 1900 it was possible to see stone-rubble foundations of at least two cottages which had stood in the S.W. of the paddock alongside the lane to Falcutt House (local inf.). Disturbed ground further S.W. may also be the sites of former buildings (SP 59504273). At the S.E. end of the area, at SP 595427, building-debris and unspecified pottery is recorded on land now under arable (OS Record Cards). Air photographs taken in 1947 (RAF VAP CPE/UK/1926, 3220–1) show ditches and banks here, prob-

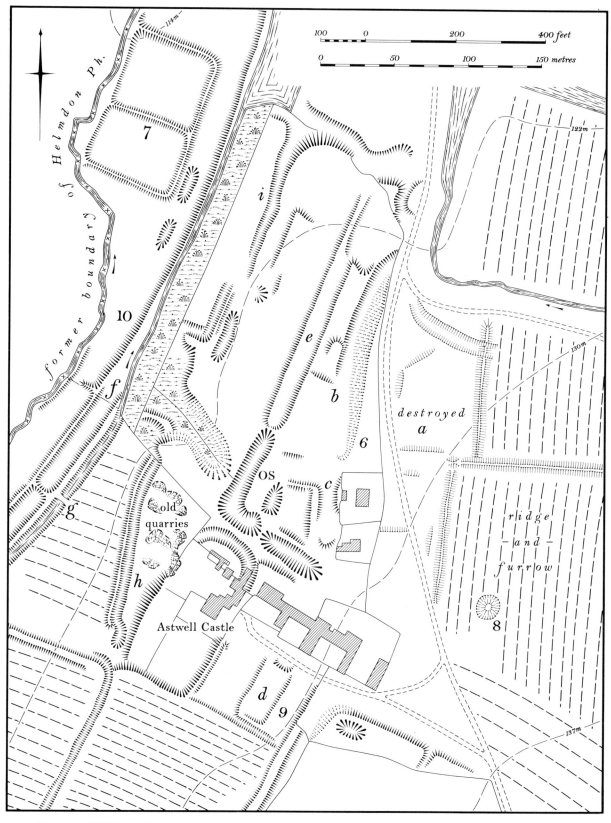

Fig. 77 HELMDON (6) Deserted village of Astwell, (7) Fishponds, (8) Windmill mound,
(9) Garden remains, (10) Mill leats and ponds

ably the sites of at least two or three former houses which had already been ploughed over. On the N. edge of the site, immediately E. of the modern farm buildings (SP 595431), are the fragmentary remains of at least three rectangular closes, bounded by low banks and scarps badly damaged by later tracks and quarrying. The easternmost close has ridge-and-furrow within it and all are edged on the N. and E. by normal ridge-and-furrow of open-field type. The 1864 map records the name Chapel Close for the paddock W. of Falcutt House (SP 593428). However, it is entirely covered by ridge-and-furrow and no possible chapel site is visible. (CUAP, ANT72)

[d](6) DESERTED VILLAGE OF ASTWELL (SP 609441; Figs. 77 and 119), lies immediately N.E. of Astwell Castle, on the E. slopes of a N.-draining valley, on limestone and clay between 122 m. and 132 m. above OD. The lands of Astwell and of the village of Falcutt (5), also now deserted, made up the old parish of Astwell and Falcutt. Astwell may once have had its own land unit separate from that of Falcutt but there is no evidence for this and the two settlements are usually listed together in the national taxation records. The relevant figures for 1086, 1301, 1334 and 1337 are given in (5) above. From these it would appear that Astwell remained in existence until after 1377.

In 1471 the manor of Astwell together with Falcutt passed to the Lovett family and the manor house was rebuilt. The embattled gate-tower as well as other parts of the building still survive and are now called Astwell Castle. By 1524 only nine people at Astwell paid the Lay Subsidy (PRO, E179/155/146) and in 1547 Thomas Lovett created a deer park, probably on the site of the village. At the same time 300 sheep were being kept on Astwell Pasture (K. J. Allison et al., The Deserted Villages of Northants. (1966), 35). In 1674 11 people in Astwell and Falcutt paid the Hearth Tax (PRO, E179/254/14) and Bridges (Hist. of Northants., I (1791), 214), writing in about 1720, recorded only four houses at Astwell. As one of these was the manor house and another the mill the village had certainly been abandoned by this date.

The remains of the village are in very poor condition and little can be learned from what survives. Indeed, the area of the former village can only be ascertained from the limits of the ridge-and-furrow on the E. This lack of identifiable earthworks is due to the varied use of the site since desertion. A small deer park was created in 1547 N. of Astwell Castle, on the site of the former village, and in the late 16th or early 17th century a formal garden was constructed (9). A landscaped park of the later 17th century also involved the construction of earthworks and further large-scale engineering works took place, perhaps in the 19th century, when new ponds and leats to Astwell Mill were constructed 450 m. to the N. of the Castle. Extensive land-drainage work in recent years has caused further damage and the E. part of the site has been completely destroyed by modern cultivation.

There is considerable evidence that the village lay N.E. of Astwell Castle. To the E. of and crossing the track to Falcutt there were, until recent destruction, two large banks running N.-S. which separated an area of disturbed ground and former closes ('a' on plan) from the ridge-and-furrow to the E. Medieval pottery of the 12th to 14th

centuries has been found in this area. Within a pasture field to the W. are traces of what may once have been a hollow-way ('b' on plan). Its E. side is a largely natural scarp still 2 m. high, but its W. side is now a low scarp only 0.25 m. high. At its N. end this appears to join the existing road to Wappenham. Further S. are a number of low banks and scarps which may be the remains of former closes ('c' on plan). The rest of the village, if it extended further W. down the valley side, has been destroyed by the gardens (9), mill leats and modern drainage works. (RAF VAP CPE/UK/1926, 3224–5; CUAP, NU94, ANT71)

[d](7) FISHPONDS (SP 607443; Fig. 77), lie N. of Astwell Castle, in the valley of a N.-flowing stream, on alluvium at 114 m. above OD. After modern drainage, ploughing and reseeding, all that remains are two roughly rectangular areas bounded by scarps and banks less than 0.25 m. high, with two small rectangular depressions at the S. end. Before destruction, however, the surrounding banks are said to have been 'very high' (local inf.) and they are clearly visible on air photographs taken in 1947, together with an inlet leat or ditch along the S. side (RAF VAP CPE/UK/1926, 3224–5). The banks are undoubtedly the remains of a set of medieval fishponds, perhaps associated with Astwell village or its manor house. Ponds of this type, set in a flat valley floor and bounded by large banks, have been noted elsewhere (e.g. RCHM Northants., II (1978), Cogenhoe (12)). (CUAP, NU94)

[d](8) WINDMILL MOUND (?) (SP 610441; Fig. 77), lay E. of Astwell Castle, on a W.-facing slope, on limestone at 132 m. above OD. Air photographs taken before total destruction by ploughing (RAF VAP CPE/UK/1926, 3224–5) show a low mound 10 m. in diam., surrounded by a shallow ditch which the adjacent ridge-and-furrow appeared to avoid. It is not certain whether this was a windmill mound or had another function.

[d](9) GARDEN REMAINS (SP 608440 and 608442; Fig. 77), lie around Astwell Castle, on limestone between 122 m. and 130 m. above OD. The manor of Astwell passed into the hands of the Lovett family in 1471 and parts of the Castle, in particular the embattled gate-tower, date from that period. The village of Astwell (6) was probably cleared away soon afterwards and in 1547 a small deer park was created over its site to the N.E. of the Castle. The manor later passed to the Shirley family and about 1606 George Shirley added a large house arranged around a courtyard, to the S.W. and W. of the earlier building. Of this house only a fragment now survives, but traces of what seem to be contemporary gardens still remain to the S. These ('d' on plan) consist of at least four rectangular areas edged by scarps between 0.5 m. and 2 m. high, set to one side of the 17th-century house and extending up the hillside to the S.E. This plan suggests a late 16th or early 17th-century date.

To the N.E. of the Castle, in the area of the former village, there are further earthworks which are also undoubtedly the remains of gardens or of landscaping. These are more difficult to date but are perhaps of the later 17th or early 18th century. The most notable feature, until it was partly destroyed, was a large roughly U-shaped pond, which was of such a size that it was shown on the OS

County Series 25 in. plans ('OS' on plan). A broad terrace some 10 m. across and bounded by low scarps ('e' on plan) continues N.E. on the alignment of the N.W. side of the pond. At its N.E. end the terrace narrows into a low bank. The feature has the appearance of a driveway leading to the Castle, but because of the existence of the pond at its S.W. end this is unlikely. A more plausible explanation is that it marks an avenue of trees which lay across the park. Between the Castle and the ponds surveyed by the OS there are further depressions but these are so mutilated that their origins cannot be ascertained. (RAF VAP CPE/UK/1926, 3224–5, CUAP, NU94)

^{d}(10) MILL LEATS AND PONDS (SP 603439–608444; partly on Fig. 77), extend along the E. side of a N.-draining valley, to the S.W., W. and N. of Astwell Castle, on clay at 116 m. above OD. The leats represent at least two separate stages in the process of supplying water to Astwell Mill which lies further N., on the Helmdon-Wappenham Road. The earliest feature is a broad leat 10 m. wide with an embanked lower side which runs off the existing stream well to the S.W. of the castle and extends N.E. roughly parallel to the stream ('f' on plan). At its N.E. end it once ran into the westernmost of the two existing mill ponds. A second leat ('g') runs parallel to and above the one already described, to a point just N.W. of the castle where it turns and continues inside the old one. This leat is shown on all except the most modern OS maps and plans as carrying water, but is now a narrow dry ditch only 7 m. across. To the W. of Astwell Castle a track crosses the new leat on a small 19th-century brick bridge. The same track crosses the old leat on a blocking causeway. Other ditches in the general area also appear to have been used to supply the mill with water. For example an embanked ditch immediately W. of Astwell Castle ('h' on plan) carried water across the hillside from a spring, and further N. at least one other ditch ('i' on plan) had the same function. (RAF VAP CPE/UK/1926, 3224–5; CUAP, NU94)

^{d}(11) MOAT AND FISHPONDS (SP 615430; Figs. 78 and 79), known as Old Mountains, lie in the E. of the parish, in the bottom of a broad shallow S.-draining valley, on Boulder Clay at 145 m. above OD. The earthworks lie near the W. edge of the deer park (12) and were perhaps the site of a park keeper's lodge. The moated site is a roughly rectangular flat island 0.5 m.–1 m. above the surrounding land and separated from the adjacent ditch on the N., E. and S. by a bank only 0.5 m. high. The ditch is 1.5 m. deep on the E. and 2 m. deep on the N., but appears to have been filled in on the S. The W. side of the site is difficult to understand and may be the result of later alterations. The ditch here is 1.5 m. deep and runs obliquely N.N.E.-S.S.W., with no trace of an inner bank. To the E. of the ditch there are two rectangular depressions, perhaps former ponds, and to the W. there is a triangular area 1.5 m. high. This may be the original W. edge of the site detached from the main part by the later ditch. At the S.W. corner is a large circular mound almost 2 m. high, linked to the corner of the moat by low causeways. The moat was apparently filled by a small stream which entered it in the N.W. corner.

To the S.W. of the moat there was a fishpond, perhaps

contemporary. The field in which it lay was called Pool Meadow in 1864 (map in NRO) and this field is bounded on the S. by a dam ('b' on plan) spanning the valley. On the E. side of the stream, which is now culverted, the dam is a massive bank nearly 3 m. high, but its E. end has been destroyed and only its outer face remains as a low scarp. To the W. of the stream the dam has been ploughed down and survives only as a broad bank 1.5 m. high. Old OS plans show a ditch at its W. end ('c' on plan) which continued the line of the dam and then returned E. before curving back N.W. This feature has now been completely destroyed by modern cultivation but the OS plans have been followed on Fig. 78. However, there is some doubt whether it was a ditch as depicted, for air photographs taken in 1947 before the destruction was complete (RAF VAP CPE/UK/1926, 3224–5) appear to show a massive E.-facing scarp. Whatever its original form the feature probably marked the W. edge of the pond. When filled this pond probably extended E. to a broad low scarp N.E. of the dam and to the S. of the moat. It also probably extended northwards beyond a low bank ('d' on plan), now ploughed down, which runs from the S.W. corner of the moat in a westerly direction. This bank can be traced for some 300 m. until it meets the W. side of the deer park. The chronological relationship of the bank to the moat and the pond is not clear. It appears to be the boundary of a close or field within the deer park (see (12) below). The probable E. boundary of this close runs N. from the N.W. corner of the moat ('e' on plan) and is now almost ploughed away but, according to old OS plans, it consisted of a low bank with a ditch on its E. side and ran N. for 460 m. until it met the boundary of the deer park near the N.W. corner of the latter.

To the S.E. of the moat a hollow-way up to 2 m. deep ('f' on plan) runs S.W. to meet the E. end of the dam ('b' on plan). At its E. end it fades out and can be traced only for 200 m. The relationship of the hollow-way to the pond is difficult to understand; the two cannot have been in use at the same time.

^{d}(12) DEER PARK (centred SP 623433; Figs. 78 and 79) occupied a large area in the E. of the parish and apparently extended eastwards into the N.W. part of Syresham parish. No record of its existence has been noted in medieval documents and the park created in 1547 by Sir Thomas Lovett of Astwell probably lay to the N. of Astwell Castle on the site of the former village (6) (K. J. Allison et al., The Deserted Villages of Northants. (1966), 35). Field names on a map of 1864 (NRO) and the modern names Astwell Park and Astwell Park Farm, as well as the surviving earthworks, prove beyond doubt that a deer park once lay here. The moated site (11) situated towards the W. edge of the park presumably represents a park keeper's lodge.

The park covers around 200 hectares, entirely on Boulder Clay, between 137 m. and 157 m. above OD. Before modern destruction it was bounded by an almost continuous bank. The bank formerly ran S.E. across the centre of a long narrow field immediately E. of Astwell Park (SP 622436). This part of it has now been destroyed, but on air photographs taken in 1947 it is clearly visible, with traces of an internal ditch. At the Syresham parish boundary (SP 627434) it fades, to recommence 200 m. to the E.,

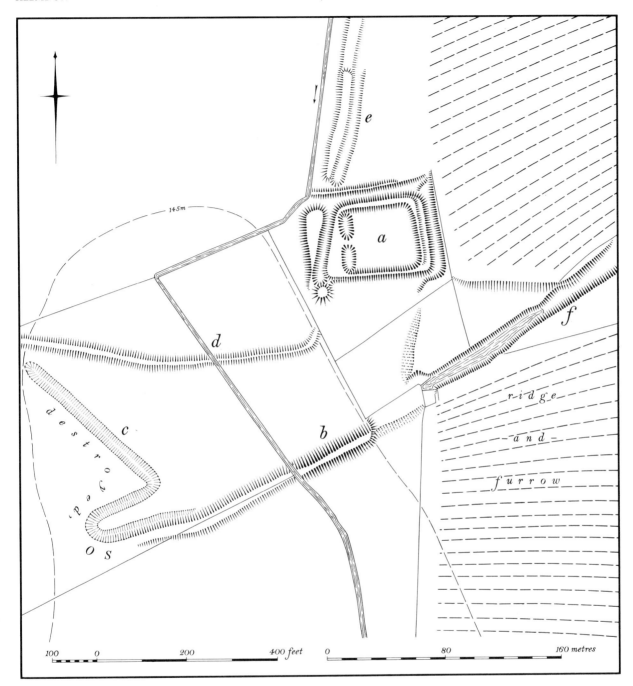

Fig. 78 HELMDON (11) Moat and fishponds

in Syresham parish, as a broad hedge-bank up to 5 m. wide and 1 m. high, curving S.E. parallel to the modern road (SP 628434–632431). The next section is lost, in a field with 19th-century broad ridge-and-furrow across it, but the boundary reappears S. of Wild House (SP 633430) as a large hedge-bank which runs S.W. to a point a little N. of Syresham village (SP 628423) and then turns until it meets the Helmdon parish boundary (SP 623426). The bank then follows the irregular parish boundary until it meets the

stream flowing S. from the moated site (11) (SP 616426). At this point the park boundary continues W. and then swings N. in a broad curve until it reaches a droveway running S.W. from Astwell Park (SP 612433). The bank, here 1 m. high, runs N.E. along the S.E. side of the droveway but, at the bend in the droveway (at SP 616435), continues N.E. in a sinuous line. Here it has again been ploughed out but it certainly once had an inner ditch. The bank met the Astwell-Syresham road (at SP 619438) where

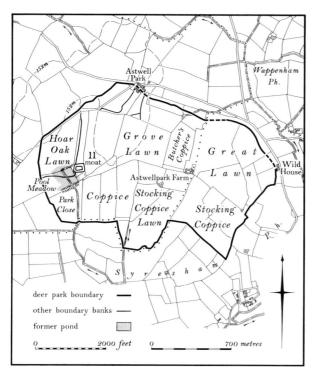

Fig. 79   HELMDON (12)   Deer park at Astwell

it turned E. and ran to Astwell Park.

The interior of the park is divided into fields, many with hedges on large banks, and a number of other banks, now either partly or completely ploughed out, are visible on air photographs. These suggest that the park was once divided into a number of large closes of unknown purpose. One bank runs N. from the N.W. corner of the moated site (11) to meet the park boundary in the N.W. corner (SP 616435) and another runs W. from the moat to the W. side of the park (SP 612430). A third can be seen on air photographs, curving S.W. and then W. from Astwell Park, and traces of another run S. from Astwell Park to meet a bank approaching from the S.W. (RAF VAP CPE/UK/1926, 3224–6, 5224–6)

(13) CULTIVATION REMAINS. The common fields of the former parish of Helmdon were enclosed by an Act of Parliament of 1758 (NRO, Enclosure Map). Nothing is known of the arrangement of these fields but it is possible that at some time there were two separate field systems, associated with the two assumed early settlements which together make up the village of Helmdon. These lands may have been two parts of the original parish, N. and S. of the main stream (Fig. 119).

Ridge-and-furrow of these fields exists on the ground or can be traced on air photographs over much of the old parish. In the S. part the pattern is almost complete, but in the N. it is less so. The ridge-and-furrow is arranged in end-on and interlocked furlongs, many of reversed-S form. A number of former headlands is still traceable as broad low banks up to 20 m. wide (SP 590445). In some places there is considerable variation in ridge width; for example

S. of Allithorne Wood (SP 585448) four blocks of relatively narrow ridges only 4 m. across are separated by single broad ridges 8 m.–9 m. wide. This is an unusual system and may indicate a late stage in strip division in this parish.

Ridge-and-furrow is also traceable within the area of land of Stocking Farm, which was formerly a detached part of Helmdon parish to the S.E. of Falcutt (Fig. 119). Here the pattern is virtually complete and it would be of considerable interest to know how this land was farmed in the medieval period and by whom.

The common fields of Astwell were enclosed by an Act of Parliament of 1761 and the common fields of Falcutt were also enclosed at this time. It is possible that each settlement once had its own field system, though this is not certain, and the assumed boundary between the two (shown on Fig. 119) has been reconstructed on the basis of two lengths of broad droveway, a footpath and a stream which form a continuous line. Ridge-and-furrow of these fields exists on the ground or can be traced on air photographs over much of the land of the old parish of Astwell and Falcutt. Around Falcutt it is arranged in interlocked and end-on blocks carefully adapted to the broken ground. To the N.E., between Astwell and Falcutt (SP 600423–615438), the furlongs run N.W., down an N.W.-facing valley side.

Ridge-and-furrow is also visible in the E. of the parish, within the area covered by the deer park (12). Much of it is of medieval form, in end-on and interlocked furlongs, but there are also considerable areas of straight ridges 7 m.–9 m. wide, fitting within the existing field boundaries (e.g. SP 617433). This is presumably the remains of late 19th-century steam ploughing. (RAF VAP CPE/UK/1926, 1217–23, 3217–27, 5218–26; CPE/UK/1994, 1093–6)

32   HEYFORD, NETHER
(OS 1:10000 [a] SP 65 NW, [b] SP 65 NE)

The small parish, covering just over 600 hectares, lies S. of the R. Nene which forms its N. boundary. Most of the N. half of the parish is low-lying ground sloping gently towards the river between 70 m. and 100 m. above OD, on gravel and Middle Lias Clay. In the S.W. the land rises more steeply across Upper Lias Clay to a high area known as the Heyford Hills, covered by Northampton Sand at 130 m. above OD.

PREHISTORIC AND ROMAN

A partly polished stone axe was found in 1941 in a gravel pit in the parish (SP 66615841; in Daventry School Museum). Two flint scrapers have also been discovered in the same area (SP 666582; BNFAS, 7 (1972), 6).

[b](1) LINEAR DITCHES (SP 651592), in the N. of the parish, just S. of the R. Nene, on gravel at 82 m. above OD. Air photographs (NCAU) show three sinuous, roughly parallel, linear ditches, visible for 75 m.

[b](2) RING DITCHES (?) (SP 653571), lie on the Heyford Hills in the S.W. of the parish, on Northampton Sand at

125 m. above OD. Air photographs in NMR show very indistinctly what appear to be two interlocked ring ditches, one about 15 m. and the other about 20 m. in diam.

[b](3) ROMAN BUILDING (SP 666583), lies in a meadow called Wonston, Horestone or Horsestone, to the E. of the village, close to the R. Nene, at 70 m. above OD. This land is said to have been regularly flooded in the past and certainly no medieval ridge-and-furrow ever existed on it. The building was discovered in 1699 when part of a polychrome mosaic with an elaborate geometrical design of boxes framing patterns of duplex knots, guilloche and lotus flowers was found. Other rooms were noted which had plaster floors with coloured borders. Slates, tiles, painted wall-plaster and pottery including samian were also recorded. In 1780 the mosaic was taken up and used for road mending. The site was re-examined in 1821 but few finds were made (J. Morton, *Nat. Hist. of Northants.* (1712), 527; J. Bridges, *Hist of Northants.*, I (1791), 519; G. Baker, *Hist. of Northants.*, I (1822–30), 191; VCH *Northants.*, I (1902), 196; A. Rainey, *Mosaics in Roman Britain* (1973), 122; P. Corder (ed.), *The Roman Town and Villa at Great Casterton, second interim report* (1954), 35–9). Roman pottery, part of the mosaic and some wall footings were found during digging on the site before 1952 (OS Record Cards). A few sherds of pottery of 3rd and 4th-century date have been noted on the site.

For Roman Road 1f, Watling Street, see Appendix.

MEDIEVAL AND LATER

A 15th-century bronze incense cup decorated with an unidentified coat of arms has been found at 'Heyford' (NM).

[b](4) SETTLEMENT REMAINS (SP 662585), formerly part of Nether Heyford village, lay on the S.E. side of the village, S. of Brook Farm, on gravel at 75 m. above OD. The site has now been built over, but on air photographs taken before destruction (RAF VAP 3G/TUD/UK/118, 6046–50) the slight remains of banks and scarps, presumably the sites of former houses, are visible. The loss of these remains means that the relationship between the green at Nether Heyford and the main part of the village which lies to the N.W. of it can never be fully understood.

(5) CULTIVATION REMAINS. The date of the enclosure of the common fields of Nether Heyford is unknown, but was certainly before 1794 (NRO). Ridge-and-furrow of these fields exists on the ground or can be traced on air photographs over most of the parish, except on the low-lying floodable land close to the R. Nene. It is arranged mainly in rectangular furlongs lying end-on or at right angles to each other except on the steep land in the S.W. of the parish where it all lies across the contours in a radiating pattern. On the top of the Heyford Hills no ridge-and-furrow is visible, probably because all trace of it has been removed by modern cultivation of the light Northampton Sand there. Much of the recoverable ridge-and-furrow is characterized by well-marked reversed-S curves. (RAF VAP CPE/UK/1994, 1170–4, 3161–3; 3G/TUD/UK/118, 6033–5, 6046–54; FSL6603, 2364–5, 2374–5, 2379–80)

The parish covers only about 370 hectares and lies on the N. side of the R. Nene which forms its S. boundary. The greater part is an extensive area of sands and gravels, sloping gently S. to the river between 70 m. and 100 m. above OD, but in the N. the land rises steeply across Lias Clay to Glassthorpe Hill, a rounded hill capped with Northampton Sand at just over 122 m. above OD.

PREHISTORIC AND ROMAN

A stone bracer or wrist guard made of a greenish-grey rhyolite was found in 1949 immediately S. of the village (SP 66445937; NM; *PPS*, 28 (1962), 263; *J. Northants. Mus. and Art Gall.*, 6 (1969), 35). A single Roman coin of 'Faustina' is recorded from the parish (NM Records).

[a](1) ROMAN SETTLEMENT (?) (SP 663599), N.W. of the village on gravel at 88 m. above OD. Roman pottery including grey wares and 4th-century Nene valley types was found in 1963. The site now lies under the M1 motorway (NM Records).

MEDIEVAL AND LATER

[a](2) SETTLEMENT REMAINS (centred SP 665595; Fig. 80), formerly part of Upper Heyford village, lie immediately S. of the existing houses, on gravel between 79 m. and 85 m. above OD. The national taxation records for Upper Heyford are very inadequate. The village is first noted in 1086 when it was listed in Domesday Book as comprising two small manors, both held by the Count of Mortain, with a total recorded population of two (VCH *Northants.*, I (1902), 322, 328). Thereafter it is always combined with Nether Heyford in the national records until the 1673 Hearth Tax Returns when 51 people are listed (PRO, E179/254/14). Bridges (*Hist. of Northants.*, I (1791), 525), writing in about 1720, said that there were 20 houses there; in 1801 the population of the area was 122. However, these figures are difficult to interpret for at that time the parish of Nether Heyford did not exist as an administrative unit and the land was in some way divided between Heyford, Flore and Bugbrooke parishes (Whellan, *Dir.*, 321).

The earliest cartographic representation of the village is a map of 1758 (NRO). This shows the village as even smaller than it is today. The two roughly parallel streets are shown extending S. from the main E.-W. route (now the A45). No buildings are depicted to the W. of the westernmost of the two streets, though the present Home Farm existed, as well as a single cottage at the junction of the street with the main road. Two other farms are depicted to the S. of Home Farm, on the E. side of the street. To the W. of Home Farm the map shows a subsidiary loop road which no longer exists. Along the eastern street only the present North Farm stood, on the W. side, with another single cottage at the A45 junction. By the early 19th century (OS 1st ed. 1 in. map, 1834) the present farm and cottages on the W. side of the western street and the farm on the E. side of the eastern street had been built, but the farms to the S. of Home Farm had disappeared.

The surviving buildings, the cartographic evidence and the earthworks together suggest that there were once perhaps two very small settlements each lying along one or both sides of two parallel streets. They may have expanded southwards along these streets and then, at an unknown period before the mid 18th century, contracted. The 1758 map shows that the settlement remained small until that date although it later grew again.

The surviving earthworks are in poor condition and not completely understood. The remains fall into two groups. To the S. of Home Farm ('a' on plan) is an area of disturbed ground including two very large roughly rectangular depressions up to 1.5 m. deep where the 1758 map depicts the two farms, with an area of narrow ridge-and-furrow

to the E. The latter is very slight and it is impossible to say whether it is earlier or later than the farms to the W. Further S. are some shallow quarry pits, with to the W. of them two rectangular sunken platforms 1 m. deep, presumably the sites of former houses alongside the existing road.

Further E., on the W. side of the eastern street, is another area of low disturbed earthworks of no coherent form, the S. part of which has been ploughed over at some time ('b' on plan). A quantity of medieval pottery was found here some years ago (local inf.). The two groups of earthworks are linked by a series of shallow ditches, scarps and low banks which may be the boundaries of former closes. Fieldwalking in the arable land S., S.W. and S.E. of the earthworks has failed to produce any evidence of former

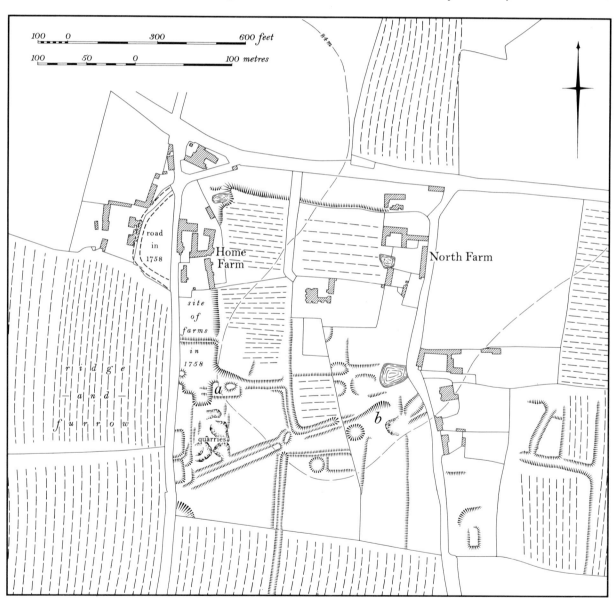

Fig. 80 UPPER HEYFORD (2) Settlement remains

occupation. (RAF VAP CPE/UK/1994, 1172–3; FSL6603, 2364–5; CUAP, AMW61)

(3) CULTIVATION REMAINS. The exact date of the enclosure of the common fields of Upper Heyford is unknown but Bridges, writing in about 1720 (*Hist. of Northants.*, I (1791), 525), said that 'about eight years ago it was enclosed by the Marquis of Powis'. Ridge-and-furrow of these fields remains on the ground or can be traced on air photographs over large parts of the parish, arranged mainly in rectangular furlongs set either end-on or at right angles to each other. Broad ditches or hollow-ways existed in a few places (e.g. SP 664591), passing between the furlongs, but their date is unknown and they may relate to a period after enclosure. (RAF VAP CPE/UK/1994, 1172–5, 1261–5; CPE/UK/1926, 4035–7; FSL6603, 2364–5, 2374–5)

34   HINTON-IN-THE-HEDGES
(OS 1:10000 ᵃ SP 53 NW, ᵇ SP 53 NE)

The parish is small, covering only 587 hectares, and lies immediately E. of Brackley. It consists of a generally flat area of Great Oolite Limestone between 120 m. and 145 m. above OD, cut into by a series of E. and S.E.-flowing streams, one of which forms the N. boundary. Along the valley sides Northampton Sand and clays are exposed.

ROMAN

ᵇ(1) ROMAN SETTLEMENT (?) (SP 569370), E. of the village on limestone at 125 m. above OD. Roman pottery was found here before 1978. A bronze axe is said to have come from the same area. (Northants. SMR)

ᵇ(2) ROMAN SETTLEMENT (?) (SP 572360), in the S.E. of the parish, on limestone at 123 m. above OD. A small quantity of large, unabraded sherds is recorded (Northants. SMR).

For possible Roman Road 56a, see Appendix.

MEDIEVAL AND LATER

ᵇ(3) MOATED SITE AND FISHPOND (SP 563370; Plate 3), lay in the angle between two streams immediately E. of the village, on clay at 118 m. above OD. The area has now been completely levelled.

The moated site consisted of a small rectangular island, 30 m. by 40 m., apparently raised slightly above the adjacent ground and surrounded by a deep ditch 12 m. wide. The ditch on the N.E. side and part of the island had already been damaged before destruction, by the realignment and deepening of the original stream. On the S.W. side was a larger rectangular island 60 m. by 45 m., surrounded by a ditch 10 m. wide with a causewayed entrance in the centre of the short N.W. side. There was a large external bank to the S.E. of both islands. In the surrounding area was a number of shallow ditches and low banks, some defining former paddocks or closes, others apparently for water. To the N.W. of the site (SP 561371) was a small rectangular embanked pond, probably contemporary with the moated site and perhaps for fish.

During the destruction of the site in 1970 short lengths of foundations and what appeared to be a central courtyard were discovered as well as traces of a large timber building lying over an earlier structure. Pottery of the 14th century was found (*Med. Arch.*, 15 (1971), 163–4; DOE, *Arch. Excavations 1970* (1971), 34). Much more pottery of the same date had been found previously (local inf.). Nothing is known of the history of the site. (VCH *Northants.*, II (1906), 416; J. Bridges, *Hist. of Northants.*, I (1791), 175; RAF VAP CPE/UK/1926, 4215–6; CUAP, AAV19 and 20, AWN77; air photographs in NMR)

ᵇ(4) SETTLEMENT REMAINS (centred SP 559369; Plate 3), formerly part of Hinton, lie in and around the village, on clay, between 122 m. and 140 m. above OD. Very little survives on the ground today and it appears that the earthworks were never very extensive or impressive. On the S.E. side of the village there was formerly an area of disturbed ground (SP 560368) but this is now built over. S.W. of the village (SP 558367), on either side of a small stream, are other very indeterminate earthworks of no coherent form.

It is not clear what the remains represent as the surviving records show no indication of shrinkage; indeed the village seems to have had a stable population since the 11th century. In 1086 Domesday Book gives a recorded population of 18 (VCH *Northants.*, I (1902), 346). In 1301, 23 taxpayers are listed in the Subsidy Roll (PRO, E179/155/31) and in 1334 the village paid 36s. 7d. in tax (PRO, E179/155/3). In 1377, 44 people over the age of 14 paid the Poll Tax (PRO, E179/155/28). The 1523 Subsidy was paid by 23 people in Hinton and Steane (PRO, E179/155/159), but by then Steane (Farthinghoe (18)) was already deserted. In 1673 23 people paid the Hearth Tax (PRO, E179/254/14). Bridges (*Hist. of Northants.*, I (1791), 175) recorded about 30 houses there in 1720. Medieval pottery from the 14th to the 17th century as well as a spur of 14th or 15th-century date is recorded from the village (*Northants. Archaeol.*, 9 (1974), 106). (RAF VAP CPE/UK/1926, 4215–6; CUAP, AAV19 and 20, AWN77)

ᵇ(5) ENCLOSURE (SP 553365), lies S.W. of the village, on sand at 137 m. above OD. Air photographs (CUAP, BV61, 62) show a small rectangular enclosure which appears to be aligned on a former headland of the common fields. A quantity of medieval pottery, probably 13th or 14th-century in date, as well as some post-medieval pottery, has been found on the site (*BNFAS*, 3 (1969), 23).

ᵇ(6) PONDS (SP 557367), lie S.W. of the village, on clay at 130 m. above OD. In 1857 (map in NRO) there were three small rectangular ponds and one circular one and the area was known as Pond Close. A very irregular pond in a small copse is all that survives. No date or function can be assigned to the site.

(7) CULTIVATION REMAINS. The common fields of the parish were enclosed by Act of Parliament of 1766. Very little ridge-and-furrow of these fields remains on the ground or can be traced on air photographs mainly because modern ploughing has removed all trace of it on the Great Oolite Limestone where it was probably always very slight. It can be seen in a few places around the village on clay, and also along the N. and N.E. boundary of the

parish, running at right angles to the contours. Former headlands survive in a few places as broad low ridges up to 10 m. across (e.g. SP 555368). (RAF VAP CPE/UK/1926, 2214–6, 4212–8; 106G/UK/1488, 4264–7)

UNDATED

[b](8) MOUND (SP 575366), lies in the S.E. of the parish, on Great Oolite Limestone at 120 m. above OD. A large rectangular mound, some 40 m. across and 1 m. high, is still visible although ploughed over. No date or purpose can be assigned to it.

[a](9) BURIALS (SP 548376), in the N.W. of the parish, on limestone at 145 m. above OD. Several human skeletons are said to have been discovered 'from time to time' in the gardens of Hinton Grounds Farm before 1848. In that year two more skeletons were found (Whellan, Dir., 484).

35 KING'S SUTTON
(OS 1:10000 [a] SP 43 NE, [b] SP 43 SE, [c] SP 53 NW, [d] SP 53 SW, [e] SP 54 SW)

The parish is large, covering some 1700 hectares, and lies against the county boundary with Oxfordshire, on land sloping generally S.W. to the R. Cherwell, but with a series of small tributary streams producing a rolling landscape of deep valleys with wide flat ridges between them. Apart from some small outcrops of Northampton Sand in the S.E. where the land rises to 130 m. above OD most of the higher parts of the parish are on Marlstone Rock. Elsewhere the underlying Lias Clay has been exposed by the down-cutting of the streams.

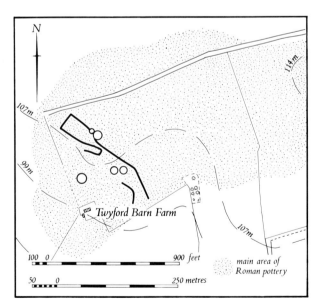

Fig. 81   KING'S SUTTON (6)   Prehistoric and Roman Settlement

The parish is particularly rich in archaeological remains of all periods. Some of these are of considerable interest in themselves, but an attempt has also been made to see them in the broader context of a continuously developing landscape (F. M. Brown and C. C. Taylor, 'Settlement and Land Use in Northants.' in BAR, International Series (Supplementary), 68 (1978), 77–89). The present boundaries of the parish are relatively modern; in the 19th century Little Purston and its surrounding land was part of Newbottle parish, and the E. part of Newbottle was a detached part of King's Sutton.

PREHISTORIC AND ROMAN

Bronze Age inhumations and a palstave often said to be from King's Sutton were in fact found in Aynho parish (see Aynho (1)).

A polished flint axe was discovered in 1966 somewhere in the parish (Oxoniensia, 33 (1968), 138; Ashmolean Museum). An iron object described as a 'cultrum or chopper' together with an 'iron knife or spatula' and a Roman coin of Vespasian were discovered at Astrop in the 19th century (JBAA, 17 (1861), 70; VCH Northants., I (1902), 216).

[d](1) ENCLOSURE (?) (SP 507336), in the S. of the parish, on Marlstone Rock at 95 m. above OD. Air photographs (NCAU) show a curved ditch which may be part of a large circular or oval enclosure about 30 m. wide.

[c](2) ROUND BARROW (SP 50193864), N. of the village and a little S.W. of Buston Farm, on the summit of a rounded hill of Marlstone Rock, at 122 m. above OD. The barrow was destroyed without excavation in about 1910 during ironstone-mining. It was about 33 m. in diam., and about 1 m. high, and apparently contained a crouched burial. (G. Baker, Hist. of Northants., I (1822–30), 703; Oxford Arch. Soc. Reps., 56 (1910), 36; OS Record Cards)

[c](3) ROUND BARROW (SP 50253860), immediately S.E. of (1) and in a similar position. It was destroyed by ironstone-mining in about 1910 but no finds are recorded from it. (G. Baker, Hist. of Northants., I (1822–30), 703; Oxford Arch. Soc. Reps., 56 (1910), 36; OS Record Cards)

[c](4) ROUND BARROW (?) (about SP 508382), described by Baker (Hist. of Northants., I (1822–30), 703) as being in a very prominent situation on High Thorn Hill above 'Buston House'. High Thorn Hill has been identified but no indication of a barrow survives. Much of the area formerly had ridge-and-furrow on it. (RAF VAP CPE/UK/1926, 5208–9)

[c](5) NEOLITHIC AND ROMAN SETTLEMENT AND BURIALS (centred SP 505387), lay on Marlstone Rock, on land sloping generally N. between 114 m. and 122 m. above OD and close to the round barrows (1) and (2). The area was worked for ironstone between 1909 and 1911 and numerous discoveries were made. In 1910 at least 12 extended skeletons were found and in 1911 four more burials, two of which were crouched inhumations. Numerous pits, Neolithic and Roman pottery, Roman coins from Claudius to Constantine the Great, flint scrapers and a polished axe were also discovered then. The Roman pottery was said

to extend over a wide area and several complete pots are recorded (*Oxford Arch. Soc. Reps.*, 56 (1910), 35–8; 57 (1911), 12–17; 58 (1912), 114–8; OS Record Cards). Some of the Neolithic pottery is said to have been found in pits and has been described as 'of Peterborough type' (*PPS*, 30 (1964), 378). Most of the finds are in the Ashmolean Museum.

For Anglo-Saxon discoveries at this site, see (8).

^a(6) PREHISTORIC AND ROMAN SETTLEMENT (centred SP 491375; Fig. 81), lies S.W. of (4), in the N.W. of the parish, on Marlstone Rock sloping S.W. towards the R. Cherwell, between 115 m. and 90 m. above OD. The area, covering some 20 hectares and known as Blacklands, has long been known as a Roman settlement, for Morton (*Nat. Hist. of Northants.* (1712), 531) recorded 'Roman money' found in Blacklands Furlong. Before 1825 skeletons 'in rude cists of sarson stones' were found in the area and in 1825 a 'cinerary urn' containing a cremation, two other skeletons and coins of Hadrian and Marcus Aurelius were discovered (G. Baker, *Hist. of Northants.*, I (1822–30), 703). Before 1841 Roman coins, including some silver ones, foundations of buildings, mill-stones and at least four more skeletons with 'rough headstones' were found and the existence of cropmarks was noted. In the W. part of the site a skeleton associated with a bone pin and 'celt of serpentine' is also recorded (A. Beesley, *Hist. of Banbury* (1841), 33). The 'celt' is probably the otherwise unlocated jade axe from King's Sutton (Ashmolean Museum; *PPS*, 29 (1963), 163, No. 34). A fragment of bronze, possibly part of a spearhead, was ploughed up in 1964 to the N. of the site (SP 48873795; *BNFAS*, 3 (1969), 1). Recent field-walking has produced Roman pottery from over a wide area but concentrated mainly at the W. end of the site (OS Record Cards). This pottery is mainly of 3rd to 4th-century date.

Air photographs (in NMR) show, rather indistinctly, at least five small circular features as well as a number of ditches which are probably parts of enclosures. Another cropmark visible on air photographs (also in NMR) passes to the N. of the site (not shown on plan) and is described as an 'early road' (*Northants. Archaeol.*, 8 (1973), 26). It appears to be an abandoned ironstone tramway.

^a(7) ROMAN SETTLEMENT (SP 496364), lies immediately N. of the N.W. part of King's Sutton village, above the flood-plain of the R. Cherwell, on clay at 85 m. above OD. Roman coins of Tetricus, Claudius II and Constans are recorded as having been found in the area known as Lake Meadow before the early 19th century (G. Baker, *Hist. of Northants.*, I (1822–30), 703). A skeleton is also said to have been found there (Whellan, *Dir.*, 486) and more recently pottery of the 3rd century has been found at the N.E. corner of the area during building work.

For Roman pottery at Walton, see (10) below.

For possible Roman Roads 56a and 161a, see Appendix.

MEDIEVAL AND LATER

^c(8) SAXON BURIAL (SP 508389), lay to the N.E. of Buston Farm, apparently on the edge of the Neolithic and Roman settlement (5). In 1910–11 a burial with spearheads, said to

be Saxon, was discovered during ironstone-working (Meaney, *Gazetteer*, 192; OS Record Cards).

(9)–(11) MEDIEVAL SETTLEMENTS (Fig. 82). In late medieval times the parish contained a number of discrete settlements, King's Sutton itself, Upper Astrop (9) and Lower Astrop, Great Purston (11), Little Purston then a detached part of Newbottle parish, and Walton (10). Each had its own associated land unit except for Upper and Lower Astrop which shared one. The possible implications of this settlement pattern have been published elsewhere (F. M. Brown and C. C. Taylor, 'Settlement and Land Use in Northants.' in *BAR*, International Series (Supplementary), 68 (1978), 77–89).

^c(9) SETTLEMENT REMAINS (SP 510374), formerly part of Upper Astrop, lie at the N. end of the hamlet, on clay at 110 m. above OD. A number of low banks, presumably abandoned closes, lie around the existing farmstead. (MVRG, *Report*, 20–21 (1972–3), 6; RAF VAP CPE/UK/1926, 2209–10)

^d(10) DESERTED VILLAGE OF WALTON (SP 506346; Fig. 83), lay in the S. of the parish, alongside a small stream on clay at 90 m. above OD. The village is first recorded in Domesday Book in 1086, but its name may be derived from *Wēala-Tun*, i.e. the farm of the serfs, Welsh or Britons (PN *Northants.*, 58). In 1086 Domesday Book lists Walton as three small manors with a total recorded population of ten (VCH *Northants.*, I (1902), 308, 324, 326). In 1301 the Lay Subsidy lists 17 people in Walton paying tax (PRO, E179/155/31) and the village is mentioned as an independent vill in the *Nomina Villarum* of 1316. In 1487 five houses there were destroyed by John Goylyn who also enclosed 200 acres of land. A few years later in 1506 there were still ten houses in existence, but in 1537 Richard Fermor was prosecuted for carrying out further enclosures and by the early 18th century Bridges (*Hist. of Northants.*, I (1791), 180) said that there were only two houses, both of which still remain. There are records of a former chapel at Walton, but this was in ruins by the 16th century and only the name Chapel Field marked it by the early 18th century (K. J. Allison *et. al.*, *The Deserted Villages of Northants.* (1960), 47). The remains of the village survived until 1960 when they were almost completely destroyed and the area ploughed up; the accompanying plan (Fig. 83) has been compiled from air photographs. From the latter it seems that the earthworks were never well preserved and that few house-sites were visible. Nevertheless the village was of considerable interest in that it appears to have lain largely on one side of its main street, a layout recorded elsewhere in the county. The principal feature of the site was the street, a broad hollow-way which ran parallel to and S. of the stream. At its N.E. end it met at right angles another track which crossed the stream from N.W. to S.E. The adjacent ridge-and-furrow extended up to the S. side of the main hollow-way so that with the exception of one small ditched enclosure all the visible earthworks of former occupation lay between the N. edge of the hollow-way and the stream. The earthworks, though much damaged by later activity and the existence of two farms, appear to have consisted of small rectangular embanked closes and long roughly parallel scarps. To the

E., beyond the 'crossroads' and close to the stream, there was a large pond 50 m. long and 15 m. wide cut down into the hillside except at its W. end where there was a large dam. On the N. side of the stream there seem to have been few remains except for parts of two hollow-ways or terrace-ways. A considerable amount of medieval pottery, mainly of the 13th and 14th centuries, together with a few sherds of Roman wares, has been discovered in the area of the former earthworks. (RAF VAP CPE/UK/1926, 4208–9; CUAP LN50, SA12, AGV33, ANT74)

^c(11) DESERTED HAMLET OF PURSTON (SP 518396; Figs. 82 and 89), lies in the N.E. of the parish, on Marlstone Rock at 114 m. above OD. Neither the situation of the hamlet nor its tenurial relationship with adjacent settlements can be fully explained. The hamlet lies against the parish boundary with Newbottle, so that the present manor house and another hamlet, also apparently called Purston (Newbottle (4)), must have been contiguous with this hamlet. Each of these settlements had its own land unit but, in addition, the settlement of Little Purston, also with its own land unit and once a detached part of Newbottle parish, lay to the W. Little Purston is and probably always was a single farm. Because of this complexity it is difficult to interpret the surviving population statistics for the medieval period.

Purston is first recorded in 1086 when Domesday Book recorded it as two small manors. One, held by William de Cahagnes of the Count of Mortain, was assessed at half a hide and had only one bordar and is perhaps to be identified as the single farm of Little Purston. The other manor, held by Robert de Statford, was assessed at half a hide and one fifth of a hide and had a recorded population of six. It may represent the other two Purstons combined, though this is not certain (VCH Northants., I (1902), 326 and 334). It is clear however, that the total figure of seven refers to three separate settlements and the same probably applies to the population given in the later records. In 1301, 16 people at Purston paid the Lay Subsidy (PRO, E179/155/31). In 1495 three land owners combined to destroy six houses and enclose and convert 280 acres of land to pasture. In 1524 only five people paid the Lay Subsidy (PRO, E179/155/134) but Bridges, writing in the early 18th century (Hist. of Northants., I (1791), 180) still described it as a hamlet. Today, with two occupied houses in the King's Sutton part of Great Purston, the manor house in the Newbottle part and Little Purston Farm, there are still some 20 people living there. (K. J. Allison et. al., The Deserted Villages of Northants. (1966), 45).

The remains of Purston in King's Sutton parish lie immediately N. of the curving parish boundary and N.E. of the Manor House. They consist of an irregular arrangement of small rectangular paddocks or closes bounded by low banks and scarps nowhere above 0.5 m. high but form

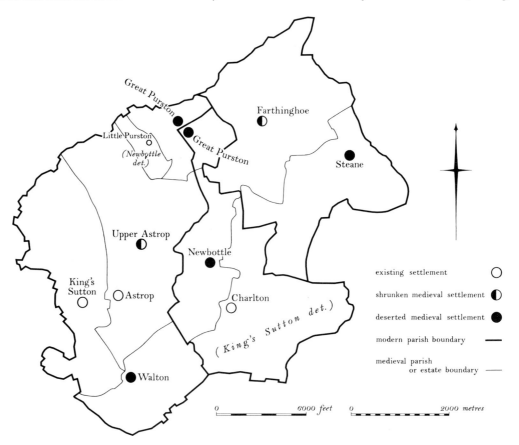

Fig. 82 FARTHINGHOE, KING'S SUTTON and NEWBOTTLE Medieval settlements and estates

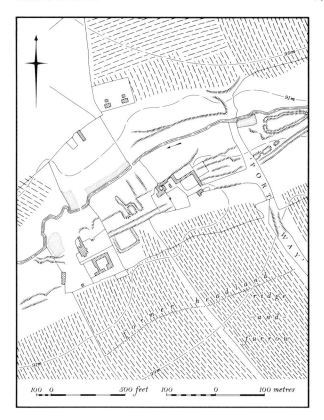

Fig. 83   KING'S SUTTON (10)   Deserted village
of Walton

no coherent pattern unless the present parish boundary was formerly a through road. There is a little evidence for this at the E. end of the site where a possible hollow-way, cut into by later quarrying, can be seen as well as what appears to be the N. side of the hollow-way further W. along the parish boundary. If this feature was indeed a street then the hamlet of Great Purston consisted of houses on both sides of a single street but the houses on each side lay in different parishes (now King's Sutton and Newbottle). Moreover, each side of the hamlet had its own land unit. For the former earthworks S. of the parish boundary, see Newbottle (4). (RAF VAP CPE/UK/1926, 4209–11)

a(12) HOLLOW-WAY (SP 495365), lies immediately N. of the N.W. part of the village of King's Sutton and N. of the Roman settlement (7). It runs E.-W. across the slope between the road to Banbury and the flood-plain of the R. Cherwell. Probably because of the Roman coins and skeletons discovered close by, the site has been described as an 'entrenchment' (G. Baker, *Hist. of Northants.*, I (1822–30), 703; A. Beesley, *Hist. of Banbury* (1841), 35) but the feature is no more than an ancient hollow-way some 12 m. across and 1.5 m. deep passing between ridge-and-furrow and presumably giving access to the river. It has now been partly destroyed by infilling. (RAF VAP CPE/UK/1926, 2208–9)

(13) CULTIVATION REMAINS (Fig. 82). The common fields of King's Sutton village were enclosed by an Act of Par-

liament of 1804 (NRO, Enclosure Map, 1805). The area affected by this Act was entirely confined to the W. part of the modern parish, the land belonging to King's Sutton itself. It is not clear from the Enclosure Map whether parts of this area were already in old enclosures before 1804. Ridge-and-furrow of these fields exists on the ground or can be traced on air photographs only in a few places. It is almost completely absent on the higher ground and can only be seen along the sides of the Cherwell valley and its tributaries N. and S. of the village where the Lias Clay outcrops. It is arranged in end-on and interlocked furlongs of normal medieval type.

The date of the enclosure of the common fields of Upper and Lower Astrop is unknown, though it was presumably before the 18th century. Ridge-and-furrow of the fields can be traced on air photographs over much of the area of the land attributable to Astrop, but little now survives on the ground. The pattern is almost entirely recoverable in the area of Astrop Park, between Upper and Lower Astrop, where large rectangular end-on furlongs are visible, many with reversed-S curves and almost all running E.-W. Among the features of interest here are the sudden changes of ridge width from 4 m. to 10 m. within one furlong (SP 505368) and a broad hollow-way passing between end-on furlongs (SP 507373). In the N. of the land of Astrop, around Buston Farm (SP 505387), there was formerly another broad track up to 40 m. wide and deeply hollowed in places, curving up the hillside. To the E. of it (SP 505388), within a normal furlong of reversed-S ridge-and-furrow 7 m. wide, was one unusual ridge 140 m. long which tapered from 16 m. wide at its S.W. end to 9 m. wide at its N.E. Elsewhere in this area ironstone-mining and later cultivation had destroyed all the ridge-and-furrow before the earliest air photographs were taken.

The common fields of the deserted village of Walton (10) were at least partly enclosed in 1487 when 200 acres of land were converted to pasture. By 1506 only 40 acres of arable existed at Walton and there were 500 acres of pasture (K. J. Allison *et. al.*, *The Deserted Villages of Northants.* (1966), 47). As a result of modern destruction, ridge-and-furrow of these fields can be traced only on air photographs. It was arranged in end-on and interlocked furlongs. To the S. of the former village (SP 502341-509343) groups of two or three former end-on furlongs had been joined together by later ploughing over the intervening headlands, producing new furlongs up to 350 m. long with triple reversed-S curves. This ploughing may be post-medieval in origin.

The exact date of enclosure of the land attributable to Great and Little Purston (11) is not known. In 1495, 280 acres of land there and in Newbottle parish were enclosed (K. J. Allison, op. cit., 45) and the rest was probably converted to pasture around the same time. Certainly most of it was divided into hedged fields by the mid 19th century (NRO, Tithe Map of King's Sutton, 1847). Very little ridge-and-furrow survives on the ground, owing to modern cultivation, but much is visible on air photographs. It is all arranged in end-on and interlocked furlongs but characterized by rather small furlongs. Evidence for the joining up of former end-on furlongs is visible as over-ploughed headlands in the N. of the area (SP 516398). (RAF VAP CPE/

UK/1926, 2208–11, 4207–10, 5204–12; CPE/UK/1929, 3165–71; 106G/UK/1488, 3231–5, 4269–73)

36 KISLINGBURY
(OS 1:10000 ^a SP 65 NE, ^b SP 75 NW)

The modern parish covers only about 560 hectares, but until recently it included all the land to the E. of the village and S. of the R. Nene now in Upton parish. It is on almost flat ground, sloping very gently N., between 90 m. and 60 m. above OD and lies on Middle Lias Clay and Boulder Clay, except close to the R. Nene on the N. boundary where there are extensive spreads of glacial sands and gravels on which the village is situated.

PREHISTORIC AND ROMAN

Roman and possibly Iron Age sherds have been found in the S.E. of the parish (SP 710577). No other details are known (BNFAS, 3 (1969), 14).

MEDIEVAL AND LATER

^a(1) SETTLEMENT REMAINS (SP 697594), formerly part of Kislingbury, lie on the E. side of Church Lane, S. of the church, on gravel at 66 m. above OD. Only two battered scarps and some disturbed ground indicate the sites of buildings which once lined the street at this point. The remains lie within the rather irregular W. part of the village, which consists of a single lane running N.-S. with the church at the N. end, and with another lane from the mill joining the first about halfway along. The E. part of the village, including the present High Street, is quite different and appears to be an almost exact rectangle of streets which on the N., W., and S. have never had buildings on their outer sides. It is possible that the W. half of the village is older, while the E. is a later, perhaps planned addition to it (NRO, Enclosure Map, 1779; RAF VAP CPE/UK/1926, 4031–4).

(2) CULTIVATION REMAINS. The common fields of the parish were enclosed by an Act of Parliament of 1779. Ridge-and-furrow of these fields exists on the ground or can be traced on air photographs over most of the old parish, except along the edges of the R. Nene, and in a number of low-lying formerly marshy areas elsewhere (e.g. SP 690590, now obliterated by the M1 motorway, 703590 and 707579). The ridge-and-furrow is arranged in furlongs set end-on or at right angles to each other in a strikingly rectangular layout. On the flood plain of the R. Nene (at SP 705597, now in Upton parish) a slightly raised circular 'island' of alluvium only 100 m. across has slight ridge-and-furrow on it. This suggests that almost every available piece of land in the parish was cultivated at some time. (RAF VAP CPE/UK/1926, 4029–36; CPE/UK/1994, 1174–6; F21 543/RAF/2409, 0138–42; F22 543/RAF/2409, 0138–43; 3G TUD/UK/118, 6028–31, 6050–5, 6112–4; FSL 6603, 2383–5)

37 LITCHBOROUGH
(OS 1:10000 ^a SP 65 NW, ^b SP 65 SW)

The roughly triangular parish, covering some 675 hectares, is bounded on the N. by an E.-flowing tributary of the R. Nene and on the S.W. by a stream flowing S.E. towards the R. Tove. Much of the higher ground in the S., above 145 m. above OD, is covered by Boulder Clay. From there the land slopes N. across Northampton Sand, Upper Lias Clay and Marlstone Rock to the stream at 100 m. above OD. Clay and sandstones are also exposed along the valley in the S.W. No prehistoric or Roman material has been found in the parish.

MEDIEVAL AND LATER

^b(1) MANOR HOUSE SITE (SP 633542), lies immediately S. of the church, on Northampton Sand at 146 m. above OD. Baker (Hist. of Northants., I (1822–30), 407) said that the medieval manor house 'stood in the inclosure called The Spinney and was taken down about fifty years ago'. On the Tithe Map of 1843 (NRO) the large paddock S. of the church is called The Spinney. The most prominent earthworks in the area are a group of large stone-pits on the N. side but these have cut through and partly destroyed a number of low banks of which fragments still survive to the S. and S.W. of the quarries. It would appear that the quarries were dug into the site of the manor house itself, perhaps for the foundation stones. In the 19th century the area was turned into a small deer park belonging to Litchborough House and was bounded by a continuous stone wall which still exists. Earthworks to the S. of the quarry may relate to this period. They include at least three shallow rectangular ponds and a rectangular enclosure 50 m. by 25 m. bounded by a low bank and ditch, as well as other shallow quarries, all cut into earlier slight ridge-and-furrow. (RAF VAP CPE/UK/1926, 5044–5; air photographs in NMR)

^b(2) SETTLEMENT REMAINS (SP 631542), formerly part of Litchborough, lie on the S. side of the main street, W. of the church, on Northampton Sand at 144 m. above OD. The village now consists of little more than a single street running N.E.-S.W. with a small green near the church and houses on both sides, except on the high bank S. of Litchborough House where there are fragmentary remains of house-sites. On the Tithe Map of 1843 (NRO) no houses are shown here except for three buildings at the N.E. end near the church. These have now gone. The street has been realigned at this point, presumably to enlarge the grounds of Litchborough House, and some of the earthworks have been cut away. This took place after 1843. (RAF VAP CPE/UK/1926, 5044–5)

^b(3) PONDS (SP 636536), lie S.E. of the village, on the N. side of the road to Cold Higham, on Boulder Clay at 162 m. above OD. The site consists of a rectangular pond with, immediately to the E., a square flat island, 20 m. by 15 m., completely surrounded by a broad water-filled ditch between 5 m. and 12 m. wide. On the Tithe Map of 1843 (NRO) neither feature is depicted, though the paddock in which they lie is called Windmill Pool. It is possible

that the moated feature is the site of a former windmill. Some unglazed sherds, presumably medieval or later, were found recently in the centre of the island (NM Records).

b(4) POND (SP 631547), lies in the valley of a small N.E.-flowing stream immediately N. of the village, on Upper Lias Clay at 122 m. above OD. The roughly rectangular water-filled pond 60 m. by 40 m. has a U-shaped island in the centre. No date or purpose can be assigned to it, though it is perhaps 18th or 19th-century in origin. It is not shown on the Tithe Map of 1843 (NRO) but is on a slightly earlier map (OS 1st ed. 1 in. map, 1834). In 1843 the area was called Paradise.

(5) CULTIVATION REMAINS. In the early 17th century there were three open fields in the parish known as Radmore, Windmill and High Cross Fields, together with an area of woodland called The Heath. Radmore Field, which occupied the E. part of the parish, was enclosed by private agreement in 1647 and all the rest, including The Heath, by another agreement in 1711 (G. Baker, *Hist. of Northants.*, I (1822–30), 404).

Ridge-and-furrow of these fields exists on the ground or can be traced on air photographs over large areas of the parish and especially in the S.W. where almost the complete layout is recoverable. It is arranged in end-on and interlocked furlongs, many of reversed-S form and some up to 400 m. in length. There is evidence of the joining together of former end-on furlongs in a number of places, notably to the N.E. of the village, S. of the Bugbrooke Road (SP 642548), where the ridges are twisted at a sharp angle as they pass over a former headland between two furlongs. Several hollowed access-ways or lanes passing between furlongs survive or can be seen on air photographs, especially W. and S.W. of the village (SP 628541, 626539 and 626536). (RAF VAP CPE/UK/1926, 4043–9, 5041–8; CPE/UK/1994, 4167–70)

38 MAIDFORD
(OS 1:10000 a SP 65 SW, b SP 55 SE)

The parish is small, less than 440 hectares, and lies on a S.-facing slope drained by streams on the S.W. and N.E. boundaries. From the stream in the S.W., flowing at some 130 m. above OD, the land rises across bands of glacial sands and gravels, and outcrops of Upper Lias Clay, Northampton Sand and Oolitic limestones to an expanse of Boulder Clay at about 170 m. above OD. No finds of prehistoric or Roman date are recorded from the parish but the earthworks of Maidford village (1) are of interest.

MEDIEVAL AND LATER

A hoard of forty silver coins dating from Elizabeth I to Charles I is said to have been found in 1910, perhaps near the parish boundary with Farthingstone (Northants SMR).

a(1) SETTLEMENT REMAINS (centred SP 610525; Fig. 84), formerly part of Maidford, lie in and around the village on Northampton Sand and Upper Lias Clay at about 150 m. above OD. The surviving records give no indication of any marked reduction of population and it is unlikely that the earthworks represent an extensive area of settlement.

Maidford is first mentioned in Domesday Book where it is listed as a single manor with a recorded population of 18, including a priest (VCH *Northants.*, I (1902), 331, 372). In 1301, 32 people paid the Lay Subsidy (PRO, E179/155/31) and in 1377, 63 people over the age of 14 paid the Poll Tax (PRO, E179/155/27). The Hearth Tax of 1673 was paid by 47 householders (PRO, E179/254/14) and this agrees with Bridges (*Hist. of Northants.*, I (1791), 247) who recorded that there were 49 houses in Maidford in about 1720.

The present village consists of a main street running N.W.-S.E. across the valley of a small stream with the church and manor house on its N.E. side, and with a rectangular arrangement of lanes on the S.W. side. It is not clear whether these lanes represent a deliberately planned addition to an earlier single-street village. The surviving earthworks on the N.W. side of the rectangular lane system consist of little more than a bank and boundary ditch. These add to the impression that this part of the village has been planned. On the N.E. side of the village, N.W. of the church, now completely destroyed by a housing estate, were other earthworks consisting of a boundary bank and traces of internal closes. The only other feature of note is a shallow hollow-way which runs from the N.E. of the ponds (2), crosses the existing main road and continues through the ridge-and-furrow to the S.E. (RAF VAP CPE/UK/1926, 3050–1; CPE/UK/1994, 4166–7; air photographs in NMR)

a(2) FISHPONDS (SP 610524; Fig. 84), lie in the centre of Maidford village in the bottom of a shallow valley draining S.W., on Upper Lias Clay between 150 m. and 146 m. above OD. Five ponds, four to the N.E. of the main street and one to the S.W., still exist though the northernmost is probably not associated with the others and may be partly natural. The other ponds are roughly rectangular with low dams up to 1.5 m. high at their lower ends. Their date is unknown but they are presumably medieval in origin, perhaps associated with the manor house to the N. They are shown much as they are now on the Tithe Map of 1846 (NRO).

a(3) MOUND (SP 60565385), stands against the Farthingstone parish boundary in the N. of the parish, on Boulder Clay at 175 m. above OD. The mound is 28 m. in diam. and 1 m. high with a slight depression in the summit, and is surrounded by a shallow ditch 5 m. wide. The adjacent ridge-and-furrow appears to respect it. It may be the site of a windmill, although there was at least one other windmill in the parish in the 19th century (SP 604531; NRO, Tithe Map).

a(4) SITE OF WATERMILL (SP 605519), S.W. of the village, on the parish boundary, on Upper Lias Clay at 130 m.

above OD. The mill buildings survived until a few years ago and their foundations are still visible. A broad mill leat or pond, now dry, to the N. of these buildings extends along the contour, well above the stream. The site is shown correctly on OS 1:2500 plans.

(5) CULTIVATION REMAINS. The common fields of Maidford were enclosed by an Act of Parliament of 1778 but no details of them are known. Ridge-and-furrow of these fields exists on the ground or can be traced on air photographs over the greater part of the parish, arranged in end-on and interlocked furlongs, many of reversed-S form. In some furlongs there appears to be considerable variation in the width of ridges, which are 2 m.–10 m. wide (e.g. SP 603527, 611530). (RAF VAP CPE/UK/1926, 1049–50, 3045–53, 5047–51; CPE/UK/1994, 4164–8, 4093)

39 MARSTON ST. LAWRENCE
(OS 1:10000 [a] SP 54 SW, [b] SP 54 SE)

The parish occupies about 660 hectares of land sloping generally S. and drained by several small streams including a S.W.-flowing brook which defines the S. edge of the parish and is a tributary of the R. Cherwell. Most of the area is covered by Upper Lias Clay between 115 m. and 150 m. above OD, but on the higher ground on the N. and E., with a maximum height of 175 m. above OD, outcrops of Northampton Sand and Oolite Limestone are capped by Boulder Clay. The parish is notable for the large number of prehistoric and Roman finds, mainly discovered by intensive fieldwork carried out by a local archae-

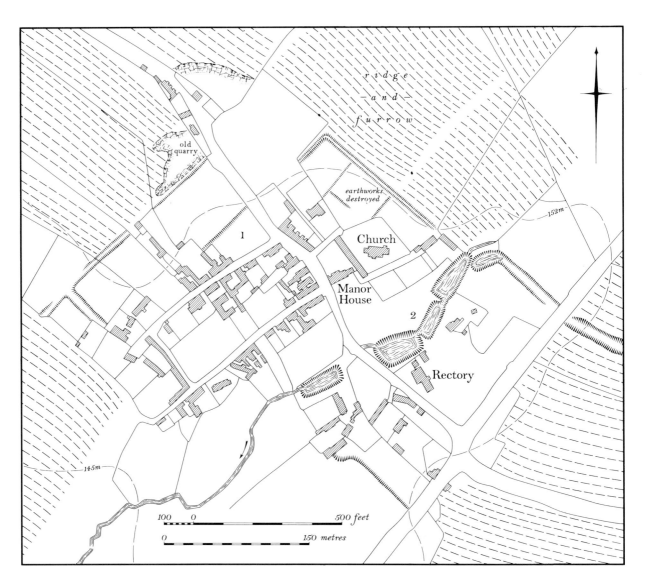

Fig. 84 MAIDFORD (1) Settlement remains, (2) Fishponds

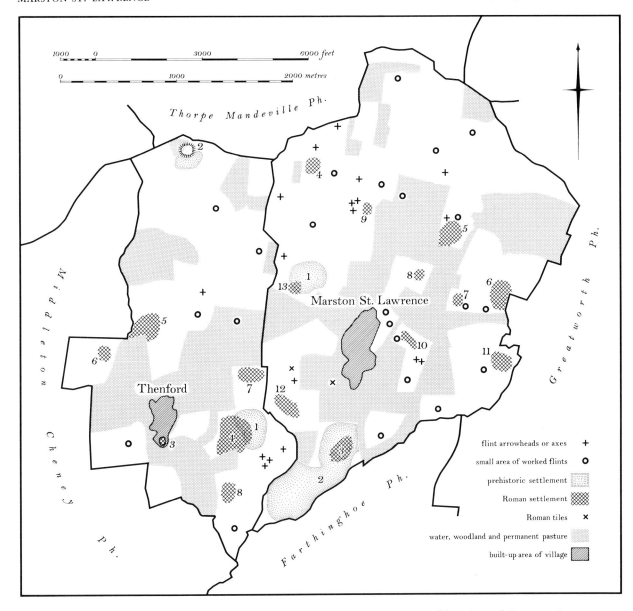

Fig. 85   MARSTON ST. LAWRENCE and THENFORD   Prehistoric and Roman sites

ologist over many years. The hamlet of Westhorp, now in Greatworth parish (8), lay in Marston St. Lawrence until the late 19th century.

PREHISTORIC AND ROMAN (Fig. 85)

The parish of Marston St. Lawrence has been intensively examined during the last 20 years by D. J. Barrett, who has kept detailed records of his field-walking. Almost all the sites and finds listed below, as well as some of those in the adjacent parishes of Thenford and Greatworth, have been found by him and most of the material is still in his possession. The implications of the results of this work, compared with the lack of knowledge elsewhere in the area covered by this Inventory, are discussed in the Sec-

tional Preface (p. xxiii). The placing of this wealth of material into numbered monuments is to a great extent arbitrary. Almost every field not under permanent pasture has produced finds, notably worked flints. These unassociated finds are here listed under categories:

(a) A Palaeolithic hand-axe (SP 532418).

(b) Flint arrowheads of various types including tranchet, leaf-shaped   and   barbed-and-tanged   (SP   53414419, 54354379,   52954360,   53614374,   52994310,   53574353, 54364340, 53074205, 54154222).

(c) Fragments of a stone axe (SP 53474413).

(d) Small scatters of worked flints of Neolithic and Bronze Age type (SP 539446, 546441, 543440, 534438, 533433, 538437, 540436, 544434, 538426, 539425, 539424, 540421, 544427, 547426, 546421, 537416, 543418).

(e) Roman tile scatters, apparently not associated with pottery (SP 530421, 534430).

[a](1) PREHISTORIC SETTLEMENT (centred SP 532429), covers some 7 hectares N.W. of the village, on Upper Lias Clay between 130 m. and 137 m. above OD. Finds from the area made over many years include some flakes, apparently of Mesolithic type, very large quantities of worked and waste flints of late Neolithic or Bronze Age type, and a small quantity of pottery described as Peterborough ware. Ten flint arrowheads of various types are also recorded. (For Roman material from the same area, see (13))

[a](2) PREHISTORIC SETTLEMENT (centred SP 533413), S.W. of the village, on Upper Lias Clay between 107 m. and 125 m. above OD. The material is spread over about 30 hectares extending about 1 km. along the N.W. side of a small S.W.-flowing stream (SP 528409–536416). The land on the opposite side of the stream, in Farthinghoe parish, is permanent grassland and thus no finds have been recorded there. The finds include a few microliths and very large quantities of late Neolithic or Bronze Age worked and waste flints. Specific objects discovered include a number of scrapers, 27 flint arrowheads of various types, fragments of three polished flint axes, and three stone axes, one of group VI, one of group XX and one of.tuff. (For Iron Age and Roman material at the extreme N.E. end of this area, see (3) and for Saxon pottery, see below).

[a](3) IRON AGE AND ROMAN SETTLEMENT (SP 534414), S. of the village, at the N.E. end of the prehistoric settlement (2) on Upper Lias Clay at 122 m. above OD. Roman tiles and pottery, mainly of the 2nd and 3rd centuries, have been found over some 4 hectares, and two Roman coins have also come from the area. In addition, five 2nd or 3rd-century urns, one containing bones, were found during pipe-laying in 1964. A small quantity of pottery tentatively described as of Iron Age type has also been found.

[a](4) ROMAN SETTLEMENT (SP 532438), in the N.W. of the parish, on Northampton Sand at 170 m. above OD. Roman pottery has been found over an area of about 2 hectares. A smaller quantity of pottery has been recorded further N. (SP 532440).

[a](5) ROMAN SETTLEMENT (SP 544433), N.E. of the village, on Northampton Sand and limestone, at 160 m. above OD. Roman pottery is scattered over about 3 hectares.

[a](6) ROMAN SETTLEMENT (SP 548427), about 600 m. S.E. of (5), on Northampton Sand and limestone between 152 m. and 165 m. above OD. Roman pottery and tile extends over about 2.5 hectares.

[a](7) ROMAN SETTLEMENT (?) (SP 544427), 300 m. W. of (6), on Upper Lias Clay at 130 m. above OD. A small scatter of Roman sherds, as well as a few worked flints, have been found.

[a](8) ROMAN SETTLEMENT (?) (SP 541429), 400 m. N.W. of (7), on Upper Lias Clay at 137 m. above OD. A few sherds of Roman pottery are recorded.

[a](9) ROMAN SETTLEMENT (?) (SP 537434), on Marston Hill, on Northampton Sand at 160 m. above OD. A small scatter of Roman sherds has been noted.

[a](10) ROMAN SETTLEMENT (?) (SP 540424), immediately E. of the village, on Upper Lias Clay at 122 m. above OD. Two small areas of Roman pottery have been found.

[a](11) ROMAN SETTLEMENT (?) (SP 548422), in the E. of the parish, immediately S. of Westhorp, on Upper Lias Clay at 145 m. above OD. A small quantity of Roman pottery and tiles has been noted.

[a](12) ROMAN SETTLEMENT (?) (SP 530418), S.W. of the village, close to the Thenford parish boundary, on Upper Lias Clay at 125 m. above OD. A small scatter of Roman pottery and tile has been found. Three flint arrowheads and part of a flaked stone axe have come from the same area.

[a](13) ROMAN SETTLEMENT (?) (SP 532429), on the same site as the prehistoric settlement (1). Small quantities of Roman sherds have been discovered.

MEDIEVAL AND LATER

Pottery, said to be of middle Saxon type, has been found to the S. of the village on the site of the Roman settlement (3) (SP 535415).

[a](14) SAXON CEMETERY (SP 542439), lay on a limestone ridge in the N. of the parish, at 170 m. above OD. After the discovery of a single skeleton in 1842, an excavation was carried out in 1843. This revealed 32 inhumations, all with their heads to the S.W. and all but three with grave goods, including two pairs of saucer brooches, four pairs of small-long brooches, a large square-headed brooch and a bronze clasp. There were also four urns, three of which definitely contained cremations. The skeleton of a horse was also discovered. The cemetery has been tentatively dated to the late 6th century. (*Archaeologia*, 33 (1849), 326–34; Meaney, *Gazetteer*, (1964), 192; J. N. L. Myres, *A Corpus of Anglo-Saxon Pottery of the Pagan Period* (1977), Nos. 800, 3126, 3127; NM)

[a](15) SETTLEMENT REMAINS (SP 537425; Fig. 14), formerly part of Marston St. Lawrence village, lay in and around the village on both sides of a small S.E.-flowing stream, on Upper Lias Clay and Marlstone Rock at 122 m. above OD. Marston St. Lawrence consists of three distinct parts. To the S. of the stream is a single street with a church, a vicarage and a few cottages. A pasture field to the S. of the church has disturbed ground which may be the site of former buildings, but nothing is shown there on the Enclosure Map of 1760 (NRO). To the N. of the stream the main street turns W. and then N. and, together with a small lane to the N. called Field View, forms a neat rectangular block with houses scattered along the main street. To the E. of the street, behind the existing buildings, are the remains of about six abandoned closes bounded by shallow ditches and low banks. At least three of these are shown as hedged on the 1760 map. At their E. ends the closes meet a continuous N.-S. scarp 1 m. high which is the W. side of a former hollow-way. The E. side of this hollow-way has been destroyed by ploughing, but it is shown as a back lane on the 1760 map. This lane, parallel to the main street, emphasizes the rectangular layout. The 1760 map suggests that at least three other lanes, already largely abandoned by the 18th century, ran E.-W. across this part of the village. On the W. side of the main street

a rather narrow lane with a series of abandoned closes along it runs S.W. to the stream.

The plan of the village, with its three constituent parts, may represent a sequence of development. It is possible that the early village lay around the church and that the rectangular block to the N. is a planned extension with subsequent growth to the S.W. Medieval pottery of 11th to 14th-century date has been found at four places in the village during building work and pipe-laying (SP 53484219, 53474230, 53564231 and 53804222; inf. D. J. Barratt). (RAF VAP CPE/UK/1926, 3212–4)

^a(16) PONDS (SP 536421–536415; partly on Fig. 14), lie S. of the village, along the valley of a stream, on Middle Lias Clay between 115 m. and 122 m. above OD. There is one large curving pond with, below it, five small rectangular ones, all with massive dams up to 2 m. high. Each of the two lowest has a long rectangular island within it. All the ponds have 19th-century sluices in their dams and appear to be the result of landscaping for Marston House which overlooks the N. pond and which was rebuilt in the first part of the 18th century. The ponds existed in their present form in 1760 (Enclosure Map, NRO), but they may have originated as medieval fishponds. (RAF VAP CPE/UK/1926, 3212–4)

(17) CULTIVATION REMAINS. The common fields of Marston St. Lawrence were enclosed by an Act of Parliament of 1760. However, all the S. part of the parish and a small part in the N. was already enclosed by that date and had been since at least the early 18th century (J. Bridges, *Hist. of Northants.*, I (1791), 181). Ridge-and-furrow of these fields exists on the ground or can be traced on air photographs around and N. of the village, but very little can be seen in the areas of Northampton Sand in the N., presumably because modern cultivation has removed the slight remains there. Where it does survive it corresponds exactly with the furlongs depicted on the Enclosure Map (NRO). It is arranged in end-on and interlocked furlongs many with reversed-S curves and is carefully arranged at right angles to the contours of any major slopes. To the N.W. of the village there are some massive headlands with the ridges ending against them in high rounded mounds (SP 532428 and 534429). Most of the S. of the parish which was already enclosed by the early 18th century also has similar ridge-and-furrow over it, showing clearly that it was once part of the common fields. (RAF VAP CPE/UK/1926, 1214–5, 3212–5; CPE/UK/1994, 1025–8)

40   MIDDLETON CHENEY
(OS 1:10000 ^a SP 44 SE, ^b SP 54 SW, ^c SP 43 NE, ^d SP 53 NW)

The parish, lying against the Oxfordshire county boundary, is of irregular shape and covers almost 1000 hectares. The rolling landscape, entirely on Lias clays and Marlstone Rock between 100 m. and 160 m. above OD, is made up of three ridges between the valleys of two small S.-flowing streams.

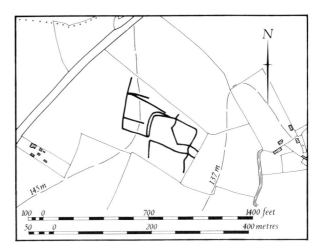

Fig. 86   MIDDLETON CHENEY (1)   Enclosures

The modern parish includes the village and lands of Overthorpe, formerly part of Warkworth parish, and the village of Middleton Cheney is in two distinct parts each lying at the head of a small valley. Apart from the prehistoric or Roman enclosures (1) little of archaeological importance has been recorded in the parish.

PREHISTORIC AND ROMAN

^a(1) ENCLOSURES (SP 49454215; Fig. 86), W. of Middleton Cheney village, on Middle Lias clays and silts at 142 m. above OD. Air photographs (CUAP, ABW87, 88) show cropmarks of a group of overlapping, sub-rectangular enclosures and ditches covering a total area of about 2 hectares.

^b(2) PREHISTORIC SETTLEMENT (SP 522406), in the extreme S.E. of the parish, on limestone at 107 m. above OD. A dense scatter of worked flints of late Neolithic and Bronze Age type covers an area of about 5 hectares. Part of a polished flint axe and a flint arrowhead have also been found (inf. D. J. Barratt).

^b(3) ROMAN SETTLEMENT (SP 517404), in the S.E. of the parish, on limestone at 122 m. above OD. Roman pottery has been found over an area of about 3 hectares (inf. D. J. Barratt).

MEDIEVAL AND LATER

(4) CULTIVATION REMAINS. The common fields of Middleton Cheney were enclosed by an Act of Parliament of 1769. On the Enclosure Map of about 1770 (NRO) most of the land attributable to the village of Middleton is shown as being under common fields. The furlongs and access-ways depicted on it agree exactly with the ridge-and-furrow which still exists or can be traced on air photographs. Large areas of ridge-and-furrow can be recovered, arranged in end-on and interlocked furlongs except along the steep-sided S.-draining valleys where it lies at right angles to the contours. There is a good example of two

former end-on furlongs being ploughed as one, with the ridges riding over the earlier headland (SP 510417).

The common fields of the hamlet of Overthorpe, which occupied the W. part of the present parish, were enclosed together with those of Warkworth by an Act of Parliament of 1764 (G. Baker, *Hist. of Northants.*, I (1822–30), 738). Ridge-and-furrow of these fields survives on the ground or can be traced on air photographs only on the low clay area around and N. of the hamlet where it is arranged in end-on and interlocked furlongs. (RAF VAP CPE/UK/1926, 1205–11, 3205–11, 5211; F21 58/RAF/1567, 0050–1, 0081–2; F22 58/RAF/1567, 0050–1)

41 MILTON MALSOR
(OS 1:10000 [a] SP 75 NW, [b] SP 75 SW, [c] SP 75 NE, [d] SP 75 SE)

The modern parish is roughly rectangular, covering only about 450 hectares. The N. part of the medieval parish N.E. of the M1 motorway is now incorporated within Northampton. The area is rather flat, sloping gently N. from 100 m. to 70 m. above OD and much of it is covered by glacial sands and gravels and Boulder Clay, apart from an expanse of Upper Lias Clay in the S. and bands of Marlstone Rock and clays and silts in the valleys W. and N. of the village. A number of finds of the prehistoric, Roman and Saxon periods have come from sand pits to the S. and W. of the village. Some of the latter may relate to the undated enclosure to the N.W. (Rothersthorpe (1)).

PREHISTORIC AND ROMAN

A polished stone axe of quartz dolerite has been found in the parish and some sherds of early Iron Age pottery were discovered during sand-extraction in 1975 at SP 728560 (NM Records).

[a](1) BRONZE AGE BURIAL (SP 72755625), discovered in a sand-pit in the W. of the parish, at 83 m. above OD. A Collared Urn of the Primary Series, with Beaker-type decoration was discovered in 1965; it contained a cremation (*Ant. J.*, 47 (1967), 198–208; OS Record Cards).

[a](2) ROMAN SETTLEMENT (?) and BURIALS (SP 727557), found during sand-extraction in 1953. Roman pottery, a quern and human skeletons are recorded (OS Record Cards; NM Records).

[a](3) ROMAN SETTLEMENT (?) and KILN (SP 731552), lies S.W. of the village at 80 m. above OD. Roman pottery and fragments of kiln bars were found in a sand-pit in 1947, together with the Saxon finds listed below (6) (NM Records; OS Record Cards).

[a](4) ROMAN SETTLEMENT (?) (SP 738556), lies on the E. side of the village at about 78 m. above OD. Rubbish pits revealed during sand-working contained Roman sherds and spindle whorls, as well as the Saxon finds listed below (5) (NM Records; OS Record Cards).

MEDIEVAL AND LATER

[a](5) SAXON SETTLEMENT (?) (SP 738556), lies on the same site as the possible Roman settlement (4), 120 m. E. of the medieval church, but outside the boundary of the old enclosures of the village as shown on a map of 1780 (NRO). Saxon sherds and loom-weights were discovered here during sand-excavation in 1964 (NM Records; OS Record Cards).

[a](6) SAXON CEMETERY (SP 731552), on the same site as the Roman material (3). Two vessels were discovered, one a footed *Buckelurne* and the other a bowl, both of 4th or 5th-century types (NM Records; *J. Northants. Mus. and Art Gall.*, 6 (1969), 47; Meaney, *Gazetteer*, 192; J. N. L. Myres, *A Corpus of Anglo-Saxon Pottery of the Pagan Period* (1977), Nos. 807, 808).

[a](7) CLOSES, MOAT AND POND (SP 735554), lie immediately N. and N.E. of the manor house, on gravel at 79 m. above OD. A small pasture field sloping E. to a stream has a number of scarps and shallow ditches within it, perhaps the boundaries of former closes. At the E. end, near the stream, is a rectangular embanked pond. A flat island, 40 m. square, surrounded by a broad ditch 10 m. wide and 1.5 m. deep, at the N. edge of the site, may be a moat. The remains are perhaps associated with the adjacent manor house. (RAF VAP CPE/UK/1926, 5027–9; FSL6565, 1798–1800; air photographs in NMR)

(8) CULTIVATION REMAINS. The common fields of the parish were enclosed by an Act of Parliament of 1799. Before that there were no definite boundaries between Collingtree and Milton Malsor (NRO, Enclosure Map, 1780; B. E. Evans, *The Story of Milton Malsor* (c. 1925), 158–9, 181). Ridge-and-furrow of these fields is visible on the ground or on air photographs over most of the medieval parish, particularly over the clay area in the S. and the N. part of the parish which is now in Northampton. Little survives in the W. It is all arranged in end-on and interlocked furlongs. In the N.E. several well-marked headlands are visible between end-on blocks of ridges (e.g. SP 741567 and 742563). Only a small area around the village appears to have been in old enclosures before 1780. No ridge-and-furrow can be traced within these limits. (RAF VAP CPE/UK/1926, 3027–30, 5026–30; 3G TUD/UK/118, 6026–7, 6055–8; F22 543/RAF/2409, 0142–4; FSL6565, 1798–1800, 1824–8)

42 MORETON PINKNEY
(OS 1:10000 [a] SP 54 NE, [b] SP 54 NW)

The parish, covering 990 hectares, lies across the valleys of several small streams flowing generally N. to join a tributary of the R. Cherwell; this W.-flowing tributary, at about 130 m. above OD, defines the N. boundary of the parish. Almost half the area is covered by Boulder Clay, but there are high outcrops of Northampton Sand rising to over 160 m. above OD, small areas of Upper Lias Clay and, immediately S. of the village, bands of limestones. Little of archaeological interest has been noted in the parish apart from the settlement remains around the village (1) and a possible deserted settlement (3).

MEDIEVAL AND LATER

[a](1) SETTLEMENT REMAINS (centred SP 572492; Fig. 13), lie W. of the village, on Upper Lias Clay at 135 m. above OD. The village of Moreton Pinkney has an unusual plan composed of two parts each centred on a green. It is not clear how such a plan has evolved unless the village is polyfocal, based on two separate settlements.

In the village there are several empty plots where houses formerly stood, but the largest area of earthworks lies immediately W. of the southern green. Long narrow closes bounded by low scarps or shallow ditches extend down the hillside towards the stream. These appear to be the abandoned gardens of houses which once stood on the W. side of the green but which had already disappeared by 1848 (NRO, Tithe Map). (RAF VAP CPE/UK/1926, 1057–8)

[a](2) POND (SP 571490; Fig. 13), lies in the bottom of a shallow W.-draining valley in the S.E. part of the village, S.W. of the church, on Upper Lias Clay at 137 m. above OD. A subrectangular pond, 50 m. by 20 m., has been formed by the cutting away of the valley side on the N. and the construction of a large bank or dam up to 2 m. high on the S. and W. The main dam on the W. has now been broken to allow water to drain from the pond. In the surrounding area there are several undatable drainage ditches. The pond is probably a medieval fishpond or mill-pond. (RAF VAP CPE/UK/1926, 1057–8)

[a](3) DESERTED HAMLET (?) (SP 567487), lies S.W. of the village, on the W. side of the road to Culworth, on Boulder Clay at 137 m. above OD. Nothing is known about the history of this site and no name can be attributed to it. Only excavation could establish whether it is an abandoned settlement.

The earthworks lie at the S.E. end of a group of small paddocks and consist of a row of rectangular ditched closes lying alongside the road, with a common boundary ditch at their N.W. ends. Some disturbed areas within the closes may be sites of former houses. (RAF VAP CPE/UK/1926, 1058–9)

(4) CULTIVATION REMAINS. The common fields of the parish were finally enclosed by an Act of Parliament of 1760. However, part of the parish, an area of unknown size apparently called The West Field, was enclosed in 1624 (J. Bridges, *Hist. of Northants.*, I (1791), 250).

Ridge-and-furrow of these fields exists on the ground or can be traced on air photographs over almost the whole parish, arranged in end-on or interlocked furlongs often of reversed-S form. Several lanes that radiate from the village appear from their hollowed form and the way the adjacent ridge-and-furrow terminates against them to be original access-ways through the common fields. Even where the ridge-and-furrow has been ploughed out the former head-lands survive as broad banks up to 12 m. wide and 0.25 m. high (e.g. SP 558489). In this parish, as elsewhere in the area, the term Banky Ground is given to well-marked ridge-and-furrow preserved in pasture (NRO, Tithe Map, 1848; SP 557478). (RAF VAP CPE/UK/1926, 1054–63; CPE/UK/ 1994, 2096–97, 3095–8)

UNDATED

(5) MOUND (unlocated). Bridges (*Hist. of Northants.*, I (1791), 250) records that somewhere in the parish there was a 'barrow of the same kind as that in Sulgrave parish' presumably meaning the mound on the N. boundary of that parish (Sulgrave (8)). No mound has been located in Moreton Pinkney and it is possible that Bridges was referring to the mound close to the parish boundary in the S.E. near Plumpton (Weston and Weedon (9)).

43 NEWBOTTLE
(OS 1:10000 [a] SP 53 NW, [b] SP 53 SW, [c] SP 53 NE)

The long parish, of irregular shape, now covers 925 hectares but has undergone several changes of its boundaries (Fig. 82). It incorporates the village and lands of Charlton and the deserted hamlet and lands of Purston as well as the territory of the village of Newbottle itself which is also now deserted. The parish slopes generally W., drained by S.W.-flowing streams. The high ground in the S. and E. between 120 m. and 150 m. above OD is an extensive outcrop of Great Oolite Limestone and Northampton Sand, which gives way to Upper Lias Clay in the W. and on the valley sides. The possible implications of the complex relationship between this parish and its neighbours, King's Sutton and Farthinghoe, have already been published (F. M. Brown and C. C. Taylor, 'Settlement and Land Use in Northants.' in *BAR*, International Series (Supplementary), 68 (1978), 77–89).

The small Iron Age hill fort known as Rainsborough Camp (1) on the S. boundary of the parish, is perhaps the most important monument, but the deserted village of Newbottle (3) and the garden remains and settlement remains at Purston (5) and (4) are also noteworthy.

PREHISTORIC AND ROMAN

A Mesolithic core is recorded from the S. of the parish (Banbury Museum; CBA *Research Report*, 20 (1977), 217) though the published grid (SP 520430) locates it in Aynho parish.

Two Roman gold coins were found in the parish in the early part of the 18th century, one of Titus from Charlton and one of Vespasian 'a little distance from Rainsborough Camp' (J. Bridges, *Hist. of Northants.*, I (1791), 190; VCH *Northants.*, I (1902), 216). Roman pottery, one complete pewter plate and a fragment of a second, are recorded as having been found in Hill Spinney. No wood of that name is known and it seems most likely that the finds were made during extensive quarrying in Newbottle Spinney (around SP 517365). (NM; VCH *Northants.*, I (1902), 218; CBA Group 9, *Newsletter*, 6 (1976), 218)

Several undated skeletons are recorded from Newbottle Spinney, and these also may have come from the stone quarries (A. Beesley, *Hist. of Banbury* (1841), 35).

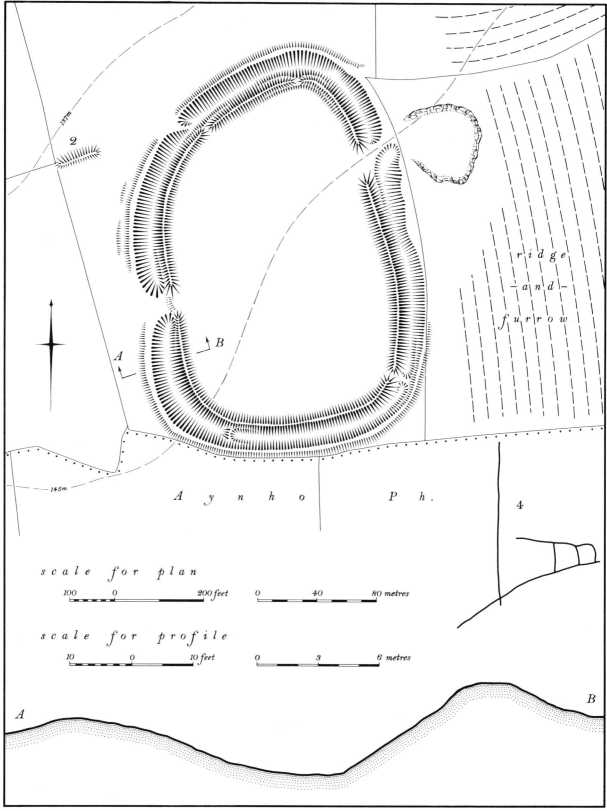

Fig. 87 AYNHO (4) Enclosures and ditches, NEWBOTTLE (1) Hill fort, (2) Mound

[b](1) HILL FORT (SP 526348; Fig. 87), known as Rainsborough Camp, lies on the northern edge of a level plateau of limestone in the extreme S. of the parish at 145 m. above OD. There are extensive views to the N. and N.W. across the Cherwell valley and over much of King's Sutton and Newbottle parishes, but to the S. and S.E. the land is flat.

The fort comprises a roughly oval area of some 2.6 hectares, bounded by a double bank and ditch. The inner bank is up to 3 m. high above the interior with an outer ditch 4 m. deep below the summit. Beyond is an outer bank, reduced by cultivation on the W. and N. to no more than 0.5 m. high and completely removed on the E. On the S. it still survives up to 1 m. high. The outer ditch has disappeared completely except for slight traces along the W. side. The main inner rampart has a dry-stone wall, in places still 0.75 m. high, set half way up the outer slope. This is visible over large lengths of the rampart and was presumably once a continuous feature.

There are several gaps through the defences. The minor ones on the N. and N.W. were made in the 17th century for local traffic, and magnetometer surveys carried out during the excavations showed that only the western entrance was original. The eastern one may be Roman. The interior is flat and featureless, having been under cultivation in the past. The site was extensively excavated between 1961 and 1965 and the prehistoric phases were published in full (*PPS*, 33 (1967), 207–306). Only a brief summary of the results is therefore given here. Eight phases of occupation were established:

1. Early Iron Age I (possibly 5th/6th centuries BC). Pre-fort occupation represented by post-holes and occupation debris.

2. Early Iron Age IIa (possibly 5th century BC). Bivallate fort constructed. Simple entrance on the W. had stone guardrooms within the inturns. One hut and two roofed working hollows in the interior also probably belonged to this phase.

3. Early Iron Age IIb (possibly early 4th century BC). A period of occupation with replacements or repairs made to the entrance, and the inner ditch cleaned out.

4. Early Iron Age IIIa (possibly early 4th century BC). Fort burnt and guardrooms destroyed.

5. Early Iron Age IIIb (4th to 2nd century BC). Fort perhaps abandoned.

6. Early Iron Age IV (late 2nd century BC). Site refortified and entrance rebuilt. One hut and a pit indicated that the interior was reoccupied.

7. Roman I (late 1st century AD). Occupation debris.

8. Roman II (3rd to 4th century AD). Stone building erected near entrance which was remodelled.

In the 18th century the inner bank was heightened and the dry-stone walling added to it. The inner ditch was deepened. This was carried out about 1772 as part of a landscaping scheme. Among the other recorded finds from the site in addition to those made during the excavation are 'broken pots, glass and ashes' found *c*. 1700 when the interior was ploughed and levelled (J. Bridges, *Hist. of Northants.*, I (1791), 190), 'numerous Roman coins, now all lost' (G. Baker, *Hist. of Northants.*, I (1822–30), 666), 'a piece of an antique Helmet' (J. Morton, *Nat. Hist. of Northants.* (1712), 86–7), 'a large quantity of gold coins' (A. Beesley, *Hist. of Banbury* (1841) 36), an iron arrowhead

(*PSA*, I (1861), 324; *JBAA*, 17 (1861), 70), and pots and glass found during the cutting of a gap in the rampart in the late 17th century (Bodleian Ms. Wood D. 18 (8563), Fol. iii and Wood F. 32 (8494), Fol. 122).

The possibility that the fort was the centre of a large Iron Age estate which remained intact into the medieval period has been suggested (F. M. Brown and C. C. Taylor, op. cit.). (RAF VAP CPE/UK/1926, 4210–1; CPE/UK/1929, 3170–2; 106G/UK/1488, 4269–70; CUAP, AAV21, AJJ16, AML59, ANT73)

[b](2) MOUND (SP 524349; Fig. 87), lies on the edge of a slope 60 m. N.W. of the N.W. corner of Rainsborough Camp (1), on limestone at 146 m. above OD. The mound is 30 m. long and 4 m. wide and only 0.25 m. high above the adjacent ground to the S., but almost 1 m. high above the ground to the N. The N. side has dry-stone walling set into it. It is traditionally known as 'The Barrow'. In its present form it appears to be a relatively modern feature and indeed the dry-stone walling must date from the late 18th century when the hill fort was given a similar wall. However it was perhaps only altered then for Morton (*Nat. Hist. of Northants.* (1712), 86) refers to a small 'piece of ground entrenched' to the S.E. of Rainsborough. As Morton appears to have reversed the compass points when describing the fort, this is probably the feature to which he refers.

For enclosures and ditches immediately S. of Rainsborough Camp (1), see Aynho (4).

For possible Roman Road 56a, see Appendix.

MEDIEVAL AND LATER

[a](3) DESERTED VILLAGE OF NEWBOTTLE (SP 524368; Fig. 82 and 88), lies around the now isolated church, vicarage and manor house, on land sloping W. on Northampton Sand and Oolite Limestone at 140 m. above OD. The village is first recorded in 1086 when Domesday Book lists it as a single manor with a total recorded population of 32 (VCH *Northants.*, I (1902), 331). However this figure certainly referred to more than the village itself for the manor is described as *cum appendiciis suis*, and the entry almost certainly includes Little Purston, now in King's Sutton parish, and perhaps part of Charlton. In 1301, 23 people at Newbottle paid the Lay Subsidy (PRO, E179/155/31) but again this figure may be inflated by the inclusion of other places. The village was recognised as an independent vill in the *Nomina Villarum* of 1316. In 1488 six houses there were destroyed and three hundred acres of land enclosed by Henry Lord Grey. In 1524 only three people paid the Lay Subsidy (PRO, E179/155/146) and by 1547 a thousand sheep were being grazed on the land of the village (K. J. Allison, *et al.*, *The Deserted Villages of Northants.* (1966), 43). By the mid 19th century the village was exactly as it is today (NRO, Tithe Map, 1844).

Very little remains of the village earthworks. There is some uneven ground S. of the church and vicarage, but parts of this are shallow quarries and the rest is the site of temporary buildings constructed during the Second World War. To the N.W. of the manor house are the ploughed-over remains of some small rectangular closes, one with ridge-and-furrow within it, bounded by low scarps and shallow ditches. Before destruction these earthworks extended further S. and medieval pottery mainly of 14th-century date has been found in the area. Further S.W. two rectangular ponds lie within a small copse. These certainly existed in 1844. A little to the N. of the manor house (SP 525373) 'sheet bronze', a clay pipe bowl, lead and medieval and later pottery have been found (*Oxoniensia*, 36 (1972), 122). (RAF VAP CPE/UK/1926, 2210–11; air photographs in NMR)

[a](4) DESERTED HAMLET OF PURSTON (SP 518395; Figs. 82 and 89), lay in the N. of the parish, on Marlstone Rock at 113 m. above OD. The hamlet was the southernmost of two settlements, both with the same name, side by side and separated only by the parish boundary with King's Sutton but each having its own associated land unit. The documented history is given under the northern settlement of Purston (King's Sutton (11)).

Nothing survives of the settlement on the ground, the area having been ploughed and returned to grassland. On air photographs taken before this destruction (RAF VAP CPE/UK/1926, 2510–11) some slight traces of embanked closes

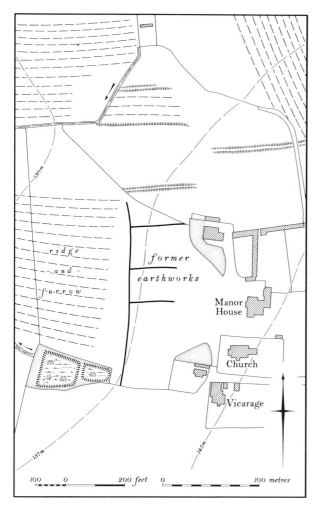

100   0   200 feet   0   100 metres

Fig. 88   NEWBOTTLE (3)   Deserted village

partly over-ploughed by later ridge-and-furrow are visible immediately S. of the parish boundary. It is possible that a street lay along the boundary.

[a](5) GARDEN REMAINS (SP 519394; Fig. 89), lay to the S.E. of the manor house of Great Purston, on Marlstone Rock between 114 m. and 152 m. above OD. Little is known of the history of the garden and almost all the earthworks have been destroyed. The site is of interest in that it appears to have covered an unusually large area.

The gardens, though apparently never finished, were clearly intended to provide a backcloth to the existing manor house extending from the main S. front of the house across generally level ground and then across the steeply rising ground further S. The house is partly of late 16th or early 17th-century date but the S. facade is of the late 17th century (N. Pevsner, *Northamptonshire* (1973), 379) and it is possible that the gardens are of the later period. The intended design appears to be more akin to mid or late 17th-century precepts.

There seem to have been three main parts to the garden. In the N., fronting the house but also extending E., was a large rectangular area covering some 8.5 hectares. At its S. end was a broad terrace ('a' on plan) which, though now ploughed down, is still 18 m. wide and 2 m. high. This terrace must have provided a walkway and a view over a formal garden between it and the house. However it is clear that the formal garden was never completed, for air photographs taken before modern ploughing (RAF VAP CPE/UK/1926, 5210–11) show that most of the area still had undamaged ridge-and-furrow on it. At the N. end of the area, close to the house, the air photographs show a rectangular layout of scarps and other disturbances which are overlaid by later ridge-and-furrow. These appear to be the remains of the deserted hamlet of Purston (4). In the N.E. corner of this section of the garden, within a small copse, is a pond with a rectangular 'moated' island in its S. part. This may also have been part of the garden design. The central section of the garden, beyond the terrace, lies on steeply sloping ground. In a typical late 16th or early 17th-century garden of this size there would have been a 'wilderness' or woodland, but the older air photographs show undisturbed ridge-and-furrow here and it seems unlikely that such a wilderness was ever laid out.

The third part of the garden lay further S., on top of the hill. On a map of Purston of 1768 (NRO) the large field here is called Mount Close and a circular feature described as 'Mount' is depicted at the N. end, overlooking the rest of the garden and the manor house. To the E., on flatter ground, is a small close called 'Bowling Green'. Both these features would be expected in a garden of the late 16th century. Again, however, the 1947 air photographs show undisturbed ridge-and-furrow in the area of the mount, though on the ground there is a low natural knoll at this point ('b' on plan). No trace remains of the bowling green, but the whole area was under cultivation in 1844 (NRO, Tithe Map of Newbottle).

[b](6) MOUND (SP 52603449), lies on Marlstone Rock, on land sloping N.E. at 130 m. above OD. The mound is now ploughed over, only 0.25 m. high and 14 m. in diam. In 1947 (RAF VAP CPE/UK/1926, 5210–11), before ploughing, it appears to have been considerably higher and was sur-

King's Sutton Ph.

107m

114 m

11

4

Manor House

N e w b o t t l e   P h.

122 m

King's

Sutton

Ph.

130 m

a

r i d g e

— a n d —

137 m

f u r r o w

145 m

152 m

'Mount'

b

M o u n t   C l o s e

1 7 6 8

100   0   300   600 feet

100   50   0   100 metres

Fig 89   KING'S SUTTON (11)   Deserted hamlet of Purston, NEWBOTTLE (4)   Deserted hamlet of
Purston, (5)   Garden remains

rounded by ridge-and-furrow. However the exact relationship with the latter is unclear.

(7) CULTIVATION REMAINS (Fig. 82). The complex pattern of settlements and land units in Newbottle makes it difficult to understand the arrangement of the medieval fields there. There were presumably at least three systems, those of Newbottle, Charlton and Purston.

The common fields of Charlton were enclosed by an Act of Parliament of 1772, but no map is known. Ridge-and-furrow of these fields exists on the ground and or can be traced on air photographs in only a few places within the land attributed to Charlton. Most of it lies S. and S.E. of the village, especially to the E. of Rainsborough Camp where it is arranged in end-on and interlocked furlongs. On the flat limestone areas N.E. of the village modern cultivation has destroyed all trace except along the valley sides where the ridges run at right angles to the contours.

The date of enclosure of the common fields of the deserted village of Newbottle is not known, except that three hundred acres were enclosed for pasture in 1488 and a thousand sheep were being kept there in 1547 (K. J. Allison et al., The Deserted Villages of Northants. (1966), 43). Only a few fragments of the ridge-and-furrow of these fields survive but air photographs show more on the broken land to the N. of the former village and in the extreme S. of the land of Newbottle. Here the apparently irregular pattern of furlongs is the result of careful construction of the ridges at right angles to the contours.

The date of the enclosure of the common fields of the deserted hamlet of Purston (4) is also unknown, though 280 acres of land either here or in the Purston of King's Sutton, or in both, were enclosed for pasture in 1495 (K. J. Allison, op. cit., 45). Although little ridge-and-furrow now exists, air photographs show the pattern of interlocked and end-on furlongs almost complete. There are two points of interest. Part of the area was apparently still ploughed in ridge-and-furrow as late as 1844, within the existing field boundaries (NRO, Tithe Map of Newbottle). Secondly, the air photographs show that on the steep N.-facing slope towards the S. of the land of Purston (SP 523394) the ridge-and-furrow had been disturbed by a comparatively modern landslip or mud-flow. (RAF VAP 106G/UK/1488, 3230–2, 4265–71; CPE/UK/1926, 2210–13, 4210–15; CPE/UK/1929, 3170–4)

44 OLD STRATFORD
(OS 1:10000 [a] SP 74 SE, [b] SP 73 NE)

The modern parish of Old Stratford is a recent creation. Until this century Old Stratford was a small hamlet beside Watling Street. The N.E. part lay in Cosgrove parish, the S.W. in Passenham and some houses in the parishes of Furtho and Potterspury. Following extensive modern development, however, a new parish was formed. This comprises all of the medieval parish of Passenham, apart from the lands of Deanshanger and Puxley which are now a separate

parish, as well as part of the S.W. corner of Cosgrove parish and the S.W. end of the old parish of Furtho, a total area of some 420 hectares. The land slopes gently between 90 m. and 60 m. above OD towards the R. Great Ouse which forms its S.E. boundary. It is mainly on Boulder Clay and glacial sands and gravels, although along the river large expanses of gravel and alluvium predominate. Many of the monuments listed below, including the important Roman hoard (2), are described in O. F. Brown and G. H. Roberts, Passenham, the History of a Forest Village (1973).

PREHISTORIC AND ROMAN

A group of circular cropmarks visible on air photographs (CUAP ZJ50–2) have been described as ring ditches, probably Bronze Age barrows (SP 779402). They are in fact the remains of a Second World War anti-aircraft battery, of a standard pattern noted elsewhere in the county (e.g. RCHM Northants., III (1981), 28, 32, 97). They are still visible as earthworks overlying ridge-and-furrow on air photographs taken in 1947 (RAF VAP CPE/UK/2097, 3185–6).

There are records of Roman coins found in the fields around Old Stratford; specifically, a 3rd-century antoninianus was found in 1976 (SP 781402; J. Morton, Nat. Hist. of Northants. (1712), 504; VCH Northants., I (1902), 220; Northants. Archaeol., 12 (1977), 213). A single sherd of Roman pottery came from the Great Ouse (SP 783393; BNFAS, 1 (1966), 12).

[a](1) DITCHED TRACKWAY (?) (SP 770417), N. of Shrobb Lodge Farm and immediately S.W. of Watling Street, on Boulder Clay at 80 m. above OD. Two parallel ditches 12 m. apart are visible on air photographs (NCAU) running N.E. towards Watling Street for almost 300 m.

[a](2) ROMAN HOARD (SP 779403), usually known as the Stony Stratford hoard, but found S. of the village of Old Stratford and thus within the county of Northampton, on Boulder Clay at 70 m. above OD. The hoard was discovered in Windmill Field in 1789 and was contained in an urn. It is now in the British Museum and comprises between 50 and 60 fragments of silver and gilt bronze plaques. Six of these have figures of deities on them. Interpretations of these have varied but one is said to show Mars and Minerva, another Mars and Victory, a third Apollo and two others Mars alone. Three of the plaques are inscribed. One is dedicated to Jupiter and Vulcan by Vassinus; the others bear a dedicatory inscription to Mars, but in all three examples the inclusion of the word Deo suggests conflation with native deities. These plaques may be parts of ritual crowns but were more probably fixed in some way, not now obvious, to the walls of a shrine. In addition there are two objects sometimes described as ensigns or head-dresses. These are constructed of bronze plates, some dish-shaped and some triangular, joined by chains. There were also several bronze plates joined by links and hinges, a group of decorated bronze discs, some silver-plated, linked by chains, and various other bronze objects including fibulae and a face mask. It has been suggested that this is a votive hoard, perhaps associated with

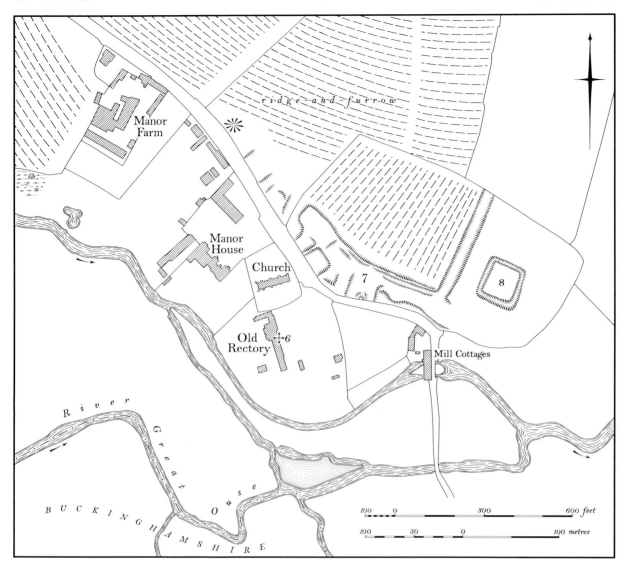

Fig. 90   OLD STRATFORD (6)   Saxon cemetery, (7)   Settlement remains at Passenham, (8) Moat

an undiscovered Roman temple, possibly the British equivalent of a *favissa*. (BM; D. Lysons, *Reliquiae Britanniae Romanae*, II (1817), Plates 34–8; Minutes of the Society of Antiquaries, 3rd June 1813, 306–11; *Corpus Inscriptionum Latinarum*, VII (1873), 81–2; *Catalogue of Silver Plate in the BM* (1921), 62–4; *VCH Bucks.*, II (1908), 11–12; J. M. C. Toynbee, *Art in Britain under the Romans* (1964), 328–30; R. G. Collingwood and R. P. Wright, *The Roman Inscriptions of Britain*, I (1965), nos. 215–7)

[a](3) ROMAN SETTLEMENT (SP 779416), N. of Old Stratford, on gravel at 75 m. above OD. Large quantities of Roman pottery, including samian and Oxford wares, were found during gravel extraction in 1978. Ditches were also noted. (Northants. SMR)

[b](4) ROMAN SETTLEMENT (?) (SP 783393), immediately S.E. of Passenham village, close to the R. Ouse on gravel

at 65 m. above OD. Roman material has been recorded (*Wolverton Arch. Soc. Newsletter*, 10 (1966), 40).

[a](5) ROMAN SETTLEMENT (SP 781412), at Firs Farm, in the E. of the village on Boulder Clay at 68 m. above OD. Roman pottery including samian, tile fragments and bone were discovered in a black layer of soil in a foundation pit (*BNFAS*, 1 (1966), 12).

For Roman Road 1e, Watling Street, see Appendix.

MEDIEVAL AND LATER

[a](6) SAXON CEMETERY (?) (SP 78033937; Fig. 90), beneath the present derelict rectory at Passenham, on river gravels, at 67 m. above OD. Seven skeletons were discovered during building work in 1873. It has also been recorded that 'human remains are everywhere to be met with just below the surface' in the field about 400 m. N. of the church, and that 50 skeletons were found when a vault was being

prepared at the church itself. In 1965 more burials, associated with 5th-century pottery, were discovered beneath the rectory. (Whellan, *Dir.* (1874), 573; VCH *Northants.*, I (1902), 236; *BNFAS*, 1 (1966), 15; *Med. Arch.*, 10 (1966), 172; OS Record Cards)

[a](7) SETTLEMENT REMAINS (SP 781393; Fig. 90), formerly part of the village of Passenham, lie on either side of the single street, immediately E. and S.E. of the church, on river gravel at 65 m. above OD. Passenham is first mentioned in *c.* 925 in the Anglo-Saxon Chronicle. It is listed in Domesday Book as two separate manors with a total recorded population of 20 (VCH *Northants.*, I (1902), 307, 321) but this figure certainly includes Deanshanger and Puxley. These settlements are listed together in all the medieval taxation returns and it is therefore not possible to ascertain the size of Passenham at any date except in 1523 when it is listed separately and ten people paid the Lay Subsidy (PRO, E179/155/140). By 1720 the village had six houses (J. Bridges, *Hist. of Northants.*, I (1791), 305) and it remains much the same size today. A map of 1600 (NRO) shows buildings S.E. of the church on both sides of the road, as well as on the site still occupied by houses.

The remains of the houses shown on the 1600 map still survive in permanent pasture. On the N.E. side of the street are at least seven building platforms defined by low banks or scarps, together with traces of former closes, and separated from the adjacent ridge-and-furrow by a bank up to 0.5 m. high. At the S.E. end a hollow-way 15 m. wide runs N.E. towards Stony Stratford. On the S. side of the road between the Old Rectory and Mill Cottages are other more indeterminate earthworks. Very slight remains also lie along the road N. of the church and immediately E. of the manor house. These may be the sites of former buildings though none is shown on the map of 1600. (RAF VAP CPE/UK/2097, 3183–4; F21 58/RAF/5517, 0004)

[a](8) MOAT (SP 782393; Fig. 90), lies immediately N.E. of Mill Cottages and at the S.E. end of the settlement remains (7), on river gravel at 65 m. above OD. The moat is presumably the site of the medieval manor house of Passenham and is probably the place described as 'Scite of Manor' in a survey of 1591 (NRO). It had certainly been abandoned by the early 18th century when Bridges (*Hist. of Northants.*, I (1791), 305), described it as an 'almost square intrenchment'. The site consists of a roughly square area, 30 m. across and level with the adjacent ground, surrounded by a shallow ditch 7 m. wide. Excavation in 1967 revealed good-quality stone buildings said to date from the late 13th century (*BNFAS*, 3 (1969), 26; *J. Wolverton Dist. Arch. Soc.*, 1 (1968), 13). (Air photographs in NMR)

[a](9) DESERTED HAMLET (SP 773422), lies in the N.E. of the parish, on Boulder Clay at 75 m. above OD. Until modern parish boundary revisions the site lay in Furtho parish. The history and indeed the name of this settlement is unknown though it is presumably listed in Domesday Book as one of the three small manors all called Furtho (VCH *Northants.*, I (1902), 324–6, 374). Thereafter there is no record of its existence; it had certainly disappeared by 1835 (map in NRO). (See also Potterspury (9)).

The site has been ploughed and all that is recoverable is stone-rubble and pottery. The latter dates mainly from the 12th to 14th centuries and includes Potterspury wares. Air photographs taken in 1947 (RAF VAP CPE/UK/1926, 4245–6) show that the area was already under cultivation then, but indicate clearly the form of the settlement. It then consisted of a broad hollow-way running N.W.–S.E. and visible for about 200 m. On the N.E. side ridge-and-furrow extended to the edge of the hollow-way, but on the S.W. there were at least four embanked and ditched closes 60 m. long and 20 m.–40 m. wide. Other deserted settlements which lay on only one side of their main streets have been recorded in the county (e.g. Braunston Cleves, RCHM *Northants.*, III (1981), Braunston (3)).

[a](10) WINDMILL MOUND (SP 777398), lies N.W. of the village, on Boulder Clay at 71 m. above OD. A low mound 20 m. across and ploughed almost flat is the site of a post mill shown on a map of 1600 (NRO).

(11) CULTIVATION REMAINS. The common fields of Passenham are traditionally said to have been enclosed by Sir Robert Banastre between 1620 and 1649 (*Northants. P. and P.*, 1 (1949), 28). On a map of 1600 (NRO) only two open fields are shown, both lying S.E. of the Buckingham road. The larger, covering the whole of the area between the village and Old Stratford, was called Little Stow Field, but Breach Field, to the N.W. of the village, was only some 12 hectares in extent.

Ridge-and-furrow of these fields survives on the ground or can be traced from air photographs, arranged in rectangular interlocked and end-on furlongs. In the former Breach Field it is almost complete. Within the latter there is a massive headland 30 m. wide and almost 2 m. high running S.W.–N.E. (SP 777397). Its size has probably been accentuated by the fact that it follows the edge of the river terrace, and has led to its identification as part of the defences of a camp constructed by Edward the Elder in 921 during his campaign against the Danes (*Wolverton and Dist. Arch. Soc. Newsletter*, 3 (1958), 23). Excavations in 1967, however, proved the earthwork to be part of the medieval field system (*BNFAS*, 3 (1969), 26; *J. Wolverton Dist. Arch. Soc.*, 1 (1968), 13). (RAF VAP CPE/UK/1926, 4244–8; CPE/UK/1929, 3181–7; CPE/UK/2097, 3184–7; F21 58/RAF/5517, 0004, 0029–30; F22 58/RAF/5517, 0030–1)

UNDATED

[a](12) MOUND (SP 777393), lies immediately S. of Passenham, on the flood-plain of the Great Ouse, on alluvium at 66 m. above OD. The mound is circular, 3 m. in diam. and less than 1 m. high. No date or function can be assigned to it. (RAF VAP CPE/UK/2097, 3183–4)

45 PATTISHALL
(OS 1:10000 [a] SP 65 NE, [b] SP 65 SE)

The parish covers 1147 hectares and lies mainly E. of Watling Street (A5) which marks part of the W. boundary, though one small area extends W. across the Roman road. The land slopes generally N. and is drained by several small tributaries of the R. Nene, one of which forms the E. boundary. The N.-S. ridges between the streams are of Northampton Sand and limestones above 122 m. above OD, but the higher ground in the S. is covered by Boulder Clay, and there are expanses of Upper Lias Clay in the N. and along the valley sides between 122 m. and 90 m. above OD.

Few archaeological remains have been noted in the parish and the main interest lies in the unusual medieval settlement pattern (2–5) (Fig. 41).

PREHISTORIC AND ROMAN

[b](1) DITCHES (SP 672535), 400 m. N.W. of Astcote on Northampton Sand at 142 m. above OD. Air photographs (NCAU) show very indistinct traces of a rectangular system of ditches covering about 0.75 hectare. These features may be modern.

For Roman Road 1f, Watling Street, see Appendix.

MEDIEVAL AND LATER

A Saxon sceatta was found in 1950 at Eastcote (*BM Quarterly*, 15 (1952), 54; *Brit. Num. J.*, 47 (1977), 39).

(2–5) SETTLEMENT REMAINS (Fig. 41), formerly part of the village of Pattishall and of the hamlets of Astcote, Eastcote and Dalscote, lie in and around the existing settlements. The remains are nowhere extensive but together they emphasise the unusual pattern of settlement in the parish, made up of four discrete units all of which are medieval in origin and two of which, Pattishall and Astcote, are mentioned in Domesday Book (PN *Northants.*, 92–3).

[b](2) SETTLEMENT REMAINS (SP 669543), formerly part of Pattishall, lie at the N.W. end of the village, on Northampton Sand at 137 m. above OD. Disturbed earthworks within a single paddock suggest that there were once houses here (RAF VAP CPE/UK/1926, 5038–9).

[b](3) SETTLEMENT REMAINS (SP 676532), formerly part of Astcote, lie in the centre of the hamlet, on Northampton Sand at 130 m. above OD. Astcote now consists of a single street bending to the E. at its N. end, and with a small triangular green towards the S. end. Between the green and the end of the curving street is a hollow-way some 12 m. wide and up to 2 m. deep, reduced to a single scarp at its N. end. It suggests either that the main street once ran almost N.-S. through the hamlet or that the green was once much larger and extended N. between the hollow-way and the existing street. Near the S. end of the hamlet (SP 677530) there was formerly another hollow-way running S.E. from the street and passing into the adjacent ridge-and-furrow. This has been completely destroyed by a housing estate. No trace has been noted of the manor house and chapel recorded by Baker (*Hist. of Northants.*, II (1836–41), 306) as having stood at the S. end of Astcote. (RAF VAP CPE/UK/1926, 3038–9; air photographs in NMR)

[b](4) SETTLEMENT REMAINS (SP 681538), formerly part of Eastcote, lie around the hamlet, on Northampton Sand and Upper Lias Clay at about 122 m. above OD. Behind the existing houses along the single street are the remains of abandoned closes edged by low banks and ditches; some

have ridge-and-furrow within them. (RAF VAP CPE/UK/1926, 3038–9, 5037–8; air photographs in NMR)

[b](5) SETTLEMENT REMAINS (SP 684541), formerly part of Dalscote, lie around the hamlet, on Boulder Clay and Northampton Sand at 138 m. above OD. Immediately W. of the main through road an area some 50 m. wide is covered by stone-rubble, brick, tiles and post-medieval pottery. The area is the site of a large building shown on a map of 1729 (NRO). Further buildings also shown on the map to the N. of the present farm are marked by low indeterminate earthworks. (RAF VAP CPE/UK/1926, 3037–8, 5036–7; air photographs in NMR)

[b](6) FISHPONDS (SP 674543), lay immediately E. of Pattishall village, in the bottom of a shallow E.-draining valley, on Upper Lias Clay at 107 m. above OD, but have now been completely destroyed. The ponds are shown correctly on the OS 25 in. map of 1883 (Northants. LI.10) and still survived in 1947 (RAF VAP CPE/UK/1926, 5037–8). There were three ponds, arranged in a line along the valley bottom. The upper one was a rectangular depression 50 m. by 15 m. and below it was a large roughly triangular pond 100 m. long and 12 m. to 60 m. wide, cut back into the valley side with a massive dam at its E. end. To the E. again was a smaller square pond, 40 m. wide, fed by a tributary stream from the N.W. Nothing is known of the history of these ponds.

(7) CULTIVATION REMAINS. The common fields of the parish were enclosed by an Act of Parliament of 1771 (NRO, copy of Enclosure Map). Nothing is known of the arrangement of these fields, and in particular it is not clear whether each of the separate medieval settlements in the parish had its own field system.

Ridge-and-furrow of these fields survives on the ground or can be traced on air photographs over most of the parish, except N. and N.E. of the village where the light Northampton Sands have been ploughed or worked for ironstone. Elsewhere a complex pattern of end-on and interlocked furlongs is visible mainly arranged to run at right angles to the contours, especially along the three small N. and N.E.-flowing streams in the N. of the parish. There are examples of over-ploughed headlands between former end-on furlongs (e.g. SP 676548), and in several places there is great variety in the width of ridges within small areas (e.g. SP 674528 and 671533). (RAF VAP CPE/UK/1926, 3035–41, 5034–41; CPE/UK/1994, 2168–71, 3162–6, 4173–4; 3G TUD/UK/118, 6032–4; FSL6603, 2379–83, 2400–4)

46 PAULERSPURY
(OS 1:10000 [a] SP 74 NW, [b] SP 74 SW, [c] SP 64 NE)

The modern parish covers some 1200 hectares including the hamlet and land of Heathencote. The higher areas in the S. and W., rising to a maximum height of 123 m. above OD, are covered by Boulder Clay. From there the land slopes generally N.E., across bands of Oolitic Limestone exposed on the steep sides of small valleys, to the valley of the R. Tove here flowing at about 80 m. above OD in a flat-bottomed valley of Upper Lias Clay and alluvial deposits.

Two Iron Age and numerous Roman settlements (1–9) have been discovered in the parish and the settlement pattern of Paulerspury village (10–14) is also of considerable interest.

PREHISTORIC AND ROMAN

The blade of a Mesolithic tranchet axe was found in 1977 (SP 70854757; NM; *Northants. Archaeol.*, 13 (1978), 180).

There are unsatisfactory records of several Roman coins from the parish, for example a possible hoard including 'several medals of Constantine, Maximillian and other Roman emperors' (J. Morton, *Nat. Hist. of Northants.* (1712), 531; J. Bridges, *Hist. of Northants.*, I (1791), 314). More recently a coin of Domitian has been found near the Roman road (SP 69924807; OS Record Cards), and an unspecified number of Roman sherds near the church (SP 71634549; *Northants. Archaeol.*, 13 (1978), 182).

[b](1) IRON AGE SETTLEMENT (SP 713442), in the extreme S. of the parish, on Boulder Clay at 129 m. above OD. Early Iron Age pottery, animal bones and burnt pebbles have been discovered (*Northants. Archaeol.*, 9 (1974), 85; CBA Group 9, *Newsletter*, 4 (1974), 27).

[a](2) IRON AGE SETTLEMENT (SP 707468), S. of Heathencote and close to the W. parish boundary, on Boulder Clay at about 125 m. above OD. Occupation-debris including early Iron Age sherds, animal bones and burnt stones has been noted (*Northants. Archaeol.*, 9 (1974), 84; CBA Group 9, *Newsletter*, 4 (1974), 27).

[b](3) ROMAN BUILDING (SP 711446), in the S. of the parish, immediately W. of Park Farm, on Boulder Clay at 130 m. above OD. The discovery of large quantities of dressed limestone, 3rd and 4th-century coins and Roman pottery including samian suggests the existence of a large Roman building or farm (*Northants. Archaeol.*, 9 (1974), 95; CBA Group 9, *Newsletter*, 4 (1974), 27; *Milton Keynes Journal*, 3 (1974), 67).

[b](4) ROMAN BUILDING (SP 713444), 300 m. S.E. of (3) and in a similar position. Much Roman pottery including samian, 3rd and 4th-century coins and dressed limestone indicate a considerable Roman building (*Northants. Archaeol.*, 9 (1974), 95; CBA Group 9, *Newsletter*, 4 (1974), 27).

[a](5) ROMAN SETTLEMENT (?) (SP 722456), in the E. part of the village, on Boulder Clay at 122 m. above OD. Roman pottery has been revealed during building development (*Northants. Archaeol.*, 10 (1975), 161).

[a](6) ROMAN SETTLEMENT (?) (about SP 713455), between the main village and Pury End, beneath the E. edge of the enclosure (13a). A trial trench across the site revealed a V-shaped ditch containing Roman coarse wares and a fragment of a mortarium (*Northants. Archaeol.*, 8 (1973), 21).

[a](7) ROMAN BUILDING (?) (SP 703461), close to the W. parish boundary, on Boulder Clay at 130 m. above OD. Roman pottery and building debris have been found in spoil from drainage trenches (*BNFAS*, 3 (1969), 1).

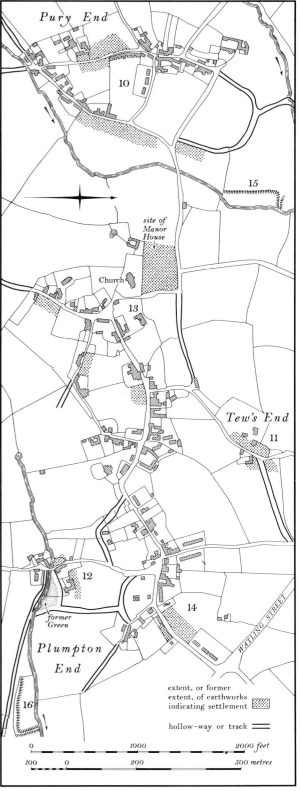

Fig. 91 PAULERSPURY (10–14) Settlement remains, (15, 16) Fishponds

ᵃ(8) ROMAN SETTLEMENT (?) (SP 722469), in the N.E. of the parish, on Upper Lias Clay at 92 m. above OD. Roman material is recorded in this area (*Northants. Archaeol.*, 9 (1974), 95; CBA Group 9, *Newsletter*, 4 (1974), 27).

ᵃ(9) ROMAN SETTLEMENT (?) (SP 717477), in the N. of the parish, on Boulder Clay at 90 m. above OD. Roman occupation debris has been noted (*Northants. Archaeol.*, 9 (1974), 95; CBA Group 9, *Newsletter*, 4 (1974), 27).

For Roman pottery and possible burials, see (24).

For Roman Road 1e, Watling Street, see Appendix.

MEDIEVAL AND LATER

(10–14) SETTLEMENT REMAINS (Figs. 91 and 92). The village of Paulerspury is dispersed over an area of 2 square kilometres and appears to consist of five separate centres joined by a network of roads many of which now survive only as hollow-ways. These are Pury End in the W., Tew's End in the N. and Plumpton End in the S.E., as well as two parts of Paulerspury itself each associated with a small triangular green. Each of these centres has evidence of former settlement and is described individually below.

The village is first mentioned in Domesday Book, listed as a single manor of three and three-fifths hides, with a recorded population of 33 including a priest (VCH *Northants.*, I (1902), 339). This figure almost certainly includes the hamlet of Heathencote (18). In 1334 the village *cum membris* paid 118s. 6¼d. for the Lay Subsidy, one of the largest sums in the area (PRO, E179/155/3). In 1673, 130 people paid the Hearth Tax but this record again included Heathencote (PRO, E179/254/14). The total population of the parish in 1801 was 859. (RAF VAP CPE/UK/1926, 3236–40, 5236–40; air photographs in NMR)

ᵃ(10) SETTLEMENT REMAINS (centred SP 710455; Figs. 91 and 92), lie in and around the hamlet of Pury End, on limestone and Boulder Clay, between 105 m. and 120 m. above OD. The surviving earthworks fall into six groups: (a) On the W. side of Careys Road (SP 70914542), a series of very slight depressions bounded on the W. by a shallow ditch, marks the sites of former houses. (b) On the E. side of Careys Road (SP 70964540) indeterminate earthworks are probably also the remains of houses. (c) On the S.E. side of Lower Street (SP 71104535–71204558) there are more low house-sites and platforms separated by a bank from the adjoining ridge-and-furrow. At the N. end of the area the ridges appear to extend almost up to the road and to have ridden over earlier house-sites now reduced to amorphous scarps and depressions. A few sherds of medieval pottery associated with very dark earth have been picked up from molehills in this area. (d) At the N.E. end of Lower Street (SP 71004566) is a group of terraces cut by a later track, together with an old pond and other more indeterminate earthworks. These remains are the site of a large farmstead which still existed in 1820 (NRO, map) and was also shown on the OS 1st ed. 1 in. map of 1834. (e) At the N. end of the village (SP 70984574–71054592) the line of Careys Road is continued N.E. as a pronounced hollow-way up to 3 m. deep. This hollow-way forks (at SP 71084585), one branch curving S.E. and then S. to meet the N. end of Lower Street. The other branch runs N.N.W. to the stream. Beyond the stream its line is con-

tinued as a terrace-way much damaged by ploughing. All these routes were shown as roads on maps of 1728 and 1820 (NRO). (f) At the S. end of the village (SP 70974520) the line of Lower Street continues as a poorly preserved terrace-way S.W. along the valley side, and Careys Road runs on as a deep hollow-way climbing the hillside to the S. Both are shown as roads in 1728 and 1820.

ᵃ(11) SETTLEMENT REMAINS (centred SP 729458; Fig. 91), lie around the existing buildings at Tew's End, on limestone at 115 m. above OD. The amorphous earthworks are sites of buildings some of which were still standing in 1820 (map in NRO). The main feature is a large hollow-way up to 2.5 m. deep at its N.E. end, which runs from the E. side of Tew's End Lane to the N. end of Longcroft Lane. This was still a through road in 1820.

ᵃ(12) SETTLEMENT REMAINS (SP 723453; Fig. 91), lie around Plumpton End, on Boulder Clay at 108 m. above OD. From the evidence of maps of 1728 and 1820 (NRO) and air photographs (RAF VAP CPE/UK/1926, 3238–9, 5238–40) the hamlet originally lay around a small triangular green immediately E. of the existing N.-S. road and on the N. side of the stream. From the N.E. corner of the green a road ran N. to the E. end of Paulerspury. The green has now been partly built over but the road survives as a hollow-way 15 m. wide (SP 72424540). Other remains include the N. boundary of the settlement, now a low bank (SP 72404536), some amorphous earthworks probably the sites of buildings on the W. side of the modern road (SP 72344533), and a terrace-way on the S. side of the stream running S.E. from the green (SP 72454525). It is recorded that in a close 'named the Hall Close, stood the old Manor-house called Plumpton Hall – foundations of buildings are said to have been dug up here' (J. Bridges, *Hist. of Northants.*, I (1791), 315).

ᵃ(13) SETTLEMENT REMAINS (centred SP 716454; Fig. 91), lie in several places around the W. half of Paulerspury village, on Boulder Clay between 110 m. and 125 m. above OD. (a) Immediately N. and W. of the church (SP 71494553) is a large area of earthworks which include some old quarries and relatively recent hedge-banks. There is also a curving terrace-way on the hillside N. of the church and this continues along the line of the modern road to the N. There is at least one house-site to the W. of this terrace-way. Immediately W. of the church are stone and brick foundations of a recently demolished farm building. The latter apparently stood on the site of the original manor house of Paulerspury which was demolished at the end of the 18th century (J. Bridges, *Hist. of Northants.*, I (1791), 311; G. Baker, *Hist. of Northants.*, II (1836–41), 120). This manor house and the associated earthworks lay within a large rectangular area bounded on the N. by the Pury End Road, on the E. by Church Lane and on the W. by a double scarp or terrace-way which runs S. from Pury Lane (at SP 71334562) along the valley side and down to a small stream (SP 71304543). Beyond the stream the S. boundary of the site continues as a well-marked bank with ditches on each side, extending E. to a point just W. of the green (SP 71004538). These boundaries may have enclosed a formal garden belonging to the manor house. In 1972 a trial excavation was carried out across the terrace-way. Two deeply cut V-shaped ditches were discovered, the

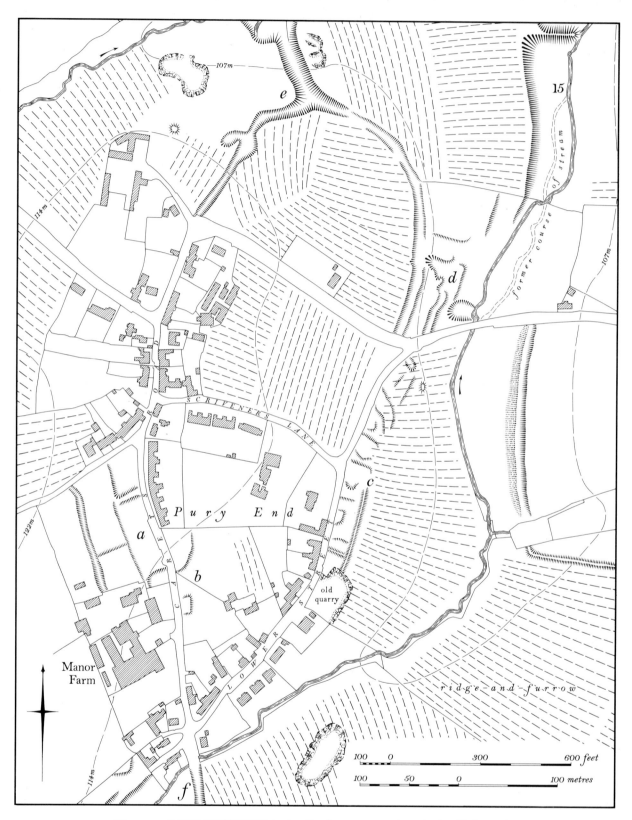

Fig. 92 PAULERSPURY (10) Settlement remains, (15) Fishpond

upper containing medieval pottery and the lower Roman (see (6); *Northants. Archaeol.*, 8 (1973), 21). (b) On the S.E. side of Park Lane (SP 71634526) are very slight earthworks, now almost ploughed out, probably the sites of former houses. (c) On the N. side of Lumber Lane (SP 71764538) slight earthworks also probably represent buildings now demolished. (d) On the S. side of High Street (SP 71884548) air photographs (RAF VAP CPE/UK/1926, 3238–9) show traces of another house-site now destroyed by the recreation ground. (e) N. of High Street and parallel to it (SP 71584562–71864566) are the remains of a broad hollow-way up to 1.5 m. deep which ran from the sharp bend in Tew's End Lane to the right-angle bend in Pury End Road N. of the church. This road had already been abandoned by 1728 (map in NRO). (f) The S. end of Park Lane (SP 71594521) formerly continued S.W. as a deep hollow-way running between ridge-and-furrow. This was still a road to Whittlebury in 1820 (map in NRO). Most of it has recently been destroyed by ploughing. (g) From the sharp bend in Lumber Lane (SP 71854531) a hollow-way continues S.E. for 100 m. Its N.W. end has been destroyed by modern housing.

[a](14) SETTLEMENT REMAINS (centred SP 723455; Fig. 91), lie in several places in the E. half of Paulerspury village, on Boulder Clay between 115 m. and 120 m. above OD. (a) On the N.W. side of Grays Lane (SP 72524563) there were formerly at least two house-sites separated from the ridge-and-furrow on the N. by a well-marked ditch. These have now been destroyed by modern housing. Immediately to the S., on the opposite side of the road, 14th and 15th-century pottery has been found (*Northants. Archaeol.*, 10 (1975), 169). (b) Fragments of a hollow-way now largely destroyed by houses and gardens can be traced running from the High Street (SP 72184547) in a broad curve to meet the road to Plumpton End (SP 72364543).

This was a through road in 1728 but had been partly abandoned by 1820 (maps in NRO). (c) A small section of an irregular hollow-way exists E. of the Plumpton End Road (SP 72454547). In 1728 this was part of a loop road which ran in a curve from the Plumpton End Road to Plum Park Lane (map in NRO). A hollow-way from Plumpton End (12) runs into it. (d) At the extreme S.E. end of Plum Park Lane (SP 72624545) is a broad hollow-way running S.E. through the adjacent ridge-and-furrow. This road is not shown on any map but it may have led to the fishpond (16).

[a](15) FISHPOND (SP 713458; Figs. 91 and 92), lies N.E. of Pury End in the bottom of the valley of a small N.-flowing stream, on clay at 100 m. above OD. A large roughly rectangular pond cut back into the valley side on the W. has a massive dam up to 3 m. high at the N. end. There is no trace of an artificial edge on the E. side; the steep natural slope seems to have sufficed. The original course of the stream is still visible in the bottom of the pond and to the S. The pond had probably been abandoned by 1728 for it is not depicted on the map of that date though the field to the N. was then known as The Fishweir. (RAF VAP CPE/UK/1926, 3237–8; air photographs in NMR)

[a](16) FISHPOND (SP 727452; Figs. 91 and 93), lies immediately N.W. of Plum Park Farm, on clay and alluvium at 99 m. above OD. A large dam 2.5 m. high spans the valley of a small E.-flowing stream. The limits of the former pond, of some 1.75 hectares, are marked on the S. side by a steep artificial scarp up to 2 m. high at the E. end but fading out at the W. end where it becomes a bank. The N. side is marked by a scarp 1.25 m. high, above which the stream now flows in a narrow artificial channel cut into the hillside. The bottom of the pond is ploughed in ridge-and-furrow which appears to be later than the construction of the dam although it is not clear whether

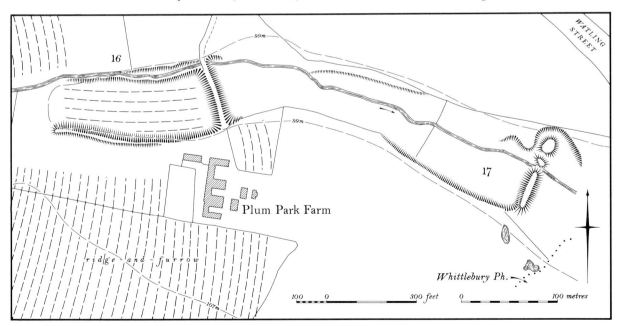

Fig. 93 PAULERSPURY (16, 17) Fishponds

the ridges were formed after the pond had been abandoned or whether the ploughing was part of a medieval rotation of fish and arable farming (RCHM *Northants.*, II (1979), Braybrooke (1) and Dingley (3)). However the land immediately to the N. has no ridge-and-furrow on it, and none was visible in 1947 when the area was still permanent pasture. It appears, therefore, that there was no obvious shortage of arable land in the area in medieval times and it is likely that the ridge-and-furrow in this pond is indeed part of a rotational system. (RAF VAP CPE/UK/1926, 5239–40)

[a](17) FISHPOND (SP 731451; Fig. 93, to the E.S.E. of and below (16), in a similar situation. The valley bottom is spanned by a dam 2.5 m. high with two later gaps in it through one of which the stream flows. At the N.E. end of the dam and cut back into the hillside is an original overflow channel. Upstream the edges of the pond are marked by low scarps. (RAF VAP CPE/UK/1926, 5239–40)

[a](18) SETTLEMENT REMAINS (SP 710473; Figs. 16 and 94), formerly part of Heathencote, lie around the existing hamlet in the N. of the parish, on Boulder Clay at 115 m. above OD. The settlement is first mentioned by name as *Heymundecot* in 1220 (PN *Northants.*, 104) but is probably much older. It is presumably included silently under Paulerspury in Domesday Book and in all medieval taxation records is listed with Paulerspury except in 1525 when 11 people at Heathencote paid the Lay Subsidy (PRO, E179/155/130). By 1720 (J. Bridges, *Hist. of Northants.*, I (1791), 314–5) it consisted of 'six farms and ten families in scattered houses'.

The hamlet is shown much as it is today on a map of 1820 except that a group of buildings is depicted to the W. on either side of a road running N. from Watling Street (SP 706474). The buildings have now been destroyed and all that remains is an area of ill-defined earthworks and part of a road surviving as a shallow hollow-way. Within the hamlet itself the probable sites of former houses survive in the S.E., and to the N.E. a broad hollow-way continues the line of the single street into the valley bottom where it is blocked by a small 18th-century cottage. Other fragmentary earthworks lie on each side of this hollow-way. Some 13th and 14th-century pottery has been found in the area (NM; *BNFAS*, 4 (1970) 21; *Northants. Archaeol.*, 13 (1978), 187). The two separate areas of settlement existing in 1820 might indicate that Heathencote was once two places. (RAF VAP CPE/UK/1926, 1236–7)

[a](19) WINDMILL MOUND (SP 70874794), lies immediately E. of Park Hall, on glacial gravel at 105 m. above OD. A circular mound 20 m. in diam. and 1.8 m. high, surrounded by a ditch 0.4 m. deep, is probably the site of a medieval windmill (*Med. Arch.*, 18 (1974), 216). The N. side and the interior have been damaged by digging, but there are traces of an original central depression. The surrounding ridge-and-furrow does not impinge on the mound.

[b](20) DEER PARK (centred SP 715445; Fig. 16), occupies just over 100 hectares of land in the S. of the parish, on Boulder Clay between 135 m. and 120 m. above OD. There is some confusion in the literature between the history of this park and Plum Park (21).

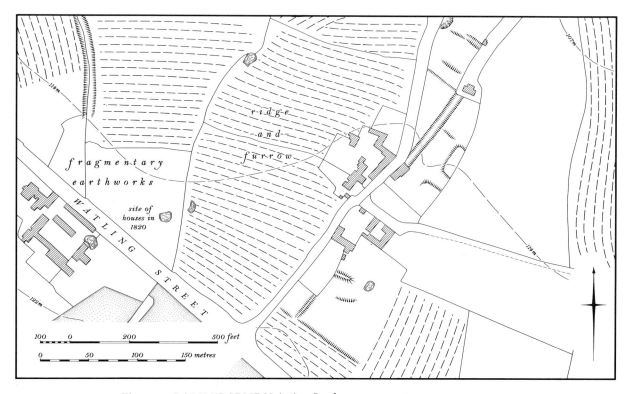

Fig. 94   PAULERSPURY (18)   Settlement remains at Heathencote

A small park of only 17 acres was created in 1363 by John de Pavely (G. Baker, *Hist. of Northants.*, II (1836–41), 204) and this seems to be the origin of the one described here. In 1410 John St. John had two parks 'called the Oldeparke and New Parke which the said John has a field called Farmsted and 100 acres of land and a wood adjoining the said field . . . containing 100 acres of land'. St. John was licensed to enclose the two parks, the field and the wood and make a new deer park (*Cal. Charter R., 1314–1417*, 442). This conversion of apparent arable land into a deer park is of interest, for much ridge-and-furrow is traceable within the park today (RAF VAP CPE/UK/1926, 5236–9). In 1541 the park was alienated to the Crown and it was disafforested in 1639 (P. A. Pettit, *The Royal Forests of Northants. 1558–1674* (1968), 14, 90, 192).

The exact location of the two pre-1410 parks is unknown, but the boundaries of the later one are clear. From the S. end of Park Lane, to the S. of Paulerspury church (SP 716452), the boundary ran S.E. until it met the lane running S. from Plumpton End (SP 723448). No trace remains here as the hedge has been realigned, but the fact that Breach Field, one of the common fields of Paulerspury, still existed to the N.E. in 1820 (map in NRO) suggests that the park boundary lay approximately along this line. It then ran S. along the W. side of the Plumpton End lane to the Paulerspury-Whittlebury parish boundary (SP 724442). No indication of the park boundary can be seen along the lane. This boundary then turned W. and followed the parish boundary for 1.75 km. to just S.W. of Park Farm (SP 709445). Again there is little indication of a park boundary, except to the S.E. of Park Farm (SP 712442–715440) where the modern hedge lies on top of or just N. of a large bank up to 1.5 m. high and 10 m. wide, and further W. (at SP 710444) where, though no hedge remains, air photographs show traces of an almost ploughed-out bank, with a broad ditch on the N. side (i.e. inside the park). To the S.W. of Park Farm the park boundary met the hollow-way or lane running S. from Pury End and ran along its E. side (SP 709445–710452). In a few places along this lane are the remains of a large bank up to 1.25 m. high. At the S. corner of Pury End the deer park boundary seems to have followed the stream. It then must have turned S.E., along the S.E. side of Paulerspury village, to reach the S. end of Park Lane. No boundary bank has been observed here. (*Northants. P. and P.*, 5 (1975), 229–30; *Milton Keynes Journal*, 3 (1974), 67–8; *Med. Arch.*, 18 (1974), 218)

[b](21) DEER PARK (centred SP 733454; Fig. 60), known as Plum Park, lies in the S.E. of the parish, on the E. side of Watling Street, on Boulder Clay between 100 m. and 115 m. above OD. It covers only 30 hectares of land, and adjoins Grafton Park (Grafton Regis (8)) and Potterspury Park (Yardley Gobion (8)).

The park is first recorded in 1328 when it was created by Richard Damory. Its later history is not well documented, but it was still known as The Park in the early 19th century (*Northants. P. and P.*, 5 (1975), 230; *Milton Keynes Journal*, 3 (1974), 68; G. Baker, *Hist. of Northants.*, II (1836–41), 213).

The S.W. edge of the park lay along Watling Street, though no indication of any boundary survives along it

today. The N. side of the park (SP 728457–734459) is marked by a scarp up to 1 m. high but a line of old quarries on the S. side has obscured any original ditch (RAF VAP CPE/UK/1926, 3240–1). The E. side coincides with the Grafton Regis parish boundary as well as with the boundary of Grafton Park. The N. part (SP 734458) of this side has been ploughed over but the original boundary, consisting of a ditch between two banks, is visible on air photographs. Within a small copse known as Grafton Park (SP 734456) a bank 1.25 m. high and 7 m. wide survives but thereafter nothing is traceable in the modern arable until the assumed boundary meets Watling Street (SP 735450). Ridge-and-furrow is visible over most of the interior of the park arranged in interlocked furlongs. It has been suggested (*Milton Keynes Journal*, op. cit.) that the park was laid out around existing common field furlongs.

[a](22) POST-MEDIEVAL POTTERY KILN (SP 722467), lies N. of the village of Paulerspury, on Upper Lias Clay, at 91 m. above OD. Excavation has revealed an oval pottery kiln, 2.13 m. by 4.26 m., constructed of tile and clay. A range of forms and fabrics was produced (*Northants. Archaeol.*, 9 (1974), 112; *Milton Keynes Journal*, 3 (1974), 28–30; *Post-Med. Arch.*, 2 (1968), 55–82).

(23) CULTIVATION REMAINS. The common fields of Paulerspury, together with those of Heathencote, were enclosed by an Act of Parliament of 1819 (NRO; Enclosure Map, 1820; map of Heathencote, 1819; map of Paulerspury, 1728). A detailed description of the arrangement of these fields and their surviving ridge-and-furrow has already been published (*Milton Keynes Journal*, 3 (1974), 67–71). This work has shown that the position in 1819, when there were no less than 11 open fields of various sizes in the parish, was only the last stage in a process of development and change which is not clearly understood.

Large areas of ridge-and-furrow survive on the ground or can be traced on air photographs. It is still particularly well preserved in the N. of the parish within the area of Towcester Racecourse where end-on and rectangular furlongs exist. This area was part of Towcester Field in 1819 and was probably one of at least three open fields cultivated by the inhabitants of Heathencote (18). Other ridge-and-furrow can be traced within the extensive old enclosures around Paulerspury village (Figs. 91 and 92) and within both the medieval deer parks (20) and (21). (RAF VAP CPE/UK/1926, 1236–41, 3236–44, 5236–41)

UNDATED

[a](24) BURIALS (SP 714465), N. of Pury End and N. of the fishpond (15). Large quantities of human bones of both sexes, including children, have been found over a number of years in this area. A few sherds of Roman pottery, including the base of an unusual 1st-century pot, have also been discovered. It has been suggested that it is the site of a Saxon cemetery but this is by no means certain. (CBA Group 9, *Newsletter*, 4 (1974), 27; *Northants. Archaeol.*, 13 (1978), 182)

47 POTTERSPURY
(OS 1:10000 [a] SP 74 SE, [b] SP 74 SW)

The modern parish covers about 780 hectares. It is long and narrow and slopes generally S.E., drained by small streams flowing towards the Great Ouse. It is almost entirely covered by Boulder Clay except around the village and in the S.E. where limestones are exposed along the valley sides.

Until 19th-century boundary changes Potterspury included the whole of the parish of Yardley Gobion, but only extended a little to the S.W. of Watling Street. It now includes what was once a detached part of Cosgrove parish, as well as the whole of Wakefield Lawn and its surrounding area. The latter was once partly common land in Whittlewood Forest though within it lay the settlement of Wakefield, first recorded in Domesday Book (VCH *Northants.*, I (1902), 329, 374). The site of the deserted village of Furtho (9) and part of its former lands occupy the S.E. of Potterspury but the rest of Furtho parish is now incorporated within Cosgrove and Old Stratford.

This parish contains a number of prehistoric and Roman sites but is most renowned for its medieval and post-medieval pottery kilns.

PREHISTORIC AND ROMAN

A large axe of white flint was found in the parish before 1903 (NM) and other flint and stone implements have been collected in the N.W. of the area. These include part of a Bronze Age perforated stone battle-axe of Group XIV (*Wolverton and District Arch. Soc. Newsletter*, 6 (1961), 2).

[a](1) RING DITCHES (SP 769423), in the S.E. of the parish close to Watling Street, on the N. side of a small E.-flowing stream, on limestone at 75 m. above OD. Air photographs (NCAU) show two ring ditches 25 m. in diam. and 35 m. apart.

[ab](2) ENCLOSURE AND DITCHES (centred SP 750434), W. of Sunnyside Farm and adjoining Watling Street, on limestone at 91 m. above OD. Air photographs (in NMR) show what appear to be two sides of a sub-rectangular enclosure with some linear ditches to the S.

[b](3) IRON AGE SETTLEMENT (SP 729435), immediately N. of the Kennels, on Boulder Clay at 120 m. above OD. Sherds of early and middle Iron Age pottery, including some of Trent Basin type, were ploughed up in 1959 (*Wolverton and District Arch. Soc. Newsletter*, 6 (1961), 2; *BNFAS*, I (1966), 5).

[a](4) IRON AGE AND ROMAN SETTLEMENT (SP 763433), in the E. of the village, on limestone at 80 m. above OD. Sherds of late Iron Age and 1st-century Roman pottery were revealed during building work on this site (*BNFAS*, I (1966), 5; *Wolverton and District Arch. Soc. Newsletter*, 10 (1966), 40).

[b](5) ROMAN VILLA (SP 736429), beneath the artificial lake in front of Wakefield Lodge, on Boulder Clay at 103 m.

above OD. Much Roman material has been dredged from the lake, including dressed limestone, brick, roof and flue tiles, tesserae, window glass and pottery (*Wolverton and District Arch. Soc. Newsletter*, 6 (1961), 3; *BNFAS*, I (1966), 12; see also Deanshanger, Prehistoric and Roman Introduction).

[b](6) ROMAN BUILDING (SP 747425), E. of Redmoor Copse, on Boulder Clay at 105 m. above OD. Ploughing has revealed disturbed floors and walls, nails, 3rd and 4th-century pottery, samian ware and mortarium sherds (*BNFAS*, I (1966), 12).

[a](7) ROMAN SETTLEMENT (SP 761420), in the S. of the parish, on limestone at 85 m. above OD. Roman tile and pottery of 1st and 2nd-century types have been found. A pronounced agger, said to be a possible Roman road, runs E. from this site towards Watling Street (*BNFAS*, I (1966), 12; 3 (1969), 1). For medieval pottery from this site, see (15).

For Roman Road 1e, Watling Street, see Appendix.

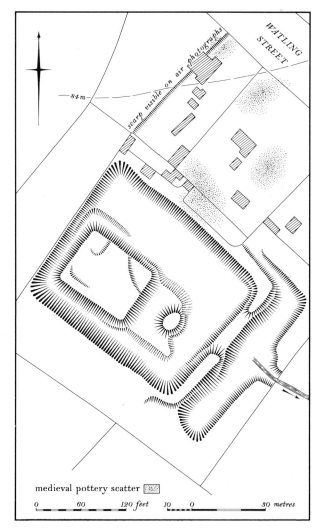

Fig. 95 POTTERSPURY (8) Moat

MEDIEVAL AND LATER

[a](8) MOAT (SP 764423; Fig. 95), lies S.E. of the village, on the S.W. side of Watling Street, on beds of the Estuarine Series, at 83 m. above OD. The site is situated on a spring line on the N. side of a shallow valley draining E. Nothing is known of its history beyond the fact that the field in which it lies was already an isolated old enclosure in 1776, lying on the E. side of an open area known as Brown's Wood Green (map in NRO).

The site has been misinterpreted in the past, notably by the OS who saw it as a large rectangular depression with an almost square island in the W. corner and a small circular one to the S.E. This situation is clearly the result of relatively recent destruction. The small island stands on a rectangular platform slightly above the level of the bottom of the surrounding ponds. It appears that there was originally one large island occupying the S.W. of the site and that the small island is the only fragment of the E. part that has survived to its original height.

This large island was asymmetrically placed, partly perhaps to provide a fishpond on the N.E. side, but also because of the natural topography of the small valley in which the site lies. The wide part of the pond occupies the lowest part of the valley. The water was retained in the pond and around the island by a massive dam on the S.E. side, up to 2 m. high. Below the dam and parallel with it is a long narrow pond, possibly once two ponds, which turns N.W. at its N.E. end, parallel with the N. side of the moat. The site is in poor condition, having been used as a nursery garden, but large quantities of medieval sherds have been revealed, particularly from the destroyed S.E. part of the island. Medieval pottery, mainly of Potterspury type, has also been noted within the gardens of the bungalows to the N.E. of the moat, suggesting that the medieval settlement extended beyond the surviving earthworks. This is confirmed by air photographs taken before the northernmost bungalow was constructed, showing a low scarp, perhaps the boundary of a former close, extending from the moat to Watling Street. (RAF VAP CPE/UK/1926, 2243–4, 4224–5)

[a](9) DESERTED MEDIEVAL VILLAGE OF FURTHO AND GARDEN REMAINS (SP 773431; Fig. 96), lie against the modern boundary between Potterspury and Cosgrove, on the S. side of a small valley, on Boulder Clay at 75 m. above OD. The medieval parish of Furtho included land to the N. and S. now in Cosgrove and Old Stratford (Fig. 16). The village is first mentioned in Domesday Book when it was divided into three small holdings with a total recorded population of 15 (VCH Northants., I (1902), 15). However, one of these manors may have been the deserted hamlet which lies to the S. in the part of Old Stratford formerly in Furtho parish (Old Stratford (9)). Furtho is named in the Nomina Villarum of 1316. No indication of its later medieval population is available as it was always taxed with Cosgrove, except in 1525 when three people paid the Lay Subsidy (PRO, E179/155/130). In 1547 200 sheep were maintained on the manor. Around 1600 Edward Furtho, a member of the family who had held the manor since the 13th century, enclosed the parish, de-populated the village, diverted the main through road and rebuilt the church. The existing building is said to be of about 1620 (N.

Pevsner, Northamptonshire (1961), 212; K. J. Allison et al., The Deserted Villages of Northants. (1966), 40).

By 1720 'only one house, with the church', survived although 'the remains of a former village' were still to be seen (J. Bridges, Hist. of Northants., I (1791), 296). The house is shown standing to the S.W. of the church, together with the remains of its formal garden, on a map of 1835 (NRO; see also Tithe Map, 1850). It was demolished in the late 19th century and replaced by the present Manor Farm to the S. A circular stone dovecote, said to be of the 15th century, is shown immediately S. of the original house and still remains.

Apart from one of the medieval fishponds, now dry, and part of the post-medieval garden, no earthworks have survived the extensive modern agricultural improvements. However, from air photographs taken before destruction (RAF VAP CPE/UK/1926, 2245–6; CUAP, XT35), more recent air photographs (in NMR) and the modern OS 1:2500 plan (SP 7743) it is possible to reconstruct a plan of the earthworks as they existed in 1947 (Fig. 96). The main feature of the site was a broad hollow-way ('a'-'b' on plan), presumably the main through road, which ran approximately E.-W. parallel with the stream. At its W. end its line is continued by a broad curving headland which once joined Furtho Lane in Potterspury village but the E. extension of the road cannot be traced. The part of this hollow-way immediately N.E. of the church was between 9 m. and 18 m. wide. Immediately to the S. of this, E. of the church ('c' on plan), there was a series of rectangular paddocks bounded by banks and ditches with, to the S. again, a large circular mound 20 m. in diam. and 1 m. high which still partly survives. To the N. of the hollow-way ('d' on plan) were two long rectangular fishponds separated by a low bank and bounded on the E. by a broad dam. Only the northern pond now survives with the dam up to 2 m. high. Along the valley side to the W. of the church and N.W. of Manor Farm there were other more indeterminate earthworks ('e').

The post-medieval garden ('f' on plan) lay immediately N. of the church and N.E. of the site of the old manor house. As its remains lie across the alignment of the medieval hollow-way, the garden must have been constructed after the road was put out of use. The 1835 map shows a long rectangular area divided into rectangular flower beds with what appears to be a shrubbery to the N. between the flower beds and a large pond. This pond, together with the scarp 1 m. high which apparently marks the division between the flower beds and the shrubbery, survives though in poor condition.

[a](10) SETTLEMENT REMAINS (SP 752434 and 754431), formerly part of Potterspury, lie on the S.W. side of Watling Street, on limestone between 85 m. and 90 m. above OD. A map of Potterspury in 1728 (NRO) shows at least six houses situated on the wide verge of Watling Street. These were presumably late encroachments on the waste. By 1776 (NRO, Enclosure Map) some of the buildings had been removed and most had disappeared by the mid 19th century (1st ed. 1 in. map of 1834). Their sites are still preserved as sub-rectangular depressions cut back into the rising ground.

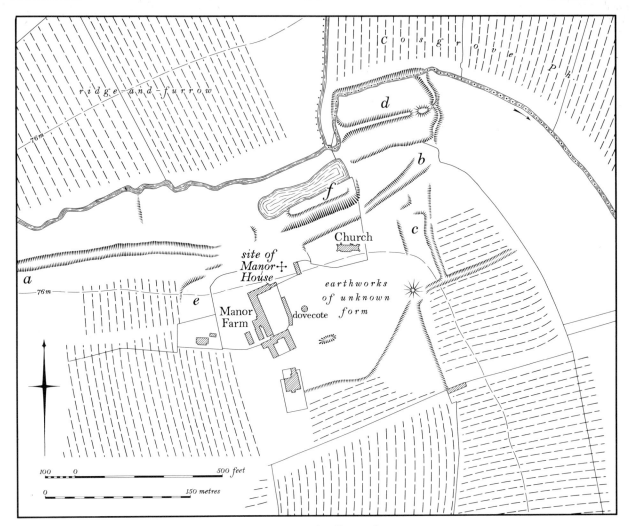

Fig. 96 POTTERSPURY (9) Deserted village of Furtho and garden remains

(11)–(14) POTTERY KILNS. Several medieval and post-medieval pottery kilns have been discovered in and around the village. The general background to the pottery industry in Potterspury has already been published (*Post-Med. Arch.*, 2 (1968), 55–81). The specific kilns are listed below.

ᵃ(11) MEDIEVAL POTTERY KILN (SP 760431), in the garden of a former farm-house in the village, on limestone at 92 m. above OD. A late 14th-century, single-flue, up-draught kiln with a circular oven and a roughly rectangular stoke-hole was excavated in 1970. It produced jugs and bowls of buff fabric with olive-green glaze. (*Med. Arch.*, 15 (1975), 177)

ᵃ(12) MEDIEVAL POTTERY KILN (SP 762433), close to the above and in a similar situation, near the vicarage. Trial excavations have been carried out on a kiln which apparently produced several different types of late medieval pottery (*Med. Arch.*, 9 (1965), 217).

ᵃ(13) MEDIEVAL POTTERY KILN (SP 76084314), N. of High Street, on limestone. A small oval single-flue kiln exca-

vated in 1949 contained wasters of many different vessels as well as roof tiles dating from the 14th or 15th century (*Arch. Newsletter*, 2 (1949–50), 156–7).

ᵃ(14) 17TH-CENTURY POTTERY KILNS (SP 76164317), in the garden of a new house constructed in the grounds of the vicarage. Excavation in 1965 revealed two kilns, a drying hut and perhaps a potter's workshop. The site has been fully published elsewhere. (*BNFAS*, 4 (1970), 24; 7 (1972), 49–51; *Wolverton and District Arch. Soc. Newsletter*, 10 (1966), 10; *Post-Med. Arch.*, 2 (1968), 55–81)

ᵃ(15) MEDIEVAL POTTERY (SP 761421), in the same area as the Roman site (7). Some medieval sherds have been found close to the stream (*BNFAS*, 1 (1966), 12).

ᵃ(16) STONE-QUARRIES (?) (SP 761433), lie on the N. side of the valley immediately N.W. of the church, on rocks of the Upper Estuarine Series, at 90 m. above OD. An expanse of what appears to be ancient stone-quarrying covers the side of the hill. At the E. end quarrying has cut through pre-existing ridge-and-furrow. A few sherds of medieval pottery have been found on the quarried areas. The proximity of the medieval kilns may be of significance in the interpretation of these earthworks. The area lay within the old enclosure around the village in 1776 (NRO, Enclosure Map). (RAF VAP CPE/UK/1926, 2244–5; air photographs in NMR)

(17) CULTIVATION REMAINS. The common fields of Potterspury and of Yardley Gobion were apparently all worked as one, and were enclosed by an Act of Parliament of 1775 (NRO, Enclosure Map, 1776). The Act also enclosed an area called Fersen Field, which was a detached part of Cosgrove parish (G. Baker, *Hist. of Northants.*, II (1836–41), 128). No details of these fields are known, beyond their general area. The Enclosure Map, as well as an earlier map of 1728 (NRO), shows that the common fields lay only to the S.E., N. and E. of the village. Ridge-and-furrow of these fields exists on the ground or can be traced from air photographs in very few places. There is a group of interlocked furlongs S.E. of the village (SP 768428) and isolated areas elsewhere (e.g. SP 767432, 770438 and 755438). Immediately N. of the village (SP 760435) is an extensive area of ridge-and-furrow preserved in permanent grassland along the valley sides. Part of this lay in the former open fields, but the rest was already in old enclosures in 1776.

Ridge-and-furrow also survives in other parts of Potterspury parish which apparently were never arable land in the common fields. In the extreme S. of the parish (SP 765421), on either side of a N.E.-flowing stream, are four rectangular interlocked furlongs which lay at the S. end of an area known as Brown's Wood Green. This was apparently common pasture land until after 1776 when it was enclosed into its present fields. This ridge-and-furrow is probably medieval in date and may be associated with the moat (8) which lies immediately to the N. Another block of ridge-and-furrow (SP 757429) lies immediately S.W. of the village and of Watling Street, within the land which was once a detached part of Cosgrove parish. This had been enclosed before 1776, apparently directly from the waste woodland. The ridge-and-furrow here fits within the modern field boundaries.

Other ridge-and-furrow, again lying within existing fields, can be seen N.W. of the village (SP 755435) on land which was also old enclosures in 1728, but which is said once to have been common grazing land shared by Potterspury and Yardley Gobion. In the W. of the parish, within Wakefield Lawn (SP 735434), further blocks of ridge-and-furrow are traceable. These may be the remains of the arable land of the former settlement of Wakefield, though it is more likely that it represents either contemporary or later ploughing of the ancient deer lawn.

The common fields of the deserted village of Furtho (9) were enclosed in about 1600 by Edward Furtho when the village itself was depopulated. Ridge-and-furrow of these fields can be traced only on air photographs around and to the S. of the site of the village where it is arranged in large rectangular furlongs set at right angles to each other (centred SP 773425). Other traces of ridge-and-furrow once part of the Furtho common fields are visible to the N.E., around Badger's Farm (now in Cosgrove parish, SP 777440) and S.E. of Knotwood Farm (now in Old Stratford parish,

SP775417). (RAF VAP CPE/UK/1926, 2240–6, 5238–45; F21 58/RAF/517, 0026–31)

For Potterspury deer park, see Yardley Gobion (8).

48 QUINTON
(OS 1:10000 [a] SP 75 SE, [b] SP 75 NE)

The parish is long and narrow and of irregular shape, covering some 350 hectares. It slopes generally N. towards a W.-flowing tributary of the R. Nene on the N. boundary. The higher ground around and S. of the village, above 100 m. above OD, is all covered by Boulder Clay. Limestones and Northampton Sand are exposed in narrow bands immediately W., N. and E. of the village and there are small areas of Upper Lias Clay as well as glacial deposits on the lower ground in the N. Two important sites have been excavated over recent years, an Iron Age and Roman settlement (5) and a medieval moated site (6), both on the S. side of the village. The latter is an element in the interesting medieval settlement pattern of the parish (6–9).

PREHISTORIC AND ROMAN

[b](1) ENCLOSURES (SP 766556), in the extreme N.W. of the parish, on alluvium at 70 m. above OD. Air photographs (not seen by RCHM) are said to show several sub-rectangular enclosures (*BNFAS*, 5 (1971), 40).

[b](2) ENCLOSURES AND RING DITCH (SP 770556), 400 m. E. of (1). Air photographs (not seen by RCHM) are said to show cropmarks of a ring ditch and two sub-rectangular enclosures (*BNFAS*, 5 (1971), 40).

[b](3) ENCLOSURE AND DITCHES (SP 771553), 450 m. S.S.E. of (2), on glacial sand and gravel at 82 m. above OD. Air photographs (CUAP, AOK36) show cropmarks of a rectangular enclosure only 0.25 hectares in area with an entrance in the E. side and a large pit in the N.W. corner. Traces of ditches are faintly visible to the E.

[a](4) RING DITCHES (?) (SP 771548 and 772547), N.W. of the village, on Northampton Sand and limestone, at 88 m. above OD. Air photographs (not seen by RCHM) are said to show cropmarks of two ring ditches. A later authority has suggested that one of these is the site of a windmill, but this is doubtful (*BNFAS*, 4 (1970), 32; 7 (1972), 60).

[a](5) NEOLITHIC (?), IRON AGE AND ROMAN SETTLEMENT (centred SP 775535), S. of the village, on Boulder Clay at 105 m. above OD. The site lies in Great Hold Field, close to a medieval moated site (6); both sites have been excavated in recent years. The prehistoric and Roman settlement was completely unrecorded and lay beneath ridge-and-furrow until modern ploughing revealed its existence. The excavations have been published fully elsewhere and only a summary is given here.

Excavation revealed evidence of possible late Neolithic occupation, including over 100 worked flints as well as leaf-shaped and barbed-and-tanged arrowheads. The main features, however, were of late Iron Age and Roman date.

The excavator distinguished three phases at the N. end of the site. In phase I, the most important feature was the ditch of a circular house 13 m. in diam. with two entrances. There were also numerous pits, ditches and depressions some of which may have been ovens or kilns, perhaps for simple pottery manufacture, but otherwise of unknown function. A cremation burial was discovered as well as late Belgic and Roman pottery including samian, spindle whorls and three brooches. This phase probably lasted from the early 1st century AD to the last quarter of that century. In phase II a stone building was constructed, overlying the circular structure of Phase I. Foundations of a rectangular stone building, 9.43 m. by 7.72 m. overall, divided into one large and two small rooms, were investigated. Hearths or ovens and pits were identified within the building, and the post-holes of a porch at the S. end. Finds included much Roman pottery, including colour-coated and samian wares, glass, building material and four coins. The latter were all of the mid 4th century, but the construction and main occupation of the building was thought to have been from the late 1st to the late 2nd century. In phase III no further construction had taken place but there was evidence from coins that the perhaps decaying building was still in use in the 3rd and 4th centuries.

Further excavations a little to the S. revealed a sequence of ditches from the mid 1st century AD culminating in a 3rd-century circular building of unusual type. The foundations of a stone building, similar to that to the N. and on the same alignment, were also uncovered. Finds included three brooches, one of the 1st century and two of the 2nd century, as well as parts of a silvered bronze mirror, a bronze needle, a paste *intaglio* of Bacchus, a bronze manicure set and a ring. Iron knives, iron nails suggesting shoe-making, iron slag, Roman coins and Iron Age and Roman pottery were also present. (*BNFAS*, 5 (1971), 25; 7 (1972), 30–31; *Northants. Archaeol.*, 8 (1973), 5, 15–16; 9 (1974), 95–6; 10 (1975), 162; 11 (1976), 193; 12 (1977), 215; 14 (1979), 103–4; CBA Group 9, *Newsletter*, 5 (1975), 17; 6 (1976), 21; 7 (1977), 13; *Britannia*, 3 (1972), 324; 6 (1975), 253; 7 (1976), 334–5; *J. Northants. Mus. and Art Gall.*, 11 (1974), 1–59)

MEDIEVAL AND LATER

[a](6) MOAT (SP 776541; Fig. 97; Plate 7), lay on the S. side of the village, on Boulder Clay, at 100 m. above OD, to the N. of a large Iron Age and Roman site (5). Excavations have been carried out at both sites since 1969: only a summary is given here. Immediately before excavation the moat consisted of a shallow ditch completely surrounding an island, but this was only part of an area of earthworks recorded on air photographs taken before destruction (Plate 7; RAF VAP CPE/UK/1926, 3021–3). These show that, in addition to the main moat, there was a smaller ditched enclosure to the N.W. and a large pond to the S.E. To the S. and S.W. were small closes or paddocks, bounded by low banks or shallow ditches, all apparently overlaid by later ridge-and-furrow. The site was a fine example of a manorial complex and was presumably the site of the main manor of Quinton which is recorded from 1086 onwards (VCH *Northants.*, IV (1937), 282–3).

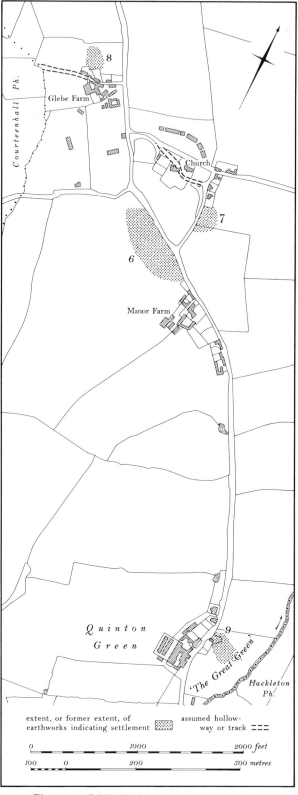

extent, or former extent, of earthworks indicating settlement

assumed hollow-way or track

Fig. 97   QUINTON (6)   Moat, (7–9)
Settlements remains

The excavations, confined to the main moat, showed that the surrounding ditch was no more than 1 m. deep and had been deliberately filled in after the 17th century. The earliest phase of building within the moat was represented by stake- and post-holes of a timber structure earlier than the 12th century. The first stone building was probably of the mid 12th century and various reconstructions took place up to the late 14th century. It was made of good-quality limestone, roofed with stone slate and green-glazed ridge tiles. Foundations of a hall and solar and of kitchen ranges were exposed. The former had a guardrobe tower on its W. side. The kitchens contained kilns, ovens and hearths, including a possible pottery kiln, a corn-drying oven and a large circular kiln with the appearance of a lime-kiln although there was no definite evidence for any of these functions. Finds included sherds of 12th to 14th-century date, two complete jugs thought to be from Brill (Buckinghamshire) and Potterspury, a Lyveden face-mask from a jug, an annular brooch, bronze pins, two seals, an iron key, nails, glass, lead, a silver penny of David II of Scotland, a 15th-century token, a pottery spindle-whorl and an unusual sculpture of a monkey with a drum. (*BNFAS*, 4 (1970), 21; 5 (1971), 34; 7 (1972), 51–2; *Northants. Archaeol.*, 8 (1973), 23; 9 (1974), 109; 10 (1975), 169; 11 (1976), 200; CBA Group 9, *Newsletter*, 4 (1974), 19; 5 (1975), 21; 6 (1976), 21; *Med. Arch*, 15 (1971), 164; 16 (1972), 195)

(7)–(9) SETTLEMENT REMAINS (Fig. 97), formerly part of Quinton village. The remains described below though scant are historically important because, together with the standing buildings and cartographic evidence, they indicate that the village was once made up of a number of distinct parts. One part lay around the medieval church (7) but probably never consisted of more than a few houses until the present century. To the N.W., around Glebe Farm (8), there seems to have been another small group of buildings. The moat (6) to the S., with the existing Manor Farm and some other houses which have left no visible trace (NRO, map of 1723), formed another distinct settlement. Further S. again lay the small hamlet of Quinton Green (9).

[a](7) SETTLEMENT REMAINS AND HOLLOW-WAY (SP 776543; Fig. 97), lie immediately W., S. and S.E. of Quinton church, at 97 m. above OD. The present drive from the Preston Deanery road to the Old Rectory occupies a broad hollow-way 13 m. wide and up to 1.5 m. deep. It continues as a hollow-way between the Old Rectory and the church, then turns E. to pass along the S. side of the churchyard and runs into School Lane. In 1723 (map in NRO) this was the main road past the church and the section of the present Preston Deanery road to the N. of the church did not exist. The modern road was constructed and the old lane abandoned at some time between 1723 and 1815 (map in NRO). On the E. side of School Lane, on the site of and to the S. of the School House, there were in both 1815 and 1723 three closes, all devoid of buildings. The area has now been built over, but air photographs taken in 1947 (RAF VAP CPE/UK/1926, 3021–2) show parts of the boundary banks, already damaged. These closes were probably the sites of houses abandoned before 1723. (Air photographs in NMR)

[a](8) SETTLEMENT REMAINS (SP 772544; Fig. 97), lie immediately N.W. of Glebe Farm at the N.W. end of the village, on limestone at 94 m. above OD. Only Glebe Farm and the modern Glebe Cottage stand today but until very recently there were derelict cottages alongside a narrow E.-W. lane to the N. of the farm. The farm, three houses on the N. side of the lane and another isolated building to the N.W. are shown on a map of 1723 (NRO). The lane ran further W. to the bottom of a valley. Apart from the rubble of the recently demolished buildings little remains on the ground. The field N. of the farm has old quarry pits over its E. part and ridge-and-furrow on its W. half. Some low banks are the sites of hedges in existence in 1723. The site of the isolated building is marked by a rectangular sunken platform and the extension of the lane to the E. is preserved as a damaged hollow-way of which only part of the S. side survives. (Air photographs in NMR)

[a](9) SETTLEMENT REMAINS (SP 783531; Fig. 97), formerly part of the hamlet known as Quinton Green, lies in the S. of the parish, on limestone and Boulder Clay at 107 m. above OD. Today the hamlet consists of one farm and a small group of cottages on the W. side of the road. However, in 1815 (NRO, Enclosure Map) these buildings lay on one side of an open triangular area known as The Great Green. On the N.E. side of this green were other houses which have now disappeared. The greater part of the area of the houses in 1815 is occupied by modern farm buildings, but further S.E. pottery of 14th to 18th-century date, together with stone and brick rubble, has been found in the modern arable land. This indicates that there may have been a larger hamlet in the area. Nothing is known of its history, but it may have been a relatively late settlement on the edge of Salcey Forest, which in medieval time extended into the parish. The fields immediately S.E. of the site (SP 788526) were known as East Assarts in 1815.

[a](10) SITE OF WINDMILL (SP 76815455), lies in the E. of the parish, on the top of a N.E.-projecting spur of Upper Lias Clay at 94 m. above OD. Air photographs taken in 1947 (RAF VAP CPE/UK/1926, 5021–3) show a well-marked mound, some 15 m. in diam., with a surrounding ditch. By 1966 the mound had been completely destroyed and only a circular cropmark 20 m. across shows on air photographs of that date (FSL6565, 1804). Nothing remains on the ground. A little to the E. (SP 76905456) is a circular patch of limestone rubble associated with large quantities of 18th and 19th-century pottery but these finds are not related to the windmill which had certainly disappeared by 1723 (map in NRO). In 1815 (NRO, Enclosure Map) the area was called Mill Closes.

(11) CULTIVATION REMAINS. The common fields of the parish were enclosed by an Act of Parliament of 1814. Immediately before that date there were three open fields occupying only the N. part of the parish (NRO, Enclosure Map, 1815). Upper Field lay to the E. of the village and Middle Field to the N.; Nether Field occupied the extreme N. of the parish. The rest of the parish to the S. of the village had already been enclosed. Exactly the same arrangement is recorded almost a century earlier, in 1723 (map in NRO).

Ridge-and-furrow of the open fields exists on the ground or can be traced on air photographs in only a few places in the N. of the parish. It is mainly arranged in rectangular furlongs set at right angles to each other which appear to agree exactly with the furlongs marked on the 1815 and 1723 maps, except at one place in the extreme N. of the parish (SP 770555). Here a block of ridge-and-furrow is identical in shape to the furlong called 'Cross Furlongs' on the maps, except that it extends beyond the 1723 and 1815 northern boundary of the furlong in what was then West Brook Meadow. In the S. of the parish a little ridge-and-furrow is visible within fields which were old enclosures in 1815 and 1723. However it is confined to those fields immediately S.W. of the village (SP 775536) which may once have been part of the common fields. No ridge-and-furrow is traceable further S., on the fields described as East Assarts on the maps or in the surrounding area of land reclaimed from the woodland. (RAF VAP CPE/UK/1926, 3020–4, 5020–4; FSL6565, 1003–5, 1802–4)

49 RADSTONE
(OS 1:10000 [a] SP 54 SE, [b] SP 53 NE, [c] SP. 64 SW)

The parish occupies only about 550 hectares and lies on land sloping generally E. bounded on the N.E. by a stream flowing towards the R. Ouse. Most of the area, from the higher ground in the W. at 160 m. above OD to the valley in the N.E., is covered by Boulder Clay, but small bands of limestone and Upper Lias Clay are exposed along this valley and that of another central stream. The main monument is the deserted village of Lower Radstone (2).

PREHISTORIC AND ROMAN

An urn containing coins, probably Roman, is said to have been found in the parish before 1900 (lost; VCH Northants., I (1902), 220; OS Record Cards).

MEDIEVAL AND LATER

[a](1) SETTLEMENT REMAINS (SP 589405), formerly part of the village of Upper Radstone, lie S.E. of the church on land sloping S., on Boulder Clay at 138 m. above OD.

There were formerly two villages of Radstone in the parish; the present one is Upper Radstone and the other, now deserted, Lower Radstone (2). The details of the population of the two places are given below (see (2)).

The remains consist of a group of ditched and embanked enclosures on the S.W. side of the main through street, separated from the adjacent ridge-and-furrow by a continuous bank and outer ditch. Along the edge of the street are disturbed areas suggesting former house-sites but a later quarry has cut through part of them. Further N.W., at the W. end of the village (SP 586406), are other earthworks now almost destroyed by ploughing. These are mostly the remains of small closes still marked on modern OS maps, the sites of houses which remained until well into the present century. However, some of the closes apparently relate to a previous period of abandonment. (RAF VAP CPE/UK/1926, 5218–9; air photographs in NMR)

[c](2) DESERTED VILLAGE OF LOWER RADSTONE (SP 601405; Fig. 98; Plate 6), lies 1 km. E. of the existing Radstone village, on the N. side of a broad open valley, on limestone of the Upper Estuarine Series at 130 m. above OD. There were formerly two villages in the parish, Upper or Over and Lower or Nether Radstone (J. Bridges, Hist. of Northants., I (1791), 191; G. Baker, Hist. of Northants., I (1822–30), 610); both were always combined in the national taxation records. In 1086 Domesday Book lists one manor of Radstone which was assessed at two hides and had a recorded population of 21. In 1260 there were 22 virgates of land in cultivation at Over Radstone, but only 2½ at Lower Radstone (PRO, C132/24(6)). The 1301 Lay Subsidy lists 30 people in Radstone (PRO, E179/155/31) and in 1524 11 people paid the Lay Subsidy (PRO, E179/155/144). In 1673 21 householders are recorded as paying the Hearth Tax (PRO, E179/254/14). In about 1720 Bridges (op. cit.) said that the present village then had 19 houses and about 100 inhabitants and that 'the footsteps of the old demolished town are still remaining'. By 1801 there were 128 people in the parish.

The earthworks suggest that the village had, in its final stages, a plan based on a T-shaped arrangement of streets. The main feature is the E.-W. hollow-way ('a'-'b'-'c' on plan). At the W. end where it is close to the stream it is up to 1.5 m. deep but as it reaches the junction with the other main hollow-way ('b'-'d' on plan) it has been damaged by later drainage works. Beyond this junction ('b' on plan) it continues E., partly as a terrace-way the up-slope side of which is 1.5 m. high, until it fades out near the E. end of the fishpond (3). On both sides of this terrace-way are foundations of stone-rubble structures up to 0.25 m. high, presumably the sites of former houses ('e' and 'f' on plan). Behind these are fragmentary remains of former closes. On the W. side of the main hollow-way is another group of similar stone-rubble foundations ('g' on plan) with, to the N., two sunken hollows ('h' on plan) which are also probably the sites of buildings. To the N. again is a large subrectangular enclosure. On the E. side of the hollow-way there are scoops cut into the hillside ('i' on plan). These may be connected with the undoubted quarry pits further E. Elsewhere on the site are rectangular closes, bounded by low scarps or shallow ditches, some of which have ridge-and-furrow within them. Towards the W. end is another stone building, possibly a long house ('j' on plan), with a larger rectangular structure to the W. ('k').

There is no indication that the village ever extended to the S. of the main E.-W. hollow-way in the S.E., but the fishpond (3) appears to have been cut through closes S. of the terrace-way. A few sherds of 14th or 15th-century pottery have been found in the modern disturbances in the main hollow-way. Further 12th to 15th-century sherds are recorded from the terrace-way to the E. (BNFAS, 3 (1969), 2; RAF VAP CPE/UK/1926; 5220–2; CUAP BLE24–6, AML64–5, AWN74)

[c](3) FISHPOND (SP 602403; Fig. 98), lies on the S.E. side of the deserted village of Lower Radstone (2), in the bottom of an E.-draining valley on alluvium at 128 m. above OD. It is subrectangular, bounded by a continuous bank which rises to 1.5 m. high at the E. end where it forms the main dam. Until recently it was dry, but it has now

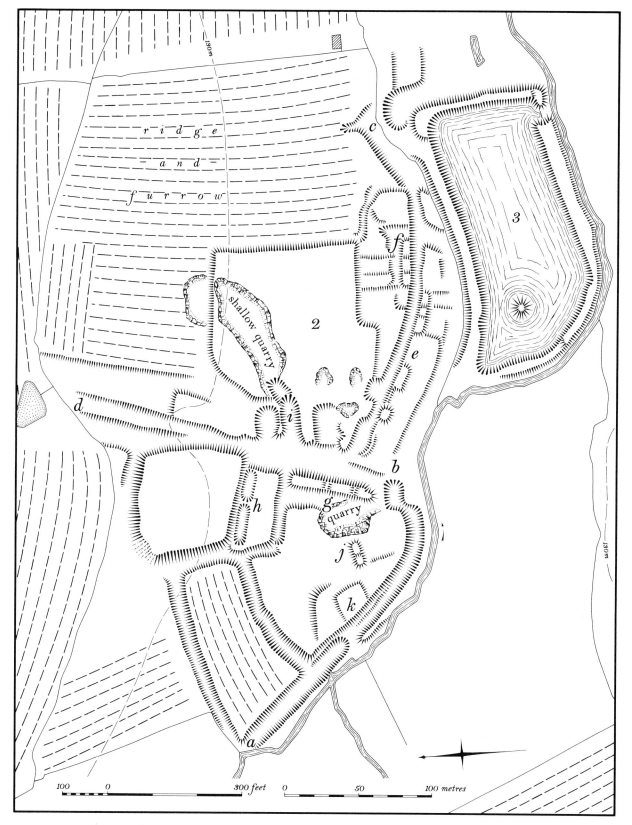

ridge

and

furrow

c

f

shallow quarry

2

e

d

i

b

h

g

quarry

j

k

a

3

100   0   *300 feet*   0   50   100 *metres*

Fig. 98   RADSTONE (2)   Deserted village of Lower Radstone, (3)   Fishponds

been repaired, filled with water and restocked with fish. Near the N.W. corner is a circular mound, which still stands 0.5 m. high above the water. The pond appears to have cut through the closes of the deserted village to the N. and may thus post-date the abandonment of the latter. (RAF VAP CPE/UK/1926, 5220–2; CUAP AML64)

[b](4) WINDMILL MOUND (SP 59513977), lies in the S.E. of the parish, against the boundary with Whitfield, on Boulder Clay at 140 m. above OD. It is a low mound 22 m. in diam. and 0.7 m. high and has been ploughed over. There is no trace of a ditch but one can be seen on air photographs (RAF VAP CPE/UK/1926, 2219–20). Some pottery of 12th to 13th-century date has been found as well as an indication of a central pit or post-hole (BNFAS, 1 (1966), 20; 3 (1969), 2; OS Record Cards).

(5) CULTIVATION REMAINS. The date of the enclosure of the common fields of Radstone is not known, nor is it certain whether each of the two villages of Radstone had its own field system, although this seems likely for the arable land of each village is described separately in 1260 (PRO, C132/24(6)). If so the long projection of the parish to the N.E. might be the land of Lower Radstone.

Ridge-and-furrow of these fields can be traced on air photographs, but little now survives on the ground as the parish is almost entirely arable. It was all arranged in end-on or interlocked furlongs, many of reversed-S form. Among the more notable features was the very wide unploughed triangular strip 220 m. long and up to 30 m. across lying between two narrow furlongs S. of the village (SP 588599), and also the joining up of former end-on furlongs with the result that two or more ridges merge to become one over an older headland (SP 600408). There was also an area of presumably 18th or 19th-century ridge-and-furrow in the E. of the parish, S. of Shortgrove Wood (SP 605407). Here ridges 10 m. wide and exactly straight lay within the existing fields. (RAF VAP CPE/UK/1926, 2217–24, 5217–23)

50 ROADE
(OS 1:10000 [a] SP 75 SW, [b] SP 75 SE, [c] SP 74 NE)

The parish is of roughly triangular shape and covers 650 hectares. It slopes generally to the S. from a ridge capped by Boulder Clay with a maximum height of 120 m. above OD. The village lies on a large expanse of Blisworth Limestone, and to the S. narrow bands of limestones and clays are exposed by the down-cutting of S.-flowing streams on the S.W. and S.E. boundaries. The medieval settlement pattern of the parish was complex. In addition to Roade itself there was a settlement a little to the W., around Hyde Farm (2), and probably another in the N.W. of the parish at the modern Thorpewood Farm. The field systems associated with these settlements are not clearly understood (3).

PREHISTORIC AND ROMAN

A flint scraper and Roman coins and pottery were found in the parish before 1904 (T. J. George, Arch. Survey of Northants. (1904), 192; OS Record Cards). This may refer to Roman material in the BM which includes pottery, a bronze strap-end and a coin of Antoninus Pius. A Roman bronze pin found in the school garden in the 1920s and sometimes said to be from Courteenhall is in NM (OS Record Cards).

[b](1) ENCLOSURES (SP 767523), close to the N. parish boundary, on Boulder Clay, at 120 m. above OD. Air photographs (not seen by RCHM) are said to show cropmarks of two small subrectangular enclosures covering just over 0.5 hectares (BNFAS, 6 (1971), 16).

MEDIEVAL AND LATER

[a](2) DESERTED SETTLEMENT OF HYDE (SP 749513; Fig. 99), lay S.E. of Roade village, immediately E. of Hyde Farm, on the N.E. side of a small S.E.-flowing stream, on Great Oolite Limestone at 110 m. above OD. Almost nothing is known of the history of the settlement and the name is not apparently recorded in documents until 1200 (PN Northants., 106). In Domesday Book one of the two entries under Roade is a manor of one hide, held by William Peveral of the Bishop of Bayeux, which was then waste and in the king's hands (VCH Northants., I (1902), 309). It is possible that the entry refers to this settlement, though this would mean that Roade itself was only a tiny manor with a recorded population of two (VCH, op. cit., 348). However, the complex pattern of minor settlements which once existed in this part of the county and which has now been partly replaced by nucleated villages (e.g. Hartwell (3)–(7)) may partly explain this problem.

The later history of Hyde is unknown and in all the national taxation records it is presumably included with Roade. The place was already reduced to a single farm by 1768 (NRO, map of Roade).

Almost nothing remains of this settlement now, most of the area having recently been built over. On air photographs taken in 1947 (RAF VAP CPE/UK/1926, 1026–8) the area immediately E. of the farm was divided into a number of rectangular closes bounded by low banks and scarps. A trackway appears to have passed between the closes, running N.W.–S.E. The whole covered about 3 hectares. On the opposite side of the valley a few indeterminate earthworks and part of a hollow-way have survived. A pond in the valley bottom appears to be modern.

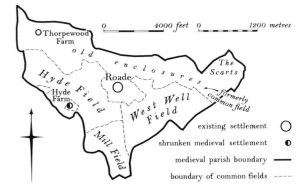

Fig. 99 ROADE Medieval settlements and fields

(3) CULTIVATION REMAINS (Fig. 99). The common fields of the village of Roade, together with those of Ashton (6), were finally enclosed by an Act of Parliament of 1816 (NRO, Enclosure Map, 1819). Immediately before that time there were four open fields in Roade, West Well Field to the S.E., Mill Field to the S., a very small Little Hyde Field to the S.E. and Great Hyde Field to the N.W. In addition there were extensive areas of old enclosures especially in the E. of the parish adjoining Salcey Forest, to the N. of the village and in the N.W. of the parish centred on Thorpewood Farm (SP 744528). An earlier map of the parish of 1768 (NRO) shows a slightly different situation and gives more information. There were then only three open fields, West Well and Mill Fields as they were in 1819 and a Hide Field which comprised the later Great and Little Hyde Fields.

In the old enclosures in the E. of the parish was a group of fields called The Scarts, i.e. assarted land (SP 781519), lying against the parish boundary, and between them and the edge of Westwell Field were three small enclosed fields, Ashwood Lays, Dobbikins Close and Middle Field (centred SP 778518) all described as 'formerly common field but now inclosed'. Immediately to the S. (SP 779514) three other fields are described as 'Part of Ashwood, Stockt up in 1747'.

It is not clear exactly how these fields relate to the medieval settlements of the parish. The old enclosures in the N.W. around Thorpewood Farm may be medieval in origin. In the 18th century the N. part of them was subdivided by three wide droveways, only one of which survives. The area may have been the land of Thorpewood Farm and perhaps was always divided into hedged fields. However, the earliest reference to the farm appears to be in 1662 (PN Northants., 106). One or two of the existing fields have traces of ridge-and-furrow within them (SP 743528 and 752525). Ridge-and-furrow is also visible in the old enclosures in the E. of the parish, both in the Scarts where it seems to fit within the existing field boundaries, and within the area of the former Ashwood. Other fields elsewhere in the parish already enclosed in 1768 also have ridge-and-furrow on them.

Little ridge-and-furrow survives in the area of the common fields. One block exists S. of the village in the old West Well Field (SP 763501), and furlongs remain in the Mill Field along the sides of a small stream (SP 757500) and in Hide Field (SP 755515). (RAF VAP CPE/UK/1926, 1020–8, 1244–5; 106G/UK/1562, 4088–9; FSL6565, 1999–2005, 2011–5)

51 ROTHERSTHORPE

(OS 1:10000 [a] SP 65 NE, [b] SP 75 NW)

The roughly triangular parish covers some 400 hectares of undulating land sloping very generally N.E. and crossed by several small streams flowing N. and N.E. to join the R. Nene. The higher parts between 75 m. and 90 m. above OD are overlaid by Boulder Clay and other glacial deposits, but on the lower ground the underlying Marlstone Rock and Upper Lias Clay are exposed. The extreme N. of the parish,

N.E. of the M1 motorway, is now incorporated within Northampton. The major monument in the parish is the unusual defensive earthwork known as The Berry (8). The settlement remains (5) are of interest as they show that the village has changed its form in recent years.

PREHISTORIC AND ROMAN

A few Iron Age sherds have been noted to the S. of the village (SP 715564; Northants. Archaeol., 13 (1978), 180). A second 'brass' of Antoninus Pius was found somewhere in Rothersthorpe before 1952 (NM).

[b](1) ENCLOSURE (SP 723564), S.E. of the village, on sand and gravel at 88 m. above OD. Air photographs (in NMR) show a small D-shaped enclosure 80 m. by 30 m., orientated N.E.–S.W. Within it and in the surrounding area are numerous other cropmarks, but these appear to be mainly natural. The site is apparently that recorded on a number of occasions, each with an incorrect grid reference (BNFAS, 5 (1971), 40; 7 (1972), 57; Northants. Archaeol., 8 (1973), 26; 12 (1977), 230). A single Iron Age sherd and some Roman pottery have been found on the site (Northants. SMR).

[b](2) ENCLOSURE AND DITCHES (SP 715564), S. of the village, on gravel at 79 m. above OD. Air photographs (in NMR) show, very indistinctly, the cropmarks of the N. part of a small rectangular enclosure with sharp corners. Immediately to the W. are two curving lengths of ditch associated with a very large pit. There are other cropmarks in the same area but these have no distinct pattern (Northants. Archaeol., 12 (1977), 230). A small quantity of worked flints has been noted in the area (Northants. SMR).

[b](3) IRON AGE AND ROMAN SETTLEMENT (SP 720560), S.E. of the village, on glacial sands at 84 m. above OD. A sand-quarry opened in 1973 has produced several worked flints, including two scrapers (SP 720561) and near by (at SP 721562) a fragment of a bar from a Roman pottery kiln has been found (Northants. Archaeol., 9 (1974), 85, 115). In 1974 a shallow ditch was exposed in the quarry face and was excavated. It appeared to be aligned E.S.E.–W.N.W. and its fill contained pottery dated to the late Iron Age and early Roman periods, as well as bone and iron slag (NM; Northants. Archaeol., 10 (1975), 162).

[b](4) ROMAN SETTLEMENT (?) (SP 713562), S.W. of the village, on a low gravel ridge at 90 m. above OD. A scatter of Roman pottery has been noted (Northants. Archaeol., 13 (1978), 182).

MEDIEVAL AND LATER

[b](5) SETTLEMENT REMAINS (centred SP 715564; Figs. 100 and 101), formerly part of Rothersthorpe, lie on the S. side of the village, on either side of The Poplars, on gravel and clay between 75 m. and 84 m. above OD. Although the village has undergone considerable shrinkage or movement, most of this appears to have taken place in relatively recent times. Rothersthorpe is first mentioned in Domesday Book where it is listed as two manors with a total recorded population of 27 (VCH Northants., I (1902), 345, 347). In 1334 the vill paid 58s. 0¼d., tax (PRO, E179/

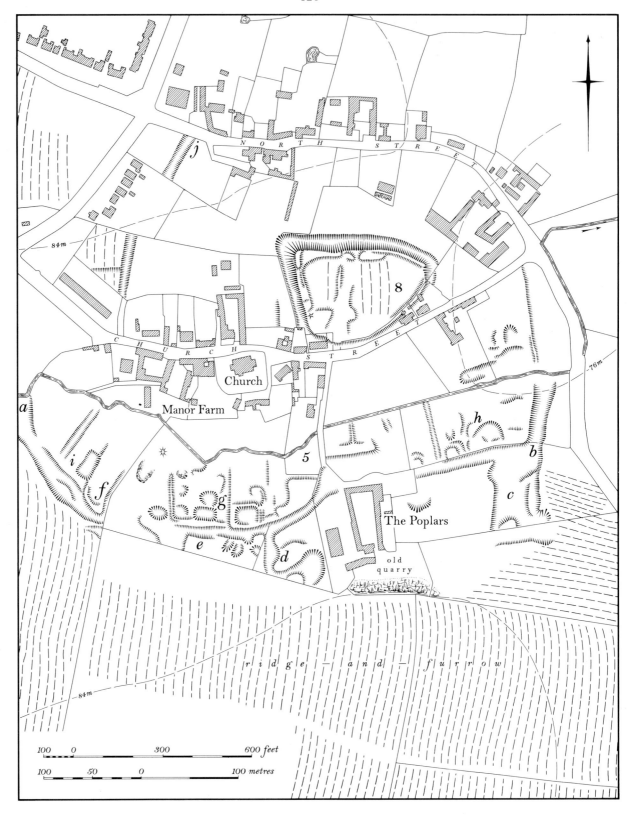

Fig. 100   ROTHERSTHORPE (5)   Settlement remains, (8)   Enclosure

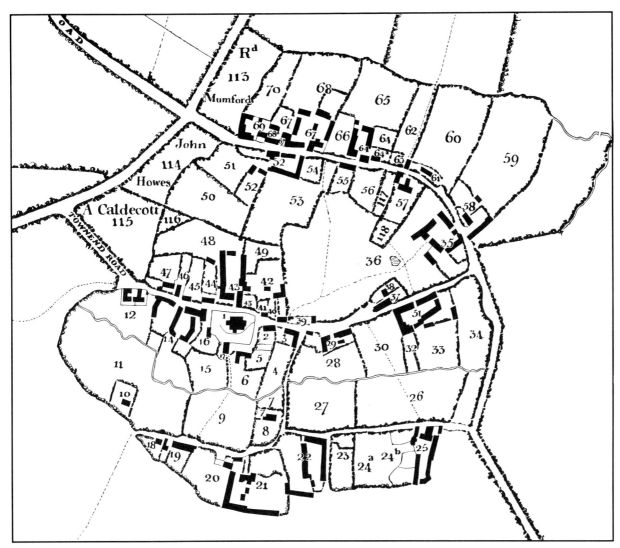

Fig. 101   ROTHERSTHORPE (5)   Settlement remains (based on the Enclosure Map, 1810, NRO)

155/3), a sum which suggests that it was much the same size as the villages in the surrounding area. There were at least 14 cottars on the main manor in 1359 when they paid rent for a common oven (VCH *Northants.*, IV (1937), 286). In 1673 47 people paid the Hearth Tax (PRO, E179/254/14) and Bridges (*Hist. of Northants.*, I (1791), 385), writing in about 1720, said there were then 54 houses at Rothersthorpe. In the 19th century the population of the parish rose from 197 in 1801 to 293 in 1871, though it fell slightly later on. These figures, especially the 19th-century ones, suggest no decline in population, and thus the cartographic evidence and the surviving earthworks have to be interpreted as the result of movement rather than of decline.

The village now consists of two main streets N. of a small E.-flowing brook and separated by The Berry (8). Church Street, with the church, Manor Farm and The Manor, lies immediately N. of the brook. North Street to the N. curves S.E. to meet the E. end of Church Street.

Two lengths of shallow ditch ('j' on plan) may be the remains of a street joining Church Street and North Street in the W. The earliest map of the village (Fig. 101; NRO, Enclosure Map, 1810) shows a more complex pattern. To the S. of the stream was another street, along which there were at least three farms and four cottages. A few years later (1st ed. 1 in. OS map, 1834) all but one of the cottages and all the farms except The Poplars had disappeared, and the street itself appears to have been abandoned. The last cottage was removed soon afterwards and by 1880 only The Poplars remained in the area.

The surviving earthworks add to the information from the maps for they show that at some time before 1810 there were other buildings along this street and that it had once been lined with houses and farms. Thus this part of the village seems to have contracted over a long period.

The main feature on the ground is the line of the original street ('a'-'b' on plan). To the W. of The Poplars it is still a well-marked hollow-way up to 1 m. deep, but at the W. end it fades out although the 1810 map shows that it continued. The drive on the N. side of The Poplars is on the line of the street and to the E. the latter is still traceable as a shallow hollow-way. Its E. end is now blocked, though it apparently once ran on to meet the present road.

The sites of all the buildings in existence in 1810 are still identifiable. The large farm-house and buildings at the E. end of the street are marked by a sunken area, much disturbed ('c' on plan). The other large farmstead immediately W. of The Poplars is also marked by an uneven area with scarps up to 1.75 m. high ('d' on plan). Further W. the sites of two of the three cottages are visible as raised platforms ('e' and 'f' on plan) though no real trace remains of the other cottages. In addition there are earthworks of the houses and closes which had already been abandoned by 1810. On the N. side of the hollow-way and S. of the church ('g' on plan) are the fragmentary

remains of two closes with some building platforms at their S. ends, and other less well-preserved remains, also perhaps former house-sites, lie further E. and W. ('h' and 'i' on plan). (Air photographs in NMR; CUAP AZV71–2)

^b(6) TRAMWAY (SP 721558), in the S.E. corner of the parish, close to the Northampton branch of the Grand Union Canal, at 90 m. above OD. The remains, which have now been totally destroyed by quarrying, were the only surviving section of a tramway built in 1804–5 to link the Grand Junction Canal at Gayton with the R. Nene at Northampton. It was used until 1815 when it was replaced by the canal. The line of the canal followed that of the tramway except at this point (A. H. Faulkner, *The Grand Junction Canal* (1972), 81–8). Before destruction there was a low curving embankment some 10 m. across and already reduced by ploughing. Its course is partly shown by the 300 ft. contour on OS 1:10560 plan SP 75 NW (1968). (RAF VAP CPE/UK/1926, 5029–30)

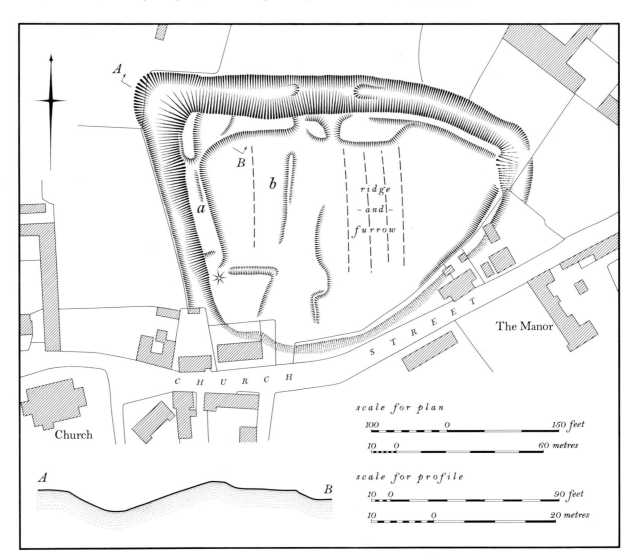

Fig. 102   ROTHERSTHORPE (8)   Enclosure

(7) CULTIVATION REMAINS. The common fields of the parish were enclosed by an Act of Parliament of 1810 (NRO, Enclosure Map). Ridge-and-furrow of these fields exists on the ground or can be traced on air photographs over large parts of the parish, arranged mainly in end-on or interlocked furlongs. It is still extremely well preserved in the W. of the parish (around SP 702563). To the S.S.W. of the village (at SP 712564) are two end-on, reversed-S furlongs which have later been ploughed together as one. This results in ridges 300 m. long, of double reversed-S form with a marked change of alignment in the centre as they ride over the original headlands. (RAF VAP CPE/UK/ 1926, 5029–34; 3G/TUD/UK/118, 6026–30, 6052–6; 1F22 543/RAF/2409, 0140–3; FSL6565, 1796–8; FSL6603, 2383–5)

UNDATED

[b](8) ENCLOSURE (SP 715567; Figs. 100 and 102; Plate 4), known as The Berry, lies in the centre of the village between North Street and Church Street, on Boulder Clay sloping gently S. between 81 m. and 77 m. above OD. Nothing is known of its history and no date can be assigned to it. To judge from its position, its name and perhaps its form, it could be a medieval structure of defensive purpose and it has been so regarded by a number of authorities (OS Record Cards; VCH Northants., II (1906), 417). However, its unusual shape and the ample evidence of secondary use both for habitation and agricultural might indicate that it is perhaps pre-medieval in origin and was reused in the medieval period, perhaps as a manorial centre. The nearest parallel to it in form, if not in situation, is Burnt Walls, Daventry (RCHM Northants., III (1981), Daventry (35)).

The remains consist of a roughly triangular area, formerly bounded by a wide, deep ditch and an inner bank or rampart. The ditch is now preserved only on the W. and N. sides where it is up to 2.5 m. deep below the adjacent land and up to 4 m. deep below the inner bank. On the S. side no trace of the ditch now survives and its line has either been built over or incorporated within modern gardens. The bank or rampart also remains on the N. and E. side, but has been much altered. The only place where it is in its original form is near the E. corner where it is a narrow-topped bank up to 1.5 m. high above the interior. Along the rest of the N. side it has been pulled down, apparently by ploughing, so that it now has a wide summit and a much-degraded inner edge. Modern footpaths pass through two gaps in the centre of the N. side. In the N.W. corner and along the W. side, the bank has also been altered and in one place appears to have a short section of a later stone-rubble wall on it ('a' on plan). There are slight traces of a bank in the S.E. corner, but along most of the S. side this has been removed and only a degraded scarp marks its outer face. No certain original entrances into the enclosure are visible, though it has been suggested (OS Record Cards) that there may have been one at the extreme E. end. The interior has a number of features all of which appear to be later than the encircling bank and ditch. In the S.W. corner is a small circular mound 0.4 m. high with a hole in the centre. To the E. of this is a length of shallow ditch which, at its E. end, turns S. and becomes a scarp. Further E. again there is a short stretch of low bank only 0.2 m. high which also

continues N. as a scarp. These features may be the sites of buildings. Part of the rest of the interior has slight traces of wide ridge-and-furrow on it. That this is later than the defences is clear from the fact that the rampart on the N. side has been pulled down as a result of its use as a headland. A low bank ('b' on plan) only 0.3 m. high crosses the interior. Its purpose is unknown, but it too seems to have been altered by later ploughing. (Air photographs in NMR; CUAP AZV71)

52   SHUTLANGER
(OS 1:10000 [a] SP 75 SW, [b] SP 74 NW)

The modern parish, which was formerly part of Stoke Bruerne, is some 500 hectares in area. The R. Tove, here flowing at about 78 m. above OD in a wide alluvial valley, defines the S. boundary. The ground rises to the N. across Upper Lias Clay and Oolitic limestones to an area of Boulder Clay with a maximum height of 128 m. above OD on the N. boundary. Little archaeological material has been noted in the parish, though the gardens (3), thought to be a 17th-century, are of some interest.

ROMAN

[b](1) ROMAN SETTLEMENT (SP 717492), in the W. of the parish, on Upper Lias Clay at 91 m. above OD. A scatter of Roman coarse wares and tile was discovered here in 1967 (BNFAS, 3 (1969), 2).

MEDIEVAL AND LATER

For the medieval deer park in the E. of the parish, see Stoke Bruerne (8).

[a](2) SETTLEMENT REMAINS (centred SP 728501), formerly part of Shutlanger, lay on the N.E. edge of the village, on limestone at 94 m. above OD. The earthworks have now been partly destroyed by modern housing, but an area of disturbed ground still remains on the E. side of a small S.-flowing stream separated from the adjacent ridge-and-furrow by a low bank and ditch. It is not clear whether these were the sites of former houses but if they were they suggest that Shutlanger once had a 'double-loop' plan of which only the S. loop now remains complete. The earthworks were already devoid of buildings in 1727 (map in NRO). (RAF VAP CPE/UK/1926, 1239–40; air photographs in NMR)

[b](3) GARDEN REMAINS AND ENCLOSURES (SP 729498; Fig. 103), lie around the isolated house known as The Monastery, on the S.E. side of the village, on Upper Lias Clay at 95 m. above OD. The house itself is of medieval origin and has much 14th-century work in it, including its original roof, porch and windows, and was probably rebuilt in the 16th or 17th century. Although usually said to be a chapel, it is almost certainly a domestic building, perhaps a manor house (Ass. Arch. Soc Rep., 22 (1894), 223–6; N. Pevsner, Northamptonshire (1973), 403).

The surviving earthworks may be a manorial enclosure though those on the S. appear to be the remains of a garden

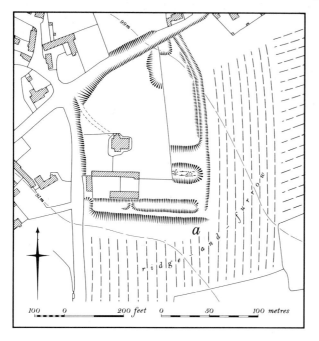

Fig. 103   SHUTLANGER (3)   Garden remains

associated with the house and perhaps of the 17th century. The house and its present gardens lie on the W. end of a low ridge, and the N. and W. sides are bounded by a steep scarp. On the E., beyond the present gardens, is a ditch 1 m. deep, apparently an earlier boundary. At its S. end this opens out into a broad depression, perhaps a former pond. On the S. side are two parallel scarps 1.5 m. high with, between them to the E., a shallow rectangular depression, also possibly a pond. These garden remains lie below the main front of the house. They appear to overlie earlier ridge-and-furrow especially in the S.E. corner ('a' on plan) for the existing ridges are too short to have been ploughed. (RAF VAP CPE/UK/1926, 1239–40; air photographs in NMR)

(4) CULTIVATION REMAINS. The common fields of Shutlanger, together with those of Stoke Bruerne, were enclosed by an Act of Parliament of 1840. Before that date there were three fields, Wood Field to the W. and N. of the village, Rowslade to the S.W. and Alderton in the S. of the parish. Within all three fields lay areas of old enclosures which appear to have been former furlongs. To the N.E. of the village, and extending across the modern parish boundary with Stoke Bruerne, was a large area of open grassland known as Stoke Plain or Shutlanger Plain. Part of Stoke Park occupied the S.E. of the parish (NRO: maps of 1727 and 1768; Tithe Map, 1842; Enclosure Map, 1844). Ridge-and-furrow survives on the ground or can be traced from air photographs in relatively few places in the parish. There are two groups of small, rectangular, interlocked furlongs in Wood Field (SP 730504 and 722498) and some end-on and interlocked furlongs in Rowslade Field (SP 718490) and in Alderton Field (SP 730481). There is no evidence that there was ever any ridge-and-furrow on Shutlanger Plain but end-on furlongs occupy much of that

part of Stoke Park which lies in this parish. The latter may be associated with the fields of a medieval settlement in Stoke Bruerne (7), for the modern parish boundary across the Park is certainly not the medieval division between Stoke Bruerne and Shutlanger. Most of the best surviving ridge-and-furrow in the parish lies around the village, within fields which were already old enclosures in 1727, although some of it (e.g. SP 730498) appears to be of open-field form. (RAF VAP CPE/UK/1926, 1029–32, 1237–42; FSL6565, 1997–9)

53   SILVERSTONE
(OS 1:10000 [a] SP 64 SE, [b] SP 64 NE, [c] SP 64 SW)

The parish covers about 760 hectares and is of irregular shape, sloping gently N. from the higher ground on the S. boundary with Buckinghamshire, at 155 m. above OD, to a N.E.-flowing stream on the N.W. boundary at about 105 m. above OD. It is entirely covered by Boulder Clay except for some small patches of glacial sands and gravels, and bands of Oolite limestone along the valley sides in the N. The most important monuments are the medieval fishponds (2) which are well documented because of their royal association.

PREHISTORIC AND ROMAN

Worked flints are said to have been found in the parish (OS Record Cards). The probable Bronze Age barrow said to be in Silverstone parish and which was excavated in 1940 actually lay just S. of the county boundary, in Buckinghamshire (Ant. J., 28 (1948), 27; W. F. Grimes, Excavations on Defence Sites, I (1960), 245–7).

[b](1) ROMAN SETTLEMENT (?) (SP 677456), in the N. of the parish, on river gravels at 105 m. above OD. The neck and parts of the handles of a large Roman amphora were discovered in the bank of a small stream, together with ashes and animal bones (OS Record Cards).

MEDIEVAL AND LATER

The Benedictine Priory of Luffield lay partly in the extreme S. of the parish, and partly in Buckinghamshire. Nothing remains on the site, which is now occupied by Abbey Farm (SP 674421; VCH Northants., II (1906), 95–7).

The site of the well-documented royal hunting lodge at Silverstone has not been located. It is mentioned as early as 1121–30 and was rebuilt and altered several times before 1317 when it was abandoned (R. A. Brown, H. M. Colvin and A. J. Taylor, History of The King's Works, II (1963), 1002–3). It may have been located near the present parish church, close to the smaller of the two fishponds (2) (SP 668443), for the area was known as Hall Garth in 1600 (NRO, map of Whittlewood Forest).

There are records of a deer park in the parish in the 13th century but this also has not been located (Northants. P. and P., 5 (1975), 231).

[a](2) FISHPONDS (SP 667446; Fig. 104), lie to the N.W. of the village, in the bottom of a broad open valley draining N.E. and in one of its tributary valleys, on alluvium be-

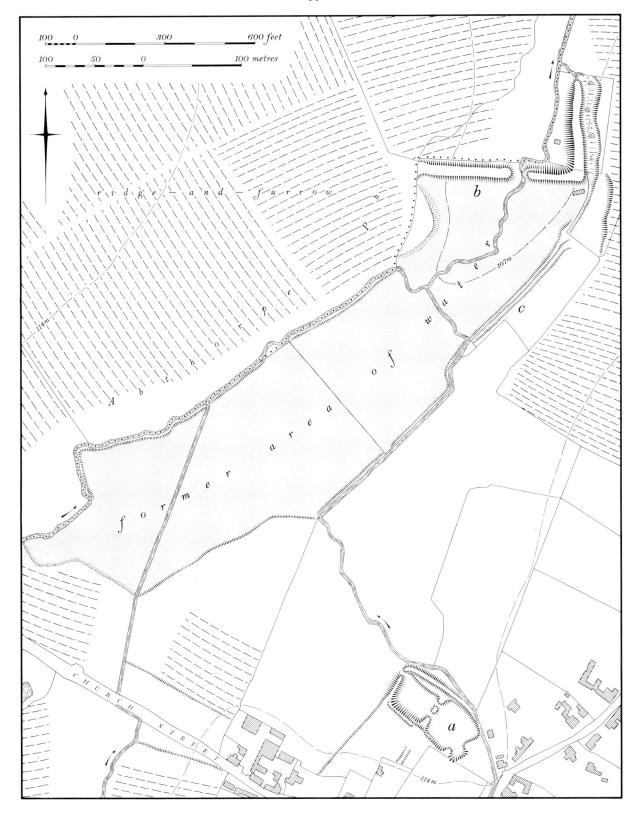

Fig. 104 SILVERSTONE (2) Fishponds

tween 105 m. and 112 m. above OD. The ponds are associated with a royal hunting lodge at Silverstone (see above) and are referred to in a number of 13th-century documents. For example in 1227 the sheriff of Northampton was ordered 'to cause the broken ponds of the Kings stews of Silverston . . . and the bays of the same to be repaired' (*Cal. Lib.* I, 23). In 1241 the bailiffs of Silverstone were asked to 'aid William the Kings fisherman, whom he is to send to fish in his stews at Silverston and to send the fish that he shall catch to the King without delay' (*Cal. Lib.* II, 31) and in 1244 the keepers of the 'stew of Silverstone' were told to 'aid Geoffrey Corburn and William the Kings fisherman, whom he is sending to fish there, to carry their fish to the King at Woodstock' (*Cal. Lib.* II, 217). Soon after, the King ordered that his servants were to 'search out nets in the town of Oxford with which William the Kings fisherman, whom he is sending to Silverstone, can fish in the Kings stews there and to carry them to Woodstock' (*Cal. Lib.* III, 83–3). In 1257 the King allocated the men of Silverstone '4 shillings spent in taking 20 pike in the Kings stews at Silverstone and in salting them and carrying them to London' (*Cal. Lib.* IV, 415). The later history of the ponds is unknown for royal interest in the hunting lodge ceased in the early 14th century. The ponds are not marked on a map of Whittlewood Forest of about 1600 (NRO).

At the S.E. end of the area ('a' on plan) are two small conjoined rectangular ponds cut back into the side of small steep-sided valley to a depth of 2.5 m. A large dam up to 3 m. high along the N.W. and N.E. sides has a later cut through it in the N. corner. The remains of a second dam 2 m. high, cut through in two places, form a division between the two ponds. These ponds were probably breeding tanks for the main pond which lies to the N. and N.W. The latter, when filled, was probably the largest artificial pond in the county in medieval times. The water was retained by a large dam spanning the open valley ('b' on plan). This is flat-topped and up to 3 m. high and has a later gap cut through the centre. At its E. end the dam turns N. and there is a large marshy depression along its E. side, perhaps where the surplus water from the pond was returned around the edge of the dam and into the stream. The depression received water from an artificial leat which ran above the former pond along its E. side ('c' on plan). However the depression is larger than it would need to be for these purposes and it may be another fishpond or a mill-pond. The area of the former pond is defined by a number of features. On the S.E. side it is marked by a high-level leat ('c' on plan) which once carried water from the tributary valley and from the small fishponds to the S.E. along the side of the pond and around the E. end of the dam. The S. side of the pond is marked by a low scarp or bank less than 0.25 m. high, now largely ploughed down or completely destroyed by the construction of a playing field at the extreme S.W. end but clearly visible on air photographs taken in 1947 (RAF VAP CPE/UK/1926, 3230–2). Most of the N.W. side of the pond is marked by another embanked leat which carries the water of the stream which occupied the valley bottom before the construction of the ponds. This leat returns the water into the valley bottom a little to the S.W. of the dam.

Another point of considerable interest is the fact that though the parish boundary between Silverstone and Abthorpe follows the stream in the valley for most of its length, in the vicinity of the pond it follows the N.W. edge of the pond as far as the dam and then returns to the original stream. This suggests that the parish boundary was moved in order to ensure that the whole pond lay in Silverstone parish. If this is so it was probably carried out by Royal Command in order to avoid the legal and administrative problems involved in having the pond in two parishes. (*Northants. P. and P.*, 4 (1970), 308; CUAP, AWN68)

[a](3) SETTLEMENT REMAINS (centred SP 662437), formerly part of Silverstone village, lie on the E. side of the road, in the S. part of West End, on Boulder Clay at 128 m. above OD. The area is under cultivation and only a scatter of stone-rubble and pottery of 13th to 18th-century date is visible. This marks the sites of at least four houses which are shown here on the map of Whittlewood Forest of about 1600 (NRO) but which had gone by 1827 (NRO, Enclosure Map). These remains contribute to an understanding of the development of Silverstone village which, before 19th-century and later changes consisted of three distinct parts. To the E., around the church, lay a compact settlement at a cross-roads. To the W. was a single long street, now known as West End, and to the S. lay another street, known as Cattle End. No explanation for this unusual settlement pattern can be suggested, except that it might be the result of piecemeal forest-edge development. (RAF VAP CPE/UK/1926, 3230–2, 5230–1)

(4) CULTIVATION REMAINS. The common fields of the parish were enclosed by an Act of Parliament of 1827 (NRO, Enclosure Map). At that time there were five open fields of very different sizes. Between the main part of the village and West End lay the small Backside Field, and to the E. lay the equally small Ridge Knoll Field. Hall Hills and Blackspit Fields were to the N.E. of the village, with Swinney Field beyond. Old enclosures surrounded the various parts of the village to the S., W. and E.

The S. part of the present parish was not in Silverstone parish in 1827 but in Whittlewood Forest and is not depicted on the Enclosure Map. An earlier map of Whittlewood Forest of about 1600 (NRO) shows a similar situation, though with some additional information. Backside Field was then known as Wood Crafts Field and all the others were grouped into two large areas known as Silson Field and Whittlebury Field. All the old enclosures S. and W. of the village are shown as on the later map but their names, for example Grindons Sart, Dancome Sart, Elms Sart and Fryers Assart, all indicate their origins as woodland clearances. These are probably some of the assarts mentioned as being in Silverstone in 1273 (*Cal. IPM* II, 49). The 1600 map also shows that all the S. part of the parish as far as the county boundary was then under woodland.

Ridge-and-furrow of these fields exists on the ground or can be traced on air photographs in some parts of the parish. A few fragments can be seen in the former Backside or Wood Crafts Field and other small areas, now built over, are visible on air photographs in the former Ridge Knoll Field. To the N.W. of the village very little ridge-and-furrow is traceable in the area of the other three former open fields and the pattern is not recoverable anywhere.

Ridge-and-furrow occurs in the old enclosure W. of the village (SP 659440 and 663433), much of it in exceptionally narrow ridges only 4 m.–5 m. across. For the most part the furlongs lie within existing fields or are bounded by shallow ditches or slight banks indicating former hedges. Further S., both in the area of old enclosures S. of the village and within the former wooded areas, wide ridge-and-furrow, exactly straight and fitted within fields of regular shape, appears to be the result of late 19th-century ploughing (e.g. SP 661429 and 673433). (RAF VAP CPE/UK/ 1926, 1231–3, 2231–4, 3228–34, 5229–32)

54 SLAPTON
(OS 1:10000 ^a SP 64 NW, ^b SP 64 NE)

The parish is small, only a little over 260 hectares, and lies to the N.W. of the R. Tove. A tributary stream forms the S.W. boundary. The high ground in the N.E. is covered by Boulder Clay and Oolitic limestones outcrop on the steep S.W. and S.E.-facing slopes between 105 m. and 120 m. above OD, with Upper Lias Clay on the lower land close to the river.

PREHISTORIC AND ROMAN

For possible barrow, see (3) below.

A coin of Trajan was found in the parish in 1878 (OS Record Cards).

MEDIEVAL AND LATER

^a(1) SETTLEMENT REMAINS (centred SP 640467; Fig. 105), formerly part of Slapton, lie in and around the existing village, on limestone and clay between 99 m. and 114 m. above OD. The surviving earthworks complement the existing pattern of streets and houses, but do not make possible any interpretation of the development of the village. The greater part of the village is arranged along a single main street running N.E.-S.W., with many gaps between the existing buildings. In most of these gaps are fragmentary earthworks indicating that buildings stood there at some time. From this street two lanes extend N.W. towards the almost isolated church and manor house, standing on high ground. Until relatively recently these lanes ran on and encircled the church, churchyard and manor house; they remain as hollow-ways or public footpaths. Immediately to the S. of the church are at least

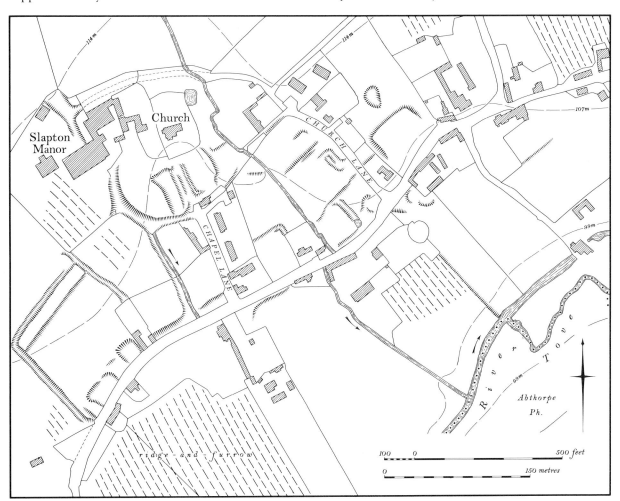

Fig. 105 SLAPTON (1) Settlement remains

four rectangular closes bounded by low scarps up to 1 m. high. These may only be abandoned paddocks, but they could be closes of houses formerly lining the old road to the S., part of which also survives as a hollow-way. Further E., along the S.W. side of Church Lane are other closes, extending down-slope from the lane with, at their N.E. ends, the remains of former buildings lining the lane.

It is not clear whether these earthworks represent a considerable reduction in village size, or are the result of changes in layout. No plans exist of Slapton before the 19th-century OS maps, which show the village much as it is today, and the surviving population statistics show no apparent reduction in its size.

In 1086 Domesday Book lists Slapton as a single manor with a total recorded population of 10 (VCH Northants., I (1902), 332), and 23 people paid the Lay Subsidy of 1301 (PRO, E179/155/31). In 1377, 60 people over the age of 14 paid the Poll Tax (PRO, E179/155/28). By 1673, 31 people in the village paid the Hearth Tax (PRO, E179/254/14) and Bridges (Hist. of Northants., I (1791), 256), writing in about 1720, said that there were about 35 families in the parish. In 1801 the population of the parish was 135.

If the earthworks do represent an alteration to the original form of Slapton village, it is difficult to see what changes were involved beyond, perhaps, a movement away from the church towards the present main street. (RAF VAP CPE/UK/1994, 3086–9; air photographs in NMR)

(2) CULTIVATION REMAINS. The common fields of the parish were finally enclosed by an Act of Parliament of 1759. However at least some enclosure had occurred long before that date for Bridges (Hist. of Northants., I (1791), 256) writing in about 1720, recorded that 'part of the Lordship is inclosed, and the rest is open field'.

Ridge-and-furrow of these fields exists on the ground or can be traced on air photographs over much of the parish, arranged in end-on and interlocked furlongs, many of reversed-S form. There appears to be very little land which has not been ploughed in ridge-and-furrow at some time and even the low-lying land in the S., along the R. Tove, has traces of it. (RAF VAP CPE/UK/1994, 3086–90)

UNDATED

[a](3) MOUND (SP 63774819), lies in the extreme N. corner of the parish, on Boulder Clay at 148 m. above OD. Here, at the highest point of the parish, a mound 13 m. in diam. and only 0.5 m. high is still visible. It has been ploughed over and there is no trace of a surrounding ditch. The suggestion that the mound is a barrow cannot be proved and it could be a windmill mound. (BNFAS, 3 (1969), 1, incorrect grid reference; OS Record Cards; CPE/UK/1994, 3088–9)

55 STOKE BRUERNE
(OS 1:10000 [a] SP 75 SW, [b] SP 75 SE, [c] SP 74 NW, [d] SP 74 NE)

The modern parish, of over 500 hectares, is roughly diamond-shaped. Up to the 19th century it included Shutlanger which is now a separate parish. From an area of Boulder Clay with a maximum height of 122 m. above OD the land slopes generally S. across outcrops of Oolitic Limestone, Upper Lias Clay and riverine deposits, to the R. Tove here flowing at 74 m. above OD. The medieval settlement in Stoke Park (7) is of some interest in that it is completely undocumented and not even a name can be assigned to it.

PREHISTORIC AND ROMAN

Worked flints of Neolithic type are said to have been found in the parish (OS Record Cards) and a Bronze Age palstave near Stoke Plain before 1904 (NM; T. J. George, Arch. Survey of Northants. (1904), 19; OS Record Cards). A Roman glass beaker, a unique import of the Flavian period, was discovered during ironstone-working before 1916, apparently with other remains (Ashmolean Museum; OS Record Cards; Burlington Magazine, No. 784, Vol. 110 (1968), 405) and a 'light-coloured urn', possibly Roman, is also recorded (OS Record Cards).

[b](1) ENCLOSURE (SP 75155085), E. of (2), on Blisworth Limestone, at 105 m. above OD. Air photographs (CUAP, ZJ60) show a D-shaped enclosure of about 0.3 hectare, with a straight ditch running roughly S.E. from its S. side. This may be the enclosure listed below (3).

[c](2) IRON AGE SETTLEMENT (SP 740497), 100 m. S. of Stoke Bruerne church, on limestone at 107 m. above OD. Several rubbish pits, containing a few sherds of Hunsbury ware, pieces of iron, mussel and oyster shells and fragments of chert, were discovered during building work in about 1957 (OS Record Cards).

[a](3) IRON AGE SETTLEMENT (?) (SP 745509), in the N. of the parish, on Boulder Clay at 112 m. above OD. Air photographs (not seen by RCHM) are said to show a D-shaped enclosure of about 0.25 hectare, with an entrance in the N.E. corner. Iron Age pottery and a scatter of limestone are reported from this site. However, the whole description may be a mislocation of (1) above. (BNFAS, 6 (1971), 17)

[b](4) ROMAN VILLA (SP 754500), midway between Stoke Bruerne and Ashton, on Boulder Clay at 96 m. above OD. Roman pottery was first noted on the site in 1945. In 1969 the foundations of a small corridor building 50 m. by 30 m., orientated N.-S., were observed as parchmarks in the pasture field and later excavations revealed foundations of walls, roof and flue tiles, pottery including samian, grey and colour-coated wares, glass, tesserae and animal bones. Recent air photographs (NCAU) show that this building is one part of a large villa. It appears to lie in the centre of the E. side of a courtyard at least 150 m. wide, with other buildings along the W. and S. sides as well as on the E. There are also indications of other well-defined structures lying obliquely to the visible buildings within the area of the courtyard. (BNFAS, 4 (1970), 12; OS Record Cards)

MEDIEVAL AND LATER

A medieval decorated floor tile was found in 1975 in the W. of the parish, some distance from any known medieval occupation (SP 73514987; Northants. Archaeol., 11 (1976), 200).

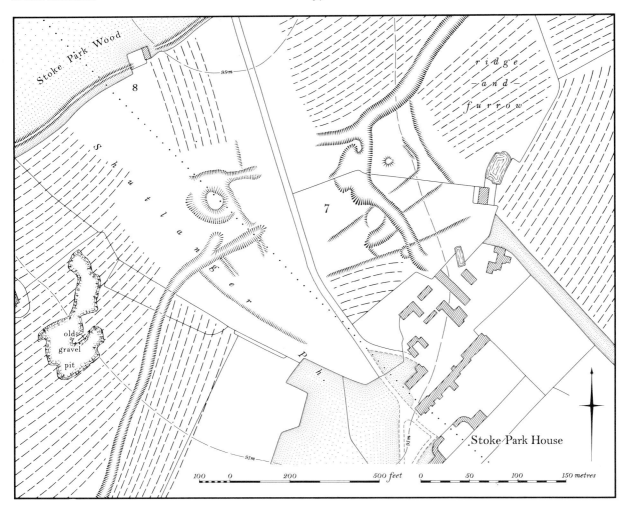

Fig. 106   STOKE BRUERNE (7)   Settlement remains, (8)   Deer park

^c(5) SAXON BURIAL (SP 740498), immediately W. of the church and close to an Iron Age site (2), on Boulder Clay at 107 m. above OD. A single inhumation, presumably Saxon, was discovered in about 1910 (Meaney, *Gazetteer*, 196).

^c(6) SETTLEMENT REMAINS (SP 742497 and 745500; Fig. 14), formerly part of Stoke Bruerne, lay in two places in the village. Although not impressive as earthworks, the remains are important in the understanding of the morphology of the village. The construction of the Grand Junction Canal through the centre of the village accentuated the two parts of Stoke Bruerne, each with its distinct plan which must be of ancient origin. On the E. side of the canal the village is laid out around a wide cross-roads, but to the W. of it there is a neat grid of lanes with the church outside it at the N.W. corner and the remains of a triangular 'green' at the N.E. The grid pattern is now very incomplete, but on a map of 1726 (NRO) a further lane is shown on the S. side of the grid, giving it a rectangular form, with two intersecting streets dividing it into four units. By 1842 (NRO, Tithe Map) this southern lane had been abandoned, except at its W. end. The remains of

this lane have recently been destroyed by modern housing, but on air photographs take in 1947 (RAF VAP CPE/UK/1926, 1242–3) part of it is visible as a rather degraded hollow-way running N.E.–S.W.

On the E. side of the village, E. of the cross-roads and behind the existing buildings on the N. side of the Ashton road, is a series of long rectangular paddocks, bounded and sub-divided by low scarps and shallow ditches, all of which have later ridge-and-furrow within them. To the W., immediately below the canal (SP 743501), a short length of hollow-way which once ran S.W. to meet the old green emerges from the buildings alongside the canal and joins another running N.W. Further S.E., on the S. side of the Ashton road (SP 746499), a small triangular field has low indeterminate earthworks within it. These may be house-sites. (Air photographs in NMR)

The morphology of Stoke Bruerne is difficult to understand. It may be that the early medieval village lay around the cross-roads, with the church isolated on the adjacent hilltop. The rectangular grid layout might then be explained as a later planned extension of the earlier village towards the church. On the other hand the village may originally have been laid out on a grid plan near the church and the E. part may thus have been a later growth beyond the 'green'. The discovery of Iron Age material (2) and a Saxon burial (5), both close to the church, may be relevant here.

^c(7) DESERTED SETTLEMENT (SP 740488; Fig. 106), lies N. of Stoke Park House, on clay at 94 m. above OD. The surviving earthworks appear to be the remains of a small hamlet, though neither its name nor any documentary proof of its existence is known. There are records that a place known as Shaw existed between the 13th and 15th centuries (PN *Northants.*, 107) and its whereabouts is unknown, but it is not certain if it is this site.

The earthworks are in poor condition. The W. part has been ploughed and returned to grass and the central part has been destroyed by the drive to Stoke Park House and by Second World War hut platforms. The settlement remains are associated with a hollow-way which can be traced from the end of an old lane from Stoke Bruerne (SP 742493), across Stoke Park and over the Shutlanger parish boundary to a small S.E.-flowing stream (SP 736486). Immediately N. of Stoke Park Farm another hollow-way leaves the main one and runs S.E. before it disappears under the farm buildings. On either side of this subsidiary hollow-way there are mutilated closes bounded by low banks and scarps; at least one of these banks crosses the hollow-way and thus must be later than it. In the N. a later drive, visible as a flat-topped bank (not shown on plan), crosses the area. To the W. of the main drive to Stoke Park House are further slight earthworks, but these have been so reduced by modern ploughing that little of their original form can be ascertained. (RAF VAP CPE/UK/1926, 1241–3; air photographs in NMR)

^c(8) DEER PARK (centred SP 736492; Fig. 106), occupies about 30 hectares in the S.W. of the parish and extends into the adjoining parish of Shutlanger, once part of Stoke Bruerne. It lies almost entirely on clay and glacial sands and gravels, between 107 m. and 90 m. above OD. The present Stokepark Wood occupies almost the same area. The deer park was created in 1270 when Pagan de Chaworth was granted permission to enclose his wood and make a park. Nothing is known of its later history except that it was still emparked in the 16th century. In the 18th century the area became part of the landscaped park of Stoke House. (*Northants. P. and P.*, 5 (1975), 231)

The roughly wedge-shaped wood is bounded on the N.W., W., S. and E. by a large bank, much altered and damaged by later copse banks, drainage ditches and trees. In many places it is now reduced to a scarp with a copse bank on its crest (e.g. SP 736495). On the N. side, E. of the drive to Stoke Park House, a long narrow strip of land has been taken out of the woodland and the original park bank on its N. side has been destroyed and replaced by a low hedge bank and external ditch.

(9) CULTIVATION REMAINS. The common fields of the parish, together with those of Shutlanger, were enclosed by an Act of Parliament of 1840. Before that date there were three fields, Wood Field to the N. of the village, Ash Hill Field to the E. and Church Field to the S. To the N.W. of the village and extending across the present parish boundary into Shutlanger was a large area of open grass-land known as Stoke Plain or Shutlanger Plain. In the extreme N. of the parish the woodland was much more extensive than it is today and there were several enclosed fields along its edges (NRO: Map of Stoke Bruerne, 1726; Maps of Shutlanger and Stoke Bruerne, 1727 and 1768; Enclosure Map, 1844; Tithe Map, 1842). Few changes took place between 1726 and 1844, apart from further encroachments on the woodland in the N. to create more enclosed fields. The whole of the S.W. of the parish was already part of Stoke Park by 1726.

Ridge-and-furrow of these fields exists on the ground or can be traced from air photographs in a few places. It is significant that no ridge-and-furrow is visible on Stoke Plain. In the former Wood Field only one block of ridge-and-furrow survives and this was known as Short Stocking Furlong in 1726 (SP 745504). Three end-on furlongs remain in Church Field (SP 742493) and a few indeterminate fragments in Ash Hill Field (SP 751497). Ridge-and-furrow is also visible along the eastern parish boundary, in areas which were already enclosed in 1726 (SP 754495 and 750492). Where clearances were made from the woodland in the N. (e.g. SP 740511 and 742518) the furlongs fit within the enclosed fields. The only extensive areas of surviving ridge-and-furrow are interlocked and end-on furlongs, mainly of reversed-S form within Stoke Park (centred SP 740488). Some of these blocks cross the parish boundary with Shutlanger. It is likely that some of this ridge-and-furrow is associated with the deserted settlement (7) which lies within Stoke Park. (RAF VAP CPE/UK/1926, 1025–30, 1241–4; FSL6565, 1999, 1001)

For the canal tramway over Blisworth Hill, see Blisworth (6).

56 SULGRAVE

(OS 1:10000 ^a SP 54 NE, ^b SP 54 SE, ^c SP 54 NW, ^d SP 54 SW)

The rectangular parish covers 815 hectares and lies across the headwaters of the E.-flowing R. Tove. The lower ground to the N. and S. of the central stream is on Upper Lias Clay but there are outcrops of limestone particularly in the S.W. around the village and Boulder Clay caps the highest part in the S. at about 170 m. above OD. The major monument in the parish is the medieval ringwork (3) which has recently been excavated.

PREHISTORIC AND ROMAN

A few worked flints are recorded (SP 574474; CBA Group 9, *Newsletter*, 8 (1978), 22). A scatter of abraded Roman sherds was found during the excavation of the medieval ringwork (3) (*Arch. J.*, 134 (1977), 109).

^a(1) FLINT-WORKING SITE AND ROMAN SETTLEMENT (SP 561472), in the extreme N. of the parish, on Northampton Sand at 175 m. above OD. Worked flints of Neolithic type and sherds of Roman pottery have been discovered (Banbury Museum; *Oxoniensia*, 36 (1971), 112).

^{ab}(2) ROMAN SETTLEMENT (SP 579450), in the S.E. of the parish, on limestone at 147 m. above OD. A scatter of

Roman sherds has been noted (*Northants. Archaeol.*, 13 (1978), 182).

MEDIEVAL AND LATER

[a](3) RINGWORK (SP 557453); Figs. 107 and 108; Plate 5), known as Castle Hill, lies at the S.W. end of the village, immediately S.W. of the church, on limestone of the Upper Estuarine Series at 155 m. above OD. The earthworks now consist of a roughly circular bank, though there are indications that this is actually made up of five approximately straight sides. The bank survives up to 3.6 m. high, with a flat top, and there are traces of a surrounding ditch 0.3 m. deep. A causeway across the ditch on the N.W. side leads through the bank and provides the only entrance.

Nothing is known of the history of the site beyond the fact that Domesday Book records that the manor of Sulgrave was held by Ghilo in 1086 and that three undertenants, Hugh, Landric and Otbert, held it of him (VCH *Northants.*, I (1902), 345). A ringwork at Culworth (1) was probably also held by Landric of Ghilo, and a ringwork or motte at Weston and Weedon (5) was held directly by Ghilo.

The site was excavated between 1960 and 1976 and during this period different interpretations of the evidence have been put forward. The most recent of these theories is presented here (*Arch. J.*, 134 (1977), 105–14).

The earliest structure, probably dating from the late 10th century, consisted of a timber building, almost certainly a hall, with a detached stone and timber building, possibly a kitchen. In the early 11th century the hall was altered and repaired and a stone building was erected to the N. Shortly afterwards a bank and ditch were constructed which perhaps surrounded the whole site. In the mid 11th century a massive rampart was added to the earlier bank and the earlier stone building was incorporated into this. This rampart may also have enclosed the adjacent church. At the same time the earlier timber structure was dismantled and replaced by a stone hall. Soon afterwards the stone building in the rampart started to collapse under the pressure and was therefore filled in. A timber tower was then raised on the rampart, using the walls of the stone building as foundations; the rampart itself was heightened and widened and it was perhaps at this stage that the present ringwork was created. In the early 12th century the rampart was

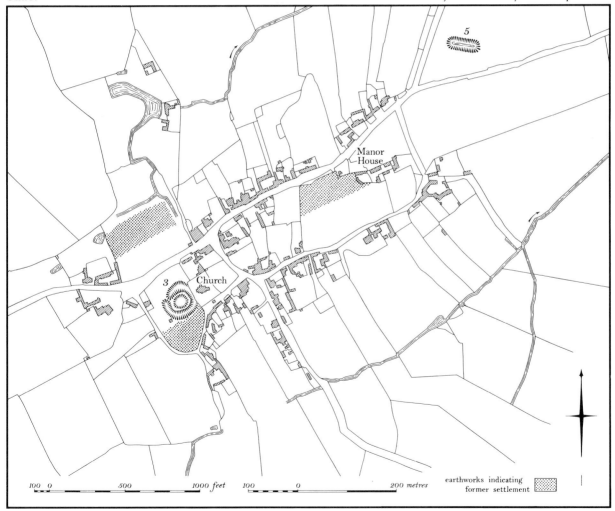

Fig. 107   SULGRAVE (3)   Ringwork, (4)   Settlement remains, (5) Pond

heightened again and the tower rebuilt. However, apart from some apparent traces of huts, the interior shows no evidence of use at this period. The whole site was abandoned by the mid 12th century. The entrance in the N.W. corner of the ringwork is a 19th-century modification. (RAF VAP CPE/UK/1926, 1215–6; CPE/UK/1994, 1028–30, 1097–8; *Med. Arch.*, 6–7 (1962–3), 333; 17 (1973), 147; *BNFAS*, 2 (1967), 28; 3 (1969), 27–9; *Northants. Archaeol.*, 8 (1973), 19; *Arch. J.*, 125 (1968), 305; 126 (1969), 131; *Current Arch.*, 12 (1969), 19–20; *Chateau-Gaillard*, 2 (1967), 39–48; CBA Group 9, *Newsletter*, 3 (1973), 20)

[a](4) SETTLEMENT REMAINS (SP 555454, 556452 and 559455; Fig. 107), formerly part of Sulgrave, lie in three places in the village, on limestone of the Upper Estuarine Series between 144 m. and 152 m. above OD. Although the remains are visually unimpressive they are potentially important since work on them may help to elucidate both the growth of the village and its relationship to the ringwork (3).

The surviving documents do not indicate any marked fall in the population of Sulgrave. The village is first men-

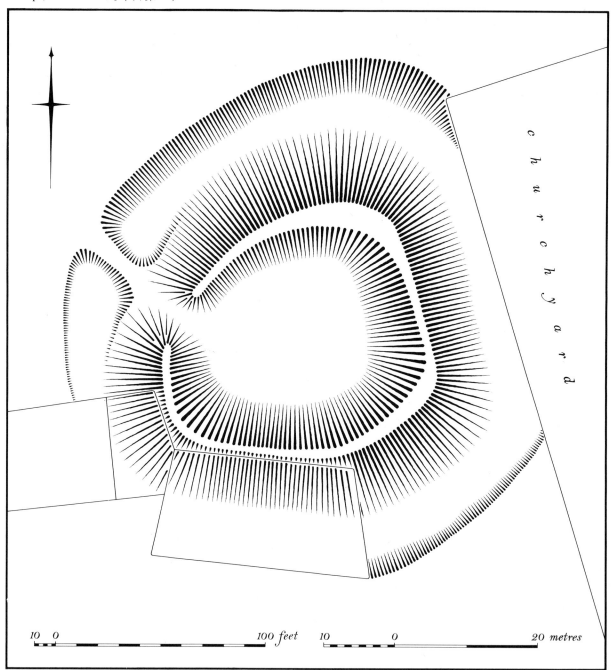

Fig. 108 SULGRAVE (3) Ringwork

tioned in 1086, in Domesday Book, as a single manor with a recorded population of 27 (VCH *Northants.*, I (1902), 345). In 1301, 42 people paid the Lay Subsidy (PRO, E179/155/31) and the village paid 60s. 2½d. for the Lay Subsidy of 1334 (PRO, E179/155/3). In 1377, 101 people over the age of 14 paid the Poll Tax (PRO, E179/155/28) and 42 people are recorded in the Lay Subsidy of 1525 (PRO, E179/155/159). In 1673, 78 people paid the Hearth Tax (PRO, E179/254/14). There were 414 people living in the parish by 1801.

The plan of the village today is a rough figure-of-eight, with the church and ringwork in the centre of the S.W. loop and the manor house at the N.E. end of the N.E. loop. In the absence of any map earlier than the 19th century it is difficult to interpret this layout. One possible explanation is that the original village lay around the church and ringwork and later expanded N.E. along the two parallel streets by gradual growth or planned development. However, the existence of earthworks on the northernmost of these two streets, together with the fact that the N.E. end of the loop did not exist as a through-road in the early 19th century (1st ed. 1 in. OS map, 1834), suggests that the village was once a single street and that the S.E. parts of the loops were originally a back lane which has become partly built up.

The remains fall into three groups. On the N.W. side of the village, behind the existing modern houses (SP 555454), are the remains of abandoned closes bounded by low banks and shallow ditches, which are presumably the former gardens of houses which once lined the street. Further S., immediately S. of the ringwork (SP 556452), on the inside of the bend of the S.W. loop, there is an area of uneven ground which contains fragments of stone walling now grassed over. These may be the sites of houses but their proximity to the ringwork suggests that they are perhaps part of a later manorial complex.

To the N.E., on the S. side of the northern street and immediately S.W. of the present manor house (SP 559455), are the fragmentary remains of sunken platforms and low scarps and banks bounded on the S. by a continuous scarp up to 1 m. high. These appear to be the sites of houses which lay along the street. (RAF VAP CPE/UK/1926, 1216–8; CPE/UK/1994, 1028–30, 1097–9)

^b(5) POND (SP 562458), lay immediately N.E. of the village, on Upper Lias Clay at 140 m. above OD. It is shown on modern OS maps as a rectangular pond orientated E.–W., 60 m. by 25 m. but has now been destroyed by ploughing. It appears to have been embanked on all sides, with a second bank on its N. side. (Air photographs in NMR)

^b(6) PILLOW MOUND (SP 56484527; Plate 7) lies in permanent pasture S.E. of the village, on Upper Lias Clay at 145 m. above OD. The mound is rectangular, 12 m. long, 7 m. wide, and less than 0.25 m. high, with a flat top. A narrow ditch only 2 m. wide surrounds it. The mound is orientated E.–W. and lies in the S.E. corner of a furlong of ridge-and-furrow running E.–W. which appears to respect it. (Air photographs in NMR)

(7) CULTIVATION REMAINS (Plate 7). The common fields of Sulgrave were enclosed by an Act of Parliament of 1767,

but no map is known to survive. Ridge-and-furrow of these fields exists on the ground or can be traced on air photographs over much of the parish, arranged in end-on and interlocked furlongs. It is particularly well preserved to the S.E. of the village where considerable areas are still under grass and a number of interesting features are visible. For example, in an area of ill-drained ground at SP 563451 a block of slight, worn-down ridge-and-furrow only 50 m. long is surrounded by well-preserved ridge-and-furrow (Plate 7). This may represent different stages of abandonment of former arable land. A circular area to the E., 30 m. in diam., where the ridge-and-furrow has been partly flattened, may be the remains of a rick stand (see RCHM *Northants.* III, Brixworth (42) and p. liii). RAF VAP CPE/UK/1926, 1214–9; CPE/UK/1994, 1027–31, 1095–1100, 3096–8)

UNDATED

^b(MOUND (SP 55934716), possibly a round barrow, lies in the extreme N. of the parish, on the summit of a rounded hill of Northampton Sand known as Barrow Hill, at 180 m. above OD. The mound is 22 m. in diam. and 2 m. high, and is rather conical. It has been damaged by ploughing round its base and no trace of a surrounding ditch can be seen, except on the N. side. It may be the site of a medieval windmill. (RAF VAP CPE/UK/1994, 1098–99; 3097–8)

57 SYRESHAM
(OS 1:10000 ^a SP 64 SW, ^b SP 64 SE, ^c SP 63 NW)

The parish is large, covering more than 1500 hectares, and includes the medieval settlements of Syresham itself (2) and of Crowfield (4). It slopes gently from 145 m. above OD in the N. to 115 m. above OD in the S., drained by a central S.-flowing stream and its tributaries. Most of the area is covered by Boulder Clay, but there are glacial sands and gravels around the main village and Oolitic limestones are exposed along the valleys of the central stream and of an E.-flowing one which forms part of the S. boundary. The area is heavily wooded in the E., being part of the former Whittlewood Forest; until the post-medieval period this forest extended further W., almost to Syresham village (NRO, maps of Whittlewood Forest; Fig. 16).

ROMAN

^a(1) ROMAN KILNS (?) (SP 632421), immediately N.E. of the village, on gravel at 134 m. above OD. 'Two small ovens' apparently associated with Roman pottery were discovered in 1926 (*JRS*, 16 (1926), 223; Northants. SMR).

MEDIEVAL AND LATER

For deer park in the N.W. of the parish, see Helmdon (12)

^a(2) SETTLEMENT REMAINS (SP 628418 and 630416; Fig. 12 and partly on Fig. 109), formerly part of Syresham, lie in two places. The village consists of two separate parts on

either side of a small valley. On the S. side is the main part, based on an oval street system; to the N. is a smaller area known as Church End, with the parish church on its E. side. The dual character of the village is perhaps a reflection of the manorial history. Domesday Book (VCH *Northants.*, I (1902), 324, 330 and 344–5) records three manors, one probably Crowfield and the others the two parts of Syresham.

The earthworks in the W. part of Church End (SP 628418) have mostly been destroyed by a modern housing estate and only a few fragmentary banks and scarps now exist. In the S. part of the village (SP 630416) a rectangular enclosure 50 m. by 30 m. orientated E.-W. and bounded by a low bank and ditch still remains. It is possibly an old paddock. (RAF VAP CPE/UK/1926, 5225–7)

[a](3) FISHPOND (SP 630417; Figs. 12 and 109), lies in the valley of a small E.N.E.-flowing stream, on clay and alluvium at 142 m. above OD. A large irregular pond is cut down into the valley sides with a large dam now much damaged at its N.E. end. The N. and S. sides have large banks 1 m.–2 m. high separating the pond from two high-level leats. The leat on the N. appears to have been an overflow channel to carry water round the pond, and the leat to the S. leads to the site of a watermill which lay immediately S.E. of the dam. Nothing is known of the

history or date of this pond. (RAF VAP CPE/UK/1926, 5225–7)

[a](4) SETTLEMENT REMAINS (SP 616416), formerly part of the hamlet of Crowfield, lie to the S.W. of the existing hamlet, in the W. of the parish, on Boulder Clay at 137 m. above OD. The name Crowfield is not apparently recorded in documents until 1287 (PN *Northants.*, 60) but it is likely that it is one of the three manors listed under Syresham in Domesday Book, perhaps the small half-hide holding with a single villein (VCH *Northants.*, I (1902), 324). The remains are visible on air photographs taken in 1947 (RAF VAP CPE/UK/1926, 5224–5; air photographs in NMR) but the area has now been partly levelled by ploughing and returned to permanent grassland. The air photographs show at least four long rectangular closes bounded by low banks and shallow ditches, extending E. from the N.-S. road S.W. of the hamlet. They had been ploughed over in slight, narrow ridge-and-furrow.

[a](5) DITCHES (SP 636420–638415), perhaps part of a former watermill, lie immediately S.W. of Kingshill Farm, on the E. side of a small S.E.-flowing stream, on glacial deposits at 122 m. above OD. Two almost parallel ditches 7 m. wide and up to 1.5 m. deep run from a sharp bend in the stream N.W. of the farm, in a curve parallel to the stream for a distance of 300 m. to a point just S. of the

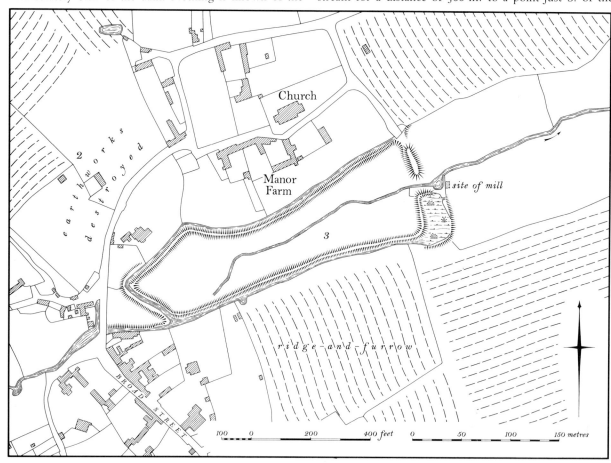

Fig. 109   SYRESHAM (2)   Settlement remains, (3)   Fishpond

farm. The lower ditch then turns W. and returns to the stream; the other continues S.E. for a further 100 m. before fading out. (Air photographs in NMR)

(6) CULTIVATION REMAINS. The common fields of the parish were enclosed by an Act of Parliament of 1765. No details are known except that there were already 460 acres of old enclosures at that time (G. Baker, *Hist. of Northants.*, I (1822–30), 676), and it is uncertain whether Crowfield hamlet had a separate field system. Ridge-and-furrow of these fields exists on the ground or can be traced on air photographs over much of the parish except in the extensive areas of woodland or former woodland. It is mostly arranged in end-on and interlocked furlongs, many of reversed-S form, and is still especially well preserved in the area between Syresham village and the county boundary to the S. (around SP 632405). Among the more notable features are well-marked hollow-ways cut into headlands and leading into the fields from the village (e.g. SP 626417), small embanked enclosures of up to 2 hectares lying over earlier ridge-and-furrow (e.g. SP 633416), and headlands which have been overploughed in ridge-and-furrow (e.g. SP 633421). The N.W. of the parish appears to have been part of the deer park (Helmdon (12)) and very little ridge-and-furrow is visible there. (RAF VAP CPE/UK/1926, 2224–30, 3226–8, 5222–30)

UNDATED

[a](7) SITE OF BUILDING (about SP 638418), E. of the village, in the vicinity of Kingshill. Bridges (*Hist. of Northants.*, I (1791), 243–4), writing in about 1720, said that somewhere to the W. of Kingshill '. . . have been found in plowing stones and foundations of buildings. And there are reports of other large stones and ruins . . . there abouts'. The site has not been located.

58 THENFORD
(OS 1:10000 SP 54 SW)

The long, narrow parish covers only 364 hectares. It slopes generally S. across Upper and Middle Lias Clay and Marlstone Rock, from a maximum height of 180 m. where Northampton Sand outcrops, and is drained by small streams on the S.E. and S.W. boundaries at about 110 m. above OD. The parish is rich in archaeological remains which include an Iron Age earthwork (2), a large Roman villa (4) and a Saxon cemetery (9).

PREHISTORIC AND ROMAN (Fig. 85)

The extensive and detailed fieldwork carried out in this part of the county by D. J. Barrett (see Marston St. Lawrence) has led to the identification of several sites and finds in Thenford parish. The finds unassociated with known settlements are here listed under their various categories: (a) four flint arrowheads of different types (SP 528413); (b) a fragment of a polished stone axe of Group VI (SP 52314277); (c) small scatters of worked flints of late Neolithic and Bronze Age type (SP 52424347, 52804310, 52264257, 52594251, 51634151, 52524078). A middle Bronze Age palstave is also recorded in the parish (BM;

copy in NM; *Arch. J.*, 110 (1953), 178). A late Bronze Age hoard found in the 19th century 'at Thenford Hill Farm' (about SP 525438) contained two swords, four spearheads, two rings and other bronze objects as well as a piece of wood (BM; *Inventaria Archaeologia*, 2nd set (1955), G.B. 12, 1–3). Its exact find spot is unknown, but it may have come from the vicinity of the Iron Age settlement (2).

(1) PREHISTORIC SETTLEMENT (centred SP 527416), to the E. of the village, on Marlstone Rock at 125 m. above OD. Worked and waste flints of late Neolithic and Bronze Age type occur over an area of some 3 hectares. Twelve flint arrowheads of various types and fragments of two stone axes, one of tuff and one of Group VI, have also been found. Part of another axe of Group VI, as well as some microliths have been found further to the E. (SP 524415). For Roman material from this area, see (4). (inf. D. J. Barrett)

(2) IRON AGE SETTLEMENT (SP 523440; Fig. 110), lies in the extreme N. of the parish, on the W. slope of a rounded hill of Northampton Sand, between 168 m. and 175 m. above OD. The site, sometimes known as Arbury or Arberry Hill, has elsewhere been described as a hill fort, but it was probably no more than a lightly defended farmstead. It was once almost circular, 150 m. across, and bounded by a bank or rampart. The area has long been under cultivation with the result that much of the rampart has been almost completely ploughed out. On the N.E. only a broad scarp survives, up to 1.5 m. high and spread by ploughing. A low bank 0.5 m. high in the S.E. and another scarp less than 1 m. high on the S.W. are all that remains of the original bank in this area. The scarp extends N. and curves N.E. and this section, outside the modern arable land, is the only well-preserved part; even here a quarry has been cut into the bank. The bank is 20 m. wide and is 2.5 m. high from the outside but only 0.5 m. from the inside. A large area of late Neolithic or Bronze Age worked and waste flints has been found in the S.E. of the site. Further scatters of flints, including microliths, lie well outside the main enclosure to the E. and S.W. (SP 52344390, 52054385). A few sherds of Iron Age and Roman pottery are recorded from the E. part of the site and the late Bronze Age hoard (see above) discovered in the 19th century may also have come from here. (A. Beesley, *Hist. of Banbury* (1841), 31; *Arch. J.*, 110 (1953), 178; RAF VAP CPE/UK/1926, 1211–2; CPE/UK/1994, 1024–5)

(3) ROMAN SETTLEMENT (?) AND BURIAL (SP 519417), lies in Thenford churchyard, on Middle Lias clays and silts at about 115 m. above OD. Morton (*Nat. Hist. of Northants.* (1712), 529) records the discovery of an urn with ashes in it at this point and also states that 'tesserae were found in the field and a medal of Constans'. In the 19th century, Baker (*Hist. of Northants.*, I (1822–30), 717) referred to fragments of Roman material 'traced in the village causeway'. These finds, apart from the burial, may relate to the villa (4).

(4) IRON AGE AND ROMAN SETTLEMENT AND ROMAN VILLA (SP 52524158), lie E. of the village, on Marlstone Rock at 130 m. above OD. Evidence of a large Roman building was first recorded in the early 19th century when foundations, a hypocaust, tesserae and coins from Tetricus

to Constans were found (G. Baker, *Hist. of Northants.*, I (1822–30), 717). A few years later there is a record of skeletons found in the garden of Thenford House (A. Beesley, *Hist. of Banbury* (1841), 32). Both these writers located the finds in the area S. of the walled garden of Thenford House (i.e. SP 524418).

Excavations between 1971 and 1973 revealed a villa with four main phases of occupation. The earliest phase was an Iron Age ditch which was overlaid by a large stone building, possibly an early villa or agricultural building. This structure later had a room and a corridor added to it.

Around A.D. 300 the main villa was erected to the N. of the earlier building. It consisted of a range of six rooms one of which contained a fine mosaic. The villa was later extended to the S. to meet the earlier building and another room was added to the W. with a bath suite to the N. The whole building was later demolished and levelled to make a courtyard. The mosaic is preserved in Thenford House. (*BNFAS*, 7 (1972), 32; *Northants. Archaeol.*, 8 (1973), 17; 9 (1974), 96; DOE *Arch. Excavations 1972* (1973), 62; *1973* (1974), 55; CBA Group 9, *Newsletter*, 2 (1972), 10; 3 (1973), 17; *Britannia*, 3 (1972), 325, 360; 4 (1973), 294; 5 (1974),

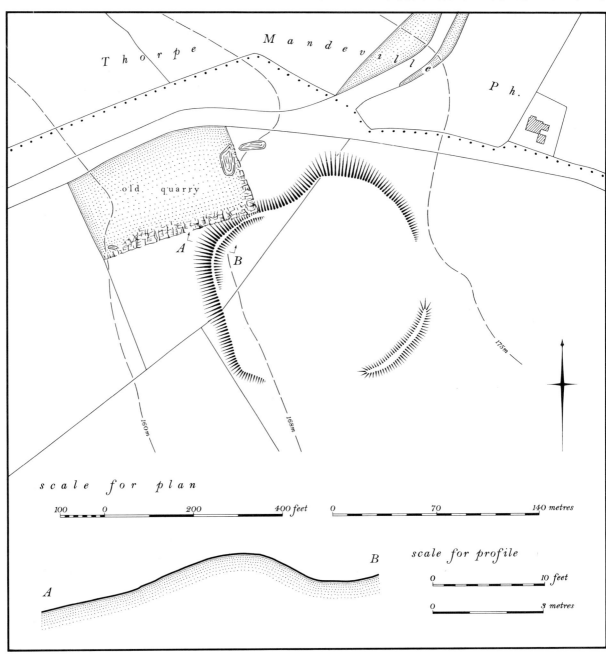

Fig. 110   THENFORD (2)   Iron Age Settlement

434; *BAR*, 41 (i) (1977), 152, No. 147).

The villa lies on the W. edge of a large area of Roman occupation debris, some 10 hectares in extent, including a dense spread of pottery and tiles (centred SP 526416; inf. D. J. Barrett). For prehistoric material from this area, see (1).

(5) ROMAN SETTLEMENT (SP 517425), N. of the village, on the E. side of a small S.-flowing stream, on Upper Lias Clay at 130 m. above OD. Roman pottery and tiles are recorded from an area of some 3 hectares. A Roman coin and two flint arrowheads have also been found. (inf. D. J. Barrett)

(6) ROMAN SETTLEMENT (?) (SP 514422), 300 m. S.W. of (5), on the other side of the stream, on Upper Lias Clay at 125 m. above OD. A small scatter of Roman pottery and tiles, and some worked flints including Mesolithic blades and a single microlith are recorded. (inf. D. J. Barrett; CBA *Research Report*, 20 (1977), 217)

(7) ROMAN SETTLEMENT (?) (SP 526421), N.E. of the village, on Upper Lias Clay at 130 m. above OD. A small quantity of Roman pottery and tiles has been found here as well as some worked flints (inf. D. J. Barrett).

(8) ROMAN SETTLEMENT (?) (SP 524411), S.E. of the village, on limestone at 107 m. above OD. A few sherds of Roman pottery, fragments of tile and some worked flints have been noted (inf. D. J. Barrett).

MEDIEVAL AND LATER

(9) SAXON CEMETERY (SP 514419), W. of the village, close to the parish boundary, on Upper Lias Clay at 122 m. above OD. Before 1830 at least seven skeletons arranged in three tiers were discovered in a large mound of earth and stones. The burials were thought to be secondary to the mound. There are references to 'many earthen urns, or drinking cups' but only one small black-ware vessel survives, accompanied by an iron knife (both in NM). Meaney gives a different location (SP 527435) but there seems no justification for this; the location given above fits the 19th-century description. Nothing now remains in the area but extensive shallow quarries. (G. Baker, *Hist. of Northants.*, I (1822–30), 717; A. Beesley, *Hist. of Banbury* (1841), 31; VCH *Northants.*, I (1902), 254; Meaney, *Gazetteer*, 196; OS Record Cards; J. N. L. Myres, *A Corpus of Anglo-Saxon Pottery of the Pagan Period* (1977), No. 811)

(10) SITE OF MANOR HOUSE (SP 519416), lies immediately N.E. of the church, on Marlstone Rock at 120 m. above OD. The area is traditionally the site of the medieval manor house of Thenford which was described in the early 18th century as being partly built in the reign of Elizabeth I (J. Bridges, *Hist. of Northants.*, I (1791), 203). It was probably pulled down soon after 1765 when the present Thenford House was built to the E. of the village (G. Baker, *Hist. of Northants.*, I (1822–30), 714). The site is now a flat pasture field with no surface features except at the N. end where there are a few low scarps.

(11) SITE OF WATERMILL (SP 517419), lies W. of the village, in the valley of a small stream flowing S.E., on Middle Lias Clay at 122 m. above OD. The mill itself stood until a few years ago, but has now been demolished.

Traces of its foundations, leats and the mill-pond to the N.W. still remain. The pond is called Mill Pond on the Tithe Map of 1851 (NRO).

(12) WINDMILL MOUND (SP 517422), lies to the N. of the village, on the side of an open shallow valley, on Marlstone Rock at 130 m. above OD. The field was known as Windmill Ground in 1851 (NRO, Tithe Map). On air photographs taken in 1947 (RAF VAP CPE/UK/1926, 3210–2) what appears to be a circular mound some 20 m. in diam. is visible. It has since been totally destroyed.

(13) CULTIVATION REMAINS. The common fields of Thenford were enclosed by an Act of Parliament of 1766, but no details of them are known. Ridge-and-furrow of these fields exists on the ground or can be traced on air photographs over large parts of the parish. It is arranged mainly in end-on furlongs running generally E.-W. across the parish. This is at least in part the result of the adaptation of the ridges to the contours, although the long runs of end-on furlongs in the centre of the parish (around SP 525425) cannot be entirely attributed to this. Especially notable in this area are two adjacent furlongs with ridges of unusual width. No explanation can be proposed for these ridges almost 20 m. wide. (RAF VAP CPE/UK/1926, 1210–11, 3210–3; CPE/UK/1994, 1024–6)

59   THORPE MANDEVILLE
(OS 1:10000 [a] SP 54 NW, [b] SP 54 SW)

The small, roughly rectangular parish occupies only some 410 hectares. Its short W. boundary lies against Oxfordshire. A rounded hill of Northampton Sand and Oolite Limestone, with Upper Lias Clay exposed on its lower slopes, rises to over 180 m. above OD in the W. of the parish. Thorpe Mandeville village lies on the E. slopes of this hill, above a small stream flowing N. and then N.W. at about 145 m. above OD. To the E. of the stream the land rises again to further outcrops of Northampton Sand and Oolite Limestone.

PREHISTORIC OR ROMAN

[ab](1) ENCLOSURES AND PITS (centred SP 546450), lie in the extreme E. of the parish, on Oolite Limestone at 190 m. above OD. Air photographs (CUAP, EY74) show cropmarks of two enclosures, one apparently oval and the other roughly rectangular, orientated E.-W. with a double ditch on its N. side. The surrounding area appears to have a large number of pits.

For possible round barrows, see (9) below.

MEDIEVAL AND LATER

[b](2) SETTLEMENT REMAINS (SP 534448; Fig. 111), formerly part of Thorpe Mandeville, lie on the E. side of the village, S.E. of the Manor House, on the S. side of the road, on Upper Lias Clay between 152 m. and 160 m. above OD. Only a few fragmentary low earthworks remain, perhaps the sites of former houses along this side of the road. The

area was already devoid of buildings in 1806 (NRO, Estate Map).

The village of Thorpe Mandeville has always been small, though it appears to have had some reduction of population in the late or post-medieval period. Domesday Book, in 1086, only lists a recorded population of nine (VCH *Northants.*, I (1902), 344). In 1301, 23 taxpayers contributed to the Lay Subsidy (PRO, E179/155/31) and in 1334 the village paid 35s. 10d., a relatively low amount (PRO, E179/155/3). In 1377, 78 people over the age of 14 paid Poll Tax (PRO, E179/155/27), but the 1523 Subsidy was paid by only 14 people (PRO, E179/155/159) and only 14 householders paid the Hearth Tax of 1673 (PRO, E179/254/14). (RAF VAP CPE/UK/1994, 1025–7)

^b(3) SITE OF MANOR HOUSE AND GARDENS (SP 531449; Fig. 111), lies in the W. of the village immediately N., W. and S. of the church, on Northampton Sand at about 170 m. above OD. The old manor house of Thorpe Mandeville, which was perhaps replaced by the present one to the E. in the early 18th century, stood here. The

earthworks were first mentioned by Bridges, writing in about 1720 (*Hist. of Northants.*, I (1791), 207); he suggested that the mounds 'still visible behind the Manor-house' were thrown up by Oliver Cromwell who traditionally kept a garrison here. The manor house to which Bridges was referring was probably the earlier one which still stood at that time.

There is no doubt that the greater part of the earthworks are the remains of a formal garden, but if Bridges did not recognise them and associated them with Cromwell they must presumably have been abandoned long before the early 18th century. This suggests that the gardens were of 16th or early 17th-century date. If this is so then the gardens were perhaps laid out by the Kirton family who held the manor of Thorpe Mandeville at that time.

The earthworks fall into three parts. In the centre ('a' on plan) is a disturbed area of ground and an amorphous mound 1.3 m. high which is undoubtedly the site of the manor house itself. To the S. is a large rectangular area bounded by scarps up to 1 m. high which is presumably

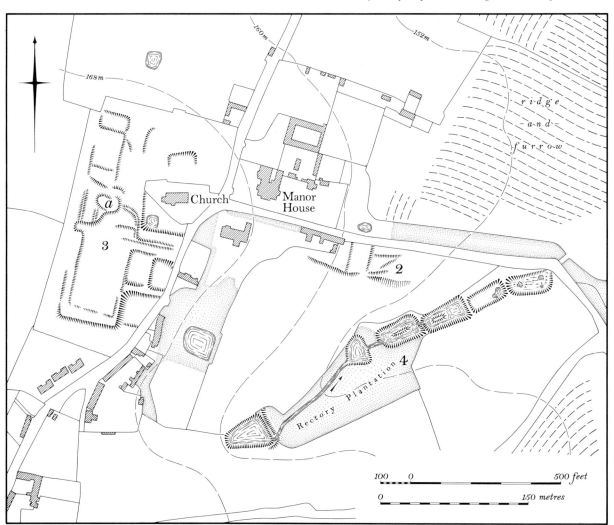

Fig. 111   THORPE MANDEVILLE (2)   Settlement remains, (3)   Site of manor house and gardens, (4)   Fishponds

Fig. 112   THORPE MANDEVILLE (4, 5)   Fishponds, (6)   Dam, (7)   Ponds

a garden court, laid out in front of the house. To the E. of it are traces of three sunken rectangular areas 1 m. deep which were presumably other parts of the garden. Other scarps to the N. of the manor house site are less well defined and may be the remains of paddocks or yards at the rear of the house. (RAF VAP CPE/UK/1994, 1025–7; air photographs in NMR)

[b](4) FISHPONDS (SP 532447–535448; Figs. 111 and 112), lie S.E. of the village in the bottom of a small valley draining N.E., on Upper Lias Clay between 160 m. and 148 m. above OD. There are six ponds, though perhaps only four or five of them are medieval in origin. The two lower ponds appear to be medieval and largely unaltered. They are rectangular depressions, 1.5 m. deep, cut down into the valley bottom. The adjacent one to the S.W. is larger, with a low rectangular island within it, and has probably been altered in the 18th century. The pond to the S.W. again has certainly been changed in outline and has a more irregular form, again with a low long island within it. The fifth pond, of roughly triangular shape, appears to be entirely of post-medieval design. The south-western-most pond, some distance upstream, is 1.5 m. deep and bounded by a massive dam 2 m. high on its N.E. side. Again, if it is medieval in origin it has been altered at a later date. All six ponds are shown on a map of 1806 (NRO) and the field to the N. was then called Fisher's Close. On a later map of 1851 (NRO) the ponds are termed 'fishponds'. (RAF VAP CPE/UK/1994, 1025–7; air photographs in NMR)

[b](5) FISHPONDS (SP 537446; Fig. 112), lie S.E. of the village and immediately S. of the Banbury to Northampton road, on Upper Lias Clay at 146 m. above OD, in the valley of a small N.-flowing stream. Both have been altered in post-medieval times but are probably medieval in origin. The lower pond is rectangular, 1.75 m. deep, with a massive dam on the N., now over 3 m. high, but presumably heightened to carry the modern road which crosses it. In 1806 (NRO, Estate Map) it was depicted with two long parallel islands within it. The upper pond is more irregular with at its S. end a small island also marked on the 1806 map. (RAF VAP CPE/UK/1994, 1025–7)

[a](6) DAM (SP 537458; Fig. 112), known locally as Giants Grave, lies E. of the village in the bottom of the valley of a N.-flowing stream, on Upper Lias Clay at 145 m. above OD. It is 2 m. high with a gap in the centre through which the stream now passes, another gap at its E. end where a modern track has cut through, and a shallow gap at its W. end which was the original overflow channel. It formerly ponded back a large area of water the limits of which are marked by a low scarp on the valley sides behind it. It is not marked on an Estate Map of 1806 (NRO) and was presumably already disused. The site is probably a medieval fishpond. (RAF VAP CPE/UK/1994, 1025–7)

[a](7) PONDS (SP 538453; Fig. 112), lie in the valley of a small W.-flowing stream, near its former junction with a N.-flowing tributary, on Upper Lias Clay at 145 m. above OD. The ponds appear to be of post-medieval date, probably of the 18th century, and were perhaps used for breeding wildfowl and for boating. The largest, lowest pond is roughly trapezoidal with a triangular extension E. up the

valley and groups of low marshy islands at each end. The central pond is the smallest and is roughly triangular and the third one has an irregular N. side with four 'bays' cut into it. The water from all three ponds passes not into the original stream but into a high-level leat which runs N.W. towards Lower Thorpe where there was once a watermill. All the ponds are depicted exactly as they are now on a map of 1806 (NRO). (RAF VAP CPE/UK/1994, 1025–7)

[b](8) PONDS (SP 531442), in the E. part of Whitnell's Spinney, in the S.E. of the parish, on Upper Lias Clay at 168 m. above OD. Two small rectangular depressions in a shallow valley are the remains of ponds which existed in 1806 (NRO, Estate Map).

[a](9) WINDMILL MOUND (SP 53704546), in the N. of the parish to the N.W. of a group of ponds (7), on Upper Lias Clay at 145 m. above OD. The mound is 20 m. in diam. and 0.7 m. high with slight traces of a ditch. It is surrounded by ridge-and-furrow, but as it has been ploughed over in recent times (local inf.) it is no longer possible to be certain whether the ridges pass under or around the mound. The field in which it stands was known as Windmill Ground in 1806 (NRO, Estate Map). It has been interpreted elsewhere as a round barrow, but is more likely to be a windmill mound. (RAF VAP CPE/UK/1994, 1026–7)

(10) CULTIVATION REMAINS. The date of the enclosure of the common fields of Thorpe Mandeville is not known, but was certainly before 1806 (NRO, Estate Map). Ridge-and-furrow of these fields exists on the ground or can be traced on air photographs over much of the parish though it occurs only rarely on the extensive Northampton Sand deposits where modern cultivation has largely destroyed it. It is arranged in end-on and interlocked furlongs, mainly of reversed-S form and is particularly well preserved to the E. of the village where a field with ridges 8 m.–9 m. wide and up to 0.75 m. high was known as Banky Grindle in 1806 (SP 536451). The term 'Banky' for areas covered by high ridge-and-furrow is common in this part of the county. (RAF VAP CPE/UK/1926, 1210–4; CPE/UK/ 1994, 1024–8, 1100–3)

60 TIFFIELD
(OS 1:10000 [a] SP 65 SE, [b] SP 75 SW)

The parish, just over 500 hectares in area, occupies the S. side of a flat-topped ridge covered by Boulder Clay, at 125 m. above OD. Only in the narrow valley in the W. of the parish, occupied by the village, are narrow bands of Oolitic limestones, Northampton Sand and clay exposed, between 125 m. and 100 m. above OD.

ROMAN

[a](1) ROMAN SETTLEMENT (?) (SP 69735293), in the N. of the parish, on Boulder Clay at 140 m. above OD. A scatter of Roman pottery was found in 1957 (OS Record Cards).

ᵃ(2) ROMAN SETTLEMENT (SP 697524), N. of the village, on Boulder Clay at 125 m. above OD. Roman pottery, including mortarium sherds, has been found (NM; *Northants. Archaeol.*, 11 (1976), 194).

MEDIEVAL AND LATER

ᵃ(3) SETTLEMENT REMAINS (centred SP 698515), formerly part of Tiffield, lie within the existing village, on limestone at about 150 m. above OD. The village appears always to have consisted of a single N.-S. street on the E. side of a small S.-flowing stream. Empty plots, containing earthworks, survived until recently but some of these have been destroyed by modern housing development. Immediately S. of the church (SP 699515) a small rectangular paddock still retains a large depression at its W. end, the site of a building which had already been removed by 1780 (NRO, Enclosure Map). At the S. end of the village (SP 699513) low banks, scarps and depressions on either side of the street are the sites of farm buildings still standing in 1780. (RAF VAP CPE/UK/1926, 1035–6; air photographs in NMR)

ᵃ(4) BANK (SP 698515), lies immediately S.W. of the church on the E. side of the stream, on clay at 102 m. above OD. A long bank 1.5 m. high and 6 m. wide spans the flat valley bottom and returns S. along the edge of the stream. No date or function can be assigned to this feature. (RAF VAP CPE/UK/1926, 1035–6)

(5) CULTIVATION REMAINS. The common fields of the parish were enclosed by an Act of Parliament of 1780 (NRO, Enclosure Map). At that time there were three open fields, Meadow Field to the S. of the village, Water Slade Field to the N. and N.W. and Full-Well Field to the E. and N.E. The Enclosure Map depicts the named furlongs of the common fields and it is of interest that each furlong is made up of a number of separate blocks of ridges, sometimes arranged at right angles to each other, an unusual system in Northamptonshire. This ridge-and-furrow survives on the ground or can be traced from air photographs in parts of all three fields and the pattern is almost complete W. of the village in the former Water Slade Field (SP 695515). There a group of rectangular furlongs, set at right angles to each other, lie around a long narrow close also containing ridge-and-furrow which was an old enclosure in 1780. To the E. of the village, in the former Full-Well Field (SP 705520), another large area of rectangular, interlocked furlongs survives. Immediately S.E. of the village, within the former Meadow Field (SP 702513), a broad hollow-way, presumably the precursor of the enclosure road to the N., passes between two blocks of reversed-S ridge-and-furrow. Ridge-and-furrow also survives around the village within paddocks which were old enclosures in 1780.

The unusual eastern projection of the parish which lay beyond Full-Well Field in 1780 was, at that date, already old enclosures. The field names there indicate that some of it had been cleared from woodland, but large parts of it have traces of ridge-and-furrow arranged in rectangular blocks. Some of the latter appear to lie within the field boundaries and may be of a relatively late date. (RAF VAP CPE/UK/1926, 1030–7, 3031–7; FSL6565, 2107–9)

UNDATED

Bridges (*Hist. of Northants.*, I (1791), 271), writing in about 1720, said 'the foundation of old buildings are said to have been formerly dug up' at two places called Oxhay and Pyesnest, but these places have not been identified today.

61 TOWCESTER
(OS 1:10000 ᵃ SP 64 NE, ᵇ SP 65 SE, ᶜ SP 74 NW)

The large parish, covering some 1500 hectares, lies on land between 135 m. and 85 m. above OD, sloping to the R. Tove which crosses its centre from W. to E. Most of the higher areas are covered by Boulder Clay but the down-cutting of the river, the Silverstone Brook and other small tributary streams has exposed large stretches of Upper Lias Clay in the valley bottoms and Oolite Limestone and Northampton Sand on the valley sides.

The major monument is the Roman town of Lactodurum (3), the site of which is occupied by modern Towcester. Though its Roman origins have long been recognized, only in recent years have excavations been carried out there and relatively little is known of its development. The extensive extramural occupation is better understood. A large number of Roman rural sites have been located in the parish, including two villas and a possible temple (5 and 7).

The shape of the present parish, that of an inverted Y, is the result of the inclusion of at least three separate medieval estates in addition to that of Towcester itself (Fig. 16). In the N. is the land and settlement of Caldecote (10); in the S.E. is the land and settlement of Wood Burcote (9), while the S.W. of the parish was once a medieval deer park, though it may have had earlier origins as a separate estate.

Little is recorded of medieval and later Towcester. The town was refortified by Edward the Elder in 917–8 and again in 1643 by Prince Rupert. Traces of both these works have been identified in excavations of the defences. The presumed 12th-century motte, Bury Mount (8) was also refortified in the 17th century but its present form is the result of later landscaping.

PREHISTORIC AND ROMAN

A Palaeolithic hand-axe is said to have been found 'near Towcester' (*PPS*, 29 (1963), 383) and a Neolithic axe is also recorded from the parish (J. Evans, *Ancient Stone Implements of Great Britain* (2nd ed.) (1897), 104; VCH *Northants.*, I (1902), 139). A stone axe of Group VI, Great Langdale type, has been found at Roman site ((5); NM Records) and another polished axe was found in 1978 (SP 68534754; NM; *Northants. Archaeol.*, 14 (1979), 104). A barbed-and-tanged flint arrowhead 'from Towcester' is in the Ashmolean Museum.

Several coins have been recorded in addition to those listed under specific monuments below. These include an Iron Age bronze coin of the North Thames Group, Mack 273 (NM; S.S. Frere (ed.) *Problems of the Iron Age in Southern Britian* (1958), 190), a silver coin of Menander of Bactria (J. G. Milne, *Finds of Greek Coins in the British Isles* (1948), 40) and a coin of Carausius (*Northants. N. and Q.*, I (1884), 99). A coin of Marcus Aurelius came from the vicinity of Rignall Farm (SP 678478); OS Record Cards). Coins of Septimius Severus, Salonina, Carausius and Magnentius are recorded from SP 698468 and two 3rd or 4th-century coins were found at an unknown date at SP 678491 (NM Records). Roman pottery found in the parish includes the following: part of a 2nd-century flagon (SP 68254825), a small number of 1st and 2nd-century sherds (SP 68554800), a thin scatter of Roman sherds together with a Bronze Age scraper and two struck flakes (SP 687479; *Northants. Archaeol.*, 13 (1978), 184–5), an unknown quantity of 1st to 3rd-century Roman pottery (SP 68584713), and Roman pottery, including a complete pot found in the 1940s (at SP 69034986; inf. T. Shirley).

^a(1) FLINT-WORKING SITE (SP 685469), beneath the Roman villa (7). Worked flints of Neolithic type including scrapers, points and cores were found during excavation of the villa; some of the small pits discovered probably date from this early period. A single flint arrowhead of Bronze Age type was also discovered (*Northants. Archaeol.*, 12 (1977), 219).

^a(2) IRON AGE SETTLEMENT (SP 689481; Fig. 114), lay close to the Silverstone Brook and a little to the W. of the main Roman extra-mural settlement alongside the Alchester road, on Upper Lias Clay at 90 m. above OD. Observations during building development in the area in 1977 led to the discovery of ditches and gullies of a 3rd-century BC farmstead (*Northants. Archaeol.*, 13 (1978), 184).

^a(3) ROMAN TOWN OF LACTODURUM (SP 693487; Figs. 113 and 114), now occupied by modern Towcester, lies on the Roman Watling Street, within a broad N.E. projecting bend of the R. Tove, on a low clay spur between the river and the Silverstone Brook at about 90 m. above OD.

The following account has been prepared by Mr. A. E. Brown and is based on work at Towcester by him and by Dr. J. A. Alexander, Mrs. C. Woodfield, Mr. G. Lambrick, Mr. D. Mynard and others.

The site has long been known to be of Roman origin. Camden commented on the discovery of Roman coins; he considered the Roman name of the place to have been Tripontium (*Britannia* (1610), 430). Both Stukeley (*Itinerarium Curiosum* (1766), II, 40) and Bridges (*Hist. of Northants.*, I (1791), 272) reported coins and remarked on the traces of the defences of the western side. Horsley (*Britannia Romana* (1732), 422) was the first to identify Towcester with the *Lactodoro* of Antonine Itinerary 470.6 and 476.11 and this is now universally accepted (*Britannia*, I (1970), 42, 49), together with the suggestion, first put forward by Richmond and Crawford (*Archaeologia*, 93 (1949), 35), that the *Iaciodulma* of Ravenna Cosmography 106.49 is a garbled version of it. It has also been shown that the correct form of the name should be *Lactodurum*, the -o- reflecting merely the Vulgar Latin of a Continental scribe: the first

element appears to be British *Lacto*-, meaning 'milk' (though the precise significance of this is obscure), the second is the very common British and Gaulish *-duro*, which should imply some form of fortification (K. H. Jackson, *Language and History in Early Britain* (1953), 259–60; *Britannia*, I (1970), 75; A. L. F. Rivet and C. Smith, *The Place-Names of Roman Britain* (1979), 382–3).

G. Baker produced a plan of the town's defences and a list of coins spanning the whole of the Roman period (*Hist. of Northants.*, II (1836–41), 318, 320) and discoveries up to the beginning of this century were summarized by Haverfield in VCH *Northants.*, I (1902), 184–6, but no systematic excavations were undertaken until 1954, when the creation of a playing field for the Sponne School led to a section being cut through the western defences by the then Ministry of Public Building and Works. The construction of large housing estates S.W. of the town prompted further excavations by the Ministry and by the Department of the Environment in 1967 and from 1974 to 1976. Excavations within the defended area were carried out in 1976 on behalf of the D.O.E. on a small area due for redevelopment in Park Street and a systematic watching brief was maintained in 1976–77 on trenches excavated within and outside the town during a major drainage scheme. The numerous casual finds reported over the years helped to augment the information derived from the excavations, most notably in the matter of the extent of occupation during the Roman period.

Historical Summary

There is no evidence of pre-Roman occupation, and certainly none of pre-Roman fortification, such as might explain the *-durum* element in the name, nor is there any hill fort in the locality from which the name might have been transferred. It has, however, been suggested (*BAR*, 15 (1975), 5) that there may have been an early Roman fort here, and the situation, well protected by streams, would be suitable, but no firm evidence for such a fort has yet been found. A thin scatter of early coins and pottery has been noted in the area of the town generally, but the only structures of the appropriate date consisted of slight traces of timber buildings found on the Park Street site, which also yielded an ornamental mount from the scabbard of a *gladius*. This remains the only definite piece of military equipment from Towcester so far known; a leaf-shaped bronze pendant (BM) is of a type which could be military but is not necessarily so.

Casual finds and excavation show that occupation intensified towards the end of the 1st century. Towcester's local importance is indicated by the fact that a large building with stone foundations, apparently public, was put up in the town at this time. Evidence of occupation in the 2nd century is abundant but the quality of construction varied. The public building was replaced by two new ones in stone, but in the N.W. of the town structures remained of timber and relatively insubstantial throughout the 2nd century. The defences were not constructed before the end of the 2nd century, obliterating some structures on the western side. There is evidence for a large timber house of the latter part of the 3rd century in the N.W. part of the town; in the 4th century this was replaced by a stone one which was finally destroyed at the end of that century or early in the 5th. Elsewhere within the town undisturbed levels belonging to the 4th century have not been discovered because of medieval and later activity, but coins and pottery have been found in residual contexts.

That there were buildings of considerable quality in Towcester or its environs is indicated by the number of architectural fragments and masonry recovered at various times from the area of the town (*Northants. Archaeol.*, 13 (1978), 77, 81, 82, 85).

Settlement outside the area which came to be defended was extensive. To the S.E. of the town, casual finds of coins and pottery of all periods indicate occupation at various points along the general line of Watling Street for a distance of 500 m. S.W. of the defended area. Intensive occupation represented by slight, mainly industrial, structures has been shown to have extended some 700 m. along both sides of the road to Alchester; they had developed certainly by the Antonine period, with a marked peak in the early 4th century. On the W. of the town, Roman material has been found along both sides of the present Brackley road for a distance of 800 m. To the N. little has been recorded from the low-lying and marshy zone extending from the presumed north gate to the R. Tove, but beyond it, much material has been found in the general area of the former railway station as well as further N.W. No evidence of extra-mural settlement exists to the N.E. but here the permanent grassland of Easton Neston Park has prevented any discoveries being made.

Apart from the fine silver sword-mount picked up as a casual find S.W. of the town (SP 68974796; *Northants. Archaeol.*, 14 (1979), 107), no material of the early Anglo-Saxon period has been recorded from Towcester. In 917 the town was occupied and fortified, almost certainly in timber, by Edward the Elder, as part of his programme of *Burh* construction; an attack by the Danes of Northampton and Leicester was successfully beaten off. In that year Edward provided Towcester with a stone wall (D. Whitelock (ed.), *Anglo-Saxon Chronicle* (1961), 64–6).

Domesday Book indicates that Towcester was a rural manor and the entry suggests that in the later 11th century it was the centre of local administration; it continued to give its name to the Hundred of Towcester for centuries. This administrative function in all probability explains the presence of the motte known as Bury Mount (8). Its situation on a much frequented length of Watling Street gave the settlement a certain commercial importance, and a market and fair are recorded in the 14th century. The military significance of the town was briefly revived in November 1643, when it was garrisoned and fortified by Prince Rupert to act as a base of operations against the Parliamentarians of Northampton; it was evacuated and the work slighted in January 1644. Its continued local importance has however meant that the area of the Roman town has been completely built over, and most of the known suburbs have been destroyed by the recent housing developments.

Roman Roads (see also Appendix, p. 178)

Towcester stands at the junction of Watling Street and of the road to Alchester. On general grounds a road N.E.

to Duston or Irchester could have been expected, but no traces of one have been recognized.

The general course of Watling Street is followed by the modern A5. On crossing the Silverstone Brook (SP 69444850) it alters its alignment towards the N.E. twelve degrees; it then runs for over 900 m. over the low ground on which Towcester is situated to cross the R. Tove (SP 68904923) where the alignment moves through fifteen degrees again towards the N.E. Within the town (SP 693487) at least three superimposed road surfaces were seen in 1950, although details of the construction are lacking (*Oxoniensia*, 15 (1950), 108). At the presumed northern gate-way (SP 69104895) a spread of orange gravel 30 cm. thick seen in 1977/8 probably represented the road. The edge of what was probably Watling Street was recorded near the southern gate (SP 69414855) in 1976; it consisted of a layer of heavy stone set in clay 28 cm. thick overlying compacted orange gravel. A series of superimposed road surfaces a little to the S.E. (SP 69434852) contained medieval pottery and were post-Roman (inf. Mrs. Woodfield).

The road to Alchester joined Watling Street within the town, just N. of the present junction of Park Street with Watling Street (SP 69254878). Within the defended area a stretch 11 m. long was uncovered on the S. side of Park Street (SP 69234872): it consisted of metalling 6 m. wide formed of large stones with gravel above, 15 cm. thick in all; above were several resurfacings. The earliest layers belonged to the last quarter of the 1st century (inf. G. Lambrick). Further S.W. (SP 69224865) the road surface was seen in 1954 (inf. J. A. Alexander).

The Defences (Fig. 113)

Only in the N.W. corner of the town do the defences survive in a recognizable form. To the S. of the present police station and running N.E. for 30 m. is a ditch 33 m. wide and 0.5 m. deep with a bank 1.5 m. high above the ditch bottom; running S.S.E. for 70 m. from the telephone exchange which sits on the presumed N.W. corner is a ditch 35 m. wide and 2 m. deep now occupied by allotments.

Information about the course of the defences elsewhere is supplied by Baker (op. cit.). His description and plan indicates that along the N.W. side the defences continued the line of the surviving fragment N.E.; recent observations confirm this. On the W., they ran along the present Queens Road, where the broad hollow in which the road sits probably represents the line of the ditch. To the S. of this, Baker's line then crossed the N.W. end of the present Richmond Road (formerly Sawpit Lane) and turned N.E. at a point S.W. of Sawpit Green to run for 190 m. to join Watling Street (SP 69404855), although his account makes it clear that the traces had been largely obliterated. From Watling Street his line ran along the southern side of the churchyard almost to the present mill leat (SP 69504870); the wall has been seen on this alignment in a water-mains trench (SP 69444864; OS Record Cards), and the ditch nearby (SP 69434857; inf. Mrs. C. Woodfield). Along the N.E. side Baker assumed that the defences coincided with the general line of the present mill leat, itself however of late 17th or 18th-century construction (J. Bridges, *Hist. of Northants.*, I (1791), 272). This conjecture is supported by

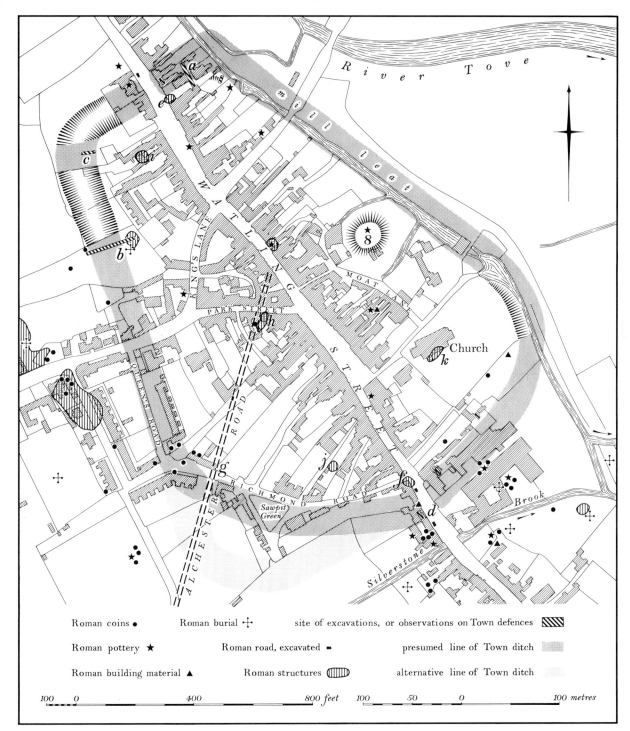

Fig. 113　TOWCESTER (3)　Roman town

a low scarp which can be seen running N.W. for 60 m. due E. of the church (SP 69494875). What has been interpreted as the tail of the rampart has been noted during drainage work near the N. corner (SP 69194896; inf. Mrs. C. Woodfield), and the rear of the rampart still exists in

a much mutilated condition immediately to the N.W.

Baker's account has been followed by most subsequent workers (e.g. a plan by Sir Henry Dryden in the Dryden Collection in the Northampton Public Library and *Arch. J.*, 110 (1953), 211), but his version of the location of the

S.W. corner can be challenged. Vertical air photographs taken in 1947 (CPE/UK/1994, 2078) show that the area S. of Sawpit Green was covered by ridge-and-furrow running N.W.–S.E. and that there were no definite traces of the defences. An alternative suggestion (OS Record Cards; A. L. F. Rivet, *Town and Country in Roman Britain* (1958), 85) would place the general line of the S.W. defences along Richmond Road. This makes better topographical sense, since this road marked the rearward termination of the medieval tenements of Towcester and the proposed line would better accommodate a gate for the Alchester road. There are a number of cracks in the brick and stone walls of properties running along the N. side of this road.

The area enclosed by the defences so defined is about 11.25 hectares. The defences have been sectioned in two places. On the N. side, just N.E. of Watling Street (SP 69174896; 'a' on Fig. 113) observation during a drainage scheme in 1977 showed a bank 10 m. wide of clay and gravel; part of the robber trench of the wall was seen but the relationship between the wall and bank could not be established. Separated from the wall by a berm 8 m. wide was a shallow flat-bottomed wet ditch at least 9 m. wide and 1.75 m.–2 m. deep. Material which had accumulated against the bank had been cut by a pit containing pottery of around 180. A straight sided wet ditch at least 12 m. wide and 3.5 m. deep cut the earlier ditch 8 m. from the outer edge of the berm; it produced largely medieval pottery. This could conceivably represent a 4th-century defensive ditch or be linked with the refortification by Edward the Elder in 917. This phase was probably represented by the rough herringbone foundations of a wall 1.3 m. wide in front of the Roman one. The shallow earlier Roman ditch was cut by another wet ditch, 4 m.–5 m. wide, V-sectioned and at least 2 m. deep; this could be attributed to Prince Rupert, who is said to have 'brought the water around the town' in 1643 (G. Baker, op. cit., 323; *Northants. Archaeol.*, 13 (1978), 182–3; inf. Mrs. C. Woodfield).

On the W. side the excavations in 1954 (SP 69104879; 'b' on Fig. 113) sectioned the defences. The results matched those obtained in 1977. The Roman defences consisted of a bank 7.5 m. wide and 2 m. high, constructed on top of an earlier well and the beam-slot of a timber building. The wall, its limestone foundations 3 m. wide, was contemporary with the bank. The ditch, which could not have been more than 2 m. deep, had been largely removed by subsequent alterations to the defences, but the yellow clay obtained from it had been spread beyond over a series of insubstantial timber buildings with gravel floors. Material from these buildings and from within and below the rampart goes down to about 175. Later alterations to the defences involved the excavation of a ditch 25 m. wide and 2 m. deep which largely removed the earlier one, the fill of which contained much medieval pottery. As before, this could represent late Roman activity or be attributable to Edward the Elder. To him could also be assigned the construction of a second wall of sandstone and limestone, 2 m. wide, in front of the Roman one and possibly also the heightening of the bank with material containing Roman pottery going down to the late 4th century. A later phase involved the addition of further material to the bank

and the excavation of a ditch of V-profile 6 m. wide and 3 m. deep, cutting through the surviving shallow ditch. This can be taken to represent the fortifications erected by Prince Rupert. The tumble of stone filling this ditch presumably represented the deliberate slighting of the defences when the Royalists evacuated Towcester in January 1644.

The defences have also been seen on the N.W. corner (SP 69044887; 'c' on Fig. 113) where observations during the building of a telephone exchange in 1967 suggested that there had been two periods of construction of the town wall, as has been noted elsewhere (*BNFAS*, 3 (1969), 18; inf. J. A. Alexander). At the S. end of the defended area (SP 69424852; 'd' on Fig. 113) what was probably the later of the wide shallow ditches was seen during drainage work in 1977 (*Northants. Archaeol.*, 13 (1978), 183).

Casual observations suggest the existence of a substantial structure containing Roman tile on the N.E. side of Watling Street (SP 69144894); this could represent the N. gate (inf. T. Shirley). Stone foundations considered to belong to the S. gate have been seen at various times (SP 69394857; inf. J. A. Alexander; *Northants. Archaeol.*, 13 (1978), 183; 'f' on Fig. 113). A third gate presumably existed on the S.W. side ('g' on Fig. 113).

Interior of the Town (Fig. 113)

Excavations at two points have established the existence of substantial buildings. Near the N.W. corner of the town (SP 69104879; 'b' on Fig. 113) the excavations of 1954 revealed some 1st-century material and the beam-slots of the S.W. corner of a late 3rd-century timber building, probably a house, at least 13 m. by 7 m. Parts of two rooms were uncovered. The structure was rebuilt once, slightly further to the N.E., away from the defences, before being replaced in the 4th century on the same alignment but further E. again by a building with limestone foundations 1 m. wide. This building had tessellated floors and walls with painted plaster; three rooms were identified. It was destroyed, possibly by fire, in the late 4th or early 5th century.

On the S. side of Park Street (SP 69234872; 'h' on Fig. 113), the foundations of a stone wall 60 cm. thick with buttresses or pilasters, were discovered. It probably belonged to a public building of uncertain purpose put up during the third quarter of the 1st century. Its W. side was aligned along the Alchester road. In the mid 2nd century it was enlarged, and then replaced by two buildings at least 7 m. by 4 m. and 5 m. by 2 m. respectively, with stone foundations 70 cm. wide, also aligned on the Alchester road. A stone-lined well belonged to this phase. Sometime in the 3rd or 4th century they were demolished to make way for a timber building represented by a row of postholes along the road frontage; this was replaced by the flimsy stone footings 40 cm. thick of a timber building, probably in the late Roman period (inf. G. Lambrick).

Elsewhere in the town the discovery of pottery and other debris in many places indicates occupation along both sides of Watling Street and the Alchester road. Stone walls were found in 1958 during excavations for a new fire station (SP 69114889; 'i' on Fig. 113) and others were recorded in the S. part of the town near Meeting Lane (SP 69314857; 'j' on Fig. 113) in the 1930s (inf. J. A. Alexander). In 1883 two pavements, one plain and the other herringbone, of tesserae cut from tiles, were found when a heating system was installed in the south aisle of the church; they lay on the same alignment as the church. A hypocaust is said to have been seen in 1937 on the S. side of the church under the porch (Ms notes by Sir Henry Dryden in Northampton Public Library; *The Antiquary*, 8 (1883), 87; inf. J. A. Alexander; 'k' on Fig. 113). Other discoveries include 1st and 4th-century material from the W. side of Kings Lane (SP 69144876), late 2nd-century pottery from a pit just inside the N. corner of the defences (SP 69194896), mid 2nd-century material from a pit on the N.E. side of Watling Street (SP 69254880) and pottery and tiles from a point just W. of Moat Lane (inf. Mrs. C. Woodfield; OS Record Cards). A marble vase was found in 1865 during the construction of The Corn Exchange (SP 69354865; illustrated in 'Broadsides', Northampton Public Library; lost). Unassociated material, including pottery of various dates as well as roofing tiles and a few coins have been recorded in a number of places. Other casual finds from the town include a hippo sandal, a bronze hand from a statue and an alabaster bottle (NM). Two small silver axes, only 4 cm. long, are recorded 'from Towcester' (private owner; *BAR*, 24 (1976), 178) while a stone female funerary head, also from the town is in the BM (*BAR*, op. cit., 112). A considerable amount of Roman pottery, all unlocated but 'from Towcester' is in the Ashmolean Museum and considerably more still remains in private hands.

Extra-mural Settlement (Fig. 114)

A large amount of Roman material has been found outside the walls of the Roman town, either as chance finds or during excavations. For convenience of presentation this has here been sub-divided arbitrarily into eight areas:

(l) Roman settlement in the area of the former railway station (SP 68924937). Several coins are said to have been found when the station was built in 1864 (inf. J. A. Alexander); many pottery fragments, including at least 100 'vessels', a few coins and pieces of glass were discovered during the excavation of the cutting to the N.E. (*The Antiquary*, 8 (1883), 87; Ms notes by Sir Henry Dryden in Northampton Public Library). A number of coins was recorded further N.W. along Watling Street (SP 68764960) in the 1950s, mainly of late 3rd and 4th centuries down to Magnentius (inf. J. A. Alexander). Skeletons, pottery, coins and a 1st-century bronze brooch were discovered on the S.W. side of Watling Street opposite the former station (SP 68774935) during the construction of a factory in 1975 (NM records).

(m) Road widening of Watling Street in the 1930s N.W. of (a) centred SP 685501; not on Fig. 114) revealed finds including pottery, two brooches and three coins of Nero, Nerva and Constantine I (*JRS*, 23 (1933), 198).

(n) Roman pottery was found during the construction of the police station, (SP 69064899) just outside the site of the presumed N. gate of the town (inf. J. A. Alexander). An 'urn' was found further N. some time between 1870 and 1880 (at SP 690492; OS Record Cards).

(o) Roman settlement, extending W. along the line of the present Brackley road (centred SP 690486). Many coins, mainly of the late 3rd and 4th centuries, and some pottery,

including a vessel containing a cremation, have been found at various times on and around Sponne School (SP 68924865). Skeletons, pottery and a building were seen on the site of the school (SP 68984872) in 1919 (OS Record Cards). The former allotments N. of the Brackley road (SP 68704860) have long been noted as productive of coins, ranging in date from Tiberius to Constantine II. A few coins have been recorded on the S. side of the road at the N. end of Pomfret Road (SP 69014868).

(p) To the S.W. of the Cemetery on the Brackley road (SP 68544829) the erection of a housing estate in 1979 brought to light ditches, a few coins and pottery ranging from the 2nd to the 4th centuries. To the S., near the Silverstone Brook (SP 68554800), a quantity of 1st to 2nd-century pottery was discovered. Further W. (SP 68444838; not on Fig. 114) road works in 1967 uncovered stone surfaces (inf. J. A. Alexander, T. Shirley and Mrs. C. Woodfield; *BNFAS*, 3 (1969), 2; *Northants. Archaeol.*, 13 (1978), 184; 14 (1979), 106; *Britannia*, 10 (1979), 302).

(q) Roman settlement, running along both sides of Alchester road to the S.W. of the town. The area S.W. of Towcester had been productive of Roman remains since the development of housing estates there in the 1950s. To the N. of the Silverstone Brook, pottery was found during the construction of a new bridge in 1953 (SP 69174837) and during flood-relief work in 1977/8 a large, probably 4th-century, ditch which cut through Antonine levels, was seen here. To the W. (SP 69154837) was a ditch containing pottery going down to the late 2nd century (inf. J. A. Alexander and Mrs. C. Woodfield). Further S.W. (around SP 690481) excavations on both sides of the Alchester road in 1967 uncovered several structures of the 4th century. At SP 69074822 was a spread of stone 10 m. by 12 m., with a smaller one to the E. of it overlying the W. ditch of the Roman road. Traces of a rectangular building, at least 6 m. by 7 m. with a sand floor containing hearths and stone post-pads, lay immediately N. of these spreads.

On the E. side of the road (SP 69084813) the stone foundations 50 cm. thick of a probably rectangular building at least 5 m. by 4 m. were discovered, cut by a ditch 50 cm. wide running parallel with the road (MOPBW, *Ann. Ex. Rep. 1966* (1967), 16; inf. D. C. Mynard). More pottery, tiles, rubbish pits, areas of stone paving and mainly 4th-century coins were reported from the area of SP 69134817 in 1966 (NM Records).

A pottery kiln making coarse grey or black ware has been reported from the area of SP 69014820 and from SP 69074804 came pottery ranging in date from the Antonine period to the mid 4th century, *opus signinum* and a silver spoon (inf. Mrs. C. Woodfield).

Further S. again, excavations in advance of housing development from 1974 to 1976 led to the discovery of more industrial structures aligned along the Roman road. On the W. side (SP 69004799) was a circular building 14 m. in diam., defined on its W. side by a gully; it contained a hearth. It was overlaid by a rectangular building with a stone floor, containing reused sculptured stones, two of which formed post bases in the interior. Facing it across the road (SP 69044798) was another circular building, defined by a gully 7 m. in diam, with opposed entrances. The E. entrance, which overlay a well-preserved wooden culvert, led via a wooden corduroy track of three phases

Fig. 114 TOWCESTER (3) Roman town

to a pond fed by a series of ditches, likewise of three phases. The hut contained three hearths and the finds, which included a complete pewter dish, indicate lead and pewter working. Both structures were linked to the road by means of stone causeways. Further S., on the W. side of the road (SP 68984795), was another probably rectangular building with a stone floor, containing a furnace, also associated with lead working. To the N.E. of this was a large sand pit marked off from the road by a wooden fence. The abundant coins indicate a date of 315–360 for this industrial activity. Observation in 1977 during the construction of houses in this area noted further round and rectangular buildings, pits and ditches, with much pottery and many coins indicating a date range from the Antonine period to the 4th century. There was also evidence of iron-working (*Northants. Archaeol.*, 10 (1975), 163; 11 (1976), 194; 12 (1977), 215; 13 (1978), 194; *Britannia*, 6 (1975), 255; 7 (1976), 355; 8 (1977), 399; inf. Mrs. C. Woodfield).

(r) Immediately outside the defences on the S. side of the town, coins, mostly 3rd and 4th-century, human bones and pottery including samian ware have been recorded at various times since the 19th century in the area of the former Brewery (SP 69504856; NM Records). A ditch parallel with the Silverstone Brook was seen at SP 69534856 in 1976/7 (inf. T. Shirley). Coins and pottery were found in 1938–9 when a car park was being constructed (SP 69434854; inf. J. A. Alexander).

(s) To the S. of the Silverstone Brook, intermittent traces of occupation in the form of coins and pottery ranging from the 1st to the 4th centuries have been found along Watling Street as far S. as Vernon Road (SP 69654832; inf. J. A. Alexander and Mrs. C. Woodfield; *BNFAS*, 3 (1969), 2).

Cemeteries

In addition to the places mentioned above, burials, presumably indicative of cemeteries, have been found in a number of places outside the defended area of the town:

(t) At SP 68914876 skeletons were found when a bowling green was levelled in 1919 (NM Records).

(u) At SP 69044854 two skeletons were found during the construction of a car park in 1968 (inf. T. Shirley).

(v) A 'Roman urnfield' was reported as having been found when the Silverstone Brook was straightened, about 1870–80 (probably SP 69244836; NM Records; inf. J. A. Alexander).

(w) Immediately S.E. of the town a skeleton was seen in 1976/7 during the flood-relief scheme (SP 69384846); others were noted to the N.W. (SP 69564854). Two skull fragments were found in 1978 to the N. (SP 69594859; *Northants. Archaeol.*, 13 (1978), 183; inf. T. Shirley).

[a](4) ROMAN SETTLEMENT (?) (SP 67634855), N.E. of Costwell Farm, on Boulder Clay at 108 m. above OD. A Roman bronze ligula and sherds probably of 2nd-century date have been found. A mid 17th-century bone-handled knife was also discovered. (*Northants. Archaeol.*, 13 (1978), 184)

[a](5) ROMAN VILLA AND TEMPLE (?) (SP 685469; Fig. 115), 1 km. W. of Wood Burcote, on limestones and clays at 107 m. above OD. Excavations between 1972 and 1976 revealed parts of a substantial villa and its outbuildings. Apart from some prehistoric activity on the site (1), the earliest occupation appears to have been a system of ditched enclosures and pottery kilns dating from about AD 40 to 60. No kilns have been found *in situ* but burnt clay debris includes a pedestal, kiln bars and a circular dome-plate

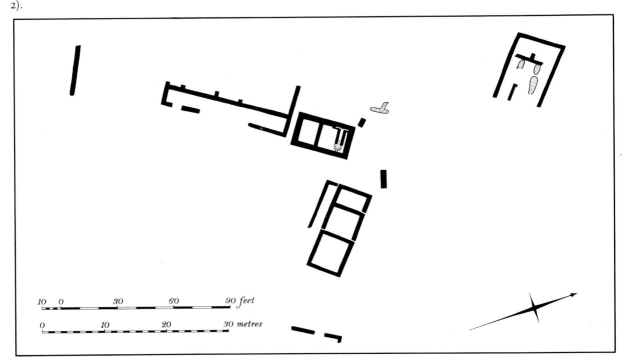

Fig. 115   TOWCESTER (5)   Roman villa (based on plan of excavation)

with a central hole. The associated pottery included jars
and bowls of late Belgic type.

The villa ('a' on plan) has not been completely excavated
and parts of only six rooms and a portico have been exposed. It appears to have been built in the late 1st century,
over earlier timber structures, and to have gone out of use
by the 3rd century. Two of the rooms had painted wall-
plaster. Adjacent to the villa on the N. lay a small rectangular stone building of two rooms ('b' on plan), erected
just after AD 200. One room contained a T-shaped corn-
drying oven and a second oven had been inserted into the
floor after the building had collapsed. To the N.E. of the
villa there was a three-celled building with a portico on
one side ('c' on plan). This was built originally as a single
room probably in about AD 130–160 over 1st-century
occupation debris and pits, and the two other rooms and
the portico were added at a later date. Tesserae and wall-
plaster were discovered around the building.

A late 1st-century rectangular stone building was discovered well to the N. of the villa, beside a small stream
('d' on plan). It had three later corn-drying ovens inside it
and considerable areas of blackened soil and carbonised
grain lay around it. The excavators suggested that this
building might have been a watermill but there is no direct
evidence for this. A Y-shaped corn-drying oven was excavated to the S. Other short lengths of walling were noted
elsewhere.

Among the numerous finds from the excavation and
from field-walking are stone mouldings, flue tiles and tesserae. A bronze scabbard-mount with Celtic decoration,
associated with pottery of the second half of the 1st century
AD, was discovered in the bottom of a ditch near the
possible mill. A small capital of limestone, a column base
and part of a shaft were also found. (*Britannia*, 5 (1974),
277–8; 6 (1975), 255; CBA Group 9, *Newsletter*, 5 (1975),
17; *Northants. Archaeol.*, 12 (1977), 218–223; 13 (1978), 79–
81)

The land on the N. side of the site is occupied by a
19th-century pumping station. It is said that when this was
constructed in about 1880 the remains of a Roman bath-
house were found. No details of this are known except for
three sculptured heads, one of which is in the British Museum (OS Record Cards). This is described as an antefix
but is more likely to be part of a funerary monument. It
shows classical influence but its treatment and expression
are entirely native (A. Ross, *Pagan Celtic Britain* (1967),
87). It has been suggested that these remains may be related
to a temple on the site.

Numerous coins, described only as 'from Wood Burcote' but probably from this site, are recorded. These include a bronze coin of Cunobelinus, Mack 242 (NM; S. S.
Frere (ed.), *Problems of the Iron Age in S. Britain* (1958),
234) and a specimen of British 'ring-money' (*Brit. Num.
J.*, 3 (1906), 388) as well as Roman coins of the 3rd and
4th centuries (NM; OS Record Cards).

ᵃ(6) ROMAN SETTLEMENT (SP 696459), in the S.E. of the
parish, S.E. of Burcote Wood, on Boulder Clay at 135 m.
above OD. Pottery of the 3rd and 4th centuries, tiles and
iron slag were found here in 1965 (*BNFAS*, 1 (1966), 13;
Wolverton and Dist. Arch. Soc. Newsletter, 10 (1966), 41).

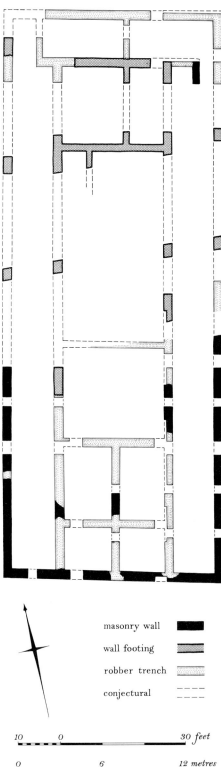

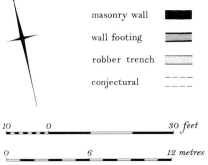

	masonry wall	■■■■
	wall footing	▨▨▨
	robber trench	▨▨▨
	conjectural	- - - -

10   0   30 feet

0   6   12 metres

Fig. 116   TOWCESTER (7)   Roman villa
(based on plan of excavation)

ᵃ(7) IRON AGE SETTLEMENT AND ROMAN VILLA (SP 669477; Fig. 116), in the W. of the parish, on Boulder Clay at 120 m. above OD. The site, sometimes known as the Foscote villa, was first discovered in 1846–8 when building material, pottery and a coin were found (VCH *Northants.*, I (1902), 199), and was partly excavated in 1955–6. Evidence of early occupation consisted of numerous hearths and post-holes, and cobbling associated with late Iron Age pottery. The main phase of occupation was represented by a rectangular stone building, 40 m. by 16 m. with a corridor on each of the long sides and containing 12 rooms. At least one mosaic, a hypocaust and a cellar were found. It was constructed in AD 65–75 and remained apparently unaltered until AD 140–160 when it was demolished. An extensive scatter of Roman pottery and other occupation debris covers the whole area. (*JRS*, 46 (1956), 134; 47 (1957), 214; *Northants. Archaeol.*, 13 (1978), 28–66)

For Roman Roads 1f and 1e, Watling Street, and 160a, see Appendix.

MEDIEVAL AND LATER

A small silver Saxon sword mount was found in 1974 (SP 68974796; NM; *Northants. Archaeol.*, 14 (1979), 107).

The S.W. part of the parish, known as Handley, was occupied by a deer park in the medieval period (*Northants. P. and P.*, 5 (1975), 225–6). The park is first recorded in 1220 and it had been abandoned before the 17th century. Although the general boundaries can be identified (Figs. 16 and 41) there is no evidence of a park pale on the ground.

For details of the late Saxon and 17th-century fortifications of the town of Towcester and a brief summary of its medieval and later history see (3). The only medieval discoveries made within the town have been part of a limestone floor and a fragment of walling associated with sherds of St. Neots ware, found in the Park Street excavation in 1954 (SP 69104879), and pottery of the 14th and 15th century, some associated with wall footings and a well, found in two places in the N.E. part of the town in 1974 (SP 692488; *Northants. Archaeol.*, 10 (1975), 171; NM).

ᵃ(8) MOTTE (SP 69344881; Figs. 113 and 117), known as Bury Mount, lies on the N.E. side of the town on land sloping gently to the R. Tove, on Upper Lias Clay at 87 m. above OD. Nothing is known of its history but it was presumably constructed in the late 11th or 12th century, perhaps by the Crown, as the centre of the extensive royal estate in this area (VCH *Northants.*, I (1902), 305). Its tactical purpose is unclear, but it is thought to have controlled the medieval road to Northampton which formerly continued the line of Church Lane across the R. Tove. This road was presumably abandoned in the 17th or 18th century when Easton Neston Park was laid out to the E. of the town (G. Baker, *Hist. of Northants.*, II (1836–41), 318, plan).

The motte was apparently altered during the Civil War by Prince Rupert, who refortified the town in 1643 and made it 'very strong and brought the water around the town' (Baker, op. cit., 322–4). In the 'Journal of Sir Samuel Luke' (*Oxford Record Society*, III (1952–3), 207, 219) it is recorded that 'They are making a mount on the further

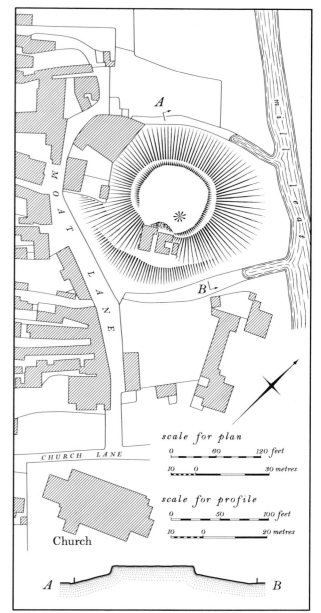

Fig. 117   TOWCESTER (8)   Motte

side of the town to plant ordnance on' and that 'There are 8 pieces of ordnance in Toster, 6 in the markett place and 2 planted on a hill towards Northampton'.

The present state of the motte may be the result of these events as much as of its later land use. The site was described by Bridges (*Hist. of Northants.*, I (1791), 272) in the early 18th century, as being 'surrounded by a mote (*sic*) which is supplied with water from the brook'. The Tithe Map of Towcester (NRO, 1843) does not show the motte at all, but depicts the site of it completely surrounded by a broad water-filled ditch running off the adjacent mill stream. The area within this ditch is called Berry Hill Garden. A slightly later and perhaps more accurate plan of

1848–55 (NRO) shows the top of the motte as circular with two buildings set on the S. side of it. The surrounding ditch is shown as made up of four almost straight lengths and these are closer to the present property boundaries than the circular ditch depicted on the Tithe Map. By the late 19th century (OS 1:2500 plan, Northants. LVI 6, 1900), the ditch had been reduced to two arms extending S.W. from the mill stream. The S.W. of the ditch is not marked and a row of buildings which still stand occupied the W.

The motte now consists of a circular mound some 65 m.–75 m. in diam. The lower slopes are occupied by modern gardens. The gradient here is slight, rising to about 3 m. above the adjacent ground. On the S. side there is then a narrow ledge, backed by a near vertical face of gravel and clay up to 3 m. high which rises to the flat top of the mound. From the lowest point on the S.E. the ledge slopes gently upwards, reaching the summit on the W. The summit itself is rather uneven, but has no marked features except for a modern pit near its S.E. edge. Traces of the surrounding ditch survive on the N. and S.E., but only their N.E. ends are now water-filled.

The unusual profile of this motte is undoubtedly the result of later alterations. The upper part seems to have been cut back at some time after the original construction of a normal castle mound either to make the summit more difficult of access or to provide a gently sloping walkway to the top. This alteration may be contemporary with the surrounding water-filled ditch. The latter appears to have been cut into the N.W. side of the mound but lies a little distance from it on the S.E. These alterations may have been made in 1643 as part of the defensive improvements of Towcester but they are more likely to be the result of later gardening activities as the name given to the area in 1843 might indicate.

[a](9) SETTLEMENT REMAINS (SP 695468; Figs. 41 and 118), formerly part of Wood Burcote, lie in and around the existing hamlet, on limestone at 122 m. above OD. Wood Burcote was formerly an independent hamlet, the lands of which seem to have occupied most of the S. part of what is now Towcester parish. The settlement is first mentioned in documents in 1200 (PN Northants., 95) but is perhaps included silently in Domesday Book under the large royal manor of Towcester (VCH Northants., I (1902), 305). In 1301 nine people in Wood Burcote paid the Lay Subsidy (PRO, E179/155/31) and the same number paid the tax of 1525 (PRO, E179/155/132). The Hearth Tax returns of 1673 list 12 people from the hamlet (PRO, E179/254/14) and Bridges, writing in about 1720 (Hist. of Northants., I (1791), 278), noted there were 25 families living there.

Wood Burcote now comprises a single street with houses and cottages lying mainly on its N.W. side. The situation was the same in the mid 19th century (NRO: map of Towcester, c. 1850; Tithe Map, 1843) but the field evidence indicates that at some time in the past the S.E. side of the street was also occupied by buildings and closes, the whole forming a small compact settlement. The surviving remains fall into three parts. At the extreme N.E. end of the hamlet the road from Towcester continues S.E. as a narrow hollow-way 2 m. deep at its N.W. end but fading out to a slight depression as it crosses the field towards Paulerspury. Within the present pasture field to the S.W., along the S.E. side of the main street, there are very slight earthworks, now almost ploughed out. These are difficult to interpret but include at least one quarry pit which has recently been filled in. Air photographs taken in 1947 before ploughing show ridge-and-furrow over part of the area (RAF VAP CPE/UK/1926, 3235–6). Nevertheless it is possible that these earthworks do include former house-sites. A large depression at the S.W. end of this area, bounded on the E. by a scarp 1.5 m. high and on the N. by the footings of a stone wall and with a small rectangular building platform at one end, may be a quarry cut into an older close. A 19th-century map (NRO) shows a short length of road at right angles to the main street running into this area. Further S.W., immediately S.W. of the only surviving house on this side of the street, the 1947 air photographs show an area of uneven ground of about 0.5 hectare. This area is now arable land and no earthworks remain, but it contains stone-rubble with post-medieval brick and tiles and, at its E. end, large quantities of medieval pottery of 13th to 14th-century date.

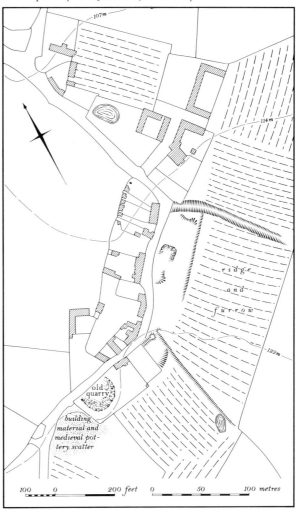

Fig. 118   TOWCESTER (9)
Settlement remains at Wood Burcote

[b](10) SETTLEMENT REMAINS (SP 687510; Fig. 41), formerly part of Caldecote, lie in and around the existing hamlet, on limestone between 115 m. and 122 m. above OD. Caldecote was formerly an independent settlement which occupied most of the N. part of the modern parish of Towcester. It is first mentioned in documents in 1203 (PN Northants., 95) but is probably included silently in Domesday Book within the large royal manor of Towcester (VCH Northants., I (1902), 305). In 1301 14 people paid the Lay Subsidy (PRO, E179/155/31) and 11 people paid the Subsidy of 1525 (PRO, E179/155/132). The Hearth Tax returns of 1673 list 14 people in Caldecote (PRO, E179/254/14). By the early 18th century there were about 20 houses there (J. Bridges, Hist. of Northants., I (1791), 278) and by the mid 19th century (NRO, Tithe Map, 1843) only some 15 buildings are depicted, much as now.

The hamlet consists of a single street with houses and farms on each side but earthworks suggest that the hamlet once extended further N. On the E. side of the street, beyond the last farm, the ridge-and-furrow terminates just short of a low bank parallel to the street. The ground between this bank and the street is uneven. On the W. side of the street, N. of the last cottage, is an area of old quarries which appear to have been cut into an embanked close, and a long narrow field to the N. again, now under grass, may be the site of other former buildings. Elsewhere the remains of the close boundaries survive as low banks in the paddocks behind the houses. (RAF VAP CPE/UK/1926, 1037–8; air photographs in NMR)

[b](11) MOAT (SP 687509), lay around Home Farm, at the S.E. end of Caldecote hamlet, on clay at 115 m. above OD. The Tithe Map of 1843 (NRO) shows the present farm-house bounded on its E., S. and W. sides by a broad water-filled ditch, apparently part of a small rectangular moat which perhaps once encircled the building. From the S.E. corner of the moat a stream led to a large rectangular pond. On a slightly later map of c. 1850 (NRO) the pond is again depicted, but the N. end of the W. side is omitted.

Apart from a shallow depression which marks the former S.E. corner, the moat has now been entirely destroyed though part of the pond to the S.E. still survives.

(12) CULTIVATION REMAINS. The common fields of Towcester, together with those of Wood Burcote and Caldecote, were enclosed by an Act of Parliament of 1762; the exact arrangement of these fields is not known.

Ridge-and-furrow exists on the ground or can be traced on air photographs over large parts of the parish, arranged in end-on and interlocked furlongs, many of reversed-S form. It is particularly well marked along the small N.E.-flowing stream which crosses the centre of the parish (SP 681470–694485) where the furlongs are all arranged at right angles to the contours. The same feature is visible along the R. Tove and beside the streams flowing S. from Caldecote. Where ridge-and-furrow no longer exists, well-marked headlands, up to 10 m. wide and 0.25 m. high can still be traced on the ground (e.g. SP 693475).

Ridge-and-furrow also survives over a large part of Handley Park, again arranged in end-on and interlocked furlongs. As some of this ridge-and-furrow appears to underlie field boundaries which are known to have been

laid out in the 16th century, it presumably dates from the medieval period but it is not possible to tell whether this ridge-and-furrow is earlier than the formation of the park itself. (RAF VAP CPE/UK/1926, 1034–6, 1230–6, 3234–7; F21 58/RAF/2316, 0065–6)

62 WAPPENHAM
(OS 1:10000 [a] SP 64 SW, [b] SP 64 NW)

The parish, covering about 950 hectares, lies across the valley of the R. Tove, here flowing at 107 m. above OD, which also forms part of the W. boundary. Tributary streams flowing generally N. or S.E. define other boundaries. Expanses of Boulder Clay cover the high areas in the N. and S. and a strip of glacial sands and gravels runs N. to S. through the centre of the parish. The valleys are floored with Upper Lias Clay, and Oolitic limestones outcrop on the valley sides.

PREHISTORIC AND ROMAN

A Middle Bronze Age palstave is recorded from the parish (VCH Northants., I (1902), 143; NM). A single late Roman pot was found in 1958, some 400 m. N. of the cropmarks listed below (1) (NM; OS Record Cards).

[b](1) ENCLOSURES (SP 622468), E. of Manor Farm, on glacial sands and gravels, at 137 m. above OD. Air photographs (CUAP, VC82, 86) show indistinct cropmarks of a D-shaped enclosure about 30 m. wide with several subdivisions. A smaller oval enclosure lies to the N.W.

[b](2) ROMAN SETTLEMENT AND KILN (SP 626453), S. of the village, on glacial gravel at 132 m. above OD. Gravel-working in 1874 revealed a Roman kiln containing 20 broken urns. Charcoal, bone, iron-slag, a silvered brooch and fragments of bronze were also found. (VCH Northants., I (1902), 221; OS Record Cards)

MEDIEVAL AND LATER

[b](3) SETTLEMENT REMAINS (SP 627457; Figs. 14 and 119), formerly part of Wappenham, once lay at the N.E. end of the village, on limestone at 115 m. above OD. There are no indications in the surviving records of any marked reduction in the village at any time and the earthworks described below have now been largely destroyed. It is difficult to understand how they related to the development of the village.

Wappenham is first mentioned in Domesday Book where it is listed as a single manor with a recorded population of 38, including a priest (VCH Northants., I (1902), 344). In 1301, 27 people paid the Lay Subsidy (PRO, E179/155/31) and in 1377, 61 people over the age of 14 paid the Poll Tax (PRO, E179/155/27). Sixty-four householders paid the Hearth Tax in 1673 (PRO, E179/254/14).

The village today falls into two distinct units at each end of a single E.-W. street. At the W. end is the church and a small triangular green, though the position of the adjacent lane suggests that this green may have once been very much larger and roughly rectangular. At the E. end is another group of houses centred on a road junction which forms another small green.

The main area of earthworks lay on ground sloping N., on the N. side of the main street, and linked the two parts of the village. The area, covering some 4 hectares, had already been ploughed in 1947 when the first air photographs were taken (RAF VAP CPE/UK/1926, 1226–7). These show that a single large field was divided into a number of small rectangular paddocks or closes, bounded by low banks or ditches, some with ridge-and-furrow within them. At the E. end was a rectangular area, apparently raised above the surrounding land, some 60 m. by 30 m., orientated E.-W. and bounded by a wide ditch. The interior was uneven. This may have been the site of a moat and manor house. No trace of these earthworks remains, though slightly uneven ground, and patches of stone rubble associated with pottery of 12th to 17th centuries lie along the S. edge of the site close to the road. This area was already devoid of buildings in the early 19th century (OS 1st ed. 1 in. map, 1834). Elsewhere in the village, behind some of the existing farms and houses, were the remains of abandoned paddocks or closes bounded by low banks and shallow ditches (e.g. SP 623657) but most of these have been destroyed.

[b](4) HOLLOW-WAYS (SP 630455; Fig. 14), lie on steeply rising ground immediately S.E. of the E. end of the village, on the S.W. side of the road to Syresham, on limestone and Boulder Clay between 114 m. and 137 m. above OD. The hillside is scored by a number of parallel hollow-ways up to 2 m. deep. To the N., near the village, they run into an area of old quarry-pits, some of which cut through the hollow-ways. (RAF VAP CPE/UK/1926, 1226–7; air photographs in NMR)

(5) CULTIVATION REMAINS. The common fields of Wappenham were enclosed by an Act of Parliament of 1761 and though nothing is known of the arrangement of these fields it is unlikely that the S.E. part of the parish, on the edge of Whittlewood Forest, was part of them.

Ridge-and-furrow may be seen on the ground or can be traced on air photographs over a large part of the parish and some exceptionally fine stretches are preserved in permanent pasture N.E. of the village (SP 633457 and 638463). It is arranged in end-on and interlocked furlongs, often of reversed-S form, and several interesting features are still visible. To the N.E. of the village (SP 633457) the furlongs are notable as they have one or two broad ridges up to 10 m. wide separating groups of four to eight ridges only 3 m. wide. The ends of the ridges here rise over the headlands between the furlongs and almost interlock with each other. The same feature occurs S.W. of the village (SP 620454) though here the underlying headland, on the edge of a natural valley, is a massive asymmetrical bank almost 2 m. high. In places where the ridge-and-furrow has been completely destroyed by modern agriculture headlands still survive as broad ridges 10 m. wide, 0.25 m. high and up to 300 m. long (e.g. SP 621452 and 620470). Hollow-ways through the ridge-and-furrow can also be seen in a few places (e.g. SP 628451). In the S.E. of the parish, although there are considerable areas of furlongs of medieval type,

most of the traceable ridge-and-furrow is very narrow, 3 m.–4 m. wide, exactly straight and fitted within the rectangular modern fields (e.g. SP 634445, 640448 and 647439). This appears to be the result of late 18th or 19th-century ploughing. (RAF VAP CPE/UK/1926, 1225–8, 3226–8; CPE/UK/1994, 1091–2)

63 WARKWORTH
(OS 1:10000 [a] SP 43 NE, [b] SP 44 SE, [c] SP 53 NW, [d] SP 54 SW)

The parish formerly extended W. into Oxfordshire and N. into the present Middleton Cheney parish and thus included the hamlets of Huscote, Nethercote and Grimsbury, now in Oxfordshire, as well as Overthorpe, now in Middleton Cheney. It covers only some 530 hectares bounded on the S.W. by the R. Cherwell at 85 m. above OD and on the S.E. by a S.W.-flowing tributary. It is entirely on Lower and Middle Lias Clay, apart from small patches of Marlstone Rock in the N. and N.E. over 120 m. above OD.

ROMAN

'Numerous coins' of the 'early Emperors' are recorded from the parish (A. Beesley, *Hist. of Banbury* (1841), 32) but these may have come from the part of Warkworth now in Oxfordshire.

For possible Roman Road 161a, The Port Way, see Appendix.

MEDIEVAL AND LATER

[b](1) SETTLEMENT REMAINS (SP 488404), formerly part of Warkworth village, lie along the single street, on Middle Lias Clay between 107 m. and 122 m. above OD. The village now consists of only five houses and farms on the E. side of the street. It is impossible to discover the size of Warkworth in medieval times because of the dependent hamlets which lay within the parish and which are included with Warkworth in all the national taxation records. The only evidence of its size is given by Bridges (*Hist. of Northants.*, I (1791), 216) in the early 18th century, when there were only five houses there, the same number as today. The relationship of the village to its now isolated church on a hilltop 300 m. to the N.W. is also unclear.

The only surviving earthworks lie behind Manor Farm (SP 48884040) where there are three small ditched enclosures covering some 0.5 hectare. These formerly extended N., behind and to the N. of Warkworth Farm (SP 48854055; RAF VAP CPE/UK/1926, 3205–6; air photographs in NMR), but have now been completely destroyed. To the W. of the street all the land is now arable, with the exception of a small quarry, and no earthworks survive, nor is there any indication on the air photographs taken in 1947 before ploughing that there were ever any earthworks here. It may be that Warkworth never consisted of more than a single main street with buildings on one side of it.

[b](2) MANOR HOUSE SITE (SP 487406), lies on a S.W.-facing slope N.W. of the village and immediately S.E. of

the now isolated church, on Middle Lias Clay at 74 m. above OD. The medieval manor house of Warkworth presumably stood on this site, but it was pulled down and rebuilt about 1595. The later house survived until 1806 when it was demolished. Two surviving illustrations and a description by Baker (*Hist. of Northants.*, I (1822–30), 741) indicate that this house was a large building arranged around a central courtyard with square projecting bays on the corners. The main front had a central entrance flanked by half-round turrets the upper parts of which were glazed. The whole building was surmounted by a balustrade (*Northants. P. and P.*, 5 (1976), 318–22).

Nothing now remains of the house apart from some uneven ground, and the whole area is now arable. Until 1970 a terraced area was preserved in pasture (OS Record Cards) and this is visible on air photographs taken in 1947 (RAF VAP CPE/UK/1926, 3205–6). These indicate that the terrace was a large curved feature, facing S. and cut back into the hillside, at least 150 m. long and 40 m. wide at its widest part.

(3) CULTIVATION REMAINS. The common fields of Warkworth were enclosed by an Act of Parliament of 1764 (G. Baker, *Hist. of Northants.*, I (1822–30), 738), but nothing is known of the arrangement of these fields except that Warkworth had its own field system separate from those of Overthorpe (Middleton Cheney (4)) and Nethercote, Huscote and Grimsbury.

The ridge-and-furrow which survives on the ground or can be traced on air photographs within the present parish is probably associated with the Warkworth common fields. None survives on the higher areas of the parish covered by Marlstone Rock, but on the lower clay land large areas of end-on and interlocked furlongs are still visible. Some fine access-ways between end-on furlongs exist (e.g. SP 490404 and 484397). To the S.W. of the village (SP 482402) ridge-and-furrow running down into a shallow valley appears once to have extended further down the slope, but the furlongs have been shortened, leaving short lengths of worn-down ridges beyond the later headland. (RAF VAP CPE/UK/1926, 3205–9, 3203–8; F21 58/RAF/1567, 0050–1, 0176–7)

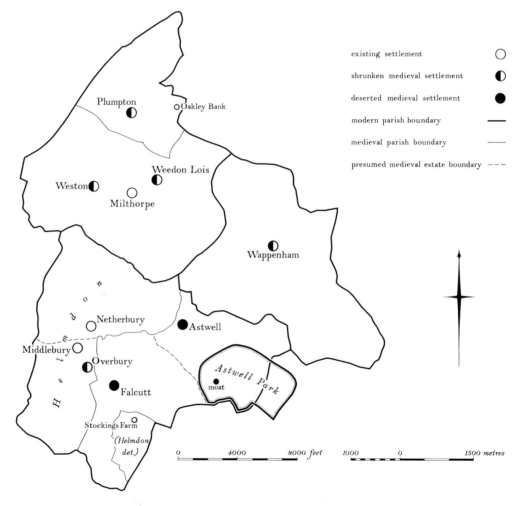

Fig. 119 HELMDON, WAPPENHAM and WESTON AND WEEDON
Medieval settlements and estates

64 WESTON AND WEEDON
(OS 1:10000 [a] SP 54 NE, [b] SP 64 NW, [c] SP 65 SW)

The modern parish is roughly triangular, covering some 1300 hectares, and contains the villages of Weedon Lois and Weston, as well as the hamlets of Milthorpe, Oakley Bank and Plumpton. The latter two settlements once lay in a separate parish of Plumpton (Fig. 119). The Banbury Lane forms the N.W. parish boundary and a small stream, one of the headwaters of the R. Tove, flows E. along the S. boundary. Another stream which joins the former flows S.E. along much of the N.E. boundary and the villages of Weston and Weedon Lois lie in the valley of a third, central stream. The ridges between the streams, and the high ground in the N.W. with a maximum height of 170 m. above OD, are covered by Boulder Clay but the down-cutting of the streams has exposed Oolite Limestone and Upper Lias Clay. There are some small patches of glacial sands and gravels.

PREHISTORIC AND ROMAN

A gold stater of Cunobelinus (Mack 206–7) was found at Weedon Lois before 1864 (BM; J. Evans, *Coins of the Ancient Britons* (1864), 298; S. S. Frere (ed.), *Problems of the Iron Age in S. Britain* (1958), 234). Many Roman coins are also recorded from Weedon Lois (T. Reynolds, *Iter. Britannia* (1799), 470). A Greek bronze coin of Sala, found at Weston in the early 19th century (G. Baker, *Hist. of Northants.*, II (1836–41), 115), is thought to be a modern loss (VCH *Northants.*, I (1902), 222).

[a](1) IRON AGE AND ROMAN SETTLEMENT (?) (SP 586478), close to the N.W. parish boundary, on Boulder Clay at 165 m. above OD. A small scatter of sherds said to be of Iron Age and Roman types has been noted, but there is some doubt concerning the identification of this pottery (*BNFAS*, 3 (1969), 2; OS Record Cards).

[a](2) ROMAN SETTLEMENT (?) (SP 578465), in the W. of the parish, on Upper Lias Clay at 137 m. above OD. A scatter of Roman pottery has been found (*Northants. Archaeol.*, 10 (1975), 163).

[b](3) ROMAN SETTLEMENT (?) (SP 602475), N. of Weedon Lois village, on Boulder Clay at 150 m. above OD. Some Roman sherds have been discovered (OS Record Cards).

[b](4) ROMAN SETTLEMENT (SP 605454), in the S.E. of the parish, on Upper Lias Clay at 122 m. above OD. Roman pottery is recorded (*Northants. Archaeol.*, 10 (1975), 163).

MEDIEVAL AND LATER

[b](5) MOTTE OR RINGWORK (SP 602470; Figs. 13 and 120), stands in the centre of Weedon Lois village, immediately E. of the church and on the W. side of The Green, on Boulder Clay at 145 m. above OD.

Nothing is known of the history of this site, but in 1086 Weedon was held by Ghilo who also held the adjoining parishes of Sulgrave and Culworth (VCH *Northants.*, I (1902), 344–5). The earthworks at Weedon may have resembled ringworks at Culworth (1) and Sulgrave (3) and the three sites may have been contemporary and constructed by the same man. Excavations at Sulgrave have indicated that the ringwork there was constructed in the late 11th century.

The remains are tree-covered and in poor condition; as a result it is almost impossible to recover their original form. They now consist of a roughly rectangular raised area, some 2 m. high, with a flat top, but with traces of a low bank along its N. side. There is no indication of a ditch and the road to the W. and the footpath to the S. both appear to have been cut back into the original mound. The gardens of the house to the S. of the site are also raised to much the same height as the castle mound, and this has led to the suggestion that there may have been a bailey here (OS Record Cards), but this idea can only be confirmed by excavation.

The relationship of the ringwork to the green and to the existing street plan is interesting. It is possible that both the ringwork and the gardens to the S. might be encroachments on an older and larger green. Alternatively the green could have evolved from the abandoned castle site in the later medieval period. In the S.W. corner of the mound are traces of stonework said to be the abutments of a feature called the Japanese Bridge and perhaps the relic of an 18th or 19th-century garden feature (OS Record Cards).

[b](6) SETTLEMENT REMAINS (SP 602469; Figs. 13 and 120), formerly part of Weedon Lois, lie on the S. side of the present through road, on Boulder Clay at 144 m. above OD. The remains are very fragmentary, but consist of low scarps and banks which bound one large and one small enclosure, with a more disturbed area which includes fragments of stone foundations at the W. end. The larger enclosure has been ploughed over with ridge-and-furrow. No date or function can be assigned to these remains. (RAF VAP CPE/UK/1994, 1092–3, 3092–3)

[b](7) FISHPONDS (SP 607467; Figs. 13 and 120), lie S. of Weedon church, in the valley of a small S.E.-flowing stream, on Upper Lias Clay between 132 m. and 137 m. above OD. Three rectangular ponds cut down into the valley bottom are edged by scarps up to 1.5 m. high and each has a dam 0.5 m.–1.5 m. high at its S.E. end. The upper dam is much degraded and the others have modern cuts through them. The stream now flows in a channel almost 2 m. deep, cut into the rising ground on the S.W. side of the valley.

Nothing is known of the history of these ponds, although they are traditionally said to have belonged to the small priory at Weedon which was established in the early 12th century as a cell of the Benedictine Abbey of St. Lucien, Oise, France. The priory was always small and poor. In 1392 it was sold to the Cistercian Abbey of Biddlesden, Buckinghamshire, but in 1440 its land passed to All Souls College, Oxford. The site of the priory is unknown, though it perhaps lay in the vicinity of the present church. (VCH *Northants.*, II (1906), 183–5; RAF VAP CPE/UK/1994, 1092–3, 3092–3)

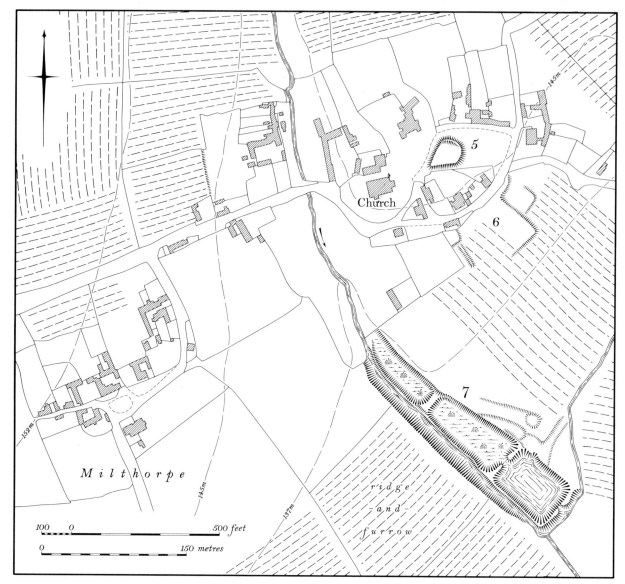

Fig. 120   WESTON AND WEEDON (5)   Motte or ringwork, (6)   Settlement remains, (7)   Ponds at Weedon Lois

[a](8) SETTLEMENT REMAINS (SP 587469; Figs. 13 and 121), formerly part of Weston, lie at the W. end of the village, on Boulder Clay at 145 m. above OD. Weston today consists of a main street running N.W.-S.E. with a side road extending S.W. from near the centre and there are indications that the main street once forked at each end. A small green still exists at the S.E. The earliest map of Weston, of 1593 (All Souls College, Oxford; copy in NRO; M. W. Beresford, *The Lost Villages of England* (1954), Plate 3), only shows part of the village but indicates that some of the houses at the N.W. end of the main street then stood on an 'island' surrounded by lanes. This suggests that there may once have been a second green at this end of the village. The village may therefore have had a layout much neater than now, and other features confirm

this idea. On the N. side of the main street the existing closes form a regular pattern which, though now disrupted by the gardens of Weston Hall to the E., are shown as continuous on the 1593 map.

On the S. side of the street, in an area not covered by the 1593 map, the pattern of closes is much less regular. To the S.E. there are small hedged paddocks. To the S.W. there is now a single large field but low banks and scarps within it indicate that a pattern similar to that in the S.E. once existed here. Ridge-and-furrow occupies some of the paddocks. The most obvious feature in this part of the village is a large rectangular pond up to 1.5 m. deep ('a' on plan). The level area bounded by scarps to the S.E. of the pond is the site of a recent tennis court (local inf.). On the N. edge of the site ('b' on plan) are the remains of at least two house-sites, indicating that the village street was once built up along this section. (RAF VAP CPE/UK/1994, 1093–5, 3093–4; air photographs in NMR; CUAP, PN73)

^a(9) MOUND (SP 58704851), lies in the N. of the parish, immediately N.W. of the old Plumpton-Weston parish boundary and within the former parish of Plumpton, on Boulder Clay at 168 m. above OD. The mound is only 0.25 m. high and 12 m. in diam., much spread, and crossed by a modern hedge. It may be the site of a windmill. (BNFAS, 3 (1969), 3)

^a(10) SETTLEMENT REMAINS (SP 597483; Figs. 119 and 122; Plate 2), formerly part of Plumpton, lie around the church and houses on a low ridge between two N.E.-flowing streams, on glacial gravel, Boulder Clay and Jurassic Clay between 137 m. and 152 m. above OD. The village was until recently the centre of an independent parish.

Plumpton is first mentioned in Domesday Book as a single manor of one hide with a recorded population of eight (VCH Northants., I (1902), 341). In the 1301 Lay Subsidy it is probably included within the entry for 'Weedon and hamlets' and it is certainly included with Weedon in the 1334 Subsidy. In 1377 60 people at Plumpton over the age of 14 paid the Poll Tax (PRO, E179/155/28) and in 1525 10 people paid the Lay Subsidy (PRO, E179/155/159). The 1673 Hearth Tax Return lists 12 people at Plumpton (PRO, E179/254/14). By 1801 only 56 people lived in the parish and though the population had risen slightly by 1831 it was down to 52 in 1871. By 1883 (1st ed. OS 25 in. plans, Northants. LV6 and 7) only the church, manor house, rectory and six cottages remained at Plumpton. Since then two of the cottages have been demolished.

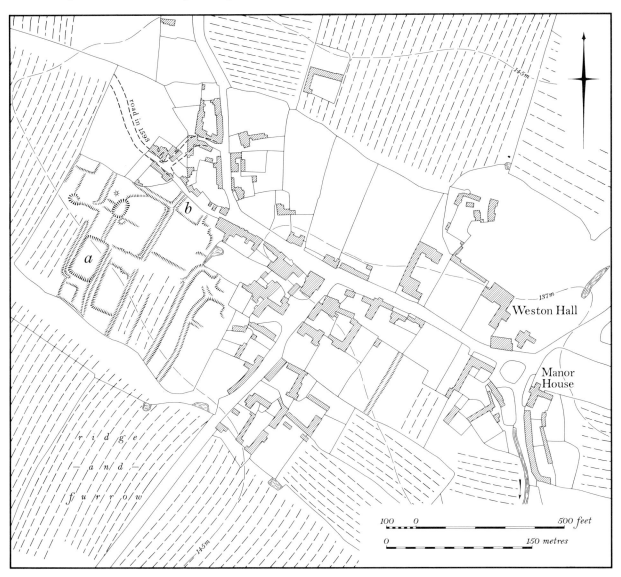

Fig. 121 WESTON AND WEEDON (8)   Settlement remains at Weston

The earthworks of the village survived undamaged until the 1960s when the whole of the S.E. part was ploughed and returned to grass. The earthworks are still visible but in poor condition. Subsequently the area W. of the church was ploughed and the fishpond to the N.W. was partly filled in. The accompanying plan (Fig. 122) is partly based on OS plans and air photographs taken before destruction in conjunction with the Commission's survey. The site is of interest for a number of reasons. The earthworks indicated that the village had extended N.E. at some time, a process that perhaps involved an element of planning. The oldest part of the village may have been the S.W. section, centred on the church and what was probably a moated manor house and associated fishponds (see below).

To the S.E. of the church and what is now the Old Rectory, on the E. side of the main through road, are areas of disturbed ground ('a' on plan) clearly representing former house-sites with long narrow closes extending down the hillside behind them. To the N.E. are further house-sites and closes ('b' on plan), but these are more regular with the ditched and embanked boundaries exactly straight. On the N.W. side of the road, the present manor house and its garden has destroyed any house-sites that existed ('c' on plan) but the fragmentary remains of evenly spaced closes suggest that the whole N.E. part of the village was a planned addition to the older S.W. part.

Immediately N. of the church is a ditch, U-shaped in plan with a broad external bank ('d' on plan). The E. side of the ditch opens out into an area of shallow quarrying. It is possible, though not certain, that this is the N.W. side of a small moat, perhaps the site of the medieval manor house, and other earthworks which lay to the S.W. and N.W. may have been part of the manorial complex. The feature to the S.W. was shown on the OS plan of 1883 as a broad trench described as Old Gravel Pits ('e' on plan). However, on air photographs taken before destruction it is clear that this trench consisted of two conjoined rectangular ponds with a broad bank or dam on the N.W. side. These were set on a spring line just below the crest of the hill. A curved length of hollow-way, also now destroyed,

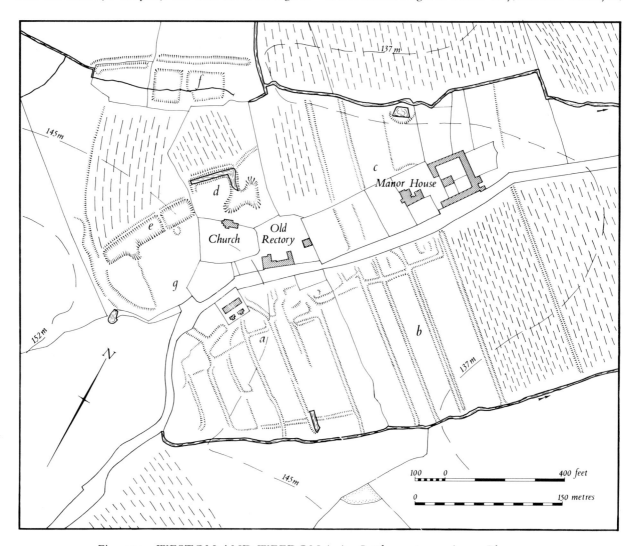

Fig. 122   WESTON AND WEEDON (10)   Settlement remains at Plumpton

lay to the S.W. of the ponds. Further N.W., in the valley bottom, the OS plan shows two roughly rectangular depressions with a ditch on the N.W., also called Old Gravel Pits ('f' on plan). Though these have been partly destroyed, enough remains on the ground to show that these too were fishponds, with an overflow channel by-passing them on the N.W. side.

No finds have been made in the area, except for a patch of limestone rubble in the modern arable land to the S. of the church ('g' on plan). This is associated with a few 13th to 14th-century sherds and considerable quantities of post-medieval pottery, glass and tile. (RAF VAP CPE/UK/ 1994, 3093–4; CUAP, NU84–5, SA42–4)

(11) CULTIVATION REMAINS. The common fields of Weston and Weedon were enclosed by an Act of Parliament of 1771. No details are known of the earlier field arrange-ments, but a map of 1593 (All Souls College, Oxford, copy in NRO) depicts the strips and furlongs which then covered most of the parish. The recoverable pattern of ridge-and-furrow fits the strips and furlongs shown on the map exactly and indicates that the strips themselves were made up of varying numbers of ridges. The map also shows that there were extensive areas of old enclosures, especially in the S.E. corner of the parish (SP 580463) and implies that the land to the N.W. of Weston village was also enclosed at that time. However normal common-field ridge-and-furrow exists in both places.

Ridge-and-furrow of these fields exists on the ground or can be traced on air photographs over most of the old parish of Weston and Weedon and except for a small area S. of Milthorpe the pattern is virtually complete. It is all arranged in end-on or interlocked furlongs; in some places there are continuous blocks of end-on furlongs running down the gentle slopes (SP 598463–603455). Large areas still survive in permanent pasture, especially N.E. of Wee-don on either side of the road to Plumpton.

A road marked on the 1593 map as 'The Way from Helmdon' is still traceable as a broad open track running N.W. from near the S.E. boundary towards Moreton Pinkney (SP 583462–579473).

The date of the enclosure of the common fields of Plumpton is not known. Ridge-and-furrow of these fields is visible on the ground or on air photographs over most of the land of Plumpton, arranged in end-on and inter-locked furlongs. It is notable that there is no traceable ridge-and-furrow within the area of Plumpton Wood (SP 604495). This suggests that this area was never ploughed in medieval times. (M. W. Beresford, *The Lost Villages of England* (1954), Plates 2 and 3; RAF VAP CPE/UK/1926, 1050–6, 1219–23; CPE/UK/1994, 2089–91)

UNDATED

[a](12) BURIALS (SP 597467), found in 1948 immediately W. of the hamlet of Milthorpe, when the area was being cleared for housing development, on gravel at 152 m. above OD. No finds were made apart from human bones, but the burials were probably Saxon or medieval. (OS Record Cards)

65 WHITFIELD
(OS 1:10000 [a] SP 63 NW, [b] SP 53 NE, [c] SP 64 SW)

The narrow parish occupies only 583 hectares, on the N.W. side of the R. Ouse which here forms the county boundary with Buckinghamshire. The higher N. part, between 140 m. and 130 m. above OD, is covered by Boulder Clay, but along the sides of the Ouse valley limestone, silts and sands are exposed.

MEDIEVAL AND LATER

[a](1) SETTLEMENT REMAINS (SP 610395), formerly part of the village of Whitfield, lie behind the existing houses on the S. side of the E.-W. main street. The remains consist of long rectangular closes bounded by low banks and ditches and are presumably abandoned gardens and pad-docks. At each end of the village there are indications that the street once ran on beyond its present extent. At the E, end (SP 614395), a long curving terrace 1.5 m. high extends E. from the bend in the street and presumably once gave access to the E. part of the parish. At the W. end rutted tracks continue the line of the street and meet a raised headland curving N.W. which joins the present road to Radstone at its junction with the A43 (SP 602395). (RAF VAP CPE/UK/1926, 2222–4; air photographs in NMR)

(2) CULTIVATION REMAINS. The common fields of the parish were enclosed by an Act of Parliament of 1796 (NRO, Enclosure Map, 1797). No details of the open fields are known. Ridge-and-furrow of these fields exists on the ground or can be traced from air photographs over wide areas of the parish, arranged mainly in interlocked and end-on furlongs, many of reversed-S form. In some places (e.g. SP 602394) it is notable for the great variation in the widths of ridges within a single furlong. A number of well-marked headlands survive (e.g. SP 614396 and 608403). (RAF VAP CPE/UK/1926, 2219–26, 4219–22; CPE/UK/ 2097, 3157–8)

66 WHITTLEBURY
(OS 1:10000 [a] SP 74 NW, [b] SP 74 SW, [c] SP 64 NE, [d] SP 64 SE)

The parish, once a chapelry of Greens Norton, cov-ers some 1000 hectares and is heavily wooded. It is almost entirely on Boulder Clay with small patches of glacial sands and gravels, and bands of Oolitic limestones in the valleys of the streams. The village lies at the highest point, in the W. of the parish, some 155 m. above OD, and from this point small streams radiate.

There are several Iron Age and Roman sites in the parish (1–4) including an important villa (4). A num-ber of these sites lie within former woodland which, in medieval times at least, was part of Whittlewood Forest (Fig. 16).

PREHISTORIC AND ROMAN

A hoard of coins, mainly Constantinian, was found before 1712 in the N. of the parish (around SP 699453; J. Morton, *Nat. Hist. of Northants.* (1712), 531; VCH *Northants.*, I (1902), 219). In 1957 a single Roman pot base was discovered N.W. of the village (SP 68474472; OS Record Cards). A number of objects were found near the church in the 1820s. These included a small palstave, two Roman tiles (NM) stamped LEG XXVV (Legio XX Valeria Victrix), part of a quern and several Greek and Roman coins. These are thought to have been part of a modern collection and not to indicate a settlement. (*Ant. J.*, 18 (1938), 45; G. Baker, *Hist. of Northants.*, II (1836–41), 73; VCH *Northants.*, I (1902), 215; NM Records; OS Record Cards)

^c(1) ENCLOSURE (SP 689431), S. of the village, within the formerly wooded area of the deer park, on Boulder Clay at about 150 m. above OD. Air photographs taken in 1947 (RAF VAP CPE/UK/1926, 2234–5) show an irregular four-sided ditched enclosure, roughly 80 m. by 50 m., with rounded corners and a small secondary enclosure attached at its S.W. corner. The feature still survived as an earthwork at that date, the ditch varying between 1 m. and 2 m. in depth, but it has since been ploughed and levelled. No dating evidence was noted but it is likely that this was an Iron Age enclosure which survived within the forested area until this century (OS Record Cards).

^c(2) ENCLOSURE (SP 687428), 300 m. S.W. of (1), in a similar situation. Air photographs taken in 1947 (RAF VAP CPE/UK/1926, 2234–5) show the earthworks of a small roughly oval enclosure, some 65 m. by 45 m. Though now totally destroyed it was probably an Iron Age settlement. OS Record Cards state that its surrounding bank was 2 m. across and 0.6 m. high with an outer ditch 1.4 m. deep.

^b(3) IRON AGE SETTLEMENT (centred SP 721432), in the E. of the parish, within Whittlewood Forest, on Boulder Clay between 120 m. and 132 m. above OD. Several discrete scatters of Iron Age material have been found over an area of at least 20 hectares, since forest clearance and deep

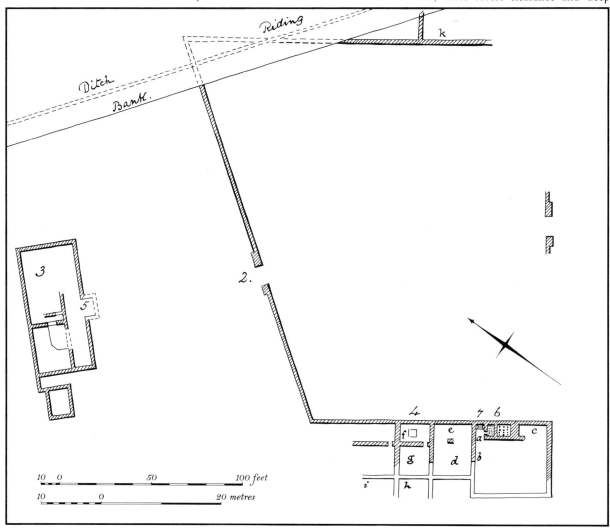

Fig. 123   WHITTLEBURY (4)   Roman villa (based on a plan in *Arch. J.*)

ploughing in 1956. Finds include areas of dark soil, burnt pebbles, cobbled floors, iron slag and worked flints associated with both early and mid Iron Age pottery (*Wolverton and District Arch. Soc. Newsletter*, 6 (1961), 2; *BNFAS*, 1 (1966), 5; *Northants. Archaeol.*, 10 (1975), 152, 175).

[b](4) ROMAN VILLA (SP 73224457; Fig. 123), lies in the centre of the small E. projection of the parish, on Boulder Clay at 117 m. above OD. The site was discovered in a stone-pit and was excavated in 1850. Only a short report was written and many details on the published plan were not mentioned.

Two buildings were discovered. One, at the S. end of the site, contained at least 12 rooms including a bath suite, and there was a mosaic pavement, apparently comprising a grid of squares outlined in red with a square of white at each intersection. This building lay to the W. of a large courtyard. The second building lay to the N. and contained two mosaics: one, in the main part of the building, had a square central panel with a bust of a winged female wearing a wreath and probably holding a spray of leaves; the other had a pattern of red crosses. Finds included painted wall-plaster, a column base, tiles, pottery including samian, and coins from Tetricus to Maximianus. More buildings debris and pottery has been found scattered over a wide area since 1950. A 'small stone pedestal', possibly an altar, is also recorded. (*Arch. J.*, 7 (1850), 172; *JBAA*, 6 (1851), 73; 7 (1852), 107, Pl. XI; *VCH Northants.*, I (1902), 199–200; A. Rainey, *Mosaics in Roman Britain* (1973), 156, Pl. 14A; *BAR*, 41 (i) (1977), 152, No. 148; A. L. F. Rivet (ed.), *The Roman Villa in Britain* (1969), 143; OS Record Cards)

For Roman Roads 1e, Watling Street, and 160a, see Appendix.

MEDIEVAL AND LATER

[d](5) SETTLEMENT REMAINS (SP 690440), formerly part of Whittlebury, lie on the W. side of the main street of the village, on glacial sands and gravels at 152 m. above OD. Most of the street has houses on both sides, but a large open space has the remains of a row of former buildings set within fragmentary closes. (RAF VAP CPE/UK/1926, 5234–5; *Northants. Archaeol.*, 10 (1975), 174)

[cd](6) MOAT (SP 688450; Fig. 124), lies in an isolated position N. of the village at Lords Field Farm, on Boulder Clay at 145 m. above OD, with extensive views to the N.W. The site now consists of a sub-rectangular island, surrounded by a broad wet moat 1 m. deep with a causeway across it on the N.E. The island is uneven but no distinguishable features remain; the present farm lies to the N.E. The earliest detailed depiction of the site is on a map of about 1726 (NRO). This shows the island as rectangular, with a large building on it, and a bridge across the ditch on the E., near the S.E. corner, leading to other buildings which appear to be barns. On a later map of about 1767 (NRO) the same details are shown and a fenced paddock is depicted to the W. of the site. The moat is traditionally the site of the manor house of Whittlebury (G. Baker, *Hist. of Northants.*, II (1836–41), 70).

[c](7) DESERTED FARMSTEAD (SP 699451), lay N.E. of the village, on the N. side of a track leading to Pury End,

Paulerspury, on Boulder Clay at 130 m. above OD. The site has been completely destroyed by modern cultivation and returned to pasture, but air photographs taken in 1947 (RAF VAP CPE/UK/1926, 3235–6, 5235–6) show a roughly rectangular enclosure, orientated N.W.-S.E., 150 m. by 90 m. bounded by a low bank and outer ditch. The interior was divided into at least two paddocks and in the N. corner there was an area of disturbed ground perhaps indicating the positions of former buildings. Ridge-and-furrow lay along the W. edge. The earthworks were probably the site of a medieval forest-edge farmstead.

[d](8) FISHPONDS (SP 689444), lie on the N. side of the village immediately N. of the church, in the bottom of a shallow valley draining N., on Boulder Clay at 147 m. above OD. Three small embanked ponds, each about 20 m. wide, are arranged in a line along the old stream bed. They are probably medieval in origin.

(9) CULTIVATION REMAINS. The common fields of the parish were finally enclosed by an Act of Parliament of 1797. In 1600 most of the parish N. of the village was under open-field cultivation but by 1726 only the area immediately E., N. and W. of the village remained unenclosed (maps in NRO). The whole of the S. and S.E. of the parish was woodland in 1600 but large areas were cleared and cultivated during the following centuries.

Ridge-and-furrow remains on the ground or can be traced on air photographs in a few places around the village itself where it is arranged in end-on and interlocked fur-

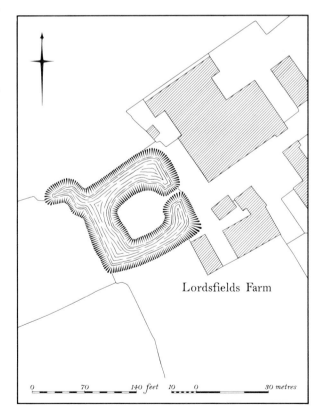

Lordsfields Farm

0   70   140 feet   10   0   30 metres

Fig. 124   WHITTLEBURY (6)   Moat

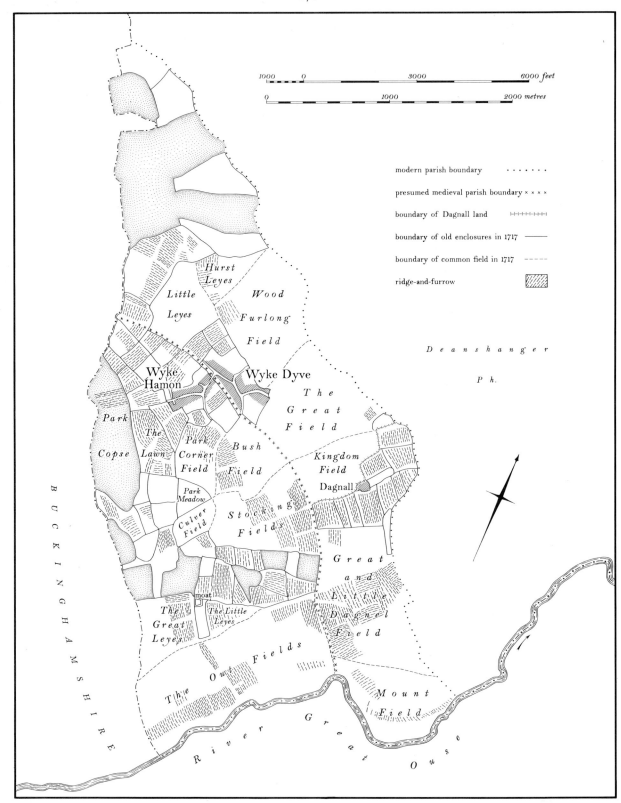

Fig. 125 WICKEN Medieval settlements, parishes, estates and fields (based on a plan of
1717, NRO)

longs of normal medieval form. There are also fragmentary pieces in the N. of the parish in the area enclosed between 1600 and 1726. (RAF VAP CPE/UK/1926, 2234–40, 3233–6, 5232–42)

UNDATED

   ᵇ(10) DITCHED TRACKWAY (?) (SP 712428) in the S. of the parish, immediately W. of Buckingham Thick Copse and close to the county boundary, on Boulder Clay at 122 m. above OD. Air photographs (NCAU) show a possible ditched trackway running S.E. from the edge of the copse and visible for some 200 m. At its N.W. end the alignment is continued by a modern ride through the copse. It is therefore unlikely to be an ancient feature.

67   WICKEN
(OS 1:10000 ᵃ SP 74 SW, ᵇ SP 73 NW, ᶜ SP 73 NE)

The triangular parish, of some 930 hectares, lies N.W. of the Great Ouse which forms the S.E. boundary. Large areas of alluvium and river gravels occupy the Great Ouse flood plain at about 68 m. above OD. The higher land to the S. of the village and in Whittlewood Forest in the W., is covered by Boulder Clay, but in the valley of a small stream which runs across the centre of the parish broad patches of Oolite Limestone are exposed.

   In the medieval period there were two villages (3), each the centre of a separate parish, but these were united in about 1586. In addition there was apparently a third settlement, now Dagnall Farm (4), and an isolated moated site (5) (Fig. 125).

PREHISTORIC AND ROMAN

   ᶜ(1) RING DITCH (?) (SP 77053775), on the flood plain of the Great Ouse at 70 m. above OD. Air photographs (not seen by RCHM) are said to show a ring ditch and linear features (BNFAS, 5 (1971), 41).

   ᶜ(2) ROMAN BUILDING (SP 761377), in the S.E. of the parish, close to the Great Ouse, on river gravel at 77 m. above OD. Building stone, roof and flue tiles, with pottery including samian and 3rd and 4th-century coarse wares all discovered in 1965, indicate the existence of a Roman building (BNFAS, 1 (1966), 14).

MEDIEVAL AND LATER

   ᵇ(3) SETTLEMENT REMAINS (centred SP 744393; Figs. 14 and 125), formerly part of Wicken, lie in and around the existing village, on limestone and Boulder Clay, between 85 m. and 90 m. above OD. The surviving earthworks, though minor, emphasize the dual character of the village. The names Wykes and Wickens Ambo (PN Northants. 107–8) reflect the existence of two separate manors, also known as Wyke Dyve and Wyke Hamon, throughout the medieval period from Domesday Book onwards (VCH Northants., I (1902), 334–349). This tenurial division corresponds with the two parts of the village on either side

of the E.-flowing stream. The N. part of the village, Wyke Dyve, is laid out along a main E.-W. street, and the S. part, Wyke Hamon, lies along a S.W.-N.E. lane. The main earthworks lie in the N. part of the village, along the N. side of Cross Tree Road, between the latter and the manor house (SP 744394). They consist of small rectangular paddocks, bounded by large banks up to 0.5 m. high and apparently made of stone rubble. They probably represent the gardens of houses which once lay along the road. To the N. and N.E. are other, more indeterminate scarps and banks as well as a roughly circular mound 0.75 m. high. The area was already devoid of buildings in 1717, and was then called The Warren (map in NRO). Earthworks to the S. of the stream, in the manor of Wyke Hamon, in a pasture field on the E. side of Leckhampstead Road, are also probably the remains of former houses and gardens. A single building still stood at the N. end of the site in 1717 and in 1841 (SP 743393; map in NRO). Other earthworks lie to the W. and S.W. on each side of Home Farm (SP 742393 and 742392); no buildings were shown in either place in 1717. The site of the parish church of Wyke Hamon, which is said to have stood at the S. end of the village and which was pulled down in 1619, has not been located. (RAF VAP CPE/UK/2097, 3179–80; air photographs in NMR)

   ᶜ(4) SETTLEMENT REMAINS (SP 759391; Fig. 125), formerly part of Dagnall, lie immediately N.E. of Dagnall Farm in the E. of the parish, on glacial sands and gravels at 80 m. above OD. The name Dagnall is not recorded until 1319 (PN Northants., 108) but the settlement is presumably much older than that. It lay in the former parish of Wyke Dyve. As it is not listed separately in any of the national taxation records there is no indication of its size until 1717 (map in NRO) when only the present farm is depicted. It is possible that the settlement never consisted of anything more than a single farmstead and that the surviving earthworks are only abandoned paddocks.

   The earthworks cover a roughly rectangular area 80 m. by 220 m., bounded on the N.E. and S.E. by modern hedges, by the farm on the S.W., and on the N.W. by a low bank and ditch which separate them from the adjacent ridge-and-furrow. Two low banks and ditches running N.W.-S.E. divide the area into three small closes. The southwesternmost of these has disturbed earthworks within it, perhaps the remains of old farm buildings (air photographs in NMR).

   ᵇ(5) MOAT (SP 749376; Figs. 125 and 126), lies in the S. of the parish, immediately S.E. of Rabbit Wood, on Boulder Clay at 85 m. above OD. The earthworks are on the S. side of a small N.E.-flowing stream and consist of a rectangular area bounded on the W., S. and E. by a ditch 8 m.–15 m. wide and up to 1.75 m. deep, cut back into rising ground on the S. The N. side is bounded by the stream and there is no trace of an original ditch. The interior is divided into two unequal parts by a subsidiary ditch which runs from the middle of the E. side and then curves towards the N. before fading out. There is a large inner bank along the N. side and the rest of the interior is uneven.

   Nothing is known of the history of this site until the early 18th century when it is shown on a map of 1717

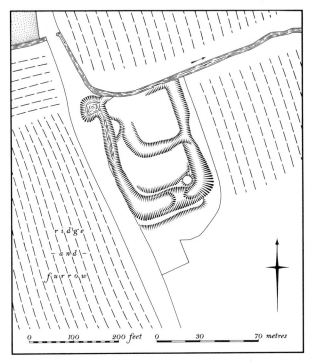

Fig. 126   WICKEN (5)   Moat

(NRO), lying at the N. end of a long, narrow field called The Grove Close and with a house standing within it. By 1841 (NRO, Tithe Map) the house had disappeared and only the W. side of the moat is depicted, as a pond. (RAF VAP 2F41, 543/RAF/1426, 0362–3; air photographs in NMR)

[b](6) DEER PARK (centred SP 738385; Fig. 125), lay in the W. of the parish, S.W. of the village, on Boulder Clay, at around 100 m. above OD. In the late 13th century John Fitzalan was granted licence to re-enclose his park which had fallen into decay. It was disparked about 1651 (*Northants. P. and P.*, 5 (1975), 233). Its exact boundaries are not known but the park presumably lay in the area of the present Wicken Park although it may have extended further S. and E. for on the map of 1717 (NRO) the names Park Meadow, Park Corner Field and The Lawn are given to this area. No definite boundary has been noted though the existing woodlands are all surrounded by large banks. This is particularly true of Park Copse.

(7) CULTIVATION REMAINS (Fig. 125). The date of the enclosure of the common fields of Wicken is unknown but was between 1717 and 1841 (maps in NRO). Before enclosure there were at least ten named common fields, which probably related to the two separate villages and parishes of Wyke Dyve and Wyke Hamon and to the third medieval settlement at Dagnall Farm (4). It may be assumed that the boundary between the parishes followed the existing stream which flows from near the county boundary W. of the village (SP 735395) to a little S. of Wicken (SP 752390) and then continued as a curving line of modern hedges as far as the Buckingham Road (SP 758381) and thence to the Great Ouse (SP 762376). If this is so, Wyke Hamon occupied the S.W. part of the modern

parish and Wyke Dyve the N.E. The land of Dagnall seems to have occupied the S.E. part of Wyke Dyve parish.

The common fields of Wyke Hamon consisted of four areas, of unequal size, immediately S. and S.E. of the village. In 1717 these were known as Bush, Park Corner, Culver and Stocking Fields. To the W., between these fields and the county boundary, lay a large area of old enclosures and woodland, part of which may have been the medieval deer park (6). To the S. of the common fields was a smaller area of copses and old enclosures and beyond them, extending to the Buckingham Road, was a large area known as Great and Little Leys. To the S.E. of the road, between it and the Great Ouse, lay an extensive tract of common arable land known as The Out Fields. Ridge-and-furrow of these fields exists on the ground or can be traced on air photographs over large parts of the medieval parish. None is visible in Culver Field but fragments of rectangular, curved and reversed-S furlongs exist in Park Corner Field (SP 744390), Bush Field (SP 748390) and Stocking Field (SP 755385). In the old enclosures to the S.E., N. and E. of Park Copse there is a continuous expanse of ridge-and-furrow arranged in rectangular interlocked furlongs many with reversed-S curves and with well-marked headlands between them. The character of this ridge-and-furrow suggests that it was formerly part of the common fields. Some of it certainly lay within woodland in 1717 (e.g. SP 736389). Ridge-and-furrow also survives within the former old enclosures S.E. of the known common fields (centred SP 753381) as well as in the Great and Little Leys (SP 749375) and in The Out Field. In the latter the ridges run downhill to the river.

Wyke Dyve appears to have had three open fields, Wood Furlong Field to the N. of the village, The Great Field to the E. of the village, and Kingdom Field further S.E. The whole of the N.W. of the parish was covered either by woodland or by open land known as Old Leys, Hurst Leys and Old Sale. Ridge-and-furrow of these fields survives or can be traced from air photographs. Only a few slight fragments are visible within the three open fields (e.g. SP 756395) but more is traceable within Old Sale and Hurst Leys to the N.W. of the village (SP 738400).

The settlement at Dagnall Farm was situated on the S.E. side of Kingdom Field. In 1717 there were old enclosures immediately to the N.E., E. and S. of it and further S. lay a large open field known as Great and Little Dagnel Field and a smaller one called Mount Field. To judge from their relative areas and their names it appears that these were formerly three open fields. Ridge-and-furrow of these fields survives on the ground or can be traced on air photographs in a number of places. In Great and Little Dagnel Field there is an expanse of end-on and interlocked rectangular furlongs (centred SP 762383) but only fragments survive in the former Mount Field alongside the Great Ouse (SP 763377–772377). Almost all the old enclosures have well-marked ridge-and-furrow lying within them. (RAF VAP CPE/UK/1926, 4233–43; CPE/UK/1929, 1184–93, 3190–4; CPE/UK/2097, 3179–83; F21, 58/RAF/5517, 0024–6; 2F41, 543/RAF/1426, 0362–6)

68 WOODEND
(OS 1:10000 [a] SP 64 NW, [b] SP 65 SW)

The modern parish, formerly part of Blakesley, contains the site and lands of the deserted village of Kirby (1) as well as the existing settlements of Woodend and Woodend Green, and covers some 700 hectares (Fig. 28). It is bounded on both the N. and S. by E.-flowing tributaries of the R. Tove at about 115 m. above OD. From these valleys the land rises across outcrops of Upper Lias Clay, Northampton Sand and Oolite Limestone to a central ridge capped by Boulder Clay, with a maximum height of 155 m. above OD.

No prehistoric or Roman remains have been found in the parish and the main monument is the deserted village of Kirby (1).

MEDIEVAL AND LATER

[a](1) DESERTED VILLAGE OF KIRBY (SP 636495; Figs. 28 and 127), lies in the E. part of the parish, on limestone and clay between 107 m. and 122 m. above OD. The boundaries of the land associated with the village can be conjectured (Fig. 28). Kirby is not mentioned by name in Domesday Book but it has been suggested that it is the small manor listed under Blakesley with a recorded population of only two (VCH *Northants.*, I (1902), 332). This manor was granted in about 1194 to the Knights Hospitallers. The village is mentioned in the *Nomina Villarum* of 1316 and in 1361 the Hospitallers' manor was described as '1 messuage and 1 carucate in Kirby'. In 1487 the Hospitallers' tenant destroyed five houses and enclosed and converted 300 acres of land to pasture, though this may not have all been at Kirby. In 1547 a thousand sheep were being grazed on the land (K. J. Allison *et al., The Deserted Villages of Northants.* (1966), 41). Bridges (*Hist. of Northants.*, I (1791), 236) recorded only one house at Kirby in the early 18th century. Its successor, Hootens Farm, is the only house in the area today.

The earthworks of the village are in good condition, though most of the site has been ploughed in ridge-and-furrow after abandonment. The remains of this ploughing, in two main blocks, are very slight and cannot represent more than one or two years cultivation.

The main feature of the site is a broad hollow-way, presumably once the main street, which crosses the area from S.W. to N.E. ('a'-'b' on plan). It is visible S. of the modern farm buildings as an uneven hollow-way ('a') with a massive scarp up to 2.5 m. high on its E. side. The next part of it has been destroyed by the farm buildings but it reappears to the N., in poor condition, in the garden of Hootens Farm. Beyond the farm the hollow-way runs down the hillside and here it is 1 m.–1.5 m. deep. At its N.E. end it divides. One branch continues N. towards the meadowland, and the other branch, now partly blocked, ran N.E. to the stream. A second hollow-way probably ran along the S. side of the site ('c' on plan) separating the village from the adjacent ridge-and-furrow, but its junction with the main one is obscured by the farm buildings. The main hollow-way is lined on both sides by subrectangular

closes bounded by low scarps, though the later ploughing seems to have destroyed parts of these. House-sites are visible within some of the closes. Immediately E. of the farm there is a long rectangular feature, bounded by low stone-rubble walls ('d' on plan) and a similar house-site lies further N. ('e' on plan). A smaller structure can be identified just W. of the point where the main hollow-way divides ('b' on plan). Shallow depressions or raised platforms elsewhere may be the sites of other buildings. A triangular depression in the N.W. of the site ('f'), with a broad ditch leading into its S.W. corner, is a fishpond. (RAF VAP CPE/UK/1926, 1045–7; CUAP, XT40–1; air photographs in NMR)

[a](2) SETTLEMENT REMAINS (SP 616493), formerly part of Woodend, lie in and around the existing village, on limestone and Northampton Sand between 137 m. and 145 m. above OD. The settlement was once known as Little Blakesley, Blakesley Parva or Wood Blakesley. The modern village consists of a single curved street running N.-S. with houses on both sides. Until recently there was a large gap on the E. side where houses had once stood. Part of this area has now been built over and no earthworks remain but the site may nevertheless be of archaeological significance. Beyond the existing gardens in the N.W. of the village at least one rectangular enclosure survives, bounded by low banks and shallow ditches. It has shallow quarry-pits within it. Other banks and ditches, perhaps indicating former buildings, lie at the N. end of the village street. (RAF VAP CPE/UK/1994, 2086–7; F21 58/RAF/2316, 0069–70; air photographs in NMR)

[a](3) MOAT (?) (SP 620498), lies S. of the site of Blakesley Hall, just within Woodend parish, in the bottom of a valley draining E., on Jurassic Clay at 114 m. above OD. The Hall, demolished in 1957–8, was traditionally said to be on the site of the manor house of the Knights Hospitallers, who acquired land in Blakesley in about 1194. The feature called a 'moat' on OS plans is now a watercourse of U-shaped plan some 10 m. wide with garden features such as bridges, waterfalls and stone revetment. It is unlikely that it was ever a medieval moat; the remains are largely the result of 18th or 19th-century landscaping. (RAF VAP CPE/UK/1994, 2086–7; air photographs in NMR)

(4) CULTIVATION REMAINS. The common fields of Woodend were enclosed by an Act of Parliament of 1788. Ridge-and-furrow of these fields exists on the ground or can be traced on air photographs over much of that part of the parish attributable to Woodend village. Although the settlement was on the edge of woodland there is every indication that the whole area has been under cultivation at some time and the pattern of ridge-and-furrow is virtually complete. It is arranged in end-on and interlocked furlongs carefully adapted to the broken terrain so that in most cases the ridges run across the contours. Ridge-and-furrow extends to within a few yards of the stream on the S. boundary of the parish, and only in the N., S. of Blakesley Hall (SP 619498), are there any large areas of meadowland without ridge-and-furrow.

The date of enclosure of the common fields of the deserted village of Kirby (1) is unknown, except that there are records of 300 acres of land, some of which lay in

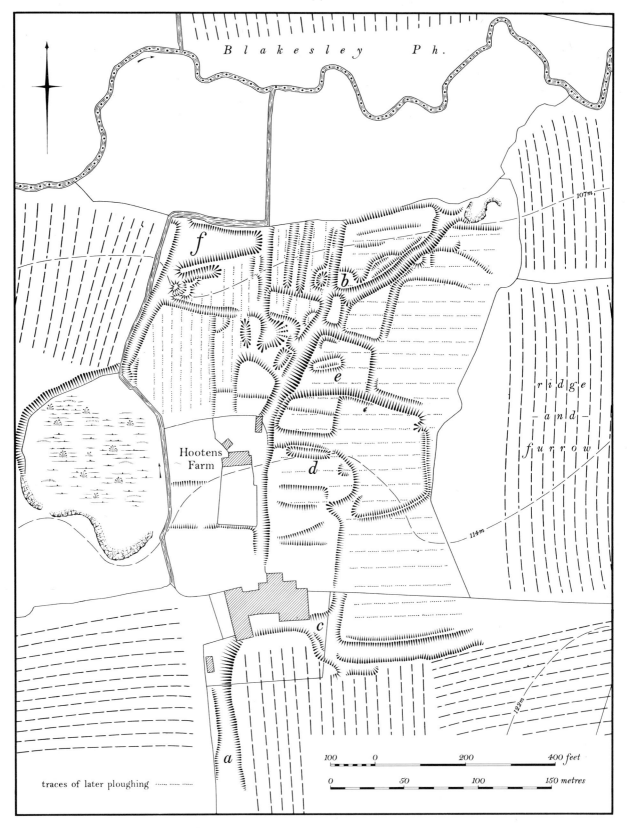

Blakesley Ph.

f

b

e

ridge

and

furrow

Hootens
Farm

d

107m

114m

122m

c

a

traces of later ploughing ......

100   0   200   400 *feet*

0   50   100   150 *metres*

Fig. 127   WOODEND (1)   Deserted village of Kirby

Kirby, being converted to pasture in 1487, (K. J. Allison *et al.*, *The Deserted Villages of Northants.* (1966), 41). Ridge-and-furrow exists on the ground or can be traced on air photographs over much of the land of Kirby, arranged in end-on and interlocked furlongs. It is particularly well preserved S. of the site of the village (SP 635492) where within a single field several interesting features are preserved in pasture. These include the overploughing of a former headland between two end-on furlongs to produce a larger furlong, the ploughing of part of a low rounded knoll which appears to be a landslip, the overploughing of part of an older N.-S. furlong by one running E.-W., and the extension of a furlong over its original headland. In addition there is evidence of temporary ploughing over the site of the deserted village itself, though the date of this is not known. (RAF VAP CPE/UK/1926, 1044–5; CPE/UK/1994, 2084–8, 3089–92, F21, 58/RAF/2316, 0069–70; air photographs in NMR)

69   YARDLEY GOBION

(OS 1:10000 [a] SP 74 NW, [b] SP 74 NE, [c] SP 74 SW, [d] SP 74 SE)

The long, narrow parish, once part of Potterspury, stretches from the R. Tove on the E. boundary to a little beyond Watling Street (A5) which forms most of the W. boundary. An E.-flowing stream flows along most of the N. side. The lower ground close to the R. Tove, below 76 m. above OD, is on Upper Lias Clay and riverine deposits. Bands of limestones are exposed on the steep slopes N.E. of the main village, and in the valley of the stream where the medieval settlement of Moor End (3) and (4) is situated. The higher ground between 95 m. and 108 m. above OD is covered by Boulder Clay.

PREHISTORIC AND ROMAN

A stone tool of unknown form is said to have been found at SP 73884435 (NM Records). A coin of Gratian and a base silver antoninianus of Valerian I have recently been recorded, the former in the village (SP 76424485) and the latter in the W. of the parish (SP 74464482; *Northants. Archaeol.*, 10 (1975), 164; 12 (1977), 222).

For Roman Road 1e, Watling Street, see Appendix.

MEDIEVAL AND LATER

The leg of a medieval greyware vessel was found in the W. of the village in 1972 (SP 76004493; *Northants. Archaeol.*, 8 (1973), 23; NM).

[d](1) SETTLEMENT REMAINS (SP 766448), formerly part of Yardley Gobion, lie behind the existing houses on the N. side of High Street, on limestone at 90 m. above OD. A group of indeterminate earthworks, some of which have now been destroyed, and a rectangular ditched enclosure probably represent abandoned buildings and closes. (RAF VAP CPE/UK/1926, 5244–5; air photographs in NMR)

[d](2) MOAT (?) (SP 761448), lay immediately S. of Moor End Road, on Boulder Clay at 102 m. above OD. The site has been entirely destroyed by modern housing, but air photographs taken in 1947 (RAF VAP CPE/UK/1926, 5244) show that it was still in existence at that time. It consisted of a rectangular area 60 m. by 40 m., orientated N.E.-S.W. and bounded on the N.W., S.W. and part of the N.E. and S.E. sides by a broad ditch which was at least 10 m. wide. The E. corner had already been obliterated. The moat was completely surrounded by ridge-and-furrow. It is said to have been the site of the manor house of Yardley Gobion (G. Baker, *Hist. of Northants.*, II (1836–41), 227).

[d](3) MOAT (SP 754446; Fig. 128), usually known as Moor End Castle, lies W. of Yardley village, within the hamlet of Moor End, in the bottom of a valley draining S., on clay at 92 m. above OD. The origins of the site are obscure but in 1327 Thomas de Ferrers was granted a licence to crenellate his dwelling place of *Le Morende*. In 1363 the manor passed to the Crown and between then and 1369 much building work is recorded. Among the structures mentioned are a royal chamber, a chapel, towers, an old chamber and inner and outer gates. It remained in royal hands during the 15th century but its subsequent history is uncertain (H. M. Colvin, *The History of the King's Works*, II (1963), 743). In the early 19th century, stone-robbing revealed foundations of a rectangular building with towers at each corner. Tiles described as 'Roman' were also uncovered (G. Baker, *Hist. of Northants.*, II (1836–41), 229; *JBAA*, 7 (1852), 111).

The site has been much altered, particularly in recent years, and now consists of a sub-rectangular island, completely overgrown, with no visible surface features. The island is surrounded by a water-filled ditch between 17 m. and 25 m. wide on the S.W., N.W. and N.E. and by a large pond 50 m. by 90 m. on the S.E. The latter may be a relatively recent widening of the ditch on this side. A small rectangular pond 40 m. by 25 m., much altered in recent times, lies to the N.W. of the site, and on air photographs taken in 1947 (RAF VAP CPE/UK/1926, 5243–4) two other smaller rectangular ponds are shown between it and the moat. These have now been destroyed.

A dry ditch 8 m. wide and up to 1 m. deep to the N.E. of the moat appears to be a former leat which carried water round the site, possibly to a mill at its S.E. end. The field on the S.W. side of the moat, in which stands the present Castle Barn, was known as Castle Yard in 1728 (map in NRO). In its S.E. corner are at least two building platforms lying at the S. ends of two rectangular closes ('a' on plan). It is not certain whether these are part of the castle or of the settlement remains (4).

[d](4) SETTLEMENT REMAINS (SP 762448; Fig. 128), formerly part of Moor End, lie between the existing houses of the hamlet, on Boulder Clay between 90 m. and 98 m. above OD. Nothing is known of the history and size of Moor End except its manorial descent and the fact that it first occurs in documents in 1168 (PN *Northants.*, 108).

The hamlet seems always to have consisted of houses arranged along a single N.E.-S.W., street with the moated site (3) on the N.W. side. The remains of former settlement exist in four places. Immediately S.E. of Castle Barn are two building platforms at the S. ends of two fragmentary closes ('a' on plan). These lie in the area known as Castle Yard in 1728 (map in NRO) and may be associated with the moat. To the S.W., on the opposite side of the road, is a strip of disturbed ground which may possibly be the site of other buildings ('b' on plan). Further N.E. and E. of the moat is a group of rectangular platforms, cut into the hillside, probably the sites of at least five houses and gardens ('c' on plan). In 1728 there were still two buildings standing here but they had disappeared by 1776 (maps in NRO). The main interest of the remains is that they appear to overlie ridge-and-furrow, fragments of which still survive on the N.W. The adjacent furlong of ridge-and-furrow ends on a well-marked headland, but at least five ridges can be traced continuing into the settlement remains. To the S. is a single raised platform, also possibly a house-site ('d' on plan). (RAF VAP CPE/UK/1926, 5243–4)

^d(5) MEDIEVAL POTTERY KILNS (SP 76254492), found in the Moor End Road during building in 1978. Two kilns and a large quantity of late 14th or early 15th-century roof tiles were noted (*Northants. Archaeol.*, 14 (1979) 111).

^d(6) MEDIEVAL POTTERY KILNS (SP 76504489), on the N. side of the village. Excavation in 1973 revealed two kilns, both of updraught type, oval in shape and constructed of limestone, with 14th-century wares of Potterspury type (*Northants. Archaeol.*, 9 (1974), 112).

^d(7) POST-MEDIEVAL POTTERY KILNS (?) (SP 766446), found a little to the S.W. of the village, during housing development in 1968. Layers of wasters of 18th-century date were discovered (*BNFAS*, 3 (1969), 30).

^c(8) DEER PARK (centred SP 745445; Fig. 60), occupies the W. part of the parish between Moor End and Watling Street, mainly on Boulder Clay between 95 m. and 110 m. above OD. The park is first mentioned in 1230 when William de Ferrers was granted a deer leap in his park of Perry and it occurs frequently in medieval documents after that. In 1537 the park was enlarged by 154 acres (64 hectares) and it appears to have gone out of use in the 17th century (*Northants. P. and P.*, 5 (1975), 230). The final boundaries of the park are depicted on maps of 1720, 1728 and 1776 (NRO) as contiguous with Plum Park (Paulerspury (21)) and Grafton Park (Grafton Regis (8)) to the N. The exact position of the earlier medieval park is not known with certainty though it is possible that it occupied the S. part of the larger park, to the S. of an E.-flowing stream.

The S.W. boundary of the later park was Watling Street (SP 735450–748438), but only a normal hedge-bank is visible today. The boundary then turned N.E. and ran along the N.W. side of the road to Yardley Gobion village, following its sharp bends to a point just S.W. of Moor End (SP 753444). Along this section there are traces of a

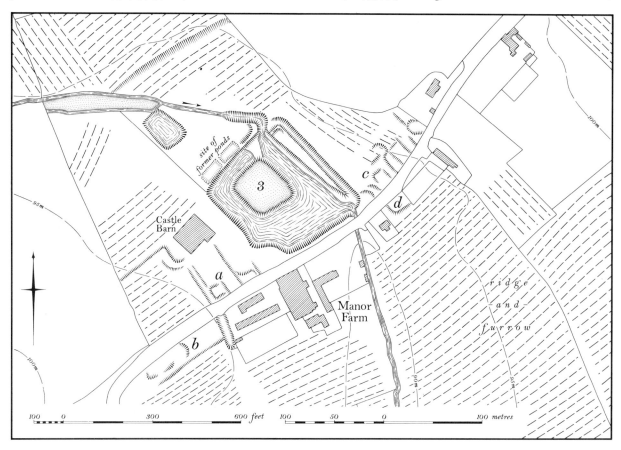

Fig. 128 YARDLEY GOBION (3) Moat, (4) Settlement remains at Moor End

large bank 1 m.–1.5 m. high and 5 m.–6 m. wide. The boundary then ran N.W. as far as a small E.-flowing stream (SP 748452) and the hedge is here in places on a bank again up to 1.5 m. high and 6 m. wide. The N. edge of the medieval park may have turned W. here and followed the stream as far as Watling Street but the boundary of the later park certainly crossed the stream and ran on N.W. until it met the S. side of Grafton Park (at SP 746454) which it followed W. to Watling Street. This assumed N. extension to the park is very close in area to the 154 acres added to the original park in the 16th century.

The interior of the park is covered with ridge-and-furrow, arranged in interlocked and end-on furlongs of reversed-S form, with well-marked headlands and at least two trackways or hollow-ways up to 12 m. wide and 1 m. deep crossing it. One of these runs from Moor End to Watling Street (SP 753444–745442) and the other from one of the bends on the Yardley Gobion road to Watling Street (SP 750440–747440). No date can be assigned either to the ridge-and-furrow or to these tracks, though they appear to pre-date the park. (RAF VAP CPE/UK/1926, 5242–3)

(9) CULTIVATION REMAINS. The common fields of the parish, together with those of Potterspury, were enclosed by an Act of Parliament of 1775 (NRO, Enclosure Map, 1776). Very little ridge-and-furrow of these fields is visible on the ground or on air photographs except on the land N.E. of the village, sloping down to the R. Tove, where the pattern of end-on and interlocked furlongs is almost complete. In this area former end-on furlongs have later been ploughed as one, with a resulting double reversed-S curve to the ridges (e.g. at SP 767451). Broad access-ways and unploughed 'greens' are also visible (e.g. SP 766452–771450 and 771453); 'greens' are depicted but the strips appear to be shown schematically on a map of 1728 (NRO).

Ridge-and-furrow of the open fields also survives N. and N.E. of Moor End (Fig. 128), running down the sides of a small valley. The furlongs on the W. side of the valley are in an area already enclosed before 1728. Within the deer park there are expanses of ridge-and-furrow of common-field type which appear to be earlier than the park (see (8) above).

There is also a little ridge-and-furrow on both sides of a stream in the far W. of the parish, to the W. of Watling Street (SP 738445). By 1720 this area was already divided into hedged fields known as Yardley Assart Grounds (map in NRO). (RAF VAP CPE/UK/1926, 5242–7)

UNDATED

(10) MOUNDS (SP 751446), W. of Moor End, on limestone at 95 m. above OD. Three 'tumuli' are described in 19th-century records, one oblong and two circular (*JBAA*, 7 (1843), 111; OS Record Cards). No trace of these exists.

APPENDIX

ROMAN ROADS

For ease of reference, all the Roman roads in the area are described here together and not separately under the parishes through which they pass. The roads are identified by the number given to them by I. D. Margary in *Roman Roads in Britain*, 3rd ed. (1973).

1e and 1f WATLING STREET. WEEDON BEC TO OLD STRATFORD (Figs. 129, 130 and 131)

This road, the main Roman route from London to the N.W., enters the area under review in the N.W. corner of Nether Heyford parish (SP 638592). The first part of the road, along the S.W. boundary of Nether Heyford, has been recorded in a previous volume (RCHM *Northants.*, III (1981), p. 208) and this description commences at the point where Watling Street meets the parish boundary between Stowe-Nine-Churches and Bugbrooke, immediately W. of Mount Farm, Bugbrooke (SP 652568). Here the Roman road is on a straight alignment running S.E. from the last change of direction S.E. of Weedon Bec. The modern A5 is in a cutting created in the early 19th century. The modern road itself appears to lie just N.E. of the assumed alignment of the Roman road and the cutting has removed all trace of any former agger.

Immediately to the S.E. the A5 swings E. in a broad arc, partly in a very deep cutting (SP 656563), in order to avoid the steep S. slopes of a broad ridge. The Roman road may have continued straight to the summit of the ridge, perhaps on the line followed by the boundary between Stowe-Nine-Churches and Bugbrooke. However, no trace of an agger exists here or further S. where the land falls steeply. It is possible that the Roman road was on the same line as the A5 at this point, and for the same reason. Whatever the exact position of the road on this ridge, the overall alignment of the Roman road changed slightly, probably about 1½ degrees further S.E.

At the bottom of the ridge the Roman road and the modern A5 are on the new alignment. The modern road crosses the valley on a raised embankment with a small culvert known as Geese Bridge (SP 658557) and the Roman road presumably crossed the stream here by means of a bridge. Beyond Geese Bridge the line of Watling Street is followed almost exactly by the modern road; the latter makes a number of minor deviations but the overall width of the present carriageway and verges has obscured or destroyed any remains of its Roman predecessor.

At the small hamlet of Foster's Booth which lies at the junction of Cold Higham and Pattishall parishes (SP 667539) the modern road swings slightly to the S.W. of the Roman alignment, but the modern houses on the N.E. side of the A5 have obscured any trace of the earlier road.

For the next 4 km. the A5 and Watling Street alignments are almost identical and there is no visible sign of the Roman road. On the N. side of the valley of the R. Tove the modern road appears to lie slightly to the S.W. of the Roman alignment (SP 684503–688494) but the widening of the road over the last 150 years and the planting of copses have again destroyed any possible remains of the Roman agger. Just before the crossing of the R. Tove (SP 689492) the modern and Roman alignments converge. The Roman road must have crossed the river on a bridge.

Beyond the river crossing, the Roman road alignment changes; the road turned 15 degrees to the S.E. to run towards and through the Roman town of Lactodurum (Towcester (3)). The details of the road as it passed through the town are described under Towcester (3) (Figs. 113 and 114). At the S.E. end of Towcester, at the point where the A5 crosses a small N.E.-flowing tributary of the R. Tove on a bridge (SP 694484), the Roman alignment changed again by a further 12 degrees to the S.E. From here to the crossing of the R. Ouse at Old Stratford, a distance of some 11 km., the Roman road remained roughly on this alignment, and is usually followed by the A5. To the S.E. from Towcester the road climbs and then, after 1 km., descends to cross the valley of a small N.E.-flowing stream at Cuttle Mill (SP 718464). Here the modern road swings slightly E., taking an easier line down the valley side. The Roman road certainly ran on and here, for the only time in this region, the original agger of Watling Street is visible. It appears from the S.W. side of the cutting of the A5 as a low bank 10 m.–12 m. wide and 0.5 m. high, running S.E. as the modern road turns slightly E. It is traceable for 200 m. halfway down the valley side but stops abruptly just above the mill-pond of Cuttle Mill (SP 71714653). It seems likely that at this point a bridge continued the line of the road across the deep valley.

Beyond the mill the A5 returns to the Roman road alignment and climbs the S.E. side of the valley. Thereafter no trace of the Roman road is visible within the county. Between Paulerspury (SP 726458) and Potterspury (SP 756432) the A5 is in places up to 40 m. to the N.E. of the direct Roman alignment but nowhere is there any trace of the Roman road to the S.W. of the A5; it seems that the actual Roman road lay off its theoretical alignment and is under the modern road, perhaps as a result of a slight surveying error.

From Potterspury to the crossing of the R. Ouse at Old Stratford (SP 781410) the A5 is exactly on the Roman road alignment. At the Ouse, which was presumably crossed at a ford, Watling Street passes beyond the boundary of Northamptonshire.

17 HARPOLE (Fig. 131)

The Roman road from the Roman town of Bannaventa to the large settlement at Duston, just W. of Northampton, crosses the N.E. corner of Harpole parish. The main part of this road has already been described in an earlier volume (RCHM *Northants.*, III (1981), p. 209). The road enters Harpole parish immediately S.E. of Oldfield Thicket (SP 689624) and runs S.E. until it crosses into Northampton at the Sand Lane cross-roads (SP 705618), a distance of 800 m. For the whole of this length the Roman road is obscured by the existing road from Duston to Newbottle and no original features are visible.

160a WHITTLEBURY TO TOWCESTER (Figs. 114 and 132)

This Roman road originally ran from the Roman town at Alchester, near Bicester, Oxfordshire, to Towcester. For much of its length in Oxfordshire and North Buckinghamshire the road is still followed by modern roads and tracks, but the part in Northamptonshire has been almost entirely abandoned.

The road enters the county near the S.W. corner of Whittlebury parish, just S.E. of Chapel Copse (SP 684420), within Whittlebury Park. Here a well-preserved agger 11 m. wide and 0.75 m. high even though ploughed over is traceable running almost exactly N. for a distance of 200 m. (air photographs in NMR). It then fades out as it crosses the line of a small E.-flowing stream, now culverted. The agger reappears on the same alignment 400 m. further N., within Cheese Copse (SP 684427), though it is much damaged by trees and is only a very slight ridge 0.25 m. high and some 10 m. wide. Nothing is visible in the modern arable land to the N. of Cheese Copse but on air photographs (RAF VAP CPE/UK/1926, 5232–3) a faint linear cropmark continues the alignment across the valley of a small N.E.-flowing stream, over a low spur and into another N.-draining valley (SP 684430–684435). Thereafter all trace of the road is lost for just over 2 km. If it continued on the previous alignment it should have crossed the Whittlebury to Silverstone road just E. of Doves Farm (SP 683444) until it reached the sharp bend in the main A43 Northampton to Brackley road (SP 684460). At this point the road turned N.E. through some 15 degrees. The short straight section of the A43, in the centre of the bend, is apparently the first 100 m. of the new alignment beyond which a pair of parallel ditches 20 m. apart visible for 700 m. on air photographs (held by Northants County Council; SP 68454610–68664677) is the continuation of this alignment. For the next 500 m. no trace has been noted but then patches of stone (at SP 68804730 and 68964778; inf. T. Shirley), still on the new alignment, probably represent the road.

To the N.E. the road has been recorded during excavations and observations on the extra-mural settlement of the Roman town in 1974–6. At a point where the road crossed marshy ground (SP 69034800) it was shown to consist of a strip of gravel 10 m. wide and up to 15 cm. thick, laid directly on the sub-soil, with a shallow ditch on the S.E. side. This was filled with material containing 1st-century pottery and efforts had been made to retain the metalling with wooden stakes. Later the width of the metalling was halved to 5 m. and again retained with stakes.

Further N.E. a length of 170 m. of the road was extensively trenched (SP 69044804–48994788). It consisted mainly of gravel 8 m.–10 m. wide, again laid directly on the sub-soil. The number of side ditches varied, there being usually two on the S.E. and three on the N.W. They contained pottery ranging from the 2nd to the 4th centuries (*Northants. Archaeol.*, 11 (1976), 194; Notes by C. Woodfield in NMR). Some 140 m. further to the N.E. a layer of hard packed gravel was seen on the same alignment during road construction in 1967 (SP 69004817) and is presumably its continuation (inf. D. C. Mynard). For the details of this road within the defended area of Towcester, see Towcester (3).

During the excavations in 1975 a short length of another road was discovered running S.E. from the Alchester road for at least 100 m. (from SP 69044803). It consisted of a thin strip of gravel 6 m. wide flanked by small side ditches. It has been suggested that it was of 3rd or 4th-century date (*Northants. Archaeol.*, 11 (1976), 194).

161a AYNHO TO WARKWORTH

A Roman road, known as the Port Way, is alleged to have run N.W. from Akeman Street at Kirtlington in Oxfordshire. There is no real proof that this was a Roman road, and if it was then it is likely to have been a minor one. The route described enters Northamptonshire near the S.E. corner of Aynho Park (SP 522322) and crosses the park as a modern track to meet the Aynho to Croughton road just E. of Aynho (SP 518333). The track lies on top of ridge-and-furrow in places and has no visible signs of antiquity. Beyond the Croughton road, the line of the Port Way is followed by an enclosure road and, beyond the Aynho to Charlton road (SP 516335), by a track, deeply hollowed in places, as far as the deserted village of Walton (King's Sutton (10)). This part is by no means straight and, whatever its origin, was in medieval times the main route S. from Walton. At Walton the hollow-way crosses a small stream and is lost. It is said to have continued N.W. to

King's Sutton and from there along the E. side of the R. Cherwell via Twyford (SP 488373) where another postulated road, 56a, is said to have crossed it. The Port Way is then assumed to have run on through Warkworth parish to Hanwell in Oxfordshire. No traces of an original road can be seen on this route N. of Walton.

166 SYRESHAM TO BODDINGTON

This is said to be part of a Roman road from Bletchley in Buckinghamshire to Wormleighton in Warwickshire. The S. part, in Buckinghamshire, has been tentatively identified (The Viatores, *Roman Roads in the S.E. Midlands* (1964), 309, 314), but its extension via Syresham, Helmdon, Sulgrave, Culworth, Aston le Walls and Lower Boddington is very doubtful (*Cake and Cockhorse*, 2, No. 7 (1964), 119).

56a KING'S SUTTON TO EVENLEY

There is good evidence that a Roman road ran S.W. across north Oxfordshire from the Fosse Way and it has been traced as far as Tadmarston, near Banbury. It is then said to have crossed the R. Cherwell near Twyford into King's Sutton parish and thence to have run eastwards via Astrop, Charlton and Evenley, crossing back into Oxfordshire at Finmere to meet the Roman Road 16a. Though a section through a Roman road is said to have been exposed in Astrop Park, the straight roads that follow much of the alleged route are enclosure tracks and show no visible signs of antiquity. (*Cake and Cockhorse*, 2, No. 7 (1964), 117)

TOWCESTER TO ?

In 1967 a trench, cut roughly N.-S. across the public footpath running immediately S. of the road, S.W. of Towcester (SP 684484), revealed a feature described as a Roman road. Four separate layers of construction were recognised and there was a sherd of Nene Valley pottery in the top layer. (*BNFAS*, 3 (1969), 2)

DEANSHANGER TO COSGROVE

There is said to be a Roman road from Water Stratford, Buckinghamshire, to Irchester, passing through Deanshanger, Old Stratford and Cosgrove. Though recorded in some detail the evidence for it is unconvincing. (*Wolverton and District Arch. Soc. Newsletter*, 5 (1960))

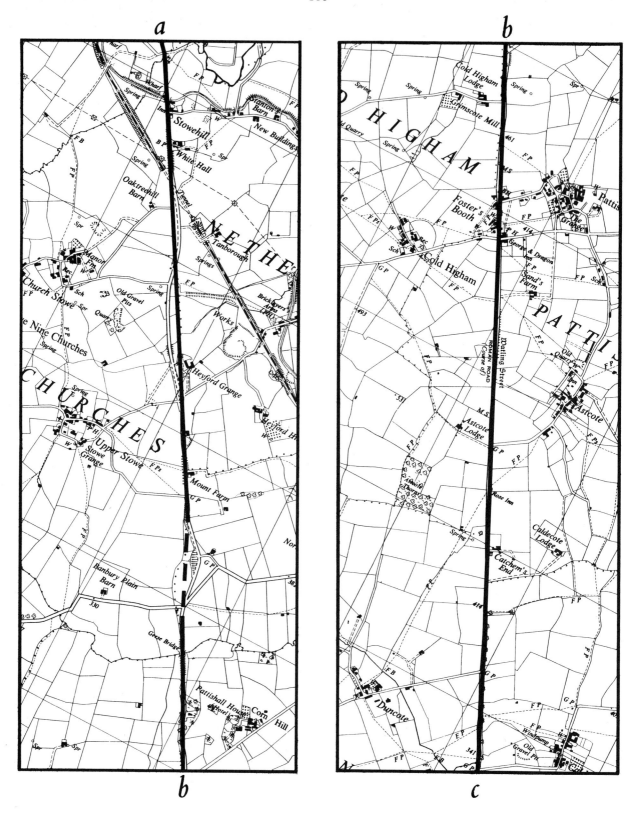

Fig. 129   ROMAN ROAD   1f, Watling Street Weedon Bec – Greens Norton

Fig. 130   ROMAN ROAD   1f and 1e, Watling Street Greens Norton – Potterspury

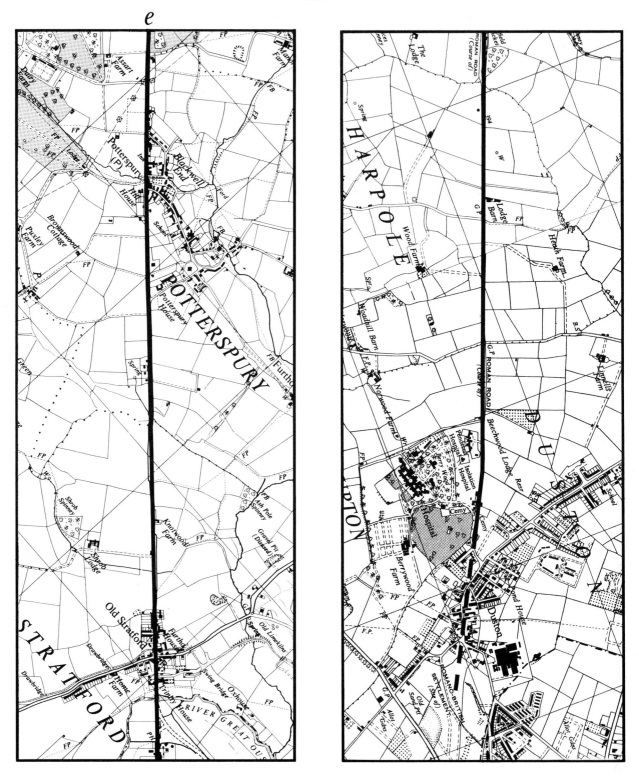

Fig. 131 ROMAN ROADS

1e, Watling Street, Potterspury – Old Stratford   17 Harpole – Duston

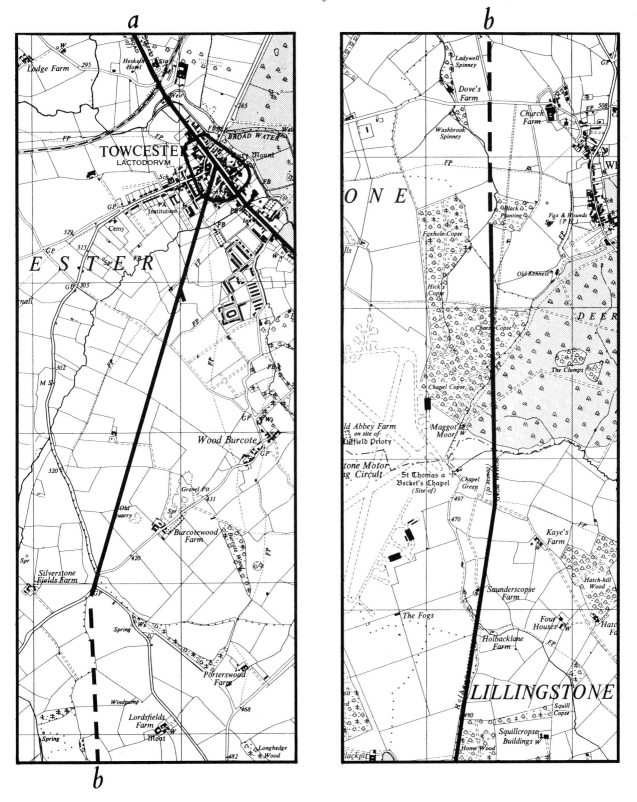

Fig. 132   ROMAN ROAD   160a, Whittlebury – Towcester

ADDENDA

These addenda contain brief summaries of new archaeological sites and finds which have been recorded from those parts of the county covered by the previous Commission Inventories since their completion. Discoveries made after 1979 are not included. New information on sites already published in the Inventories is also noted. The material is listed under the parishes in the earlier Inventories. Additional information to a monument already published is given the original number of the monument. New sites are given new numbers and to facilitate the identification of the latter they are prefixed by an asterisk (★).

VOLUME I

1 ADDINGTON, GREAT

PREHISTORIC AND ROMAN

A Neolithic stone axe of tuff has been found (SP 95997496; Kettering Museum).

[a](3) ROMAN SETTLEMENT (SP 947756). Recent fieldwork has produced more evidence of a stone building, and the associated pottery is said to range from the 1st to the 4th centuries. The building may have been a villa (CBA Group 9, *Newsletter*, 2 (1972), 23).

MEDIEVAL

★[d](9) MEDIEVAL POTTERY (SP 959749), at the N. end of the village. Late 15th-century pottery has been found in a rubbish pit exposed by building work (*Northants. Archaeol.*, 9 (1974), 105).

2 ADDINGTON, LITTLE

ROMAN

A Roman bronze handle was found somewhere in the parish before 1899 (BM).

MEDIEVAL

★[b](8) MEDIEVAL DITCHES (SP 95657350), within the old enclosures on the W. side of the medieval village, on limestone at 65 m. above OD. Building work in 1973 revealed several shallow ditches and one pit associated with medieval pottery. A single Saxon sherd was also found (NM; *Northants. Archaeol.*, 9 (1974), 106).

3 ALDWINCLE

PREHISTORIC AND ROMAN

An Iron Age sword with decorated scabbard mounts (Piggott's Group V or 'Battersea' type) was found in 1968 in the dried-up river bed close to the R. Nene (SP 998800; *Northants. Archaeol.*, 11 (1976), 165–70). A coin of Augustus was discovered before 1712 (J. Morton, *Nat. Hist. of Northants.* (1712), 532).

[b](1–11) HENSLOW MEADOW COMPLEX (centred SP 997803). Full reports of excavations on monuments (1–5), (8), (9) and (11) have been published (*Northants. Archaeol.*, 11 (1976), 12–70; 12 (1977), 9–47, 52; *Britannia*, 7 (1976), 39–72). A single radio-carbon date of 4560∓170 B.P., has been obtained for the Neolithic mortuary enclosure (1), which corresponds to an uncalibrated date range of 2690–2540 b.c. (*Northants. Archaeol.*, 12 (1977), 183). An important small find from the excavation has now been identified as a link from a mid 1st-century military horse harness (*Northants. Archaeol.*, 13 (1978), 169).

★[c](24) ENCLOSURES AND DITCHES (TL 003815), S.W. of the village, on river gravel at about 40 m. above OD. Air photographs (in NMR) show indistinct cropmarks of at least one rectangular enclosure and a number of short ditches.

MEDIEVAL

[b](18) SAXON SETTLEMENT AND BURIAL (centred SP 997803). A full report of the excavations at this site has been published (*Northants. Archaeol.*, 12 (1977), 47–54).

4 APETHORPE

PREHISTORIC AND ROMAN

A stone axe is said to have been found in the parish in 1954 (OS Record Cards; lost).

^b(3) ROMAN VILLA (TL 02639493). Contemporary accounts of the excavation were published in *The Stamford Mercury*, 15 April, 27 May and 2 September, 1859.

MEDIEVAL AND LATER

^b(4) DESERTED VILLAGE OF HALE (centred TL 015943). The earliest description of the site occurs in 1551: 'Within this manor the land has a freehaye which was sometime a hamlet called The Hale and was inhabited as there remayneth a mention of old walls at this day: The inhabitants whereof were decayed by report of divers ancient persons long before the remembrance of any man living . . .' (NRO, Westmorland Collection, W4 xiv 5).

(6) CULTIVATION REMAINS. Although the date of enclosure of the greater part of the common fields is still unknown there are records that the demesne land was already enclosed by the early 16th century (NRO, Westmorland Collection, 11/46).

5 ASHTON

PREHISTORIC AND ROMAN

A stone mace (near Group I) is said to have come from this parish or from Polebrook (Peterborough Museum).

^b(1) PREHISTORIC SETTLEMENT (TL 048890). Among the worked flints found here are a core and a blade of Mesolithic type (CBA *Research Report*, 20, (1977), 216; Peterborough Museum).

^{bc}(2–4) ROMAN SETTLEMENT (TL 046892). Among the finds made in 1844 when the railway was constructed was a Roman coin hoard, apparently in more than one vessel, associated with human bones, pottery and pins. The hoard contained a few early coins and over 1200 antoniniani (*Num. Chron.*, 5 (1945), 193–5; *BAR*, 40 (1977), 5). It has been suggested that part of the site was a cemetery (*Archaeologia*, 32 (1847), 1–3). Excavations between 1974 and 1978 in the S.E. of the area (TL 050892) revealed a Roman road running N.W.–S.E. across the area, with a minor road adjoining it at right angles from the W. Three rectangular stone buildings, one of which appeared to have been a smithy, were investigated near the road junction. The smithy contained at least five identifiable furnaces and a stone trough which may have been a quenching tank. Among the finds were a smith's hammer, an anvil, nails and other iron objects. A stone-lined well behind the smithy contained a large lead tank decorated with a Chi-Rho monogram. A circular hut, probably constructed AD 60–80, and two small kilns have also been found, all lying within a ditched enclosure. (*Northants. Archaeol.*, 10 (1975), 153; 12 (1977), 210–11; 13 (1978), 181; 14 (1979), 105; *Durobrivae*, 3 (1975), 12–15; 5 (1977), 6–11; *Britannia*, 6 (1975), 253; 8 (1977), 433–4; 9 (1978), 442.

Small-scale excavations further S. in 1976 led to the discovery of a late Iron Age ditch, containing pottery which included imported fine wares such as terra rubra, terra nigra, Lyon cups and beakers. A bronze coin of Tasciovanus, minted at Verulamium, of a type previously unrecorded was also discovered. (*Durobrivae*, 5 (1977), 9).

As well as the many Roman finds from field-walking over the whole area a Bronze Age transverse arrowhead (*Northants. Archaeol.*, 10 (1975), 149) and a sherd of Ipswich-type ware (*Northants. Archaeol.*, 12 (1977), 223) have been discovered.

Air photographs (NCAU) shows cropmarks extending to the N.W. of the area previously illustrated. These include a ring ditch and enclosures (TL 043897).

★^b(7) IRON AGE SETTLEMENT (?) (TL 046899), in the extreme N.W. of the parish, on river gravel at 18 m. above OD. Fragments of Iron Age pottery and three flint scrapers have been found. Air photographs (not seen by RCHM) are said to show a sub-rectangular enclosure (*Northants. Archaeol.*, 13 (1978), 180). Other photographs (NCAU) show a pit alignment and linear ditches to the S.E.

★^c(8) ROMAN SETTLEMENT (TL 078884), in the E. of the parish, on Boulder Clay at 66 m. above OD. An extensive scatter of 3rd to 4th-century pottery has been found (*Northants. Archaeol.*, 13 (1978), 181).

★^c(9) ENCLOSURES AND LINEAR DITCHES (TL 057891), N.E. of the village, on Cornbrash at 32 m. above O.D. Air photographs (Northants. SMR) show indistinct cropmarks of enclosures and ditches.

MEDIEVAL AND LATER

^c(5) DESERTED VILLAGE OF ELMINGTON (TL 053896). Deep ploughing has revealed an extensive scatter of late medieval pottery and building material (*Northants. Archaeol.*, 12 (1977), 226).

6 BARNWELL

PREHISTORIC AND ROMAN

^d(3) ROMAN SETTLEMENT (TL 074836). Details of the excavation of a Roman building on this site have now been published (*Northants. Archaeol.*, 9 (1974), 86; *Durobrivae*., 2 (1974), 27–8; *Britannia*, 5 (1974), 434).

★^b(12) ENCLOSURE (TL 051857), N. of Barnwell Castle, on Cornbrash at 35 m. above OD. Air photographs (NCAU) show, very indistinctly, a possible rectangular enclosure.

★^a(13) RING DITCH (TL 04708545), N.W. of Barnwell Castle, on limestone at 30 m. above OD. Air photographs (NCAU) show a ring ditch 12 m. in diam.

7 BENEFIELD

PREHISTORIC AND ROMAN

A barbed-and-tanged arrowhead is recorded (SP 983903; *Northants. Archaeol.*, 13 (1978), 178).

[b](2) ROMAN SETTLEMENT (SP 969868). Recent finds from this site include more pottery, roof-tiles and a saddle quern (*Northants. Archaeol.*, 11 (1976), 185).

★[b](15) FLINT-WORKING SITE (SP 96808735), on a S.-facing slope, on Boulder Clay at 88 m. above OD. Worked flints and a leaf-shaped arrowhead have been found (*Northants. Archaeol.*, 10 (1975), 149).

MEDIEVAL AND LATER

★[b](16) SETTLEMENT (SP 996886), 300 m. S.E. of Lower Benefield village, on Boulder Clay at 83 m. above OD. Medieval pottery including St. Neots and Lyveden wares has been found as well as two iron arrowheads (*Northants. Archaeol.*, 11 (1976), 196).

★[b](17) PILLOW MOUNDS (SP 987889), in the bottom of a valley, close to the stream, on clay at 60 m. above OD. There are eight scattered mounds, three of which lie on top of ridge-and-furrow. One is circular, only 2 m. in diam. and 0.25 m. high. The others are all rectangular, 1.25 m.-1.5 m. wide, 3 m.-7 m. long and 0.25 m.-0.5 m. high (*Northants. Archaeol.*, 10 (1975), 174).

9 BRIGSTOCK

PREHISTORIC AND ROMAN

A polished stone axe is said to have been found in 1969 on the Iron Age and Roman settlement (4) (OS Record Cards).

[c](1, 2) ENCLOSURE AND BARROW (SP 925842). Recent ploughing of these earthworks has revealed late Iron Age pottery and other occupation debris. Field-walking immediately to the W. has led to the discovery of further late Iron Age material covering about 3 hectares (*Northants. Archaeol.*, 13 (1978), 178).

[b](4) ROMAN TEMPLE (SP 961858). Details of two bases, a shaft and another fragment of masonry have been published (*Northants. Archaeol.*, 13 (1978), 79-81).

★[a](14) BRONZE AGE BURIALS (?) (SP 933857), found in 1928 in a sand-pit N.W. of Brigstock village, on glacial sand at 65 m. above OD. The records are inconsistent. According to the *Kettering Leader*, 24 March 1928, a single crouched inhumation was discovered but local information states that there were five or six skeletons as well as pottery and bone needles.

★[a](15) ROMAN SETTLEMENT (?) (SP 940865), N.N.W. of the village, within Old Dry Hills Wood, on Boulder Clay at 86 m. above OD. According to local information, 'pots and coins' and stone were found here some years ago. More recently, Roman pottery has been discovered in some quantity in the wood.

★[c](16) ROMAN SETTLEMENT (SP 913835), in the extreme S.W. of the parish, on Boulder Clay at 100 m. above OD. Recent field-walking has led to the discovery of a small quantity of 1st-century pottery and a scatter of burnt stone (*Northants. Archaeol.*, 11 (1976), 186).

MEDIEVAL AND LATER

[acd](11) DEER PARKS (centred SP 9283). Further details of the history of these parks have now been published (*Northants. Archaeol.*, 9 (1974), 103-4; CBA Group 9, *Newsletter*, 4 (1974), 24; *Northants. P. and P.*, 5 (1975), 217, 220).

★[a](17) SAXON SETTLEMENT (?) (SP 932857), N.W. of the village, on Great Oolite Limestone at 69 m. above OD. A small quantity of early Saxon pottery has been found (*Northants. Archaeol.*, 14 (1979), 107).

★[b](18) DEER PARK (centred SP 975857), in the extreme E. of the parish, immediately W. of the deserted village of Lyveden (Pilton (6)), on Boulder Clay between 62 m. and 92 m. above OD. A licence was given to Robert de Wyvill in 1328 to enclose, empark and hold in fee simple his wood of Lytelhawe by Lyveden. Nothing is known of its later history, but this area is called the Old Park on the 18th-century maps of Brigstock (NRO). The N. boundary of the park is the present Harley Way between Oundle and Brigstock, but no trace of a bank is visible. The W. side is bounded by a large bank up to 1.5 m. high which follows the E. edge of Cherry Lap Wood and the E. side of Sling's Nook Wood. The boundary then apparently followed the present Brigstock-Aldwincle boundary to a point just W. of the gardens of Lyveden New Bield (Aldwincle (22)). It then ran N. along the Brigstock-Benefield boundary, back to Harley Way. There is no trace of a boundary bank on this alignment. In 1540 Sir Thomas Tresham was given licence to enclose 320 acres of land to the S. in Aldwincle parish (*Northants. P. and P.*, 5 (1975), 227-8).

10 BULWICK

ROMAN

★[c](6) IRON-WORKING SITE (SP 929939), S. of Mavis Wood on Estuarine Clay at 90 m. above OD. Two shaft furnaces and two groups of channel hearths have been excavated after their discovery during ironstone-quarrying (*Northants. Archaeol.*, 14 (1979), 32-5).

★[c](7) IRON-WORKING SITE (SP 926937), S.W. of (6) in a similar position. A single shaft furnace, a group of channel hearths and some ditches have been excavated during ironstone-quarrying (*Northants. Archaeol.*, 14 (1979), 34-6).

★[c](8) BUILDING (SP 934935), S.E. of (7), was destroyed by quarrying in 1957. No details known. Large quantities of slag around the site suggests that iron-working was carried out there (*Northants. Archaeol.*, 14 (1979), 37).

MEDIEVAL AND LATER

[a](4) SETTLEMENT REMAINS (SP 958942), formerly part of the hamlet of Hinwick. No precise date has been suggested for the abandonment, but several tenements were still recorded there in the late 15th century (NRO, Tryon Ms. TB 24/2-4). Medieval pottery has been noted in a pit exposed by a service trench at the N. end of the hamlet (SP 959945; NM; *Northants. Archaeol.*, 9 (1974), 104).

11 CHELVERSTON-CUM-CALDECOTE

PREHISTORIC AND ROMAN

★[c](13) IRON AGE SETTLEMENT (TL 000686), in the E. of the parish on Boulder Clay at 85 m. above OD. Probable ditches containing early Iron Age pottery and part of a quern have been revealed during reclamation of wartime runways on the airfield (*Northants. Archaeol.*, 13 (1978), 178).

★[b](14) ROMAN SETTLEMENT (?) (SP 989696), on the W. side of Chelverston, on Cornbrash at 61 m. above OD. A small quantity of colour-coated pottery has been found on a building site (*Northants. Archaeol.*, 12 (1977), 211).

13 COLLYWESTON

MEDIEVAL AND LATER

[a](8) FISHPONDS (centred SK 991029). Documents in St. John's College, Cambridge (St. John's Coll. Ms. 62–9, 91–7, 13, 14, 102–9) throw considerable light on the management and maintenance of the fishponds in the early 16th century when the manor was held by Margaret, Countess of Richmond, and suggest that some of the ponds may have been constructed at that time. Of the works listed the following are of particular interest: 1 Feb. 1500, 'Paid towards breaking of the old sluice in the pondyard and making a new sluice there. Making a new gutter from the fish house, through the pondyard and the covering of the gutter'. 14 March 1500, 'Expenses making a new frame and paling about the new ponds in the nether part of the park'. 21 March 1500, 'Payment towards the parrging of the little pond in the pondyard with clay'. 2 July 1500, 'Robert Freeman of Ketton three days to make a hovell for the Herons . . . '. 1502, 'New stew in pondyard with frame of timber and new house made over the same 16 ft. long x 10 ft. New door made from house to fishouse'. 11 May 1504, 'Making a new frame of timber for the end of one of the new ponds'. 17 May 1504, 'Making three new ponds next to the garden in the park'. 24 August 1504, 'Making a new house at the ponds in the park 28 ft. long x 12 ft.'. 1506, 'Ponds in the park. Repairs of the ponds in the park and the new house there: for squaring and levelling of the floors in the same house and for emending and scouring of the dykes that convey water to the ponds'.

14 COTTERSTOCK

PREHISTORIC AND ROMAN

A Neolithic leaf-shaped arrowhead has been found (TL 040915; *Northants. Archaeol.*, 13 (1978), 178).

[a](2) ROMAN VILLA (TL 03269107). Air photographs taken in the drought of 1976 show the greater part of the villa in considerable detail as parchmarks. It appears to have been unusually large, over 200 m. long and some 60 m. wide, and consisted of buildings arranged round two courtyards with other possible buildings to the N. (*Nor-*

thants. Archaeol., 12 (1977), 211–2; *Durobrivae*, 5 (1977), 24–5).

★[a](4) ROMAN SETTLEMENT (?) (TL 04359065), at the E. end of Cotterstock village, on Great Oolite Limestone at 20 m. above OD. A few sherds of Roman pottery have been found in an abandoned garden and there are local reports of more pottery having been noted in the area (inf. Mrs. J. Johnston).

18 DUDDINGTON

ROMAN

★[a](5) IRON-SMELTING FURNACE (SK 99050038), S. of the village, on limestone at 60 m. above OD. A furnace, almost certainly of Roman date, has been found in a pipeline trench. A charcoal-filled pit lay to the S.E. (SK 99470025). (*Northants. Archaeol.*, 13 (1978), 181)

UNDATED

A bell, spearheads, swords and a 'celt' are said to have been discovered near the W. of 'Duddington Lock' at an unknown date (perhaps SK 987008; *Broadsides*, Central Library, Northampton).

19 EASTON-ON-THE-HILL

PREHISTORIC

★[c](7) FLINT-WORKING SITE (TF 02470120), in the S. of the parish, on Lincolnshire Limestone at 75 m. above OD. A scatter of worked flints has been discovered, but no details are known. An implement described as a Mesolithic axe is recorded from a point a little to the S. (TF 02450115). (Northants. SMR)

20 FINESHADE

ROMAN

★(6) ROMAN SETTLEMENT (?) (SP 974971), in the extreme S. of the parish, on clay at 83 m. above OD. A small quantity of Roman pottery including samian has been noted (*Northants. Archaeol.*, 14 (1979), 105).

21 FOTHERINGHAY

PREHISTORIC AND ROMAN

★[c](41) RING DITCH AND LINEAR DITCHES (TL 051942), N.W. of the Walcot Lodge Complex, on gravel at 23 m. above OD. Air photographs (NCAU) show a small ring ditch and some indeterminate linear features.

★[c](42) ROMAN SETTLEMENT (?) (TL 059931), near Fotheringhay Church, on river gravel at 15 m. above OD. Roman pottery has been found in this area (Peterborough Museum).

MEDIEVAL AND LATER

^c(35) FOTHERINGHAY COLLEGE (TL 05919311). The 1926 excavations were published in *Oundle School Commemoration Book* (1927), 38–40. Trenches revealed the foundations of the severely robbed walls of the cloister and showed its internal dimensions to be about 20 m. square. Many glazed floor tiles were recorded. Walls of buildings attached to the W. and E. sides of the cloister were also noted. (*Northants. Archaeol.*, 11 (1976), 177)

^{ac}(36) DEER PARK (centred TL 062944). Additional information on the history of this park has been published (*Northants. Archaeol.*, 9 (1974), 105; *Northants. P. and P.*, 5 (1975), 225).

22   GLAPTHORN

PREHISTORIC AND ROMAN

Worked flints, including scrapers, have been found N.W. of the village (TL 01979067; *Northants. Archaeol.*, 14 (1979), 102).

★^b(4) RING DITCH (TL 04009035), in the E. of the parish, on limestone at 29 m. above OD. Air photographs (Northants. SMR) show a small ring ditch.

★^b(5) ROMAN SETTLEMENT (TL 02059005), S.W. of the village, on Cornbrash at 37 m. above OD. Roman pottery, mainly of Nene Valley type, and several blocks of limestone have been found (inf. Mrs. J. Johnston).

★^b(6) ROMAN SETTLEMENT (TL 02909017), E. of the village, on Cornbrash at 37 m. above OD. A large quantity of Roman pottery, including Nene Valley and samian wares, and several fragments of hypocaust tiles have been found. Worked flints including scrapers have also been noted in the area. (*Northants. Archaeol.*, 14 (1979), 105; inf. Mrs. J. Johnston)

★^b(7) ROMAN SETTLEMENT (TL 01439110), on the S. side of Short Wood, on Boulder Clay at 62 m. above OD. An area of Roman pottery, including Nene Valley types and samian, and fragments of roof-tiles have been noted (inf. Mrs. J. Johnston).

MEDIEVAL AND LATER

★^b(8) SETTLEMENT REMAINS (TL 024900), formerly part of the southern nucleus of Glapthorn village, lie to the S. of the church, on Great Oolite Limestone at 37 m. above OD. The earthworks consist of a well-marked hollow-way running E.-W. immediately S. of and parallel to the present gardens with, on its S. side, traces of at least three closes bounded by shallow ditches or low scarps. Some indeterminate earthworks lie to the W. (*Northants. Archaeol.*, 14 (1979), 108).

23   HARGRAVE

MEDIEVAL AND LATER

^a(3) SETTLEMENT REMAINS (TL 034707). A quantity of

13th-century pottery, including Lyveden wares, has been found in a pit exposed during building work (*Northants. Archaeol.*, 9 (1974), 106).

24   HARRINGWORTH

PREHISTORIC AND ROMAN

A quartzite macehead has been found (SP 93419489; NM Records). A 1st-century Roman brooch (NM) came from ironstone-workings before 1960 (SP 91279533) and a 4th-century Roman coin came from the E. end of the village in 1978 (*Northants. Archaeol.*, 14 (1979), 105).

^b(1) ENCLOSURE (SP 94139475). A section was dug across the bank of the enclosure before destruction but no dating evidence was found (*Northants. Archaeol.*, 14 (1979), 111–12).

^a(4) ROMAN SETTLEMENT (SP 935980). Further excavations led to the discovery of a Roman building 30 m. by 14 m., probably a barn. Remains of other buildings lay beneath it and in the vicinity. Pottery dating from the whole of the Roman period and evidence of iron-working were found (*Northants. Archaeol.*, 9 (1974), 89–90; 13 (1978), 181; CBA Group 9, *Newsletter*, 4 (1974), 10; *Britannia*, 5 (1974), 434).

^a(5) ROMAN IRON-WORKING SITE (SP 924959). Ironstone-mining in 1973 revealed further ditches and a number of iron-smelting furnaces (*Northants. Archaeol.*, 9 (1974), 90).

★^a(13) NEOLITHIC AND BEAKER PITS (SP 934977), on the S. side of the Welland valley, on limestone at 90 m. above OD. Ironstone-working has revealed a small pit containing 180 sherds of Beaker pottery which came from not less than ten different vessels and a second pit containing early Neolithic pottery and worked flints (*Northants. Archaeol.*, 11 (1976), 183; 13 (1978), 3–7).

★^a(14) IRON AGE SETTLEMENT (SP933967), in the E. of the parish, on limestone at 110 m. above OD. Ironstone-mining has recently revealed several Iron Age features over an area of 1 hectare. The features appeared to be of two periods and included two parallel ditches of the 3rd or 4th century BC and pits and ditches of a later date (*Northants. Archaeol.*, 14 (1979), 102).

★^a(15) IRON-SMELTING FURNACE (SP 934979), in the N.E. of the parish, on limestone at 91 m. above OD. Recent ironstone-working has exposed a smelting furnace, probably pre-Roman in date, which was cut by a ditch containing early Roman pottery (*Northants. Archaeol.*, 14 (1979), 102).

★^a(16) IRON-WORKING SITE (SP 941969), in the E. of the parish, W. of Town Wood on Estuarine Clay at 100 m. above OD. Furnace lining and slag have been found over a wide area. No dating evidence but probably Roman (*Northants. Archaeol.*, 14 (1979), 37).

★^a(17) IRON-WORKING SITE (SP 925951), in the S. of the parish, N. of Hollow Wood, on limestone at 95 m. above OD. Furnace lining and slag have been found. No dating evidence but probably Roman (*Northants. Archaeol.*, 14 (1979), 37).

★[a](18) IRON-WORKING SITE (SP 934951), E. of (17), on Estuarine Clay at 95 m. above OD. Furnace lining and slag have been found. No dating evidence but probably Roman (*Northants. Archaeol.*, 14 (1979), 37).

★[a](19) IRON-WORKING SITE (?) (SP 908953), in the N.W. of the parish, on limestone at 100 m. above OD. Descriptions by quarrymen suggest that an iron-working site existed here (*Northants. Archaeol.*, 14 (1979), 37).

MEDIEVAL AND LATER

[a](6) SETTLEMENT REMAINS (SP 918971), formerly part of Harringworth village. A recently discovered map of the village, dated 1630, (copy in NRO) shows that there were at that time at least six houses or farmsteads occupying the area of the earthworks. However, three closes were already empty and the earthworks probably represent gradual abandonment over a long period.

[a](7) SETTLEMENT REMAINS (SP 926972), formerly part of the hamlet of Shotley. On a map of 1630 (copy in NRO) the two branches of the hollow-way are shown as existing roads with at least three buildings alongside them.

[a](8) FISHPOND (SP 918975). A map of 1630 (copy in NRO) shows the original shape of the pond with a second basin, of which no evidence survives on the ground, to the N.W. parallel with the river. The depiction on the map of a formal garden further S. suggests that the area around the manor house may have been landscaped in the early 17th century.

[ab](9) DEER PARK (centred SP 922953). Further details of the history of the park have been published (*Northants. P. and P.*, 5 (1975), 226).

25 HEMINGTON

PREHISTORIC

A Palaeolithic handaxe has come from the parish (Cambridge Museum; CBA *Research Report*, 8 (1968), 243).

26 HIGHAM FERRERS

PREHISTORIC AND ROMAN

A barbed-and-tanged arrowhead was found in 1975 (SP 950687; NM; *Northants. Archaeol.*, 11 (1976), 184).

[c](2) ROMAN SETTLEMENT (SP 955690). Details of part of a capital have been published (*Northants. Archaeol.*, 13 (1978), 79).

★[c](14) ROMAN TRACKWAY (SP 950688–951688), on the N. bank of the R. Nene on alluvium at about 45 m. above OD. During gravel-working in 1973–4 a trackway 2 m.– 2.5 m. wide and over 50 m. long was discovered, running E.–W. It was constructed of thin layers of limestone fragments and brushwood and in some places was reinforced with substantial vertical timbers placed at intervals along the edges. A Roman sherd, some human bones and a fragment of roof-tile were found on the track. Other finds

came from a layer of black clay which passed both beneath and over the track, and included Roman pottery, an unidentified antler tool, many animal bones, and part of a leather shoe possibly of late Roman or early Saxon date (*Northants. Archaeol.*, 10 (1975), 154–5).

Subsequent gravel-working has revealed the continuation of the track W. into Irthlingborough parish for a further 400 m. after which it turned S.W. and was visible for a further 250 m. At its E. end a second metalled track was observed running N.N.W. for 600 m. (*Northants. Archaeol.*, 11 (1976), 192).

MEDIEVAL

A late Saxon or medieval eel-trap weight was found in 1974 near the R. Nene (SP 951688; *Northants. Archaeol.*, 10 (1975), 167).

★[c](15) MEDIEVAL POTTERY KILN (SP 959692), at the N. end of the town on Great Oolite Limestone at 60 m. above OD. The remains of a kiln have been discovered, lying on top of earlier occupation debris. Little of the kiln structure survives but a large quantity of pottery was found in the flue. The kiln has been tentatively dated on documentary grounds to the mid 15th century (*J. Northants. Mus. and Art Gall.*, 10 (1974), 38, 55–7).

27 IRTHLINGBOROUGH

PREHISTORIC AND ROMAN

[b](7) IRON AGE AND ROMAN SETTLEMENT (SP 958715). Field-walking on this site has led to the discovery of further Iron Age and Roman pottery, as well as worked flints (*Northants. Archaeol.*, 11 (1976), 184, 192).

28 ISLIP

PREHISTORIC AND ROMAN

A pebble macehead with hour-glass perforation, said to be Mesolithic, has been found (SP 979785; NM; CBA *Research Report*, 20 (1977), 216).

[b](4) TRACKWAY AND ROMAN REMAINS (SP 992799). A few pieces of Roman pottery and one Iron Age sherd have been found on this site (OS Record Cards).

★[b](11) IRON AGE SETTLEMENT (SP 985793), at the N. end of the village, on limestone at 61 m. above OD. Ditches discovered during housing development contained late Iron Age pottery (*Northants. Archaeol.*, 13 (1978), 179).

29 KING'S CLIFFE

PREHISTORIC AND ROMAN

A large polished stone axe of Group VI, Great Langdale type, was found in the parish before 1952 (NM; OS Record Cards) and a gold coin of Maximus was found before 1862 (*Stamford Mercury*, 19 September 1862).

★ᵇ(8) FLINT-WORKING SITE (TL 018965), S.E. of the village, on limestone at 40 m. above OD. A quantity of worked flints of Bronze Age type has been found (CBA Group 9, *Newsletter*, 7 (1977), 27).

★ᵇ(9) ROMAN SETTLEMENT (TL 017992), N.E. of the village, on limestone at 70 m. above OD. Roman pottery is recorded (CBA Group 9, *Newsletter*, 7 (1977), 27).

★ᵇ(10) ROMAN SETTLEMENT (TL 010990), 700 m. S.W. of (9), on limestone at 75 m. above OD. Roman sherds have been found (CBA Group 9, *Newsletter*, 7 (1977), 27).

★ᵇ(11) ROMAN SETTLEMENT (TL 021968), S.E. of the village, on limestone at 60 m. above OD. A scatter of Roman pottery has been discovered (CBA Group 9, *Newsletter*, 7 (1977), 27).

★ᵇ(12) ROMAN SETTLEMENT (TL 014980), N.E. of the village, on limestone at 63 m. above OD. A large quantity of Roman material, some of which is said to have been kiln debris, was found some fifty years ago when this area was ploughed (inf. E. Standen).

MEDIEVAL AND LATER

ᵇ(6) DEER PARK (centred TL 025980). Further details of the history and boundaries of this park have now been published (*Northants. P. and P.*, 5 (1975), 227).

(7) CULTIVATION REMAINS. Ridge-and-furrow in the N. of the parish (TL 014993) is now known to date from after the mid 19th century. It is exactly straight, 15 m. wide and was formed by steam ploughing after the clearance of woodland (D. N. Hall, *Wollaston* (1977), 138).

31   LILFORD-CUM-WIGSTHORPE

PREHISTORIC

★ᵃ(7) RING DITCHES (TL 04558508), immediately N.W. of Barnwell Station, on Cornbrash at 34 m. above OD. Air photographs (NCAU) show two adjacent ring ditches about 10 m. in diam.

32   LOWICK

PREHISTORIC AND ROMAN

★ᵇ(9) ENCLOSURES (SP 965808), N. of Drayton Park, on Boulder Clay at 70 m. above OD. Air photographs (in NMR) show a small rectangular enclosure only 15 m. by 25 m., orientated N.W.–S.E., with a circular feature 25 m. in diam. lying against its S.E. side.

★ᵇ(10) ENCLOSURES (SP 963803), immediately N. of Drayton House, on limestone at 70 m. above OD. Air photographs (in NMR) show a rectangular enclosure 20 m. by 50 m., orientated N.W.–S.E., with subsidiary enclosures in the W. and E. corners. A second enclosure only 12 m. square is visible 70 m. to the N.E.

★ᵇ(11) ROMAN SETTLEMENT (?) (SP 975805), S. of the village, on Northampton Sand at 45 m. above OD. A

small quantity of Roman pottery was found during the construction of pylons (*Northants. Archaeol.*, 11 (1976), 192).

MEDIEVAL AND LATER

ᵃᵇ(6) DEER PARK (centred SP 955815). Further details of the history of the park have now been published (*Northants. Archaeol.*, 9 (1974), 110; *Northants. P. and P.*, 5 (1975), 221).

★ᵈ(12) SETTLEMENT REMAINS (SP 801790), formerly part of Slipton, lie at the S. end of the village, on limestone at 63 m. above OD. Low banks and scarps, presumably the sites of former houses and gardens, still survive.

35   NASSINGTON

PREHISTORIC AND ROMAN

★ᶜ(30) LINEAR DITCHES (TL 055949), S.W. of the village, on Great Oolite Limestone at 42 m. above OD. Air photographs (NCAU) show, very indistinctly, a group of intersecting linear ditches.

★ᶜ(31) ROMAN IRON-WORKING (TL 058968), N.W. of the village, on Northampton Sand at 30 m. above OD. A small area of iron slag 5 m. in diam. has been noted. Within it a small iron anvil of Roman type was discovered (*Durobrivae*, 7 (1979), 21–2).

MEDIEVAL AND LATER

ᵇ(27) SAXON CEMETERY (TL 071956). Further details of the spearheads from this cemetery have now been published (M. J. Swanton, *The Spearheads of the Anglo-Saxon Settlements* (1973), 199; *BAR*, 7 (1974), 69–70).

★ᵇ(32) FISHPOND (TL 063960), immediately S. of the village, on clay at 28 m. above OD. A small rectangular pond, 30 m. by 15 m., orientated E.–W., is cut into the hillside and is fed by springs. The field in which it lies was called Fish Pond Close in 1778 (NRO, Enclosure Map).

36   NEWTON BROMSHOLD

MEDIEVAL AND LATER

A silver coin of Offa was found in the parish before 1878 (*Arch. J.*, 35 (1878), 270).

ᵇ(9) DEER PARK (centred SP 990640). Further details of the history and boundaries of the park have now been published (CBA Group 9, *Newsletter*, 4 (1974), 26; *Northants. P. and P.*, 5 (1975), 226–7).

37   OUNDLE

PREHISTORIC AND ROMAN

Two polished stone axes, both of Group VI, have come from the parish (NM; Bristol City Museum). A leaf-shaped arrowhead and a scraper are in the Ashmolean Museum (J. Evans, *Ancient Stone Implements* (1897), 301,

373) and a barbed-and-tanged arrowhead is also recorded (TL 021871; *Northants. Archaeol.*, 13 (1978), 180). Three late Bronze Age socketed axes were found before 1948 somewhere near Oundle. They are said to have been discovered 'with about eighty other axeheads in an earthenware jar', but this seems unlikely (Birmingham City Museum; *Northants. Archaeol.*, 12 (1977), 209). Three other socketed axes found before 1866 are in BM. A bronze bust of Minerva is recorded from Oundle (*BAR*, 24 (1976), 206).

★ᵃ(15) IRON AGE SETTLEMENT (TL 035893), N.W. of the town, on sand and clay at 42 m. above OD. Iron Age pottery of the 2nd and 1st centuries BC has been found on a cropmark of a small enclosure observed from the air. The site has now been built over (*Northants. Archaeol.*, 14 (1979), 103; *Durobrivae*, 7 (1979), 26).

★ᵃ(16) ROMAN SETTLEMENT (?) (TL 042886), N. of the town on limestone at 30 m. above OD. A small quantity of Roman pottery and a few medieval sherds have been found on a building site (*Northants. Archaeol.*, 11 (1976), 193, 199).

38 PILTON

PREHISTORIC AND ROMAN

A coin of Hadrian is recorded from the parish (VCH *Northants.*, I (1902), 219).

ᵃ(4) IRON AGE AND ROMAN SETTLEMENT (SP 99858602). Iron Age material has now been noted as well as the Roman finds previously recorded (*Northants. Archaeol.*, 11 (1976), 184).

★ᵃ(13) IRON AGE SETTLEMENT (?) (SP 992867), in the N. of the parish, on Oxford Clay at 63 m. above OD. Iron Age pottery has been noted here (*Northants. Archaeol.*, 11 (1976), 184) and further pottery is recorded to the S. (SP 992864; Northants. SMR).

★ᵇ(14) IRON AGE SETTLEMENT (?) (TL 003859), in the N. of the parish, on Boulder Clay at 75 m. above OD. Iron Age sherds have been found (*Northants. Archaeol.*, 11 (1976), 184).

★ᶜ(15) IRON AGE SETTLEMENT (?) (TL 022841), immediately S. of the village, on limestone at 32 m. above OD. Iron Age material has been discovered (*Northants. Archaeol.*, 11 (1976), 184).

★ᵇ(16) ROMAN SETTLEMENT (?) (TL 001851), W. of Pilton Lodge, on Oxford Clay at 60 m. above OD. Roman pottery is recorded (*Northants. Archaeol.*, 11 (1976), 193).

MEDIEVAL AND LATER

ᵃ(6) DESERTED VILLAGE OF LYVEDEN (SP 984860). Further details of the excavations have now been published (CBA Group 9, *Newsletter*, 2 (1972), 17; 3 (1973), 21; 4 (1974), 12; *Med. Arch.*, 17 (1973), 183; 18 (1974), 220; DOE *Arch. Excavations 1973* (1974), 92; *J. Northants. Mus. and Art Gall.*, 12 (1975); V. L. Evison *et al.* (ed.), *Medieval Pottery from Excavations* (1974)).

39 POLEBROOK

PREHISTORIC AND ROMAN

A 'tanged lancehead' is said to have been found in about 1958 (TL 076876; OS Record Cards).

★ᵃ(7) ROMAN SETTLEMENT (TL 084855), in the S.E. of the parish, on Boulder Clay at 67 m. above OD. Roman pottery is recorded in the area (Northants. SMR).

MEDIEVAL AND LATER

ᵃ(5) SETTLEMENT REMAINS (TL 061859), formerly part of the village of Armston. Excavations were carried out in 1927 by pupils of Oundle School inside the ditched enclosure on the E. side of the site. All the finds were of the 17th century and included stone walls of buildings, floors, drainage channels and a 'road' (*Northants. Archaeol.*, 11 (1976), 177).

40 RAUNDS

PREHISTORIC AND ROMAN

Two barbed-and-tanged arrowheads were found during the excavations at (27). A coin of Gallienus was discovered in 1918 (TL 003728; OS Record Cards).

★ᵃ(23) RING DITCH (SP 983726), W. of the village, on Northampton Sand at 40 m. above OD. Air photographs (NCAU) show a ring ditch 17 m. in diam.

★ᵃ(24) RING DITCH (SP 980709), S. of Stanwick village, on Great Oolite Limestone at 67 m. above OD. Air photographs (Northants SMR) show a ring ditch 16 m. in diam. with traces of a central pit.

★ᵃ(25) ENCLOSURE (SP 985709), S.E. of Stanwick, on Cornbrash at 67 m. above OD. Air photographs (Northants. SMR) show very indistinctly what appears to be a roughly circular cropmark 15 m. in diam. with several internal features.

★ᵃ(26) LINEAR DITCHES (SP 990717), S.W. of Raunds village, on Cornbrash at 63 m. above OD. Air photographs (Northants. SMR) show very indistinct cropmarks of intersecting linear ditches covering about 5 hectares.

MEDIEVAL AND LATER

★(27–29) SETTLEMENT REMAINS, formerly part of Raunds village, have been noted in three places. These indicate a complex history of development and it seems likely that the village evolved from a number of centres.

★ᶜ(27) SETTLEMENT REMAINS (TL 002720), known as Thorpe End, lie on either side of the road running S. from the village, on clays and sands at 60 m. above OD. A plan has been made of a group of closes bounded by low banks and scarps and containing building platforms, with a hollow-way running E. into ridge-and-furrow. Building work in 1976 on part of these earthworks exposed a few early to mid Saxon sherds and much Saxo-Norman and later medieval pottery. Excavations which began in the same year have revealed the remains of a manor house and associated dovecote which were finally demolished in the late 13th or early 14th century. Beneath the E. end of the house lay the foundations of a small Saxon church only 8 m. long, with a graveyard to the S. (MVRG *Report*, 23 (1975), 13–14; 24 (1976), 26; *Northants. Archaeol.*, 12 (1977), 225; 13 (1978), 188–9; 14 (1979), 97–100; *Med. Arch.*, 22 (1978), 149, 181; 23 (1979), 242; Northants. SMR).

★[c](28) SETTLEMENT REMAINS (TL 004733), lie immediately N. of the village, on clay at 52 m. above OD. An area of some 3 hectares is occupied by several rectangular closes marked by low scarps and banks, some of which contain the sites of former buildings.

★[a](29) SETTLEMENT REMAINS (SP 999733), lie at the N. end of the village, on limestone and sand at 55 m. above OD. Several closes covering about 1 hectare have been noted. Excavations in 1975 exposed 13th-century occupation debris associated with the closes. Below this lay a late Saxon graveyard from which came three decorated tombstones and below this again there was evidence of extensive early to mid Saxon occupation (MVRG *Report*, 24 (1976), 26).

UNDATED

★[a](30) BURIALS (SP 977705), S. of Stanwick village, on Great Oolite Limestone at 61 m. above OD. Shortly before 1938 'a large number of cup-shaped pits', some containing human bones, were discovered during quarrying (*Northants. Natur. Hist. Soc. and FC*, 29 (1938), 60).

41   RINGSTEAD

PREHISTORIC AND ROMAN

[b](4) IRON AGE SETTLEMENT AND ROMAN VILLA (SP 976748). Continued gravel-working on this site in 1975 revealed part of a stone drum decorated with scales, from a large Roman column. It had been buried in a shallow pit and appeared to be on the E. side of the main villa site. (NM; *Britannia*, 3 (1972), 322; *Northants. Archaeol.*, 11 (1976), 193; 13 (1978), 82–3).

★[b](10) BRONZE AGE BURIAL (SP 981749), discovered W. of the village during gravel-working in 1975. A small Bronze Age vessel was found in a pit, with cremated bones. Several other pits and shallow ditches in the same area could not be dated but were probably of Neolithic or early Iron Age date (*Northants. Archaeol.*, 11 (1976), 184; inf. D. A. Jackson).

★[a](11) FLINT-WORKING SITE (SP 982751), N.E. of (10) and discovered during gravel-working in 1975. Worked flints including an axehead were found (*Northants. Archaeol.*, 11 (1976), 184).

★[ab](12) PIT ALIGNMENT (SP 979750), immediately N.E. of (4) on gravel at 37 m. above OD. Gravel-extraction has exposed a pit alignment made up of square or rectangular pits. This was overlaid by a shallow ditch on the same alignment. One of the pits contained a complete vessel of late Bronze Age or early Iron Age date (*Northants. Archaeol.*, 13 (1978), 168–80).

MEDIEVAL AND LATER

[b](8) DESERTED SETTLEMENT OF MILL COTTON (SP 969744). Excavations just outside the northern enclosure in 1973, before destruction by gravel-working, revealed a 14th-century bakehouse and 11th and 12th-century ditches. Excavations in 1974 within the enclosure showed no trace of any building; the surrounding moat was found to be revetted at one point (*Med. Arch.*, 18 (1974), 218; *Northants. Archaeol.*, 10 (1975), 170; DOE *Arch. Excavations 1974* (1975), 103).

UNDATED

★[a](13) MOUND (SP 977751), lay W. of the village, on gravel at 39 m. above OD. A low mound 36 m. in diam. was destroyed by gravel-working in 1976. Beneath it was a ring ditch 20 m. in diam. and 1.4 m. deep. No evidence of its date or function was recovered (*Northants. Archaeol.*, 12 (1977), 209).

42   RUSHDEN

PREHISTORIC

A fragment of a stone macehead has been found in the parish (NM).

43   SOUTHWICK

PREHISTORIC AND ROMAN

Part of a polished stone axe of Group VI, Great Langdale type, was found in 1974 (SP 980933) and part of another polished axe of greenstone, probably of Cornish origin, was found in the parish in about 1969 (*Northants. Archaeol.*, 14 (1979), 104). A hoard of about 150 Roman silver coins, of Galba, Vespasian, Domitian and Trajan, was found in a pot somewhere in the parish before 1879 (NM Records; lost).

[b](10) ROMAN SETTLEMENT (centred SP 982932). Details of the 1st-century kiln have now been published (*J. Northants. Mus. and Art Gall.*, 10 (1974), 6–12) as well as a full description of the Saxon strap-end previously noted (*Durobrivae*, 3 (1975), 28).

[b](11) ROMAN SETTLEMENT (SP 997914). A few sherds of Iron Age pottery have recently been found at this site (OS Record Cards).

★[d](17) ROMAN SETTLEMENT (TL 022922), immediately N.E. of Southwick Hall, on clay at 30 m. above OD. Roman pottery, mainly of Nene Valley type including part of a Castor box and some rouletted sherds but also with some samian, has been found. The pottery lies around a wide earthen bank which contains iron slag (inf. Mrs. J. Johnston).

MEDIEVAL AND LATER

A silver coin of Harold, unique in this country, has been found immediately E. of the village (TL 024923; *Northants. Archaeol.*, 10 (1975), 166).

★[d](18) DAM (TL 025920), E. of the village, on the N. side of Wych Spinney. A low dam 45 m. long and 1.7 m. high spans the valley of a small E.-flowing stream. The modern road runs on top of it. In 1834 the dam ponded back a small lake which extended N.W. and formed part of the landscaped park of Southwick Hall (map in NRO).

44   STOKE DOYLE

PREHISTORIC AND ROMAN

[b](6) ROMAN SETTLEMENT (TL 033865). The existence of this Roman settlement has now been confirmed by the discovery of considerable amounts of building stone and pottery. A subrectangular ditched enclosure has also been noted in the area (TL 035865) (*Northants. Archaeol.*, 10 (1975), 162).

★[b](14) LINEAR DITCH (TL 001869), in the N.W. of the parish, on Oxford Clay at 60 m. above OD. Air photographs (in NMR) show slight traces of a linear ditch some 200 m. long, running N.W.-S.E.

★[b](15) ENCLOSURES (TL 001862), 700 m. of S. of (14), on Boulder Clay at 70 m. above OD. Air photographs (in NMR) show very indistinctly what appears to be either a large subrectangular enclosure covering about 2 hectares with interior subdivisions or a series of small conjoined rectangular enclosures.

MEDIEVAL

A hoard of medieval silver coins, some of Edward IV, was found in a pot in 1873, apparently within the village (*Northampton Mercury*, 1 Feb. 1873).

46   TANSOR

ROMAN

Roman pottery and coins were found in the parish in the 18th century (W. Stukeley, *Carausius*, I (1757), 170).

★[b](9) ROMAN SETTLEMENT (?) (TL 075903), E. of Tansor Grange, on sandstone at 25 m. above OD. A scatter of 3rd-century Roman pottery has been found (*Northants. Archaeol.*, 13 (1978), 182).

47   THORPE ACHURCH

MEDIEVAL

★(9) THORPE WATERVILLE CASTLE (TL 022814), immediately S. of Thorpe Waterville, on gravel at 25 m. above OD. Records have now come to light of an excavation carried out in 1929–30 on the site of the medieval manor house. A large rectangular building with walls 3 m. thick, possibly a hall, was discovered as well as fragments of other walls (*Northants. Archaeol.*, 11 (1976), 178). The fea-possibly a hall, was discovered as well as fragments of other walls (*Northants. Archaeol.*, 11 (1976), 178). The fea-

ture described as a moat on the W. edge of the site is in fact an old gravel-pit.

48   THRAPSTON

PREHISTORIC AND ROMAN

A Neolithic stone axe of Group VI has been found in the parish (SP 99717847; NM Records).

★[b](8) ROMAN SETTLEMENT (TL 024779), in the extreme E. of the parish, on Cornbrash at 54 m. above OD. Roman pottery, a stone scatter and a 4th-century coin were discovered in 1978 (*Northants. Archaeol.*, 14 (1979), 106).

MEDIEVAL AND LATER

[a](6) OCCUPATION SITE (SP 996787). Further details of the mound and its structure have now been published (*Northants. Archaeol.*, 10 (1975), 175; 12 (1977), 190–1).

49   THURNING

PREHISTORIC

★(4) FLINT-WORKING SITE (?) (perhaps TL 096831), from a gravel-pit probably in the extreme E. of the parish. A group of unspecified Neolithic flint tools is said to have been found before 1928 (Peterborough Museum Records). A polished flint axe in the same museum, also found before 1928 in the parish, may be from the same site.

50   TITCHMARSH

PREHISTORIC AND ROMAN

A coin of Domitia Longina (81–96) was found in about 1962 at the S.E. end of the village (TL 02917945; NM).

[b](11) ENCLOSURES AND DITCHES (TL 01657985). Roman pottery has been found on the cropmarks previously recorded (*Northants. Archaeol.*, 13 (1978), 185). For Saxon and medieval finds, see (32).

[b](19) ROMAN SETTLEMENT (TL 024795). More Roman pottery has been found within the village, E. of the church (TL 023798; *Northants. Archaeol.*, 13 (1978), 185). For Saxon and medieval finds, see (33).

[b](22) ROMAN SETTLEMENT (centred TL 005794). Two skeletons in stone-lined graves, associated with 4th-century pottery, have been discovered in the area of the known cemetery W. of the settlement (TL 004795; *Northants. Archaeol.*, 10 (1975), 163). Details of a capital have been published (*Northants. Archaeol.*, 13 (1978), 77).

★[b](29) DITCHED TRACKWAY AND ENCLOSURES (TL 037777), S.E. of the village and immediately E. of Wood Lodge, on Boulder Clay at 70 m. above OD. Air photographs (in NMR) show very indistinctly a slightly curved ditched trackway, running. E.-W. and traceable for 150

m. Parts of possible enclosures lie on either side of it.

★^b(30) IRON AGE AND ROMAN SETTLEMENT (TL 037775), in the S.E. of the parish, on Boulder Clay at 63 m. above OD. An extensive spread of Iron Age and Roman pottery and burnt pebbles is recorded (*Northants. Archaeol.*, 13 (1978), 180).

★^b(31) ROMAN SETTLEMENT (TL 035798), E. of the village, on Oxford Clay at 35 m. above OD. Unspecified Roman material, said to represent a possible villa, is recorded. A 3rd-century coin has also been found (*Northants. Archaeol.*, 13 (1978), 182).

MEDIEVAL

★^b(32) SAXON SETTLEMENT (?) (TL 018798), on the same site as (11). Pottery of Saxon and early medieval types has been found (*Northants. Archaeol.*, 13 (1978), 185; 14 (1979), 107).

★^b(33) SAXON SETTLEMENT (?) (TL 023798), on the same site as (19). Pottery of Saxon and early medieval types has been noted (*Northants. Archaeol.*, 13 (1978), 185).

51 TWYWELL

PREHISTORIC AND ROMAN

Several flint arrowheads have been found in the parish (NM). Roman pottery of Nene Valley type in BM may have come from (5).

^b(4) IRON AGE SETTLEMENT (SP 952788). The full report of excavations at this site has now been published (*Northants. Archaeol.*, 10 (1975), 31–93).

52 WADENHOE

ROMAN

★^c(8) ROMAN SETTLEMENT (TL 009837), immediately N.W. of the village, on Cornbrash at 53 m. above OD. Roman pottery associated with an area of dark soil has been recorded (*Northants. Archaeol.*, 10 (1975), 163).

53 WAKERLEY

PREHISTORIC AND ROMAN

^a(1) BRONZE AGE SETTLEMENT (?) (SP 939982). Details of the pottery from this site, including Beaker and Collared Urn sherds, have been published (*Northants. Archaeol.*, 13 (1978), 8).

^a(2) IRON AGE AND ROMAN SETTLEMENT (SP 940983). Further details of this extensive site have now been published (*Britannia*, 4 (1973), 294; 5 (1974), 434; 6 (1975), 255; 9 (1978), 115–242; *Northants. Archaeol.*, 9 (1974), 85; 10 (1975), 163; 11 (1976), 194; CBA Group 9, *Newsletter*, 3 (1973), 14, 17; 4 (1974), 8; 5 (1975), 16; *BAR*, 24 (1976), 181). Part of a stone axe of Group VI has come from this site (NM Records).

MEDIEVAL AND LATER

^a(3) SAXON CEMETERY (SP 941983). Further details of this cemetery have now been published (*Northants. Archaeol.*, 10 (1975), 163).

^b(4) REMAINS OF HOUSE AND GARDENS (SP 956995). Immediately to the W. of this site and E. of the road to Barrowden there is a large rectangular fishpond with inlet and outlet channels still visible. This is unlikely to be directly associated with the 17th-century house and may relate to an earlier use of the site.

54 WARMINGTON

ROMAN

Part of a Roman rotary quern has been found immediately S.W. of the village close to the line of the Roman Road 570 (TL 074907; *Northants. Archaeol.*, 10 (1975), 163). Two pottery spindle whorls, each made from the base of a 3rd-century pot, came from the N. side of the village (TL 079914; *Northants. Archaeol.*, 12 (1977), 223).

^b(15) ROMAN SETTLEMENT (TL 071913). Two Roman spindle whorls have been found on this site (*Northants. Archaeol.*, 12 (1977), 223).

MEDIEVAL AND LATER

^b(19) SETTLEMENT REMAINS (TL 077907), formerly part of the hamlet of Southorpe. Additional information concerning the abandonment of the site has now come to light. A plan of the parish of 1622 (NRO) shows that Southorpe was then almost exactly the same as it was in 1775. This shows that no desertion occurred between these two dates although some had taken place before 1622. The major depopulation was in the early 19th century.

^c(21) DESERTED VILLAGE OF PAPLEY (TL 105888). Details of a small building, apparently of 12th and 13th-century date, which was excavated before 1972, have been published (*Med. Arch.*, 17 (1973), 183).

(22) CULTIVATION REMAINS. A map of the parish of 1622 (NRO) provides additional detail concerning the common fields. All the traceable ridge-and-furrow agrees with the strip system that then existed.

★^b(23) MOUNDS (centred TL 095907), E.S.E. of the village, in an area of ridge-and-furrow. Several rectangular mounds lie on headlands between furlongs. They are 12 m. long, 3 m. wide and 0.4 m. high, with flat tops. Their purpose is unknown.

55 WOODFORD

PREHISTORIC

Part of a Neolithic polished stone axe of Group VI, together with some fragments of tiles, possibly Roman, were found associated with a medieval pit (14).

★^b(13) BARROW (?) (SP 974756), in the S.E. corner of the parish, on alluvium at 36 m. above OD. A circular mound 15 m. in diam. and 0.25 m. high has been described as a barrow (CBA Group 9, *Newsletter*, 2 (1972), 23).

MEDIEVAL

★ᵇ(14) MEDIEVAL PIT (SP 96907681), found at the S.E. end of the village in 1971. It was interpreted as a cess-pit and contained a large quantity of pottery dated to the mid 12th century, including over 50 sherds of Stamford ware (*Northants. Archaeol.*, 12 (1977), 191–5).

56 WOODNEWTON

PREHISTORIC AND ROMAN

A few isolated worked flints have been found within, to the S.W. and to the N. of the village (*Northants. Archaeol.*, 14 (1979), 104).

★ᵇ(4) FLINT-WORKING SITE (centred TL 039933), covers about 20 hectares on either side of the parish boundary with Southwick and immediately N.W. of the Stone Pit Lodge Complex (Fotheringhay (21–25), Southwick (1–9)), on limestone and clay at 22 m. above OD. A thin scatter of worked flints, including Mesolithic and Neolithic types, has been noted (inf. Mrs. J. Johnston).

★ᵇ(5) ROMAN SETTLEMENT (TL 035936), S. of the village, on Great Oolite Limestone at 30 m. above OD. Roman pottery, mainly of Nene Valley type but including some samian, has been found over an area of almost 3 hectares. Near the centre some 30 sq. m. has fragments of Colly-weston tesserae. One leaf-shaped and one tanged arrow-head have also come from the site and waste flakes have been noted to the N.E. (inf. Mrs. J. Johnston).

★ᵃ(6) ROMAN SETTLEMENT (TL 034953), N. of the village, on Cornbrash at 45 m. above OD. A scatter of Roman pottery, including Nene Valley and samian wares, has been found (inf. Mrs. J. Johnston).

57 YARWELL

PREHISTORIC AND ROMAN

Two stone axes (both lost) are said to have been found in the N.E. of the parish in about 1925 (TL 06649868, 07109888; OS Record Cards).

ᵇ(3) ROMAN BUILDING (TL 066979). Further details of the excavation of this site, and a description of a capital, have now been published (*Northants. Archaeol.*, 11 (1976), 178; 13 (1978), 77).

★ᵇ(11) ROMAN SETTLEMENT (TL 056985), in the W. of the parish, W. of Old Sulehay Forest, on Lower Lincolnshire Limestone at 44 m. above OD. A scatter of pottery of the 3rd and 4th centuries, together with building stone and tile, has been noted (*Northants. Archaeol.*, 10 (1975), 164).

★ᵇ(12) ROMAN KILN (TL 060991), a little to the S.W. of the Roman building (5), on Lower Lincolnshire Limestone at 52 m. above OD. The remains of a pottery kiln were revealed and excavated during stone-quarrying. Large quantities of kiln furniture and dome plates were discovered and the associated colour-coated wares have been dated just before AD 150 (*Northants. Archaeol.*, 10 (1975), 164; *Britannia*, 6 (1975), 255; *Durobrivae*, 3 (1975), 15–18).

★ᵇ(13) ROMAN SETTLEMENT (?) (TL 06609900), close to (8), on limestone at 32 m. above OD. Roman pottery was found here in 1930. Prehistoric worked flints are also known to have come from the area (OS Record Cards).

VOLUME II

1 ASHLEY

ROMAN

ᵃ(1) VILLA (SP 788917). Details of a moulded limestone shaft have been published (*Northants. Archaeol.*, 13 (1978), 79).

3 BOZEAT

PREHISTORIC AND ROMAN

ᵈ(5) IRON AGE AND ROMAN SETTLEMENT AND KILN (SP 911579). In addition to the Iron Age material recorded from the site, subsequent fieldwork has revealed Roman occupation and kiln debris (OS Record Cards).

MEDIEVAL

'Several Saxon coins' are said to have been found in Bozeat (J. H. Marlow, *History of Bozeat* (1936), 36).

UNDATED

A small piece of limestone with a carving of a face on one side was found in 1976; no date can be assigned to it (SP 90455895; NM; *Northants. Archaeol.*, 12 (1977), 231).

4 BRAFIELD-ON-THE-GREEN

PREHISTORIC AND ROMAN

A Mesolithic core has been found (SP 816593; NM; CBA *Research Report*, 20 (1977), 216).

★[b](34) IRON AGE SETTLEMENT (?) (SP 826589), N.E. of the village, on Boulder Clay at 99 m. above OD. A few sherds of Iron Age pottery were found in 1976 (*Northants. Archaeol.*, 12 (1977), 208).

7 BROUGHTON

ROMAN

★[a](5) ROMAN SETTLEMENT (SP 847770), in the N.E. of the parish, on Northampton Sand at 95 m. above OD. Roman pottery, quern fragments and a scatter of stone are recorded (Kettering Museum Records).

8 BURTON LATIMER

PREHISTORIC

Four Mesolithic cores and two flakes have been found (SP 900740; NM; CBA *Research Report*, 20 (1977), 216).

MEDIEVAL

★[a](13) SAXON SETTLEMENT (?) (SP 89347565), in the N.W. of the parish, on Northampton Sand at 60 m. above OD. A small quantity of early or mid Saxon pottery is recorded (*Northants. Archaeol.*, 11 (1976), 195).

10 CASTLE ASHBY

PREHISTORIC

[a](1) FLINT-WORKING SITE AND DITCHED TRACKWAY (SP 856609). Part of a polished stone axe of Group VI and additional worked flints have been found (*Northants. Archaeol.*, 13 (1978), 178).

★[a](13) FLINT-WORKING SITE (SP 855604), N.W. of the village, on Northampton Sand at 75 m. above OD. A scatter of worked flints, including a plano-convex knife, and a single sherd of Saxon pottery were found in 1977 (Northants SMR).

★[a](14) IRON AGE SETTLEMENT (?) (SP 857604), S.E. of (13), on Northampton Sand at 84 m. above OD. Iron Age pottery and worked flints were discovered in 1977 (CBA Group 9, *Newsletter*, 8 (1978), 21). For Saxon finds from this site, see (15).

MEDIEVAL

★[a](15) SAXON SETTLEMENT (?) (SP 857604), on the same site as (14). Early Saxon sherds have been noted (CBA Group 9, *Newsletter*, 8 (1978), 21).

11 COGENHOE

PREHISTORIC AND ROMAN

Among the worked flints previously recorded, Mesolithic cores, flakes and scrapers have now been identified

(SP 826606, 830604; CBA *Research Report*, 20 (1977), 216). A stone flake of Group VI was found on the Roman site (4) (SP 838599; NM). A 4th-century Roman coin has been discovered (SP 83026069; *Northants. Archaeol.*, 13 (1978), 180).

[a](4) IRON AGE AND ROMAN SETTLEMENT (SP 839600). Three additional 4th-century coins have been found on this site (*Northants. Archaeol.*, 13 (1978), 180).

[a](5) IRON AGE AND ROMAN SETTLEMENT (SP 826607). A decapitated burial with the head placed between the legs, associated with an iron knife, has been found on the eastern side of this site (SP 828607). It was identified as late Roman (*Northants. Archaeol.*, 11 (1976), 191).

★[b](16) IRON AGE SETTLEMENT (?) (SP 853602), S.E. of Whiston Church, on Northampton Sand at 90 m. above OD. Iron Age pottery and worked flints were found here in 1977 (CBA Group 9, *Newsletter*, 8 (1978), 21). For Saxon finds from this site, see (18).

★[b](17) ROMAN SETTLEMENT (SP 852606), immediately N. of Whiston Church, on Upper Lias Clay at 75 m. above OD. A small scatter of Roman sherds and tile fragments has been noted. Three pieces of early or mid Saxon pottery have also been found (*Northants. Archaeol.*, 11 (1976), 191).

MEDIEVAL

[a](9) SETTLEMENT REMAINS (SP 850605), formerly part of Whiston. Medieval pottery, traces of walling and a possible hearth have been found S.W. of the church (SP 849604) and other medieval sherds have been recorded from elsewhere in the vicinity of the village (*Northants. Archaeol.*, 11 (1976), 191; 12 (1977), 233).

★[b](18) SAXON SETTLEMENT (?) (SP 853602), on the same site as (16). Early Saxon pottery has been found (CBA Group 9, *Newsletter*, 8 (1978), 21).

★[b](19) SAXON SETTLEMENT (?) (SP 854600), immediately S.S.E. of (18) on limestone at 85 m. above OD. Early or mid Saxon sherds have been noted (Northants. SMR).

12 CORBY

PREHISTORIC AND ROMAN

A leaf-shaped arrowhead has been found (SP 881906; *Northants. Archaeol.*, 12 (1977), 208).

[b](2) IRON AGE SETTLEMENT (SP 863869, ref. incorrect in RCHM II). Further pits, ditches and Iron Age pottery have been discovered (*Northants. Archaeol.*, 13 (1978), 178).

[a](12) ROMAN SETTLEMENT (SP 88149039). Pits and ditches containing a few Roman sherds have now been found (*Northants. Archaeol.*, 12 (1977), 211).

★[b](22) IRON AGE SETTLEMENT (SP 880868), N.E. of Great Oakley village, on Boulder Clay at 115 m. above OD. Part of an early Iron Age round hut and several pits have been excavated in advance of ironstone-working. Further quarrying in 1978 exposed additional Iron Age features, including a bowl-shaped iron-smelting hearth (*Northants. Archaeol.*, 12 (1977), 209; 13 (1978), 180; 14 (1979), 103).

★[b](23) ROMAN SETTLEMENT (SP 865863), N.W. of Great Oakley village, on Boulder Clay at 106 m. above OD. Several pits have been discovered. One contained an iron mattock, a tanged spearhead and an iron ferrule, and others held 3rd and 4th-century pottery and animal bones (NM; *Northants. Archaeol.*, 12 (1977), 212).

★[b](24) ROMAN BURIAL (SP 885867), in the S.E. of the parish, on Boulder Clay at 110 m. above OD. An isolated cremation accompanied by parts of an amphora and about 200 nails was discovered during ironstone-mining (*Northants. Archaeol.*, 14 (1979), 106).

MEDIEVAL AND LATER

A silver coin of Richard I is known to have come from Corby (NM Records).

[b](18) FISHPONDS (SP 866859). A plan of the site has now been published (CBA Group 9, *Newsletter*, 9 (1979), 46–7).

14   CRANFORD

PREHISTORIC

★[c](9) RING DITCH (SP 90907718), in the W. of the parish, on Northampton Sand at 69 m. above OD. A small ring ditch 12 m. in diam. with an entrance on the E. side is visible on air photographs (Northants. SMR).

17   DESBOROUGH

PREHISTORIC AND ROMAN

A Food Vessel and a small Collared Urn have recently been given to NM. They were probably found in about 1908 in ironstone-quarries W. of the town (*Northants. Archaeol.*, 13 (1978), 178).

★(13) ROMAN STRUCTURE (?) (perhaps SP 805832), described as 'a Roman latrine', was found during ironstone-mining in 1874 (J. R. Moore, *A History of Desborough* (1910), 4).

18   DINGLEY

MEDIEVAL

A Saxon sceatta of series E type was found in the parish before 1712 (*Brit. Num. J.*, 47 (1977), 39).

19   DODDINGTON, GREAT

PREHISTORIC AND ROMAN

[a](2) IRON AGE AND ROMAN SETTLEMENT (SP 882658). A limestone loom-weight and some Roman sherds have been found to the W. of the enclosure previously recorded (SP 880658). A large quantity of Iron Age and Roman pottery and a flint hammerstone have also been recorded in the

vicinity (SP 883659) (*Northants. Archaeol.*, 11 (1976), 183).

★[a](15) ENCLOSURE (?) (SP 888654), N.E. of the village, on limestone at 75 m. above OD. Air photographs (Northants. SMR) show part of what may be a rectangular enclosure 40 m. wide.

★[b](16) FLINT-WORKING SITE (SP 872640), in the S.W. of the parish, on limestone at 72 m. above OD. The numerous worked flints, previously recorded, have now been identified as probably Neolithic. They include 43 cores, 120 flakes or blades, a scraper and an arrowhead (*Northants. Archaeol.*, 11 (1976), 183).

20   EARLS BARTON

PREHISTORIC AND ROMAN

A large rolled Palaeolithic flaked tool has been found in gravel close to the R. Nene (SP 8662; *Northants. Archaeol.*, 11 (1976), 183). A leaf-shaped arrowhead and a scraper (SP 84436257; Northants. SMR) and a Roman bronze coin (SP 870634; *Northants. Archaeol.*, 14 (1979), 105) are also recorded.

[cd](6) ENCLOSURE, PIT ALIGNMENT AND DITCHES (SP 850627). A coin of Constantine I has been found in this area (*Northants. Archaeol.*, 14 (1979), 105).

[c](7) RING DITCHES, PIT ALIGNMENTS AND IRON AGE AND ROMAN SETTLEMENT (SP 845625). Excavations in advance of road construction have revealed part of a circular Iron Age enclosure containing traces of occupation including at least two buildings. Iron Age pottery, a loom-weight, a spindle whorl, bronze fragments and slag, and animal bones have been found. Field-walking has produced early and late Iron Age pottery, worked flints, a limestone block with cupmarks and a few early Saxon sherds (NCAU; *Northants. Archaeol.*, 14 (1979), 102).

★[d](18) IRON AGE SETTLEMENT (SP 85586388), N.E. of the village, on Northampton Sand at 83 m. above OD. Soil-stripping has revealed ditches and pits associated with pottery, including several sherds with geometric and curvilinear decoration perhaps of the 1st or 2nd century BC. Quantities of daub and traces of a hearth were also noted within one of the pits (*Northants. Archaeol.*, 13 (1978), 178).

MEDIEVAL

Some medieval pottery has been found within the village (SP 85286365; *Northants. Archaeol.*, 11 (1976), 197).

[d](15) FISHPONDS (SP 854638). The dam of the northernmost fishpond still survives (SP 85576403; *Northants. Archaeol.*, 13 (1978), 186).

★[c](19) SAXON SETTLEMENT (?) (SP 843625), in the S.E. of the parish, on river gravel at 52 m. above OD. Sherds of early to mid Saxon type were found in 1968 (*Northants. Archaeol.*, 14 (1979), 107).

22 ECTON

PREHISTORIC AND ROMAN

A partly perforated quartzite macehead has been found within the North Ecton Complex (SP 82136535; NM) and a few worked flints, including two scrapers, are also recorded (SP 830628; Northants. SMR).

★[b](24) ENCLOSURE (SP 838629), N.E. of General Spinney and of (17), on gravel at 58 m. above OD. Air photographs (Northampton Development Corporation Archaeological Unit) show a D-shaped enclosure of approximately 0.5 hectare, orientated E.-W. and with a well-marked entrance in its E. side.

★[b](25) ENCLOSURE AND DITCHES (SP 839625), 300 m. S. of (24), on gravel at 52 m. above OD. Air photographs (Northampton Development Corporation Archaeological Unit) show a small trapezoidal enclosure 0.25 hectare in extent with no visible interior features or entrances. Other features, including possible linear ditches, are indistinctly visible to the N. and N.E..

★[b](26) ENCLOSURES (SP 837641), N.E. of the village, on Upper Lias Clay at 78 m. above OD. Air photographs (Northants. SMR) show two oval conjoined enclosures, each 20 m. wide. Other indistinct features are visible in the area.

MEDIEVAL AND LATER

★[b](27) SETTLEMENT REMAINS (SP 831633), formerly part of Ecton village, lie S. and S.E. of Ecton Hall within the park, on clay sloping S. between 84 m. and 75 m. above OD. The present village of Ecton consists of little more than a single N.-S. street with the church and hall to the W. of it. To the E. of the S. end of this street and roughly parallel to it are two hollow-ways (SP 830633, 832633). Both are 10 m. wide and up to 2 m. deep and are cut at their N. ends by the ha-ha bounding the gardens of the hall. The E. hollow-way is lined on its W. side by rectangular closes separated by low banks and scarps and with a slight bank defining their W. edge. Within the closes, near the hollow-way, are depressions and uneven ground which may be the sites of former houses. The E. side of the hollow-way is now under cultivation; large quantities of medieval and post-medieval pottery and areas of stone have been found here. The W. hollow-way has no obvious house-sites or closes alongside it, perhaps because the land has been ploughed and returned to grass. There are, however, some very slight depressions and scarps which may indicate that this hollow-way too was once lined with buildings.

If these depressions are indeed part of the village then Ecton once consisted of three roughly parallel streets, perhaps as a result of planning. The N. ends of these streets have presumably been destroyed by the gardens of Ecton Hall, though the old drive to the hall and a track to the W. (SP 829639 and 828638) may follow their original alignments. The date of the abandonment of the central street is unknown. In his *History of Ecton* (1825) J. Cole stated: 'It appears that Ecton has formerly been more extensive, as a farm-house, with several other dwellings, under the name "Little Ecton", situated to the east of Mr. Isted's House, were standing in the memory of some of the inhabitants now living'. This must refer to the group of eight houses set within small closes which, in the mid 18th century, lay on the E. side of the E. hollow-way (NRO, map of Ecton, 1759). These were removed later in the century when the park was laid out (NRO, late 18th-century maps of Ecton).

23 GEDDINGTON

PREHISTORIC AND ROMAN

A flint core and several worked flints have been found (SP 89908565; Northants. Archaeol., 11 (1976), 183).

[a](4) IRON AGE AND ROMAN SETTLEMENT (centred SP 875824). Excavation in advance of ironstone-working has revealed several early Iron Age pits and ditches, as well as a circular enclosure, 11 m. in diam., with an E.-facing entrance. This feature may have been a drainage gully encircling a hut (Northants. Archaeol., 12 (1977), 208; 13 (1978), 179; 14 (1979), 10–16).

MEDIEVAL AND LATER

Some medieval pottery is recorded from the S. end of the village (SP 89128263; Northants. Archaeol., 13 (1978), 187) and a silver coin of Charles the Bold, Duke of Burgundy, 1486–74, has been found further N.E. (Northants. Archaeol., 11 (1976), 197).

★[a](9) SAXON SETTLEMENT (?) (SP 87688272), immediately N. of (4), on limestone at 90 m. above OD. A small scatter of Saxon sherds has been noted (Northants. Archaeol., 12 (1977), 224).

★[b](10) SAXON SETTLEMENT (?) (SP 897856), in the extreme N. of the parish, on limestone at 72 m. above OD. A small scatter of Saxon pottery associated with areas of iron slag has been noted (Northants. Archaeol., 11 (1976), 195).

★[c](11) SAXON SETTLEMENT (?) (SP 900837), N.E. of the village, on limestone at 90 m. above OD. An extensive area of burnt earth 35 m. in diam. contained ironstone, slag and Saxon pottery (Northants. Archaeol., 11 (1976), 195).

★[a](12) SETTLEMENT REMAINS (SP 896829), formerly part of the village, lie in the S.E. of the village at the S. end of Chase Road, on Northampton Sand at 80 m. above OD. An area of about 1 hectare is occupied by low, indeterminate banks and scarps. On the E. a well-marked bank separates the area from the adjacent ridge-and-furrow. According to local tradition this is the site of a manor house but it is more likely to represent small houses and gardens.

25 GRENDON

PREHISTORIC AND ROMAN

A Mesolithic core has been found (SP 880600; CBA Research Report, 20 (1977), 216).

[a](7) Ring Ditches, Enclosures and Pit Alignments (centred SP 879622). The large cropmark site has now been almost completely destroyed by gravel extraction. The following observations have been made. The large ring ditch proved to be a Bronze Age barrow with a stone kerb. Iron Age pottery and two iron-smelting pits, probably of Iron Age date, were found in the vicinity. One of the pit alignments were exposed and excavation showed that the pits were of two periods. At one point the pit alignment was cut by the ditch of an Iron Age enclosure. Other finds included four early Bronze Age Urns, probably from barrows (*Northants. Archaeol.*, 12 (1977), 209; 13 (1978), 179).

MEDIEVAL

[a](14) Saxon Settlement (SP 877623). The Saxon material previously recorded lies on the prehistoric site (7). Recent gravel-working revealed extensive evidence of early Saxon occupation including three sunken huts, post-holes and pits (*Northants. Archaeol.*, 12 (1977), 224; 13 (1978), 179).

26 GRETTON

PREHISTORIC AND ROMAN

★[d](12) Iron Age Trackway and (?) Settlement (SP 907943), E. of the village, on Great Oolite Limestone at 110 m. above OD. A large amount of Iron Age pottery has been recovered from two parallel ditches 6 m. apart, possibly bounding a trackway. No evidence of settlement was found in the adjacent area (*Northants. Archaeol.*, 14 (1979), 102).

★[d](13) Roman Iron-Working Site (SP 909945), E. of the village, on limestone at 107 m. above OD. A shaft furnace, hearth and a ditch were discovered during ironstone-quarrying. Further evidence of iron-working has been noted 380 m. to the W. (*Northants. Archaeol.*, 14 (1979), 36).

27 HACKLETON

ROMAN

[d](7) Roman Settlement (SP 800558). Recent air photographs (Northants. SMR) show a rectangular enclosure bounded by very broad ditches, with a smaller enclosure attached to one side, the whole covering 0.5 hectare.

[b](11) Roman Villa (SP 79785414). Further discoveries include a wall 22 m. long, running E.-W. with projecting walls on each side, as well as part of a tessellated pavement (*Northants. Archaeol.*, 14 (1979), 106).

28 HANNINGTON

PREHISTORIC AND ROMAN

[a](2) Iron Age and Roman Settlement (SP 811712). More Roman pottery and a few Iron Age sherds and worked flints have been recorded from the site (*Northants. Archaeol.*, 11 (1976), 183).

[a](3) Ring Ditches, Enclosures and Ditches (SP 807712). A scatter of worked flints, including scrapers and a core, has been recorded (*Northants. Archaeol.*, 11 (1976), 183).

30 HARRINGTON

ROMAN

A few sherds of Roman pottery have been found near the site of the deserted village of Newbottle (4) (local inf.).

MEDIEVAL

[a](4) Deserted Village of Newbottle (SP 777815). A quantity of early Saxon pottery has been noted on the site of the village (local. inf.).

33 HOLCOT

PREHISTORIC

★[a](9) Ring Ditch (SP 792706), in the N. of the parish, on Northampton Sand at 115 m. above OD. Air photographs (Northants. SMR) show a ring ditch about 15 m. in diam.

35 HOUGHTON, LITTLE

PREHISTORIC AND ROMAN

Two Mesolithic cores as well as blades and flakes have been identified (SP 800590; NM; CBA *Research Report*, 20 (1977), 217). A large flint tanged spearhead and a lozenge-shaped arrowhead were found in 1975 (SP 80696055; NM; *Northants. Archaeol.*, 11 (1976), 184).

[d](14) Roman Settlement and Kilns (SP 812596), within the East Houghton Complex. Five Roman coins of 1st to 4th-century date and a 1st-century bronze brooch have been found (*Northants. Archaeol.*, 11 (1976), 192).

(15–20) South Houghton Complex (centred SP 802593). Construction of the by-pass around Little Houghton village in 1978 produced additional evidence of prehistoric and Roman occupation in this area, including a pit containing Beaker sherds and charcoal (SP 80665926), a ditch containing Iron Age sherds (SP 81005927), pits and a ditch with Roman pottery (SP 80225929), a pit containing Roman sherds and two pits with sherds of either Bronze Age or late Iron Age type (SP 80265930) and undated pits and ditches (SP 79825931, 80025929) (*Northants. Archaeol.*, 14 (1979), 102–3).

36 IRCHESTER

PREHISTORIC AND ROMAN

A small flint axe was found in about 1966 within the Roman town (SP 917666; Northants. SMR).

[a](7) ROMAN TOWN (SP 917667). A detailed description of the architectural masonry from the town has been published (*Northants. Archaeol.*, 13 (1978), 81, 82, 85). Further references to a Roman lead coffin found in 1876 are listed in *BAR*, 38 (1977), 38 no. 142.

★[a](13) FLINT-WORKING SITE (SP 921673), immediately N. of the R. Nene, on alluvium at 40 m. above OD. Over 130 worked flints including at least 30 cores as well as scrapers and other tools are recorded (NM; Northants. SMR).

MEDIEVAL

A Saxon sceatta of series K type was found in the Roman town (7) before 1898 (*Brit. Num. J.*, 47 (1977), 41).

[a](8) SETTLEMENT REMAINS (SP 920669), formerly part of the hamlet of Chester-on-the-Water. A full history and description of the site has now been published (*Northants, P. and P.*, 6 (1978), 15–19).

38   KETTERING

PREHISTORIC AND ROMAN

A Bronze Age axe (BM) is said to have come from Kettering.

[b](7) IRON AGE AND ROMAN SETTLEMENT (centred SP 886780). Further details of the excavations have now been published (*Northants. Archaeol.*, 11 (1976), 170–7, 192).

UNDATED

★[b](18) BURIAL (perhaps SP 876795), in 'Rectorial Allotment Field, near Avondale Road' in 1905. A skeleton orientated E.-W., without grave-goods, was discovered in a stone-lined grave (*Northants. N. and Q.*, 1 (1905–7), 209).

40   MEARS ASHBY

PREHISTORIC AND ROMAN

Worked flints or scrapers have been found at three new locations (SP 849649, 841664, 853654; *Northants. Archaeol.*, 11 (1976), 184). A polished flint axe (SP 83256665), part of another (SP 854665) and a leaf-shaped arrowhead (SP 849659) have also been discovered (*Northants. Archaeol.*, 12 (1977), 209).

[ab](6) IRON AGE AND ROMAN SETTLEMENT (centred SP 850663). Further discoveries on or near this site include a flint plano-convex knife (SP 848662; *Northants. Archaeol.*, 13 (1978), 179), scrapers and worked flints (SP 852663, 85156565, 849663; *Northants. Archaeol.*, 11 (1976), 184) and a Roman coin, AD 251–3 (SP 850662; *Northants, Archaeol.*, 11 (1976), 192).

[a](7) ROMAN SETTLEMENT (SP 850652). Two Roman coins have been found, one of Gallienus and one of Crispus (*Northants. Archaeol.*, 12 (1977), 213; 13 (1978), 181).

42   MOULTON

PREHISTORIC OR ROMAN

★(12) ENCLOSURE (?) (SP 781693), in the extreme N.E. of the parish, on Northampton Sand at 94 m. above OD. Air photographs (Northants. SMR) show some very indeterminate cropmarks 0.5 hectare in extent which may represent a roughly circular area of settlement.

43   NEWTON

ROMAN

★[a](14) ROMAN SETTLEMENT (SP 89308637), N. of Little Oakley village, on limestone at 90 m. above OD. A large quantity of Roman pottery, stone roof slates and quernstones has been found (*Northants. Archaeol.*, 11 (1976), 193, listed under Oakley).

MEDIEVAL

[b](7) SETTLEMENT REMAINS (SP 879835), formerly part of Great Newton. A small quantity of medieval pottery has been found at the E. end of the village (SP 883834; *Northants. Archaeol.*, 11 (1976), 197).

47   OVERSTONE

PREHISTORIC AND ROMAN

[a](2) ROMAN SETTLEMENT (SP 797657). An antoninianus of Victorinus was found in 1974 (*Northants. Archaeol.*, 11 (1976), 193).

★[a](9) IRON AGE SETTLEMENT (?) (SP 795674), in the N. of the parish, on limestone at 115 m. above OD. Iron Age pottery and a scatter of stone associated with a dark area of soil have been found (inf. D.N. Hall).

★[a](10) IRON AGE SETTLEMENT (?) (SP 793672), S.W. of (9), in a similar situation. Iron Age pottery, a scatter of stone and an area of dark soil are recorded (inf. D.N. Hall).

★[c](11) ROMAN SETTLEMENT (?) (SP 803670), in the N. of the parish, on limestone at 107 m. above OD. Roman pottery has been noted, with an area of dark soil (inf. D. N. Hall).

49   ROCKINGHAM

PREHISTORIC OR ROMAN

★(15) ENCLOSURES (SP 860918), in the N.W. of the parish, close to the R. Welland, on gravel at 54 m. above OD. Air photographs (not seen by RCHM) are said to show a group of enclosures (*Northants. Archaeol.*, 12 (1977), 230).

50   ROTHWELL

PREHISTORIC

A pebble macehead with hour-glass perforation, tentatively identified as Mesolithic, has been found (SP 815812; CBA *Research Report*, 20 (1977), 217; Leicester Musuem). A flint core and some flakes are also recorded (SP 82638080).

51   RUSHTON

PREHISTORIC AND ROMAN

A leaf-shaped arrowhead has been found (SP 84068105; *Northants. Archaeol.*, 14 (1979), 104).

^d(3) IRON AGE SETTLEMENT (SP 850837). Excavations in 1970 revealed more ditches containing pottery and a small quantity of animal bones. The pottery appeared to be mainly of Iron Age date (*Northants. Archaeol.*, 11 (1976), 83–7).

★^c(14) FLINT-WORKING SITE (SP 845829), immediately E. of Rushton All Saints, on Northampton Sand at 90 m. above OD. Pipeline construction in 1976 exposed a large quantity of flint scrapers, blades and waste flakes (*Northants. Archaeol.*, 13 (1978), 180).

★^d(15) FLINT-WORKING SITE (SP 86328077), in the extreme S.E. of the parish, on Northampton Sand at 87 m. above OD. Several flint flakes, and a number of small cores have been noted (*Northants. Archaeol.*, 11 (1976), 184).

★^d(16) ROMAN SETTLEMENT (SP 85158140), in the S. of the parish, E. of Glendon Hall, on Northampton Sand at 107 m. above OD. A large quantity of Roman pottery has been discovered (*Northants. Archaeol.*, 11 (1976), 193).

MEDIEVAL AND LATER

^c(8) SETTLEMENT REMAINS (SP 845829), formerly part of Rushton All Saints. Pipe-laying at the E. end of the village revealed areas of burnt stonework, iron slag and fragments of a furnace, associated with 13th to 14th-century pottery. Other stonework and pottery of 11th to 18th-century date including Stamford ware was found a little to the S. (*Northants. Archaeol.*, 13 (1978), 189; 14 (1979), 107).

52   STANION

PREHISTORIC AND ROMAN

A polished flint axe has been found in the S.W. of the parish (SP 90958540; *Northants. Archaeol.*, 14 (1979), 104). Further scatters of Iron-Age and Roman pottery have been noted in the S. of the parish in the vicinity of (2–7) (*Northants. Archaeol.*, 11 (1976), 184, 194; 13 (1978), 182; 14 (1979), 104; 106, OS Record Cards; Northants. SMR).

★^a(13) IRON AGE SETTLEMENT (SP 913857), S. of the village, on limestone at 67 m. above OD. A scatter of occupation debris and late Iron Age pottery is recorded (*Northants. Archaeol.*, 14 (1979), 104).

MEDIEVAL

^a(11) MOAT AND ENCLOSURES (centred SP 923863). A small quantity of early Saxon pottery has been found at the extreme E. end of this site (SP 926862; *Northants. Archaeol.*, 14 (1979), 107).

★^a(14) SAXON SETTLEMENT (?) (SP 913860), S. of the village, on Cornbrash at 83 m. above OD. A small scatter of Saxon pottery has been discovered in association with Roman material. A medieval iron hunting arrowhead was also found (*Northants. Archaeol.*, 11 (1976), 194, 196).

★^a(15) SAXON SETTLEMENT (SP 90458645), S.W. of the village, on limestone at 86 m. above OD. Excavation of a sand-pit revealed two hearths and a post-hole containing Saxon pottery. Similar pottery was found in the surrounding fields (*Northants. Archaeol.*, 13 (1978), 185).

★^a(16) SAXON SETTLEMENT (?) (SP 928863), in the S.W. of the parish, on limestone at 66 m. above OD. Early Saxon pottery and some worked flints have been found here (*Northants. Archaeol.*, 14 (1979), 107).

★^a(17) IRON-WORKING SITE (?) (SP 90778675), S.W. of the village, on Northampton Sand at 78 m. above OD. An extensive area of iron slag is associated with pottery of the 13th and 14th centuries (*Northants. Archaeol.*, 13 (1978), 189).

53   STOKE ALBANY

PREHISTORIC

★^a(6) ENCLOSURE (SP 795885), N.W. of the village, on Middle Lias Clay at 84 m. above OD. Air photographs (Northants. SMR) show very indistinctly an almost square enclosure some 50 m. wide.

56   SYWELL

ROMAN

★^b(11) ROMAN SETTLEMENT (?) (SP 822673), S. of Sywell Hall, on Northampton Sand at 79 m. above OD. Roman pottery, some of it associated with an area of stones, and a few worked flints were discovered in a trial trench (*Northants. Archaeol.*, 14 (1979), 108).

MEDIEVAL AND LATER

^b(7) SETTLEMENT REMAINS (SP 821673). Trial excavation on the N. side of the village (SP 822673) revealed early medieval pottery including St. Neots and Stamford wares, as well as late medieval and post-medieval sherds (*Northants. Archaeol.*, 14 (1979), 108). For Roman finds, see (11).

59   WARKTON

PREHISTORIC

^b(1) ENCLOSURE (SP 90728050). A scatter of stone, bone and late Iron Age pottery has been found on this cropmark (*Northants. Archaeol.*, 11 (1976), 184).

60 WEEKLEY

PREHISTORIC AND ROMAN

[a](1) IRON AGE AND ROMAN SETTLEMENT (centred SP 875812). Full details of the recent excavations have been published (*Northants. Archaeol.*, 11 (1976), 71–82).

[a](2) IRON AGE SETTLEMENT AND ROMAN BUILDING AND KILNS (SP 884818). Further details of the recent excavations have been published (*Northants. Archaeol.*, 11 (1967), 194; 12 (1977), 210; 13 (1978), 180). Petrological analysis of late Iron Age sherds with curvilinear decoration has shown that the raw materials used are from the Lizard, Cornwall (*Northants. Archaeol.*, 12 (1977), 183–4). A Belgic coin, possibly Trinovantian, of Addedomaros, has been found (*Northants. Archaeol.*, 14 (1979), 104). In the early 19th century a 'Roman pavement' was discovered in this area and later destroyed (letter of November 1809 in *Broadsides*, Central Library, Northampton).

★[a](13) ROMAN WELL (SP 870817), within Weekley Hall Wood, on Boulder Clay at 110 m. above OD. A well about 25 m. deep was discovered during ironstone-mining. Two complete jars found at the bottom suggest that the well was in use during the 2nd century (*Northants. Archaeol.*, 12 (1977), 223).

61 WELDON

PREHISTORIC

★[b](11) IRON AGE SETTLEMENT (?) (SP 912889), discovered during ironstone-mining, on limestone at 90 m. above OD. A quantity of early Iron Age pottery was found in some shallow pits (*Northants. Archaeol.*, 12 (1977), 210).

MEDIEVAL

[b](9) IRON-WORKING SITE (SP 928895). Additional finds from this site have now been published (*Northants. Archaeol.*, 12 (1977), 227).

62 WELLINGBOROUGH

PREHISTORIC AND ROMAN

A pebble macehead with hour-glass perforation, said to be Mesolithic, has been found in Finedon (SP 920720; NM; CBA *Research Report*, 20 (1977), 217), and a scatter of worked flints has been noted (SP 910683; *Northants. Archaeol.*, 11 (1976), 184). A coin of Constantine I and some undated Roman sherds have been reported from the N.E. end of Finedon (SP 923726; *Northants. Archaeol.*, 12 (1977), 223) and a silver Roman coin was found on the W. side of Wellingborough (SP 888679; J. Cole, *Hist. of Wellingborough* (1837), 176; lost). Objects described as 'a potter's wheel and stands of unbaked clay', and perhaps a Roman kiln, have been found somewhere in the parish (*Arch. J.*, 35 (1878), 88).

(3) BRONZE AGE BURIALS (unlocated). A Collared Urn of the Primary Series (in Ashmolean Museum) may be one of the three Urns previously recorded (*PPS*, 27 (1961), 297, No. 129).

[d](13) IRON AGE AND ROMAN SETTLEMENT (centred SP 875680). Full details of the excavations have now been published (*Northants. Archaeol.*, 11 (1976), 89–99; 12 (1977), 55–96, 210).

[d](18) ROMAN SETTLEMENT (SP 885695). Air photographs (Northants. SMR) show indistinct cropmarks covering 0.5 hectare, perhaps bounded on two sides by a ditch, close to the Roman material previously recorded.

★[d](36) FLINT-WORKING SITE (SP 893668), S. of Wellingborough, on Upper Lias Clay at 45 m. above OD. Worked flints including scrapers and points are recorded (Northants. SMR).

★[d](37) ROMAN SETTLEMENT (?) (SP 898692), N.E. of Wellingborough, on Northampton Sand at 25 m. above OD. Roman material including coins and pottery is said to have been found at Ladyswell (VCH *Northants.*, I (1902), 221).

63 WESTON-BY-WELLAND

ROMAN

★(3) ROMAN SETTLEMENT (SP 786916), in the N.E. of the parish, on gravel at 66 m. above OD. Roman pottery, tesserae and tiles from this area are in Market Harborough Museum. The material probably represents the western extension of the large Iron Age and Roman site immediately to the E. (Ashley (1)).

65 WILBY

PREHISTORIC AND ROMAN

Part of a moulded shaft was ploughed up in 1972, in an area where Roman material had not previously been recorded (*Northants. Archaeol.*, 13 (1978), 79; NM).

★[b](9) FLINT-WORKING SITE (SP 860658), W. of the village, on Northampton Sand at 83 m. above OD. A wide scatter of worked flints has been found, including cores, flakes, scrapers, an arrowhead and a point (*Northants. Archaeol.*, 11 (1976), 185).

66 WOLLASTON

PREHISTORIC

★[a](37) FLINT-WORKING SITE (SP 896646), in the N.E. of the parish, close to the R. Nene, on alluvium at 45 m. above OD. Worked flints said to be of Mesolithic type have been found (CBA Group 9, *Newsletter*, 8 (1978), 2).

MEDIEVAL

A Saxon sceatta was found in the parish in 1967 (*Brit. Num. J.*, 47 (1977), 50). Many details of the archaeology and history of the parish are given in David Hall's *Wollaston* (1977). An interpretation of the village plan has also been published (*Med. Arch.*, 21 (1977), 189–193).

[b](34) MANOR HOUSE SITE (SP 905624). A plan of the site has now been published (CBA Group 9, *Newsletter*, 9 (1979), 49–50).

VOLUME III

4 BADBY

PREHISTORIC AND ROMAN

A quartzite pebble-hammer with hour-glass perforation was found N. of the village in 1968 (SP 55925977; *Northants. Archaeol.*, 14 (1979), 102).

★[b](10) ROMAN SETTLEMENT (SP 559598), N. of the village, on Middle Lias Clay at 134 m. above OD. A very large quantity of Roman pottery, mostly grey ware but including samian, mortarium sherds and colour-coated wares, a bronze coin, fragments of quernstones and a dense scatter of stone were found in 1976–8 on a site where a pottery scatter had previously been recorded (*Northants. Archaeol.*, 14 (1979), 105).

6 BOUGHTON

★[b](12) FLINT-WORKING SITE (SP 756667), in the extreme N. of the parish, and extending into Pitsford parish, on Northampton sand at 91 m. above OD. A large area of worked flints is recorded (Northants. SMR).

8 BRAMPTON, CHURCH

ROMAN

Roman pottery has been discovered in a pipeline trench immediately N.W. of the village (SP 717660; Northants. SMR).

11 BRIXWORTH

PREHISTORIC

Part of a Mesolithic or Bronze Age perforated stone implement was found in 1977 (SP 74107139; NM; *Northants. Archaeol.*, 13 (1978), 178).

13 BYFIELD

ROMAN

A Roman altar has been recorded from Byfield but it may have been brought to the parish from elsewhere in recent times (Northants. SMR).

18 CLIPSTON

PREHISTORIC

A few worked flints, including a core and a scraper, have been found in the parish, mainly in the W. and S.W. (inf. A. E. Brown).

MEDIEVAL

A detailed description of the ridge-and-furrow in Clipston, together with further details of the history of the parish have been published. (CBA Group 9, *Newsletter*, 9 (1979), 21–31)

19 COLD ASHBY

PREHISTORIC

More than 50 worked flints, including three cores, have been found at SP 665782. Other flints have been noted at SP 643768. (inf. A. E. Brown)

21 CREATON

PREHISTORIC

More than 50 worked flints have been found, mostly in the N. and S.W. of the parish. They include thirteen cores and six scrapers and are mainly of Neolithic or later type although there are a few Mesolithic forms. (inf. A. E. Brown)

26 ELKINGTON

PREHISTORIC

At least 110 worked flints have been discovered in the parish, almost all to the N. and N.E. of the village. They include several microliths as well as thirteen cores and three scrapers of Neolithic and later type. (inf. A. E. Brown)

28 FARNDON, EAST

PREHISTORIC

About 20 worked flints have been found in the S. and N.E. of the parish. They include a blade and a flake of Mesolithic type and a core and two scrapers of Neolithic or later date. (inf. A. E. Brown)

MEDIEVAL

A silver short-cross penny of King John was discovered in the village in 1977 (SP 716848; *Northants. Archaeol.*, 13 (1978), 186).

31 FLORE

ROMAN

Two Roman coins, both probably of the 2nd century, were found S. of the village in 1978 (SP 64085953; *Northants. Archaeol.*, 14 (1979), 105).

32 GUILSBOROUGH

PREHISTORIC

Some 30 worked flints have been found in the parish. Most are of Neolithic or later type but there are some Mesolithic forms. At least ten cores and five scrapers are recorded (inf. A. E. Brown).

34 HADDON, WEST

ROMAN

A coin of Gratian was found in about 1863 within the village (SP 630718; Northants. SMR).

36 HASELBECH

PREHISTORIC

More than 60 worked flints have been found, including thirteen scrapers and a large number of cores. They are mainly of Neolithic or Bronze Age types, with a few Mesolithic forms (inf. A. E. Brown).

39 HOLLOWELL

PREHISTORIC

About 60 worked flints, of Mesolithic and Neolithic or later forms have been found in the parish, mainly in the S. round Teeton. They included seven cores, seven scrapers and a leaf-shaped arrowhead (inf. A. E. Brown).

40 KELMARSH

PREHISTORIC AND ROMAN

Some 30 worked flints have been found mainly in the S. of the parish. They include four cores and four scrapers, all of Neolithic or later type (inf. A. E. Brown).

^c(7) ROMAN SETTLEMENT (SP 745793). The reported cropmarks are now known to cover about 20 hectares and, though very indistinct, include a ditched trackway running N.E.–S.W. (SP 748795) and a group of irregular enclosures (SP 744794) (NCAU).

41 KILSBY

PREHISTORIC

A few worked flints, some of Mesolithic type, were discovered during excavation of the Roman road in 1977 (SP 57397234; *Northants. Archaeol.*, 13 (1978). 89–90).

44 LONG BUCKBY

PREHISTORIC AND ROMAN

★^a(10) FLINT-WORKING SITE (SP 650679), in the E. of the parish, on Northampton Sand at 152 m. above OD. A scatter of flints of Neolithic type and part of a polished stone axe are recorded (CBA Group 9, *Newsletter*, 8 (1978), 22).

★^a(11–13) FLINT-WORKING SITES. Scatters of worked flints, said to be mainly of Bronze Age type, have been found (CBA Group 9, *Newsletter*, 8 (1978), 22).

★(11) FLINT-WORKING SITE (SP 647684), 600 m. N.W. of (10), on Northampton Sand at 164 m. above OD.

★(12) FLINT-WORKING SITE (SP 646688), 400 m. N.N.W. of (11) on Northampton Sand at 167 m. above OD.

★(13) FLINT-WORKING SITE (SP 633695), in the N. of the parish, on glacial gravel at 128 m. above OD.

★^a(14) ROMAN SETTLEMENT (SP 625685), N. of the village, on Boulder Clay at 125 m. above OD. An area of dark soil containing occupation debris has been noted (*Northants. Archaeol.*, 13 (1978), 181).

45 MAIDWELL

PREHISTORIC AND ROMAN

A few worked flints, including two cores and two scrapers, all of Neolithic type, have been found at SP 730772 (inf. A. E. Brown).

^a(3) IRON AGE AND ROMAN SETTLEMENT (centred SP 747772). At some time before 1901 objects described as 'Roman bricks' and 'a path paved with cobble stones' were found at the E. end of the village (SP 750770; *Broadsides*, Central Library, Northampton).

46 MARSTON TRUSSELL

PREHISTORIC

About 30 worked flints have been found in the parish, all of Neolithic or later form, including one arrowhead, five scrapers and three cores (inf. A. E. Brown).

47 NASEBY

PREHISTORIC AND ROMAN

A partly polished flint axe was found on Naseby Field in 1973 (SP 68117945; *Northants. Archaeol.*, 14 (1979), 103), and about 40 worked flints, all Neolithic or later types including four scrapers and eight cores, are recorded from the parish (inf. A. E. Brown). A Bronze Age spearhead of unknown provenance and a hoard of 57 Roman coins of the early 4th century, discovered in 1924 'at Naseby Hall', are in Market Harborough Museum.

★ᵃ(6) ROMAN SETTLEMENT (SP 693789), N.E. of the village, on Upper Lias Clay at 185 m. above OD. A dense scatter of Roman pottery including samian, Nene Valley and Oxfordshire wares has been found (*Northants. Archaeol.*, 13 (1978), 181).

★ᵃ(7) ROMAN SETTLEMENT (?) (SP 693778), S.E. of the village, on Boulder Clay at 190 m. above OD. A scatter of Roman pottery is recorded (*Northants. Archaeol.*, 13 (1978), 181).

49 NORTON

ROMAN

A single coin of Constantine I has been found (SP 602637; *Northants. Archaeol.*, 13 (1978), 181).

50 OXENDON, GREAT

PREHISTORIC AND ROMAN

Some 20 worked flints have been found in the parish, mainly S.W. and N.E. of the village. They include five cores, and two scrapers of Neolithic or later types and some blades which may be Mesolithic (inf. A. E. Brown). A coin of Postumus has come from the parish (Market Harborough Museum).

51 PITSFORD

ROMAN

★ᵃ(10) ROMAN SETTLEMENT AND WELL (SP 742672), S. of Boughton Grange, on Northampton Sand at 105 m. above OD. A well, Roman pottery and 'leather' are said to have been discovered in this area in about 1936. The site has been quarried away. Two quernstones, upper and lower, of local stone and probably of Iron Age date, came from the same area (OS Record Cards, grid reference incorrect).

53 RAVENSTHORPE

PREHISTORIC

Nearly 80 worked flints have been found in the parish. Most are of late Neolithic or Bronze Age type though some may be Mesolithic. They include thirteen cores and ten scrapers (inf. A. E. Brown).

54 SCALDWELL

PREHISTORIC AND MEDIEVAL

The following finds are said to have been made during ironstone-quarrying somewhere in the parish in the 1920s: a stone axe, up to 200 silver pennies of Henry I, burials and gold objects, and a 'series of trenches up to 40 ft. long filled with human bones' (*Northampton Independent*, 4 September 1926).

55 SIBBERTOFT

PREHISTORIC

More than 80 worked flints have been found, mainly in the N.W., N.E. and S.E. of the parish. They include part of an axe, twelve cores and several scrapers and are mainly of Neolithic or later types with a few Mesolithic forms (inf. A. E. Brown).

57 STANFORD-ON-AVON

PREHISTORIC

Some 20 worked flints of Neolithic or later type, including four cores and one scraper, have been found in the parish (inf. A. E. Brown).

60 SULBY

PREHISTORIC AND ROMAN

A few worked flints of Neolithic or later type, including four scrapers, have been found in the parish (inf. A. E. Brown).

★ᶜ(6) ROMAN SETTLEMENT (?) (SP 663797), in the S. of the parish, on Upper Lias Clay at 142 m. above OD. A small scatter of Roman sherds has been noted (*Northants. Archaeol.*, 13 (1978), 182).

61 THORNBY

PREHISTORIC

A few worked flints, including two scrapers, have been found at SP 675766 (inf. A. E. Brown).

64 WELFORD

PREHISTORIC

About 80 worked flints of Neolithic or later type, including 17 cores and 18 scrapers, have been found in the parish (inf. A. E. Brown).

62 WATFORD

ROMAN

★[b](7) ROMAN SETTLEMENT (?) (SP 596703), in the N. of the parish, on Marlstone Rock at 135 m. above OD. Unspecified Roman material is recorded (Northants. SMR).

★[b](8) ROMAN SETTLEMENT (?) (SP 599704), 300 m. E. of (7), on Middle Lias Clay at 135 m. above OD. Roman material is said to have been found (Northants. SMR).

65 WELTON

ROMAN

★(6) ROMAN SETTLEMENT (?) (unlocated, possibly in Watford parish). Roman material was discovered in the 19th century, possibly in the vicinity of the Saxon burials (1) (Dryden Collection, Central Library, Northampton).

68 WOODFORD-CUM-MEMBRIS

MEDIEVAL

★[a](4) DAM (SP 513513), in the extreme W. of the parish, on Upper Lias Clay at 147 m. above OD. The shallow valley of a S.E.-flowing stream is spanned by a large earthen dam 100 m. long and 2 m. high. It is breached in the centre. (RAF VAP CPE/UK/1926, 3067–8).

ROMAN ROADS

1f, WATLING STREET

A section has been cut through the Roman road in Kilsby parish (SP 57397234), in the part where the alignment is no longer followed by a modern road. The excavation revealed at least two, and perhaps three separate parallel carriageways, of which the central one was twice the width of each of the flanking ones. (*Northants. Archaeol.*, 13 (1978), 87–92; *Britannia*, 9 (1978), 442).

57a MIDDLETON TO STANION

Excavations have been carried out on the Roman road in Hazel Wood, Corby (SP 879883; *Northants. Archaeol.*, 13 (1978), 92–4), and in South Wood (SP 897873; *J. Northants. Nat. Hist. Soc. and FC*, 33 (1959), 259–60).

FROM ALDWINCLE TO ?

Further details of this road, running N.E. from the road 57a have now been published (*Northants. Archaeol.*, 12 (1977), 47).

FROM ASHTON TO ?

During excavations of the Roman settlement at Ashton (3) a Roman road was discovered running N.–S. across the site. Parchmarks to the S. and a short length of agger to the N. (TL 048895) indicate the continuation of this road over a total distance of 800 m. At the S. end (TL 047888) an area of stonework was found in the bed and bank of the R. Nene during drainage work. It is possible that the road crossed the river at this point. Within the settlement a second road was discovered, running W. for 25 m. from the main one (*Durobrivae*, 3 (1975), 12–15; 5 (1977), 6–7; *Northants. Archaeol.*, 11 (1976), 185).

PLATES

PLATE I

EVENLEY (9). Deserted village of Astwick, from N. (CUAP)

PLATE 2

ASTON LE WALLS (1). Deserted village of Appletree, from N. (CUAP)

WESTON AND WEEDON (10). Settlement remains at Plumpton, from E. (CUAP)

PLATE 3

GRAFTON REGIS (5–7). Motte or ringwork, site of manor house and garden remains and settlement remains, from N. (CUAP)

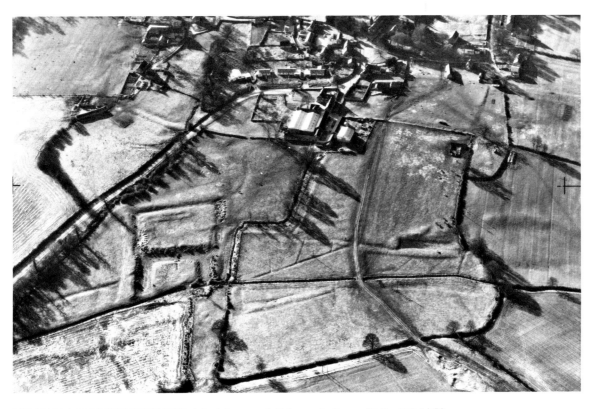

HINTON-IN-THE-HEDGES (3). Moat and fishpond, from N.E. (CUAP)

PLATE 4

EDGCOTE (1). Deserted village of Edgcote, from N.W.

ROTHERSTHORPE (8). Enclosure, N.W. corner from S.E.

PLATE 5

CULWORTH (1). Ringwork, from N.W.

SULGRAVE (3). Ringwork, from N.E.

PLATE 6

RADSTONE (2). Deserted village of Lower Radstone, from N.W. (CUAP)

PLATE 7

QUINTON (6). Moated site, before destruction. (RAF)

SULGRAVE (6, 7). Pillow mound and cultivation remains. (NMR)

PLATE 8

CROUGHTON. Roman pewter plates. (NM)

INDEX

In this Index the numbers in brackets refer to the monuments as listed in each parish. References to the Sectional Preface and to material not associated with a particular monument are provided with page numbers. The letters 'a' or 'b' after a page number indicate the first or second column of text. The classified lists, arranged chronologically, are selective.

BRONZE AGE: Sectional Preface, p. xxiv; p. 11b; p. 27a; p. 27b; p. 73a; p. 118a; Addenda to vol. I: p. 191a; vol. II: p. 200a.
ROMAN: Towcester (3).
SAXON: p. 29b.

Photoset by Input Typesetting Ltd
Printed for H. M. Stationery Office by McCorquodale Printers Ltd London
HM(C)1134 Dd699036 C15 4/82 McC56–2110